THE HISTORIC LANDSCAPE OF CATALONIA

THE MEDIEVAL COUNTRYSIDE

VOLUME 23

General Editor
Phillipp Schofield, Aberystwyth University

Editorial Board
Laurent Feller, Université Paris 1 Panthéon-Sorbonne
Paul Freedman, Yale University
Thomas Lindkvist, Göteborgs universitet
Sigrid Hirbodian, Universität Tübingen
Peter Hoppenbrouwers, Universiteit Leiden
Piotr Górecki, University of California, Riverside
Sandro Carocci, Università degli Studi di Roma Tor Vergata
Julio Escalona, Consejo Superior de Investigaciones Científicas, Madrid
Pere Benito i Monclús, Universitat de Lleida

Previously published volumes in this series
are listed at the back of the book.

The Historic Landscape of Catalonia

Landscape History of a Mediterranean Country in the Middle Ages

by
JORDI BOLÒS

BREPOLS

British Library Cataloguing in Publication Data
A catalogue record for this book is available from the British Library.

© 2023, Brepols Publishers n.v., Turnhout, Belgium.

All rights reserved. No part of this publication may be reproduced,
stored in a retrieval system, or transmitted, in any form or by
any means, electronic, mechanical, photocopying, recording,
or otherwise without the prior permission of the publisher.

ISBN: 978-2-503-60305-6
e-ISBN: 978-2-503-60326-1
DOI: 10.1484/M.TMC-EB.5.131926

ISSN: 1784–8814
e-ISSN: 2294–8430

Printed in the EU on acid-free paper.

D/2023/0095/22

Table of Contents

List of Illustrations 7

Chapter 1
Introduction 11

Chapter 2
Houses Become a Village: The Villages of the Pyrenees 31

Chapter 3
Churches, Monasteries, and Villages: In Each Village a Church 49

Chapter 4
Castles and Castral Villages: The *incastellamento* of the Landscape 77

Chapter 5
New Towns and Complex Settlements 107

Chapter 6
Hamlets and Farmsteads: The Dispersal of the Population 133

Chapter 7
The Medieval Towns and Cities: The Other Side
of the Medieval Landscape 161

Chapter 8
Cultivated Land: The Relevance of Pre-Medieval Past 187

Chapter 9
Coombs, Terraces, Concentric Forms, and Land Strips 201

Chapter 10
Irrigated Land, Rivers, and Lakes 227

Chapter 11
The Importance of Mills, Iron, and Salt 243

Chapter 12
Woodland and Pastureland: Changes in Vegetation and
Environment 257

Chapter 13
Roads and Pathways, the Network that Organizes the Landscape 279

Chapter 14
Boundaries and Territories: A Country Full of Old Borders 293

Chapter 15
The Importance of Toponymy 321

Chapter 16
Mapping the Historical Landscape 333

Conclusion 353
Studying Historic Landscapes Bridges Gaps
Between the Past and the Present 353

Glossary 365

Works Cited 373

Index of Personal Names 427

Index of Place Names 430

Index of Subjects 447

List of Illustrations

Chapter 1 — Introduction

Figure 1. Topographic map of Catalonia. — 12

Figure 2. Map of historic Catalonia with the boundaries of the *comarques* (or regions). — 15

Chapter 2 — Houses Become a Village

Figure 3. Village of Olopte (Cerdanya). — 38

Figure 4. Village of Senet (Alta Ribagorça). — 39

Figure 5. Village of Espot (Pallars Sobirà). — 41

Figure 6. Necropolis of La Tossa de Baix (Rosselló, Segrià) and its surroundings. — 45

Chapter 3 — Churches, Monasteries, and Villages

Figure 7. Map of historic Catalonia showing the churches, monasteries, and villages mentioned in this chapter. — 51

Figure 8. Village of Vilaür (Alt Empordà). — 55

Figure 9. Village of Pesillà (Roussillon). — 58

Figure 10. Village of Bages (Roussillon). — 59

Figure 11. Village of Sant Vicenç dels Horts (Baix Llobregat). — 60

Figure 12. Town of Organyà (Alt Urgell). — 68

Figure 13. Abbey of Poblet (Conca de Barberà). — 70

Chapter 4 — Castles and Castral Villages

Figure 14. Map of historic Catalonia showing the location of the castles and villages mentioned in the text. — 79

Figure 15. *Castrum* of El Roc d'Enclar (Andorra). — 80

Figure 16. Castle and fortification of Siurana (Priorat). — 84

Figure 17. Tower of the castle of Vallferosa (Segarra). — 86

8 LIST OF ILLUSTRATIONS

Figure 18. Village of Aguiló (Santa Coloma de Queralt, Conca de Barberà). 93

Figure 19. Castral village of Palau-sator (Baix Empordà). 95

Figure 20. Castral village of La Roca d'Albera (Roussillon). 96

Figure 21. Village of Montfalcó Murallat (Les Oluges, Segarra). 97

Figure 22. Village of La Guàrdia de Noguera (Pallars Jussà). 102

Chapter 5 — New Towns and Complex Settlements

Figure 23. Map of historic Catalonia with the new towns mentioned in the text. 109

Figure 24. Town of Vilagrassa (Urgell). 114

Figure 25. Town of La Selva del Camp (Baix Camp). 116

Figure 26. Town of Ulldecona (Montsià). 119

Figure 27. Town of Torroella de Montgrí (Baix Empordà). 121

Figure 29. Town of Santa Coloma de Queralt (Conca de Barberà). 129

Figure 30. Town of Àger (La Noguera). 131

Chapter 6 — Hamlets and Farmsteads

Figure 31. Hamlets of the valley of Sant Joan de les Abadesses (Ripollès). 136

Figure 32. Parish of Ordino (Andorra). 138

Figure 33. Farmstead of Les Heures (La Quar, Berguedà). 141

Figure 34. The *almunia* of Vensilló (Els Alamús, Segrià). 145

Figure 35. Parish of Sant Vicenç del Sallent (Santa Pau, Garrotxa). 152

Figure 36. Farmhouse of Mas B de Vilosiu (Cercs, Berguedà). 156

Figure 37. Inhabited cave of L'Esplugallonga (Conca de Dalt, Pallars Jussà). 158

Chapter 7 — The Medieval Towns and Cities

Figure 38. The city of Lleida (Segrià). 164

Figure 39. The city of Tortosa (Baix Ebre). 169

Figure 40. The town of Granollers (Vallès Oriental). 172

LIST OF ILLUSTRATIONS   9

Figure 41. The town of Cervera (Segarra).   174

Figure 42. The town of Puigcerdà (Cerdanya).   176

Chapter 8 — Cultivated Land

Figure 43. Fields of Sant Joan de Mollet (Gironès).   196

Figure 44. Village of Fortià (Alt Empordà).   197

Chapter 9 — Coombs, Terraces, Concentric Forms, and Land Strips

Figure 45. Coma de Barbó or Borbó (L'Espluga de Francolí,
Conca de Barberà).   204

Figure 46. Comes de Maldà and Maldanell (Urgell).   207

Figure 47. Coma de Matxerri (Castelldans, Les Garrigues).   207

Figure 48. Terraces of Aranyonet (Gombrèn, Ripollès).   211

Figure 49. Bellvei (Baix Penedès).   215

Figure 50. Vilajuïga (Alt Empordà).   218

Figure 51. Els Ofegats (Agramunt, Urgell).   219

Figure 52. Llenguaderes (Capçanes, Priorat).   221

Figure 53. Between El Badorc and El Freixe (Piera, Anoia).   224

Chapter 10 — Irrigated Land, Rivers, and Lakes

Figure 54. *Hortes* of Sant Vicenç de Jonqueres
(Sabadell, Vallès Occidental).   231

Figure 55. Ditches around Lleida.   233

Figure 56. *Horta* of Menàrguens (La Noguera).   235

Figure 57. *Huerta* of Estadilla (Aragon).   236

Chapter 11 — The importance of Mills, Iron, and Salt

Figure 58. Carolingian mills in the Riera de Merlès (Berguedà).   245

Figure 59. Molins de la Vila (Montblanc, Conca de Barberà).   248

Figure 60. Mills of Empordà.   251

Chapter 12 — Woodland and Pastureland

Figure 61. Map of historic Catalonia with the location
of the places mentioned in this chapter. 259

Figure 62. Pollen analysis of Banyoles (Pla de l'Estany). 263

Figure 63. The pastures of Enveig (Cerdanya). 270

Chapter 13 — Roads and Pathways, the Network that Organizes the Landscape

Figure 64. Map of historic Catalonia with a depiction
of the main roads mentioned around 1000. 281

Figure 65. Road from La Granada to Sant Martí Sarroca
(Alt Penedès). 285

Figure 66. Paths of Vilanova de Raò (Roussillon). 285

Chapter 14 — Boundaries and Territories

Figure 67. The parish of Vila-sacra (Alt Empordà). 298

Figure 68. The village of Polinyà (Vallès Occidental). 301

Figure 69. The Àneu valley (Pallars Sobirà). 305

Figure 70. The parish of Solsona (Solsonès). 309

Figure 71. The territory of Olèrdola (Alt Penedès). 312

Figure 72. The municipality of Gelida (Alt Penedès). 314

Chapter 15 — The Importance of Toponymy

Figure 73. Pre-Roman place names in Pallars Sobirà and Ribagorça. 323

Figure 74. Roman place names in Roussillon. 325

Figure 75. Germanic place names in the Alt Berguedà and Ripollès. 328

Chapter 16 — Mapping the Historical Landscape

Figure 76. Fragment of a map of toponyms. 336

Figure 77. Historic Landscape Characterisation map. 347

CHAPTER 1

Introduction

Travelling across Catalonia, we discover landscape contours gradually drawn over centuries, an indelible imprint of human activity. Villages, farmsteads, fields, pastures, ditches, and roads all bear witness to the past. This book aims to provide guidelines for the interpretation of these landscapes. Sometimes, when visiting a country, one tends to concentrate on its main monuments or towns. In Catalonia, tourists typically visit the cities of Barcelona, Girona, Perpignan, Tarragona, or Lleida, the monasteries of Sant Pere de Rodes, Ripoll, Cuixà, Sant Cugat del Vallès, Gerri, Alaó, Poblet, or Santes Creus, the churches of the Boí Valley — World Heritage sites, without realizing that to make their way there, they pass through landscapes that, thanks to recent research, historians have just begun to understand and date. Realizing the variety of these landscapes has allowed us to appreciate their significance as historic documents, and as part of the heritage of their people.

Research on landscape history has been thriving across Europe over the last few years in both northern, central European and the Mediterranean countries. These studies have consolidated our knowledge of the origins of our immediate surroundings and have, in turn, delved into their respective histories. Such research has strengthened the bonds between the landscape and its changing social and economic reality across the centuries. These studies have also attracted other disciplines to their fold in an attempt to gain new knowledge and have helped, or *should* help, to bring Catalonia and its history closer to the people who live there and to anyone curious about the origins of the Catalan and European landscapes.

Studying the historic landscape also involves digging into an everyday space that bears the traces of previous settlers, including wealthy or poor peasants, secular lords, powerful or humble ecclesiastics, city dwellers, Christians, Muslims, and Jews. The landscape was made up of numerous elements, which were created, maintained, and used by lords but also by peasants and city dwellers. Many of these elements bring us closer to the holders of power; others allow us to understand social relations; still, others zoom in on the economy, people's mindsets, or religion. Overall, studying the landscape helps us to gain an insight into our current world and our surroundings. I believe, as will be emphasized in this volume, that the possibility of revisiting unwritten 'documents' around us enables us to understand that our past is important not only to those who dwell but also, obviously, to everybody else. It is of interest for anybody who visits a place to be able to 'read' landscape elements and learn about why and when they were created. This will in turn be explained at length in this volume.

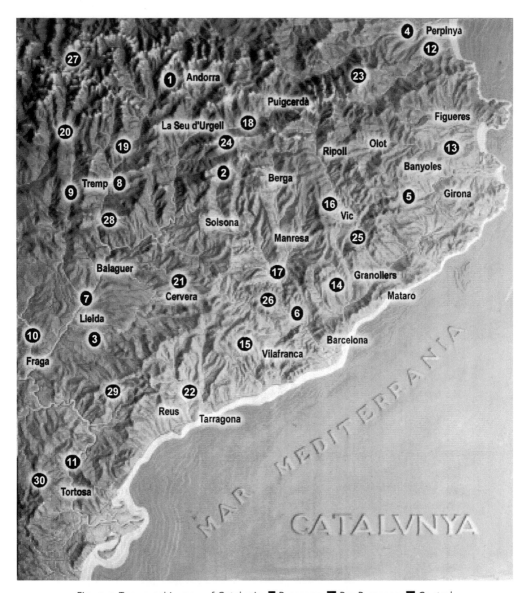

Figure 1. Topographic map of Catalonia. 1. Pyrenees. 2. Pre-Pyrenees. 3. Central Depression. 4. Tet. 5. Ter. 6. Llobregat. 7. Segre. 8. Noguera Pallaresa. 9. Noguera Ribagorçana. 10. Cinca. 11. Ebro. 12. Rosselló / Roussillon. 13. Empordà. 14. Vallès. 15. Penedès. 16. Osona. 17. Bages. 18. Cerdanya. 19. Pallars. 20. Ribagorça. 21. Segarra. 22. Camp de Tarragona. 23. Canigó. 24. Cadí. 25. Montseny. 26. Montserrat. 27. Vall d'Aran. 28. Montsec. 29. Montsant. 30. Els Ports. Map: Institut Cartogràfic i Geològic de Catalunya (1932, 1936–1939). Reproduced with permission.

All figures are by the author, and sources indicated where appropriate.

The Area Under Discussion

The scope of the present work is Catalonia and its history, which not only comprises the territory now governed by the Catalan government (the *Generalitat*, in Catalan), but also the historic Catalan regions, now part of the French department of Pyrénées-Orientales: Roussillon, Conflent, Vallespir, and Alta Cerdanya, separated from Catalonia and ceded to France as a result of the Treaty of the Pyrenees in 1659. Historical Catalonia also includes the independent state of Andorra and regions just west of Catalonia that are also Catalan-speaking, although they now belong to the Autonomous Community of Aragon.

Catalonia is a diverse country with striking differences as regards landscape, climate, and vegetation, with mountains of over 3,000 metres in height and extensive plains almost at sea level, e.g., Roussillon and Empordà (Fig. 1). There are also interior plains surrounding the city of Lleida. One can find a wide variety of rainfall levels ranging from 1,029 mm in Olot or 788 mm in Puigcerdà and a mere 351 mm in Lleida, through 626 mm in Perpignan, 598 mm in Barcelona, 548 mm of rainfall in Tortosa, and 475 mm in Tarragona. This diversity certainly has a marked impact on vegetation and crops in Catalonia from fir tree forests (*Abies alba*) and beeches (*Fagus sylvatica*) to the lands where evergreens holm oaks struggle to get by (*Quercus ilex rotundifolia*). In many *comarques*,[1] the predominant trees are oaks (e.g. *Quercus pubescens*), evergreen oaks (*Quercus ilex*), and pine trees. Inevitably, such an assortment of climates has had an effect, over the centuries, on crops; thus, in drier lands, regular and abundant crops are guaranteed only if the land can be properly irrigated.

Nowadays, the Catalan mainland currently governed by the *Generalitat* is made up of forty-two *comarques*. To these should be added the five historic *comarques* of northern Catalonia, *Catalunya del Nord* (in the French department of the Pyrénées-Orientales), Andorra, and the five *comarques* under Aragonese administration. The *comarques* are mostly administrative divisions, yet they can also be economic entities and reflect a frame of mind and, sometimes, even a historic reality. Some tribes in the Iberian period, before the arrival of the Romans, had already settled in the current *comarques* (e.g. *Ausetani* in Osona, *Ceretani* in Cerdanya, *Bergistani* in Berguedà, *Laietani* in Maresme or in Barcelonès, and *Sordones* in Roussillon). Also, a few medieval counties coincided, approximately, with the current *comarques*: e.g. Roussillon, Conflent, Vallespir, Empúries, Peralada (*comarques* of Alt and Baix Empordà), Besalú (Garrotxa), Osona, Manresa, Cerdanya, Berga, Urgell (Alt Urgell), Pallars, Ribagorça. In the coming pages, to ensure easier geographical positioning,

---

1 A comarca (plural *comarques*) is a territorial subdivision, like a district, that brings together several populations with a sense of unity due to the natural conditions, history, or neighbourhood relations between its main town and the smaller villages that make it up.

The Medieval Period

The chronological framework of this book largely coincides with that of the Middle Ages, from the political, social, and economic transition that followed the end of Roman rule to the beginning of the modern age. At this point, it is also worth noting that studying the historic landscape is a long-term process. Therefore, in-depth knowledge of the medieval landscape requires a profound knowledge of Roman and even pre-Roman landscapes, the latter being little known in Catalonia, unfortunately. On the other hand, gaining expertise in the field of medieval landscapes requires a preliminary evaluation of the changes after the fifteenth century and the proper identification of every landscape feature that, since the Middle Ages, has been preserved to the present day, five centuries later.

I argue that, apart from studying the past, one of the purposes of research on historic landscapes is to understand more accurately the current landscape. These studies should help to emphasize its value adequately and, as a result, to manage it better. We need to bridge the gap between the past and the present, and by so doing, discover the traces of the past in many of the landscape elements around us. Our neighbouring landscape is a living space of historic interest. Thus, the scenery, as a silent witness to our history, becomes part of our heritage. Recently, our interest in learning about and disseminating the past encouraged us to embark on the project PaHisCat (short for 'Paisatge Històric de Catalunya', in English, Historic Landscape of Catalonia), a similar project to the English HLC project (Historic Landscape Characterisation). Although we failed to achieve our initial objective to map the entire territory of Catalonia, not only did PaHisCat lay out a few methodological principles but also triggered an interest in the study of past landscapes and provided an insight into some aspects of Catalan history. This will be discussed at length in Chapter 16.

Catalan history has a long tradition, partly similar to that of the rest of Europe yet different in a few aspects. Catalonia's origins go back to the early Middle Ages. The Carolingian period saw the creation of the Hispanic 'March' (meaning frontier), made up of those counties ruled by Charlemagne which bordered Hispania, as those territories under Islamic rule were named (hence, they remained on the other side of the frontier). In the Carolingian Empire, there were other marches (e.g. the marches of Brittany and Pannonia); later on, to the west of England, the march of Wales was also created.[3]

---

2 This refers to *País Valencià* or, during the Middle Ages, the Kingdom of Valencia.
3 Lieberman, *The Medieval March of Wales*; Rowley. *The Welsh Border*.

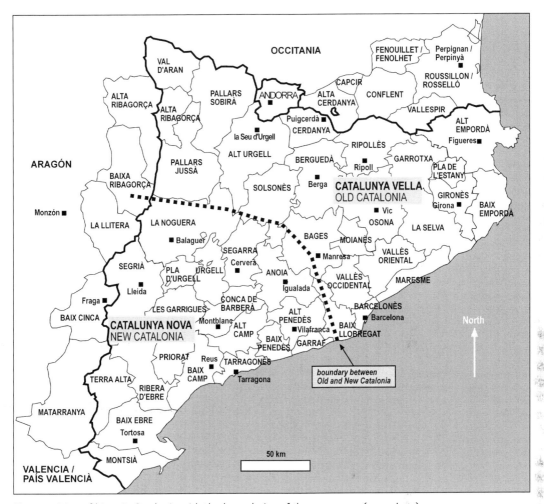

Figure 2. Map of historic Catalonia with the boundaries of the *comarques* (or regions).

The Carolingian Catalan counties spread across the Eastern Pyrenees and stretched to Barcelona. In 801, the river Llobregat acted as the natural frontier between the Carolingian Empire and the Cordovan Emirates. Gradually, the territory under the rule of the Catalan counts extended across the south and the west. A few centuries later, in 1148, the count of Barcelona conquered Tortosa and, shortly after, in 1149, the cities of Lleida and Fraga (the latter currently in the Autonomous Community of Aragon). This variety in the history of the Catalan south-western regions had an impact on some landscape features of these territories conquered in the mid-twelfth century, added to the fact that, as pointed out above, the climate is drier. The so-called 'Old Catalonia' (*Catalunya Vella*, in Catalan) (i.e., the Carolingian counties) covers the mountainous land of the Pyrenees and the eastern *comarques*, which are closer to the coast and therefore more humid, that extend from Perpignan to Barcelona. The landscape of 'New Catalonia' (*Catalunya Nova*, in Catalan) includes the drier lands of the plains of Lleida and Camp de Tarragona as well as the *comarques* surrounding the final course of the river Ebro. This territory was under Muslim rule until the mid-twelfth century.

A significant number of books have been written on the history of Catalonia, most of which are in Catalan.[4] In Catalonia (and also the Balearic Islands and Valencia), from the Middle Ages, the language spoken was, and is, Catalan. It is a Romance language close to Occitan, the language used by medieval troubadours to write their poems. Likewise, it is in the Catalan language that hundreds of literary and scientific works have been written, from the Middle Ages to the present.

In order to delve into the medieval history of Catalonia, we begin with a brief account of the links between Catalonia and its neighbouring countries. This will make it easier to understand the focus of this book on the Catalan historic landscape.

One of the first contacts that shaped the future of Catalonia — and that of the Catalan language — occurred between the Catalan territory and the Occitan lands beyond the Pyrenees.[5] Catalonia originally had numerous, strong connections with the surrounding territories of Languedoc, Gascony, and Provence, all of which have had a significant impact on Catalan history. In the Visigothic period, both the land later to be known as Catalonia and the land of Languedoc, around Narbonne, were part of the Visigothic kingdom of Toledo. Between 713 and 719, all of these lands fell under Muslim rule. After 759, gradually, the future Catalan counties were conquered by the Carolingian Frankish kings. In 801, the city of Barcelona was besieged and conquered by Charlemagne's son. In these counties, — i.e., those from Old Catalonia — the decades under Islamic rule did not break up their population, laws, or, eventually, their authorities. Two centuries later, around the year 1000, the counts of Barcelona became sovereign and, as such, mainly searched for spouses in the Occitan lands. This resulted in an expansion of their dominions to the north, mainly the counties of Carcassonne, Provence, and other territories beyond the Pyrenees.[6]

Secondly, it is worth noting the links between Catalonia and other countries in the Iberian Peninsula, principally Aragon. Ramon Berenguer IV, the count of Barcelona, became the king of two independent states, albeit *de facto*: one

---

4 Salrach, *Història de Catalunya: El procés de feudalització*; Batlle, *Història de Catalunya: L'expansió baixmedieval*; Bolòs, *Catalunya medieval*; Sabaté, *Història de Catalunya: Catalunya medieval*.

5 Occitania is a region where Occitan was historically the dominant language. This country encompasses the southern part of France, as well as part of Catalonia, the Aran Valley, and some valleys of Italy. It should not be confused with the current administrative region of Occitanie.

6 Aurell, *Les noces du comte*.

of them was constituted by the counties of Catalonia and the other by the Kingdom of Aragon. Ramon Berenguer IV then decided to conquer Tortosa (1148) and Lleida (1149), which resulted in the establishment of boundaries to the south and west of a country that was already known as Catalonia. It extended from Salses to the north of Roussillon, to the river Cinca, a natural frontier with Aragon, and all the way down to Sénia, a watercourse that marked the northern border of Valencian territory, which was not conquered by the Catalan-Aragonese kings until the thirteenth century.[7]

The lands of Tortosa and Lleida were for several centuries subject to Islamic rule before they were captured by the count of Barcelona.[8] These territories were initially ruled from the city of Córdoba to the south of the Iberian Peninsula. It was not until the *fitna* or civil war in the eleventh century that the unified Caliphate of Cordoba broke up into independent kingdoms, *taifas*, two of which had as their capitals the cities of Lleida and Tortosa. The tenth and eleventh centuries (the years of the Caliphate and the taifa kingdoms) brought prosperity to both cities. The Islamization of their population and the abandonment of the Romance language (or vulgar Latin), widely spoken in the eighth century, mainly accelerated in the tenth and eleventh centuries. This caused the counts' conquests of the twelfth century (of Tortosa and Lleida) to be different from those in the eighth and ninth centuries (of Girona and Barcelona), when their Islamized populations were still a minority, hence most probably considered foreign. In the twelfth century, the inhabitants of these conquered lands, commonly known as *sarraïns* (Saracens), were expelled, or segregated in marginal urban spaces, within clear boundaries, or in certain streets of some villages. Although many of these so-called Saracens were descended from inhabitants from the Visigothic period, they were indeed different as they spoke Arabic and were Muslims.

After the defeat of the Catalan-Aragonese King Pere I in Muret, in 1213, the French managed to conquer Occitania from the north. The northwards expansion project, pursued by the counts of Barcelona for centuries, came to a halt. As a result, the monarchs of Catalonia and Aragon were forced to seek to expand their kingdoms to the south and to the east. In the thirteenth century, King Jaume I — son of Pere I — conquered Mallorca and, subsequently,

---

7 Forcadell, 'El rio Sénia: origen y fosilización de la frontera entre Cataluña y el reino de Valencia'.

8 We never use the term 'reconquest', as we believe it to be inappropriate for two reasons. First, because those who literally 'conquered' Elna, Girona, La Seu d'Urgell, Barcelona, or La Ribagorça were the Frankish kings, who had never had any right over these lands, or their counts. Later on, the Catalan counts continued to depend on these monarchs, although, in fact, towards the end of the tenth century, they became independent. Secondly, because most of the inhabitants who lived in Lleida or Tortosa in the middle of the twelfth century were the descendants of those who lived there in the seventh century. Eventually, they would have, slowly but inexorably, become Islamized throughout the eighth to tenth centuries. About the borders of Catalonia see Ortí, 'La primera articulación del estado feudal', p. 975.

the Kingdom of Valencia, which is currently Valencia (*País Valencià*). This resulted in the migration of many Catalan families to these lands, as well as the expansion of the Catalan language across most of the *comarques* of these neighbouring countries. The process of colonization that had started one hundred years earlier in New Catalonia now extended to Majorca and the rest of the Balearic Islands, as well as the irrigated plains of Valencia.[9] Some regions of the inland of Valencia were mainly populated by Aragonese people.

Likewise, it is worth noting the links established in the second half of the thirteenth century, with the Mediterranean territories which are currently part of the Italian state, particularly the islands of Sicily and Sardinia. As a result of the events that took place at that time, a variant of old Catalan is still spoken nowadays in L'Alguer (It. Alghero), one of the towns in Sardinia.[10] By the end of the Middle Ages, in the fifteenth century, the kings of Catalonia, Aragon, and Valencia also became kings of other states, like Castile and, for a while, Portugal.[11] This is the backdrop against which the modern era began.

Why Study Catalonia?

Catalonia is an interesting territory for the medieval historian because it was a march or borderland. In the ninth century, part of the future Catalonia lay in the Carolingian Empire and another part belonged to Al-Andalus, the Emirate of Córdoba. We find, therefore, various realities. While the Carolingian counties — i.e. Old Catalonia — have many elements that resemble the lands of Languedoc, those of New Catalonia have many landscape features encompassing both physical and human characteristics, similar to those towards the south in Valencia. To understand more about the interest in studying this country, we need to consider that the count of Barcelona became king of the Catalan-Aragonese Kingdom, which in turn played a remarkable role from a political and economic point of view in southern Europe throughout the whole of the high Middle Ages. Within the approximately 40,000 square km of Catalonia, we find a great diversity of landscapes and landscape components, from farmsteads to ecclesiastical villages, coombs, *hortes* or irrigated land, etc., a fact that has attracted the attention of Catalan researchers over the last few years. Likewise, the history of the Catalan counties has caught the attention of many historians from all over the world, such as Pierre Vilar, John Elliott, Pierre Bonnassie, Thomas Bisson, Paul Freedman, John Shideler, Stephen Bensch, Christian Guilleré,

---

9 Furió, *Història del País Valencià*, pp. 37–56.

10 Milanese, *Alghero. Archeologia di una città medievale*.

11 In relation to Catalan national identity throughout the Middle Ages, see Sabaté, 'Catalan Identity Discourse in the Late Medieval Mediterranean'.

INTRODUCTION 19

Jonathan Jarrett, Adam Kosto, Brian Catlos, Alan Ryder, Jeffrey Bowman, Gregory Milton, Thomas Barton, Cullen Chandler, etc.[12]

There is yet another aspect that makes us especially value this research. As mentioned above, the people of Catalonia, a country with a strong and marked identity in medieval Europe, spoke Catalan, a Romance language. Some linguists point out that Catalan and Occitan form a group that must be differentiated from the group of Hispanic languages and from French dialects.[13] This Occitan-Catalan linguistic and cultural space obviously developed in the early Middle Ages. The language spoken a thousand years ago in the Catalan counties, and also perhaps in the lands of Lleida, was the one used in this Occitan-Catalan linguistic space.[14] The similarities with the language used in Languedoc were remarkable, although no one disputes the fact that Catalan and Occitan are two different languages.[15] This tight link reflects the common history that existed in the early Middle Ages, which lasted until the thirteenth century. And, as said above, this link, which we also find in social and political realities, is also more or less reflected in the landscapes of these territories.

In fact, the anthropic landscape of Old Catalonia is very similar to the one we would have found to the north of the Pyrenees, for example, in the Occitan lands of Languedoc. Both territories belonged to the Carolingian world. Catalonia was a march of the Carolingian Empire, a land bordering Hispania. But our study goes beyond Old Catalonia. As we have seen, this original territory, which extended from the Llobregat to Roussillon and to Ribagorça, expanded to the south, where it occupied lands with a strongly Islamized population. This process created a territory, New Catalonia, whose newly arrived population had to adapt to a country that already had slightly different characteristics. Some of the original, Islamic inhabitants stayed, but most of them fled and headed south.

Thus, the study of Catalonia, a unified territory but one conquered in two stages, will be the subject of the next few pages, in which we will see the contrast between Old and New Catalonia, between such cities as Girona or Barcelona, and others, like Lleida or Tortosa, between lands where farmsteads or ecclesiastical villages predominate, and lands with a more concentrated

---

12 Vilar, *La Catalogne dans l'Espagne moderne*; Elliott, *The Revolt of the Catalans*; Bonnassie, *La Catalogne du milieu du Xᵉ siècle à la fin du XIᵉ siècle*; Bisson, *Fiscal Accounts of Catalonia*; Freedman, *The Diocese of Vic*; *The Origins of Peasant Servitude*; Shideler, *A Medieval Catalan Noble Family: The Montcadas*; Bensch, *Barcelona and its Rulers*; Guilleré, *Girona al segle XIV*; Jarrett, *Rulers and Ruled in Frontier Catalonia, 880–1010*; Kosto, *Making Agreement Medieval Catalonia*; Catlos, *The Victors and the Vanquished*; Ryder, *The Wreck of Catalonia*; Bowman, *Shifting Landmarks*; Milton, *Market Power*; Barton, *Victory's Shadow*; *Contested Treasure*; Chandler, *Carolingian Catalonia*.
13 Colón, *El lèxic català dins la Romania*.
14 Coromines, *Estudis de toponímia catalana*, vol. I, p. 29.
15 Clear similarities have also been noted between Catalan and Arpitan or Piedmontese. Castellanos, *Els cosins del català*.

settlement, or between castral and new towns. Catalonia, together with Occitania, stood between France and the Hispanic lands. In the thirteenth century, the French monarchy, based in the north, conquered the Occitan lands, while the Catalans captured the southern territories, then in the hands of the Islamized Andalusians. This was the case during the Middle Ages; then, throughout the modern period, we find different political realities, caused by the fact that, from the end of the fifteenth century, the same monarch was at the head of the Catalan-Aragonese Crown and the Crown of Castile (and many other countries). The northern Catalan *comarques*, with their capital at Perpignan, were ceded to France by the 1659 Treaty of the Pyrenees.

Be that as it may, the characteristics of Catalonia, a country linked to the lands of the north and the south and, at the same time, culturally very different, are the reasons why this territory is worth studying. We analyse the characteristics of its landscape and the changes that have occurred over the centuries. However, in the following pages, we also consider the close links between Catalonia and its neighbouring countries to the north and south, which may often help us to better understand its characteristics. We will focus on, for example, research done on the Occitan lands and the Valencian *comarques*.

This book delves into the historic landscape of a Mediterranean country. Throughout these chapters, I will make constant comparisons with landscapes of other European territories and, in particular, those on the Mediterranean coast. If we want to fully understand the breakthroughs in research on the Catalan historic landscape, we need to consider the similar research on nearby countries. Here is a brief presentation of the topics under analysis in this volume.

Transition from the Ancient to the Medieval Period

Research carried out in the last decades across most of Europe has been significant.[16] Simultaneously, archaeological excavations in some Catalan *comarques* have led to remarkable advances in our knowledge of the settlements in the early Middle Ages, like the layout of the houses, the materials they were made of, or the existence of silos, and of *trulls* (in Catalan, from *torcularia* (Latin), 'wine presses' or 'oil presses'), and burials. Nevertheless, the novelties we are most keen to discover are those that might reveal such data as the position of villages, how many houses there were in each of them, the division of rural territories, or the links between medieval hamlets (*vilars*, in Catalan) and the Roman *villae*.

---

16 Brogiolo and Chavarría, *Archeologia postclassica*.

Open Villages

The book by Benoît Cursente on the society of Gascony in the high Middle Ages was key in raising our awareness and curiosity about so-called 'open villages', or 'villages of houses' (those comprised simply of an agglomeration of houses, in French: *villages à maisons*).[17] Cursente depicted a complex society with a strong emphasis on the peasants, but with differences among village communities. In the Catalan Pyrenean *comarques*, where there is a predominance of this type of open village, we have discovered evidence of confrontation, after 1000, between rural communities and lords who intended to build castles and control pre-existing communities (Chapter 2).

Ecclesiastical Villages

The books on ecclesiastical villages edited in France in 1989 and 1994 by Michel Fixot and Elisabeth Zadora-Rio had an impact on studies conducted to the south of the Corbières Massif.[18] In fact, in some Catalan *comarques*, at the time of the creation of population clusters, one of the main determining factors was the possibility of building *sagreres*, houses clustered closely for protection within a perimeter of sacred space surrounding a church (a phenomenon known as *ensagrerament*, as coined by Ramon Martí in 1988). These are also termed *celleres*.[19] This process can also be found in other European countries. As will be seen in Chapter 3, this process can be analysed in more detail, for example, by undertaking archaeological excavations. On the other hand, it should be said that while studying ecclesiastical villages brings us closer to the peasants who inhabited them, it is most revealing about the power relationships between ecclesiastical and secular lords.

Castles

Research carried out in Europe in the last few years on castles in the early Middle Ages has changed our view of this period; it shows a process of fortification which was much earlier than was previously assumed based on written sources.[20] Unfortunately, major studies published in Europe on medieval fortifications hardly refer to the exceptional buildings created in Catalonia before 1000, like the castles of Vallferosa and Santa Perpètua de Gaià, or after this date, the feudal castles of Mur, Viacamp, Llordà, and Lluçars. Despite this, in the book by Oliver Creighton, which very rightly defends the need

---

17 Cursente, *Des maisons et des hommes*.
18 Fixot and Zadora-Rio ed., *L'église, le terroir*; Fixot and Zadora-Rio ed., *L'environnement des églises et la topographie religieuse des campagnes médiévales*.
19 Martí, 'L'ensagrerament: l'adveniment de les sagreres feudals'.
20 Christie and Herold ed., *Fortified Settlements in Early Medieval Europe*.

CHAPTER 1

to carry out studies that go beyond the borders of the different countries.[21] This will be analysed at length in Chapter 4.

Castral Villages

Research on castral villages in Languedoc, carried out by Dominique Baudreu, facilitates our understanding of many Catalan villages still clustered around a castle.[22] The interest in villages next to castles dates back a long time, in view of the studies of *incastellamento* (concentration of the population within walls), a process carried out in Italy.[23] Nevertheless, we now know that, as shall be seen in Chapter 4, castral villages could have originated as a result of the following three factors: a tradition much earlier than 1000 (perhaps as a consequence of the peasants' contribution), the need to protect oneself when the frontier with the Muslims was too close, and the desire of the lords to attract population from the district to their castles. This awareness facilitates understanding the processes of *encimbellament* (a Catalan term for the process of moving a village to a higher level for security reasons) and the ensuing abandonment of such villages, moved to a lower level, away from the castle.

New Towns

Studies on Occitan *bastides* (an Occitan term which means 'to build', 'to construct', hence *vilatges bastits*, 'constructed villages' triggered an interest in the study of Catalan new towns. As will be seen in Chapter 5, many studies and books on new towns in Europe have lately been published. What we should be seeking in such towns is not only their exceptional planning but also the fact that they provide an insight into the power relations as well as the economic situation. In Catalonia, new towns should be related to town charters of privileges, franchise jurisdictions, and the creation of new sites for marketplaces, but in certain other European places, new towns are often related to colonization processes and land control (e.g., Occitania, Wales, or Slavic countries).

Hamlets

In English, the word '*hamlet*' or, in French, the word *hameau*, corresponds to the word *vilar* in Catalan, used in the Middle Ages (and surviving as a fossilized place name).[24] To better understand the settlement processes in the early Middle Ages, mainly those of Pyrenean lands, *vilars* play an essential

---

21 Creighton, *Early European Castles*, p. 24; Creighton, *Castles and Landscapes*.
22 Baudreu, 'Une forme de villages médiévaux concentrés'.
23 Toubert, *Les structures du Latium médiéval*.
24 Roberts, *Landscapes of Settlement*, p. 16.

role, since as many as half a dozen families could live in them. Chapter 6 deals with this semi-dispersed settlement process.

Farmsteads

We can find dispersed settlements in many European countries.[25] The reasons for scattered versus concentrated settlement are related to relief, vegetation, climate as well as specific social relations and even traditions. There were farmsteads on marginal lands and on flat and fertile lands. Farmsteads were located within village territories or parishes (Chapter 6). It has also been pointed out that the creation of many farmsteads should be related to the lords (at least they did not raise any objections). Many years ago, Jaume Vicens Vives studied the *remences* war in which relatively rich peasants from the late Middle Ages, who lived in farmsteads and, backed up by the monarchy, revolted against their lords.[26] Although the outcome of this confrontation should not be overstated, this clash ended in victory for the peasants and their release from legal servitude.

Towns

Researching references to towns (*viles*, in Catalan) entails delving deep into the central centuries of the Middle Ages, as these settlements came into being and grew around a marketplace, the result of an economic and demographic reality and also a social one. Some of these towns arose as a result of the issuing of a population charter (*Carta de poblament*, in Catalan). The origin of towns was tightly linked to the beginning of a different social model, in which merchants and craftsmen were very significant. This will be seen in Chapters 5 and 7.

Cities

To understand the urban landscape, it is essential to become familiar with the origins of cities, often from a Roman or Muslim past. Furthermore, studying cities involves discovering a society with traits different from those of the rural world. This knowledge has spurred us to delve into urban planning and zoom in on streets, squares, and central places (Chapter 7). According to recent research, full awareness of the evolution of urban space planning can be achieved by defining 'plan units'.[27] More recently, in the European context, a fair number of studies on the urban world have been published.[28]

---

25 Roberts, *Landscapes of Settlement*, 76; Roberts, *Lost Farmsteads*.
26 Vicens Vives, *El gran sindicato remensa*.
27 Conzen, *Alnwick, Northumberland*; Gauthiez, *Atlas morphologique des ville de Normandie*.
28 Simms and Clarke ed., *Lords and Towns in Medieval Europe*.

Old Fields

The last few decades have seen the publication of a wide range of studies on fields created or reorganized in the Roman period.[29] Such research points to two conclusions. On the one hand, pre-medieval continuities in some places are complex. On the other hand, many Roman-looking landscape features are, in fact, the result of later transformations, especially from the Middle Ages. As will be seen in Chapter 8, in many Catalan cultivated lands there is evidence of the influence of their pre-medieval past, despite the existence of profound transformations dating back to the end of the Western Roman Empire. We often find more remnants of the Roman past on roads rather than on fields, as these were usually organized according to a pre-existing network of roads.

Coombs and Valley Bottoms

In Mediterranean countries, the utilization of valley bottoms has been significant throughout the centuries, even before the Middle Ages. This flat floor space in a valley was often divided into slotted strips or plots. This phenomenon has been studied in North Africa and the eastern Mediterranean region of Palestine.[30] In Catalonia, as will be seen in Chapter 9, we can find valley bottoms furrowed by a river as well as valley bottoms deprived of any visible watercourse. The latter have come to be known as *comes* ('combes' or 'coombs') or valley bottoms. Many places, especially on land with no considerable rainfall, were in all probability the first cultivated and inhabited places. Studying medieval *comes* can lead us to focus our attention on the so-called *New Catalonia*.

Terraces

Terraces existed long before the Middle Ages on the Mediterranean coast, in among other places, Israel,[31] Greece, Cyprus, and the south of Gaul. A full understanding of the Mediterranean landscape requires a proper appraisal of their significance. Recently, in the north of the Iberian Peninsula, some archaeological excavations have provided evidence that by the early Middle Ages, terraces already existed close to inhabited places.[32] In western Catalonia, I have collaborated on projects to date dry farming terraces by Optically Stimulated Luminescence (OSL), which has enabled us to date accurately dry farming terraces to the high Middle Ages. Additionally, as will be seen

---

29 Chouquer, *L'étude des paysages. Essais sur leurs formes et leur histoire*.

30 Fenwick, *Early Islamic North Africa*, p. 90.

31 Gadot and others, 'The Formation of a Mediterranean Terraced Landscape'.

32 Ballesteros and Criado, 'El paisaje agrario medieval en Galicia'; Ballesteros, 'La arqueología rural y la construcción de un paisaje agrario medieval'.

in Chapter 9, an excavation conducted in Cerdanya has produced accurate dating from before then.[33]

Cultivated Land Strips

The ancient fields, i.e., those with a Roman past, often were divided into land strips. This is true of many *comarques*, as confirmed by documentary evidence. Nevertheless, in Chapter 9, our focus will be on land strips found in colonized lands. In Germanic countries, medieval historians have for many years been interested in *Waldhufendörfer* (literally 'forest villages'): rural settlements built on both sides of the road. Farming or cultivation was done on the land behind them, which formed long strips of land that ran up to the forest.[34] Other examples of such practice can be found in other places, e.g. regular plot divisions in a few new towns in the region of Gascony, in the southwest of France.[35] These are coaxial field systems (or coaxial *bands*), which were very common in many European places in the Middle Ages.[36] In Catalonia and Valencia, many places have been discovered, especially after the Christian conquest, whose land was divided into strips and designated by drawing lots between farmers. Overall, this leads us to infer the existence of land surveyors (Cat. *agrimensors*) in charge of mapping out the land with accurate precision.[37]

Irrigated Lands

Research on hydraulic systems carried out in the Balearic Islands and Valencia has been the basis for further studies on irrigated lands, for example, in Catalonia, specifically in the regions of Tortosa and Lleida. It should be said at this point that the topic of irrigated spaces has been a source of controversy and discussion among scholars and experts in the historic landscape. We particularly need to know more about irrigation systems before the arrival of the Muslims as this practice, to a greater or lesser extent, must have existed by then.[38] We should study clearly how irrigated spaces evolved over the centuries

---

33 Rendu and others, 'Reconstructing Past Terrace Fields in the Pyrenees'.

34 Ennen and Jansen, *Deutsche Agrargeschichte vom Neolithikum bis zur Schwelle des Industrie-zeitalters*, p. 11.

35 Lavigne, *Essai sur la planification agraire au Moyen Âge*.

36 Chouquer, *Les parcellaires médiévaux en Émilie et en Romagne*, p. 219.

37 Recent studies also suggest that not all coaxial strips of land had been organized after the year 1000 and that some of them had been organized in the early Middle Ages and were closely related to old roads. See Bolòs, *El paisatge medieval del comtat de Barcelona*.

38 This note translated from Catalan reads as follows: 'The existence of aqueducts or ditches that carried water from distant points to their destination, in the Roman past, in the Camp de Tarragona, has been identified around Constantí, on the bridge of Les Caixes'. Prevosti, 'Els estudis de paisatge al territori de la ciutat romana de Tarraco', p. 209.

26   CHAPTER 1

under Islamic rule (eighth to twelfth centuries) and assess the impact of the growing significance of cities. At that time, large *hortes* (irrigated and intensively cultivated spaces) were created, for example in Lleida and Tortosa.[39] It is also important to discover what happened after the Christian conquest, as many aspects changed, but in some places, there was, in all probability, continuity. All these things are important for understanding the historic landscape, particularly in the regions of New Catalonia (Chapter 10).

Mills

Studying mills means studying construction, landscapes, and social relationships. Much research has been done across Europe on hydraulic mills, and human-operated mills, mainly vertical and horizontal wheel water-powered mills.[40] In Catalonia, all types of mills can be found, although horizontal wheel mills are the predominant type. In the Carolingian period, there was a significant increase in the use of water-operated millstones, possibly caused by a social change. On the other hand, the likely influence of Muslim tradition favoured the spread of horizontal wheel mills powered by a vertical storage tank that delivered water under pressure (*molins de cup*, in Catalan). This will be seen in Chapter 11. Another interesting factor to consider is the close relationship between mills and irrigated spaces.

Forests

Across Europe, in the last few years, there have been important contributions to the study of vegetation from the past. Such research has allowed, for example, the release of ground-breaking volumes on the environmental history of medieval forests in Europe.[41] As indicated in Chapter 12, the studies on vegetation from medieval Catalonia have followed a methodological approach whose search for information is not based only on written documents or archaeological excavations but on pollen analysis as this technique affords a considerable amount of information on what the plant landscape was like and how it changed throughout the medieval period. From this information, we can then compare the written documents on, for example, the use (and often abuse) of natural resources.

---

39 I use the Catalan word *horta*, which has a meaning like that of the Castilian *huerta*, i.e., a set of irrigated land.

40 Mousnier ed., *Moulins et meuniers dans les campagnes européennes*; Jaccottey and Rollier ed., *Archéologie des moulins hydrauliques, à traction animale et à vent*.

41 Hoffmann, *An Environmental History of Medieval Europe*; Bépoix and Richard ed., *La forêt au Moyen Âge*.

Livestock and Pastures

For some time, we have been aware of the importance of *transhumance* (or 'migratory herding') for Cistercian monasteries. We have also learned that, for example, a few large Carolingian abbeys (like Sant Miquel de Cuixà), well before 1000, also owned a great number of animals.[42] However, in the last few years, there has been a change in relation to the assessment of livestock history in the medieval economy. Principally, pollen analysis has verified the significant role of livestock and pastureland in the early Middle Ages.[43] This discovery, in all probability, can also be applied not only to Catalonia but also to many other lands in Mediterranean Europe (Chapter 12).

Roads

Eric Vion published a study on communication routes in western Switzerland in 1989, which changed our perspective on how to study historical roads. Roads are extremely important elements of the landscape.[44] These will be analysed in Chapter 13. This analysis cannot be limited to studying a few main roads, as was the traditional practice. Instead, we need to imagine a closely-knit network of roads and paths. On the one hand, many roads were inherited from the past, and on the other hand, the *raison d'être* of these roads was their frequency of use. Some research has been done recently in Cerdanya, Pallars Jussà, Baix Llobregat, and Alt Penedès that leads us to conclude that studying such routes provides information on many other aspects of the past landscape.

Large Territories

Kingdoms, counties, and bishoprics were limited by boundaries whose location, relative positions, and changes over time are worth studying (Chapter 14). In the last few years, across Europe, boundaries, and frontiers have become the theme of numerous research efforts.[45] We also need to study their impact on neighbouring territories. On the other hand, it is worth considering at this point that Catalonia was divided between the eighth and the twelfth centuries by a frontier that separated the land ruled by Frankish kings and Christian counts, from the land controlled by the Islamic authorities of Al-Andalus. As will be seen in this volume, whenever we refer to castles, castral districts, or

---

42 *Catalunya carolíngia, vol. VI: Els comtats de Rosselló, Conflent, Vallespir i Fenollet*, ed. by Ponsich, docs. 55, 126, pp. 115, 172 (years 864 and 879).

43 Riera and Palet, 'Aportaciones de la Palinología a la historia del paisaje mediterráneo'.

44 Vion, 'L'analyse archéologique des réseaux routiers'.

45 Bartlett and MacKay ed., *Medieval Frontier Societies*; Sénac, *La frontière et les hommes*; Abulafia and Berend ed., *Medieval frontiers*; Baron and others ed., *Ériger et borner diocèses et principautés au Moyen Âge*; Rippon, *Kingdom, Civitas, and County*; Gasc and others ed., *Las fronteras pirenaicas en la Edad Media*.

repopulation, this practice influenced how the territory was organized and also determined the shape of some counties (like Berga and Manresa) and a few bishoprics (like Vic and Roda).

Smaller Territories

One of the most interesting topics to investigate and understand is the boundaries of small districts, basically, villages or parishes. As far as the origins and the features of these territories are concerned, three factors need to be considered: a farming tradition, based on the economic needs of a specific community, a pre-medieval tradition, stemming from the Roman *fundi*, and lordly impositions intended to preserve or sometimes even modify boundaries. Traditionally, the significance of knowing about village boundaries was largely minimized and even disregarded, even though some of them could provide significant information as they may be quite ancient. Research carried out in France or England has proved the importance of studying village boundaries.[46] In Catalonia, recent research has raised awareness of the importance of village territories that extend far back into the past, e.g., Vila-sacra (Fig. 67). This will be dealt with in Chapter 14.

Place names and Cartography

In Chapter 15, we focus on toponymy. Recent research has revealed the importance of the study of place names in order to learn about the past landscape; from knowing when these names were created, to seeing them according to the farmers' point of view since they were the ones who often created these place names. Finally, Chapter 16 will be devoted to cartography as a science that allows us to represent the past landscape and, at the same time, discover its characteristics. This leads us to understand and appreciate current and old aerial photographs. The chapter includes a commentary on the characteristics of projects such as the English HLC (Historic Landscape Characterisation) and the Catalan PaHisCat.

Final Remarks

One brief note should finally be made on the naming of people and places. As regards people, principally counts and kings from the Middle Ages, their names will be their usual vernacular Catalan version (e.g., Jaume I or James I, Guifré el Pilós or Wilfred the Hairy). Place names will be referred to by their Catalan form, except for larger cities with a long historic tradition of

---

46 Rouche, *L'Aquitaine des Wisigoths aux Arabes*; Baron and others ed., *Reconnaître et délimiter l'espace localement au Moyen Âge*.

nomenclature and a widely accepted translation into English. I use this formula for all the Catalan-speaking areas where Catalan is an official language. Only in the *comarques* from the French Département des Pyrénées-Orientales, to avoid misunderstandings, I will include the official French form alongside the Catalan counterpart, for example, Pesillà or Cuixà (Catalan names) will also be written in French as Pézilla and Cuxa. As regards Occitan toponymy, we will provide the official place name plus its Occitan counterpart in brackets, as this formula brings us closer to the medieval setting and language of the epoch.

Other aspects are worth considering, as regards terminology. According to research from recent years, we can distinguish between the early Middle Ages, defined as the period from the sixth to the tenth century, the high Middle Ages, from the eleventh century to the mid-fourteenth century, and the late Middle Ages, from the mid-fourteenth century to the late fifteenth century.

In the contents of several chapters in this book, I have added a description of the main aspects of each topic with a commentary on specific cases, as this will enable us to explore each topic further and bring the reader closer to specific realities of the Catalan *comarques*. In these case studies, I have attempted to reflect on, if not all, most of the *comarques* (Fig. 2). Despite that, I acknowledge that, for practical purposes, I have had to shortlist the examples; there are certainly many other cases of villages, fields, irrigated land (*hortes*), boundaries, and cities that could have been cited and mentioned, but I have opted to leave them out of this volume to ensure conciseness.

As indicated in this introduction, the contents of this book owe a great deal to recent studies from the last few years in Europe. I am also deeply indebted to a sizeable amount of research work carried out in Catalonia. *The Historic Landscape of Catalonia* aims to disseminate the origins of a country in Mediterranean Europe endowed with a long historic tradition.

Before concluding, I would like to thank Paul Freedman for the support I received from him as a great scholar of the medieval history of Catalonia. His advice has been of paramount importance in defining some content, as well as in the publication of this text. I am also grateful for the translation by Mariona Sabaté Carrové, who has always shown great enthusiasm in her work. I am also indebted to Brepols Publishers for their interest in the publication of this book. Finally, I would like to send a warm thank you to my wife, Imma Sànchez-Boira, for her comments and suggestions on the content of the text and, especially, her patience with my long working hours under a messy pile of books and papers. Her support has seen me through months in which, too often, COVID-19 has forced us to stay locked up at home.

Lleida, December 2021

CHAPTER 2

Houses Become a Village

The Villages of the Pyrenees

Introduction

Villages and farmhouses occupy a central position in any settled, rural landscape. They are inhabited by men and women who organize and use the space around them. These individuals work the cultivated land, walk their roads, remember where the boundaries are and also recall the names of places. In the following pages, we will study villages, especially their constituting features such as houses, churches, castles, or any deliberate plan for a living space. In this chapter, we will focus on the so-called 'open villages', where houses constitute a village that does not depend on proximity to a church or castle. Such villages can be considered the oldest and most basic. In Catalonia, we find open villages mainly along the valleys of the Pyrenees, on the northern and southern slopes. Here, in addition, we present the findings from a few archaeological sites and how they contribute to our understanding of medieval settlements. At the end of the chapter, we can expand our vision to other *comarques* and I will also focus on early medieval necropolises, which often provide more information about the inhabitants of the place than the few preserved remains of houses. Finally, we comment on the results obtained from two sites excavated in fortified places, inhabited in the Islamic period, and located near Lleida and Fraga.

What Do We Know About Medieval Villages?

From the first chapters of this volume to Chapter 7, we discuss inhabited settlements, particularly what they were like in the Middle Ages and how they were formed and transformed over the centuries. To this end, we have consulted written documents, become familiar with and interpreted current maps, and analysed the results of excavations conducted to the present. These three sources of information combined can allow us to better understand facts that are far from simple.

Over the last few decades, a typology of Mediterranean medieval settlements has emerged that can be applied to the current volume: open villages made up solely of houses (in French: *villages à maisons*), ecclesiastical villages, castral villages (or hilltop villages), and new towns. This will be our focus in the next few chapters. However, despite the convenience and usefulness of this general classification, some cases deserve special attention. Taken to extremes, one may even argue that there are as many cases as there are inhabited settlements. For example, recent archaeological findings have challenged some ideas about castral and ecclesiastical villages.[1] Contrary to many historians' claims,[2] Aymat Catafau states that the dialogue between written sources and archaeological findings becomes a constantly humbling experience for historians, as they need to re-read and re-interpret documents whenever new evidence emerges.[3] This position is a far cry from that of those who reject, wrongly in our view, the relationship between archaeology and history.[4] Nowadays, the scientific community fosters closer communication between archaeologists, historians, and geoscientists.[5]

Having analysed settlements, from Chapter 8 onwards, our study will focus on how settlers and farmstead dwellers used what was around them and adapted it to their needs. For example, we will explore how villagers worked fields and irrigated land, how they used forests and pasturelands, how they organized the network of roads, and even how they established the boundaries of usable land. Sometimes, it was the feudal lords who acted as catalysts in the transformation of the surroundings of inhabited settlements; more often, it was the peasants who struggled to preserve their inherited lands, transform them, and, by so doing, create new landscapes.

The Morphogenesis of Villages

As said above, recent studies have enabled us to establish a classification of medieval settlements, making it possible to identify the origin of nearly all Catalan villages. In broad terms, villages in northeast Catalonia created from a *sagrera* (that is, villages that grew around the parish church) are ecclesiastical villages; Pyrenean villages are made up of groups of houses, and the villages in New Catalonia are most commonly castral villages. Finally, new towns (*viles noves*) can be found everywhere. Although this overview is generally correct, further explanations and analyses are necessary, as there are many exceptions to the general rule.

In the twentieth century, the geographers Griffith Taylor and Michael Robert Conzen started talking about morphogenesis as applied to the study of both rural and urban settlements.[6] Nevertheless, the earliest precedents for the current morphogenetic studies of villages date back to research carried

---

1 Catafau and Passarrius, '"Village ecclésial" et cellera en Languedoc-Roussillon'.
2 Bourin and Zadora-Rio, 'Pratiques de l'espace: les apports comparés des données textuelles et archéologiques'.
3 Catafau, 'Le modèle de "village ecclésial" en Languedoc, Roussillon et Catalogne', p. 122.
4 Austin and Alcock ed., *From the Baltic to the Black Sea. Studies in Medieval Archaeology*.
5 Izdebski and others, 'Realising consilience'.
6 Taylor, 'Environment, Village and City'; Conzen, 'Morphogenesis, morphological regions, and secular human agency in the historic townscape'.

out in France at the end of the twentieth century.[7] Awareness, across southern Europe, of the existence of villages that grew around a castle, a church, or were simply made up of houses, was heightened by many studies carried out in the 1980s and 1990s by Michel Fixot and Elisabeth Zadora-Rio, Dominique Baudreu, Benoît Cursente, and Aymat Catafau.[8] For example, Catafau's doctoral thesis focused on villages from the region of Roussillon at the northernmost end of medieval Catalonia.[9] These early studies have greased the wheels in recent decades for further studies on medieval inhabited settlements in Catalan *comarques*. The groundwork for such research is based on written documents and, mainly, modern cadastral maps. Although the use of modern maps may have caused a few errors — it may be difficult sometimes to identify all the changes to the landscape over the centuries — such maps continue to be an optimal tool for the study of high medieval villages. Additionally, the full understanding of the dissemination of this research involves comprehending the close relationship between these studies of medieval settlements and research by historians such as Pierre Toubert and Pierre Bonnassie from the last quarter of the twentieth century focusing on the importance of social changes that took place around the year 1000.[10]

The Contribution of Archaeology

To begin with, we will focus on the conclusions reached as a result of archaeological excavations of early medieval sites. Then, our attention will turn to the so-called *villages à maisons*, villages made up of houses, usually open villages, without walls.

Archaeological excavations are a mainstay of historical landscape research. The archaeology of the medieval past allows us to understand where the inhabited settlements were located, what the houses and spaces for storing cereals or keeping cattle were like, as well as identifying areas of industrial activity or places intended for religious services. Archaeology also helps us learn about cemeteries, fortifications, mills, forges, and can even allow us to date cultivated lands. Certainly, excavations have given us new insights into what existed in the early medieval period. In this respect, it is worth mentioning Gian Pietro Brogiolo and Alexandra Chavarría-Arnau whose archaeological

---

7 Fixot and Zadora-Rio ed., *L'église, le terroir*; Fabre and others ed., *Morphogenèse du village médiéval*.

8 Fixot and Zadora-Rio ed., *L'église, le terroir*; Fixot and Zadora-Rio ed., *L'environnement des églises et la topographie religieuse des campagnes médiévales*; Baudreu, 'Une forme de villages médiévaux concentrés'; Cursente, *Des maisons et des hommes*; Cursente, 'Le village pyrénéen comme "village à maisons"'.

9 Catafau, *Les celleres et la naissance du village en Roussillon*.

10 Toubert, *Les structures du Latium médiéval*; Bonnassie, *La Catalogne du milieu du Xe siècle à la fin du XIe siècle*.

Early Medieval Settlements

The transition between the Roman and medieval periods is a long-standing issue that continues to attract the attention of historians and archaeologists.[12] To fully understand this transition period, it is essential to discover the changes in the places where peasants and feudal lords lived. To this end, the following questions will be answered: firstly, we need to know the chronology of these transformations, and whether this chronology was uniform everywhere. We also need to figure out whether there was a noticeable loss of population and if, as a result, any areas were left empty. Similarly, it is also important to understand the relationship between the Roman *villae* and the new spaces where medieval peasants lived, known as *vilars* (hamlets, in English), a settlement often formed by sunken featured buildings, or pit-houses (*Grubenhauser*), or made of rammed earth, or even stone. We also need to verify the places where feudal lords who held most of the power in the new medieval society lived, as their philosophy differed considerably from that of the members of the Roman senatorial class. Concerning all of the above, written documents reveal very little, therefore it is only data provided by archaeology that will facilitate the answers to these questions. In the next few paragraphs, we will consider this issue, and demonstrate the main results of research carried out over the last few years.

Excavations have allowed us to obtain valuable information on early medieval settlements. According to recent results, we know of the existence of plain villages, often next to former Roman *villae*, and also hilltop villages (*vilatges encimbellats*, in Catalan). The houses were made mainly of wood or rammed earth. There were often a large number of silos (*sitges* in Catalan) next to the houses. According to Jordi Roig, in the *comarca* of Vallès, there are archaeological sites from the sixth to eighth centuries of Visigothic period as well as sites from the Carolingian era, the ninth to eleventh centuries.[13]

The plains were home to the majority of the excavated villages from the sixth to eighth centuries. Some of them were set up on the same spot, or close to, a former Roman *villa* (e.g. Plaça Major in Castellar del Vallès, L'Aiguacuit,

---

11 Brogiolo and Chavarría-Arnau, *Aristocrazie e campagne nell'Occidente da Costantino a Carlo Magno*; Brogiolo and Chavarría-Arnau, *Archeologia postclassica*.
12 Wickham, *Framing the Early Middle Ages*; Christie, *The Fall of the Western Roman Empire*.
13 Roig, 'Asentamientos rurales y poblados tardoantiguos y altomedievales'; Roig, 'Vilatges i assentaments pagesos de l'Antiguitat tardana'; Roig, 'Formas de poblamiento rural'.

Can Palau de Sentmenat, Santiga [Vallès] or Vilauba [Pla de l'Estany]).[14] However, other houses were built far from the former settlements before the Middle Ages (Can Gambús 1 and Ca l'Estrada [Vallès], La Solana [Garraf]).[15] Sometimes the houses were wooden huts (e.g. Can Gambús [Vallès], La Solana in Cubelles [Garraf], or Ca l'Estrada in Canovelles [Vallès]) whereas other houses had walls of stone or rammed earth (El Bovalar [Segrià], El Serradar [Empordà], and Vilaclara [Bages]). As mentioned above, these houses were accompanied by silos for storing cereals (e.g., Can Gambús had 232 silos, Els Mallols [Vallès], 139, or the settlement of La Solana, 87).[16] In addition, at many of these early medieval sites, wine presses (*torcularia*) have also been found, as well as, surprising though it may seem, silos containing skeletons, probably of male and female slaves.[17] In sum: there was an abundance of settlements, of small *vilars*, and of society under lordly rule, plus, as evidenced by the laws of the time, plenty of slavery (see the ninth book of the Visigothic *Liber iudiciorum*).[18] In Chapters 12 and 13 there is an analysis of how important livestock farming must have been in tandem with cereal cultivation (silos) and vineyards (wine presses). And, as has been pointed out, in a way, we can refer to villages through the identification of collective spaces, such as a church, a cemetery, a place with silos, a press, a mill, a well, a cattle enclosure, and streets, squares, and fortifications.[19]

As regards the Carolingian era, there were many hilltop villages (e.g., Castellar Vell, in Vallès), and many other villages were on the plains. The latter could even be located in the same spot as their preceding site (e.g. L'Aiguacuit [Vallès]). Additionally, other settlements that are worth mentioning are those that could be considered detached single-family farmhouses, later known as farmsteads (*masos*, in Catalan) (e.g., Ca l'Estrada and Can Gabús [Vallès]).[20] In the Carolingian period, hilltop villages were enclosed within walls like Santa Creu de Llagunes (Pallars Sobirà) or Caulès (La Selva). These will be further analysed in the chapter devoted to castles and castral villages (Chapter 4). We will find that many of these villages, enclosed behind walls, were built on far older, ancient remains. In general, after studying several excavated Carolingian sites, these findings reflect a social and economic change concerning the Visigothic period: the sites from before the eighth century reveal the existence of a production centre, despite differences, linked to the

---

14 Regarding Vilauba: Castanyer and others, 'Després de les *villae*'.
15 Roig, 'Formas de poblamiento rural', pp. 124–28.
16 Roig, 'Silos, poblados e iglesias', p. 147.
17 Folch and others, 'Les explotacions rurals tardoantigues i altmedievals a la Catalunya Vella', pp. 96, 100.
18 *Llibre dels judicis. Traducció catalana moderna del* Liber iudiciorum, ed. and trans. by Bellés, pp. 265–74.
19 Maufras and others, '*Villae* — Villages du haut Moyen Âge en plaine du Languedoc oriental', p. 99.
20 Roig, 'Silos, poblados e iglesias', p. 159.

CHAPTER 2

tradition of *fundi* from the late Roman Empire, whereas Carolingian sites are often rather associated with housing.[21] In England, lately, there has been recognition of the importance of changes during the 'long eighth century' (*c.* 700–830), a time of remarkable economic development, an increase in worked land, a growth in commercial relations, and, above all, changes in the placement of settlements.[22] In Catalonia, this century coincided with the years under Islamic rule, which may have made these developments less obvious, while these changes transformed the economic milieu and social relationships of western Europe, as Chris Wickham has pointed out.[23]

The Houses Become a Village: The Pyrenean Settlements

One of the main topics dealt with at a congress held in Toulouse in 1997 was that of open villages made up of houses.[24] Following earlier studies by Benoît Cursente on Gascony,[25] it was important to figure out whether it was possible to find this form of settlement in other Pyrenean regions and *comarques*. Certainly, in the last few years, several studies have unveiled open villages, made up of houses, in several Catalan *comarques*, from Ribagorça to Conflent[26] and Ripollès.

Characteristics of Open Villages Made Up of Houses

The main character trait of this type of village is the fact that it was the houses alone that shaped the village's urban planning. As will be seen in the following chapters, in contrast to castral or ecclesiastical villages, open villages were not built around a castle or a church. The houses stood apart from each other and, often, were lined up on either side of a street that could also be a communication road. They can be named *'pobles de cases'* (initially, Benoît Cursente referred to them as *'villages casaliers'*).[27] According to studies of Gascony, the layout of these villages in the high Middle Ages was drawn up in relation to the houses owned by the most influential families in the village. Another characteristic

---

21 Folch and others, 'Les explotacions rurals tardoantigues i altmedievals a la Catalunya Vella', p. 103.

22 Astill, 'Understanding the identities and workings', p. 46; Hansen and Wickham ed., *The Long Eighth Century*.

23 Wickham, 'Overview: Production, Distribution, and Demand'.

24 Berthe and Cursente ed., *Villages pyrénéens*.

25 Cursente, *Des maisons et des hommes*.

26 Catafau, 'Le rôle de l'église dans la structuration de l'habitat sur le versant français des Pyrénées'.

27 Cursente, 'Le village pyrénéen comme "village à maisons"', p. 166.

of these settlements was that they were open and had no walls around them to enclose or protect them (hence 'open villages'). Other defining traits allow us to differentiate them from other types of villages.

One of the most obvious distinguishing features is the location of the church. In villages made up of houses, churches were not built in the middle of the inhabited settlement (which, perhaps, already existed), but rather at one end of the village, sometimes quite far away from the houses. This could be because the churches were built on land owned by the founding family or families or perhaps they were built with the idea of Christianising a previously pagan place. Finally, one of the last aspects of these villages is that they lacked any fortification, castle, manor or fortified house (*domus fortis*; Fr. *maison forte*); as will be seen below, which, if they exist nowadays, it is thanks to their construction during a later phase, either at the end of the Middle Ages or well into modern times.

Some Examples of Villages Made Up of Houses

As explained above, villages made up of houses abound in mountainous areas, especially all over the Pyrenees. In Catalonia, many of them were built in the *comarques* of Conflent and Ripollès, Cerdanya, Alt Urgell, Pallars, and Ribagorça, and also in Andorra. Studies of Sobrarbe in western Ribagorça also reveal the importance of this form of settlement.[28] Certainly, in other European regions, there is a similar form of high-altitude settlement. Some of them are on the northern side of the Pyrenees. In Gascony, the village of Louvie-Soubiron (Oc. Lobièr Sobiran or de Haut)[29] is one prime example. There are other examples in the Massif Central, in the middle of France, and in the Alps.[30] Others have been documented in Navarre and the Basque Country.[31] A few villages in the Pyrenean sector of the Camino de Santiago have similar characteristics.[32]

Next, we will explain a few cases that will illustrate this topic by zooming in on villages that, although transformed to a greater or lesser degree, still exist today.

---

28 Domergue, 'La diversité morphologique des habitats du Sobrarbe', p. 454.
29 Cursente, *Des maisons et des hommes*. It is certainly necessary to relate this place to a place where wolves abounded and to a process of division of population, as we also find in the region of Pallars Sobirà.
30 Grélois, 'Pourtour et quartiers périphériques'.
31 Jusué, *Poblamiento rural de Navarra en la Edad Media*.
32 Passini, 'Habitat villageois médiéval le long du chemin vers Saint-Jacques de Compostelle', pp. 221–25.

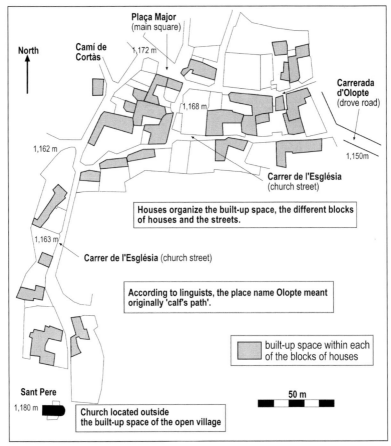

Figure 3. Village of Olopte (Cerdanya). Example of an open village, without a castle and with the church separated from the houses.

Olopte (Cerdanya)

In this village on the sunny side of Cerdanya, 1,170 m high, the houses and groups of houses line two streets, *Carrer Major* (Main Street) and *Carrer de l'Església* (Church Street) (Fig. 3). Its Romanesque church, dedicated to Saint Peter, stands 200 m further south, next to a small hill. *Carrer Major* runs along a former, more ancient path, a drove road (i.e., an animal herding path). The name of the village, pre-Roman in origin, comes from *orots bide*, 'calf road'.[33] The former language of Cerdanya, which was similar to Basque, ceased to be spoken in the transition from the Roman to medieval periods. This settlement was organized by its residents, and has lasted, probably with

---

33   Coromines, *Onomasticon Cataloniae*, vol. VI, p. 34.

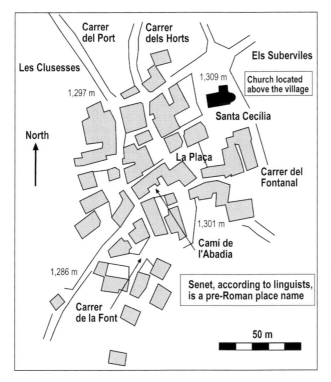

Figure 4. Village of Senet (Alta Ribagorça). Example of an open village. The church is above the set of houses (some *capmasos*) that formed this settlement.

many changes, to the present. It should be noted that the toponym may have been coined before the houses were even built. In this case, we can see that it was the houses, together with the buildings associated with them, that set up the village, probably long before the church was built.

Sorpe (Pallars Sobirà)

The village of Sorpe, located at 1,260 m high, also extends along a 200-metre-long street, currently called *Carrer Major* (Main Street). Its Romanesque church, dedicated to Saint Peter, was built 60 m away from this main street to the northeast of the village. Its main houses, about a dozen of them, are almost certain to have existed in the Middle Ages, although they would have been smaller than their current modern versions. Despite changes over the centuries, the current village has, in many respects, inherited most of the traits from the former 1000-year-old village. Its layout is medieval, although it would be unwise to state that Sorpe has undergone continuity with no changes whatsoever since the early Middle Ages. This is an issue which needs further study as we do not know what its houses before 1000 were like or even where they were located.

Senet (Vilaller, Alta Ribagorça)

The village of Senet stands on the left side of the river Noguera Ribagorçana, around 1,300 m high. Senet is made up of several houses, around 200 m from the mountain stream (which drains into the Noguera). In this case, the village is not built along a road but is laid out on a network of streets and one main square. Outside the village, the main housing area, stands the Romanesque church dedicated to Saint Cecilia (Fig. 4). Logically, we must assume that the houses were built in the early Middle Ages and, later, before the year 1000, the pre-Romanesque church was built in the upper part of the village. In this case, the continuity, which undoubtedly exists between the current houses and the *capmasos* from the high Middle Ages, is obvious. It should be noted, at this point, that the village holds an interesting document from 1118, which reports on thirty-three *capmasos* dating back to the early twelfth century.[34] Perhaps, if the site were ever excavated, the remains of the foundations of some of the current houses could be revealed.[35]

As regards the term *capmàs*, it should be noted that in territories of clustered settlements, the term *capmàs* (*caput mansus*, in Latin) was used, especially in relation to the house in the village, rather than the term *mas* (*mansus*, in Latin; *farmstead*, in English), which, as will be seen in Chapter 6, after the year 1000, was the usual nomenclature in territories of dispersed settlements.

Later Transformations

In some villages of houses, hence open villages, there had been significant changes by the end of the Middle Ages. Violence during the later Middle Ages or the mere existence of mighty feudal lords led villages to build fortifications, enclose houses within walls, or even create, at a certain distance, a new, fortified village.

In Pallars Sobirà, these villages of houses abound, as reported in studies carried out in this *comarca* on settlements. They underwent significant transformation from the end of the fifteenth century onwards, particularly following the long war of conquest suffered by the last count of this Pyrenean territory, Hug Roger III.[36]

Espot (Pallars Sobirà)

According to Joan Coromines, Espot is a toponym written in a pre-Roman language, originating from the word *ezpotu* (a pair of separate neighbourhoods),

---

34 *Col·lecció diplomàtica de l'Arxiu Capitular de Lleida*, ed. by Bolòs, doc. 240.

35 Bolòs, 'La vila de Senet (Alta Ribagorça) al segle XII'.

36 Bolòs, 'Un territori en temps de guerra'.

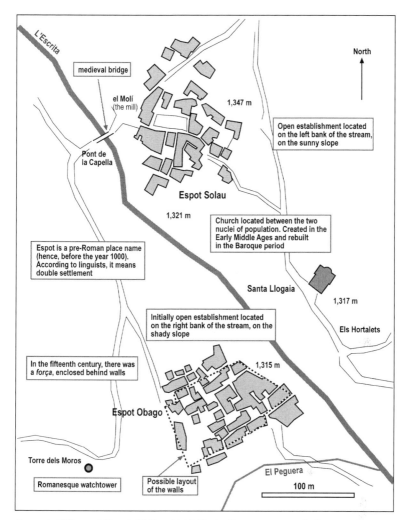

Figure 5. Village of Espot (Pallars Sobirà). A village composed of two neighbourhoods. In the middle is the church. The southern neighbourhood was walled in the late Middle Ages.

most possibly coined before the year 1000.[37] This word describes the fact that this was a double village, made up of two populated areas, one for each side of the river Escrita. Initially, this was, in all probability, an open village. Amidst these two areas, next to the watercourse, there is a church, dedicated to Saint Leocadia (an ancient dedication, of Visigothic tradition) (Fig. 5). It seems that, perhaps due to the pressure of the lord of the place in the later Middle Ages,

---

37 Coromines, *Onomasticon Cataloniae*, vol. IV, pp. 137–39.

the areas located on the right bank of the river, called Espot Obago, became a 'força', a fortification (in Latin *fortitudo*) or a walled town. In 1487, following a siege and under threat of setting the village on fire, it was agreed that one side of the wall would be pulled down. Four days later, the doors on the gateway were opened and the king's army was allowed into the village.[38] Espot had shifted from being an open village to becoming a fortified one, like most of the ecclesiastical or castral villages we will analyse in the next few chapters.

Àreu (Alins, Pallars Sobirà)

Àreu, located at the northernmost end of the Vallferrera valley, is a twin village in the same *comarca* as Espot. A text from the sixteenth century records the village of Àreu and alludes to a *força* and a *vila*, a village.[39] The text points out that in the *força* there was a castle, a tower, a church, and houses, the walls of which acted as defensive barriers. To the south, there was the *vila*, without walls but with a church, dedicated to Saint John.[40] The current distance between the two villages is around 400 m. The current church of the village, dedicated to Saint Clement, stands out against the background of the valley, and is located amidst the houses. But initially, the church may have stood at one end of the village, which, over the centuries, expanded towards the north. On the other hand, it is not certain whether the modern church of Saint Clement stands on the same site as the former Saint John's church. What really matters is that, after the year 1000, the lord of the place decided to build a new fortified hilltop village, far from the open village made up of houses on the plain. In any case, there was no relocation, unlike what happened in other *comarques*. In fact, this 'splitting-into-two' process has been associated with the process of *incastellamento* described in Chapter 4.

A Few Other Details about the Villages Made Up of Houses

Some questions remain unanswered as a result of what has been said in the paragraphs above. For example, can we date back the origin of this form of settlement to before 1000? According to written documents from the Carolingian period, the origins of many of these open villages belong in the period before 1000.[41] It is uncertain what exactly was there before *c.* 806.

---

38 Bolòs, 'Un territori en temps de guerra', pp. 55–57. In 1484, Ferdinand the Catholic commissioned the Count of Cardona Joan Ramon Folc III to conquer the Pallars. After several years of war, in June 1487, the castle of València d'Àneu, the count's last fortress, surrendered.

39 Tragó, *Spill manifest de totes les coses del vescomdat de Castellbò*, ed. by Baraut, p. 58.

40 Bolòs, *Els orígens medievals del paisatge català*, p. 212.

41 Bolòs and Hurtado, *Atles dels comtats de Pallars i Ribagorça*; Bolòs and Hurtado, *Atles dels comtats de Cerdanya i Berga*.

Nor do we have enough evidence of continuity in the location where the houses stood, before or after the year 1000. These structures are frequently documented in the late Middle Ages, and they were most likely renovated and expanded, but they remained on the same site later on. We should remember that in the high Middle Ages, the dwellings of these open villages, usually detached from each other, often created clusters of buildings around them. It was precisely in this cluster, in Gascony, where, according to Cursente, the main family and those families dependent on the main household (so-called *botoys* in Bearn) lived.[42] But while the origin of this society, which was highly stable and often linked to livestock farming activities, can probably be dated to the early Middle Ages, the location of these houses is uncertain before the late Middle Ages. This issue should be addressed in the future. But it is worth considering that, as will be pointed out in the later chapter on hamlets (Chapter 6), inhabited settlements in the early Middle Ages were unstable.

The Necropolises from the Early Middle Ages

It may often seem that we find more evidence of settlements from the early Middle Ages in necropolises, found everywhere, than in the rather scarce remains of inhabited places studied so far.[43] We shall skip this detail and instead briefly mention some facts about tombs that will also allow us to know and understand other aspects of the early medieval landscape. For simplicity's sake, we can point out that there were the following types of burials in Catalonia in the early Middle Ages: rock-cut graves and slab tombs and, more rarely, graves dug into the soil, sarcophagi, and *tegulae* tombs. It should also be noted that we usually find these burials before the year 1000 or in a prominent place, for example, on top of a rock, or next to a church. The former, those located on a rock or hill, tend to be the most ancient. Digging a tomb into a rock required a considerable amount of effort (i.e., possibly specialists were assigned this task), even more so if we consider the characteristic poor housing where people lived. This leads us to infer that they could have the symbolic value of marking territory[44] or showing the social dominance of a person or group of people, or could be the result of tradition, stemming from the end of the Roman Empire and extending to the twelfth century.

We can date the tombs next to churches generally to around the year 1000 while those on hills or rocks may well be early medieval. Therefore, since the necropolis could not be far from the inhabited area, the appearance of isolated

---

42 Cursente, *Des maisons et des hommes*, p. 388; Cursente, 'Le village pyrénéen comme "village à maisons"', p. 163.

43 Bolòs, 'L'estudi de les necròpolis medievals catalanes, entre l'arqueologia i la història'.

44 Martín Viso, '¿Datar tumbas o datar procesos?'; Martín Viso, 'Espacios funerarios e iglesias'; Martín Viso, 'Ancestors and landscape: early medieval burial sites'.

44   CHAPTER 2

burials far from a church bears witness to a nearby settlement from the early Middle Ages. This is common practice in other European countries.[45]

Despite this, it is worth noting that, according to several studies, the process of *inecclesiamento* (as reported by Lauwers),[46] of attraction between churches, tombs, and even inhabited settlements, existed in some places long before the eleventh-century Peace and Truce of God movement.[47] The research allows us to conclude that, in certain places, the churches soon attracted the tombs of the most powerful men from the area and, in turn, the rest of the population (therefore in France, from Larina, Jau-Dignac or Saleux, and also several places in the Iberian Peninsula). In Catalonia, there are also examples of the orientation of tombs towards churches, long before the second millennium AD, perhaps in relation to the churches of Sentmenat (Vallès Occidental), Artés (Bages), Creu de Sant Salvi de Casserres (Berguedà), Obiols (Berguedà), Camps (Bages),[48] Porqueres (Pla de l'Estany), Empúries (Alt Empordà), Sant Feliu de Guíxols, Santa Cristina d'Aro (Baix Empordà)[49] or Sant Sadurní de Pesillà (Roussillon).

With regard to medieval necropolises, we shall refer to the excavations of the cemetery of the village of Vilarnau (Roussillon) and the ensuing detailed research on burials, which date between the ninth to the fourteenth centuries.[50] The tombs were all located within thirty steps of the church, although for some, it could be stated that they were excavated long before the eleventh century, back when the inviolable perimeter (*sagrera*) was created. Later, the space close to the church was used to dig silos, and this indicates its connection with *cellers* or *sagrers* created after the year 1000 and, possibly, the existence of a few houses.[51]

Pertegàs (Calders, Moianès)

In the years 2007–2009, a large section of the necropolis of Pertagàs was excavated.[52] The thirty-seven tombs studied were made of slabs dated between the seventh and eighth centuries. Pertegàs was not documented until 965.[53] This document from the tenth century refers to around two hectares of vineyards. In the tenth century, this place, Pertegàs, appeared to have been connected

---

45 Chavarría Arnau, 'The topography of early medieval burials', p. 107.
46 Lauwers, 'De l'*incastellamento* à l'*inecclesiamento*'.
47 Treffort ed., *Le cimetière au village dans l'Europe*; Maufras and others, '*Villae* — Villages du haut Moyen Âge', p. 97.
48 Gibert, *La fi del món antic i els inicis de l'edat mitjana*, pp. 45–51.
49 Burch and others, 'Formas de poblamiento y ocupación en el ámbito rural del Nordeste catalán desde el Bajo Imperio romano hasta la época visigoda'.
50 Passarrius and others, *Vilarnau: un village du Moyen Âge*, pp. 145–257.
51 Catafau, 'Le modèle de "village ecclésial"', p. 43.
52 Gibert, *La fi del món antic i els inicis de l'edat mitjana*, pp. 62–66.
53 *Catalunya carolíngia, IV: Els comtats d'Osona i Manresa*, ed. by. Ordeig, doc. 967.

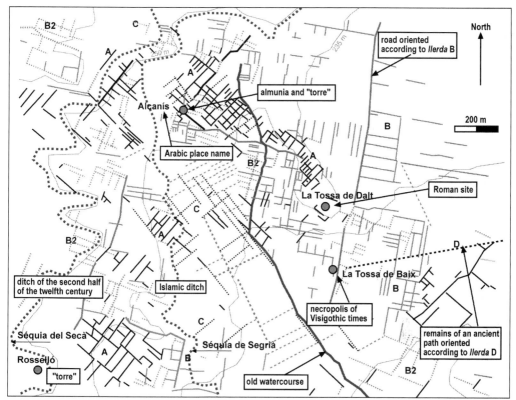

Figure 6. Necropolis of La Tossa de Baix (Rosselló, Segrià) and its surroundings. In the same agricultural area, in the Roman period there was one settlement, then another Visigothic one, and in the Islamic era a different one.

with the south along a road that must have followed the ridge separating the terms of Calders and Talamanca; to the west, Pertagàs bordered on the district of Viladecavalls. Even to date, close to this place, there is evidence of the *mas* (farmstead) of L'Estrada. According to its toponym, Pertegàs must have been a place for cutting wood.[54]

The necropolis stands on an elevated place on the isthmus of a meander of the Calders stream. It must be assumed that, in the Visigothic period, this settlement was the place where the Pertegàs farmhouse was later built, about 260 m away from the tombs. Studies of the bones of the men, women, and children who were buried there demonstrated that people from that time were accustomed to hard work. In one of the northernmost tombs, a pottery pitcher was found, possibly connected to a pagan ritual, a type common in burials in the early Middle Ages. It is unknown whether there was any church

---

54 Coromines, *Onomasticon Cataloniae*, vol. VI, p. 210.

46   CHAPTER 2

nearby. Even though around the seventh century, burials close to churches were possible, this, as I have said, was not recorded as a common practice until a date closer to the year 1000.

La Tossa de Baix and its Surroundings (Rosselló, Segrià)

The necropolis of La Tossa de Baix was excavated in 2000. Fifty-five empty tombs were discovered in the rock, almost all facing east to west.[55] There must have been many more of them. They were ^{14}C-dated to the Visigothic period (AD 645–782).[56] The location of the village where people lived is yet unknown, although it was probably not very far from the rock where the dead were buried. Be that as it may, we can state that all the space around this place is intensely populated land worked for many centuries (Fig. 6). Suffice it to say that around 300 m north of this necropolis, on a higher position, lies the archaeological site of Tossa de Dalt, a former Roman *villa*. Besides, around 700 m northwest towards Tossa de Baix, within the same cultivated space, the *almúnia* of Alcanís was built in the Islamic era;[57] possibly, in this Islamic period, there must have been a large ditch called Séquia de Segrià.[58] This *almúnia*, after the feudal lords' conquest in 1149, became a *torre*. Further explanations of Islamic *almúnies* and *torres* from after the Christian conquest will be given in Chapter 6.

Our interest in the surroundings of the necropolis of Tossa de Baix is based on the possibility of discovering essential information that goes beyond tombs excavated from 1,300-year-old rock. Certainly, this necropolis aids us in the definition of *terroir*, an agricultural economic space,[59] and it also allows us to ensure its continuity of use over the centuries, despite milder or more violent transitions. The political and social upheavals that occurred between the second and twelfth centuries AD were so dramatic that the location of the settlement changed; however, this agricultural space was always well-tilled in the Roman period, during the Visigothic and Islamic eras, and after the Christian conquest of 1149. A similar situation can be found in many other Catalan locations, as well as in Languedoc, and also in Italy and the north of France.[60]

---

55   Graells, 'Dues noves necròpolis del Segrià: Escalç (la Portella) i la Tossa de Baix (Rosselló)'.
56   Folch and Gibert, 'L'ús de datacions radiocarbòniques en jaciments altmedievals', p. 297.
57   *Almúnia* is an agricultural settlement from the Muslim era. This type of settlement was generally linked to the ruling leadership of the cities that owned it.
58   This canal must have been built in the eleventh century to bring water to the northern sector of the city (the *medina*) of Lleida. It also enabled the fields along its course to be watered. After the count's conquest (in 1149), the canal was enlarged.
59   See: Leturcq, *Un village, la terre et ses hommes.*
60   Gentili, 'L'archéologie au village en Île-de-France', p. 96.

Islamic Villages

While in Valencia[61] and Aragon[62] several non-fortified villages from the Islamic period have been studied, in Catalonia, for the time being, none of them has been excavated. On the other hand, as shall be seen in the coming pages, significant urban excavations have been carried out in Lleida, Balaguer, and Tortosa, as well as two inhabited towers or ʾabrāǧ (pl. of burǧ), in Solibernat and Safranals. Despite this, we believe that a few existing towns may still retain the remains of urban planning from before the Christian conquest; this was our assumption in the case of the town of Ascó.[63] Certainly, this has also been suggested for the Portuguese town of Mértola.[64] Recently, a doctoral thesis has reconstructed the location of the sector of the village of Aitona, after the Christian conquest, where a Muslim community lived.[65] The space occupied by the Islamic quarter extended along three nearly parallel, barely straight streets, organized along a small valley and its western side. Indeed, many Muslim towns pivoted around a central gorge or stream, whose main street ran along with them. Others may have stretched along a slope or a flatter terrain.

To look for examples of settlements larger than small ʾabrāǧ or towers, which we will analyse in Chapter 6, we must go further south. Worth mentioning are the dispersed houses located on a mountain slope, supposedly of Berber origin, located in La Vall d'Uixó.[66] Also, in Valencia, an excavation in the Torre Bofilla (Bétera) revealed a part of the tower and an enclosed space or albacar, a residential area made up of forty-six houses.[67] There were houses of many different sizes: the largest 270 sq m and the smallest nearly 190 sq m. The urban network delimited around ten blocks of houses. There were walls, wells, and baths. Further to the south, in Murcia, we find the alqueria of Calasparra, with a similar structure and around sixty houses.[68] In all likelihood, some of the inhabited settlements in the Islamic period in New Catalonia may have been quite similar to it.

---

61 Bazzana, *Maisons d'al-Andalus*.

62 Sénac, *La frontière et les hommes*; Sénac, *Un 'village' d'al-Andalus aux alentours de l'an Mil*.

63 Bolòs, *Els orígens medievals del paisatge català*, pp. 214–17.

64 Boissellier, *Le peuplement médiéval dans le sud du Portugal*, pp. 403, 653.

65 Monjo, 'Sarraïns d'Aitona, el tresor de la família Montcada', p. 107.

66 Bazzana and others, *Les château ruraux d'al-Andalus*; Bazzana, 'Maison-bloc, maison-enclos et maison agglutinante'.

67 López Elum, *La alquería islámica en Valencia*. It should be borne in mind that, in principle, the *albacar* was a walled enclosure, not suitable as a habitual residence but used as a refuge by the inhabitants of a village or the immediate territory on those occasions of threat from an enemy.

68 Pozo, 'La alquería islámica de Villa Vieja', p. 169.

Conclusions

In this chapter, we have come a few steps closer to the earliest medieval settlements, *vilars* sometimes located near the former Roman *villae*, often built near new churches or fortifications. For now, little is known about them. Perhaps one of the main points we have learned is that there were many of them; this has been confirmed in Vallès and Roussillon.[69] But, overall, these *vilars* were unstable; many of them disappeared or, perhaps, were moved hundreds of metres. Others — sometimes referred to in written documents as *villae* — ended up becoming villages in the high Middle Ages, consisting of a church and, sometimes, a fortification. Added to that, other *vilars* became dispersed farmsteads. In Chapter 6, further details will be provided on both *vilars* (hamlets) and *masos* (farmsteads).

In this chapter, we have analysed in detail the characteristics of villages made up of houses, which were nearly always open villages. The *villages à maisons* are well documented in the high Middle Ages, but assuredly, whether with a similar morphology or not, they already existed before the year 1000. These are villages that must have originated before the creation of feudal castles and before many of the churches were built, which we systematically find outside the centre of these settlements. Unfortunately, based on our present knowledge, we still cannot pin down the origins of how these open villages made up of houses were planned any earlier than the late Middle Ages. However, we know that, nowadays, this type of settlement is found almost exclusively in the Pyrenean region.

---

69   Kotarba, 'Les sites d'époque wisigothique de la ligne LGV', p. 63.

CHAPTER 3

Churches, Monasteries, and Villages

In Each Village a Church

Introduction

In most of Europe, villages are built around churches. In some parts of Catalonia, the number of villages which grew up around churches is remarkable. Aymat Catafau's doctoral thesis shows the spread of this phenomenon in the diocese of Elna (in Roussillon) and its importance shortly after the year 1000. We can find a similar process in other bishoprics, such as Girona, Vic, or Barcelona. It is certainly necessary to relate this fact to the influence of the Church at that time and to the creation of the institution of the Peace of God. We need to consider that in every medieval village there was a church, which, however, in open or castral villages, was often at some distance from the inhabited centres. In this chapter, we will also mention other religious institutions, such as the Benedictine or Cistercian monasteries, collegiate churches, or the commanderies of military orders, as well as the possibility of inhabited places close to these buildings. Finally, we will briefly focus on the continuation of pagan forms of religion well into the Middle Ages.

What Do We Know About the Church and the Landscape, and About Villages Built Around a Church?

In the Middle Ages, across Europe, the influence of churches and monasteries on the population was remarkable, and not only for purely religious reasons. Together with cathedrals, collegiate churches (communities of canons), convents, and commanderies of military orders, churches and monasteries became everyday institutions, present in almost every aspect of life. This allows us to understand their impact on the territorial organization. On the other hand, the close relationship between churches and inhabited settlements continued throughout the medieval period, even before AD 1000. Lately, there has been much discussion about the long process of *inecclesiamento*, concerning the polarization of space around the church, a process that began well before the year 1000.[1] Archaeological excavations have made it possible to relate, from a very date, churches, burials, and houses. Additionally, in the high Middle Ages, the existence of Benedictine or Cistercian monasteries had an impact

---

1 Lauwers, 'De l'*incastellamento* à l'*inecclesiamento*'.

50 CHAPTER 3

on the society around the territory where they were built, as well as on their economy, and, in turn, altered the landscape of other areas.

On this issue, the church within the landscape, two pioneering works should be cited. One of the earliest books to focus on the impact of churches on the European landscape was a volume edited by Michel Fixot and Elisabeth Zadora-Rio called *L'église, le terroir*, published in 1989. On monasteries, it is worth recalling Mick Aston's ground-breaking work called *Monasteries in the Landscape*, first edited in 1993 (and re-edited in 2000).[2] In both cases, attention was drawn to how specific elements of the landscape, a church, or an abbey, were able to transform their entire environment.

While the original elements of open villages, dealt with in the previous chapter, were probably the houses themselves, ecclesiastical or *sagrera* villages, as the name suggests, had a church as their initial element. The desire to find out the origin of the currently inhabited settlements motivated, at the end of the last century, a growing interest in this type of ecclesiastical village. In France, as pointed out above, Fixot and Zadora-Rio, in 1989 and 1994, published two collections of works that define the characteristics of this form of settlement in much of western Europe.[3] Shortly after, for Catalonia, the doctoral thesis by Aymat Catafau (published in 1998), on *cellera* or *sagrera* villages from the Roussillon, made a fundamental contribution to extending our knowledge of ecclesiastical villages.[4] Further research has been conducted, even a book on this topic, that has pushed forward our knowledge of medieval settlements.[5]

Churches

The earliest churches date back to the end of the Roman period and the beginning of the Middle Ages. Initially, we find mainly oratories, funeral churches, and baptismal churches. In many parts of Europe, most of the earliest churches were close to the cathedral, located in the city. Some of them were built in the countryside: parish churches built by the bishop as well as chapels (in some cases, considered almost as parishes) by local lords.[6] As regards the territory under study, it is worth noting the *villa Fortunatus*, located north of Fraga (Baix Cinca), where a church was built, is related to the Christianization of the ruling classes at the end of the Roman era (Fig. 7). It has been noted that the end of the fifth century marked the beginning of conflicts between the bishop and secular landowners over the jurisdiction

---

2 Aston, *Monasteries in the Landscape*.
3 Fixot and Zadora-Rio, *L'église, le terroir*; Fixot and Zadora-Rio, *L'environnement des églises et la topographie religieuse*.
4 Catafau, *Les celleres et la naissance du village en Roussillon*.
5 Farías and others, *Les sagreres a la Catalunya medieval*.
6 Codou, 'Dans les campagnes aussi, des monuments chrétiens', pp. 126–30.

CHURCHES, MONASTERIES, AND VILLAGES 51

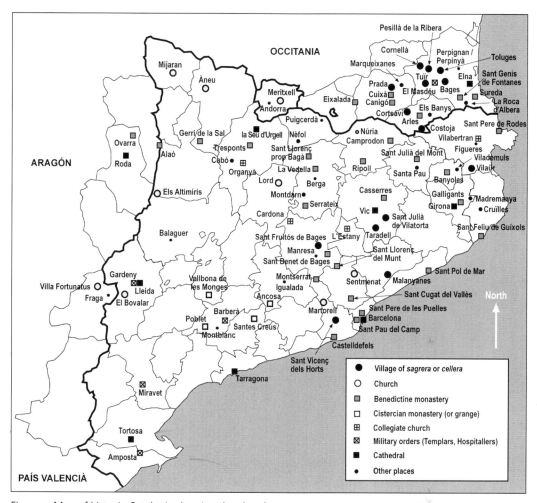

Figure 7. Map of historic Catalonia showing the churches, monasteries, and villages mentioned in this chapter.

of churches.[7] A constant confrontation between the bishops and the secular nobility persisted throughout the Middle Ages and, as we shall see, even affected the layout and organization of some villages.

In Catalonia, during the Visigothic period, studies have concluded that there must have been a remarkable growth in the number of churches located near *vici*,[8] near former *mansiones* located next to the main roads of communication,

---

7 Brogiolo and Chavarria, *Aristocrazie e campagne nell'Occidente*, p. 127.
8 One of the senses of the word *vicus* (plural *vici*) was that of a village located in a rural area (*pagus*). It also had other meanings, such as the neighbourhood of a larger settlement.

52   CHAPTER 3

near strongholds (or *castella*), and also in many other settlements. The church of Santa Margarida de Martorell (Baix Llobregat) was sited precisely where the Roman *mansio Ad Fines* had once stood.[9] We also believe that in the centre of valleys and territories in general, where previously pagan temples may well have existed, churches were built, which were often dedicated to the Virgin Mary.

Furthermore, over the centuries under Carolingian rule, a significant number of churches were certainly built. Thanks to the numerous records preserved from the ninth and tenth centuries, we can now document most of them. It suffices to browse through the maps published in the ten volumes of *Atles dels comtats de la Catalunya carolíngia* (Atlas of Counties in Carolingian Catalonia) to realize their importance. As regards Charlemagne's empire, some capitularies point out the need to reconstruct or restore churches (or should there be too many of them, destroy them). Certainly, in 895, it was established that there should be no more than four or five miles (about six or seven and a half kilometres) between the parishioners' homes and their place of worship.[10]

Characteristics of Sagreres

Studies carried out in recent decades have made it possible to define the characteristics of *sagreres* and point out the diverse importance of *sagrera* villages in different *comarques*. According to the historical scholarship, after the year 1000, the thirty-step space around the church became a protected space (at least this was so for the ecclesiastical authorities) to prevent (or at least discourage) access by violent people. From then onwards, the immediate vicinity of many churches was used not only for burying the dead but also to store grain and wine. Silos and cellars were fitted, and, shortly after, housing even began to be built. They were therefore used not only for storing wine (hence their name, *cellera*, cellar) but also cereals or tools.[11] It should be noted that, according to what we see now, some of these *sagreres* or protected areas, were circular (Fig. 9), while others had a slightly rectangular shape (Fig. 11). Given the size of medieval houses, there were plenty of them, although this would mean that in some places, after a few years, they started to run out of space for burying the dead. It should also be noted that the size of the *sagrera* space depended, as some documents state, on the length of the legs of the person walking the thirty steps, starting from the four walls of the church. Sometimes, the consecration act itself established that, due to the topography, some of the sides fell short of thirty steps. But in general, most *sagreres* were

---

9   Sales, *Las construcciones cristianas de la* Tarraconensis, p. 185–87.
10   Lauwers, 'De l'*incastellamento* à l'*inecclesiamento*', p. 321.
11   Catafau, 'Les celleres du Roussillon, mises au point et discussions', p. 26.

of a similar size. There were exceptions like the churches of Costoja and Sant Llorenç de Cerdans, with only twelve steps, or *sagreres* around some collegiate churches, monasteries, or important churches like in Vilabertran, Sant Miquel de Fluvià, Breda, Castelló d'Empúries, and Guissona, with as many as sixty steps.[12] The chronology of the transformations was not exactly the same everywhere, nor was the space used inside the *sagrera* the same (sometimes perhaps only a part of it was built on).

There is, however, one important aspect: *sagreres* are, in principle, well-dated. This protected space surrounding the church was a consequence of the Church's attempting to impose assemblies to establish an ecclesiastical Peace and Truce. The Peace and Truce of God movement began in Gaul and soon reached the Catalan counties.[13] In 1027, an assembly held in Toluges (Roussillon) (in French, Toulouges) established the protection of the land surrounding the churches, and again in 1030 and 1033 in two council meetings held in Vic (Osona).[14] Nevertheless, as mentioned above, much earlier than that, there were not only tombs, as many excavations have proved, but even buildings around churches, dating to the early Middle Ages. This is the case, for example, in the *comarques* of Roussillon and Berguedà.[15] In the next few pages, these phenomena will be analysed in depth.

Dissemination

We might wonder why some *comarques* were peppered with so many ecclesiastical villages, while in others there were so few of them, particularly in Old Catalonia. A few years ago, we established a contrast between the creation of *sagrera* villages and castral villages and sought to identify whether the reason for these differences was the lords of these villages. We need to consider the difference between secular lords, who built castles and aimed to control the population, and ecclesiastical lords, particularly bishops, who wanted to protect and perhaps control villagers and sometimes owned castles.[16] From this, we came to the conclusion that in places with a powerful bishop, like Abbot Oliba (971–1046), the son of a count and a count himself, from a very early age, the number of *sagreres* grew significantly, and these remained intact for decades. On the other hand, in places whose bishops could not override a count or secular lords, even though at first there might

---

12 Morelló, 'Singularitats (o no) d'un fenomen "català": l'ensagrerament'.

13 Koziol, *The Peace of God*.

14 *Les constitucions de Pau i Treva de Catalunya*, ed. by, Gonzalvo. There are historians who consider that the document of the assembly of the year 1027 is false (Martí, 'L'ensagrerament: utilitats d'un concepte', p. 94).

15 Catafau, '"Village ecclésial" et cellera' p. 122; Gibert, *L'expressió material del poder durant la conquesta comtal*, p. 53.

16 Bolòs, 'Pobles de sagrera i pobles castrals'; Freedman, *The Diocese of Vic*.

54 CHAPTER 3

have been *sagreres*, these were destroyed and nearly all the villages became castral villages or new towns created by a lord. For example, there is a stark contrast between the county of Vic, where Abbot Oliba, considered one of the spiritual founders of Catalonia, was highly influential, with a virtually total absence of castral villages, and the county of Pallars (in the diocese of Urgell), with no ecclesiastical villages.

As regards the Catalan bishoprics, the dioceses with the highest number of ecclesiastical villages were Elna, Vic, Girona, and Barcelona. On the other hand, even in some of these bishoprics, the reality of marchlands, organized as castles with a surrounding district (in Catalan, *castells termenats*, 'castles with a territory or district'), where, logically, secular lords held most of the power, was significantly different from those of remote areas, far from the borders. This is the case for the county of Manresa, in the diocese of Vic, or that of Penedès, in the diocese of Barcelona. Also, as previously mentioned, as regards the dioceses of Urgell and Roda, the number of ecclesiastical villages is low. Certainly, we know that during the feudal wars in Pallars, in the eleventh century, many *sagreres* were destroyed, as documents which report complaints of violent acts demonstrate. Moreover, *sagreres* hardly existed in the regions of Lleida, Tarragona, and Tortosa, as in the eleventh century they were under Islamic rule. Besides, as pointed out by Catafau, in the bishopric of Elna, ecclesiastical villages were located mainly on low plains and valleys, and were rarely on land over 600 m high.[17]

The *sagreres* facilitated the power exerted by bishops over the territory. Often, ecclesiastical *sagrera* villages were controlled by a bishop, while the farmsteads (*masos*, in Catalan) within the village boundaries were ruled by a secular lord who, in some cases, at the end of the Middle Ages, even dared to plunder *sagreres*.[18] On the other hand, apart from bishops, according to Catafau, monasteries also sometimes utilized *sagreres* to protect their ownership rights in remote places. This was the case, for example, for the Occitan abbey of Lagrasse (in Occitan, La Grassa), with respect to *sagreres* or *celleres* in the villages of Pesillà de la Ribera, Cornellà de la Ribera (in French, Corneilla-la-Rivière) or Prada de Conflent (in French, Prades).[19]

As we mentioned, in many areas of Europe we can find ecclesiastical villages. In some cases, around the church, until the modern era, there were barns instead of houses, a reminder of the original *raison d'être* of Catalan *sagreres* or *celleres*, i.e. protected spaces around a church. Two villages near the Rhine should be noted: Dossenheim an der Zinsel, in Alsace, or the fortified church (*Kirchenburg*) of Riehen, in Switzerland, near Basel.[20]

---

17 Catafau, 'Petites, nombreuses, isolées?', p. 82.
18 Pladevall, *Taradell. Passat i present d'un terme i vila d'Osona*, p. 216.
19 Catafau, 'Le modèle de "village ecclésial"', p. 21.
20 De Meulemeester, 'Même problème, même solution', pp. 105–12.

CHURCHES, MONASTERIES, AND VILLAGES

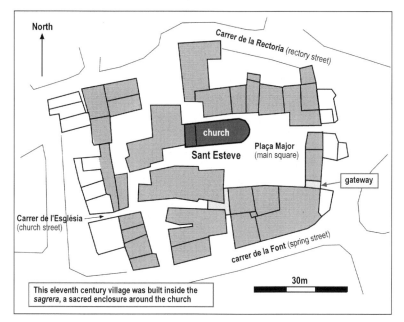

Figure 8. Village of Vilaür (Alt Empordà). The village was created inside the thirty steps established as the *sagrera* around the church. It has changed over the centuries.

Some Examples of Sagrera Villages

Examples of *sagrera* villages abound. Some villages in the space of a former *sagrera* have been well preserved and it is even possible to identify them in the current *parcellation* (or land plot division), while others have been dramatically transformed, while others display no evidence of their medieval layout. It must be said, though, that some *sagreres* were only partially built (for example, on the southern part of the church) and others continued to be used as cemeteries and had no houses. Next follows a description of some of the *sagrera* villages from several *comarques*.

Vilaür (Alt Empordà)

Vilaür, a village in the *comarca* of Alt Empordà, is a magnificent example of a *sagrera* village (Fig. 8). The settlement of *Villadur* was recorded first in 1017, although its origins are further back (maybe an early medieval *Villa Auguri*).[21] Vilaür is in the bishopric of Girona. Nowadays, the church of Saint Steve faces an open square, accessible along with the inside of the *sagrera*, through

---

21 Coromines, *Onomasticon Cataloniae*, VIII, p. 55.

56 CHAPTER 3

a gateway located to the east of the village.[22] The thirty-step boundary of the original holy protected space is still noticeable in the land plot division. Most probably, later on, this village became fortified with a gateway at the entrance in the sixteenth century. In Vilaür the boundaries of the medieval *sagrera* are fossilized in the current town planning, despite the reconstruction of contemporary houses, which often stand on the same site as the older houses.

Sant Julià de Vilatorta (Osona)

Sant Julià de Vilatorta is in the bishopric of Vic. The place was already recorded in 935 (*Villa Torta*) and its church had existed at least since the beginning of the tenth century (901–914). In the diocese of Vic, there were a significant number of *sagreres*, and Sant Julià de Vilatorta is one of them. The documents describe it as a *sagrera* and also a *cellera*. Nowadays, we find a church amidst houses, which were possibly bult on the sites of those constructed in the second half of the eleventh century. In 1028, there is evidence of the existence of a *sagrer*, a piece of land within the *sagrera*. This is believed to be the earliest written reference to a *sagrera*.[23] To the east, the *sagrera* extended along a street, called Carrer del Pont (Bridge Street, in English); beyond this street, there must have been more houses within the protected space of the church's surroundings.[24] On the other hand, to the south-east, the main square (Plaça Major, in Catalan) was under the control of the secular lord of the territory. In the second half of the fourteenth century, eighteen families, apart from the parish rector, lived inside the *sagrera*.

As explained above, the *sagrera* village and the dispersed farmsteads within the municipal district often reflect different realities, but, despite this, they seemed to complement one another. A village depended on a bishop, whereas its surroundings and its parish often relied on a secular lord. Peasant male heirs would sometimes live in farmsteads, while their younger sons (known as *cabalers* in Catalan) lived in ecclesiastical villages. We have found evidence of this practice in many villages in the plain of Vic, e.g. Taradell.[25] There was a duality between *sagrera* villages and dispersed farmsteads in many other *comarques* with a predominance of dispersed settlements, like Garrotxa (in Sant Esteve d'en Bas or Montagut de Fluvià)[26] or Gironès (e.g. Sant Martí Vell).

---

22 Bolòs, 'Aportació al coneixement de la morfogènesi dels pobles del comtat d'Empúries', p. 267.

23 Morelló, 'Singularitats (o no) d'un fenomen "català": l'ensagreLrament'.

24 Puigferrat, *Sant Julià de Vilatorta després de la Pesta Negra*, pp. 117–34.

25 Pladevall, *Taradell. Passat i present d'un terme i vila d'Osona*.

26 Bolòs, 'Le rôle du château et de l'église', pp. 90–97.

Sant Fruitós de Bages (Bages)

There are a few *sagreres* which were partially abandoned or transformed over the centuries; others, as pointed out above, were not even built on. In the village of Sant Fruitós de Bages, we find a *sagrera*, where there is currently only construction in the southern part of its holy space. It can only be accessed through a gateway that opens into the southern side of the *sagrera*. While nearly all of the villages in Osona are ecclesiastical, most of the villages in Bages, to the west of the river Llobregat, were castral in the tenth century as they were situated in march or frontier territory. In this place, the church dedicated to Saint Fructuosus was documented in 942; it is likely, though, that it is earlier in origin. Although it cannot be ruled out completely that before 1000 there were houses around the church, it was only after this date that a thirty-step *sagrera* was set up, and with minor changes, this layout has remained untouched to the present.

Pesillà de la Ribera (Roussillon)

As explained above, in 1998, Aymat Catafau published his doctoral thesis on the *celleres* (cellar spaces) of Roussillon.[27] This research showed the possibility and the importance of the morphogenesis of villages, particularly villages originating around a church. Mainly in the bishoprics of Elna and Girona, the fact that *sagreres* were often used to store wine and cereals, hence utilized as *cellers*, explains the alternative use of the term *cellera*, rather than *sagrera*.[28] Also, as will be seen below, the term *cellera* was used by many secular lords to refer to inhabited areas surrounding a castle. Also, in Roussillon, there are still a few of the prettiest *sagreres* or *celleres* in Catalonia.

The place of Pesillà (Fr. Pézilla-la-Rivière) was first documented in 876 but the name goes back to the Roman period (Fig. 74). The church of Saint Felix was already recorded before 1000, and, in the eleventh century, an inhabited *sagrera* or *cellera* probably developed. This *cellera*, according to Catafau, was soon enclosed within a rammed earth wall.[29] Later, in the thirteenth century, there was a stone and lime wall, hence becoming known as a *força* (a fortress). Documents also indicate that, before the demographic crisis of 1348, there was even an external neighbourhood or quarter.

Currently, there is an almost perfect circle of houses surrounding the church of Saint Felix (Fig. 9). There is a fortified door to the northeast, possibly corresponding to the *Portal d'Amunt* (Upper Gateway) referred to

---

27 Catafau, *Les celleres et la naissance du village en Roussillon.*
28 Catafau, *Les celleres et la naissance du village en Roussillon*; Mallorquí, 'Les celleres medievals de les terres de Girona'.
29 Catafau, *Les celleres et la naissance du village en Roussillon*, pp. 490–94.

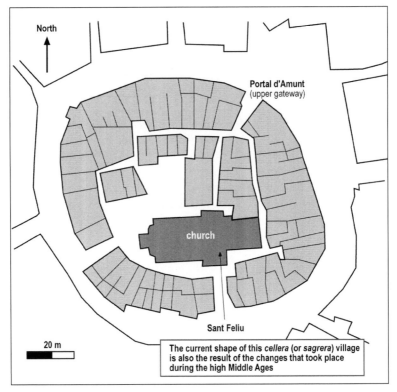

Figure 9. Village of Pesillà (Roussillon). In Pesillà there were two churches: one had only a funerary function, while the other, Sant Feliu, represented on the map, was the centre of a *sagrera* or *cellera*.

in the thirteenth century. Still, it should be noted that, at first, this circular space was thought to have belonged to the former ecclesiastical village from the eleventh century, perhaps slightly enlarged due to the construction of boundary walls. Nevertheless, recent excavations have proved that this boundary, now quite noticeable, is situated a few metres beyond the original boundary of the holy space and therefore does not stand on the earlier smaller *cellera*.[30] This circle of houses then dates back to the expansion of the thirteenth century, when there was a *cellera* and even several lordly houses.

Additionally, in the former territory of Pesillà (formerly, there was a *fundus* from a man called *Pedilius*),[31] there was another church, situated 370 m away from that of Saint Felix. This church, dedicated to Saint Saturnin, was built between the fifth and eighth centuries, and always maintained its exclusively funerary function. Excavations have revealed *tegulae* tombs, which date back

---

30 Passarrius and Catafau, 'Autour de quelques villages du Roussillon', p. 260.
31 Coromines, *Onomasticon Cataloniae*, vol. VI, p. 213.

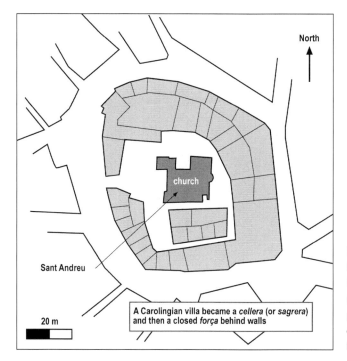

Figure 10. Village of Bages (Roussillon). Research carried out in recent years has made it possible to discover the evolution of this village, built around a church.

to Late Antiquity.[32] Whereas, excavations around the church of Saint Felix only found children's tombs from the seventh and eighth centuries.

As Catafau points out, excavations often conclude that churches are older than the written documentation claims. Nor can we rule out the possibility that, sometimes, churches were built on places with earlier tombs.[33] This practice has also been reported in Sant Andreu de Sagàs (Berguedà).[34] It was even possible for the church to have been built on an earlier inhabited settlement, as could well have been the case in Santpedor (Bages).[35]

In studying the *sagrera* of Pesillà, three essential sources of information have been used: written documents, the cadastre (land registry) from the nineteenth century (unfortunately, only undertaken in France), and archaeological excavations. In this case, the excavation results have required us to amend our preliminary conclusions, which were based on the analysis of maps from the cadrestral research. However, we cannot forget that thanks to this two-century-old official land registry, twenty years ago there was a significant breakthrough in our knowledge on how villages were formed.

---

32 Catafau and Passarrius, '"Village ecclésial" et cellera', p. 119; Passarrius and Catafau, 'Autour de quelques villages du Roussillon', pp. 258–59.
33 Catafau and Passarrius, '"Village ecclésial" et cellera, p. 122.
34 Gibert, *L'expressió material del poder durant la conquesta comtal*, p. 53.
35 Gibert, *L'expressió material del poder durant la conquesta comtal*, p. 31.

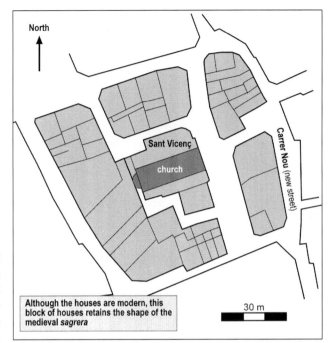

Figure 11. Village of Sant Vicenç dels Horts (Baix Llobregat). In the present town we can still see the quadrangular shape of the *sagrera* around the church.

Then, other in-depth studies on specific places, have allowed — and so will in the future — increasing accuracy.

Bages (Roussillon)

The village of Bages in Roussillon was established as an ecclesiastical village in the eleventh century. However, the place dates to 922 (and it might have existed even much before then). The church of Saint Andrew was not documented until the following century, although it must have been much older. As pointed out by Catafau, until the thirteenth and fourteenth centuries, the area surrounding the church retained its function as the places where the harvest was collected and, accordingly, preserved the term *cellera*.[36] There were also houses. In the twelfth century, this was an enclosed space (perhaps by houses or a wall), with a gateway. We know that in the thirteenth century, the former *cellera* was surrounded by dry moats and a wall; specifically, it is referred to as a *villa* and as a *castrum*. Then, in the fourteenth century, there are references to a defensive wall. Currently, we can still observe an enclosed village, with one access point and a slightly rounded shape (Fig. 10). Certainly, just as an open village (such as Espot) could became a *força*, or fortified village, some

---

36 Catafau, *Les celleres et la naissance du village en Roussillon*, pp. 194–98.

ecclesiastical villages (such as Bages) became *forces* (*fortitudines*): Bages transitioned from being a *sagrera* (or *cellera*), formerly defended by a bishop, to becoming an enclosed village, protected by walls.

Tuïr (Roussillon)

In 956, the *villa* of *Tecorio* was already documented. This place probably owes its name to the presence of huts in the early Middle Ages.[37] Indeed, in a document from 960, there is a reference to a *puig* (hill, in English) with houses, located near — not around — the church of Saint Peter, which could not have been too far from this hilltop *vilar* (or hamlet). There must have been another hamlet like the one accidentally found recently in an excavation within the limits of this township.[38]

Even so, there are remarkable differences between the settlements before and after 1000. Currently, Tuïr (Fr. Thuir) has a quarter called La Cellera around the church. Incidentally, the *sagrera* or *cellera* of Tuïr was not documented until the thirteenth century, when the village became fortified by a wall, enclosing a space wider than that of the former *sagrera*; it was recorded that the wall of the *cellera* had to be reinforced with lime and finished with merlons.[39] In this case, the settlement belonged to the counts of Besalú, and later to the kings of Catalonia and Aragon. It should also be noted that, despite the absence of documents bearing witness to that, the earliest ecclesiastical settlement must have originated, like in many other places, in the eleventh century.

Sant Vicenç dels Horts (Baix Llobregat)

There is also evidence of *sagreres* in the bishopric of Barcelona, for example in the *comarques* of Vallès and Baix Llobregat.[40] In 936, the place of Garrosa had already been recorded. Shortly afterwards, in 955, written records mention a road leading to the church of Sant Vicenç.[41] Currently, it stands in the middle of a block of houses, possibly standing, with very few changes, on a former ecclesiastical *sagrera*. Its total area is 8,750 sq. m, including a church and a few nearby streets (Fig. 11). On the other hand, it must be noted that the current church of Sant Vicenç is larger than that of the eleventh century. At the time when this *sagrera* was defined, the thirty steps around the temple were measured with regard to each of its four walls. As can be seen, the ground plan of this ecclesiastical village must have been square-shaped.

---

37 Coromines, *Onomasticon Cataloniae*, VII, p. 358.
38 Dominguez, 'Les Espassoles'.
39 Catafau, *Les celleres et la naissance du village en Roussillon*, pp. 631–37.
40 Vilaginés, *El paisatge, la societat i l'alimentació al Vallès Oriental*.
41 *Catalunya carolíngia, vol. VII: El comtat de Barcelona*, ed. by Baiges and Puig, docs. 191, 358.

Transformations and Evolution of Sagreres

In 1994, Pierre Bonnassie published an enlightening study on the evolution of *sagreres* in Catalonia. In the first phase, *sagreres* were used as shelters; Bonnassie dates this phase between 1020–1035, coinciding with the Assemblies of Peace and Truce in Toluges and Vic. In 1028, there is documentary evidence of the thirty ecclesiastical steps. Later a stage of the institutionalization of *sagreres* began, which Bonnassie dates to between 1030 and 1060.[42] During these decades, many churches were consecrated, and many houses were built within the holy protected space. In Sant Boi de Llobregat — a village close to Sant Vicenç dels Horts —, in 1054, it seems that there were so many houses within the burial ground that the dead could no longer receive an appropriate burial.[43] In Sant Martí de Cortsaví (Vallespir; Fr. Corsavy), analysed further in the next chapter, there were forty-three *sagrers* within the sagrera. The term *sagrers* refers to each plot of land into which the holy space was divided, used to store cereals or wine and, maybe, build a house. Usually, *sagreres* would contain between five and twenty houses.

Let's now go into the second half of the eleventh century. According to the chronology proposed by Bonnassie, from 1060, a process that altered the fundamental nature of *sagreres* occurred. The most serious event of that time was that many members of the nobility defied ecclesiastical authority by building manors and castles either next to the *sagrera* or even within the holy protected thirty-step area. For example, the lords of Vilademuls and Cruïlles settled within the *sagreres* of these villages. Likewise, in many villages from the *comarques* of Empordà, Osona, and Roussillon, the castle or manor (in fact, in Latin, *domus fortis*) was built next to the initially protected thirty-step space.[44] A few secular lords, Ramon Sunifred being one of them, possibly lord of Rubí, managed to create, before 1080, a *sagrera* in Santa Maria de Malanyanes, in the *comarca* of Vallès Oriental. Gradually, the secular lords lost their fear of spiritual punishment, and there were even acts of violence against people living inside the *sagreres*. Such violence, found clearly in Pallars (between 1060 and 1080), caused the population in this *comarca* to abandon the space around the church. In other places, from 1060, the *sagreres* became fortified, as explained above. In fact, in the Assembly of Peace and Truce of 1173 there are already references to '*ecclesias incastellatas*', or fortified churches.

In some *comarques*, the term *cellera*, originally synonymous with *sagrera*, in the twelfth century, designated housing around a castle, organized under the protection of a secular lord. According to Aymat Catafau, this evidences

---

42 Bonnassie, 'Les sagreres catalanes', p. 73.
43 Catafau, 'Les celleres du Roussillon, mises au point et discussions', p. 24.
44 Bolòs, 'Aportació al coneixement de la morfogènesi dels pobles del comtat d'Empúries', pp. 269–72; Catafau and Passarrius, '"Village ecclésial" et cellera', p. 121.

a process of *incastellamento*.[45] In the next chapter, the examples of La Roca d'Albera (Roussillon) or the new town of Santa Pau (La Garrotxa) will be studied in depth.

Benedictine Monasteries

To understand the organization of the territory in the Carolingian era, it is worth noting the importance of monasteries that, after a few years of uncertainty, ended up being governed by the rule of Saint Benedict. The spiritual and cultural functions of the monasteries, as well as their role in governing and organizing the territory, deserve special consideration, as they were one of the mainstays of the power of the Carolingian kings over the country, as evidenced by the large number of diplomas they received from Frankish monarchs.[46] Indeed, the abbeys themselves became centres of landed domains.[47] Below, we will focus on one aspect of monasteries: their location. Only occasionally shall we refer to the impact and influence of the changes they caused in the surrounding landscape. To assess their relevance, each type of monastery will be illustrated with one example.

Sant Cugat del Vallès (Vallès Occidental): Plain Monastery

Initially, one assumes that the best location for a monastery would be on a plain, with fertile land around it for cultivation, and close to a crossroads. This was precisely the location of Sant Cugat del Vallès. Additionally, this place had a long history behind it, as the monastery was built on the former location of a *castrum* from the late Roman period and a paleo-Christian church.[48] Other monasteries had similar locations: Sant Genís de Fontanes and Sant Andreu de Sureda (Roussillon), Sant Miquel de Cuixà (Conflent), Sant Esteve de Banyoles (Pla de l'Estany), the latter positioned, as its name indicates, next to the well-known lake of Banyoles, Sant Pere de Casserres (Osona), on a meander of the river Ter, Sant Benet de Bages (Bages), next to the river Llobregat, or Santa Maria de Serrateix (Berguedà), right in the middle of a plateau.[49]

---

45 Catafau, 'Le modèle de "village ecclésial"', p. 21.

46 *Catalunya carolíngia, II: Els diplomes carolingis a Catalunya*, ed. by Abadal. Recently, research have been carried out on the monastic domains in Ripollès and the county of Urgell: Costa, *Poder, religió i territori*; Miró, 'Territori i economia als monestirs del comtat d'Urgell'.

47 Lauwers, 'De l'*incastellamento* à l'*inecclesiamento*', pp. 323–27.

48 Sales, *Las construcciones cristianas de la* Tarraconensis *durante la Antigüedad Tardía*, pp. 208–13.

49 *Diplomatari del monestir de Santa Maria de Serrateix*, ed. by Bolòs.

64   CHAPTER 3

Santa Maria de Ripoll (Ripollès): Valley Monastery

In mountainous counties, such as those found in Old Catalonia, it is logical that many monasteries were built at the bottom of the valleys, often near the confluence of two rivers. A notable example is that of Santa Maria de Ripoll, built by Count Guifré I around 880; initially, one of his sons was to become its first abbot. The female monastery of Sant Joan de les Abadesses, created about five years later by the same count for his daughter, is located about nine kilometres east of Ripoll, also on the banks of the river Ter. The monastery of Camprodon (Ripollès, in the county of Besalú) and that of Sant Llorenç prop Bagà (Berguedà) are in similar locations. Next to the latter have been found, on a cliff, caves that were inhabited, which suggests some even older hermit precedents (before the first date on which the abbey is mentioned, in 898).[50]

Santa Maria d'Alaó (Ribagorça): Gorge Monastery

In the Carolingian period, many monasteries were built at the end or in the middle of a gorge (in Catalan, *congost*), a narrow, enclosed pass, furrowed by a river and surrounded by mountains. We find abbeys located in gorges next to the rivers Isàvena (Ovarra), Noguera Ribagorçana (Alaó), Noguera Pallaresa (Gerri), Segre (Tresponts), Llobregat (La Vedella) or Tet (Eixalada). Most surprisingly, some of these monasteries were built in places that were, at the time, very dangerous, because they were very close to the lands still controlled by the Muslims. This is very evident, for example, in the case of the monasteries of Alaó and Ovarra. Despite this danger, many of these abbeys slowly gained a vast patrimony, especially farmland, and sometimes also acquired control of the livestock routes that connected the lowlands with the high mountainous pasturelands, located to the north of the gorge where they were built. Recent excavations have been carried out at the site of the Altimiris, apparently a former Visigothic monastery dedicated to Saint Cecilia.[51] This site is above the Mont-rebei gorge, furrowed by the river Noguera Ribagorçana (flowing over 325 m downstream). This is a hilltop location near a gorge and is, possibly, related to livestock farming activities.

Santa Cecília de Montserrat (Bages): Hilltop Monastery

Some monasteries were built on top of mountains, as these were, in principle, much safer places, but there was a downside that they did not have easy access to water, and this was an essential feature of any inhabited place. A good example of this is the monastery of Saint Cecilia in Montserrat, located on the northern slope of this mountain range, near the site of a castle, probably

---

50   Bolòs and Pagès, *El monestir de Sant Llorenç prop Bagà*, pp. 229–31.
51   Sales and Sancho, 'Monastic Networks and Livestock Activity'.

built in the Islamic period. We can also mention those of Sant Julià del Mont (La Garrotxa), Sant Llorenç del Munt (Vallès Occidental) and Sant Martí del Canigó (Conflent). Surely, in some cases, the choice of location weighed heavily on the holy character that these mountains could have had, even before the Christianization of society around the end of the Roman period. Perhaps their foundation should be related to the set of processes that pursued the Christianization of pagan festivals or temples and of stones, trees, and fountains where non-Christian religious ceremonies were performed. Next, I will discuss the place of Madremanya or the Roc de Sant Urbici of Serrateix, where the pagan past and the Christian religion also coincide.

Sant Pere de Rodes (Alt Empordà): Maritime Monastery

In the Carolingian period, there was a land border with Al-Andalus (near which some of the gorge monasteries mentioned above were located), and there was also a maritime border. The Mediterranean Sea was a source of wealth through fishing, but its shores were often attacked by the Saracens and even by the Vikings.[52] Despite these dangers, several monasteries were built along the Catalan coast, such as Sant Pere de Rodes, Sant Andreu de Sureda (six kilometres off the shore), Sant Feliu de Guíxols, Sant Pol de Mar, and Santa Maria de Castelldefels. Some were short-lived, such as the abbey of Castelldefels while others, which were more sheltered on top of a mountain, such as Sant Pere de Rodes, were consolidated and fared well throughout the Middle Ages.

Sant Pere de les Puelles (Barcelonès): Urban Monastery

Monasteries were built all over Europe outside the city walls, which were often important for urban growth. For example, the abbey of Saint-Sernin, in Toulouse, was the centre of an important suburb in this Occitan city.[53] In Catalonia, in relation to Barcelona, it is worth noting the monastery of Sant Pere de les Puelles, a feminine name in Catalan for a feminine monastery, and the abbey of Sant Pau del Camp, both of which were built outside the city walls. Near Girona, the monastery of Sant Pere de Galligants was built, where, after the year 1000, one of the suburbs of the city was constructed.[54]

---

52 Bonnassie, 'Le littoral catalan durant le Haut Moyen Âge'.
53 Wolff, *Regards sur le Midi médiéval*, pp. 201–12.
54 Canal and others, *Girona, de Carlemany al feudalisme*, p. 104.

66   CHAPTER 3

Monasteries and Villages

Further on, we will focus on the new monastic villages, with special emphasis on Sant Joan de les Abadesses, a well-planned town located to the north of this abbey, created in the time of Count Guifré el Pilós (870–897). However, close to many other Catalan monasteries, we also find settlements which were established more spontaneously. At Santa Maria de Ripoll (Ripollès), there was an abbey, the parish church of Saint Peter, a church dedicated to Saint Eudald, and a marketplace, located at the confluence of two rivers, Ter and Freser. There are other well-planned monastic neighbourhoods, probably from the Middle Ages. In Sant Cugat (Vallès Occidental), the settlement was built between the monastery and the parish church of Saint Peter. In Banyoles (Pla de l'Estany), the village also extended alongside the abbey, towards the church of Saint Mary and the lake. In Gerri de la Sal (Pallars Sobirà), a small village was set up on the other side of the river Noguera Pallaresa where artisans and labourers who worked in the salt ponds collecting salt lived. Santa Maria d'Arles, an abbey in Vallespir, will be discussed further below. At Roses (Alt Empordà), excavations and the study of some *capbreus* (land terriers, in English) have made it possible to reconstruct the settlement next to the abbey of Santa Maria.[55] In other places, the town was further away from the monastery. Thus, concerning Sant Pere de Rodes, the town of Santa Creu de Rodes (now, Santa Helena), currently under excavation,[56] was built 600 m away from this remarkable monastery that rises above the sea.

Banyoles (Pla de l'Estany)

Before 822, the monastery of Sant Esteve de Banyoles had been founded a few hundred metres from a large lake, where, according to the documents, it was possible to fish. The monastery stood at the end of a fertile plain that was worked intensely throughout the early Middle Ages, as demonstrated by pollen analysis. In 1017, a parish church in the town of Banyoles, dedicated to Saint Mary, was mentioned; possibly it was much older. In addition, in 1086, a weekly market was held in the town of Banyoles, which was documented. According to the research undertaken, the first town, Vila Vella, was established between the monastery and the church of Santa Maria dels Turers.[57] Later, probably in the twelfth century, an outer town was created, Vila Nova, which involved extending the settlement about 250 m further west. In this westernmost sector, which passed the *Rec Major* (i.e., a drainage channel of

---

55 Pujol, *La vila de Roses*.
56 Mataró and others, 'Santa Creu de Rodes'; Ollich and others, 'Dos exemples d'urbanisme medieval a Catalunya'.
57 Moner, 'La vila de Banyoles'.

the lake), there was a square where the market was held, where there were also leather and textile industry activities.[58]

Arles (Vallespir)

In Arles (Fr. Arles-sur-Tech), there was a monastery, dedicated to Saint Mary, recorded in 934, after the transfer of the community from the place where it was originally settled, about three kilometres down the river Tec (in a place where Roman remains were preserved). There was also a parish church dedicated to Saint Stephen, documented in 993 on the occasion of its consecration. In 1159, a new consecration document shows that the church was granted a thirty-step cemetery.[59] In this town, however, it was the Benedictine abbey that organized the settlement. The documents recording the consecration of the church of Saint Mary in 1046 and again in 1157 refer to marks that delimit the area of immunity and protection around the monastery (*immunitatis signum*). This must have favoured the creation and consolidation of the settlement. In the thirteenth century, there were references to dry moats (in Latin, *valla*) that surrounded the town.[60]

Looking at the maps from the early nineteenth century against the current ones, we see three aspects worth highlighting.[61] First, there was an organized southern sector relating to the abbey. Second, the northern and western sectors were organized into slightly orthogonal shapes. And, thirdly, there was a space that surrounded the settlement, with a predominance of curved forms, which must probably stand on the site where the dry moats were created as protection. This space, enclosed by dry moats and probably by walls, must have been the protected area established by the monks and marked at the beginning with signs.

Collegiate Churches and Villages

We cannot focus only on monasteries. Along with the Benedictine abbeys, we find collegiate churches, not only in the cities but also in the countryside. The ecclesiastics dedicated to the canonical life were initially those who assisted the bishop. During the reign of Charlemagne, in Aachen, in the year 816, the *Institutio canonicorum* was drafted. It is not until the eleventh century that the canonical reform movement spread, found in Saint-Ruf d'Avignon and imposed on the Lateran Council in 1059.[62] The secular canons were

---

58 Farías, *El mas i la vila a la Catalunya medieval*, p. 254.
59 Catafau, *Les celleres et la naissance du village en Roussillon*, p. 186.
60 In Catalan, the dry moats are called 'valls' or, currently, also 'fossats'.
61 Catafau, *Les celleres et la naissance du village en Roussillon*, p. 192.
62 It should be borne in mind that, from 1113, the county of Provence became dependent on the count of Barcelona.

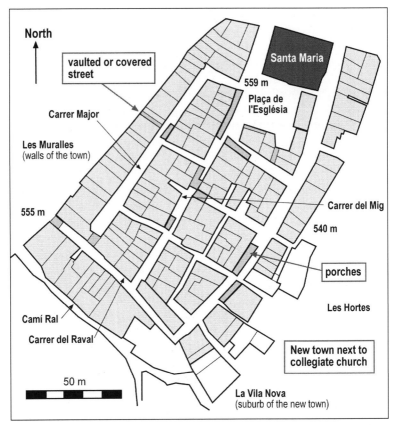

Figure 12. Town of Organyà (Alt Urgell). New town founded next to the collegiate church of Santa Maria.

differentiated from the regular canons who were governed by the so-called Rule of Saint Augustine. In Catalonia, we find several collegiate churches in L'Estany, Organyà, Vilabertran, Mur, Cardona, Àger, Ponts, etc.

Likewise, there were towns created near or next to collegiate churches, such as Vilabertran (Empordà), L'Estany (Moianès), or Organyà (Alt Urgell); the latter will be analysed in depth below. In Cardona, there was also a notable collegiate church dedicated to Saint Vincent, next to a very old castle and extensive salt mines.[63] Below the hill, where the castle had been first built and then the collegiate church, was the village (which must have existed long before the community of canons was established).

---

63 Casas, *Història de Cardona, vol. III: La canònica de Sant Vicenç de Cardona*.

Organyà (Alt Urgell)

Organyà, first documented in 993, was surely a place inhabited long before (there appears to have been a *fundus Organianus*).[64] Santa Maria d'Organyà is a collegiate church documented in 1090. As for the town of Organyà, in 1233, a pariage or lordship-sharing agreement (*pariatge*, in Catalan)[65] was established between the counts of Foix and the canons of this place, in which the new town and its marketplace was referred to; the old town was also mentioned.[66] To the south of the church of Santa Maria (Saint Mary), we still find the remains of a new town, planned and organized perhaps around the main street and a secondary one that went from northeast to southwest, and perhaps in involving two or three cross-streets (Fig. 12). It is possible that this medieval town evolved in several stages. On the other hand, there was probably a perimeter wall, which must coincide with the layout of the houses that now enclose this built-up area to the west, east, and south. Around 1200, the so-called *Homilies d'Organyà* were composed here, a collection of sermons that forms one of the oldest literary documents written in Catalan. However, the Catalan language was already in use several centuries earlier.[67]

Cistercian Monasteries and Granges

In Europe, a few notable studies have been undertaken on Cistercian monasteries and their landscapes.[68] The Cistercian order had a long tradition of carefully selecting suitable places to settle. Simultaneously, Cistercian communities transformed the environment where the abbey had been built. In addition, around the various monasteries, a set of granges were created, a clear sign of the desire of these monks, at least at the beginning, to directly manage their estates.[69] Examples from Catalonia include the great monasteries of Poblet (Conca de Barberà), Santes Creus (Alt Camp), and the female community of Vallbona de les Monges (Urgell).

The estates of the Catalan Cistercian monasteries have been widely researched. At their creation in the twelfth century, the abbeys of Poblet or Santes Creus were located in places that, a few years before, were across the border in Islamic lands.[70] In addition, they stood in places close to major roads.

---

64 Coromines, *Onomasticon Cataloniae*, VI, p. 69.

65 A *pariage* is a feudal law contract of association between two or more lords, ensuring them equal rights and joint ownership of the same land.

66 Gascón, 'Els acords de Pariatge al Bisbat d'Urgell', pp. 88–90.

67 see Alturo and Alaix, *Lletres que parlen. Viatge als orígens del català*.

68 Williams, *The Cistercians in the Early Middle Ages*.

69 In the twelfth century, the Cistercian monks created monastic granges, which were large, isolated buildings intended to house collective agricultural or industrial activity carried out on site by a group of monks detached from an abbey.

70 Altisent, *Història de Poblet*; *Diplomatari de Santa Maria de Poblet*, ed. by Altisent; Carreras,

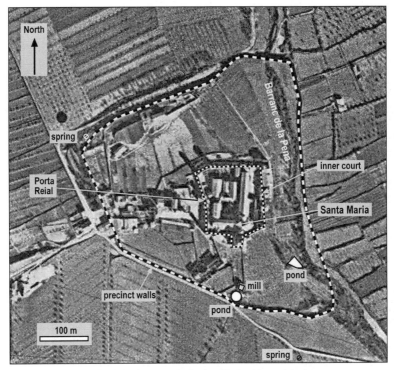

Figure 13. Abbey of Poblet (Conca de Barberà). In this aerial photograph taken in 1946 we see the abbey, the inner court, and its precinct walls. Source: © ICGC. Reproduced with permission.

Poblet was next to the road that connected Lleida with Tarragona, and Santes Creus was next to the river Gaià and to the road that connected the Penedès (and Barcelona) and the Conca de Barberà (and Lleida).[71]

The Abbey of Poblet and its Enclosed Area (Conca de Barberà)

In 1150, the monastery of Santa Maria de Poblet was founded. Like most Cistercian abbeys, it has an enclosed precinct around it. We can still observe and see it in aerial photographs (Fig. 13). It covers an area of 17.9 hectares. In the rest of Europe, there are precinct walls that enclose up to 30 ha, as at Clairvaux, and others that only enclose up to 3.85 ha, as at Pilis. Many of these enclosed areas in England cover about 24 ha (e.g., at Fountains, Furness, and Garendon).[72] In Valencia, the abbey of Santa Maria de Valldigna (La Safor),

---

El monestir de Santes Creus, 1150–1200; Papell, 'El domini del monestir de Santes Creus'.
71 Bolòs, 'La implantació del Cister al territori'.
72 Williams, *The Cistercians in the Early Middle Ages*, p. 199.

created much later in 1298, had an enclosure of 5 ha (and the enclosure area, the inner court, extended along 1.14 ha).[73]

In Poblet, closer to the monastic buildings, there was still another enclosure, like the one we also find in many other Cistercian monasteries: the inner court.[74] Until the fourteenth century, this inner court was enclosed by a low wall. However, due to the wars of King Pere III of Catalonia and Aragon with the king of Castile, it was fortified and a high wall, as well as an external dry moat.[75] Work on this wall was not completed until the fifteenth century. The only gateways to this inner enclosure were the Royal Towers, consisting of a polygonal floor plan that protected access to the abbey. This inner wall was 608 m long, with a remarkable height of about eleven metres.

Studies carried out in recent years have revealed ditches and underground aqueducts that brought water to the eastern sector of the abbey, located next to the Barranc de la Pena where there are also several springs. The internal circulation of water has been noted, resembling what we find in the abbey of Fontfroide (Oc. Fontfreja), an Occitan monastery where the monks of Poblet came from.[76] It is known that in the fifteenth century, the main canal that carried water was rebuilt and repaired.

The Grange of Ancosa (La Llacuna, Anoia)

The monks who settled in Santes Creus had previously dwelt in Valldaura (Vallès Occidental) and subsequently went to live for a few years in Ancosa, a place that eventually became just a grange in the abbey of Santes Creus, next to the river Gaià. A few years ago, an archaeological excavation carried out in Ancosa revealed the walls of the main medieval buildings and a large and significant deep well. The pipes that, for 1 km, carried water from the springs on a nearby mountain slope to the grange *horts* were also documented.[77] Certainly, the main problem with the site of Ancosa, which prevented it from becoming the site of a large Cistercian monastery, was precisely a lack of water.

Military Orders and Commanderies

The importance of military orders in New Catalonia was remarkable. There are numerous orders, especially of the Templar and Hospital brethren. Ramon Berenguer IV, count of Barcelona (*de facto* the sovereign of Catalonia), became king of Aragon, but to achieve this he had to agree to make important

---

73 Garcia-Oliver ed., *El Císter, ideals i realitat d'un orde monàstic.*
74 Williams, *The Cistercians in the Early Middle Ages*, p. 204.
75 Gonzalvo, 'La muralla de Poblet'.
76 Juan-Villanueva, 'Hidraulisme històric del monestir de Poblet i del seu hinterland immediat'.
77 Bolòs and Mallart, *La granja cistercenca d'Ancosa*. The *horts*, which were probably irrigated, could not have been too extensive.

72   CHAPTER 3

concessions to the military orders, due to clauses in the will of King Alfonso I of Aragon. This was one of the reasons for the creation of notable Templar commanderies in New Catalonia, such as the castle of Gardeny, next to Lleida, Miravet, on the banks of the river Ebro, or Barberà, in the Conca de Barberà, and also some Hospitaller commanderies, such as that of Amposta. In Old Catalonia, El Masdéu (Roussillon), an important Templar commandery, was also created.

Many documents have been published from the commanderies of Barberà, El Masdéu, and Gardeny.[78] Gardeny's documentation records the organization of the estates depending on the Templars on the Segrià plain. At the top of the hill of Gardeny, to the west of the city of Lleida, the Templar twelfth-century castle and an adjoining church still stand.

Templar Segrià

Thanks to the preserved documentation, we understand the process of colonization and distribution of the lands of the Templar area in the north of Lleida, irrigated by the so-called Séquia (ditch) de Segrià (currently the Canal de Pinyana). On the one hand, this region, much smaller than the current *comarca* of Segrià, exploited many elements of the landscape that existed before the conquest of 1149 (e.g., the *almúnies* or hamlets, and the irrigation canals) and, on the other hand, a new landscape was created as a result of a process of conquest, repopulation, and reorganization of space. The *almúnies* became 'torres' (towers), and at the head of many of these settlements, a member of the lower nobility settled. The irrigated space was probably enlarged, the land was parcelled out again and plots of land of regular sizes, the *parellades*, were created and distributed among the newcomers.[79] The institution of 'heirs' (a single male successor to property) was established. They received the plots of land and were assisted by partners who collaborated in the fieldwork. I believe that these plots of land, the *parellades*, comprised an area of about ten hectares. The reorganization also established what the rent for the Templars should be, which varied depending on whether the land was irrigated or dry. Certainly, the yield of the land varied greatly depending on whether it could be irrigated or not; in irrigated lands, a good harvest was guaranteed, even in years of drought.

---

78 *Col·lecció diplomàtica de la casa del Temple de Barberà*, ed. by Sans Travé; *Diplomatari del Masdéu*, ed. by Tréton; *Col·lecció diplomàtica de la Casa del Temple de Gardeny*, ed. by Sarobe.

79 Bolòs, 'Paisatge i societat al "Segrià" al segle XIII'; Bolòs, 'Changes and survival: the territory of Lleida'.

Pagan Background

In Catalonia, it is unusual to find a menhir (a tall, upright stone erected for pagan religious purposes) next to a church, unlike in England.[80] However, there are exceptions, as later on we will discuss the church of Santa Maria de Mijaran (Val d'Aran), which is located next to a large rock. However, other aspects allow us to identify links between the pagan and Christian eras. First, toponymy, which, as we will discuss in Chapter 15, speaks volumes, and can illustrate many aspects of our past. Let's focus on two toponyms: Madremanya and Marqueixanes. The former, a village located in the Gironès, reminds us of the existence of a *Mater magna* or Cybele. In the case of Marqueixanes (Conflent; Fr. Marquixanes), according to philologists, this place name is reminiscent of 'mother-oaks', a cult of trees.[81] There are other examples; remains dating back to the Middle Ages have been found in the church of Mosoll (Cerdanya), a place name that may derive from a mausoleum. Also, some names related to Jana (such as Fontjanina, and Ribagorça) point us towards the goddess Diana.[82] Or the place name Nèfol (also in Cerdanya) reminds us of forest nymphs. In the Carolingian period, the whole valley of Cabó (Alt Urgell) was called *pagus Nempetano*, the land of nymphs. The early medieval process of the Christianization of the landscape has been studied in many European countries and it has allowed us to understand better not only the changes that took place in mentality and religion, but also some components of the current landscape.[83]

Other pieces of evidence take us back to pre-Christian times. In Berguedà, near Sant Joan de Montdarn and also near Serrateix (on the rock of Sant Urbici), there are large monoliths with religious significance for the local population over the centuries, to the point that, as a sign of respect for the first emptied niche, there is still an annual procession. In the Aran Valley, as said above, we also find the Mijaran stone (2.4 m high), close to a church dedicated to the Virgin Mary. As the name suggests, it is in the middle of the valley and was probably a symbolic place long before Christianization began.

Certainly, the link between the pagan past and the medieval Christian world is evident in many churches dedicated to the Virgin Mary, located halfway through a valley, at places like Santa Maria d'Àneu (Pallars Sobirà), the church of Santa Maria de Mijaran (Val d'Aran), or Santa Maria de Lord (Solsonès). The latter sanctuary rises to 1,160 m high, on top of a large rock or prominent *mola*, in the middle of of the valley of Lord (it must be borne in mind that Lord is a pre-Roman place name).[84]

---

80 Semple, 'In the Open Air'.
81 Coromines, *Onomasticon Cataloniae*, V, p. 205.
82 Coromines, *Onomasticon Cataloniae*, IV, p. 248.
83 Sánchez-Pardo and others, *Ecclesiastical Landscapes in Medieval Europe*.
84 Coromines, *Onomasticon Cataloniae*, V, pp. 108–10.

74   CHAPTER 3

At the same time, a process of Christianizing pagan sites took place. This was the case of mountains considered sacred, such as Montserrat and Canigó, places of passage or pasturelands, such as Núria (Ripollès) or Meritxell (Andorra), or even places of thermal waters, such as Els Banys d'Arles (Fr. Amélie-les-Bains) (Vallespir). As mentioned above, monasteries were built (in Montserrat, Canigó, or Els Banys d'Arles) or even sanctuaries, as a result of the discovery of a statue of the Virgin Mary (e.g., in Núria, Meritxell, or also in Montserrat).

Despite these pagan remains, the imagery from the Carolingian Catalan counties is that of a fully Christianized country. Each village had its own church for baptisms, mass services, and, perhaps, burials. We find that during the ninth and tenth centuries, some lords and even communities of parishioners took part in the construction of their churches; later on, in Chapter 14, we will illustrate this practice with Santa Maria d'Olvan and Santa Maria de la Quar (Berguedà). In addition, as evidenced by archaeological excavations, especially in the plains of Roussillon, Empordà, or Gironès, there were many very old churches, built long before the Carolingian era.[85] We have also found them in the *comarques* of Vallès (Sant Menna, in Sentmenat), Bages (Artés), Camp de Tarragona, or in the plain of Lleida (El Bovalar) and even on the northern slope of the Montsec, at the site of Els Altimiris.[86] Surely, the sacralization of space had already begun even before the Middle Ages, as we see in *Villa Fortunatus*.

Conclusions

As has been illustrated in this chapter, the influence of the Church in the Middle Ages was significant and ecclesiastical institutions had a strong impact in many areas, apart from the purely religious. For example, they determined the characteristics of many villages, organized around the church within the space called, after 1000, a *sagrera* or *cellera*. These villages, created in the eleventh century, have survived to the present day, sometimes without much change (even if the current houses were built in the last few centuries). On the other hand, even though archaeological excavations from recent years call for minor amendments, we believe that overall, the result of studies from the last decades remains almost unchanged.

There was also a considerable growth in the number of Benedictine monasteries, often founded in the Carolingian period. Adjoining some of these abbeys, new towns were created, as we have seen in the cases of Sant Joan de les Abadesses, Ripoll, Banyoles, Gerri, and Sant Cugat del Vallès.

---

85   Palol ed., *Del romà al romànic*.
86   Alegria and Sancho, 'Els Altimiris, enllaços i confluències entre la Tardoantiguitat i l'Alta Edat Mitjana'.

In the Middle Ages, the collegiate churches (e.g., Organyà, Vilabertran, or Cardona), the Cistercian monasteries (e.g., Poblet and Santes Creus), and the commanderies of military orders (e.g., those of the Templars of Gardeny, Miravet, Barberà, or El Masdéu) became important. Their existence not only affected the landscape of the place where the central buildings stood, but also the landscape of the whole area, where the domains of these abbeys or military orders extended.

Walking through the valley of Boí (Alta Ribagorça), we can admire the beauty of the extraordinary Romanesque churches and bell towers that pepper this valley, now a UNESCO World Heritage Site. However, we must consider that, in the eleventh and twelfth centuries, all the counties of Old Catalonia had plenty of Romanesque churches, with bell towers that were almost always higher than any of the peasant houses in the villages where they stood. This wealth of construction produced, between 1984 and 1998, no less than twenty-eight thick volumes of *Catalunya Romànica* (Romanesque Catalonia), which includes many studies, maps, and photographs of churches built between the ninth and thirteenth centuries.[87] If we mapped all the Romanesque ecclesiastical buildings studied in this work, we would find hundreds of dots. In the Middle Ages, however, castles formed another network of buildings that was almost as dense and widespread as that of churches, and it is precisely this topic that will be discussed in the next chapter.

---

87 Vigué and Pladevall ed., *Catalunya Romànica.*

CHAPTER 4

Castles and Castral Villages

The incastellamento of the Landscape

Introduction

We now know that many fortifications were built during the early Middle Ages, some of which had peasants and other inhabitants who were not part of the seigneurial military entourage. Archaeological research in recent years has changed the way we view these centuries after the fall of the Roman Empire. During the Carolingian period, many castles were built in Catalonia, especially along the march or border. During the high Middle Ages, all members of the upper and lower nobility owned castles or fortified houses. These political and social realities led to the construction of villages alongside fortifications, the construction of castles next to villages, and the relocation of some settlements to elevated sites, often somewhere close to a castle. Sometimes we can talk about the process of deliberate population concentration, *incastellamento*, a process described by Pierre Toubert, but at other times the reality is much more complex. In any case, we can point out that the Middle Ages were centuries with a strong *incastellamento*, at least in the sense that this word also has in Italian: they were a period in which many castles were built everywhere and the local population were concentrated within the castle sites, nominally for their protection, but also to control them. Here in Chapter 4, we will discuss the villages and the castles, both those built in the early medieval period and those constructed by Muslims or Christians after 1000. We will also see examples of the relocation of the local population to the proximity of a fortification as well as the removal of a community away from an old border castle. Certainly, the changes in politics and in society had an obvious impact on the medieval landscape.

What Do We Know About the Villages Built Around a Castle?

Often, when we think of a medieval landscape, we picture a castle on top of a hill with a neighbouring village and fields cultivated by peasants. To understand the territorial organization in the Middle Ages, we should recall the importance of castles. In the coming pages, we will analyse castles and castral districts, castles and borderlands, and castles with towns next to them. We will also discover that the fortifications of the sixth century differed from the towers of the eighth century, the feudal castles of the eleventh century, and the castle-palaces of the fourteenth century. Nowadays, one might feel more connected to peasants who worked the land than to medieval lords who lived primarily through battles and ostentation. But to understand the society and landscape of the Middle Ages, we inevitably need to figure out who built the castles and how their existence affected the landscape around the fortifications.

Dozens of books on medieval castles have been published in Europe. Here, only five of them will be cited. First, a few years ago, a book on the castles of the early Middle Ages showed us the importance of these fortifications in northern Italy before 1000.[1] Second, an in-depth analysis of this issue is revealed in a collection of works published by Christie and Herold entitled *Fortified Settlements in Early Medieval Europe*, which includes a study of the Catalan site of L'Esquerda (Osona).[2] A third study worth noting is Creighton's work on castles and the landscape in which they were built; this is one of the earliest studies of both features.[3] Fourth, another remarkable study is the volume on the fortifications of western Occitania, which consists of a description of numerous castles and their relationships with the landscape, settlements, and power, and also with their inhabitants.[4] Finally, a classic work on the castles of the Islamic era *Les châteaux ruraux d'al-Andalus* is worth mentioning.[5]

Castles of the Early Middle Ages

Our knowledge of fortifications from the early Middle Ages has changed significantly in recent years. For a long time, it was believed that the castles of the early medieval period consisted merely of large enclosures protected by landscape features, and that, in general, they were uninhabited places.[6] However, the excavations carried out in the Occitan lands, for example in Roc de Pampelune, have altered this view and raised our awareness of the complexity and diversity of early medieval castle-building.[7] At the same time, this research has helped to better understand the society of this period.[8] Even in recently published studies, it has been suggested that there was more than one stage for the building of castles, and there has been much debate on

---

1 Brogiolo and Gelichi, *Nuove ricerche sui castelli altomedievali in Italia*.
2 Christie and Herold ed., *Fortified Settlements in Early Medieval Europe*; Ollich and others, 'The Southern Carolingian Frontier'.
3 Creighton, *Castles and Landscapes*.
4 Bourgeois and Remy ed., *Demeurer, défendre et paraître*.
5 Bazzana and others, *Les château ruraux d'al-Andalus*.
6 Fournier, *Le château dans la France médiévale*, p. 46.
7 Schneider, 'De la fouille des villages abandonnés à l'archéologie des territoires locaux', p. 139; Catafau, 'Del poble al paisatge. Elements per a una historiografia recent del poblament medieval de l'Europa occidental', p. 33; Zadora-Rio, 'Early medieval villages and estate centres in France', pp. 81–83.
8 Diarte-Blasco, *Late Antique and Early Medieval Hispania*, pp. 70–75.

CASTLES AND CASTRAL VILLAGES

Figure 14. Map of historic Catalonia showing the location of the castles and villages mentioned in the text.

who built these fortifications.[9] In this respect, in principle, it is believed that they were mostly made and owned by the powerful, who left the residential inhabited *villae* at the end of the Roman world to settle in these fortified places which served as refuges but also as control mechanisms over the territory. However, some of these *castra* or *oppida* were also built by monarchs and, perhaps, in some areas of Europe, even by local communities.

As regards Catalonia under Visigothic rule, one of the few texts preserved concerning this period, written on account of the episode of the uprising of

---

9 Catalán and others, *Las fortificaciones en la tardoantigüedad*.

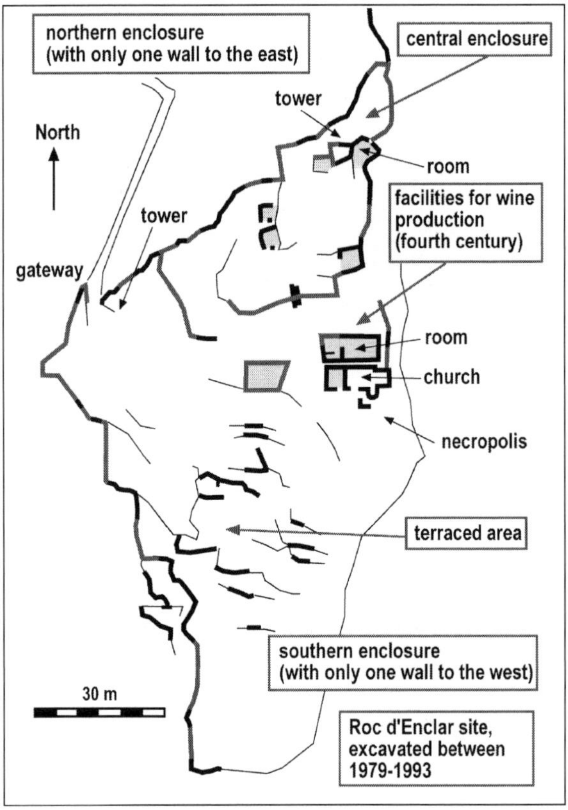

CHAPTER 4

Figure 15. *Castrum* of El Roc d'Enclar (Andorra). An extensive stronghold built on a hilltop at the end of the Roman era and abandoned in the thirteenth century. Source: Llovera and others, *Roc d'Enclar.*

Labels within figure: northern enclosure (with only one wall to the east); central enclosure; tower; North; room; facilities for wine production (fourth century); tower; gateway; room; church; necropolis; terraced area; southern enclosure (with only one wall to the west); 30 m; Roc d'Enclar site, excavated between 1979-1993

Duke Paulus, in the second half of the seventh century, already mentions *castra* at Llívia (Cerdanya), Ultrera, and Cotlliure (Roussillon; Fr. Collioure). Certainly, there were others, for example, Puig Rom (Alt Empordà) and Roc d'Enclar (Andorra). Surely, a long list of names should be added, as each Catalan comarca had one or more of them. In the Carolingian period, some of these *oppida* continued to serve as refuges for the ruling classes. Even on the march, or the border with the Islamic lands, some of the fortifications had these characteristics, for example, the castle of Tarabau (Noguera), analysed later on in this volume. In addition, thanks to archaeological excavations, we know that, for example, the castles of Olèrdola, Castellví de la Marca (Penedès), Roda de Ter (L'Esquerda, Osona) and Can Maurí (Berga, Berguedà), already existed before the medieval period (Fig. 14).

Roc d'Enclar (Andorra)

Excavations carried out by the government of Andorra on the Roc d'Enclar hill have revealed a notable early medieval fortification (Fig. 15).[10] It has been possible to ascertain how this lofty place was used for many centuries from

---

10 Llovera and others ed., *Roc d'Enclar. Transformacions d'un espai dominant.*

the end of the Roman era to the end of the thirteenth century. In the fourth or fifth centuries, a fortified castle was built on this site. An area of 5600 square metres was created. During the sixth to the eighth centuries, this *oppidum* was probably a centre of administrative power. It appears that in the Carolingian period, in the eighth and tenth centuries, Roc d'Enclar became the symbol of the power of the Frankish kings and their representatives, the counts of Urgell. At this stage, three enclosures were created: the main enclosure, another to the south with a church and a necropolis, and an enclosure to the north with a single longitudinal wall located in the more vulnerable and unprotected area. Enclar served as the central place of the valley, inhabited, and located very close to the church of Santa Coloma and the town of Andorra la Vella (it initially meant 'Andorra the villa').

L'Esquerda (Roda de Ter, Osona)

The University of Barcelona has been carrying out excavations at the uninhabited L'Esquerda site for several decades. Its research started off by studying tombs excavated in the rock, located next to a Romanesque church dedicated to St Peter. The team went on to excavate a few medieval houses, and ended up with ambitiously uncovering an entire important village located on the meander of the river Ter, near Vic. L'Esquera shows a chronological framework that extends, as a fortification and inhabited place, from the Iberian period to the high Middle Ages.[11] At the end of the Roman era and during the Visigothic period, it regained its function as a settlement and fortified place and the stones of the Iberian wall were re-used for construction. Silos and a necropolis show that it was inhabited in the early Middle Ages. In the Carolingian period, the documents allude to *Rota Civitas*, the city of Roda, destroyed in 826, because of an anti-Frankish uprising led by Aissó (perhaps Ayxun) and Guillemundus. The role of this fortification, next to the river Ter, was to control the territory. It extended over a large area of about twelve hectares, making it easy to defend because this area is cut by the course of the river Ter.

Tarabau (La Baronia de Rialb, Noguera)

When the art history encyclopaedia 'Catalunya Romànica' came out, references to Tarabau castle were already known from an early document of 892 referring to a *castro Tarabaldi*.[12] Initially, it can be considered a *castrum*. It is located on top of a large and steep, flat-topped hill, so the place was easy to

---

11 Ollich and others, 'Visigots i carolingis a Osona. Novetats arqueològiques des del jaciment de l'Esquerda'; Ollich and others, 'The Southern Carolingian Frontier in *Marca Hispanica* along the River Ter'; Pratdesaba, *El procés de fortificació i reocupació del territori a Catalunya*.
12 *Catalunya carolíngia, vol. VIII: Els comtats d'Urgell, Cerdanya i Berga*, ed. by Ordeig, doc. 97.

82   CHAPTER 4

defend. It was a fortification at the end of the county border. Later, probably after 1000, a feudal castle at its highest point and a church dedicated to Saint John were built.

In the early Middle Ages, there was a large enclosure, defended by the topography and some sections of the wall (probably rebuilt later), which are still visible. On the south side, where the wall is most evident, its gateway is still untouched. This large enclosure covers an area of 1.5 ha. As said above, it must have been a Carolingian *castrum*, plausibly occupied in the ninth century by a man bearing a Frankish name, Tarabald. However, without an excavation, it is impossible to verify what was there before the ninth century.

Certainly, these are not unique cases. Near Girona there was the *castrum* of Sant Julià de Ramis, excavated in recent decades.[13] The *castellum* of Casserres from the Visigothic and Carolingian periods can be found in Berguedà.[14] In Osona, the castle of Cabrera, also documented before 1000, is now being excavated. In the Penedès, as mentioned, we find the castles of Olèrdola and Castellví de la Marca. In Pallars, the castle of Toló shares similar characteristics with that of Tarabau. Even Llimiana (Pallars Jussà) must not have been very different from all these high medieval *castra*, although, in this case, there has been continuity in the settlement of this place. And, in La Ribagorça, the early castle of Viacamp, which we will discuss later, must have been similar. Also, further examples include the castle of Fontova (in Castilian, Fantova) and even the fortification of Roda d'Isàvena, where an episcopal seat was built in the middle of the tenth century, and later a set of houses and then a feudal castle. These are just a few names from a list that, as I said, could be long.

Castles from the Islamic Era

While several synthesizing works on the Islamic fortifications of Valencia and Aragon have been completed, there has been no overall study of castles from the Islamic era in Catalonia to date.[15] There are remains of notable fortifications, such as those in Castell Formós in Balaguer, El Castellàs (Baix Cinca), Castelldans (Les Garrigues), Castellot de Sant Joan (La Noguera), Torre de la Força (La Noguera), Siurana (Priorat), etc. Some were rammed earth towers (such as La Força), others were palace castles (such as Castell Formós), there were also fortifications, possibly located next to a pass (such as Castellot de Sant Joan) or an inhabited place (such as Castelldans),[16] and yet others were constituted, mostly, by a large enclosure, which could serve

---

13 Burch, *Excavacions arqueològiques de la muntanya de Sant Julià de Ramis.*
14 Gibert, *L'expressió material del poder durant la conquesta comtal*, p. 80.
15 Guichard, *Les musulmans de Valence et la Reconquête*; Sénac, *La frontière et les hommes (VIIIᵉ–XIIᵉ siècle).*
16 See: Vigué and Pladevall ed., *Catalunya Romànica*. In its volumes, it contains a detailed study of the history and characteristics of all these medieval buildings.

as a place from which the territory could be controlled and possibly also as a refuge for people and even animals; it was commonly known as an *albacar*.[17] In some of these fortifications, there could be a cistern, the remains of a residential building (in some documents referred to as *celòquia*, from Arabic *salūqiya*), and there could also be houses. Some of these *ḥuṣūn* (plural of *ḥiṣn*) were quite similar to the European medieval *castra* or *oppida*. Perhaps some Islamic *ḥuṣun* were built by the villagers of nearby towns, although on land near the border, many were probably built by the authorities. On the other hand, we do not know whether, in some *comarques*, the creation of *ḥuṣun* attracted a population living in dispersed settlements, as Philippe Sénac believes.[18] This typology is very similar to that proposed by Sénac for the northern Aragonese lands. He identifies castles located at the top of a rocky cliff (such as Sen and Men), and others erected on fortified hills above an inhabited and fortified place (such as Gabarda or Tubo). He also alludes to large enclosures. Finally, he refers to the existence of fortified settlements.[19]

El Castellàs (Vilella de Cinca, Baix Cinca)

In a small mountain range located 283 metres high, above the River Cinca (its riverbed is 125 metres above sea level), there was a fortification from the Islamic era. It was a large enclosure, with an area of about 700 square metres and about ninety metres in length. On the southern end was a large cistern (about ten metres long). Further north from the cistern, chambers were built. Everything had to be enclosed within a seventy centimetres-wide wall, which followed the upper platform of the mountain range, at the top of the slope. Possibly, this *ḥiṣn* originated in the eleventh century before the advance of the Aragonese kings down the river Cinca.

Later on, in Chapter 6, we will consider towers or *ʾabrāǧ* (pl. of *burǧ*), such as Solibernat (Segrià) or Els Safranals (Baix Cinca), small fortified settlements which were probably built at the same time, in the late eleventh–early twelfth century, as a result of the imminent threat of the Christian conquest.

Siurana (Priorat)

The fortification of Siurana was the last place in the hands of the Muslims in Catalonia; unconquered until 1154 when Tortosa and Lleida had already fallen.[20] Siurana is on top of a steep mountain at an altitude of 750 metres. The natural drop of more than 270 metres to the nearby river Siurana makes

---

17 Guichard, *Les musulmans de Valence et la Reconquête*, pp. 215–21.
18 Sénac, *La frontière et les hommes (VIIIᵉ–XIIᵉ siècle)*, p. 231.
19 Sénac, *La frontière et les hommes (VIIIᵉ–XIIᵉ siècle)*, pp. 222–50.
20 Tortosa was conquered by Ramon Berenguer IV in 1148 and Lleida by the count of Barcelona and by the count of Urgell the following year.

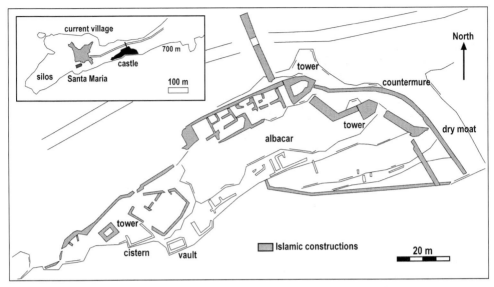

Figure 16. Castle and fortification of Siurana (Priorat). The Islamic stronghold of Siurana, with a castle, a thick wall, and a settlement, was not conquered until 1154. Source: Menchon, 'Algunes fortificacions (islàmiques?) al sud de Catalunya'.

it an easy place to defend. We see a large enclosure with an area of 3.6 hectares (Fig. 16). This space was enclosed on the eastern end by a thick wall (250 centimetres wide), which also blocked the passage to the main access road. On this eastern wall, there was a solid tower and a large hollow tower, both with a pentagonal plan.[21] These towers and the wall that closes off access are made with large ashlars and have been dated to a time close to 900. At the eastern end of the enclosure, there is another outer wall, thinner and above the margin of the moat. To the west of this wall was the castle, with a rectangular tower, also from the Islamic period, built on formwork. Further on, to the south-west, lies the current village of Siurana and a Romanesque church; before 1154, all this space was also part of the enclosure, with houses, cisterns, silos, and a necropolis.

Castles of the March

From the eighth to the twelfth century, the territory we now call Catalonia was divided by a wide border that separated the lands controlled by the Frankish kings or the Catalan counts from the lands under Islamic control, the Emirate

---

21 Piera and Menchon, 'El castell de Siurana (Cornudella de Montsant, el Priorat)'; Menchon, 'Algunes fortificacions (islàmiques?) al sud de Catalunya', pp. 71–75; Bolòs, 'Castell de Siurana', pp. 385–88.

and the Caliphate of Córdoba or the *taifas* (i.e. the independent Muslim principalities of the Iberian Peninsula) of Lleida and Tortosa. Between 801 and 1149, according to the documents made in the Catalan counties, this strip of land was a march or border area extending from just south of Barcelona to the Ribagorça for about 180 kilometres. This fact had an important influence on the organization of the territory. One word of warning at this point: we should not confuse the Hispanic March or set of counties on the border between the Carolingian Empire and Hispania (or Al-Andalus), with the land of the march of each of the counties.

Within the march territory of each county, the space was not organized according to the valleys (as we find in the Pyrenees), villas, or parishes. All the space near the border was organized into district castles, or castles with a territory (*castells termenats*, in Catalan). Documentation indicates the existence of numerous fortifications. In each of these castles, there could be one or more settlements and one or more churches. This will be further discussed in Chapter 14.

One can easily be misled into thinking that everything that is documented on a given date was built on precisely the date indicated. This was not necessarily always the case. For example, in the Carolingian ninth and tenth centuries, not everything mentioned in the many preserved texts was built during that precise period, despite the absence of written documents granting this certainty that may certify its exact dating. As a result, it is critical to remember that some fortifications from the Carolingian and comital eras must have stood in the same or a similar location to those from the previous Islamic or Visigothic periods.

The importance of controlling territory and, especially, of having its roads well-guarded implied that, in the ninth and tenth centuries (and perhaps before), the watchtower (*torre de guaita*, in Catalan) became a key landscape element, often accompanied by an enclosure. From the top of the tower, messages could be sent to other fortifications, employing smoke during the day and fire signals at night. This is a communication system that, for example, was still used by Muslims in the thirteenth century (and is very well described in the chronicle of King Jaume I (James I), following the conquest of Valencia) and by Christians throughout the high Middle Ages.

At first, numerous fortifications with towers in the frontier lands, such as those of Vallferosa and Santa Perpètua de Gaià, were conventionally dated to this Carolingian period. However, recent analyses of timber used in these constructions have concluded that they were built earlier, in the Islamic period (or perhaps even earlier than that). According to written documents and preserved remains, there were many other castles and towers that, for the most part, are very likely to have been built during the ninth and tenth centuries, such as perhaps those in Viver, Fals, Ardèvol, Coaner, Castellví de Rosanes, Subirats, Sant Pere de Ribes, Font-rubí, Montbui, Vilademàger, Lloberola, Ponts, etc. Before 1000, there were circular towers, while others had a square (supposedly, the oldest) or a quadrangular plan with rounded corners. It should be borne in mind that there was probably an enclosed space next to the tower, as we can see in the case of Santa Perpètua de Gaià or the excavations carried out in the castle of Ardèvol. There were also a few larger rectangular buildings, such as those at Montbui and Miralles.

Vallferosa (Segarra)

The tower of the castle of Vallferosa was not documented until the eleventh century, but it is certainly much older. It is an exceptional, over thirty-metre-high tower (Fig. 17). It is located almost at the bottom of a valley that connects La Segarra with the city of Solsona. At first, it looked as if it was conceived as an inner tower, covered, and raised with an outer one. The door is about seven metres from the outside floor. There is a chimney-shaped narrow hole embedded in the outer wall on the inside part, which allows access

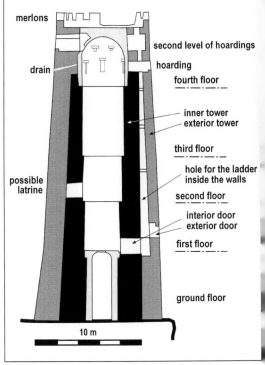

Figure 17. Tower of the castle of Vallferosa (Segarra). Tower of over 30 m high, located next to a road, built in the eighth or ninth centuries. Plan by the author. Source: Menchon, 'Algunes fortificacions (islàmiques?) al sud de Catalunya'; Menchon, 'Dos torres y un relato histórico en revisión'.

to the different floors, up to the fifth level or higher. On the upper level, there is a set of holes behind which would have been wooden individual scaffolds (like hoardings or *bretèches*). Recent studies have concluded that interior and exterior construction are contemporary. There was only one renovation back in the thirteenth–fourteenth centuries which mainly affected the upper part. The rest of the construction is much older. Until recently, it was supposed to be from the end of the tenth century.[22] However, the radiocarbon analyses from recent years date it back to the eighth and ninth centuries, therefore under Islamic rule.[23] These dates are quite surprising, but similar to those established for the tower of Santa Perpètua de Gaià

---

22   Cabañero, *Los castillos catalanes del siglo X*; Bolòs, *Castells de la Catalunya central*.
23   Menchon, 'Dos torres y un relato histórico en revisión'; Menchon, 'Una torre, dues anelles i unes analítiques impertinents'.

CASTLES AND CASTRAL VILLAGES   87

(Conca de Barberà), dated even earlier to the seventh or eighth centuries.[24] This has led to the construction of Vallferosa being attributed to the need to control a livestock path, reflecting the society of the 700s or 800s (i.e. the end of the Visigothic period or early Islamic decades), rather than the Carolingian march of the tenth century. Still, this construction may have been used when, in the tenth and eleventh centuries, this place became the border of the county of Urgell. We can consider ourselves fortunate to see it preserved in its entirety. Recent restoration work has allowed a thorough examination of this structure.

In fact, if we compare these towers with others in the rest of Europe, we find that in other countries, early medieval towers were located along the roads, possibly for defensive purposes, but also for their use to control passage and to collect fees, such as the *teloneum*.[25] There is still a lot of work to be done. It is essential to carry out comparative studies now that remarkable progress in research is being made everywhere and there is quick and easy access to contributions written around the world.

Tona (Osona)

While the castles of Vallferosa and Santa Perpètua de Gaià may well date back to before the Carolingian period, it is harder for us to establish a date for the construction of the castle of Tona.[26] I had previously dated it to 888 (*castro Tonda*), when this castle on the Vic plain was documented for the first time.[27] After what we have seen concerning Vallferosa, however, I leave open the possibility that the tower at the top of the enclosure could be much older.[28]

Now follows a brief description of the two main elements at the top of the castle hill. Firstly, there is a square tower and, secondly, a flat and wide enclosure, which extends over about three hectares, probably a remnant of a *castra* from the early Middle Ages. There is also a Romanesque church, built on top of the pre-Romanesque counterpart (where very old tombs have been found, perhaps from before the ninth or tenth centuries). The tower is built on a formwork made up of sections, reminiscent of that used to make rammed earth walls, a building system widely used in the early Middle Ages, especially in fortifications. Its sides are 4.30 m in length, and its formworks are about ninety centimetres high.

---

24 Menchon, 'Algunes fortificacions (islàmiques?) al sud de Catalunya', pp. 80–85.

25 Brogiolo and Chavarria, *Archeologia postclassica*, pp. 105–11. The teloneum was first a tollhouse and then became a tax on goods transport and sale.

26 Tona is located to the south of the Vic plains. This place was first conquered before the year 801. After the revolt of Aissó, it was conquered again, at the end of the ninth century, during the reign of Count Guifré el Pilós (Count Wilfred I the Hairy).

27 *Les Dotalies de les esglésies de Catalunya (segles IX–XII)*, ed. by Ordeig, doc. 10; Bolòs, *Castells de la Catalunya central*, pp. 61–64.

28 Gibert, *L'expressió material del poder durant la conquesta comtal*, p. 77.

88   CHAPTER 4

This fortification is part of the network of district castles or castles with a territory (*castells termenats*, in Catalan) in the county of Osona. This county, whose capital was Vic, after the uprising of Aissó (or Ayxun) and Guillemundus, in 826, was conquered again by Count Guifré el Pilós (Count Wilfred I the Hairy) at the end of the ninth century.[29] It was one of the first territories to implement the typical organization of the country as regards marches of Catalan counties: the division into castral territories. This will be dealt with in-depth in Chapter 14.

Castell de Ribes (Garraf)

As noted above, areas close to the coast were especially dangerous, as they were for monasteries. The site of Sant Pere de Ribes is about four kilometres from the seaside. In 990, the bishop of Barcelona granted a settlement charter to encourage its repopulation. A tower about fourteen and a half metres high must have been built at the end of the tenth century. The access door to this building opened about eight metres from the outside floor; this door was finished with a horseshoe arch.[30] Although there is no evidence nowadays, there were probably other outbuildings next to the tower. In principle, we can consider this to be a typical construction of the period before 1000.

In summary, recent studies have confirmed the existence of an exceptional set of buildings from the early Middle Ages. The documents show that most of these fortifications contributed to defending the marches of the different Carolingian counties. However, this research has also highlighted the challenge of accurately dating many of these constructions built before 1000.

Feudal Castles

Mur, in the *comarca* of Pallars Jussà, is a magnificent example of a feudal castle, considered to be one of the most typical examples of eleventh-century Catalan fortifications. It was built by the Catalan Viscount Arnau Mir de Tost (*c.* 1000–1072) who is credited with constructing many other fortifications such as those of Viacamp and Lluçars (Ribagorça) or Llordà (Pallars Jussà). Arnau Mir de Tost came to possess about seventy castles in the counties of Urgell, Pallars, and Ribagorça, either in full control or through infeudation by the counts of Urgell, Barcelona, or the king of Aragon.[31]

---

29 In 870, Count Guifré el Pilós (Wilfred I the Hairy) received the counties of Urgell and Cerdanya from the Frankish monarchs. In 878, he became count of the counties of Barcelona and Girona. This made it easier for him to regain control of the lands of Osona and Baix Berguedà, located between these two territories.

30 Adell and Riu, 'La torre de l'alta edat mitjana de Ribes'.

31 Fité, *Reculls d'història de la Vall d'Àger*.

CASTLES AND CASTRAL VILLAGES   89

Hundreds of castles were built in Catalonia in the eleventh and twelfth centuries. Unfortunately, many of them have been destroyed or badly damaged over the centuries. We can, however, list a fair number of fortifications with a tower and an enclosure, such as those of Farners (La Selva) and Cruïlles (Baix Empordà) or keeps (*donjons*, in French; *torrasses*, in Catalan) from the twelfth century, such as the Templar castle of Gardeny (Segrià). The encyclopaedic work 'Catalunya Romànica' is a comprehensive study of all the fortifications of this Romanesque period.[32] We should also mention the six volumes 'Els castells catalans', which has an extensive description of all the castles based only on the study of the written documents.[33]

Mur (Pallars Jussà)

The castle of Mur consists of a tower and an enclosure with rooms, a cistern, barns, etc. It was made of stone ashlar. This was one of the castles of Viscount Arnau Mir de Tost, who, as mentioned above, was a powerful lord on the frontier in the first half of the eleventh century.[34] This castle was excavated from 1997–2002.[35] The complementarity between the tower, almost always of a circular plan, and an adjoining enclosure is one of the characteristic features of most feudal castles of the eleventh century. In this case, a collegiate church and, probably, some houses were built next to the castle.

Lluçars (Ribagorça)

In Romanesque Catalonia, almost all the main towers of the castles were made of stone and had a circular plan. From the eleventh century, we find very few towers that were not cylindrical. However, within the domains of Arnau Mir de Tost, we discover the castle of Lluçars (Ribagorça) with a magnificent pentagonal tower and six wooden trestles separating the different levels.[36] While most of the towers were simple watchtowers from where smoke or fire signals could be sent, the castle of Lluçars was a residence for its lords. There is a chapel and a latrine. Upstairs, there were also several wooden scaffolds (or hoardings). The tower stood on a hill above the village.

The castle of Lluçars resembles the fortification we find in Viacamp (Ribagorça), where there is a large circular tower and, around it, an even wider enclosure. In both cases, but especially in the one in Viacamp, as we have said, there was probably a fortification, a *castrum*, long before the tower was built in the eleventh century.

---

32 Vigué and Pladevall ed., *Catalunya Romànica*.
33 Català i Roca dir., *Els castells catalans*.
34 Fité and González, *Arnau Mir de Tost. Un senyor de frontera*.
35 Sancho, *Mur, la història d'un castell feudal*.
36 Bolòs and Busqueta, 'Castell de Lluçars'.

90 CHAPTER 4

For this Romanesque period, we can also mention the large rectangular residential castle that Arnau Mir de Tost, owned in Llordà (Pallars Jussà).[37] And, as stated above, from the twelfth century we find some keeps with rectangular floor plans and halls inside. The castle of Gardeny (Segrià) and the keep of Riner (Solsonès) are prime examples of residential castles. Then in the thirteenth century, the castles were formed by four wings around a large central courtyard, with towers at the four corners, such as the magnificent (and unfinished) castle of Montgrí (Baix Empordà), located at the top of a mountain, or that of Balsareny (Bages), by the river Llobregat.

The Creation of a New Frontier

In 1213, King Pere I (Peter I), King of Catalonia and Aragon, died close to the Occitan town of Muret, fighting against the French crusader Simon de Montfort. In 1258, the Catalan-Aragonese monarch, Jaume I (James I), had to accept the loss of the rights that his ancestors had held over much of Occitania and granted them to the king of France. This led to the creation of a border in northern Catalonia that separated Roussillon from Languedoc; in other words, the lands where Catalan was spoken from the lands where Occitan was spoken at the time. This constituted a border between the two kingdoms and motivated the construction of fortifications on the southern side with the extension of the castle of Talteüll (Fr. Tautavel) and the fortification of many churches. On the north side, numerous castles were rebuilt in the region of Fenouillèdes (now part of France), which previously depended on the Catalan counts, castles such as Puilaurens (Oc. Puèglhaurenç), Fenouillet (Oc. Fenolhet), Quéribus (Oc. Querbús), Peyrepertuse (Oc. Pèirapertusa) and Aguilar.[38] It seems that while the borders of the counties were easy to cross, this new demarcation between two opposing states was much less permeable. We will talk about it again when we study the borders of Catalonia in Chapter 14.

Precedents of Hilltop Villages

Let's go back again to settlements, and in turn, move back a few centuries. Excavations in recent decades in Europe have been instrumental for under-

---

37 In Llordà we find one of the best examples of Romanesque residential architecture. It contains innovative elements with respect to the traditional military architecture of the border. It consisted of three successive enclosures, at the top of which was the palace of Arnau Mir de Tost. This residential palace had three halls, one on top of the other, and a few other rooms, among which its kitchen stands out.

38 Alessandri and Bayrou, 'Sur quelques fortifications de la frontière de 1258'; Bolòs, *Els orígens medievals del paisatge català*, p. 91.

standing the characteristics and chronology of many castral villages. As is well known, in Montarrenti or Poggibonsi, below the castral villages after 1000, evidence has been found of houses from the Carolingian period and even of the most modest homes from the early medieval period.[39] Before a village controlled by the Carolingian lords or feudal lords was created, there was already a hilltop village probably built by peasant communities. This finding reflects the change of opinion that has taken place in recent years in how we view early medieval society and the current assessment of the role that peasants played in this context.[40]

Although in Catalonia, there is, to my knowledge, no synthesizing work on the contribution of the archaeology to the study of early medieval society, some interesting research has been done in this area. Analysing the results of archaeological excavations, we realize that not all the hilltop fenced-in villages can be dated to sometime after 1000. We find early medieval villages whose steep topography and a wall delimited their living space within which the houses were crowded. The most notable examples are Santa Creu de Llagunes (Pallars Sobirà) and Caulès (La Selva).[41] In the former, it seems clear that the church was built later. This type of village corresponds to an early medieval settlement that prioritizes defence. We could also add to these L'Esquerda (the old town of Roda, near Vic). Certainly, the origin of these villages precedes the feudalization of the year 1000. In all three cases, much older precedents have been noted: prehistoric in the case of Santa Creu de Llagunes, dating perhaps from Late Antiquity in the case of Caulès, and Iberian in L'Esquerda (with precedents in the late Bronze Age). In any case, long before1000, there were already fortified and hilltop medieval villages. They were certainly not the only ones; surely there are still inhabited towns today that could be included in the first villages of houses, despite being protected by their topography and perhaps by walls (for example, Moror or Llimiana in Pallars Jussà, Montclar in Berguedà, or Vilamitjana in Alt Urgell). Further research and archaeological excavations are still needed, such as those undertaken during the twentieth century by Manuel Riu, Albert Roig, and Jordi Roig.

Santa Creu de Llagunes (Soriguera, Pallars Sobirà)

This site has been excavated beginning in 1993. It is a magnificent example of a medieval mountain village, enclosed by walls located at about 1620 metres high. Its precedents date back to the Bronze Age and we know that it was inhabited in the Middle Ages but abandoned around the thirteenth or fourteenth centuries, at the time of the late medieval demographic crisis

---

39 Francovich and Hodges, *Villa to Village*.
40 Wickham, *Framing the Early Middle Ages*.
41 Roig and Roig, 'L'ocupació del territori de muntanya'; Riu, *Excavaciones en el poblado medieval de Caulers*; Riu, *L'arqueologia medieval a Catalunya*, p. 52.

CHAPTER 4

when a colder period began.[42] It was a walled village, with an area of about 2800 sq. m. There were even deep moats around the walls, perhaps inherited from pre-medieval phases. Inside, there were several stone-walled houses. Later, after 1000, it seems that a tower and a Romanesque church were added, located in the north-east corner.

Despite the differences, mention should also be made of the village of Bolvir, which has recently been excavated.[43] It was a walled village, located in the middle of Cerdanya. Most of the excavated houses were attached to the perimeter wall. Bolvir dates back to between the eleventh and twelfth centuries, although it was built on an *oppidum* from the fourth–first centuries BC. We find, therefore, a link with the pre-medieval past and a fortified settlement, which, according to researchers, may have been created again under the protection of the counts of Cerdanya, at a date very close to 1000. This case is a link to what we will see in the next section.

Characteristics of Castral Villages

A wide variety of books and studies have been published in Europe on castral villages. We will name just a few. First, there is Dominique Baudreu's article on the Occitan castral villages of Bas-Razès.[44] Second, some research was done a little earlier, which helps us understand both castral villages and new towns.[45] Also worth noting are the proceedings of two congresses: one at Flaran, dedicated to castles and settlements in western Europe; and a more contemporary congress dedicated to towns built in the shadow of castles.[46] Finally, there is an innovative volume on castles and *incastellamento* in Tuscany and other Italian regions.[47]

Below, we will focus mainly on castral villages created in Catalonia. These were small villages originally set up in the high Middle Ages close to a castle. In many cases, they have not changed much since then. However, as far as we know, it is impossible for us to confirm — or to deny — that before then, in the same place, there was a settlement dating back to the early Middle Ages. Surely, if we did further research, we would possibly find examples of both. For example, Palau-sator is quite different from Aguiló.

As we will see when describing the examples, there were settlements organized next to a castle in all the Catalan counties. However, while *sagrera* villages were very common in north-eastern Catalonia, castral villages

---

42 Roig and Roig, 'L'ocupació del territori de muntanya'.

43 Cubo and others, 'El Castellot de Bolvir. Un vilatge cerdà dels segles XI-XII'.

44 Baudreu, 'Une forme de villages médiévaux concentrés'.

45 Cursente, *Les Castelnaux de la Gascogne médiévale*.

46 Higounet, *Paysages et villages neufs du Moyen Âge*; Chédeville and Pichot, *Des villes à l'ombre des châteaux*.

47 Francovich and Ginatempo, *Castelli. Storia e archeologia del potere*.

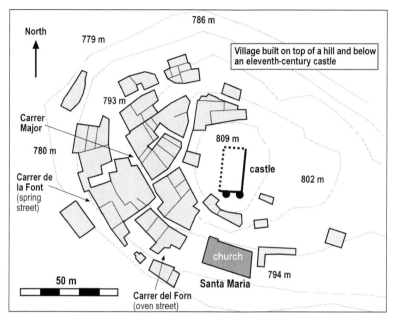

Figure 18. Village of Aguiló (Santa Coloma de Queralt, Conca de Barberà). Perched village built below an eleventh-century castle.

predominated in New Catalonia. This was not due to insecurity so much, as has sometimes been claimed, but to the characteristics of society at a given time. It has been verified for the diocese of Vic that the construction of ecclesiastical or castral villages depended largely on the relative influence of clergymen, especially bishops, and secular lords, as seen above with regard to *sagrera* villages.[48]

Castles were often built on top of a hill, in a prominent, easy-to-defend place. The village next door, therefore, would extend along the hillside, often on the southern side, which is the sunniest. Many of its streets follow the contours of the hills. These villages were frequently surrounded by ramparts or walls constructed from the exteriors of the houses. The village church was often outside the built-up area, next to the medieval walls or even at some distance. Sometimes, but not very often, the castral church became the village church. Whenever there was a process of *incastellamento* (e.g. Cortsaví), the former church, located quite far from the inhabited centre, over time retained only its burial function.[49]

---

48 Bolòs, 'Pobles de sagrera i pobles castrals'.
49 Catafau, 'Petites, nombreuses, isolées?', p. 83.

Aguiló (Santa Coloma de Queralt, Conca de Barberà)

To begin with examples of castral villages, we have singled out two places in New Catalonia to illustrate some of the characteristics of these hilltop settlements. Sometimes these were eagles' nests, whose protection was sought in a rugged topography; in fact, in this case, the name Aguiló (perhaps from an *eagle, àguila*, in Catalan) could account for the origin of its name (although it may derive from the fact that it is located to the north, *aquilone*, of the plain of Santa Coloma de Queralt).[50] As we shall see below, sometimes the position of a village, too far from the cultivated land, could not be maintained for very long, especially by peasants who worked the land, and when the dangerous situation disappeared, its population would move to a flatter position. But that was not always the case. At Aguiló, we find an eleventh-century castle, some of whose walls can still be seen. Below was the church dedicated to Saint Mary, and next to it, houses were organized along four or five streets (Fig. 18). This is a typical lofty castral village.

Granyanella (Segarra)

Granyanella is a hilltop village built around a castle. A set of houses surrounded a fortification, of which there are no remains, despite our certainty of its location. Further east, outside the gateway, is a second-half ring of houses, perhaps the result of a late extension of the original core. About 120 metres to the east of the castle — with a drop of thirty metres — is the parish church of Sant Salvador, documented in 1112. This separation between the church and the castle is very common in many castral villages. We know that there was a chapel in the castle, dedicated to Saint Matthew, which, however, did not become the parish church. The fact that the town was under the jurisdiction of the lords of the fortification, the Anglesola family, and that the parish church depended on the bishop of Vic, caused this distancing, which resembles, although the motivations were probably different, what we find in the villages of houses of the Pyrenees. In addition, it must be borne in mind that in the diocese of Lleida in the twelfth century, there were notable clashes between great secular lords and the bishop, due to tithes; at times, these disagreements ended in excommunications.

Palau-sator (Baix Empordà)

Although the *sagrera* or ecclesiastical village predominates in the Empordà area, occasionally we find castral villages, like Palau-sator (Fig. 19). This is a very interesting case. The tower that gives the place its name (in this case, 'sa' in Sator is an article) is an old building, probably from the pre-Romanesque

---

50 Coromines, *Onomasticon Cataloniae*, vol. II, p. 24.

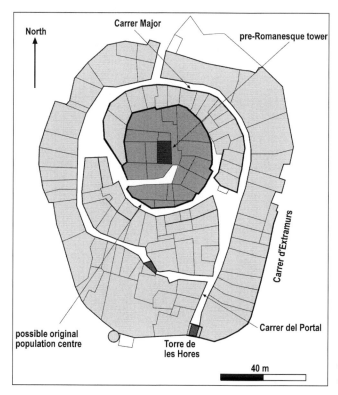

Figure 19. Castral village of Palau-sator (Baix Empordà). Enclosed village built around a tower in different phases.

period. It is already mentioned in a document from 994, although it may well have originated before, so the first settlement was certainly from much earlier than 1000.[51] In fact, cist tombs and *tegulae* graves, possibly from the Visigothic period, were found to the south and east of the church.

A closed village was built around the tower, probably in two phases. In the first phase, houses were built, forming circles of houses that extended around the building.[52] Then, in the second phase, there was an expansion to the south, with the extension of *Carrer Major* (main street), which reached the *Torre de les Hores* gateway. About 160 metres south of the tower, outside the built-up area, the church, dedicated to Saint Peter, was built. Although it is very difficult to confirm without archaeological evidence, we can propose to date the first phase to a time close to 1000 (with possible older precedents) and the second to the twelfth or thirteenth centuries.

---

51 Bolòs, 'Castell de Palau-sator', p. 231.
52 Bolòs, 'Conèixer el paisatge històric medieval per poder planificar i gestionar el territori', p. 156.

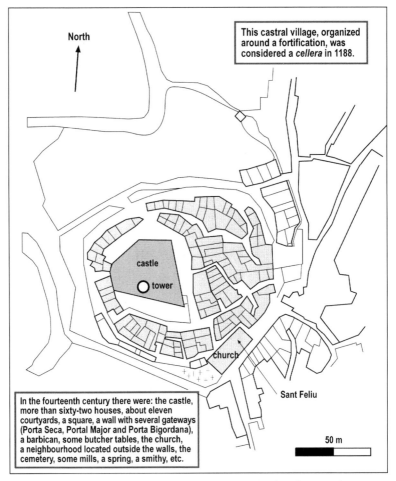

Figure 20. Castral village of La Roca d'Albera (Roussillon). Village established around a castle, referred to as a *cellera* in medieval documents. Source: Catafau, *Les celleres et la naissance du village en Roussillon*.

La Roca d'Albera (Rosselló)

Aymat Catafau, in his book on the origin of ecclesiastical villages in Roussillon, describes the village of La Roca d'Albera (Fr. Laroque-des-Albères) whose castle, La Roca, dates from the eleventh century.[53] This fortification had already become a construction that attracted the population in the late eleventh century. Interestingly, in 1188, according to documents preserved, a concession for a cellar was granted inside the *cellera* of the castle of La Roca d'Albera (Fig. 20). As Catafau points out, this apparent incompatibility — the ecclesiastical *cellera* and the surroundings of a castle — may be surprising, but

---

53 Catafau, *Les celleres et la naissance du village en Roussillon*, pp. 371–94.

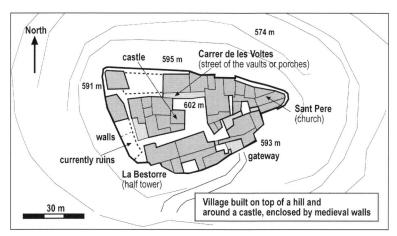

Figure 21. Village of Montfalcó Murallat (Les Oluges, Segarra). Example of a 'perched' or hilltop village built around a castle and enclosed by remarkable walls.

this contradictory situation can also be seen in many other castral villages.[54] Finally, it is worth noting that, in this case, the parish church, Sant Feliu de Tanyà, was about 600 m away to the east.

Then, in the fourteenth century, the castral village of La Roca d'Albera was already considered a *fortalicium*, a fortified place, enclosed by a wall, where, at the end of this century, there were ninety-five separate properties. The *capbreus* (in Latin, *caput breve*, land terrier) from this period provide enough data to reconstruct the streets, the square, and the butchers' tables; there are even references to a sewer. In La Roca d'Albera, we see a village built around the place where the castle once stood. Despite having a circular plan, we can see an extension on the eastern side, with several streets leading onto the square and other gateways (medieval documents already mention the *Portal Major* or main gateway).

Sort (Pallars Sobirà)

The town of Sort is currently the capital of the Pallars Sobirà *comarca*. In the Middle Ages, there was, in the upper part of the town, the castle of the counts of Pallars. Our focus on this place revolves around two aspects. First, the church of Saint Felix is to the south of the old town. It is now situated in a marginal position; at the beginning of the eleventh century, this church had a *sagrera*, which could have become a village. But this never happened because it was destroyed as a result of fighting in the second half of the eleventh century among feudal lords associated with different branches of the count's house.

---

54 Catafau, *Les celleres et la naissance du village en Roussillon*, p. 376.

98   CHAPTER 4

Secondly, we are interested in the fact that in the high Middle Ages a castral village developed, which is currently visible to the east of the counts' castle, and was organized around three streets almost parallel to each other, and which follow the same contour (Carrer de Sant Ot, Carrer del Mig, and Carrer Major).[55]

Montfalcó Murallat (Les Oluges, Segarra)

Montfalcó Murallat is a well-preserved, walled town on a hilltop (Fig. 21) enclosed by a rampart made from right-angled ashlars. The gateway, finished with a voussoir arch, is on the southern side of the wall. In the centre of the village, there is a square, under which there is a cistern. From the square, a street leads to the Romanesque church of Sant Pere (Saint Peter) and another, Carrer Rodó, which goes around the inner face of the wall. In the middle of the town of Montfalcó Murallat, next to the square, was the square tower of the castle. In studying its planning, we have observed the existence of extensions, which motivated the construction of a new wall to the south and the construction of another tower. The castle must have been built in the eleventh century; in 1043, the term *Monte Falconi* was already cited.[56] The town walls are predominantly medieval, but parts may well be from a later period.

In the Middle Ages, many Catalan villages were enclosed by walls with one or more gateways. Sometimes they were enclosed by ramparts, made of good ashlars, possibly with half towers (*bestorres*, in Catalan) or corner towers (*torres d'angle*). In other cases, Catalan villages were only protected by the external walls of houses. Occasionally, although not often, they were enclosed within rammed earth walls, as evidenced in the population charter of Vilanova de Segrià from 1231.[57]

Overall, we can find walls in almost every castral village, as seen in previous examples. There were also walls in new towns, as will be seen in Chapter 5, such as Montblanc, Vilafranca del Penedès, and La Selva del Camp. As mentioned above, some house or open villages (e.g. Espot) and *sagrera* villages (e.g. Bages de Rosselló) ended up becoming a *força*, enclosed by walls. In some border counties at the end of the Middle Ages, there were also fortified churches, a good example being the church of Ropidera (Conflent), which since the thirteenth century was near the border with the kingdom of France.[58]

---

55   Bolòs, 'Un territori en temps de guerra'.

56   The place name may come from the name of the bird of prey, the hawk (Cat. *falcó*). However, it probably derives from the Germanic name of a person, *Falco*, documented before the year 1000, for example in the county of Manresa. Coromines, *Onomasticon Cataloniae*, vol. IV, p. 184; Bolòs and Moran, *Repertori d'Antropònims Catalans*, p. 288.

57   *Cartas de población y franquicia de Cataluña*, ed. by Font Rius, doc. 256.

58   Leclerc, 'Les églises fortifiées du Roussillon'; Passarrius and Catafau, 'Ropidera: un poble medieval en els seus territoris'.

Incastellamento and Hilltop Villages

A chapter on castral villages would not be complete without considering the process of concentrating the population within fortifications, *incastellamento*, and perhaps the best way to start is with reference to Italy and the early works of Pierre Toubert.[59] After the publication of Toubert's thesis, which had a significant impact and influence on research carried out in Italy and in much of Europe, several conferences were held on this topic, introducing some variety to certain aspects of the characteristics and chronology of changes around 1000.[60] Again, thanks to archaeological excavations, it has now been discovered that under many of these castral villages in northern Italy, originally believed to have been established as a result of *incastellamento*, there were pre-existing hilltop villages from the early medieval period created not by lords but rather by local peasants seeking a safe place.[61] In addition, in Italy, it has also been pointed out that there was a phase prior to the *incastellamento* of the year 1000, related to the construction of lordly homes (*curtes*, in Latin) in the Carolingian period.

Despite all this, around 1000, in many regions of Europe, there was indeed an increase in the number of hilltop villages next to castles. The well-known excavations of Rougiers (Oc. Rotgiers) should be mentioned.[62] Lately, this is seen as a process that began around 1000 and developed in the twelfth and thirteenth centuries.[63] In Catalonia during the tenth, eleventh, and twelfth centuries, many hilltop villages were created, often located next to a fortification. And, perhaps more importantly, especially in the eleventh century, there were numerous relocations of families, for example, from the side of a church to the side of a castle of the lord of the place. In sum, there was more than one motive for the creation of hilltop villages.

There are mainly two reasons for this phenomenon. On the one hand, safety was a concern in the lands that were close to frontiers during the tenth and eleventh centuries. Later there are references to settlements like Vilademàger in the county of Barcelona, and the castle of La Guàrdia in the county of Pallars. Maybe then we should talk about hilltop villages. Keep in mind that many of these villages built on top of a mountain or hill were created well before 1000.

On the other hand, lordly pressure also played a part. Although there may be exceptions to this practice, in Old Catalonia we find clear testimonies of *incastellamento*, for example in Cortsaví (Vallespir), as will be seen later. In New Catalonia, we can mention Verdú (Urgell), whose lady of the castle

---

59 Toubert, *Les structures du Latium médiéval*.
60 Barceló and Toubert ed., *L'incastellamento*.
61 Francovich and Hodges, *Villa to Village*.
62 Démians d'Archimbaud, *Les fouilles de Rougiers*.
63 Maufras and others, '*Villae* — Villages du haut Moyen Âge', p. 95.

encouraged people to settle in front of the fortification and next to the church of the place, as evidenced by a document from 1184.[64] Closer to Lleida, the Templar lords of Vilanova de la Barca and Vilanova de Segrià wanted to concentrate in one place the population, who until then had been living in dispersed 'towers', which were probably fortified hamlets, as we will see in Chapter 6, that often had roots in the Islamic era. This process of *incastellamento* favoured the creation of castral villages as well as new towns, which can be easily confused.

There are also many surprising cases: in the settlement charter of Civit (Segarra), its lord authorized twelve families to settle in this border place, build their houses, work the land, and build a castle (Latin, 'faciatis castro et turre cum muros').[65] Here, in 1051, the fortification was built by the peasant settlers themselves. We must keep in mind that this village was located in the *marca* (a march) of the county of Manresa, and at an exceptional moment when the lord of the settlement perhaps prioritized his need to occupy territory over his desire to build a castle.

Population Relocation

Above, we have already commented on Àreu (Pallars Sobirà) and the phenomenon of its twin settlement: a few hundred metres from the older, open village, a *força* was built, a castral village, enclosed by walls. In this case, in a region of villages of houses, its lord decided to create a newly fortified and better-located settlement but did not push for or force the abandonment of its original location. However, in many other cases, in eleventh-century Catalonia, the population was relocated and the old village was deserted. A very interesting case, studied by Aymat Catafau, is that of Sant Joan de Pladecorts (Vallespir; Fr. Saint-Jean-Pla-de-Corts) where the population was relocated from an ecclesiastical to a castral village, about 400 m to the west.[66] This castral village was considered, in the fourteenth century, to be a *cellera* and, in the sixteenth century, a *força*. In the same region, the case of Cortsaví stands out, which we will discuss below.

Further south, we also find other examples of relocations. This was the case in Foixà in Empordà.[67] In a flat place, at a crossroads dating back to the Roman era, was the church of Saint John (where plausibly there was a *sagrera*); on a nearby hill, further to the south-east, a castle was built and at its foot there are a cluster of houses still called La Vila.

---

64 *Cartas de población y franquicia de Cataluña*, ed. by Font Rius, doc. 174.

65 *Cartas de población y franquicia de Cataluña*, ed. by Font Rius, doc. 24.

66 Catafau, *Les celleres et la naissance du village en Roussillon*, pp. 574–78.

67 Bolòs, 'Aportació al coneixement de la morfogènesi dels pobles del comtat d'Empúries', pp. 273–74.

Much further to the southwest, inside marchland, we find another good example of *incastellamento*-related population relocation. The village of La Curullada (its name coming from *cruïllada*, crossroads in Catalan), located in La Segarra, was initially, at a date close to 1000, next to the river Ondara, where the church was; then a castle was built about 500 m further north on a higher location; gradually, everybody moved to the vicinity of the fortification, including eventually even the church.

Catalonia provides many other cases, such as Mosset, Eus, and Vallestàvia (Fr. Baillestavy) in Conflent and Vallfogona de Ripollès (Ripollès). The relocation of the latter does not seem to have occurred until the fourteenth century when a manor (*casa forta*, in Catalan) was built 350 m from the church.[68] It should be noted that the earliest research on relocations from an ecclesiastical to a castral village was undertaken in the Occitan region.[69] In Lansac (in the Occitan region of Fenouillèdes; Oc. Lançac), there was a double relocation process: its population first left the church precinct to settle next to the castle. Then, at the end of the Middle Ages, they returned next to the church, close to their land. In Loupian (Oc. Lopian), on the other hand, the inhabitants moved from the early medieval settlement (between the fourth century and the tenth or eleventh centuries) to the castral village (eleventh century); in this case, though, there was a baptismal church between the original settlement and the castral village.[70]

Cortsaví (Vallespir)

In the village of Cortsaví (Fr. Corsavy) we find a very interesting case of *incastellamento* or the transfer of a population next to the castle.[71] Shortly after 1000, there was a thirty-step *sacraria* (or sacred circle) around the church of Saint Martin of Cortsaví. A document made in 1090 mentions the forty-three *sagrers* (*sacrarii*, plots of land) in the cemetery of Saint Martin, which, we must assume, were occupied by the living and the dead. However, the lord of Cortsaví obliged those who lived there to pay for oppressive levies known as 'bad customs' (*malos usaticos*, in Latin). Soon, people had to move. In 1159, a chapel dedicated to Saint James was built in the castle of Cortsaví. This castle is located about 900 m west of the church of Saint Martin of Cortsaví. Therefore, even though in the eleventh century a group of *sagrers* and, plausibly, houses were built around the church of Saint Martin, throughout the eleventh century and especially in the twelfth century, through lordly pressure, the families had to move to around the castle, where the village is located nowadays.

---

68 Bolòs, *Els orígens medievals del paisatge català*, p. 279.
69 Baudreu and Cazes, 'Le rôle de l'église dans la formation des villages médiévaux'.
70 Schneider, 'De la fouille des villages abandonnés à l'archéologie des territoires locaux', p. 150.
71 Catafau, *Les celleres et la naissance du village en Roussillon*, pp. 305–11.

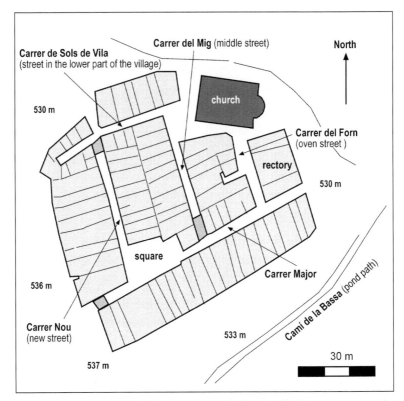

Figure 22. Village of La Guàrdia de Noguera (Pallars Jussà). New town created as a result of the relocation of the people who lived next to a 'perched' or hilltop castle.

Decastellamento

In Catalonia, there was an *incastellamento* (or in Catalan *encastellament*) brought about by the lords (e.g. Cortsaví or Verdú) and, perhaps earlier, there was also an increase in the creation of hilltop villages, as a result, mainly, of the proximity to the border with the Islamic lands (e.g. Vilademàger). After the year 1000, some of the sites selected for safety because of the threat from the Muslim territories were gradually abandoned because these higher locations were inconveniently far away from the fields. For this reason, we use *decastellamento*, a term coined by Settia to refer mainly to the dismantling of fortifications.[72] This process may account for the creation of new villages near the fields or the growth of existing settlements. Two examples are worth mentioning: Vilademàger is on the border between the counties of Barcelona and Manresa, and La Guàrdia is at the southern end of the county of Pallars.

---

72 Settia, *Castelli e villagi nell'Italia padana*, p. 287.

La Llacuna (Anoia)

In the municipality of La Llacuna, we find a very clear example of *decastellamento*. In the Carolingian period, the castle of Vilademàger is already mentioned, one of the many fortifications at the centre of a district of a march castle, very close to the border with the lands controlled by the Muslims. As the name suggests, there was a *villa* and a church, apart from a fortification, which has been recently excavated.[73] However, during the high Middle Ages, the population moved from this hilltop village to a village on the plain, La Llacuna, next to a Benedictine priory and where a marketplace was soon set up every week. However, in the village of La Llacuna there was no parish church until the eighteenth century. Vilademàger is 740 metres high in a steep area, while La Llacuna is 615 metres above sea level on a plain next to a spring and an *horta* that extends over a slope; the two villages are around 1.4 kilometres apart.[74]

La Guàrdia de Noguera (Pallars Jussà)

Around 1000, a settlement and a church were built next to the castle of La Guàrdia, at 710 metres above sea level. It was a hilltop location far away from farmland. Centuries later in the high Middle Ages, the inhabitants moved one kilometre to the south to a newly-organized settlement which was located at 530 metres above sea level. The new town of La Guàrdia has the characteristics of a planned village; in the higher southern part, there is a street running from east to west, plus three streets from north to south (Fig. 22). To the north there is another street going east and west with the church located at the northeast corner.

Fortifications Move Closer to the Crops

There was also another reality: the relocation of the lords from a hilltop castle, inhabited in the early Middle Ages, to a castle located in a flatter place, which was closer to people, roads, and cultivated land. This could even lead to a concentration of the population in this flatter area and, in turn, the creation of a new castral village. Three obvious examples stand out. Some *veguers* (Latin, *vicarii*, viguiers), which initially depended on the count, from the castle of Finestres (Garrotxa), who around 1000 became feudal lords, lived in an inaccessible place, situated at 957 metres high, on top of a peak surrounded by cliffs. This fortification, created in the Carolingian period, was located on the southern border of the county of Besalú; this was a good lookout point (hence its name). In the high Middle Ages, these lords from Finestres moved

---

73 Sabaté and Folch, 'El castell de Vilademàger'.
74 Bolòs, *El paisatge medieval del comtat de Barcelona*, pp. 190–202.

104 CHAPTER 4

to Santa Pau, where they built a Gothic castle-palace located in the middle of a valley, 496 metres high. As we will discuss later, a new town was built around the castle in 1300, and it even had a square with arcades where the market was held. The castle of Finestres was an early medieval fortification, while the castle of Santa Pau was a high medieval castle-palace.

In the nearby valley of Bas, we find a very similar situation: the lords of the valley moved from the hilltop fortification of Castelló, which was on a cliff at 953 metres above sea level, to the top of the hill of El Mallol, which was only 524 metres high. In fact, the village of El Mallol grew up around this new castle; it is a castral village that is also slightly elevated. It represents a transition from an early medieval *castrum* to a feudal castle. Finally, in previous references to the creation of a castral village in Vallfogona de Ripollès, we assume that it dates from the fourteenth century as a result of the creation of a manor located 350 metres from the church (at an altitude of 995 m). Before 1349, the lords of this village lived in the castle of Milany, which was on top of a mountain at 1530 metres above sea level; this fortification is currently being excavated.[75]

Conclusions

A high percentage of Catalan villages are built below or next to a castle. A few years ago, we sought to visualize these villages by mapping both castles with neighbouring settlements and hilltop castles remote from settlements.[76] There was a clear difference between Old and New Catalonia; in the former, a minority of villages were within fortifications, whereas in the latter a majority of villages were fortified. However, as we have pointed out, it is also important to differentiate between castral villages resulting from a process of *incastellamento* caused by pressure from a lord, and those undergoing an *encimbellament* (hilltop settlement), caused by the desire to move away from danger. We have mentioned two examples: Cortsaví, far from the march, and Vilademàger, which in 1000 was very close to the border with Islamic lands.

Rediscovering castral villages has also made us aware of another reality, to which all the other elements of the historical landscape can be applied. We have found that, sometimes, landscape features may be much older than we assumed at first. For example, the castle of Vallferosa is not documented until the eleventh century, and it was believed to have been built at the end of the tenth century, but according to recent work, it could date back to the eighth century. We have learned that we cannot rely blindly on the dates recorded in written documents, as they only certify the date of their documented existence, but they seldom prove whether or not they existed before.

---

75 Fàbregas, 'Sota l'enderroc: les restes del castell de Milany'.
76 Bolòs, 'Fortificacions de la marca i organització del territori a Catalunya', p. 80.

Another lesson is that change was constant. People who lived around the churches of Sant Joan de Pladecorts or Cortsaví in the eleventh century were forced to move and live around the castle, probably due to lordly pressure. On the other hand, sometime later, people who lived next to the castle of Vilademàger went down to La Llacuna, near their farmland, while the parish church was not built until the eighteenth century. Or the lords who lived in the old castle of Milany in the fourteenth century decided to move down to La Sala, next to the church of Vallfogona de Ripollès, where a small castral village was created.

Many villages were built in New Catalonia during the eleventh and twelfth centuries as a result of conquest and colonization. However, in many cases, we would almost certainly find the remains of older houses if we excavated deep enough (unless they were destroyed over the centuries). Be that as it may, whether it is due to people searching for a safer place to live, trying to avoid a temperature inversion, or by the pressure of a lord having built a castle on top of a hill, many counties of Catalonia are sprinkled with hilltop villages (*pobles encimbellats*) and villages near castles (*encastellats*). They have become a remarkable element of the Catalan landscape since the Middle Ages.

CHAPTER 5

New Towns and Complex Settlements

Introduction

One component of the medieval landscape that long ago caught the attention of historians was the creation of new towns. Their populations were economically dynamic, with significant artisanal and trading activity, and they were, in particular, places with urban planning. The forms of urban planning of the Occitan *bastides* were of particular interest to French and English historians. New towns have been found all over Europe, often with regular urbanism. Different typologies of the various forms of organization of urban space have been established. In Catalonia, both in the north and in New Catalonia we also find many new towns, often well planned, possibly related to the new towns discovered further north or further south, for example in Valencia and the Balearic Islands. In studying these newly built villages, however, it must be borne in mind that they were often the result of the ambition of a lord, sometimes of a sovereign, to consolidate his power over a territory. At the end of this chapter, we will also comment on the existence of more complex polyfocal villages, such as the beautiful examples of Santa Coloma de Queralt and Castelló d'Empúries.

What Do We Know About New Towns

Studies of European medieval new towns (*viles noves*, in Catalan) started earlier than those of castral and ecclesiastical villages. Significant contributions to this type of settlement have been made by studying Occitan new towns or *bastides*,[1] the new towns of Wales and England,[2] Germany and Slavic countries,[3] the territory of Valencia, and the Balearic Islands, to mention just a few.[4] Studies have been conducted on Italian new towns or settlements from the former kingdoms of Castile or Portugal.[5] From the high Middle Ages onwards, new towns (*viles noves*) often planned, were an important landscape feature in Catalonia too.

New towns across Europe reflect a period of population growth. They are also evidence for a process of economic expansion and, very often, of

---

1   Higounet, *Paysages et villages neufs du Moyen Âge*; Beresford, *New Towns of the Middle Ages Gascony*; Guidoni, *Storia dell'urbanistica. Il Duecento*, pp. 33–49.
2   Beresford, *New Towns of the Middle Ages*; Aston and Bond, *The Landscape of Towns*, p. 79.
3   Higounet, *Les Allemands en Europe centrale et orientale au Moyen Âge*.
4   Rosselló, *Viles planificades valencianes*; Mas, 'Les Ordinacions d'en Jaume II'.
5   Guidoni, *Storia dell'urbanistica. Il Duecento*, pp. 83–96; Martínez and Urteaga ed., *Las villas nuevas medievales del suroeste europeo*; Paio, 'As noves vilas medievais portuguesas'.

the colonization of previously conquered lands. They may be the result of an attempt to control territory, sometimes to counteract the military or economic influence of the surrounding lords, or sometimes to dominate the population in the area. This was the case of the Occitan lands conquered by the northern French. The construction, after the crusade against the Cathars, of the new town of Carcassonne (1247) or the planned settlement of Aigues-Mortes (1240) merit special attention.[6] The same phenomenon applies to the English-controlled Welsh march, German-colonized lands in Eastern Europe, and a few repopulated areas of Valencia.[7] The processes of conquest and colonization, as shown by Robert Bartlett, were present across Europe all through the high Middle Ages.[8] Elsewhere, for example, in Italy, the creation of *borghi nuovi, borghi franchi, or terre nuove* was more closely linked to the desire to expand cities in hitherto marginal and sometimes even dangerous lands.[9]

The Process of Conquest

Before considering the characteristics of the new villages, it is worth referring briefly to the process of the conquest of New Catalonia, which took place in the eleventh and twelfth centuries. Although not all new towns are in New Catalonia, they are numerous in the plains of Lleida and in the vicinity of the cities of Tarragona and Tortosa. Many received population charters, which were published by Josep M. Font Rius in 1969.[10]

In 801, the border between the lands that belonged to Charlemagne's empire and the lands that depended on the Emir of Córdoba was the river Llobregat, only about eleven kilometres west of Barcelona. It was not until the tenth century that the boundaries of the march's lands reached the Gaià, at the gates of Tarragona. The same applies to other counties. The southern boundary of the county of Urgell must have initially extended perhaps as far as Oliana, where there is a castle called Castell-llebre (the name is understood to come from old Catalan. It is related to *vedre*). In the tenth century, on the other hand, the mountainous land was already differentiated from the lands of the march or border. In this first stage of the conquest, there were a few population charters. We find them, for example, in relation to the town of Cardona (Bages) and the castles of Montmell (Baix Penedès) and Sant Pere de Ribes (Garraf).

---

6 Bocchi, *Per antiche strade*, p. 143.
7 Beresford and St Joseph, *Medieval England. An aerial survey*, pp. 231–38; Higounet, *Les Allemands en Europe centrale et orientale au Moyen Âge*; Torró, 'Arqueologia de la conquesta'.
8 Bartlett, *The Making of Europe*.
9 Bocchi, *Per antiche strade*, pp. 146–64.
10 *Cartas de población y franquicia de Cataluña*, ed. by Font Rius.

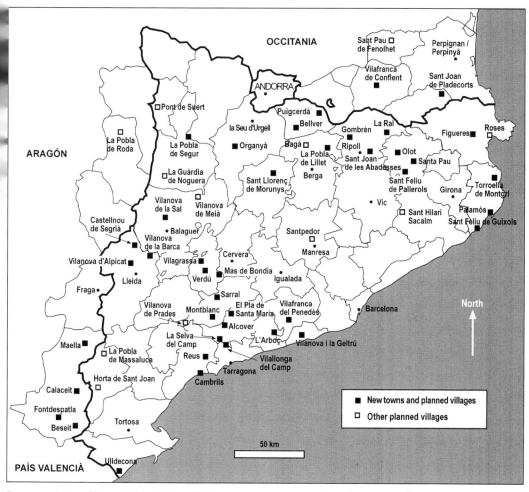

Figure 23. Map of historic Catalonia with the new towns mentioned in the text.

Throughout the eleventh century, the political situation changed radically, because of the creation of the various *taifa* kingdoms and the ensuing break in the balance of power that had prevailed until then to the benefit of the Christian sovereigns. The new political reality allowed further expansion to the west and south, with the occupation of such towns as Guissona (before 1024), Cervera (1026), Àger (1034), Agramunt (c. 1050), Camarasa (1050), Tàrrega (before 1056), L'Espluga de Francolí (c. 1087), etc. It was not, however, until the first half of the twelfth century that the conquest of the main cities of New Catalonia took place: Balaguer (1110), Tarragona (1116), Tortosa (1148), Lleida and Fraga (1149).[11]

---

11 All these population charters were published in 1969 by Font Rius, *Cartas de población y franquicia de Cataluña*.

With the conquest of Siurana, a fortified eagle's nest, around 1153 or 1154, the conquest of Catalonia ended, during the rule of Ramon Berenguer IV, who was also the prince of Aragon, following his marriage to the daughter of the king of Aragon.[12]

The process of conquest and colonization of New Catalonia was linked to the granting of many population charters, such as those of Calders (1037), Albinyana (1040), Granyena de Segarra (1054), El Talladell (1067), Gerb (1082), Penelles (1084), Tàrrega (1116), Tarragona (1129), Bellcaire d'Urgell (1139), Almenar (1147), L'Espluga Calba (1148), to name but a few. In some of these newly created towns, we find planned urbanism. In 1148 and 1149, after the conquest, population charters were granted to Tortosa and, in 1150, to the city of Lleida. From then on, the granting of concessions ensued. This was the case with, for example, L'Espluga de Francolí (1151), Vinaixa (1151), Castelldans (1151), Vimbodí (1151), Cambrils (1152), Siurana (1153), Constantí (1159), Agramunt (1163), Menàrguens (1163), and Ulldemolins (1166). We can even mention the population charter granted by Ramon Berenguer IV, in 1149, to the Jews of Tortosa, authorizing them to build sixty houses.[13]

Typology and Distribution Map

Although new villages are more frequent in New Catalonia than in Old Catalonia, we see them all over Catalonia. In Figure 23, we find just a few of them. Recently, notable efforts have been made to establish a typology of this type of village, for example concerning the numerous *bastides* of the Occitan lands.[14] These contributions have been used as references when proposing a typology of new Catalan towns. We can therefore establish the following types of planned villages:

– First, new towns were organized along one or more lengthwise road axes. There is a distinction between villages whose houses follow a single axis and those with a main street and one or more parallel streets. In all these cases, there may be some less important cross-streets since the main facades of the houses face the main axes.

– Secondly, new towns with a main axis or street and several rather long perpendicular streets branching out. These settlements have a pattern reminiscent of a herringbone, i.e. cross-streets forming right angles. It should be noted that the houses, in this case, are not oriented around the main street, as seen in the previous case, but around the various cross-streets.

---

12 Menchon, 'Algunes fortificacions (islàmiques?) al sud de Catalunya', pp. 71–75.
13 *Cartas de población y franquicia de Cataluña*, ed. by Font Rius, doc. 76.
14 Abbé and others, 'Les villes neuves médiévales du sud-ouest de la France'.

- Third, new towns are organized according to an orthogonal grid pattern. There are several possibilities. We need to differentiate between, for example, house blocks with a square pattern and house clusters with a rectangular pattern. In small towns, only a few streets were sometimes organized, often orthogonally.

- Fourth, new towns with more irregular shapes. The lack of regularity can be attributed to an irregular topography or the fact that they were, after all, small settlements. There could also be irregularities in some new villages because, before their creation, there could have been a building or a road that caused a distortion in the urban organization. An illustrative example of this is the town of Ulldecona (Montsià) (Fig. 26). Another reason for their irregular shape could be their construction in different phases.

It is also essential to check whether these new towns have a square. The square used to be a space dedicated to celebrating the market, hence market squares (*mercadal*, in Catalan). The markets often had arcades in order to provide shelter for people. Next to the square could be the church or the town hall. These well-planned squares used to be organized according to an orthogonal grid pattern; in this case, the square could be the same size as one of the blocks of houses (Fig. 27).

Table 1 shows many of the new towns in Catalonia, created in the high Middle Ages, and records the name of the village and its region, or *comarca*, as well as its date of creation, often coinciding with the year in which the village was granted a population or privilege charter. The next column gives the lord of the town. The last column of the table details the shape of the village and its surface. In terms of shape, we have used the typology described above. As for the surface, we have taken as a reference what we see in current aerial photographs. It should be borne in mind that there is a difference between the early new town and the medieval settlement (this is the case, for example, of Figueres, Maella, Vilanova del Penedès, etc.); in these cases, we have included in brackets the extension from the latter. In this table, we have not included neighbourhoods of houses found in a few large towns, with shapes reminiscent of new towns because of a previous planning design (e.g., Girona, Tarragona, Balaguer, Ripoll, Tàrrega). On the other hand, we do include new monastic villages such as Sant Joan de les Abadesses and Sant Llorenç de Morunys.

Most of these villages originated when a lord promoted houses for families to settle in. Therefore, when these new towns were originally created next to a castle, they did not differ much from the castral villages. This is the case, for example, of Santa Pau, Sant Joan de Pladecorts, Verdú, and Montblanc. However, this was not always the case. As a result of the settlement transfer that took place in Ulldecona, which was founded by a master Hospitaller, the new town was built far from the castle. Nor can we forget cases of new towns created next to a monastery, for example in Sant Llorenç de Morunys or, as we will see below, in Sant Joan de les Abadesses. Above, we have already

CHAPTER 5

Table 1. New towns in Catalonia created during the high Middle Ages.

Name	Comarca	Date
Alcover	Alt Camp	1166
L'Arboç	Baix Penedès	12th century
Bellver	Cerdanya	1225
Beseit	Matarranya	12th century
Calaceit	Matarranya	12th century
Cambrils	Baix Camp	1155
Castellnou de Segrià (now Vilanova de Segrià)	Segrià	1231
Figueres	Alt Empordà	1267
Fondespatla	Matarranya	1232
Gombrèn	Ripollès	1278
Maella	Matarranya	1181
Mas de Bondia	Segarra	12th and 13th centuries
Montblanc	Conca de Barberà	1163
Olot	Garrotxa	1427
Organyà	Alt Urgell	1233
Palamós	Baix Empordà	1279, 1336
El Pla de Santa Maria	Alt Camp	1173
La Pobla de Lillet	Berguedà	1297
La Pobla de Segur	Pallars Jussà	13th century
Puigcerdà	Cerdanya	1178
La Ral	Ripollès	1248
Reus	Baix Camp	1184, 1186
Sant Feliu de Guíxols	Baix Empordà	1181
Sant Feliu de Pallerols	Garrotxa	12th and 13th centuries
Sant Joan de les Abadesses	Ripollès	1206, 1243
Sant Joan de Pladecorts	Vallespir	1188
Sant Llorenç de Morunys	Solsonès	1297
Santa Pau	Garrotxa	1300
Sarral	Conca de Barberà	1180
La Selva del Camp	Baix Camp	1164
Torroella de Montgrí	Baix Empordà	1237, 1265, 1272
Ulldecona	Montsià	1274
Verdú	Urgell	1184
Vilafranca de Conflent	Conflent	1088–1090
Vilafranca del Penedès	Alt Penedès	12th century
Vilagrassa	Urgell	1185
Vilallonga del Camp	Tarragonès	1285
Vilanova d'Alpicat (now Alpicat)	Segrià	14th and 15th centuries
Vilanova de la Barca	Segrià	1212
Vilanova de la Sal (or de Privà)	Noguera	1154–1166
Vilanova de Meià	Noguera	11th and 12th centuries
Vilanova i la Geltrú (Vilanova de Cubelles)	Garraf	1274

rd	Shape	Surface (in ha)
ng and archbishop	A grid pattern with rectangular blocks and a square	2.11
ng	Two lengthwise streets with crosswise streets	3.58
unt	A grid pattern with rectangular blocks and a square	1.26
ng	Three streets and a grid pattern	0.72
ng	Polyfocal and irregular	5.34
unt	Main street, cross-streets, and the square	3.51
mplars	Two streets	0.47
ng	A grid pattern and rectangular blocks	3.27 (5.31)
rd	A grid pattern and rectangular blocks	1.36
rd	Irregular and three streets	0.29
ng	Irregular grid pattern	2.17 (3.67)
mplars	Street	0.51
ng	With two streets, a square, and one expansion district	13.37
lod	A grid pattern and rectangular blocks and a square	1.79
llegiate church, count	A grid pattern	1.24
ng	A grid pattern and rectangular blocks	1.89
ng and archbishop	Herringbone	3.67
rd	Irregular, and four streets	0.64
scount	Two streets	0.98
ng	Two streets and one expansion district	1.78 (3.94)
ng	Street	0.48
hamberlain	A grid pattern and rectangular blocks and a square	3.91 (11.6)
onastery	A grid pattern and rectangular blocks and a square	3.53
rd	Street and square	0.62
onastery	Herringbone and square	2.07
rd	Street and three side streets	0.47
onastery, viscount	Herringbone	1.38
rd	Square	0.39
ng	A grid pattern and rectangular blocks	4.29
chbishop	Herringbone	4.30 (7.56)
rd, King	A grid pattern and rectangular blocks and a square	3.13
ospitallers	A grid pattern and blocks originally rectangular	8.74
rd	Four streets	2.07
ount	Two main streets	2.22
ount	A grid pattern and expansion	4.75 (15.26)
ing	Main street and side streets	0.85
ing	Main street and side streets	1.70
-	Main street	0.33
emplars	Main street	0.91
ount	A grid pattern	0.79
rd	Irregular, with four streets	1.28
ing	Three streets and one square	2.37

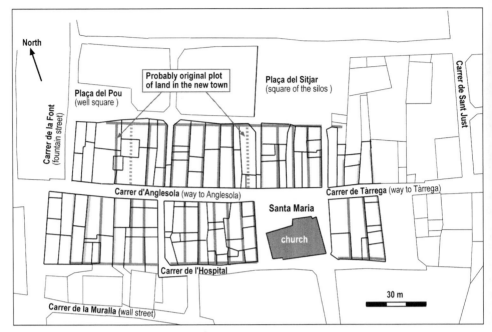

Figure 24. Town of Vilagrassa (Urgell). New town created by the monarch in 1185 along an important communication route.

mentioned Organyà, a town built next to a collegiate church. And, certainly, in many new towns, there were no fortifications or abbeys that they were attached to, as in the case of Olot.

We will now focus on various examples of planned new towns in Catalonia, which will help us to explain the characteristics of the different types of these villages and compare them with new towns from the rest of Europe.

The Main Street and Possibly a Few Parallel Side Streets

Several new towns, e.g. Vilagrassa (Urgell) and Mas de Bondia (Segarra), were just organized along the main street. In Vilagrassa, the street coincided with an important communication route. It was also common to find a street running parallel to the main one, possibly added later; this is the case of Vilafranca de Conflent (Conflent). From the main street or the lengthwise streets, several side streets branched off, although the facades of the houses used to look onto the main streets. When we look closely at these villages, we realize they were rarely created spontaneously and were the result of careful planning.

Vilagrassa (Urgell)

The settlement charter of Vilagrassa, from 1185, granted by Alfons I, King of Catalonia and Aragon, has been preserved. According to this document, the new settlement (*nova populatione*) was made up of houses with *horts*.[15] As explained above, it was organized along the main road that connected Barcelona and Tàrrega with Lleida. The current houses, located on both sides of the road, allow the reconstruction of the original land plot (about seven or eight metres wide by about thirty metres long). On the north side, there may have been about fifteen plots to build on, and on the south side, where the church of Saint Mary stood, perhaps fewer (Fig. 24).

There are other examples of towns outside Catalonia consisting of the main street and one or more streets running parallel to it. In Catalonia, we do not find many cases with more than one parallel street. In Occitania, there is the *bastida* of Vic-en-Bigorre (Oc. Vic de Bigòrra) and Puymirol (Oc. Puègmiròl), whose main street is quite distinctive since it is wider than its parallel side roads.[16] Morlaàs (Oc. Morlans) is also worth mentioning; it was a town that received a settlement charter in 1101 and developed along a road with several phases of growth.[17] In Italy, the town of Rubiera was built on both sides of the main road, as was the case in Vilagrassa.[18] In the Basque Country, a few interesting examples have also been preserved, for example, Arrasate-Mondragon, Azpeitia, and later Azkoitia.[19] In Navarre, we can highlight Puente la Reina-Gares.[20] In all these cases, the central street coincides with an old medieval road. Sometimes the pattern is complicated and, thus, in Viana, also in Navarre, we discover a reality that brings us closer to the type analysed below.[21]

One Main Street and Several Crosswise Streets (Herringbone Shape)

There are new towns whose houses were built mainly along a series of side streets running crosswise to the axial road. One beautiful example of this type of new town is La Selva del Camp (Baix Camp). The model of this kind of village, reminiscent of a herringbone pattern, is the new town of Sant Joan de les Abadesses, which will be mentioned later in connection with monastic settlements which were constructed on new sites.

---

15 *Cartas de población y franquicia de Cataluña*, ed. by Font Rius, doc. 176.
16 Abbé and others, 'Les villes neuves médiévales du sud-ouest de la France', p. 13.
17 Abbé and others, 'Les villes neuves médiévales du sud-ouest de la France', pp. 18–19.
18 Bocchi, *Per antiche strade*, p. 153.
19 Urteaga, 'Censo de las villas nuevas medievales en Álava, Bizkaia y Gipuzkoa', pp. 72–73; Arizaga, *Urbanística medieval (Guipúzcoa)*, pp. 68–69.
20 Jusué and Unzu, 'Villas nuevas en Navarra (siglos XII–XIV)', pp. 149–51.
21 Jusué and Unzu, 'Villas nuevas en Navarra (siglos XII–XIV)', pp. 155–56.

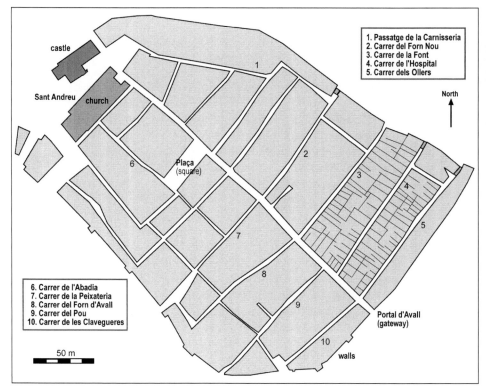

Figure 25. Town of La Selva del Camp (Baix Camp). New town created following the granting of a settlement charter in 1164, with a herringbone-shaped ground plan.

La Selva del Camp (Baix Camp)

This town, located about fourteen kilometres north of Tarragona, received a settlement charter in 1164 from the archbishop of Tarragona.[22] At that time, it was called *Vila Constantina*. The main axis of La Selva del Camp is *Carrer Major*, which acts as the town's backbone. From this central axis, on both sides, five side streets branch off, which probably constituted the original centre.[23] Then, in a second phase, perhaps as early as the thirteenth century, a set of streets was built between this early town and the castle, located further north, with an organization like that found in the first phase, and which, therefore, also extended on both sides of the main street. It was a well-planned settlement (Fig. 25).

---

22 *Cartas de población y franquicia de Cataluña*, ed. by Font Rius, doc. 125.
23 Bolòs, 'Els pobles de Catalunya a l'edat mitjana', p. 111; Bolòs, *Els orígens medievals del paisatge català*, p. 225.

NEW TOWNS AND COMPLEX SETTLEMENTS   117

This type of settlement is also found in many other places in Europe, such as San Damiano d'Asti in Italy.[24] In medieval Ragusa, now the Croatian city of Dubrovnik, after an intermediate phase in which blocks of nearly square or rectangular houses were built during the last phase of urban planning of the enclosed space behind the walls, a set of houses were organized according to a system of double-row blocks, reminiscent of the form we are now discussing.[25] In the town of Korčula in Croatia, we find a similar herringbone-shaped layout.[26]

In Valencia, the town of Vinaròs shares similar features, having been planned in 1241.[27] Also, in the medieval Kingdom of Valencia, we discover a more complex reality in Vistabella: to the north of the town was a castle from the Islamic era; to the south, we see the main street, from which four crosswise streets lead to the southern wall and five streets went north.[28]

A Grid Pattern Plan with Square-Shaped Blocks of Houses

This type of new town with a plan arranged according to an orthogonal grid pattern is perhaps the most noticeable and striking feature and the one that most easily relates to a newly planned and created settlement. We find the same organization of urbanized space in some Occitan *bastides*, such as that of Mirande (Oc. Miranda).[29] Most clusters of houses in the new town of Carcassonne (Oc. Carcassona) are square-shaped.[30] We can also discover other examples of this type in distant lands, such as the city of Krakow and other Polish settlements or Italian cities, such as Cittadella, in Veneto.[31]

In Catalonia, one example worth mentioning is Ulldecona, in the Montsià *comarca*, where, despite a few minor changes, an orthogonal grid was created, possibly with a few square-shaped blocks of houses.

Ulldecona (Montsià)

The current settlement of Ulldecona is the result of the 1274 relocation process. The inhabitants who lived next to the castle settled in a new town, then called Sant Lluc d'Ulldecona, located 1.2 kilometres to the east of the fortification.[32] Ulldecona is a prime example of a process of *decastellamento*

---

24   Guidoni, *Storia dell'urbanistica. Il Duecento*, p. 84.
25   Slukan Altić, 'The Medieval Planned Towns in Croatia', pp. 308–09.
26   Slukan Altić, 'The Medieval Planned Towns in Croatia', pp. 313–15.
27   Rosselló, *Viles planificades valencianes*, p. 57.
28   Rosselló, *Viles planificades valencianes*, p. 215.
29   Guidoni, *Storia dell'urbanistica. Il Duecento*, p. 112.
30   Bocchi, *Per antiche strade*, p. 144.
31   Czaja, 'Polish Town Plans', p. 241; Guidoni, *Storia dell'urbanistica. Il Duecento*, pp. 86–87.
32   *Cartas de población y franquicia de Cataluña*, ed. by Font Rius, doc. 324.

(despite its dependence on a lord, the Hospitallers of Amposta) or, rather, of *desencimbellament* or descent from the top of the hill. In this village, we still see fossilized traces of a regular grid. Right in the middle stands the church dedicated to Saint Luke, at the intersection between Carrer de Sant Lluc (Saint Luke Street) and Carrer Major (Main Street).[33] There were perhaps five more streets, parallel to Carrer Major, and seven more streets, parallel to Carrer de Sant Lluc (Fig. 26). The settlement charter established the sizes of the plots to be used to build the houses: they correspond to a square of sixteen royal *braces* (a measurement) on each side, about thirty metres ('pro statica sexdecim braças regales ex utroque latere'); we still find some blocks of houses which fit with these sizes. It must be said that, within the walls that enclosed this orderly settlement, there are several irregular features, the most important of which is a street that runs from south to north for 200 metres, the more than likely fossilized evidence of an old road, part of the route preserved from when the settlement was planned.[34]

Before describing the following type of settlement, we shall stop for a moment in Valencia, specifically in Almenara, as this is a perfect example of this type of settlement.[35] In some new towns, we see two phases that are well reflected in the current plot, the plot that is there now. Thus, in Nules, there was the first phase of square-shaped blocks of houses and open houses in Carrer Major (Main Street), and a second phase with rectangular blocks where the main facades of the houses faced the six streets running perpendicular to this Carrer Major.[36] We can also mention the remarkable new town of Vila-real, where we find that many of the blocks of houses today are almost square, although the original organization tended to have rectangular islands. It was a very well-planned town, with three longitudinal streets: Carrer d'Amunt (up), Carrer Major (Main Street), and Carrer d'Avall (down), according to the medieval names, crossed by three more streets: Borriana and Enmig (in the middle) and the current Carrer de Colom, in the northeast.[37] Finally, on the island of Mallorca, Petra is a prime example of a settlement organized according to an orthogonal grid pattern, as is Sa Pobla.[38]

---

33 Bolòs, 'Els pobles de Catalunya a l'edat mitjana', p. 100; Bolòs, *Els orígens medievals del paisatge català*, pp. 227–29.

34 The old road went from the village of Amposta to the village of Godall. Martí and Negre, 'Assentaments i espais agraris medievals al Baix Ebre i al Montsià', p. 84.

35 Rosselló, *Viles planificades valencianes*, p. 170.

36 Rosselló, *Viles planificades valencianes*, p. 159.

37 Rosselló, *Viles planificades valencianes*, pp. 148–49.

38 Mas, 'Les Ordinacions d'en Jaume II'; Andreu, *L'Ordinació de Petra, any 1300*.

NEW TOWNS AND COMPLEX SETTLEMENTS   119

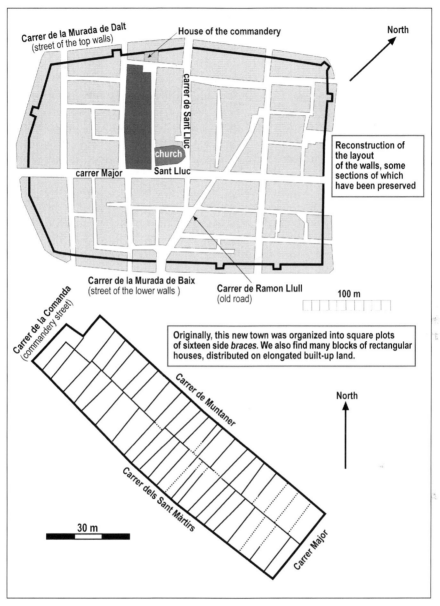

Figure 26. Town of Ulldecona (Montsià). A new town created in 1274. The regular grid pattern of its streets is still maintained today. It was enclosed by ramparts.

120   CHAPTER 5

A Grid Pattern Plan with Rectangular-Shaped Blocks of Houses

There may be an even larger number of settlements whose orthogonal grid pattern indicates the creation of rectangular-shaped blocks of houses. There are abundant examples of this phenomenon throughout Europe. In the Occitan lands, Sainte-Foy-la-Grande (Oc. Senta Fe la Granda) was founded in 1255, Grenade-sur-Garonne (Oc. Granada) in 1290, Marciac in 1288, and Monpazier (Oc. Montpasièr) in 1284.[39] However, Grenade shows a complex reality, as the blocks of houses become longer as they separated from the central axis, running from east to west. In England, there are villages of rectangular-shaped blocks in New Winchelsea, and in Wales, in Flint and Caernarfon.[40] In the Basque Country, it is worth mentioning Zarautz, Getaria, and Donostia.[41] In Tuscany, we find several *terre nuove* with similar characteristics, such as San Giovanni Valdarno.[42] Elsewhere in Italy, there is Frossasco, established in 1288, or Cherasco, in 1248.[43] In Andalusia, the new fifteenth-century town of Santa Fe has a remarkable square grid pattern of blocks of houses with a rectangular ground plan, well into the modern era.[44] In some cases, rather than rectangles, the grid pattern is more trapezoidal, as with New Salisbury in England.[45]

Catalonia also has plenty of examples of such grid patterns, like the monastic settlement of Sant Feliu de Guíxols, as well as the towns of Palamós and Olot. The new town of Olot was built relatively late in the fifteenth century, after much of the old town collapsed due to an earthquake in 1427.[46] The construction of this new town from scratch allowed the people of Olot to free themselves from the shackles of their lord, the monastery of Ripoll.[47]

Let us now turn to another interesting plan, that of Torroella de Montgrí, a town set up on an orthogonal plan of rectangular blocks, as well as a square, planned at the same time as its streets.

Torroella de Montgrí (Baix Empordà)

This is an outstanding example of a new town organized according to an orthogonal plan. We can identify at least two sectors. The earliest, further to the north, was built around a church dedicated to Saint Genesius (Fig. 27).

---

39 Guidoni, *Storia dell'urbanistica. Il Duecento*, pp. 114–26; Leguay, *La rue au Moyen Âge*, p. 28.

40 Lilley, *Urban Life in the Middle Ages, 1000–1450*, p. 161; Lilley, 'Urban Landscapes and their Design', pp. 234–42.

41 Arizaga, *Urbanística medieval (Guipúzcoa)*.

42 Francovich and others, 'Archeologia delle terre nuove in Toscana'.

43 Guidoni, *Storia dell'urbanistica. Il Duecento*, pp. 84–85.

44 Malpica and Martín, 'Las villas nuevas medievales del reino de Granada', pp. 381–88.

45 Beresford, *New Towns of the Middle Ages*, p. 148.

46 Puigvert, *L'època medieval*; Puigvert, *La reconstrucció de la vila d'Olot després dels terratrèmols*.

47 Bolòs, *Els orígens medievals del paisatge català*, p. 230.

NEW TOWNS AND COMPLEX SETTLEMENTS 121

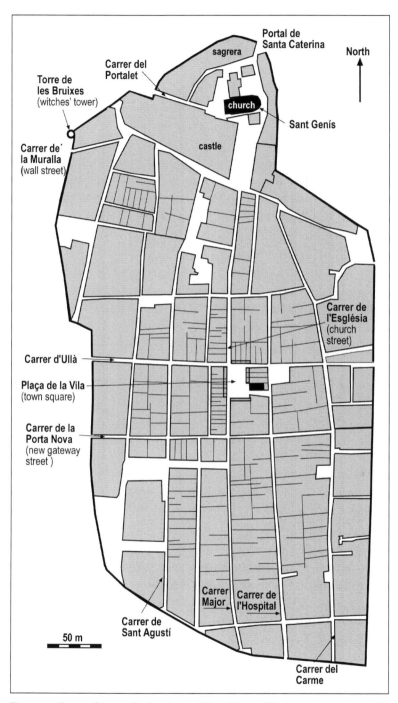

Figure 27. Town of Torroella de Montgrí (Baix Empordà). A new town, created in the thirteenth century, consisted of rectangular blocks and a central square.

CHAPTER 5

This is where the Carolingian *villa* stood, documented in 888.[48] This sector, still known as *La Sagrera*, the precinct immediately surrounding the church, was probably created after 1000. Near the church, as in many other places in the *comarca* of Empordà at the end of the eleventh century, there was a castle (documented from 1085), which later became the royal palace. In 1298, a *cellera* is mentioned, perhaps resembling those in Santa Pau or La Roca d'Albera.[49]

Let's now focus on the new town. In the thirteenth century, there were important changes: two settlement charters were drawn up in 1237 and 1265 and again in 1272, Torroella came under the rule of the Catalan-Aragonese monarch, and, in all probability, it was in this century that the new town was planned. In a study carried out a few years ago, I concluded that the growth of this planned village was perhaps in two phases.[50] In the first phase, at least four streets were laid out from south to north, cut by possibly three cross-streets; a square was formed in the middle. The blocks of houses were quite elongated (about eighteen metres wide by about sixty-five metres long). At a later stage, the town must have expanded westwards, eastwards, and even southwards. In this town, there was a convent and a Jewish quarter or neighbourhood. It was enclosed within walls, as stated in its settlement charter of 1265 that references a 'murum ville Turricellae'.[51]

A New Town with a Square

Several studies on medieval town planning indicate the importance of the creation of public squares in new towns and cities.[52] Squares were located opposite the town hall, the cathedral, next to a church, or facing a convent; however, as previously stated, the most common type of square in Catalonia was the *mercadal* (in English, market square), a space for the weekly market. In the case of the new town of Torroella de Montgrí, we have already seen the significance of its square. For the late Middle Ages, we find many towns with a market square with arcades that provided shelter for the stalls.[53] We will now move on to the new villages of Santa Pau and Montblanc, whose main square also occupies a central position. Later, in Chapter 7 we study the historical landscape of towns and cities, and there is a reference to, for example, the great market of the city of Balaguer. We also find a large market square in the medieval town of Vic. Squares were important spots for commerce and social interchange in most new towns built in the Middle Ages.

---

48 *Catalunya carolíngia, vol. V: Els comtats de Girona, Besalú, Empúries i Peralada*, ed. by Sobrequés, Riera and Rovira, doc. 63.

49 Bolòs, 'Aportació al coneixement de la morfogènesi dels pobles del comtat d'Empúries', p. 278.

50 Bolòs, 'Aportació al coneixement de la morfogènesi dels pobles del comtat d'Empúries', p. 278.

51 Pladevall ed., *L'Art Gòtic a Catalunya. Arquitectura III*, p. 30.

52 Guidoni, *Storia dell'urbanistica. Il Duecento*, pp. 163–73; Bocchi, *Per antiche strade*, pp. 169, 213–25.

53 Farías, *El mas i la vila a la Catalunya medieval*, p. 289.

New Towns with Other Shapes

There are still other types of new towns. Some of them have simple but fairly regular shapes. La Pobla de Segur was organized along four streets enclosing blocks of houses recalling Occitan settlements such as Plaissan or Canet.[54] Other new towns have more irregular shapes. Santa Pau was built in 1300, around a market square and next to the castle. The parish church was originally in Els Arcs, a place just over a kilometre to the east. Below, we explain in more detail the cases of Santa Pau and Montblanc; the latter was a town created by the monarch in the middle of the *comarca* of Conca de Barberà. Many of these towns were market towns, so they will be further analysed in Chapter 14.

Santa Pau (La Garrotxa)

The new town of Santa Pau could be considered a prime example of a settlement resulting from a process of *incastellamento* or incastellation (additionally, as mentioned above, its lords moved downwards from the top of the peak of Finestres).[55] In 1300, shortly after building the castle, the lord granted a settlement charter to create a *cellera* (a word used with a similar meaning to what we saw in the case of La Roca d'Albera).[56] Currently, in the town of Santa Pau we can still discern three sectors. One is located to the east, next to the gate of Vila Vella (the old town). A second residential area was located to the southwest, around the arcaded square, where the market was held, constituting the Vila Nova (the new town). The third sector is a row of houses that unites the two other sectors. It is located to the north of the castle and next to where there used to be dry moats (currently there is a square precisely called Els Valls).

Montblanc (Conca de Barberà)

Although Montblanc was built next to a castle, it was a new town, created by King Alfons I. In 1163, this Catalan-Aragonese king granted a charter to build a town located at a junction of roads. The original core was probably constructed along with Carrer Major (Main Street), to the east of the castle and to the north of Saint Mary's church.[57] A square was soon created, which served as a marketplace to the south of the church. The importance of commercial activity must have favoured the expansion of the population to the south and west. Thus, houses began to be built on the extension between the main street (Carrer Major) and the church of Saint Michael and the church and hospital of Sant Marçal (or Saint Martial); it was also in this sector that the Jewish

---

54 Schneider, 'Villes et villages du Languedoc central', pp. 125–27.
55 Bolòs, *Els orígens medievals del paisatge català*, pp. 233–34.
56 *Cartas de población y franquicia de Cataluña*, ed. by Font Rius, doc. 364.
57 Bolòs, *Els orígens medievals del paisatge català*, pp. 285–88.

124   CHAPTER 5

quarter, as well as the royal palace, were established. During the fourteenth century, all of this built-up space was enclosed within ramparts which have fortunately survived to the present without much change.

Monastic New Towns

Some planned towns were built next to monasteries, often under the auspices of the monastic community itself. Sometimes such towns received a settlement charter. See above for references to sites of Benedictine monasteries and descriptions of some of the towns created, perhaps spontaneously, next to these abbeys, such as Arles (Vallespir), Banyoles (Pla de l'Estany), and Gerri de la Sal (Pallars Sobirà). As mentioned above, the planning of some new monastic towns was carefully thought out. This is the case with Sant Joan de les Abadesses and Sant Feliu de Guíxols. In other instances, the planning is limited to a few neighbourhoods of neatly structured new towns; this is true, for example, of Ripoll.[58] In Roses (Alt Empordà), it has been possible to reconstruct the appearance of the monastic settlement thanks to excavations and thorough research on several *capbreus* (land terriers).[59] This evidence reveals that this monastic settlement was enclosed within walls in the thirteenth century, and its streets were arranged following a carefully planned pattern, with a high street and at least four cross-streets heading west.

Sant Joan de les Abadesses (Ripollès)

In 1243, the abbot of this monastery, which formerly had been a female community, granted the inhabitants of the town a charter of privileges, at a time when the walls and dry moats had already been built ('ista villa fuit muris et vallibus munita').[60] Possibly some decades earlier, the construction of the new town that we can see to the north of the abbey began.[61] At present, we can identify, to the north of the Plaça Major, several blocks of houses, elongated and arranged on both sides of Carrer de Corriols.[62] The streets are narrow, and the blocks are about seventy metres long by ten metres to sixteen metres wide (Fig. 28). To the east of the main street are eight blocks of houses, to the west, only seven. This layout corresponds to the type of new village whose houses were arranged along the streets, transversal to the main axis, following a herringbone structure.

---

58 Bolòs, *Els orígens medievals del paisatge català*, p. 199.
59 Pujol, *La vila de Roses*; Pujol, 'L'urbanisme de la vila de Roses'.
60 *Cartas de población y franquicia de Cataluña*, ed. by Font Rius, doc. 282.
61 *Cartas de población y franquicia de Cataluña*, ed. by Font Rius, doc. 220.
62 Bolòs, *Els orígens medievals del paisatge català*, pp. 235–37.

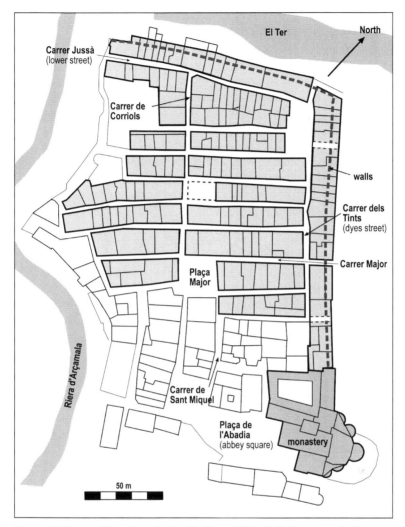

Figure 28. Town of Sant Joan de les Abadesses (Ripollès). New town built next to a monastery with a herringbone shape and perimeter walls.

Sant Feliu de Guíxols (Baix Empordà)

We can find other interesting examples of new monastic villages. In the town of Sant Feliu de Guíxols, to the northeast of the monastery, a new town was built consisting of two streets to the northeast and three streets crossing them. The rectangular blocks of houses were about twenty-four metres wide and fifty-seven metres long. This whole space was enclosed by walls fitted with five gateways. The market square was on the south side. In 1181, the abbot of its monastery granted a franchise charter to the inhabitants of the town,

126 CHAPTER 5

and in 1227, new privileges were granted. In 1354, during the reign of King
Pere III (Peter III), the Ceremonious, of Catalonia and Aragon, part of the
settlement became a royal town. Perhaps the planned village dates back to the
fourteenth century. To the southwest, closer to the monastery, there are a few
more streets which have a disorganized layout; they are probably older than
the new town. The Jewish quarter was also in this sector. On the other hand,
it should be borne in mind that the town was set on fire in 1285, following the
crusade of the King of France against Catalonia, and also that the town was
badly damaged at the end of the seventeenth century, again by the French army.
As said above, it corresponds to the type of new town organized according
to a grid pattern consisting of blocks of rectangular houses.

The castellnous *of Lleida*

According to documentation from the city of Lleida in the second half of the
twelfth century, a significant percentage of the people who emigrated to this
city, after its conquest in 1149, came from the Occitan lands, especially from
Gascony and Languedoc.[63] This fact may have had an impact on the appearance
of new villages called *castellnous*, similar to what we find in Gascony, for which,
a few years ago, Benoît Cursente studied the appearance of numerous castral
burgs, which received the same name (*castelnaux* or *castèthnaus*).[64] Most
of these Gascon *castelnaux* from the twelfth and thirteenth centuries were
basically formed by an urbanized street, very often located next to a castle.[65]
We can mention several examples, such as Poyaller (Oc. Pojalèr), Montaut,
Lembeye (Oc. Lenveja), and Garlin.

Some of these *castellnous* in the vicinity of Lleida were, in fact, new towns
designed to bring together the population which, until then, lived half-scattered
across the territory, in the so-called *torres*, which, as we will see in the next
chapter, were small villages, perhaps with some fortification, a reminder, in
many cases, of the *almunias* or *'abrāǧ* (pl. of *burǧ*, tower) from Islamic times.
A good example of this phenomenon is the town of Vilanova de Segrià, which
was initially called *Castellnou* and received a settlement charter in 1231.[66]

Markets and Town Centres

Market towns developed around a square where the market was held or,
more often, they were already inhabited before 1000 in places whose space,
from a certain point, was designated as a meeting place of traders, mainly
agricultural and also artisans coming from the region and, as a consequence,

---

63 Bolòs and Moran, *Abusos comesos a Lleida per Peire de Lobeira*.
64 Cursente, *Les Castelnaux de la Gascogne médiévale*.
65 Berdoy and Jean-Courret, 'Castelnaux du bassin de l'Adour (Landes et Béarn)'.
66 *Cartas de población y franquicia de Cataluña*, ed. by Font Rius, doc. 256.

NEW TOWNS AND COMPLEX SETTLEMENTS   127

acquired great significance. There is evidence of the importance of this trading activity and settlements developed around marketplaces throughout Europe, a phenomenon related to the expansion of commerce and the increasing economic relevance of towns.[67] One illustrative example is the Rhenish city of Freiburg im Breisgau (commonly referred to as Freiburg), a new town with a herringbone street pattern, founded in 1175 as a free market town near the river Rhine. In other countries, on the other hand, there was more continuity. In Italy, cities such as Brescia held the medieval market at the site of the forum, just as in the Roman period.[68]

In the Catalan context, after 1000, towns emerged in places where a whole set of new activities related to trading and handcrafts was concentrated. These towns not only held markets but also were inhabited by artisans, together with, possibly, a notary, perhaps since the thirteenth century. This was a place where, in addition, as evidenced by documents, credits were granted. On the outskirts of these market towns, there used to be pottery kilns as the archaeological evidence has revealed. This was the case in the *comarca* of Berguedà as we can see from the analysis of ceramics fired in the high Middle Ages in the kilns of Casa-en-Ponç (located on the outskirts of Berga).[69] This pottery must have been sold in the market to people who lived tens of kilometres away in all directions, within the area of this central place's economic influence.[70] In the region of Vallès, we have studied, for example, the localities where there are references to the *mesura* (medieval measuring system) of Granollers or that of Sant Celoni, a town located a few kilometres further east, at the foot of the Montseny Massif.[71]

Further on in this volume, we will discuss at length some of these market towns, such as Granollers and Vilafranca del Penedès; we will now turn our attention to a good example, Martorell.

Martorell (Baix Llobregat)

We have seen the importance of the market in some of the places studied so far, such as Balaguer, La Llacuna, Santa Pau, and Montblanc. Sometimes, the existence of a market was the reason behind the foundation of a new settlement. However, there are very few examples of that. One of such case is Martorell. The old town of Martorell is a one-road village. Along the street, which corresponds to a Roman main road, we can still make out the various phases of its growth. The initial phase, dating back to the eleventh century,

---

67 Curtis, 'The Emergence of Concentrated Villages in Medieval Western Europe', p. 248.

68 Bocchi, *Per antiche strade*, pp. 165, 168.

69 Riu, *L'arqueologia medieval a Catalunya*, pp. 107–08. I will refer to it again in Chapter 11.

70 López and others, 'Difusión de las cerámicas grises/oxidadas medievales en las comarcas de Barcelona'. Salrach, 'El mercat de la vila, mercat de productes', pp. 445–50.

71 Vilaginés, *El paisatge, la societat i l'alimentació al Vallès Oriental*, p. 204; Aventín, 'Le rôle du marché dans la structuration de l'habitat catalan au Bas Moyen Âge'.

128 CHAPTER 5

includes the first section of this urban road of about 180 m in length. At its centre, the road widened to form a market square; on the north side, there was a church. A document from 1032 reports on the church of Saint Mary of Martorell, located '*in foro Martorelio*'. Surely the word *forum*, in the classical tradition, referred to the market square.[72] Many of the facades of the houses on this street are still between 3.7 m and 5.5 m.

In a second phase, the road was extended to the east, about 175 m further. Finally, in the late medieval period, this built-up road with houses on either side still extended about 155 m more, until it reached the eastern gateway, located only about 325 m from the Devil's Bridge (*el Pont del Diable*, in Catalan), an old bridge (with ashlars from the Roman period on its lower part) over the river Llobregat. It should be noted that, in 1282, apart from the weekly market venue, an annual fair was held in Martorell precisely near the Devil's Bridge, next to the chapel of Saint Bartholomew. All this built-up space, which stretched along both sides of the street, was enclosed within walls with several gateways in the walled enclosure.

More Complex and Polyfocal Settlements

So far, we have studied relatively simple settlements, that is, villages created around a church or a castle, villages organized around the houses that made them up (open villages), or around streets or roads that determined their main structure and subsequent expansion (new towns). But we have already seen the existence of more complex examples, such as the monastic new towns like Sant Joan de les Abadesses and Sant Feliu de Guíxols and the *sagrera* villages that became towns, like Torroella de Montgrí. Certainly, we can easily find many other examples of complex settlements.

Even some newly created towns were built in several stages. This was probably the case of Montblanc and Vilafranca del Penedès, as will be seen in subsequent chapters. Town planning does not necessarily have to be regular. Sometimes irregular patterns can reflect different phases of planned development, as evidenced in the case of Coventry in England.[73]

In most Catalan large towns, such as *comarca* capitals, it is easy to see the several stages of growth that took place during the medieval period, which can be related to different central constructions or various extensions. We will now turn our attention to settlements that we believe are representative of the so-called '*polyfocal towns and villages*', studied in England many years ago.[74]

---

72 Bolòs, *Els orígens medievals del paisatge català*, pp. 237–38.
73 Lilley, 'Mapping the Medieval City', p. 276.
74 Taylor, 'Polyfocal Settlement and the English village'.

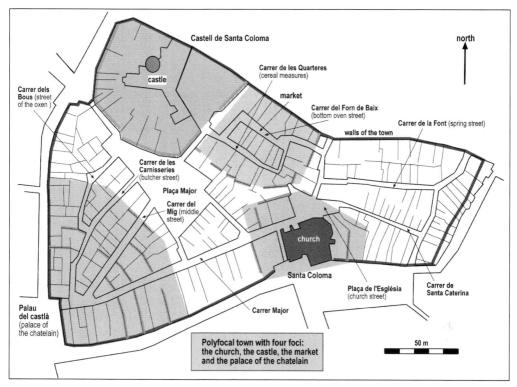

Figure 29. Town of Santa Coloma de Queralt (Conca de Barberà). Polyfocal town, founded around a church, a castle, the Castellan palace, and a new neighbourhood.

Santa Coloma de Queralt (Conca de Barberà)

This is a magnificent example of a polyfocal town.[75] Due to there being only a few changes over the last few centuries, it is easy to follow the traces of its phases of construction. It is noticeable that at an early stage a church dedicated to Saint Columba was built (Fig. 29). This town is situated in an area that, around 1000, was close to the border, the march. However, the church could well have been built before, and even long before, the county's conquest. After the turn of the millennium, around the church, a cluster of houses may well have been built within a space conceived as a *sagrera*. A castle may have been built at a later stage, surely built later than the temple because it is dedicated to Saint Columba (*Santa Coloma*, in Catalan). It is located at the north-western end of the town. In a third phase, to the east of the castle, there

---

75 This town has attracted the attention of several historians: Milton, *Market Power: Lordship, Society, and Economy in Medieval Catalonia*; Segura, *Història de Santa Coloma de Queralt*; Assis, *Els jueus de Santa Coloma de Queralt*.

CHAPTER 5

must have been a sort of a quadrangular new town and, at the south-western end, the castellan's palace, which triggered the creation of several streets that, in a fan-shaped structure, led to the northeast, towards the future *Plaça Major* (main square, in English). Finally, at the end of the Middle Ages, all these streets and houses were enclosed within walls whose perimeter can still be easily traced. This settlement is, at the same time, an ecclesiastical, castral village and shares many of the features of new towns; this settlement started from at least four foci.[76]

Àger (La Noguera)

The town of Àger is situated in the centre of a wide valley, which stretches between the Montsec, in the north, the Montclús mountain range, in the south, the Noguera Ribagorçana, in the west, and the Noguera Pallaresa, in the east. In 1034, Arnau Mir de Tost first conquered this border town, where, in the Islamic period, there was an important Christian community. The medieval town of Àger was organized in the eleventh century in relation to the castle and the collegiate church of Sant Pere (Fig. 30). Around this lofty space, there were several churches, some of which had existed since before the conquest, while others were possibly built shortly afterward: Santa Coloma,[77] Sant Joan, Sant Martí, and Sant Vicenç. It is precisely around the latter that we find the eastern sector of the medieval town. An elongated square was built, where the market was regularly held, between the urban sector organized to the east of Sant Pere and the organized area around Sant Vicenç; this square was enlarged in the fourteenth century.[78] All this space around Sant Pere and Sant Vicenç was enclosed within walls with four access gates: the Pedró gate (leading to Sant Joan and Santa Coloma), the Sant Martí gate (leading to Saint Martin's church and towards the west), the Soldevila gate (to the east of Sant Vicenç), and the Sant Pere gate, below the collegiate church. The walls around the hill of Sant Pere, where the fortification stood, were probably built in the early Middle Ages; the easternmost part of the wall must have been built later (perhaps after the Christian conquest).[79] Outside the walls, towards Sant Joan and towards Sant Martí, two suburbs were built. In the previous case, we have seen the role played by the church of Santa Coloma de Queralt. In Àger we see that the high medieval town was organized around a castle and two churches (Sant Pere and Sant Vicenç); the churches of Sant Joan and Sant Martí stood at the centre of two suburbs outside the walls, while Santa Coloma remained on the outskirts.

---

76 Bolòs, 'Conèixer el paisatge històric medieval per poder planificar i gestionar el territori', p. 155.

77 A necropolis from the early Middle Ages has been excavated. See the words 'Àger' and 'Santa Coloma' in: http://invarque.cultura.gencat.cat/ [accessed 10 December 2021].

78 Fité, *Reculls d'història de la Vall d'Àger*, pp. 370–75.

79 Fité and Bolòs, 'Vila d'Àger', pp. 107–11; Fité and Masvidal, 'Restes subsistents del recinte fortificat del castell d'Àger, d'època andalusina'.

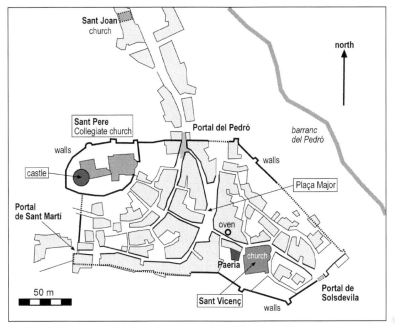

Figure 30. Town of Àger (La Noguera). The town was created in the high Middle Ages based on precedents prior to the conquest of Arnau Mir de Tost. It was organized in relation to the castle, the collegiate church, the parish church (Sant Vicenç), and the market square (Plaça Major). Source: *Reculls d'història de la Vall d'Àger*.

Castelló d'Empúries (Alt Empordà)

In Catalonia, several settlements have originated from the merger of two nuclei, initially belonging to two different lords. A good example is Vilanova i la Geltrú (Garraf), whose current name reflects this duality. In the case of Castelló d'Empúries, the settlement dates to the high Middle Ages with the union of two inhabited nuclei. On the one hand, a nucleus was organized around Saint Mary's church named *Puig Salner* (salt hill), which depended on the cathedral of Girona. On the other hand, the nucleus where the castle of the Count of Empúries stood was located about 300 m to the south-west of the church. It was called *Puig del Mercadal* (market square hill). Initially, there were two walls, one for each nucleus. Over time, the sector between the two walled enclosures was urbanized, especially on both sides of the road to Peralada, north of the Puig del Mercadal. In addition, the Jewish quarter (*call*, in Catalan) was built to the east of this suburb. Around 1300, walls were built to enclose the entire built-up area, with eight gateways on either side of the walled enclosure. Around 1336, the castle was demolished, and the site became known as *Plaça del Gra* (grain square). Commercial and artisan

132   CHAPTER 5

activity was concentrated in Puig del Mercadal, while Puig Salner became the ecclesiastical and residential district.[80]

Conclusions

In the Occitan lands, the *bastides* represent a symbol of the medieval past, like the castles supposedly of Cathar origin. Across Europe, studies of new towns have flourished in recent years. As regards Catalan-speaking areas, it is worth mentioning a recent study carried out in Valencia on planned medieval and modern Valencian towns.[81] In Catalonia, we may not find as many new towns as in other European countries, but such as they are, they deserve to be known and appraised.

The new towns are a symbol of the new mentality from the high Middle Ages (eleventh–fourteenth centuries). Their creation is related to the lords' initiatives or grants of settlement charters. They are also associated with control of the territory and the people, though their inhabitants may have enjoyed certain privileges. But these new towns were also symbols of new economic activities in an era of thriving trade. Therefore, many of these towns were built, for example, at a crossroads (as in the case of Montblanc) and many of them had at their core a square where the market was held every week (as in Torroella de Montgrí and Santa Pau).

This chapter has also illustrated the fact that the urban planning of many villages is not limited to understanding the morphology of ecclesiastical or castral settlements that have not changed much over the centuries. In many medieval towns, we discover various focal elements and, in almost all of them, we can distinguish various stages of growth. The larger the settlement, the more complex it may be to decipher. This will be analysed in-depth in Chapter 7, which deals with towns and cities, and their complex planning. Vilanova i la Geltrú originated from a merger of two towns, a new town, and a castle town. In Vilafranca del Penedès, Martorell, Puigcerdà, and Cervera we can distinguish several stages of growth. Tàrrega also shows complex growth. In Balaguer, the town planning from the Islamic period and that following 1105, when it became the capital of the counts of Urgell, merged. Certainly, although we are on the right track, there is still a lot of work to be done on this issue.

---

80 Puig, 'La vila de Castelló d'Empúries'; Farías, *El mas i la vila a la Catalunya medieval*, p. 251.
81 Rosselló, *Viles planificades valencianes.*

CHAPTER 6

Hamlets and Farmsteads

The Dispersal of the Population

Introduction

In many European countries, there are areas with a concentrated population and others where a more dispersed population predominates. In Catalonia, there are many counties in which most of the population lives in scattered farmhouses, a few hundred metres apart. This is typical in *comarques* such as Osona, La Garrotxa, Berguedà, and Vallès Oriental. Several studies have been carried out to find out their main characteristics and origin. However, the existence of a scattered settlement of isolated houses cannot be ruled out even before 1000. On the other hand, the population that predominated in the early Middle Ages consisted of semi-scattered hamlets. It should be noted that these hamlets, especially in mountainous areas, have survived to the present day. Similarly, in the *comarques*, which were part of Al-Andalus, there were also semi-scattered settlements, although they were given other names (such as *almunia* or *burg̊*, and more rarely, *alqueria* or *rafal*). Based on what the written documents reveal, what we can still see and what has been found in archaeological excavations in recent decades, we have learned more about hamlets and farmsteads, as will be seen in this chapter.

What Do We Know About Medieval Hamlets and Farmsteads?

All over the world, regions feature predominant settlements concentrated in villages and towns, while other regions feature hamlets (defined as fewer than eight houses) and still others are characterized by scattered settlements or farmsteads, inhabited by only one family.[1] These three forms of settlement are found all over the European continent.[2] This has been a topic of study for decades. For example, in England, evidence shows the predominance of scattered farms in some regions, such as Cornwall, Devon, or Essex, at least since the early Middle Ages.[3] In Catalonia, since the Middle Ages, these detached houses have been named *mas*, a term also found in the eastern areas of Occitania, especially in Provence, in some valleys in the north of Italy, and

---

1 Roberts, *Landscapes of Settlement*.
2 Engel and others, *Grosser Historischer Weltatlas. II: Mittelalter*, pp. 38–39.
3 Taylor, *Village and Farmstead*, pp. 175–200.

in southern Aragon.[4] With respect to the Catalan lands, the characteristics of farmhouses have been studied for years, as well as the reasons why in some *comarques* almost the entire population is geographically dispersed.[5] In recent years, several conferences and books have been published on this topic.[6]

Dispersed settlements are a landscape feature of almost half of the Catalan *comarques*. The Carolingian *mansus*, found in the central territories of the Charlemagne Empire, was a one-family home, located on a lord's villa.[7] However, the *mas* of Old Catalonia, in the high Middle Ages, despite bearing the same name, was almost always a farmhouse built in the middle of the farmland and separated by a few hundred metres from other neighbouring farmhouses.[8] If we walk across *comarques* such as La Garrotxa, Gironès, Osona, Bages, Berguedà, and Solsonès, we find that they are still made up of dispersed settlements.

However, before focusing on this type of dispersed settlement, we will first zoom in on half-dispersed settlements, hamlets, and settlements known in Catalan documents as *vilars* (in Latin, *villares*). It was common to find a relevant *mas* after 1000, especially in the early Middle Ages, where there had been a hamlet (e.g., *mas* Les Heures of Berguedà (Fig. 33), *mas* Corbs del Sallent of Garrotxa (Fig. 35), and *mas* Gurri of Osona, to name just a few).

The Hamlets of the Early Middle Ages in Old Catalonia

Documents from the Carolingian period often mention the existence of villas and hamlets (*vilars*). Generally, the villa was the place where the parish church was located, as well as being the centre of land for villagers, and often for a jurisdictional territory, sometimes with a long tradition; many of these villas have now become villages, within their municipal district. Within the district of the villa, it was not uncommon to find smaller clusters, hamlets. However, it should be said that in the Middle Ages, these features were not always regular; sometimes, as we will see in the case of the valley of Sant Joan de les Abadesses, there may not be a great difference in the number of inhabitants between villas and hamlets. In general, however, the impression is that villas were older than hamlets, judging by the place names. *Vilars* often received the names of their first settlers (for example, Vilartolí, Vilargonter,

---

4 Mastrelli Anzilotti, 'Osservazioni in margine al lessico alpino', p. 58; Hernández Sesé, *Mases y masoveros*.

5 Vilà Valentí, *El món rural a Catalunya*, pp. 63–78.

6 To and others, *El mas medieval a Catalunya*; Ferrer and others, *El mas català durant l'edat mitjana i la moderna*.

7 In the Carolingian period, it corresponded to an inhabited place and the territory that depended on it. These villas had different characteristics to those from villas in northern France; they did not always correspond to a lordly domain.

8 Freedman, *The Origins of Peasant Servitude*, p. 26.

or Vilarsendre) and, therefore, perhaps, in many cases, we may infer that they were created in the Carolingian period. This is also true for other areas of Europe.[9] In any case, to understand the settlements of the early Middle Ages — not only of the Carolingian era — it is important to consider the spread of hamlets, often inhabited by five to about eight families.

An important aspect should also be noted: the settlements of the early Middle Ages were generally unstable. Usually, throughout the early medieval period, there was continuity in the occupation of large areas of good farmland, dating to the Roman era. It has also been argued that there could be several inhabited sites within each of these territories and that these settlements could easily vary in location. Archaeological work has revealed that in the north of France during the early Middle Ages hamlets could often be displaced by a few hundred metres from their original location.[10] This mobility has also been verified in excavations in Languedoc and by other archaeological surveys in north Italy.[11] Further south, in Roussillon, similar examples have been found.[12] In this same region, the site of Les Espaçoles is a case in point, a possible hamlet located 1.3 kilometres northeast of the current town of Tuïr.[13] Over seventy-five silos, some burials, and remains of the foundations of houses, among other evidence, were found there. This place began to be inhabited around the seventh century and was abandoned in the tenth century. As Aymat Catafau points out, in this region of Roussillon, it was not until around 1000 that a process of the concentration of settlements around churches and castles started; before then, there were half-dispersed settlements.[14] In other *comarques* though, from the turn of the millennium, there was the opposite process of dispersal.

We know, therefore, that one territory could be made up of several hamlets, as shown in excavations and in documents such as acts of consecration.[15] But before focusing on the valley of Sant Joan de les Abadesses, there is another aspect of hamlets worth mentioning. We cannot be sure that hamlets were always formed by a set of clustered houses. Where the dispersed settlements predominated later, we believe that there were formerly, perhaps even before 1000, several houses separated by hundreds of metres. Therefore, although calling them *masos* would be a misnomer, it cannot be ruled out that, in some places what we would have found before 1000 may have been a reality similar to the dispersed settlements that were the rule in the eleventh and twelfth centuries. This issue will be further analysed concerning the excavation of the

---

9 Pichot, *Le village éclaté*, p. 189.
10 Gentili, 'L'archéologie au village en Île-de-France', p. 97.
11 Schneider, 'Dynamiques spatiales et transformations de l'habitat en Languedoc', p. 309; Vaccaro, 'Il popolamento rurale tra fine v e inizi x nella Maremma Grossetana'.
12 Kotarba, 'Les sites d'époque wisigothique de la ligne LGV', p. 63.
13 Dominguez, 'Les Espassoles'.
14 Catafau, *Les celleres et la naissance du village en Roussillon*.
15 *Les Dotalies de les esglésies de Catalunya (segles ix–xii)*, ed. by Ordeig.

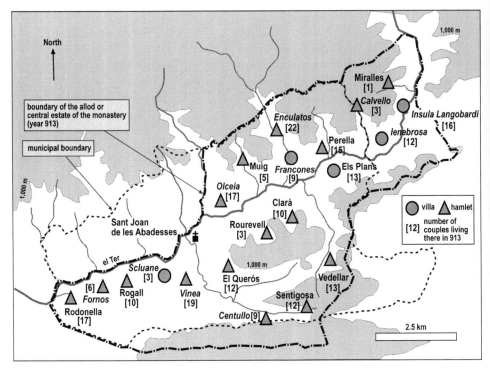

Figure 31. Hamlets of the valley of Sant Joan de les Abadesses (Ripollès). A document from 913 gives us the names of the hamlets inside this monastic allod and the names of their inhabitants.

vilar of Montclús (Berguedà). Keep in mind that, for example, in Portugal (in Castelo de Vide), single household farmsteads have been related to rock-cut graves, dated to before the eighth century.[16]

La Vall de Sant Joan de les Abadesses (Ripollès)

In 913, there was a lawsuit between the community of nuns at Sant Joan de les Abadesses and the peasant families living in the valley over the ownership of lands from different settlements (Fig. 31).[17] This document is important, and not only for the monastery, as the community of nuns won the lawsuit. For us, this is a remarkable discovery because it bears witness to the fact that in this valley, which was a monastic allod,[18] there were twenty-one settlements,

---

16 Prata, 'Post-Roman Land-Use Transformations', p. 67.
17 *Catalunya carolíngia, vol. IV: Els comtats d'Osona i Manresa*, ed. by Ordeig, doc. 119.
18 An allod is a piece of land over which the allodial landowner (allodiary) had full ownership and right of alienation. We must keep in mind that this land, the allod, may correspond to a piece of land owned by a farmer and also, for example, to a villa owned by a lord.

HAMLETS AND FARMSTEADS 137

Table 2. Settlements in the valley of Sant Joan de les Abadesses (Ripollès)

Settlement	Place name in 913	Current place name	Couples	Male	Female	Total
Villa	*Insula Langobardi*	[Sant Pau de Seguries?]	16	16	16	32
Hamlet	*Miralias*	Miralles	1	1	1	2
Villa	*Ienebrosa*	[El Callís?]	12	12	15	27
Hamlet	*Calvello*	[La Forcarà]	3	4	3	7
Hamlet	*Perella*	Perella	15	15	15	30
Villa	*Francones*	[El Reixac?]	9	9	10	19
Hamlet	*Enculatos*	[Can Batlle?]	22	22	23	45
Hamlet	*Mogio*	Muig	5	5	6	11
Villa	*Olceia*	[La Batllia?]	17	17	19	36
Villa	*Scluvane*	[L'Òliba?]	3	5	3	8
Hamlet	*Rodebaldencos*	Rogall	10	10	11	21
Hamlet	*Fornos*	[El Guillot?]	6	6	6	12
Hamlet	*Puio Redundo*	Rodonella	17	17	18	35
Hamlet	*Vinea*	[Les Llances?]	19	20	21	41
Hamlet	*Centullo*	[Caramelles?]	9	9	9	18
Hamlet	*Boscharones*	El Querós	12	13	12	25
Hamlet	*Sintigosa*	Sentigosa	12	12	12	24
Hamlet	*Clarano*	Clarà	10	10	12	22
[Hamlet]	*Roverbello*	Rourevell	3	3	3	6
Hamlet	*Vedellare*	Vedellar	13	14	14	28
Villa	*Planas*	Els Plans	13	15	16	31
			227	**235**	**245**	**480**

and there is evidence of the names of its former inhabitants.[19] This makes it possible to know the number of people who lived in each of these villas and hamlets, or *vilars* (in this case, the difference between them was not very obvious), which ranged from twenty-two couples in *Enculatos* to one couple in *Miralles* (hence, a farmstead, see Table 2). Additional data can also be obtained through research on the linguistic origins of the anthroponyms of these settlers; interestingly enough, we have noticed an abundance of anthroponyms of Frankish origin.[20] This document also allows us to estimate that, in these mountainous lands, there was a high population density. If we

19 Bolòs, *Els orígens medievals del paisatge català*, p. 251.
20 Kremer, 'Zur Urkunde A. 913 des Archivo Condal in Barcelona'.

Figure 32. Parish of Ordino (Andorra). This parish had a half-dispersed population. In the high Middle Ages, there were about twelve hamlets.

estimate that, according to the limits carefully defined in the document, this territory had an area of 51.8 square kilometres and, considering that they lived there with children and other relatives, at least about a thousand people, we must conclude that, in 913, there was a density of close to twenty inhabitants per square kilometre, a remarkable figure if we compare it against that of many other places in western Europe before 1000.

Muig (Sant Joan de les Abadesses, Ripollès)

Mas Muig still exists today. It is located at an altitude of 970 metres. A little further down, at about 750 metres, is the *mas* of La Sala de Muig. It is almost certain that the lands of these two farms coincide with the territory of the *vilar* of *Mogio*, first recorded in 913, where we have evidence, as we have seen, of five families. The territory of this hamlet probably extended for about ninety-five hectares and occupied a valley furrowed by the Muig stream.[21] There were, of course, cultivated lands and meadows, and a large extension of forest land. According to what we can see in the aerial photographs from the mid-twentieth century, the farmland of *mas* Muig covered an area of about nine hectares; we see about five terraces under the house, slightly differentiated from each other, and, around them, terraced land in the middle of the forest. On the other hand, around the *mas* of La Sala de Muig, there were about fifteen hectares of cultivated land, and about ten braided terraces extended under the farmhouse and more terraced land nearby. We do not find wide fields, however. In short, we have a well-dated and, above all, precisely located Carolingian hamlet. However, it is difficult to know exactly what this small valley of Muig was like a thousand years ago; some features may have changed, but there are many others that we assume have remained unchanged.

The Parish of Ordino (Andorra)

In Andorra, despite the great changes that have taken place in recent decades, we can still find evidence of dispersed settlements and the creation of many small hamlets that existed in each of the six medieval parishes. In 1176, there was an agreement between the bishop of Urgell and the men from the different parishes of Andorra. In the parish of Ordino, located at the northern end of Andorra, a text from the twelfth century mentions at least twelve hamlets distributed along the valley furrowed by the river Valira (Fig. 32).[22] Apart from the churches of Sant Corneli and Sant Cebrià d'Ordino, there were two more chapels in this northern valley: that of Sant Martí de la Cortinada and that of Sant Serni de Llorts. In addition, among the names of the hamlets mentioned in the twelfth century, apart from the name of Ordino, there are three pre-Roman place names (Sornàs, Arans, and Llorts). This document allows us to learn about the organization of a settlement created in the early Middle Ages. Similarly, Ordino, like Lòria, Andorra, and the other three parishes, was inhabited in the early Middle Ages. It has been confirmed by

---

21 Bolòs, 'Cartografiar el paisatge medieval de Catalunya'.

22 'Els Documents, dels anys 1151–1190, de l'Arxiu Capitular de la Seu d'Urgell', ed. by Baraut, doc. 1,711.

140   CHAPTER 6

archaeological excavations that *Lauredia* (Sant Julià de Lòria) existed already in the sixth century.[23]

This is not a unique case of a half-dispersed settlement organized along a valley. We can find many other examples in the Catalan Pyrenees and on the northern slopes of this mountain range. In the Occitan lands, in Casaux (Oc. Casals) and Campan, we also discover numerous villages distributed at the bottom of a valley, spread out across ten or twenty kilometres, forming a single parish.[24]

Corbs (Santa Pau, La Garrotxa)

In the parish of Sant Vicenç del Sallent, about eight or nine Carolingian hamlets became about thirty-five single-family farms (about twenty-seven *masos* or farmsteads, two *bordes*, and about six *masoveries*) (Fig. 35). We will now shine a spotlight on one of these *vilars*, split into two farmsteads. The hamlet of Corbs, documented shortly after 1000 (although it was much older), may well have been fragmented into the higher *mas*, Corbs d'Amunt, and a lower *mas*, Corbs d'Avall, shortly after this date.[25] At present, this place still exists and it is the higher *mas* that is now inhabited; on the other hand, the other *mas* is empty (*rònec*, in Catalan), deserted at the end of the Middle Ages, and all that remains of its existence are heaps of stones in the middle of the forest. The original site of the Corbs perhaps consisted of a group of three or four small, clustered houses. However, we cannot rule out completely that before 1000, this *vilar* was already made up of several houses a few hundred metres apart. As we have pointed out, we will reconsider this theory by analysing the structure of the *vilar* of Montclús (Berguedà) in the Carolingian period.

We estimate the total extent of the lands of the old *vilar* (hamlet) to be about thirty hectares, partly crop fields, terraces, and wooded areas, covered with evergreen oaks (Quercus ilex ssp. ilex). In the eleventh century or perhaps the twelfth century, the lower farmstead of Corbs d'Avall had an area of only about ten hectares, while the higher farmstead of Corbs d'Amunt was about twenty hectares. In front of the old hamlet, there was a spring, next to the stream, about 200 metres from the farmstead of Corbs d'Amunt. Later, we will revisit the analysis of the parish of Sant Vicenç del Sallent.

Les Heures (La Quar, Berguedà)

The farmstead of Les Heures was already mentioned in the Carolingian era; it was a hamlet. In 899, a document refers to the *villare Lodovese*.[26] At that time, it was probably named after settlers from Languedoc, who settled there after

---

23 Fortó and Vidal, 'En los orígenes de Sant Julià de Lòria (Andorra)', p. 261.

24 Catafau, 'Petites, nombreuses, isolées?', p. 84.

25 Bolòs, *El mas, el pagès i el senyor*.

26 *Diplomatari del monestir de Sant Pere de la Portella*, ed. by Bolòs, pp. 150–53.

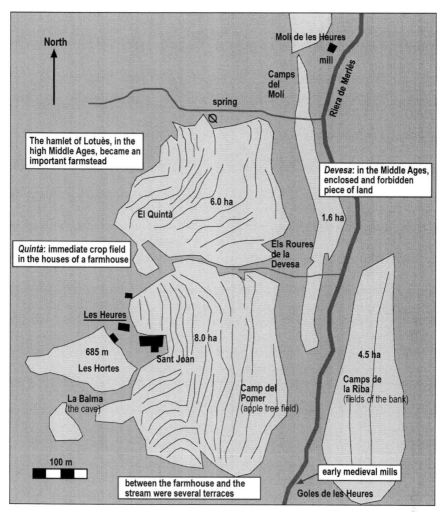

Figure 33. Farmstead of Les Heures (La Quar, Berguedà). In the Carolingian period it was a hamlet, possibly inhabited by several families. In the high Middle Ages, the original hamlet became a farmstead.

the Carolingian conquest a century earlier. According to the current cadastral boundaries, the total area was about 150 hectares, of which about fifteen and a half hectares were probably cultivated, covered with fields and especially terraces; the rest was forested land (Fig. 33). After 1000, this Carolingian *vilar* (hamlet) became the *mas* (farmstead) of Les Heures, which probably soon had *masovers* (someone who farmed land rented from the peasants of the main farmhouse). There was even a chapel dedicated to Saint John. About 350 metres to the east of this place, we find the Merlès stream, fitted with several mills. In the so-called *Goles de les Heures* — gorge where this

142   CHAPTER 6

watercourse runs through — we notice on both sides of the stream holes drilled into the rock to support the wooden dam of a mill, probably around 1000; in Chapter 11, we shall analyse mills in depth.

The Contribution of Archaeology: The Hamlets

Medieval history studies usually neglect the results of archaeological excavations. Unfortunately, there have been fewer archaeological excavations in Catalonia than those in other European countries. We have already mentioned the studies carried out in Les Espaçoles (Tuïr, Roussillon). At this point, three more sites will be analysed; one from the Visigothic period and two from the Carolingian era, which most likely correspond to what the documents call a *vilar* or hamlet. These sites are of a certain significance, although we have no evidence that every hamlet from the early medieval period was exactly like these. While these are open, there were also hamlets enclosed within walls, such as that of Santa Creu de Llagunes (Pallars Sobirà). If we look at the early medieval sites, such as the ones excavated in the *comarca* of Vallès, many inhabited places located on the plain were probably open and lacked protective walls, while others were perched (i.e., located on a hilltop) and defended by the topography and perhaps by some walls. Also, in all probability, what we would have found in the marchland, near the border with Al-Andalus, would have been quite different.

Vilaclara (Castellfollit del Boix, Bages)

Between 1989 and 1991, several excavation campaigns were carried out in a small hamlet from the early Middle Ages in the south-west of the *comarca* of Bages.[27] Three dwellings were discovered in the excavated space, each consisting of one, two, and three rooms, respectively, attached to each other. All three had an open courtyard in front of them. There are remains of grindstones for the manual grinding of cereals, a lever wine press, an oven for baking bread, and various fireplaces. Around 500 metres away, there used to be a spring (where, later, the farmstead of Can Prat was built). About twenty-five metres to the west of the early medieval settlement, a necropolis was discovered. Despite precedents, the excavated remains were dated to the seventh century. It is considered to correspond to a *vilar* from the early Middle Ages, from the Visigothic period.[28]

---

27 Enrich and others, *Vilaclara de Castellfollit del Box (El Bages)*.
28 In Catalonia, the Visigothic period ended around 713 or 714.

La Coma Peironella (Angostrina and Vilanova de les Escaldes, Alta Cerdanya)

This settlement from the early Middle Ages was excavated in 2001 and again in 2014–2017.[29] It was formed by around two dozen constructions separated from each other. It was built at an altitude of 1250 metres. It was inhabited between the seventh and tenth centuries. The importance of metallurgy-related activities has been pointed out, especially following the findings made in the northernmost sector of the site and the existence in this same place of precedents from the Iron Age. In the southern sector, where the houses were located, we have been able to discover several kinds of seeds: rye (*Secale cereale*), wheat (*Triticum aestivum/durum/turgidum*), barley (*Hordeum vulgare*), and a variety of pulses. This hamlet was close to the ancient capital of the Cerdanya territory, the city of Llívia.

Montclús (Santa Maria de Merlès, Berguedà)

In the Carolingian documentation, there are references to the hamlet of Montclús (893: 'villare qui dicitur Monte Cluso'). In 2003, excavation revealed the location of two areas of built-up spaces: a small house and, next to it, a space intended perhaps for livestock and food handling.[30] The ceramic materials date from between the eighth and eleventh centuries. In addition, in a collection of pottery made in the lower fields of the lands of the current *mas* of Montclús, numerous pottery fragments from the tenth and eleventh centuries were found. It should also be noted that, not far from the excavated site, there were three scattered houses like this one. In fact, here we may be dealing with a Carolingian hamlet formed by dispersed settlements, which we can consider as a precedent for the farmsteads that, according to written evidence, predominated in this region in the high Middle Ages. There does not seem to be much difference between what appears to have existed in Montclús and the four *masos* excavated in Vilosiu (a villa also from the early Middle Ages) that are documented at the end of the tenth century; this issue will be further analysed below.

---

29 Campmajó and others, 'Un atelier de traitement du fer sur le site du Haut Moyen Âge de la Coume Païrounell'; Luault, 'Angoustrine-Villeneuve-des-Escaldes (Pyrénées-Orientales). Coume Païrounell'.

30 Folch and Martí, 'Excavacions arqueològiques al vilar de Montclús'.

144   CHAPTER 6

Half-Dispersed Settlements in New Catalonia: *almúnies* and *ʾabrāǧ* (or *torres*)

Documents in Arabic, written after the Christian conquest, and especially archaeological excavations reveal information about the characteristics of settlements in New Catalonia before 1148 and 1149, the dates of the counts' conquest of Tortosa, and Lleida. While in other areas, such as Valencia or the Balearic Islands, the documents after the conquest of King Jaume I (James I) in the thirteenth century allude to *alqueries* and *rafals*, in the regions of Lleida and Tortosa, there are references to *almúnies*. This Arabic term refers to an inhabited location or an estate frequently held by a landowner living in a major city or town. Their existence has been linked to the last stage of Islamic rule and the increasing importance of cities, but we cannot rule out the existence of *alqueries* at an earlier stage.[31]

According to the Arabic documents, when Christian armies were nearby, the *almúnies* became fortified with towers and underground shelters; as a result, they were frequently referred to as *ʾabrāǧ* (pl. of *burǧ*, tower).[32] These settlements from the Islamic period, after the conquest, often came to be called *torres* (towers), which, as we shall see, were small settlements, often mentioned in documents from the second half of the twelfth century and later centuries.[33]

In the medieval documentation of the *comarques* of Segrià, Llitera, and Baixa Ribagorça, we find abundant references to *almúnies*. After the conquest of 1148, around Tortosa, some *almúnies* are also documented, which were obviously created before this date. In this city, located on the banks of the river Ebro, they were located mainly to the south of the town, near the coast, on land dedicated to livestock farming.[34] As mentioned, in New Catalonia, the terms *alqueria*, *aldea* or *rafal* are much rarer. However, near the Ebro delta, there is the village of L'Aldea and, within the municipality of Esplús (La Llitera; in the Middle Ages, Esplucs), the now deserted place of Ràfels.

Two types of *almúnies* have been differentiated: irrigated and dryland.[35] In the latter, livestock must have been important, since we have noticed, often in the contemporary period, in the middle of the territory or often coinciding with its limit, the existence of a drove track (*cabanera* or *carrerada*, in Catalan), which we assume existed in the Middle Ages. However, despite the presumed importance of livestock in the Islamic era, dryland growing cereals, also had remarkable economic importance.[36] Certainly, not everything was irrigated,

---

31 Brufal, 'L'espai rural del districte musulmà de Lleida', p. 385.

32 *De quan érem o no musulmans*, ed. by Bramon, p. 113.

33 There are still the villages of Torrefarrera, Torre-serona, Torrelameu, Torres de Segre, etc.

34 Negre, *En els confins d'al-Andalus*, p. 386.

35 Eritja, *De l'almunia a la* turris: *organització de l'espai a la regió de Lleida*, pp. 27–29.

36 Sabaté and Brufal ed., *Arqueologia medieval IV: Els espais de secà*.

HAMLETS AND FARMSTEADS   145

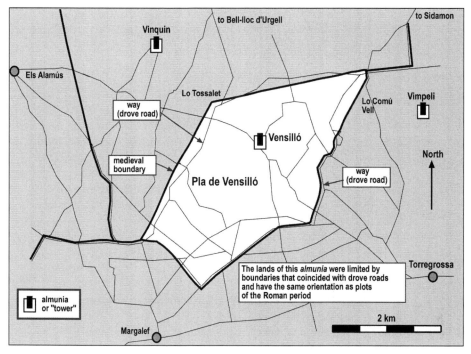

Figure 34. The *almunia* of Vensilló (Els Alamús, Segrià). Islamic settlement on dryland probably partly devoted to grazing. We can define the boundaries of this territory.

as documents show and as can be seen from the study of the territory. On the other hand, sometimes, in these rainfed lands, there could be a small valley of a *reguer* (an old watercourse), of a *clamor* (also a watercourse especially when it rains heavily) or a *coma* (or coomb), a small valley with a small, sometimes irrigated, space. In Chapter 9 we will return to this topic, particularly concerning the possible *almúnia* of Matxerri (Castelldans, Les Garrigues). Here are two examples of *almúnies* displaying different characteristics. We first learned about them thanks to documents written after the Christian conquest.

Vensilló (Els Alamús, Segrià)

This place name reveals the existence of a settlement from the Islamic era. The current territory of Vensilló probably coincides with the old territory for livestock and agricultural exploitation.[37] We can assume that it occupied an area of about 770 ha (Fig. 34). What is more interesting, however, is that these boundaries also fit with ancient livestock roads which have been used until the present. In addition, some of these boundaries, curiously enough, display

---

37 Eritja, *De l'almunia a la turris: organització de l'espai a la regió de Lleida*, pp. 73–76.

146   CHAPTER 6

the same orientation as the Roman plot divisions (possibly centuriations) from the vicinity of Lleida.[38] This is a farm located on dryland where livestock must have been of paramount importance.

Orriols (Tamarit de Llitera)

A document from 1160 mentions the 'almuniam de Horriols', which the bishop of Lleida reports to be in the municipality of Tamarit (La Llitera). Almost five kilometres west of the town of Tamarit de Llitera, there is still the place of Orriols, next to a flat valley, furrowed by a ravine. According to aerial photographs from 1946, there were regular strips of irrigated farmland, about thirty-five metres wide, distributed transversely on both sides of the watercourse; they had a total length of about 500 metres. There are about seventeen of them along about a kilometre; all of them are, of course, perpendicular to the ravine. We believe that what we saw in the middle of the last century was already created after the Christian conquest, in the eleventh and twelfth centuries, and, despite this, does not coincide with what we would have found in the Islamic era.

We can assume that before the Christian conquest there was an *almúnia*, a few houses with an irrigated space. Surely, the plots of land at that time were more irregular and smaller than those we see in aerial photographs, as has been shown in Valencia.[39] In the eleventh century or perhaps in the twelfth century, this space had to be redistributed and organized, perhaps in *parellades* (the land worked by a pair of oxen), similar to what we find in El Segrià, to the north or east of Lleida. Therefore, these strips must be contemporary with the strips of irrigated land that still exist, for example, in Almenar,[40] Torrefarrera (Segrià), and Menàrguens (La Noguera) (Fig. 56); we will discuss this further in Chapter 10.

The Contribution of Archaeology: *Almúnies*

Thorough knowledge of the past requires careful study of the written documentation and the archaeological data as two complementary sources. Indeed, written sources on their own are often insufficient when we seek to reconstruct the structures of early medieval settlements.[41] Since, in the region of Lleida, the documents from after the counts' conquest of 1149 allude to *almúnies* and *'abrāğ* (plural of *burğ*, tower), which, we know, had their origins before the conquest; excavating these settlements became an essential requirement.

---

38 Bolòs, *Els orígens medievals del paisatge català*, p. 106.
39 Esquilache, *Els constructors de l'Horta de València*.
40 Bolòs, *Els orígens medievals del paisatge català*, p. 318.
41 Francovich, 'The Beginnings of Hilltop Villages in Early Medieval Tuscany', p. 78.

As seen above, the *almúnies* consisted of a group of buildings inhabited by several families. They were probably called *'abrāǧ* when they were fortified. Up until now, two *'abrāǧ* have been excavated, and these have shed relevant information on the settlement of the Islamic era. Both *almúnies* date to a late period, when the fear of an attack by Christian rulers weighed heavily, which made defence an essential issue at these sites.

Solibernat (Torres de Segre, Segrià)

Very few archaeological excavations have been carried out on Islamic sites. Solibernat is one of them, and quite an interesting case too. Excavations from between 1983 and 1986 revealed an inhabited hilltop space, surrounded by a wall with two towers at both ends.[42] The southern sector was considered to be the one that included two dwelling places. The northern sector likely served as a warehouse. In addition, below the north-eastern slope of the hill, there was an enclosure for the livestock. Solibernat dates from the first half of the twelfth century, at a time when the written sources refer to the need to build *'abrāǧ* (plural of *burǧ*) or *torres*, due to the threat posed by Christian rulers, as they were gradually approaching.[43] This perched and fortified settlement was about fifty-five metres long and about twelve and a half metres wide. This place is suitable for the twin purposes of defence and livestock raising. The former was highly valued; however, the latter was also significant.[44]

Els Safranals (Fraga, Baix Cinca)

This site resembles Solibernat (incidentally, it is located only about sixteen kilometres to the west). It was built one kilometre to the north of Fraga, a town on the left bank of the River Cinca, about sixty metres above the level of the river. It dates to the final stage of Islamic rule in Fraga which was handed over to the count of Barcelona on the same day as Lleida (i.e., at the end of 1149). According to the results of the excavation of this site, this space was inhabited and enclosed by walls.[45] A central courtyard led to the north of this *burǧ*, where there was a storage and kitchen area, and to the south, a space divided into four or five rooms. Beyond that, at the southern end, there was a tower, like the one found in Solibernat. The walls were formed by rows of stones, topped by a wall made of rammed earth. The houses were covered by flat roofs. Also, as found in Solibernat, this space had a defensive

---

42 Rovira and others, 'Solibernat (Lleida). Un asentamiento rural islámico'.
43 *De quan érem o no musulmans*, ed. by Bramon, p. 113.
44 Eritja, *De l'almunia a la turris: organització de l'espai a la regió de Lleida*.
45 Montón, *Zafranales. Un asentamiento de la frontera hispano-musulmana*; Montón, 'El poblamiento de la frontera hispano-musulmana en al-Andalus'.

148 CHAPTER 6

purpose, but, in this case, the people who lived there were mainly dedicated to agricultural activities.

To these constructions must be added, in all probability, *almúnies* or perhaps *'abrāğ* as studied by Jesús Brufal.[46] In many of these constructions, there are remains of walls, sometimes located at the top of the hill or on its slope (Matxerri, Mas de Melons, Timorell, Vallseca, Vinfaro, Tabac); in some of them, silos were discovered (Matxerri, Mas de Melons) and in all of them, fragments of pottery from the Andalusian period. In Chapter 9, we will study in detail the space where one of these possible *almúnies* was located.

The *torre*, a type of hamlet

In the region of Lleida, the documentation from after the 1149 Christian conquest reports on *almúnies* as well as *torres* (towers). In this case, when we refer to 'towers', the sense of this word does not correspond to a fortification but to a small village with the likely presence of a tower. It is very likely that this name, *torre*, derives from the Arabic name *burğ*, which, as we have seen, is what some settlements in the last decades of Islamic rule received. In the documents of Gardeny's commandery, there are references to fifteen 'towers'.[47] Beyond this large Templar estate there were other *torres* such as Torre Pallaresa (nowadays, Torre-serona), Torrelameu, or Torregrossa. In many cases, they had irrigated land and sometimes smaller pieces of dryland. We estimate that in the estate where the Segrià *torres* were located, more than 80 per cent of the farmland was irrigated. Some of these *torres*, such as Torrefarrera or Rosselló, became larger villages, with a church (and are now the centre of a municipality), while others were abandoned. It should be noted that most of these 'towers' were ceded to knights as members of the lower nobility who had participated in the military conquest. We will now look at 'towers' as inhabited places and, above all, as centres of agricultural space.

Torrefarrera (Segrià)

In the current municipality of Torrefarrera there are at least two *torres*: Torrefarrera and La Grallera. In 2013, we analysed the characteristics of *parellades* discovered in this territory.[48] As pointed out above concerning the Templars in Segrià, these *parellades* were the result of the distribution of the lands that took place after the counts' conquest. They covered an area of about ten hectares and were often irrigated, located next to the Séquia de

---

46 Brufal, 'L'espai rural del districte musulmà de Lleida'.

47 Bolòs, 'Paisatge i societat al "Segrià" al segle xiii'; Bolòs, 'Changes and Survival'.

48 The territory arranged in *parellades* is made up of strips of land, often of a considerable length. On the irrigated land, at one end, we see the ditch.

Segrià (Segrià ditch) or one of its irrigation branch channels.[49] Thus, in the *partida* (a set of rustic lands) of Els Trullets, we managed to reconstruct the shape of five strips of land, plausibly organized in the twelfth century. Water was drawn from a canal, the Sèquia del Secà, which was most likely built after the conquest of 1149. Further south, towards Conillars and Marimon, it was also possible for us to reconstruct several *parellades*, taking the water from the Sèquia Major (or of Segrià), which, already existed in the Islamic period.

Dispersed Settlements: The Farmsteads

In many *comarques* of Catalonia, there abound scattered *masos* or farmsteads inhabited by one family of peasants. This type of settlement, in some territories the majority, dates back to the Middle Ages.[50] The creation and spread of these farms depended on several factors.

–   Formerly, topography and vegetation were determining factors. There were, however, changes over the centuries. I believe that, in the beginning, perhaps before 1000 in mountainous areas (such as Vilosiu in Berguedà) the appearance of farmsteads was tightly linked to the need to occupy marginal lands. Farmsteads in cleared formerly forested land were common around 1000. The word *mas* (*mansus*), which means farmstead, was not always used, and the location was referred to as *domus* (house). However, in the eleventh and twelfth centuries, in eastern Old Catalonia, dispersed settlements also spread across flat and cultivated lands, not only marginal areas. It was therefore a slightly different process from what happened in Languedoc, where the dissemination of farmsteads was associated with the occupation of hillsides and high valleys, which could date back to the mid-eleventh century and throughout the twelfth century.[51]

    In the late Middle Ages (before the demographic crisis of 1348), in areas of New Catalonia where clustered settlements predominated, we find new family farms often located on the margins of some districts.[52] In the municipality of Rocallaura (Vallbona de les Monges, Urgell), a castral village, according to the *capbreu* (land terrier) of 1483, there had been nine farmsteads, some on the outskirts of the municipality and others, perhaps, in the opinion of Jacinto Bonales, as a fragmentation of the lord's demesne.[53] In general, however, I believe that in these *comarques* interspersed settlement predominated, between the various districts.

---

49 Bolòs, 'El paisatge de Torrefarrera cap a l'any 1200 i als darrers segles medievals'.
50 Some recent studies point out that in the Roman period, alongside the large *villae*, there were also numerous small settlements, where peasants lived, which we can call hamlets or farmsteads. See Grau, 'A Peasant Landscape in the Eastern Roman Spain'; Revilla, 'On the Margins of the Villa System?'.
51 Durand, *Les paysages médiévaux du Languedoc*, p. 200.
52 Argilés, 'Paisatge, societat i organització del territori a Rocallaura'.
53 Bonales, *Història de Rocallaura*, p. 122.

150   CHAPTER 6

As we will see later, there were many *bordes* (secondary farmsteads) and *masoveries* (farmhouses separated from one another) at that time in the lands where a dispersed settlement pattern predominated, in Old Catalonia.

– Secondly, the construction of a farmstead in a certain place depended on the existence of a minimum amount of arable land, pastures, forestland, and, above all, water. Generally, next to each secluded farmhouse there was some kind of watercourse, either a river, a torrent, or a spring. Water is, of course, an essential requirement in any place inhabited by a family or community.[54] On the other hand, in many cases, the arable extent of some farmsteads, and especially of most of the *bordes* and *masoveries*, was almost insufficient for a family to survive. This was the case when the family only had a few terraces and had no wide extension of the land. Certainly, as I said, when the demographic crisis of the fourteenth century kicked in because of the Black Death, these *bordes* and *masoveries* were the first farms to be abandoned.

– Third, the spread of dispersed settlements also depended on a collective tradition and mentality which made it possible and desirable. The importance of a common mindset has also been significant in other European countries.[55] This required a minimum degree of security; insecurity surely favoured the concentration of the population in specific nuclei, even in some cases, enclosed behind walls, as reported in many countries.[56] Perhaps the shift of hamlets from the early Middle Ages, based on several families living close by, to the farmsteads from the high Middle Ages could well reflect the beginning of a less insecure stage. Being at a safe distance from the Islamic border and the end of looting raids from the eleventh and twelfth centuries may have instilled in the inhabitants the idea of tranquillity. Still, violence, a chronic disease in feudal society, as reflected in the complaints of twelfth-century peasants, seems to contradict the idea of a much safer environment.[57] Perhaps we can speak of an external danger that everyone had to protect against an internal danger that was much more difficult to avoid. Be that as it may, after 1000, there was a sharp increase in dispersed settlements in many *comarques*.

– Fourth, probably because of the approval granted by the lords or even, as has been proposed, the pressure of these lords, in some places, the dispersal was promoted to facilitate the management of the census.[58] In some *comarques*, this practice has been considered fundamental for comprehending the dispersal process of many cases, throughout the

---

54 Roberts, *The Making of the English village*, p. 105.
55 Pichot, *Le village éclaté*, p. 351.
56 Vaccaro, 'Il popolamento rurale tra fine V e inizi X nella Maremma Grossetana', p. 190.
57 Bisson, *Tormented Voices*.
58 To, 'Le mas catalan du XIIe siècle', p. 176.

eleventh and twelfth centuries. It is believed that the years between 1100 and 1125 became the period of maximum increase in the number of farmsteads.[59] In a study on the territory of Vilamajor (Vallès Oriental) Mercè Aventín pointed out that although all the names of the farmsteads of this parish were known by the thirteenth century and even sometimes from the mid-twelfth century, a few of them were documented as early as the second half of the eleventh century.[60] Many of them had precedents in villas, and especially in Carolingian hamlets.

It should be noted, however, that this practice may seem to go against the tide. In most of western Europe, between the eighth and twelfth centuries, there was a process of concentrating rural inhabitants into villages.[61] This process, in many European countries, may have been favoured by various circumstances such as the growing power of lords, the communal use of land or the use of resources by the community, the consolidation of the territories, changes in the organization of the fields, and even the general trends of urban planning and the creation of markets. Despite all this, in many *comarques* of Catalonia, the pressure that led to dispersal prevailed, to the point that, in some territories, the population living, say, near the church accounted for a tiny percentage of all the people who lived in the parish, a fact, nevertheless, in line with some other European countries.[62]

Although this issue will be discussed later, at this point we can establish a chronology of the different stages of the dispersal process. In the so-called Old Catalonia, especially the easternmost sector, there was a process of fragmentation that began with the shift of hamlets to farmsteads, some examples of which will be analysed below. Then there was the appearance of the so-called *bordes*, small and secondary farms, which sometimes only paid half of the census assigned to a *mas*. Finally, there appeared the so-called *masoveries*, or farmhouses inhabited by a peasant who depended on another peasant (and on a lord). Understanding social relations is essential for comprehending the evolution of settlements. On the other hand, it must also be noted that the lands of some of these family farms, created as a result of demographic pressure in the thirteenth and fourteenth centuries, as I have noted above, were too small and poor to support the needs of a family over generations.[63]

Taradell (Osona)

While in the parish of Ordino, in Andorra, until the contemporary era, there was a predominance of half-dispersed settlements in hamlets, in many Catalan *comarques*, very soon, the former hamlets became farmsteads, as a result of

---

59 Farías, *El mas i la vila a la Catalunya medieval*, p. 27.
60 Aventín, *Vilamajor 872–1299. De la fi del sistema antic a la consolidació del feudalisme*, pp. 86–87.
61 Curtis, 'The Emergence of Concentrated Villages in Medieval Western Europe', pp. 225–26.
62 Pichot, *Le village éclaté*, p. 279.
63 Freedman, *The Origins of Peasant Servitude in Medieval Catalonia*, p. 149.

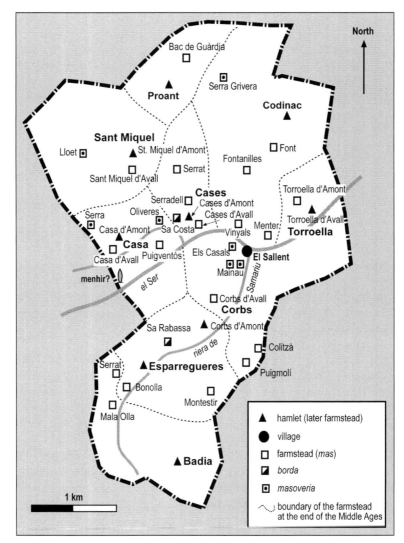

Figure 35. Parish of Sant Vicenç del Sallent (Santa Pau, Garrotxa). The preserved land terriers allow us to determine the number of farmsteads, *bordes* and *masoveries* that existed in the territory that depended on this parish.

a process of population dispersal. In Taradell, to the south of Vic, within a district in an area of 26.5 square kilometres, a document from 977 alludes to eight hamlets, to which six more should be added, as cited in other texts.[64]

---

64 *Catalunya carolíngia, vol. IV: Els comtats d'Osona i Manresa*, ed. by Ordeig, doc. 1,235, pp. 1329–1330; Bolòs, *Els orígens medievals del paisatge català*, pp. 252–53; Pladevall, *Taradell. Passat i present d'un terme i vila d'Osona*.

Most of these hamlets, in the high Middle Ages, were fragmented into farmsteads.[65] Thus, the lands of the former hamlet of Gurri were divided into four *masos*, Gurri d'Amunt, Gurri d'Avall, Gurri Mitjà, and even Gurri Curt (the latter two, very small, were deserted by the sixteenth century). A similar process can be seen in many other *comarques* and can be studied, for example, in La Garrotxa.

El Sallent (Santa Pau, Garrotxa)

A few years ago, I wrote a book about the landscape and society in the parish of Sant Vicenç del Sallent in the Middle Ages.[66] The preserved documentation and several *capbreus* (i.e., land terriers) made it possible to reconstruct the evolution of the settlement before and after the Black Death of 1348. In this parish with an area of 11.5 square kilometres, before 1000, there must have been eight or nine hamlets. Between the eleventh and mid-fourteenth centuries, there were significant changes in the population, as will be explained below (Fig. 35). This process should be carefully narrated, as it coincides with what was happening in many other places.

- The processes of the appearance of farmsteads and the splitting into two. The eight or nine villages of the early Middle Ages, after 1000, became about twenty-seven farmsteads. There were several cases of splitting, with the creation of a *mas* above and another one below. For example, the farmsteads of Torroella d'Amunt and Torroella d'Avall, where formerly there must have been a hamlet of Torroella (called this way because of the possible existence of a small tower). We have already mentioned above the splitting of the hamlet of Corbs.

- Appearance of *bordes*. In the twelfth century, in marginal areas, so-called *bordes* were created, built on the boundaries of the parish or uncultivated land located between the various *masos*. At the end of the territory of Sallent de Santa Pau, we find references to two *bordes*, one on a coast or slope and the other, as its name suggests, as the result of a clearing (bordes of Sa Costa and Sa Rabassa). These medieval *bordes* should not be confused with the *bordes* found in the modern period (since the seventeenth century) as temporary summer homes, in the high mountain lands of the Pyrenees (and also the French Massif Central) and, therefore, closely linked to livestock activities.[67] Rather, we must relate the medieval Catalan *borda* to *borda* or *bordaria*, which, in France and England in the Middle Ages, referred to a farm held by a *bordarius* (bordar or boarder).[68]

---

65 Pladevall, *Taradell. Passat i present d'un terme i vila d'Osona*, pp. 273–300.

66 Bolòs, *El mas, el pagès i el senyor*.

67 Fau, 'Les monts d'Aubrac: approches d'un habitat médiéval montagnard', p. 175.

68 Faith, *The Moral Economy of the Countryside*, p. 66; Darby, *Domesday England*, pp. 69–70.

CHAPTER 6

- Appearance of *masoveries*. A *masoveria* was a farm separated from a *mas* or farmstead, as a result of an agreement between the lord and the farmer who had the usufruct of the farmstead. This process probably took place in the thirteenth century or the first half of the fourteenth century. It involved the *sub-establishment* of a whole farm.[69] In this case, the peasants who lived in the *masoveria* no longer paid a census only to the lord, but also 'helped' the peasants of the main *mas* from which their lands had been separated. In the parish of Sallent, there were about six (or seven) *masoveries*. They were small, and their soil was of very low quality. As a result of the demographic crisis of the fourteenth century, they were the first farms to be abandoned.

Serrateix (Berguedà)

The parish of Serrateix has an area of 24.8 sq. km and is located to the south of Berga. There is a *llevador de comptes* (a rental, in English) of the monastery of Santa Maria de Serrateix, put together around 1400 which allows us to reconstruct the settlement of the parish of Serrateix from the high Middle Ages.[70] The situation must have been quite similar to that described at Taradell (Osona) and Sallent de Santa Pau (La Garrotxa).

Several sets of graves cut into the rock have been discovered, bearing witness to the fact that Serrateix was inhabited already in the early Middle Ages. In 798, it was conquered by Count Borrell I of Cerdanya. In the ninth and tenth centuries, there were probably at least six hamlets. After 1000, there was a process of settlement dispersal. In the late Middle Ages, in this well-defined parish, there were about twenty-four farmsteads and seven *masoveries*. Some of these farmsteads were also the result of a process of splitting, and in others, the place name still included the name 'vila' or 'vilar', a clear reminder of their origin. Sometimes, thanks to preserved documentation, the history of a current farmstead can be traced back over the centuries: the current *mas* Cebers corresponds to the former hamlet of Xeixelans, recorded in 990 (*vilare de Cixilani*); there was also a watchtower in this hamlet, located above Cardona, before 1000.[71]

Neighbourhoods

According to Elvis Mallorquí, in *comarques* of dispersed settlements it is common to find, throughout the high Middle Ages, dispersed farmsteads grouped into neighbourhoods (in Latin *vicinati*, in Catalan *veïnats*).[72] In many

---

69 Freedman, *The Origins of Peasant Servitude in Medieval Catalonia*, p. 150.

70 *Diplomatari del monestir de Santa Maria de Serrateix*, ed. by Bolòs, doc. 395, pp. 544–58.

71 *Diplomatari del monestir de Santa Maria de Serrateix*, ed. by Bolòs, docs. 23, 31 and 395.

72 Mallorquí, 'Els veïnats: orígens i evolució d'una demarcació territorial'.

parishes of the diocese of Girona there were several neighbourhoods. This practice requires research on the origin of these neighbourhoods precisely because, in the tenth and eleventh centuries, large parishes were organized that included old villas and hamlets (*vilars*). For example, in 904, the church of Santa Maria de la Bisbal (Baix Empordà) was consecrated and extended over a territory that included three villas and three hamlets. In 1062, in the aftermath of the consecration of the parish of Cruïlles, in the same *comarca*, there is written evidence of nine villas and four hamlets.[73] In the fourteenth century, people referred only to neighbourhoods and no longer remembered their former origins as villas or hamlets. Sometimes they consisted of a single farmhouse, and other times they may have included as many as twenty-five farmsteads. Mallorquí found as many as 208 medieval neighbourhoods in the archdeaconries of Girona and La Selva. He claims that over 35 percent of them originated from a Carolingian villa or hamlet. In the high Middle Ages, in the centre of the neighbourhood could be, for example, a suffragan church or a manor (*domus fortis*) or even a castle.

The Contribution of Archaeology: Farmsteads

In recent decades, a few medieval farmsteads have been excavated. The earliest site to be excavated was *mas* A de Vilosiu in 1960–1961, an effort led by Albert del Castillo and Manuel Riu. In the years 1984–1986, excavations were undertaken in *mas* B de Vilosiu, located about 210 metres above the previous one.[74] Other single-family farms have also been excavated near Guixers (Solsonès), Esparreguera (Baix Llobregat), near Artés (Bages), Collsacabra (Osona), Colera (Alt Empordà), etc.[75]

The farmhouses of Vilosiu only have one level, on level ground. However, during the high Middle Ages, there were already farmhouses of more affluent farmers with two levels, with a higher floor. Sometimes a natural margin was leveraged with access to the upper level through the back door. In addition, *post-mortem* inventories from the late Middle Ages indicate that some farmhouses from this period already had a higher level, with access through an interior staircase.[76] We know that in the late Middle Ages, there were *masos torre*, tower-shaped farmhouses (as seen elsewhere in Europe).[77] In the sixteenth century, we find examples of the typical two-story modern *masia*; on the upper floor, there was a room or hall around which the various chambers were distributed;[78] however, life revolved around the kitchen, which was usually where the fireplace was located.

---

73 Mallorquí, 'Els veïnats: orígens i evolució d'una demarcació territorial', p. 366.

74 Bolòs ed., *Un mas pirinenc medieval: Vilosiu B.*

75 Riu, *L'arqueologia medieval a Catalunya*, p. 45.

76 Benito, 'Casa rural y niveles de vida en el entorno de Barcelona a fines de la Edad Media'.

77 Remacle, 'Les maisons rurales en pierre au Val d'Aoste', p. 206.

78 Barbany and others, *De la balma a la masia.*

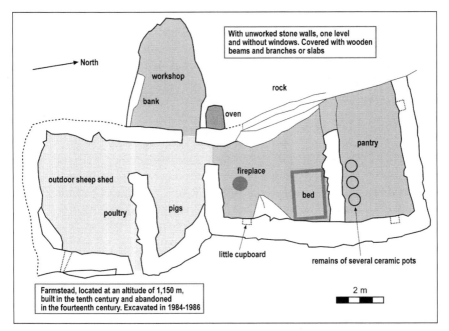

Figure 36. Farmhouse of Mas B de Vilosiu (Cercs, Berguedà). An archaeological site consisting of a room for eating and sleeping, a pantry, a room with an oven, and some courtyards for livestock. It was built in the tenth century and abandoned in the fourteenth century.

Mas B de Vilosiu (Cercs, Berguedà)

Mas B de Vilosiu was a poor farmhouse, probably built before 1000 and located at an altitude of 1150 metres. The house consisted mainly of a bedroom-dining room, and a pantry at the back. At the entrance, there was a courtyard and, on the left, a chamber for the oven (Fig. 36). Further out, there was another court, uncovered, perhaps for sheep. Everything was on ground level. There were probably no windows (just a hole at the top of the wall). The roof was made of tree branches and rested on a rock behind it. This house was probably inhabited from the end of the tenth century until it was abandoned in the fourteenth century when the demographic crisis of the end of the Middle Ages arose everywhere. Nearby there were small fields, a few *horts* (next to a stream), a pasture area, and a forest area. At about 210 metres, we find a farm similar to this one (mas A de Vilosiu), excavated in the 1960s. In this valley of Vilosiu, it seems, according to the documents, that there were at least four farmhouses. At this point, it is worth noting previous references to Montclús, a place located in this same region, but perhaps that was not always the case since, in the early Middle Ages, the documents allude to villas and hamlets being clustered settlements. But, in this villa of Vilosiu, a few years before 1000, there was a church dedicated to Saint Mary as well as a set of dispersed single-family homes.

A similar type of detached farmhouse can be found just outside Catalonia. In the French Massif Central, in parts of Quercy and Agenais, from the Middle Ages, farmsteads, as well as dispersed settlements, abounded.[79] In Aubrac, in this same massif, medieval farmhouses have been studied whose perimeter walls, as in the case of Vilosiu, were made of stone. However, the internal partition that separated the area for animals from the space for people must have been made of wood.[80] The farmhouses have been dated to around 1000; perhaps the fact that this was a warmer period, as we will discuss in Chapter 12, facilitated the colonization of places located at an altitude of 1200 metres. Certainly, these constructions are much poorer than the increasingly comfortable farmhouses from the twelfth century onwards, which, as we have said, mark a precedent for modern farmhouses.[81]

Caves and *esplugues*

Let's go a little further back in time. Between the sixth and eleventh centuries, people, looking for security, sometimes settled in high places, which were easy to defend. It was also common for them to sometimes settle in caves or *balmes*, often called *esplugues* (*speluncas*, in Latin). Some of these troglodytic settlements have been studied. Special mention should be made concerning those of L'Esplugallonga (Pallars Jussà), those of Oroners (La Noguera), and those of Can Ximet (Alt Penedès).[82] The latter is located close to the Olèrdola site, the capital of the Penedès in the early medieval period. The Oroners' site is also particularly interesting because within the *balma* there is not only a set of houses but also a castle and an eleventh-century church. We could refer to the many churches built under a rock; we can even mention the Carolingian monastery of Les Maleses (Pallars Jussà), which was also built using a rocky shelter.[83] This type of troglodytic settlement was very common in many countries on the shores of the Mediterranean.[84]

L'Esplugallonga (Conca de Dalt, Pallars Jussà)

The Esplugallonga site is in an elongated *balma*; it is about 120 metres long by about ten or fifteen metres wide (Fig. 37). Around eleven buildings were attached to the rocky wall at the bottom, which probably corresponded to

---

79 Hautefeuille, 'Limites, paroisses, mandements et autres territoires…', pp. 77–82.
80 Fau, 'Les monts d'Aubrac: approches d'un habitat médiéval montagnard'; Fau ed., *Les Monts d'Aubrac au Moyen Âge*.
81 Barbany and others, *De la balma a la masia*.
82 Bolòs and others, 'Els habitatges de Can Ximet'.
83 Bolòs, 'Grottes habitées, ermitages troglodytiques et châteaux bâtis dans des grottes'.
84 Guillot ed., *De la spelunca à la roca*.

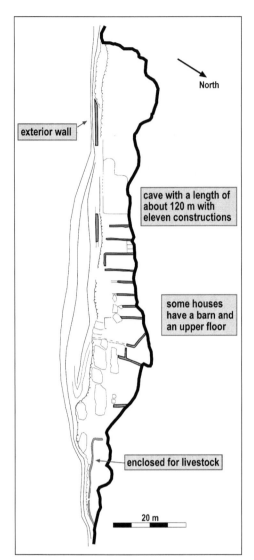

Figure 37. Inhabited cave of L'Esplugallonga (Conca de Dalt, Pallars Jussà). Shallow cave with several dwellings. It was inhabited throughout the high Middle Ages.
Source: Roig, 'Despoblat d'Esplugallonga'.

a smaller number of family homes.[85] At the north-eastern end there was a cattle enclosure. At the back of one of the houses was a stone barn; no silos were found, unlike at the Can Ximet site (Alt Penedès).[86] These homes in L'Esplugallonga could have had more than one level. They are dated, based on the ceramic materials found there, between the ninth and tenth centuries and the thirteenth or fourteenth centuries.

Conclusions

It is impossible to study the medieval landscape without assessing the importance of the hamlets in the early Middle Ages and the farmsteads, especially in the high Middle Ages, for many of the *comarques* located in the north-east of Catalonia. The current landscape, in this respect and in others, is strongly indebted to the landscape created in the medieval period.

The hamlets had their origins in the early Middle Ages, when the Roman *villae* were abandoned. They were everywhere. Some progressed and became villages, others became farmhouses, and eventually many were abandoned. As I have said, the hamlets were unstable; they often moved from one place to another close by. On the other hand, despite the differences, this type of half-dispersed settlement also existed in the Catalan *comarques* under Muslim rule, and documentation confirms the existence of *almúnies* and ʾ*abrāǧ* (plural of *burǧ*). In the previous

---

85 Bolòs, 'Grottes habitées, ermitages troglodytiques et châteaux bâtis dans des grottes', pp. 133–35.
86 Casquete and Salvadó, 'Les balmes obrades de Can Ximet'.

pages, through our knowledge of the *vilars*, *almúnies*, and *torres*, we have tried to establish links between the work extracted from written documents, archaeological excavations, and the regressive study (working back in time from modern sources) carried out while consulting contemporary aerial photographs. The same process was applied when studying farmsteads.[87]

In the early medieval period, there were probably farmsteads in the middle of fields or forests (Carolingian documents sometimes allude to houses, *domus*). It was, however, shortly before 1000, when the word mas (*mansus*) started to spread. Slowly, in the eleventh and twelfth centuries, its use began to reflect the fact that there was a single-family house, with its lands, built no longer in the middle of a village (sometimes when this was so, it was called a *capmàs* or *caput mansus*), but in the middle of fields, meadows, and forests, and located a few hundred metres from the nearest farmhouse.

We know that the word manse (*mansus*) in Carolingian Europe mainly leads us to think of large twofold estates, with a demesne and fragmented land in *mansi* and, perhaps, one single fiscal account unit.[88] However, as we have seen, in Catalonia, beginning in 1000, *mas* reflects a dispersed form of settlement.[89] As pointed out, after the first wave of farmstead creation, in the twelfth and thirteenth centuries, the second wave of settlement dispersal came, as the demographic pressure grew, which led to the creation of *bordes* and also *masoveries*. In the aftermath of the demographic, economic, and social crises of the late Middle Ages, this process of dispersal came to a grinding halt. With the outbreak of the Black Death and the crisis, the parish of Sallent de Santa Pau went from more than thirty-five farms to only six (apart from some houses located in the *sagrera* of Sant Vicenç). It was not until the seventeenth and eighteenth centuries that the population numbers again reached the levels of 1348, the year in which the Black Death broke out.

---

87 In relation to landscape archaeology studies and retrogressive analyses, see Rippon, 'Historic Landscape Analysis: Understanding the Past in the Present', pp. 158–61.

88 Bonnet and Descatoire, *Les Carolingiens (741–987)*, pp. 120–21; Chouquer, *Dominer et tenir la terre dans le haut Moyen Âge*, p. 349.

89 Recent studies show the spread of the word mas (*mansus*), already before the year 1000, especially in lands that depended on the counts of Besalú and Cerdanya, and in relation to rural farms.

CHAPTER 7

The Medieval Towns and Cities

The Other Side of the Medieval Landscape

Introduction

Having studied the landscape of the villages and farmsteads, we now turn our attention to the landscapes of towns and cities. To understand the medieval landscape, we cannot separate the rural from the urban world, as if they were different realities. We find cities rooted in the Roman past and others in the Islamic Andalusian past. You need to see their features. The origins of Tortosa were different from those of Girona; we will discuss it in detail in this chapter. They are organized along streets and also in relation to churches (or mosques), castles, palaces, or a marketplace. In addition, the walls, which enclosed the urban space, and the handicrafts practised inside, were important. On the other hand, we must differentiate neighbourhoods inhabited by Jews or Muslims. Medieval towns were places of coexistence or sometimes of confrontation. It is also important to distinguish between the cities of the early Middle Ages and those created after 1000. Cities are often the complement to the rural world, evident when studying the many towns within almost every *comarca*. These towns, often newly created as we saw in Chapter 5, were of great importance in the growth of artisanal and trading activity and had a strong impact on the population living in rural areas.

What Do We Know About the Landscape of Medieval Towns?

All too often, it is the history of the rural landscape that is subjected to analysis while little or no attention is paid to the urban world. Either that or the history of the urban landscape is analysed quite separately from everything else. However, the common features between both landscapes are manifold. People did not live in seclusion and isolation within city walls.[1] The relationship between the urban inhabitants and their immediate rural environment was constant and seamless, whether they were artisans, peasants (of which there were many), merchants, or lords (who lived in the city but had estates in the countryside). For this reason, we consider that adding cities and towns to this volume on the history of the medieval landscape of Catalonia is more than appropriate.

---

1 Gauthiez, 'La transformation des villes au Bas Moyen-Âge', p. 31.

162   CHAPTER 7

After all, in the previous chapters of this volume, we already devoted a few pages to aspects related to the development of villages and towns.

Gaining knowledge of the stages of development and the social and economic organization of European cities is a traditional field for medievalists. Many books have brought us closer to medieval cities, both Christian and Muslim. In this section, we want to highlight those that allow us to better understand the urban landscape. In 1976, Mick Aston and James Bond published a synthesis on this subject in *The Landscape of Towns*.[2] In addition, numerous atlases of European cities have been published in recent years,[3] one of which stands out is the *Atlas de Paris au Moyen Âge*, which represents the European capital city's urban space, settlements, society, religion, places of power, and economic centres.[4] These are perhaps the main aspects we need to address in a study on the development of a city. Other remarkable works have been done on housing, such as the volume directed by Yves Esquieu and Jean-Marie Pesez or Jean Passini's research about the city of Toledo.[5] However, our focus of interest in this chapter is to understand how the urban space was organized.

In 1960, Michael R. G. Conzen published a study of the town planning of the English town of Alnwick.[6] He investigated the town based on defining the plan units of the oldest part of the town and the modern extensions. These plan units were made up of streets, blocks of houses, and housing, differing from each other by reason of their size, shape, and street orientation. This was a very important contribution, which made it possible to figure out the different stages of the creation of urban space. Other English towns, such as Coventry, were subsequently analysed.[7]

This methodology has also been applied in studies on Normandy, France, and Upper Brittany.[8] Gauthiez defines 'plan unit' as an urban space with a common internal organization different from that around it, which leads us to assume that this space has a shared history.[9] Likewise, in a similar way to what we said when studying the rural plot division on the formation and foundation networks, so too concerning the cities, we can distinguish between 'spontaneous' and 'deliberate' urban planning.[10] Finally, it should be noted

---

2   Aston and Bond, *The Landscape of Towns*.
3   Simms and Clarke ed., *Lords and Towns in Medieval Europe*; Lavaud, 'The Atlas històriques de Bordeaux'.
4   Lorentz and Sandron, *Atlas de Paris au Moyen Âge*.
5   Esquieu and Pesez, *Cent maisons médiévales en France*; Passini, *Casas y casas principales urbanas*.
6   Conzen, *Alnwick, Northumberland*.
7   Lilley, 'Mapping the medieval city'.
8   Gauthiez, *Atlas morphologique des villes de Normandie*; Gauthiez and others, *Village et ville au Moyen Âge: les dynamiques morphologiques*; Bachelier, *Villes et villages de Haute-Bretagne*.
9   Gauthiez, *Atlas morphologique des villes de Normandie*, p. 10; Gauthiez and others, *Village et ville au Moyen Âge: les dynamiques morphologiques*, p. 481.
10 Gauthiez, *Atlas morphologique des villes de Normandie*, pp. 11–12.

THE MEDIEVAL TOWNS AND CITIES

163

that the interactions between the various plan units should help establish a relative chronology.

Cities with a Roman Heritage

The Roman influence is highly visible in three Catalan cities: Barcelona, Girona, and Tarragona. It is also present in other cities or towns, such as Lleida, Vic, Elna, Guissona, Isona, Llívia, La Seu d'Urgell, and Empúries, where important remains of buildings from before the medieval period have been found. However, it is only with the former three cities that medieval town planning owes much to development from the Roman period. In these cities, the early walls and even some of the main roads were created more than 1500 years ago.

Barcelona (Barcelonès)

When comparing the urban planning of Barcelona (*Barcino*) from the Roman period with its planning from the early Middle Ages, we find remarkable continuities, the most obvious being the layout of the walls. The Roman urban planning of the fourth-century area was not outgrown until the thirteenth century, during the reign of King Jaume I (James I). Then there was a new extension, in the fourteenth century, during the reign of Pere III (Peter III) the Ceremonious.[11] However, despite this urban continuity, in the Visigothic, Islamic, and Carolingian eras, the organization of the streets, squares, and the distribution of the most important buildings probably differed slightly from the Roman period. Christianization led to the building of a cathedral and several churches (Saint James, Saint Michael, and Saint Justus). In the Visigothic period, an Aryan cathedral must have been created. New power-related buildings were probably built. We know that in the northern corner of the city next to the cathedral in the Carolingian period, the count's palace was built where the royal palace would later be situated. We also know that, despite occasional changes, the fundamental axes of the Roman city, organized orthogonally, remained. However, over the Middle Ages, some streets moved or changed locations, while others simply disappeared or were created anew.[12] From the tenth century, the city began to grow beyond its Roman walls, with the emergence of several suburbs, built around places where the market was held or near the main roads outside the walled-in space.[13]

---

11 As pointed out, I use the numbering system used in Catalonia in relation to this monarch of the Catalan-Aragonese Crown. As king of the kingdom of Aragon, he is the fourth monarch bearing that name.

12 Bolòs and Hurtado, *Atles del comtat de Barcelona (801–993)*.

13 Banks, 'El marc històric', pp. 21–104.

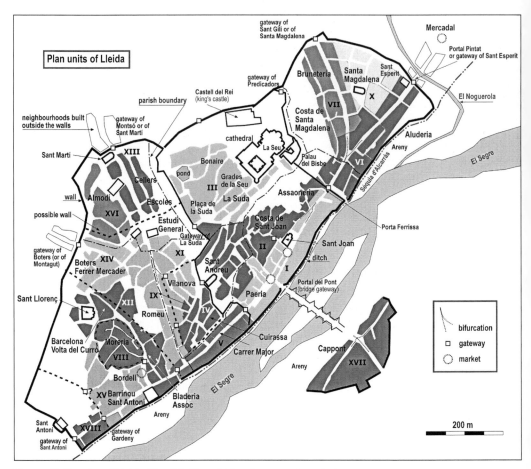

Figure 38. The city of Lleida (Segrià). The city has Roman antecedents, was planned in the Islamic period, and was reorganized into five parishes after the conquest of the counts of Barcelona and Urgell in 1149. Suggested reconstruction of the plan units. Source: Author.

The city behind the tenth-century walls stretched out to reach about 11.5 hectares; the walled-in area in the fourteenth century occupied about 214 hectares. However, the hectares corresponding to the enlargement from the time of King Peter III, located south-west of the Rambla, was partly left unbuilt due to the demographic crisis of the late Middle Ages.

Islamic Cities

Lleida and Tortosa were the capitals of two taifa kingdoms in the eleventh and twelfth centuries. The organization of these cities owes much to the urban planning of the Islamic era, although there may have been earlier antecedents. We also find clear evidence of the Muslim era in other towns, such as Balaguer (Noguera) or Fraga (Baix Cinca). First, we will focus on Lleida, both the Islamic city and the city that was organized after the count's conquest in 1149.

Lleida (Segrià)

Lleida has some antecedents from the Roman era, which are quite noticeable when looking at the orientation of its main street or, for example, the buildings found where the Auditorium now stands. However, the structure of the medieval city is that of the city created during the Islamic era (*madīna Lārida*). According to al-Himyarī, around 883–884, the city of Lleida began to be fortified. Its mosque was built in 901. As in many Muslim cities, there was a kasbah (*qaṣaba*), or citadel, called *Suda*, where the main mosque was built (despite this being a rare occurrence, we also find a similar case in Palma de Mallorca).[14] The *Suda* stood on an area of about six hectares and was possibly the residence of city rulers (Fig. 38). At the southern end of the Suda stands the *Cuirassa* (from Arabic *qawraŷa*), after the Christian conquest, the Jewish quarter, a fortified space that allowed, from the kasbah, access to the river Segre (and thus, in case of siege, ability to obtain water).

The second sector of Islamic cities was the medina or *al-madīnah* (the old walled part of the former town). In Lleida, the medina stood between the *Suda* hill and the river Segre. It was enclosed by walls and stretched along the main street (Carrer Major). Thirdly, at each end of medina, there were several suburbs or *ravals* (from Arabic *rabaḍ*). After the conquest of the counts of Barcelona and Urgell in 1149, this original layout was essentially maintained. At the top, in the *Suda* district, the cathedral of Santa Maria and the King's castle were built. From 1168, where the old medina was located, the parish of Sant Joan began its expansion. To the north-east and south-west of this core, several more parishes were built (Santa Magdalena, Sant Andreu, Sant Llorenç, and Sant Martí), where surely, before the Christian conquest, there were various suburbs (as can be seen in Santa Magdalena as revealed by archaeological excavations) (Table 3).

---

14 Mazzoli-Guintard, *Ciudades de al-Andalus*, p. 141.

166   CHAPTER 7

Table 3. Types of spaces in the City of Lleida (twelfth–fifteenth centuries)

Secular
Castell del Rei (King's Castle)
Paeria (formerly, Palace of the Sanaüja family)
Palaces of the Montcada, Cervera, Òdena families etc.
Home to some important person (which gave name to a street)
Bridge (over the river Segre)
Prison
Hospitals (often under the Catholic Church's protection)
Baths (possibly some of them of Islamic origin)
Brothel (initially in Santa Magdalena, and later in Sant Llorenç)

Religious
Seu Vella: Saint Mary's Cathedral
Bishop's Palace, Archdeacons' Houses, and other dignitaries of the chapter
Parishes of Sant Joan, Sant Llorenç, Santa Magdalena, Sant Andreu, and Sant Martí. Parishes outside the wall: Sant Pau and Sant Gili
Mosque (in the Muslim quarter)
Synagogue (in the Jewish quarter, or *Cuirassa*)
Christian cemeteries, one Islamic cemetery, and one Jewish cemetery (outside the city walls)
Chapels
Convents and monasteries (outside the city walls)

Economic
Mercadal (the merchants' gathering spot), and later, market on the Sant Joan's square
Pes de l'oli (Oil weighing), *Pes de la llana* (Wool weighing), etc.
Assoc (market of Muslim tradition)
Almodí (building for cereal storage and sale)
Mills and ditches (outside the city walls). Boat mills (on the riverbank)
Ovens or bakeries (at least one for each parish)
Butcher shops and *maell* (or slaughterhouse)
Tanneries for elaboration of hides (near the ditch or Séquia d'Alcarràs)
Hostels and taverns
Houses of different trades or crafts

Urban development
Quarters or parishes. Quarter (or district) on the other side of the bridge (Cappont)
Portals or gateways (del Pont [of the bridge], de Sant Esperit, de Montsó, de Montagut, de Gardeny, etc.)
City walls (several stages)
Streets (linking gates, linking main buildings, leading to a house, etc.)
Squares (next to a church or on a crossroads). The Mercadal square was abandoned at the end of the Middle Ages
Arcades (on streets or squares where the market activity took place)
Ponds (in Suda), wells, fountains

Cultural
Estudi General (in 1300) or university

Plan Units of Lleida

In the book *Dins les muralles de la ciutat* (Within the city walls) we first drew plan units of this city (only from the medieval period).[15] Then, for a map of Lleida from the end of the Middle Ages, we discovered, as Keith Lilley points out, that establishing a relative chronology showing the oldest and newer plan units is not always an easy task.[16] In addition, drawing the development units for Lleida is especially difficult for two reasons. Firstly, because some neighbourhoods experienced heavy destruction in the modern era (for example, in La Suda or Santa Magdalena), it is impossible to recreate the plot division of the original houses. Secondly, it is not possible to see the links between what was created after the conquest of 1149 and what was created before. Despite these difficulties, this is my proposal (Fig. 38):

I. Lower sector of the parish of Sant Joan, which extends along with Carrer Major (the main street). It corresponds to the ancient medina of the Islamic era. It was largely redeveloped after the conquest of 1149. Carrer Major was already a street in the Roman period.

II. Slope of Sant Joan. The slope of the Cathedral hill, which was probably also part of the ancient Islamic medina.

III. La Suda. It corresponded to the ancient Islamic kasbah (*al-qaṣabah*) or citadel. After the Christian conquest, the King's Castle and the Cathedral (where a former mosque was located) were built. We do not know whether in 1149 there was anything left of the original buildings that existed before the conquest or, as a result, at what time the town's development was organized as it was according to the documents of the late Middle Ages. Currently, there are no remains of any building, apart from Seu Vella, (the former cathedral) and the castle.

IV. *Cuirassa* or Jewish quarter. The term *cuirassa* comes from the Arabic *qawraỹa*, which means an extension of the *kasbah* to the river and access to water in case of siege. As in the previous case, we are unsure whether or not the whole complex was built after 1149. After that date, it was ceded to the Jews.

V. Sector of the Carrer Major located beneath the Jewish quarter. It extended along this street, to the southwest of the gate of the old medina and to a gate near Carrer del Romeu (nowadays, Carrer de Cavallers). According to written sources, there were old buildings, from before the conquest, and many others built after 1149.

---

15 Bolòs, *Dins les muralles de la ciutat. Carrers i oficis a la Lleida dels segles XIV i XV*, sheet 10.
16 Lilley, 'Mapping the Medieval City'.

VI. Carrer de l'Aluderia and Portal Pintat. After 1149, it became a street populated by hide and leather workers. Its urban development must have been similar to that in Sector VII.

VII. Carrer de la Bruneteria and Portal de Santa Magdalena. It was an inhabited street in the Islamic period (as excavations have shown) and after 1149. Initially, after the Christian conquest, as its name suggests, it was a community of weavers.

VIII. Moreria. After 1149, a quarter was built, formerly outside the city walls, to be inhabited by Muslims who had decided to stay. It must have been urbanized at that time.

IX. Carrer del Romeu. The important pivotal point most probably corresponded to a former road. It was developed after 1149, to the west of the Jewish quarter; we do not know, however, what was there originally.

X. Santa Magdalena. The sector is located around the church of Santa Magdalena, between Carrer de l'Aluderia and Carrer de la Bruneteria (sectors VI and VII). It must have been inhabited shortly after 1149.

XI. Carrer de Vilanova. The space is located between Carrer del Romeu, the church of Sant Andreu (next to the Suda wall), and the Jewish quarter.

XII. Carrer de Barcelona and Carrer de la Bladeria. Urbanized space along the street that connected the Bladeria (the grain market) and the church of Sant Llorenç. It was probably built after the construction of Sector VIII, although it is impossible to know what was there before 1149.

XIII. Carrer de les Escoles and Portal de Sant Martí. This space is located on both sides of the street that leads to the Portal de Montsó or of Sant Martí. Some houses were probably built after 1149; we do not know what was there originally.

XIV. Carrer de Boters and Portal de Montagut. This space is located on both sides of the street that leads to the Portal de Boters or of Montagut. By 1200, we know that there were even houses outside this gate.

XV. Barrinou. This sector is located around the extension of the Carrer Major towards Gardeny.

XVI. L'Almodí. The sector is located between Portal de Sant Martí and Portal de Boters, next to Almodí, a place for the storage and sale of cereals.

XVII. Cappont. This quarter is on the other side of the bridge. It was attached to the parish of Sant Joan. It was organized around three streets or three old roads.

XVIII. Portal de Sant Antoni. The last section of Carrer Major is located near the convent of Sant Antoni (where there was a hospital of the Order of Saint Anthony). It was built at the end of the Middle Ages.

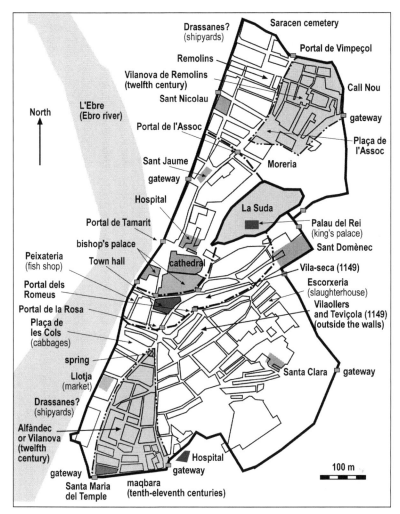

Figure 39. The city of Tortosa (Baix Ebre). A city planned in the Islamic period, formed by a *suda* or kasbah (citadel), the madinah, and several suburbs, as well as a shipyard. Tortosa was conquered by the count of Barcelona in 1148. Source: Kirchner and Virgili, 'De Turṭûša a Tortosa. La ciutat abans i després de la conquesta catalana'.

After 1149, the city of Lleida was built with walls and gates, main buildings, as well as core streets. As we will see later, there was a distinctive urban planning policy for the so-called *places* (squares) or land without housing within the walls. To conclude this section, it must be said that, in the modern period, the population has decreased, and wars have caused the destruction of entire buildings and neighbourhoods, such as those of Cappont, Santa Magdalena, and finally the Suda.

Balaguer (Noguera)

The city of Balaguer owes a great deal to the Islamic city from before the 1105 Conquest and to the city created after that date, which became the capital of the counts of Urgell. The Islamic city of Balaguer (*Madīna Balagī*) was made up of a large fortification, a well-planned district (Pla d'Almatà), and another one mainly organized along a stream that flowed into the Segre. The Pla d'Almatà initially seems to have been a military camp (*miṣr*); it had an area of about twenty-five hectares. The kasbah (later 'Castell Formós') may be dated to 897–898. Back then, Balaguer must have had several mosques. After the Christian conquest, the castle became the residence of the counts of Urgell. The district organized formerly according to an orthogonal grid (Pla d'Almatà) was abandoned, and the lower part of the city expanded downstream, with the construction of new streets, a large *mercadal*, or market square, and a new town that included a synagogue and the Jewish quarter.

Tortosa (Baix Ebre)

Tortosa (*Madīna Ṭurṭūša*) had a similar organization to Lleida. There was the *Suda* (citadel) or kasbah, where the rulers lived (Fig. 39). To the west of the Suda, between this fortified sector and the river Ebro, was a walled-in medina with four gates. The fortifications had been rebuilt around 940.[17] Most Islamic cities entered a phase of development in the late tenth century and throughout the eleventh century, at the time of the Caliphate of Cordoba and the taifa kingdoms.[18] However, in the cases of Lleida and Balaguer, the first reforms must date to the end of the ninth century.

In Tortosa, the most important mosque stood in the area of the medina, yet close to the Suda (citadel). According to al-Ḥimyarī, it had 'a five-nave mosque with a large and spacious courtyard, rebuilt in 345 (956–57)'. There were also several baths in this medina, apart from bazaars and houses. To the north and south, in a similar way to what we find in Lleida, there were suburban areas where many of the artisanal and mercantile activities took place. To the north, Remolins, outside the first wall, was a trading district. The Jewish quarter was established in this place.[19] In the south, before 1148, there were some outlying areas that after the Christian conquest were called Vila-seca and Vilaollers. Remolins and Vila-seca, to the north and south of the medina, were also walled in.[20] On the riverbanks to the north, according to some, or, according to others,[21] to the south of the city, there were shipyards

---

17 Negre, *En els confins d'al-Andalus*, p. 299.
18 Gutiérrez Lloret, 'Ciudades y conquista', pp. 155–56.
19 Barton, *Contested Treasure*, map 3.
20 Kirchner and Virgili, 'De Turtûša a Tortosa. La ciutat abans i després de la conquesta catalana'.
21 Negre, *En els confins d'al-Andalus*, pp. 301–03.

THE MEDIEVAL TOWNS AND CITIES 171

in the Islamic period where, as stated by al-Ḥimyarī, 'big boats were made with the wood of their mountains', used at the Ports of Tortosa and Beseit.

The Contributions of Archaeology

There are two excavations of particular significance for understanding the urban landscape of the Islamic era. One is the so-called Portal de Magdalena (on land now occupied by the Municipal Auditorium of Lleida). As a result of the excavations carried out between 1984 and 1987, it was possible to reconstruct a district of the city of Lleida. What was found, relating to the late medieval period, was remarkable. But perhaps even more so, was material unearthed from the Islamic era. At least four streets were located, and the sewer system (public and domestic), numerous silos, and a few water wells were excavated. Above all, it became clear what the structure of some houses was like. In the houses of Lleida before 1149, as in many other Islamic cities, there used to be a hallway, a central courtyard, and one or two side rooms.[22]

The other important excavation was in Pla d'Almatà (Balaguer, La Noguera), a very interesting site that has been studied for some years. In Pla d'Almatà during the eighth century, shortly after the Islamic conquest, there was possibly a military camp. The whole space was walled in using rammed earth of which some sections are still preserved. Then, in the second half of the tenth century and throughout the eleventh century, numerous houses were built until the conquest by the counts of Urgell in 1105.[23] We find many more houses larger than those in Lleida ranging from between 80 and 150 square metres compared to 50–100 square metres of those in the district of Santa Magdalena, in Lleida. A stone base supported a rammed earth wall. They were also organized around a porched courtyard. The courtyard was accessible through a vestibule. Several silos have also been dug out. All these homes correspond to the type of house found in many other places in the Iberian Peninsula or North Africa, as, for example, the remarkable remains of *Siyāsa* (Cieza, Murcia), where eighteen Islamic-era houses were excavated.[24]

---

22 Loriente, *L'horitzó andalusí de l'antic Portal de Magdalena*; Loriente and Oliver, *L'antic Portal de Magdalena*.

23 Alòs and others, 'Les cases andalusines del Pla d'Almatà (Balaguer, Noguera)'; Monjo, Alòs, and Solanes, 'El Pla d'Almatà (Balaguer, La Noguera): vint anys de recerca arqueològica'.

24 Valor and Gutiérrez, *The Archaeology of medieval Spain*, pp. 74–85; Gutiérrez Lloret, 'Coming back to grammar of the house: social meaning of medieval households'; Jiménez and Navarro, 'El urbanismo islámico y su transformación después de la conquista cristiana'.

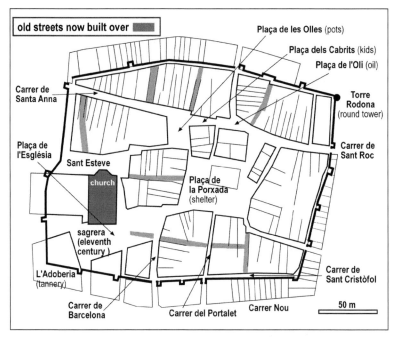

Figure 40. The town of Granollers (Vallès Oriental). Market town created in the high Middle Ages. Granollers contains a square, a church, and a walled enclosure. Source: Vila and Pancorbo, 'La topografia urbana de Granollers'.

Towns

In previous chapters, we have already mentioned the importance of market towns after 1000, the process of revitalizing trade, artisanal production, and the emergence of central sites. Sometimes they were new towns (such as Martorell or Montblanc), and other times they were old early medieval settlements that had grown and become a commercial draw (such as Granollers). Their common feature was a regular market, which attracted the population of the surrounding villages or farmsteads once a week. These towns also attracted a community of artisans, merchants, and even notaries.[25] They were a new urban reality that reflected, in fact, a new society, a new economy, and even a different mindset. In previous chapters, especially those on new towns, we have alluded to Montblanc; later, we will talk about Vilafranca del Penedès, Reus, and Puigcerdà, which could also have been included in Chapter 5.

---

25 Aventín, 'Le rôle du marché dans la structuration de l'habitat catalan au Bas Moyen Âge', p. 276.

THE MEDIEVAL TOWNS AND CITIES   173

Granollers (Vallès Oriental)

In the tenth century, references are made to the district of a villa called Granollers, where there was a church dedicated to Sant Esteve. In 1089, there is written evidence that a house was to be built on a plot of land located in the *sagrera* of Granollers. In recent years excavations have been carried out near the church of Sant Esteve, which have revealed tombs from the ninth to eleventh centuries and silos, reminding us of the existence of this *sagrera*. However, the marketplace was the true pivotal point of the town, probably more important than the church. The market must also have been created in the eleventh century as it is already documented in 1074.[26] In the twelfth century, there are references to a marketplace (*mercadallo* or *forum*). In 1316, Granollers became a royal town.

The medieval perimeter of Granollers was very regular (Fig. 40). The built-up area, about four hectares, had a slightly rectangular plan, with long sides of about 220 metres. It was organized, first, around the church, and later with regard to the space dedicated to the market and various streets. The church had a *sagrera* around it. The arcaded market square (*Plaça de la Porxada*) where the market was held is in the middle of the town. Nearby, there are smaller squares that remind us of commercial activities, probably from the Middle Ages: *Plaça de les Olles* (square of the pots), *Plaça dels Cabrits* (square of the kids, or young goats), *Plaça de l'Oli* (square of the oil) and, also, *Plaça del Blat* (square of the wheat, or perhaps of the cereals).[27] We can find similar examples in many other places. For example, in the town of Peralada (Alt Empordà), *c.* 1300, around the main square, there were also spaces intended, in this case, to sell cereals, meat, fish, cabbage, oil, shoes, and haberdashery products.[28] We find the same situation further south, for example in the city of Valencia.[29]

All this space, with the church, the squares, the streets, and the houses, was walled in, and was only accessible through gates. Around 1366, the perimeter wall was built, and it was about 800 metres long, although it is possible that there was a previous wall. On the other hand, if we study the road network, we find that the roads crossing or entering the medieval village had a long-standing tradition, possibly connected to Roman paths. This is the case, for example, with the street that ran from the Caldes gate, on the west, to the Bell-lloc gate, on the east.

---

26   Vila and Pancorbo, 'La topografia urbana de Granollers', pp. 15–17.

27   Vila and Pancorbo, 'La topografia urbana de Granollers', p. 19.

28   Farías, *El mas i la vila a la Catalunya medieval*, pp. 289–91.

29   García Marsilla, 'De la plaza a la tienda', p. 75.

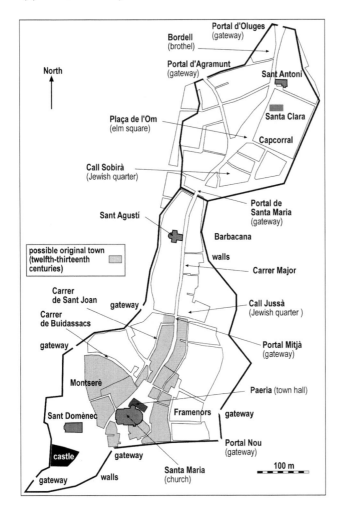

Figure 41. The town of Cervera (Segarra). A market town built along a main street. Initially, it was a castral village. In the high Middle Ages, the Paeria (town council building), a square, and several suburbs were built. Source: Verdés and Turull, 'La vila de Cervera'.

Vilafranca del Penedès (Alt Penedès)

It was probably created in the first half of the twelfth century, with a market venue in 1177. In 1188, there was, according to documents, a parish church. In 1191, we know that an annual fair was also held. In the thirteenth century, a palace was also built by the Catalan-Aragonese King, Jaume I (James I). In 1274, the Jews of Vilafranca received a privilege; the *call*, or Jewish quarter, was at the westernmost end of the town. At the time of King Pere III (Peter III), in the fourteenth century, as in many other towns and cities, some of the old defences were demolished and new walls were put up. According to the *fogatge* (a hearth tax) of 1358, immediately after the Black Death, there were 873 *focs* (hearths or inhabited houses).

The outline of this town at the end of the Middle Ages, walled in with several gates, was peculiar. Clearly, it can only be understood on the basis of the assumption that it saw several phases of growth. It shows a former core extending from *Plaça del Vall del Castell* (dry moat of the castle) to *Carrer de Clascar* and from *Carrer de la Cort* to at least *Carrer del Marquès d'Alfarràs*; this was an area of about 3.3 hectares. Perhaps, in a second phase, the town expanded from this former core to the south-east, all the way to *Rambla de Nostra Senyora*. On the north side, it may not have extended beyond *Carrer de la Parellada*. In a third phase, the medieval town was completed by extending itself northwards, along the *Carrer dels Ferrers* (blacksmiths) and the *Carrer de la Font* (spring). Altogether, it spread over an area of more than thirteen hectares. The different orientations of the streets help us understand the existence of the different development stages of this new medieval town.

Cervera (Segarra)

Around 1026, Cervera must have been a small town around a castle. In the fourteenth century, on the other hand, we would have found more than 1,200 *focs* (hearths or inhabited houses). It expanded basically along a single street, which curiously followed the ridge of a mountain range, the current Carrer Major (Fig. 41).[30] Near the castle, northbound, the church of Santa Maria was built, and then the seat of the Paeria (the town council), located in front of a square. Beyond this square, we find the first expansion (twelfth to thirteenth centuries), which extended about 185 metres along the main street up to Portal Mitjà (middle gateway). During a second stage (thirteenth to fourteenth centuries), the town was extended another 250 m, reaching the Portal de Santa Maria. Simultaneously, three suburbs were built: on the east, towards the convent of Sant Francesc (or Framenors); on the west, surrounding the convent of Sant Domènec; and, on the north, on the so-called Capcorral, by the convent of Sant Antoni. All this space, in the fourteenth century, was walled in, as was the case in many other towns during the Kingdom of King Pere III (Peter III), ruler of Catalonia and Aragon.[31]

As noted in other European countries, the location of towns and villages depended largely on the priorities of their inhabitants.[32] Should they be seeking a protected and easy place to defend, they would choose a hill or a mountain range (as in the case of Cervera) or a river meander (as in the case of L'Esquerda, in Osona). If what they were looking for was a convenient location for a market, they would choose a flat place located near a crossroads (such as Vilafranca del Penedès or Montblanc). It should be noted that the

---

30 Verdés and Turull, 'La vila de Cervera', pp. 96–99.

31 It was largely due to the danger that existed between 1356 and 1375, during the so-called Two Peters War, which pitted the kingdom of Castile against the Crown of Catalonia and Aragon.

32 Aston and Bond, *The Landscape of Towns*, p. 85.

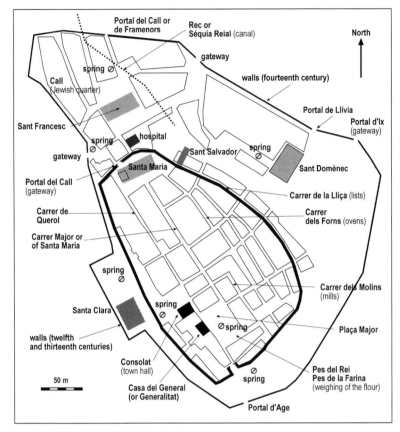

Figure 42. The town of Puigcerdà (Cerdanya). In 1181 the charter of privileges for a new town was granted. Soon there was a square, several orthogonally organized streets, some suburbs, and the walls. Source: Mercadal and Bosom, 'La vila de Puigcerdà'.

decision of the lord of the place was surely decisive when choosing a site (as in the cases of Puigcerdà and Bellver de Cerdanya, and their hilltop new towns).

Reus (Baix Camp)

The two lords of this town were the chamberlain of the church of Tarragona and the castellan of the castle of Reus. Two settlement charters were granted, that of the castellan in 1183, and that of the chamberlain in 1186. Around the year 1150, there was already a parish dedicated to Saint Mary, which was later dedicated to Saint Peter. Before 1310, it seems that a market was held every Monday in the main square (next to the church). Since 1343 merchants have also gathered once a year in Reus to hold a fair.

In the twelfth century, a settlement was probably planned to the south-west of the church and the castle.[33] The streets of this older town constitute a grid made up of rectangular blocks of houses. Around 1240, this central core expanded with the creation of a new town or a suburb to the north, beyond the existing walls. In the fourteenth century, new walls were built that enclosed this new town and the existing hospital. In the fifteenth century, the market square was built, taking advantage of the former location of the castle.

Puigcerdà (Cerdanya)

Since 1094, there has been a castle in Puigcerdà. Thanks to the monarchy, between 1178 and 1181 a new town was created at the top of the hill, where some buildings were erected. In 1181 Puigcerdà received a charter of privileges, establishing the need to build a wall. A weekly market was already being held there.[34] The original core centre, the *Vila Vella* (old town), was organized around the Plaça Major where people going to the market gathered, and an almost orthogonal grid of streets (Fig. 42). From the square to the east onto Carrer d'Ix to the north-west ran the Carrer de Querol, and that of Santa Maria, forming the basic structure of this walled-in town. In the fourteenth century, to the north and east, an extension was made, known as *Vila Nova* containing the Jewish quarter (the *Call*), the convents of Sant Francesc and Sant Domènec.[35] This extension was, subsequently walled in. To the north of the town, there was a pond, referred to in Chapter 10, in the section on ditches. It seems that a new Jewish quarter was built between the wall and the lake. Puigcerdà was an important economic, commercial, and artisanal production centre, and it progressed despite the fires that raged through the town in 1281 and 1308.

Despite the differences among all these towns, we can easily identify common elements. The most important ones were their status as commercial and artisanal centres and their central position in the economy of the region. They all had a space to hold a market. Other common aspects were their walls, a church, a palace or a castle, a planned plot division, convents, or a *call*, a Jewish quarter.

Walls and Gates

One of the hallmarks of medieval cities was their walls. Their value as a material reality, but also a psychological one, has been pointed out. In Catalonia, there were ramparts from the Roman period, the Islamic period, and the late medieval period (especially from the reign of King Pere III (or Peter III)).

---

33 Morelló, 'La vila de Reus'; Gort, *Reus al segle XII*.
34 *Cartas de población y franquicia de Cataluña*, ed. by Font Rius, doc. 166.
35 Mercadal and Bosom, 'La vila de Puigcerdà'.

178   CHAPTER 7

All the cities and towns had protective walls. In most cities, the ramparts were built in several stages. In Barcelona, we can differentiate between the walls of the late Roman Empire, those from the time of King Jaume I or James I (1213–1276), and walls from the time of King Pere III (1336–1387). In Lleida, the ramparts from the Islamic period have been differentiated from the walls built after the conquest of 1149 or those built in the late Middle Ages. In Girona, one can even identify the extensions made in the Carolingian period based on Roman walls.[36]

The gate also had symbolic importance. Their location could sometimes recall the orthogonal structure of the Roman era, as was the case in Barcelona, where there were four gates surrounding the Roman *cardo* and *decumanus*. In this city, it was near these gates that the palaces of the counts (or kings) and viscounts were built; outside the gates, markets were held and suburbs were built up. In Lleida, along the *Carrer Major* (main street), many gates were built in relation to the various enclosures and the different phases of the city's expansion. Often, the names of the gates are related to the last destination of their roads. In Lleida, there are references to, for example, Portal de Corbins, Montsó, or Montagut.[37]

Streets

Many of the urban streets may have originated in the Roman period, despite changes over the centuries. For example, the street network in early medieval Barcelona dates back to before the sixth century. We know that in the Visigothic era these streets were curtailed with a house in the middle, while others became narrower or were diverted. However, for example, in Lleida the high street, Carrer Major, despite the transformations that took place in the Islamic era, coincides with the *decumanus* of the ancient period (and with the orientation of the *Ilerda A* centuriation).

The main streets would start from the gates and link with the principal places of the city. Thus, we find streets from the cathedral to the different parishes, to the palaces, or to the market. In Lleida, in the twelfth century, we find that according to the documents preserved, there were roads to Santa Maria (the cathedral), others to Santa Magdalena, others to Sant Andreu, etc. Alleys led to private houses and can therefore be considered dead ends.

Some streets corresponded to old roads. As noted with respect to other countries, it is common to come to forks in a road beyond a gate. It is also possible that over time houses or a suburb were built on both sides of these roads. This is what we find, for example, in the streets of the Aluderia (nowadays, Carrer del Carme) and the Bruneteria (nowadays, Carrer de la Magdalena),

---

36 Canal and others, *Girona, de Carlemany al feudalisme*, p. 109.
37 Bolòs, *Dins les muralles de la ciutat. Carrers i oficis a la Lleida dels segles XIV i XV*.

THE MEDIEVAL TOWNS AND CITIES 179

to the north of Lleida, where this process of forks and town planning must have occurred before 1149, the date of the Christian conquest.

Furthermore, understanding medieval streets involves knowing their size, whether they were cobbled, or if they were fitted with sewers, what the houses on either side were like (for example, whether they had protruding upper floors), or what the workshops looked like. The streets were public spaces, as opposed to the private spaces of the houses lining them. There were also public spaces such as squares or markets, and others that we can consider half-public, such as churches, hospitals, hostels, or bakeries, and houses containing a public oven.

An aspect still little studied is the issue of dirty water and sewers. We know that in Islamic Lleida there were sewers. However, after the conquest of the count in 1149, they stopped being used.[38] However, in other Catalan cities, such as Girona, there are documents from the thirteenth and fourteenth centuries that mention them.[39]

Central Sites and Trading and Artisanal Activities

When understanding the organization of a city, the location of its central sites is essential. First, we need to consider castles, palaces, and cathedrals. These are usually referred to by the collective term 'topography of power.'[40] In Barcelona, the king's palace and the cathedral stood at the north-east end, on the side facing the mountain. In Lleida, in the late Middle Ages, the cathedral, the bishop's palace, and the king's castle were at the top of the hill. In Tarragona, the seat of the archbishopric was also situated in a high place, formerly occupied by Roman temples.[41] Likewise, the various parish churches in every sector of the cities can also be considered central places. In the case of Lleida, the city in the late Middle Ages was organized, even from an administrative point of view, around its five parishes (apart from the cathedral, nowadays the Seu Vella, dedicated to Santa Maria).

The building from which urban power was exercised also became a central place, although in general, this occurred late. In Barcelona, during the second half of the fourteenth century, the *Consell de Cent* moved to Carrer de la Ciutat, next to Plaça de Sant Jaume. In Lleida, an old seigneurial palace became the building of the *Paeria*, where the *paers* (or town councillors) held their meetings from 1383. We must keep in mind, however, that these municipal institutions often had their origins in the twelfth century and were consolidated in the thirteenth century.

---

38 Loriente and Oliver, *L'antic Portal de Magdalena*, pp. 109–11.
39 Gerez, 'Ús i abús de l'aigua a la Girona baixmedieval'.
40 Bocchi, *Per antiche strade*; Bocchi, 'The Topography of Power in the Towns of Medieval Italy'.
41 Menchon and Piñol, 'La ciutat de Tarragona', pp. 63–67.

180   CHAPTER 7

Second, it is worth noting the importance of markets and places where trading activities were carried out. In some cities, new and large markets were built (such as Vic or Balaguer); in others, the market might be held in squares near a church or an important building. Sometimes, there was a specialization concerning the products sold in each place (e.g., poultry, cabbages, pottery) as we have seen in Peralada and Granollers. Arcades were built in many of the market squares, usually in front of the houses around the square or along a street.[42] Certainly, we find arcades or porches in many other Mediterranean cities, such as Genoa (which eventually, in the fifteenth century, closed down).[43] The importance of trading activities changed the appearance of many cities. In Girona, according to an official register from 1354, forty-six shops were built next to the space where the market was held.[44]

The places where the products such as wheat, straw, wool, or oil were weighed could also be used as city landmarks. In some cities with strong commercial activity, there were auction markets (*llotges* in Catalan) dedicated to specific trade-related activities, e.g., Barcelona, Perpignan, Castelló d'Empúries, Tortosa, and also, outside Catalonia, in Valencia or Palma de Mallorca. Bridges outside the town walls were important for the organization of town planning.[45] This is the case for Lleida where the Cappont district, located on the other side of the river Segre, is mentioned at the end of the Middle Ages. Port cities, such as Barcelona and Tortosa had shipyards (*drassanes* in Catalan). These have also been present, since the tenth century, in Palma de Mallorca.[46]

Thirdly, hospitals, convents, bakeries, and houses with an oven, hostels, prisons, or brothels should be analysed. These constructions were distinguishing features of some of the streets or some sectors of the urban space. We cannot underestimate the great importance of the Franciscan and Dominican convents in the growth of many towns or cities (such as Cervera, Puigcerdà, or the main cities in the country). Even the home of a rich or well-known local citizen could serve as a point of reference; many streets were named after a person who lived or had lived there. Also, many dead-end streets were known by the names of the owners of the houses where the alley ended. We have already talked about the importance of the creation of a university in Lleida (*Estudi General*, in Catalan), in 1300, with the buildings of its various faculties.[47]

Finally, it should be noted that, over time, some streets specialized in certain trades. We find this phenomenon in many other European countries.[48] The existence of streets dedicated to shoemakers, weavers, saddlers, belt makers, boilermakers, silversmiths, etc., is well known. Inevitably, some trades, such

---

42   Vinyoles, 'Veus i sensacions dels mercats medievals', pp. 77–97.
43   Gauthiez, 'La transformation des villes au Bas Moyen-Âge', p. 40.
44   Canal and others, *La ciutat de Girona en la 1ª meitat del segle* XIV.
45   Gauthiez, 'La transformation des villes au Bas Moyen-Âge', p. 39.
46   Barceló and Rosselló, *La ciudad de Mallorca*, p. 105.
47   Lladonosa, *L'Estudi General de Lleida*.
48   Leguay, *La rue au Moyen Âge*, pp. 130–33.

THE MEDIEVAL TOWNS AND CITIES   181

as those related to the working of leather goods, were located in marginal spaces due to the stench caused by their work as well as the need to have a watercourse nearby (such as a river or a canal). Blacksmiths would also settle in marginal urban areas due to the danger of fires.

Jewish and Muslim Quarters

In many Catalan cities and towns, there was a Jewish quarter, known as a *call* of *jueria* and, in Lleida, as *Cuirassa* (after the term for the fortified space, near the citadel, allocated to the Jews) (Fig. 38). In Barcelona, there was a *Call Major*, next to Plaça de Sant Jaume, and a *Call Menor*, on the other side of the modern Carrer de Ferran. In Girona, a considerable effort has been made to establish what the plot division of the Jewish quarter along with Carrer Major del Call was like. One of the most important *aljames* was that of Perpignan.[49] The *aljames* were self-governing communities of Jews or Muslims. In the Jewish quarters or communities, there were one or more synagogues. In Catalonia, there were thirty-six *aljames* and over a hundred groups of Jews living in smaller settlements.[50]

Likewise, in other cities and towns in New Catalonia, there was also a quarter where the Islamic population lived. In the city of Lleida, the Muslim community that did not flee was installed outside the primitive walls, a quarter that was initially called *Vila dels sarraïns* (or *villa Sarracenorum*). There was a mosque in this community. In twelfth-century Lleida, there was also a Muslim butcher (*carnizeria sarracenorum*).[51] Also, in Lleida, the cemeteries of Muslims and Jews were further north, outside the city walls.

The study of urban *aljames*[52] leads us to inquire into coexistence among the various religious communities. It must be borne in mind that relations among the Christian, Jewish, and Islamic communities varied greatly over time. There were periods without much tension, but there were also stages of confrontation and considerable violence, especially after the Black Death.[53] There were technological and cultural exchanges and contributions, which we will discuss later in studying such aspects as irrigated areas or the introduction of certain crops and constructions in the Islamic world (and subsequently

---

49 Daileader, *De vrais citoyens. Violence, mémoire et identité dans la communauté médiévale de Perpignan*, pp. 117–52.

50 Forcano and Hurtado, *Atles d'història dels jueus de Catalunya*, p. 62. A number of studies have been published on Jewish communities, for example: Batlle, *L'aljama de la Seu d'Urgell medieval*; Denjean, *Juifs et Chrétiens*.

51 *Fiscal Accounts of Catalonia under the Early Count-Kings (1151–1213)*, ed. by Bisson, doc. 146.

52 Aljama is a term of Arabic origin used to designate the self-governing communities of Moors and Jews living under Christian rule.

53 Forcano and Hurtado, *Atles d'història dels jueus de Catalunya*, pp. 142–43.

182 CHAPTER 7

under Christian rule).[54] We also note the existence of notable Jewish medical specialists, scientists, and writers living in the Jewish quarters.[55] In the rural world far from the cities and towns, there were examples of forced coexistence between Christians and Muslims from the twelfth century, as we find in the villages of the Baix Segre or the river Ebro.[56] Outside of Catalonia, we should mention the study of the call or Jewish quarter of the city of Mallorca.[57] And, for Valencia, Ferran Garcia-Oliver has made a remarkable contribution to our knowledge about the daily life and relations between the Islamic and Christian communities at the end of the Middle Ages, as documented for the domains of the Cistercian abbey of Valldigna.[58]

Suburbs

All cities had a core nuclear space, the Roman city or the Islamic medina, and peripheral towns or suburbs (*burgs* or *ravals* in Catalan).[59] In Old Catalonia generally, these outer suburbs were created around 1000.[60] They could be built around a road, a market, a monastery, a church, or a port area. Barcelona had several suburbs outside the gates before the turn of the millennium.[61] In Girona, one outer suburb was created next to the church of Sant Feliu and near the monastery of Sant Pere de Galligants and another further south, in the Areny.[62] In this city, expansion began in the eleventh century but flourished mainly in the twelfth and thirteenth centuries. Then, from the late thirteenth century, there was an expansion in the *Mercadal* (market) district, to the south-east of the river Onyar. In Tortosa and Lleida, the organization of the Islamic suburbs took place before the conquest of 1148 and 1149, and was inherited by the subsequent reorganization.

---

54 Based on previous studies, we can point out the contributions made in assessing the positive aspects of the coexistence of the three religious communities in the Iberian Peninsula. In this sense, worth mentioning is the volume *Convivencia*, published in 1992, with works by Thomas F. Glick, Benjamin R. Gampel, Dwayne E. Carpenter, Juan Zozaya, etc. Special note should be made of: Glick, 'Coexistence. An Introductory Note'.

55 Forcano and Hurtado, *Atles d'història dels jueus de Catalunya*, pp. 132–33, 146–49.

56 Monjo, *Sarraïns sota el domini feudal*; Monjo, 'Sarraïns d'Aitona, el tresor de la família Montcada'.

57 Bernat, *El call de ciutat de Mallorca*.

58 Garcia-Oliver, *The Valley of the Six Mosques*. See also, in relation to Jews: Garcia-Oliver, *Els murs fràgils dels calls*; Rich, *La comunitat jueva de Barcelona*.

59 Lilley, *Urban Life in the Middle Ages, 1000–1450*, p. 181.

60 Sabaté, *El territori de la Catalunya medieval*, pp. 149–66.

61 Banks, 'El marc històric'; Banks, 'The topography of Barcelona and its urban context in eastern Catalonia from the third to the twelfth centuries'; Espuche and Guàrdia, *Espai i societat a la Barcelona pre-industrial*.

62 Canal and others, *La ciutat de Girona en la 1ª meitat del segle XIV*, p. 10; Palahí and Nolla, *Entre l'hospici i l'hospital*, p. 16; Nolla and Sagrera, 'Girona a l'edat mitjana. L'urbanisme', p. 59.

THE MEDIEVAL TOWNS AND CITIES   183

Perpinyà (Perpignan in French) became one of the most important cities in medieval Catalonia, despite having no antecedents as a Roman or Muslim city. A *cellera* was created around the church of Sant Joan, perhaps walled-in in the twelfth century. In the second half of the twelfth century, a second city wall was built to the south-west of the former wall. Between 1150 and 1270, a set of suburbs were built outside the city walls, towards the churches of Sant Jaume (Saint James), to the east, and Sant Mateu (Saint Matthew), to the south-west. The planning of these new communities followed an orthogonal grid pattern, with rectangular blocks of houses. These suburbs remained within the third enclosure of walls built between 1277 and 1344. Within this third enclosure, located south of the second, there were also several convents and the Jewish quarter.[63]

An Ecclesiastical Quarter, A University Quarter, and the Urban Hospitals

As happened elsewhere, in many Catalan cities with an episcopal seat the late medieval centuries saw the creation of an ecclesiastical district.[64] In Lleida's Suda or neighbourhood next to the cathedral and the episcopal palace became in the late Middle Ages the sector of the city where the canons and church dignitaries lived.

Also, as I said, in Lleida, in 1300, a university or college (*Estudi General* in Catalan) was established. Buildings were put up to host the faculties of civil and canon law, medicine, philosophy, and the arts; in 1426, a faculty of theology was also established. In 1328, the boundaries of the university space within which the various faculties and college lodgings stood were delineated.

In almost every city and town there were centres of assistance for the 'solemn' poor and the shameful poor (*pobres de solemnitat* and *vergonyants*).[65] We find them next to the cathedral, where the ecclesiastical institution of *Almoina* (episcopal Almshouse) was, and in relation to some parishes.[66] Also, in the urban centres we would have found several hospitals, where the sick and the poor were cared for and sheltered. Recently, a book has been published about the network of numerous hospitals that existed in the city of Lleida in the high Middle Ages.[67]

---

63 Passarrius and Catafau, 'Trois décennies d'archéologie à Perpignan', pp. 21–47; Catafau, 'Les cases dels eixamples medievals de Perpinyà', p. IX fig. 12.
64 Esquieu, *Quartier cathédral. Une cité dans la ville*.
65 Claramunt, 'El bací dels pobres vergonyants'.
66 In relation to Barcelona: López, *La Pia Almoina de Barcelona*.
67 Roca, *Pobresa i hospitals a la Lleida baixmedieval*. In relation to the Santa Creu hospital in Barcelona: Castejón, *Aproximació a l'estudi de l'Hospital de la Santa Creu de Barcelona*.

184   CHAPTER 7

Developing the Towns and the Cities

In many towns and cities, there were quarters or blocks of newly created houses. Sometimes the streets fit into a very regular grid, perhaps even orthogonal. We find a very interesting case in Tarragona, where, after the conquest of the twelfth century, the highest district of the city became planned, urbanized, and eventually located next to the metropolitan seat.[68] In Girona, the new quarters, known as *establiments* (settlements), were also meticulously planned; in some ways, they resemble new rural towns.[69] Concerning the first half of the fourteenth century, these quarters have been found in at least fourteen different parts of the city. If we want to learn about the organization of an urbanized space in the thirteenth century, the excavations in Carrer de Savaneres are highly illustrative.[70] The excavations discovered a series of terraced houses; each had a width that ranged from four to five metres and a length of fifteen to twenty metres. Initially, they had a ground floor, an upper level, and, in all probability, an attic.

Above, I have alluded to the creation in Perpignan of planned new communities in Sant Mateu and Sant Jaume, similar to the Girona *establiments*. Urban development near the church of Sant Mateu took place between 1240 and 1280. There are as many as 311 land grant deeds to authorize building houses on that land. These communities were made up of rectangular blocks of houses, arranged according to an orthogonal grid pattern.[71] Within the area enclosed by the third walled enclosure, other areas called *colomines* (or *coromines*) were also built; these were previously used for crops, such as those of En Pere Comte de Salses, En Bisbe, or En Pere Roig.[72] The study of the buildings on these blocks of newly built houses has allowed us to analyse their characteristics.[73] We can relate the *establiments* of Girona or Perpignan to the *pobles* studied in the city of València, documented since 1283, such as La Pobla de l'Almoina (year 1307), La Pobla de Fijac (at least since 1309), also called Butsènit, La Pobla d'en Cervató (before 1327), and La Pobla d'en Mercer (around 1299).[74] It shows the years of growth of artisanal and mercantile activities and of the different population groups before the crisis of the fourteenth century.

Another interesting urban planning process is the one undergone in Lleida after 1149 (the date of the Christian conquest), concerning land where there were only the crumbling remains of the former houses. The documents reveal the existence of squares or land (*places* in Catalan) that required proper

---

68 Riu, *L'arqueologia i la Tarragona feudal*; Bolòs, *Els orígens medievals del paisatge català*, p. 431.
69 Canal and others, *La ciutat de Girona en la 1ª meitat del segle XIV*, pp. 17–19.
70 Palahí and Nolla, *Entre l'hospici i l'hospital*, p. 45.
71 Catafau, 'Les cases dels eixamples medievals de Perpinyà'.
72 Passarrius and Catafau, 'Trois décennies d'archéologie à Perpignan', pp. 35–39.
73 Rémy and Catafau, 'Maisons urbaines à Perpignan dans les lotissements du XIIIᵉ siècle'.
74 Torró and Guinot, 'De la *madīna* a la ciutat'.

planning, including such valuable information as to the sizes of the houses designed for construction (two or four *braces* wide, between 3.3 to 6.6 metres, by eight *braces*, about 13.3 metres long). Even today, the sizes of some facades in the city of Lleida's Carrer Major (main street) and Carrer de la Magdalena (then Bruneteria), Carrer del Carme (then Aluderia), and Carrer de Cavallers (then El Romeu) are reminiscent of the shapes of houses built in the twelfth and thirteenth centuries.[75] We should not be surprised by urban medieval procedures as similar cases have been studied in many cities, towns, and villages throughout Europe.

Conclusions

In this chapter we have seen some of the features of the history of the landscape of cities, often called the townscape, in Catalonia. Proper treatment of these would deserve an entire volume. In fact, on this subject, great contributions have been made throughout Europe over the last fifty years. Today's cities owe much to the Roman cities and especially to those of the Middle Ages. Therefore, understanding them entails considering their origins, particularly what they were like and why their streets, squares, walls, and gates were the way they were. It is also necessary to discover the central places and how trade was distributed in the different streets and sectors of the city. We need to relate the urban landscape to the economy and, above all, to society, which is made up not only of artisans and merchants but also of clergymen, members of the nobility, and many peasants. In addition, the city was also a space where members of different religious communities lived together. Finally, we have seen that cities changed greatly throughout the Middle Ages and became larger and more complex.

75 Bolòs, 'Ciutat de Lleida', p. 134.

CHAPTER 8

Cultivated Land

The Relevance of Pre-Medieval Past

Introduction

In Mediterranean areas such as Catalonia, the impact of what was created in pre-medieval and even pre-Roman times is significant. Studies so far have shed particular light on centuriations which are grid patterns on land, usually dating from the Roman period. As medievalists, however, we are primarily interested in finding out whether the Roman centuriation persisted into the Middle Ages. We want to know the degree to which what was done during the medieval era copied pre-medieval forms or orientations. Recently, a few notable contributions have been made, mainly establishing old, i.e., Roman, and new, i.e., medieval land division patterns for the many landscapes bordering the Mediterranean. We also intend to find out about other orientations related to early parcellations (networks of land subdivisions), such as those also discovered in other European countries dating to the pre-Roman periods. Roads orientated according to the networks of original centuriations often give us a false sense of security as they hide from us a more intricate reality of many stages from our past. Below, we will discuss some examples of these issues.

What Do We Know About the Pre-Medieval Origins of Medieval Fields?

Research in recent decades has shed considerable light on the history of cultivated landscapes. Studying arable land makes one realize the great importance of long-term studies.[1] To understand the medieval (and contemporary) landscape, it is essential to have a sense of the pre-medieval plot distribution. In this chapter, unlike previously, we will focus on discovering what existed in the Middle Ages but had its origin in a previous stage or at least owed much to what was done before the sixth century. The agricultural landscape created in the ancient period that has survived to the present is also a medieval landscape and also the product of the modern and contemporary eras. Likewise, we must also consider that a Roman road is often at the same time a medieval road. If people from the Middle Ages had not worked the fields, for example, and organized them according to centuriations, or had not travelled by an ancient route, neither fields nor roads would exist nowadays.

---

1 Watteaux, 'Archéogéographie de l'habitat et du parcellaire', p. 116.

188   CHAPTER 8

In many European countries, studies have been carried out on foundation networks, such as centuriations, and on formation networks, dating to the pre-Roman period (although there may also be medieval ones).[2] This research provides us with a lot of information about landscapes that were used and transformed in the Middle Ages, and which have slowly formed over the last millennia. Plot division networks, while they may seem simple at first, are far from obvious. There has been much controversy and discussion among scholars on this issue, and many viewpoints and approaches.[3] In these introductory paragraphs, as in other chapters, various works and studies will demonstrate the complexity of the foundation or formation of land division.[4] The first work to be discussed, and one of the most recent contributions, is an ambitious project that has clarified many aspects of centuriations in the lower Rhône valley and the survival of some forms despite significant breaks.[5] Second, there is an accurate and rigorous study on the plain of the river Po, pointing out the possibility that during the early Middle Ages plot division was still made in the 'Roman' way.[6] Third, new research on the survival of orthogonal plots in medieval England has recently been published.[7] A study of Roman plot division in Hispania also alludes to the possible survival of surveying activity throughout the early Middle Ages. Thus, in the town of Brimeda (located near Astorga), in 878, signs were made (*fecit suas signas*), houses and courts were built, the place was ploughed and sown, and cattle were brought in.[8] In the twenty-first century, we can still see that the boundaries of the municipality of Brimeda — a space organized in the ninth century — and the margins of the cultivated plots, next to the river and on both sides of a road, have the same orientation, certainly in a way that is not accidental. As we shall see later, similar cases can be found in Catalonia. We will later explain how, in the ninth century, surveying texts whose ideas originated in the Roman period were copied in the monastery of Ripoll (Ripollès), and some new ones may even have been written.[9] Finally, beyond the Pyrenees, it is worth mentioning a pioneering study that relates Gascon medieval new

---

2   Watteaux, 'Archéogéographie morphologique de la plaine sud-vendéenne', p. 279; Favory, 'Les parcellaires antiques de Gaule médiane et septentrionale', p. 114; Chouquer, 'La morphologie agraire et les paysages de la plaine des Tilles et de l'Ouche'; Georges-Leroy and others, 'Les vestiges gallo-romains conservés dans le massif forestier de Haye'.

3   Leveau, 'Compte rendu de: Gérard Chouquer, L'étude des paysages'; Chouquer, *Les parcellaires médiévaux en Émilie et en Romagne*, pp. 114–17.

4   Chouquer, *Dominer et tenir la terre dans le haut Moyen Âge*, pp. 138–39.

5   Favory, *Le Tricastin romain: évolution d'un paysage centurié*; Chouquer and Jung, 'La dynamique du réseau: vers un autre objet', p. 179.

6   Franceschelli and Marabini, *Lettura di un territorio sepolto*; Gelichi, 'Agricoltura e ambiente nell'Italia tardo-antica e altomedievale', pp. 127–30.

7   Blair and others, *Planning in the Early Medieval Landscape*.

8   Ariño and others, *El pasado presente. Arqueología de los paisajes en la Hispania romana*, pp. 205–07.

9   Andreu, 'Edició crítica, traducció i estudi de l'*Ars Gromatica sive Geometria Gisemundi*'.

CULTIVATED LAND   189

villages from the Middle Ages to contemporary networks.[10] Coaxial bands abound in many other countries of western Europe as well.

Roman Centuriations

Much research has been done in recent years on Roman centuriations. Across Europe, it is worth mentioning the contributions, mainly in France, by Chouquer and Favory.[11] In the Italian and Iberian peninsulas, interesting studies have also been published.[12] It should be noted that not every finding can always be easily interpreted. By delving deeper into the study of a territory, one realizes the complexity of the evidence preserved and the possible coexistence of several centuries in the same *comarca*. In the township of Vistrenque (Oc. Vistrenca), located near Nimes, a thoroughly studied area, the remains of two centuriations in Nimes have been found, one centuriation in Orange (Oc. Aurenja) and one formation network related only to this *comarca*.[13] In the Catalan *comarques*, this complexity of pre-medieval networks is a regular feature. We find these networks everywhere, from Roussillon to Camp de Tarragona and, to the west, to the plain of Lleida. This proliferation of pre-medieval forms may provoke surprise and scepticism, but we believe that they must be properly assessed to evaluate their actual impact.

In Catalonia, the *comarques* most frequently under study have been those in Camp de Tarragona, a region that hosted the capital of Hispania Citerior, Tarraco.[14] The coexistence around this great city of at least three centuriations sprawled across the whole territory of Tarragona and divided it. There is also a doctoral thesis on the landscape and the centuriation of Barcino, the ancestor of the current city of Barcelona.[15] The Roman plot division of the Empordà region, with its main trading city Empúries, the Roman *Emporiae*, has also been analysed in depth.[16] It is claimed that in this coastal plain of the Empordà region, there were several centuriations whose orientations went from south to north, partly because of the orientation of the Via Augusta that crossed this region, from Girona to El Pertús and La Clusa (where the Via Domitia began). Detailed contributions have also been made on Roussillon, where there is evidence of the centuriations of *Ruscino* (now Castellrosselló) and others

---

10 Lavigne, *Essai sur la planification agraire au Moyen Âge*; Lavigne, 'Parcellaires de fondation et parcellaires de formation à l'époque médiévale en Gascogne'; Chouquer, *Les parcellaires médiévaux en Émilie et en Romagne*, p. 119.

11 Chouquer, 'Etude morphologique du cadastre B d'Orange'; Favory, 'Les parcellaires antiques de Gaule médiane et septentrionale'.

12 Settis, *Misurare la terra*; Ariño and others, *El pasado presente*.

13 González Villaescusa, *Las formas de los paisajes mediterráneos*, pp. 85–172.

14 Palet and Orengo, 'Les centuriacions de l'*Ager Tarraconensis*'.

15 Palet, *Estudi territorial del Pla de Barcelona*.

16 Palet and Gurt, 'Aménagement et drainage des zones humides du littoral emporitain (Catalogne)'.

190   CHAPTER 8

that may well be related to the city of Narbonne (*Narbo Martius*).[17] Research in all of these countries has shown the importance of the transformations undergone by the landscape in the Roman period.

Centuriations and plot divisions from the Roman period have also been carefully studied in other territories in Catalonia. Some Pyrenean territories, such as Cerdanya or Pallars Jussà, with the Roman cities of Llívia (*Iulia Lybica*) and Isona (*Aeso*), are worth noting respectively.[18] We can expand this list further with centuriations in western Catalonia around the Roman cities of Lleida (*Ilerda*) and Guissona (*Iesso*). As a result of excavations carried out recently in Guissona, the orientation of a centuriation has been clearly outlined.[19] The PaHisCat project in Ilerda has delineated two reliable plot divisions (*Ilerda A* and *Ilerda C*), which coincide with the city's decumanus and cardo, as well as several other possible pre-medieval plots.

Despite being a controversial topic, it can be confirmed that there were also plot division systems which were probably created in the Roman period in many other *comarques*, such as Vallès, Penedès, Maresme, Osona, Solsonès, Bages, Conca de Barberà, and possibly Baix Berguedà and Baix Ebre. By and large, almost every ancient city corresponded to centuriation or another planned network. Moreover, it seems that, at a later stage, perhaps during the late Roman Empire, the landowners, owners of *fundi* and *villae*, often organized their domains 'in the Roman style' and divided them into an orthogonal design, possibly like the one used in the territory itself or neighbouring *comarques*.

We believe that a full understanding of the imprint left by the pre-medieval period on the landscape requires a series of clarifications. Firstly, a centuriation often did not affect the whole territory. There were cultivated lands that, for some reason (perhaps because they belonged to people friendly to the colonizers), were not parcelled out, or lands that were, perhaps, covered by forest and, at least initially, were not cultivated and parcelled out. They could be organized later, though. This means that, in the same territory, one can find evidence of two or more centuriations alternating over space, and this, over the centuries, can lead to complex realities, difficult to interpret. Even on land already parcelled out, in the late Roman Empire, a landowner may have parcelled it out again, following a new orientation.

In addition, when studying the territory, we find, on the one hand, cultivated land divided according to one centuriation, and on the other, roads organized according to the orientation of the same centuriation, or sometimes failing to coincide with the orientation altogether. We often find paths that follow the orientation of a Roman plot division and are located far from the area that was initially plotted following this orientation. Therefore, in short, we should

---

17   Chouquer and Comps, 'Centuriations et organisation antique de l'espace'.
18   Aguilar and others, 'Cadastres romans a Catalunya'; González Villaescusa, *Las formas de los paisajes mediterráneos*.
19   Rodrigo, 'L'estructuració del territori de *Iesso* en època romana'.

CULTIVATED LAND 191

consider that copies of a centuriation could be made either when organizing new *fundi* or when establishing the orientation of new paths. This was the case throughout the Roman era and perhaps even during the early medieval period. Only by considering this complexity can we understand our findings when studying the territory.

Second, when understanding the landscape, pre-Roman remains should also be evaluated with the proviso that they have not been planned globally and are often called formation networks (*réseaux de formation*, in French, as opposed to foundation networks). In fact, Chouquer prefers to differentiate symmetrical plots like a chess board, symmetrical plots with coaxial bands, and asymmetrical plots. In the Middle Ages we find the three types, although the last two predominate, as studied by Cédric Lavigne in Gascony, or as considered by Gérard Chouquer in northern Italy.[20] If we focus again on the pre-Roman period, we must point out that we find extensive territories organized according to formation networks or plots asymmetrical, as discovered in France and England.[21] Above all, they are frequently related to the network of communication roads. On the other hand, in Catalonia and some other European countries, we believe that pre-Roman roads must have, more than once, served as a point of reference when organizing Roman centuriation networks, as they probably followed orientations adapted to the land topography. In this respect, one interesting proposal is that presented by Chouquer, in which he advocates the likelihood of 'discrete planning' at times even prior to the centuriation.[22]

One must tread carefully on such issues as the permanence of Roman orientations after the Roman Empire came to an end. For example, we may well find cases, which we will study later, with regard to slope strips, of a path being pre-medieval and oriented according to a former orientation while the coaxial plots on either side, with the same orientation, were organized throughout the early Middle Ages.

Pre-Roman and Post-Roman Formation or Foundation Networks

For a given territory with a large number of different plot divisions (or rather, *orientations*), which had an impact on the organization of the road network and, directly or indirectly, on the distribution of fields, one can assume

---

20 Lavigne, *Essai sur la planification agraire au Moyen Âge*; Chouquer, *Les parcellaires médiévaux en Émilie et en Romagne*, pp. 238–40.

21 Chouquer and Favory, *Les paysages de l'Antiquité*; Chouquer, 'L'émergence de la planimétrie agraire à l'Âge du Fer'; Watteaux, 'Le bocage. Un paysage rural à la lumière des études archéologiques et archéogéographiques', p. 68, 70; Oosthuizen, *Landscapes Decoded*, pp. 69–71; Fleming, *The Dartmoor Reaves*; Rippon and others, *The Fields of Britannia*, pp. 214–17.

22 Chouquer, *L'étude des paysages*, p. 141.

192   CHAPTER 8

that not all of the units and divisions were Roman, and some of them are likely to have been drafted earlier. One example of this has been described above, in the Occitan region of Vistrenque. In the *comarca* of Pallars Jussà, around Isona, a centuriation and an older formation network may also be differentiated.[23] However, a full guarantee, yet difficult to confirm, may be achieved if we manage to relate these networks and excavated sites to the pre-Roman, Iberian period. For example, an orientation, referred to as VP5 when studying the landscape of the county of Barcelona, in some cases and places, is likely to be pre-Roman due to its coincidence with the orientations we find in some sites from the Iberian period.[24] Other places around Catalonia (Isona, in Pallars Jussà) or Valencia (Llíria, in Camp de Túria) show evidence of a prior agricultural orientation of Iberian tradition of 525 m.[25] On the other hand, for the rest of Europe, mainly the north, numerous pre-Roman formation networks have been identified and studied (often they are symmetrical plots with coaxial bands or asymmetrical plots).

There are also post-Roman plot divisions, made after the fall of the Roman Empire. First, it has often been claimed that evidence of a centuriation is more likely to be from the medieval rather than the Roman period. On this issue, Brigand states that on land near Venice, traces of centuriations still visible now are mainly the result of two thousand years of land use, despite their origin as a Roman initiative.[26] In Italy, again, it is believed that plot division networks were reorganized after the end of the Roman Empire.[27] In Catalonia, some of these plot divisions may date back to the Visigothic period. For the time being, the only case of plot division that may exhibit these features is in the municipality of Fraga, a Catalan-speaking town in Aragon, very close to the city of Lleida.

Buars (Fraga, Baix Cinca): In the Early Middle Ages

In a book published in 2018, Jacinto Bonales raises the possibility that the remains of the orthogonal plot division in Buars (or Venta del Rei), a place located twelve kilometres west of Fraga, correspond to a local centuriation organized in this territory.[28] Buars is likely to have been a stopping place on

---

23 González Villaescusa, *Las formas de los paisajes mediterráneos*.
24 Bolòs, 'Història del paisatge i mapes de Caracterització del Paisatge Històric'; Bolòs, *El paisatge medieval del comtat de Barcelona*, pp. 781–84.
25 González Villaescusa, 'Essai de définition d'un module agraire chez les Ibères'.
26 Brigand, 'Les paysages agraires de la plaine venitienne', p. 21; Brigand, 'Centuriations romaines dans la plaine alluviale du Brenta'; Brigand, 'Archaeogeography and Planimetric Landscapes', pp. 200–01; Chouquer, *Les parcellaires médiévaux en Émilie et en Romagne*, p. 120.
27 Franceschelli and Marabini, *Lettura di un territorio sepolto*, p. 156. In France, we also find that regular agrarian forms were created throughout the early medieval centuries. Lauwers and others, 'Lieux et dynamiques du peuplement rural', p. 97.
28 Bonales, *Traces d'un passat llunyà*.

an important road in the transition period between the Roman and medieval worlds. In Buars the plot division overlaps with one from the time of Augustus with an orientation from south to north.[29] According to Bonales, the later plot division, perhaps created around a *fundus*, could well be from the Visigothic period. As has been pointed out in other places, these plot division networks with the *cardo* oriented almost from north to south may well date to a very late period. We know, however, that during the Roman Empire, these plot subdivisions had at first a fiscal purpose and then their aim became planning the space and most probably controlling their inhabitants.[30]

As noted above, recent studies, even in less-Romanized zones such as England, have shown plot division networks created throughout the early Middle Ages which had an impact on the organization of settlements and agricultural land.[31] Scholars and researchers emphasize the importance of the Church. For example, Georges Duby pointed out years ago, when studying the ways of thinking during the early Middle Ages, the relevance to the early medieval people of recalling the Roman past, arguing that the desire to evoke it was reflected in gold coins, marble, and stone, the Latin language, and even the spread of Christianity.[32] Now, we might add, given this research carried out in England, that this desire to recover the classical past was also reflected in the organization of the territory planned by surveyors.

In Catalonia, in the second half of the ninth century, an *Ars Gromatica sive Geometria Gisemundi* was written. As the title indicates, it was written by Gisemund, someone acquainted with surveying, who sought not only to preserve ancient knowledge but also to apply it to a landscape whose many elements of the past were still recognizable.[33] The text was stored in the noted library of the monastery of Ripoll. This abbey was an important cultural centre and its monastic community strove to recover knowledge from the classical period. Gisemund's book includes many texts on the establishment of land boundary markers, the distinction between public and private property, the Roman land cadastre, and the technical procedures of agrarian planning.[34] This was by no means the only work with this content in Charlemagne's Europe. Similar books have been found elsewhere in the Carolingian Empire, also in the ninth century, in Corbie, northern France, or Bavaria.[35]

---

29 Bonales, *Traces d'un passat llunyà*, pp. 225–26.
30 Chouquer, *Cadastres et Fiscalité dans l'Antiquité tardive*.
31 Blair and others, *Planning in the early Medieval Landscape*.
32 Duby, *Guerriers et paysans, VIIᵉ-XIIᵉ siècle*.
33 Olesti, 'Héritage et tradition des pratiques agrimensoriques', p. 258.
34 Andreu, 'Edició crítica, traducció i estudi de l'*Ars Gromatica sive Geometria Gisemundi*';
    Olesti, 'Héritage et tradition des pratiques agrimensoriques'.
35 Chouquer, *L'arpentage romain*, p. 272.

194   CHAPTER 8

Continuity and Change

When studying the forms and shapes of fields, roads, and boundaries, we must value the evidence from the past and assess the transformations across centuries. The problem lies in deciding what has remained from what has changed. Nevertheless, according to recent research, a few current forms may seem unchanged, and others even overlap with those from the Roman period, despite a break of decades or even centuries. This issue has been thoroughly studied in France and Italy.

As discussed above, research in the Rhone Valley and the Po plain has shown that sometimes coincidences can occur in the orientations of modern and older plots, even after long temporary breaks.[36] This has been seen in places with medieval fields on a higher level than the ground level of the Roman period, and therefore well above the Roman farmland, due to erosion and sedimentation. As has been pointed out, there is a high possibility of transmission of form in the same place (*isotopie*, in French) or even a displacement of form, while maintaining the same orientation (*isoclinie*, in French).[37]

To understand continuity, two landscape components must be considered: roads and settlements. The roads have often endured over the centuries and may have been the basis that has allowed the maintenance of field organization or may even have served as the basis for restructuring the plot division system. If the road followed the orientation of a centuriation, all the adjoining fields along the route were probably similarly oriented even if they had been organized later, for example in the medieval period. As said above, this practice makes it possible to understand many Roman-looking agricultural plot divisions that should actually be dated as medieval (or even more modern). This is probably the case with some coaxial strips, often located on one side of a road or on both sides.

On the other hand, we must point out the importance of settlements influencing networks of plot divisions for at least two reasons. Firstly, there was probably more intense continuity in the use of farmland around the settlement. Therefore, it is easier to follow a similar orientation from centuries ago. It has sometimes been suggested that the fact that a place was inhabited during the Islamic era prevents us from finding evidence of pre-medieval plot divisions. In some cases, however, the result might be quite the opposite. Where there has been long-term continuity in settlement it is much easier for ancient forms to survive (e.g., fields or roads). Let us consider that there must have been a break in plot division if there was a total reorganization of plots, caused, for example, by the transition from being rainfed to becoming irrigated land.

---

36 Berger and Brochier, 'Paysages et climats en moyenne vallée du Rhône'; Chouquer and Jung, 'La dynamique du réseau: vers un autre objet'; Franceschelli and Marabini, *Lettura di un territorio sepulto.*

37 Chouquer, *L'étude des paysages.* 2000; Chouquer, 'Glossaire', *Études rurales*, 2003.

The second aspect, which will be further discussed in the chapter on communication routes, is that often the outward-bound roads of a town have orientations that coincide with the various ancient, traditional plot divisions found in the *comarca*. This raises many unresolved questions about the changes that occurred in a settlement at the transitional stage between the Roman and medieval worlds and how this process affected the organization of space. As we will see in Chapter 9, this phenomenon may even have led to the creation of radio-concentric shapes: the plots appear to be organized in a circle around an inhabited place.

Old Fields in Some Catalan *comarques*

Next, we will attempt to interpret the forms of the fields of several Catalan *comarques*. Using several examples, we will zoom in on different landscapes and consider some of the problems raised in the previous sections.

Sant Joan de Mollet (Gironès)

The reason for selecting Sant Joan de Mollet, a town located east of Girona next to the river Ter, is that this is one of the few examples with sufficient evidence of a centuriation on account of two different sources: written documents from the Carolingian period and what we can see in contemporary aerial photographs. According to a document from 926, in this place located south of the river Ter, we can contrast rectangular pieces of land, with a predominating ratio of 1:2, with elongated fields of up to twelve *destres* wide (about thirty-three metres) by 340 *destres* long (about 959 metres), i.e., with a ratio of 1:28 between the short and the long sides.[38] Observation of the aerial photograph of this municipality taken in 1956 reveals that it is still possible to understand this double reality recorded in documents written before 1000 (Fig. 43). The farmland along the Moredell stream (or Monadell) shows evidence of the Carolingian hamlet of Moredell (in fact, a diminutive of Mollet) and whenever we see a *coma* (a combe or coomb, in English) or a hollow, these may coincide with the former lands mentioned, which have a slightly rectangular shape. Instead, to find a space to accommodate the elongated field of about 959 metres long, we need to go to the river plain of Sant Joan de Mollet (located further north). This long piece of land must have extended, from north to south, from the edge of the old course of the river Ter to the foot of the mountain range. To understand this plot division, our best bet is to assume the existence of ancient precedents. As mentioned above, the basis of this plot of land had as its remote origin a Roman centuriation,

---

38 *Catalunya carolíngia, vol. V: Els comtats de Girona, Besalú, Empúries i Peralada*, ed. by Sobrequés and others, doc. 199.

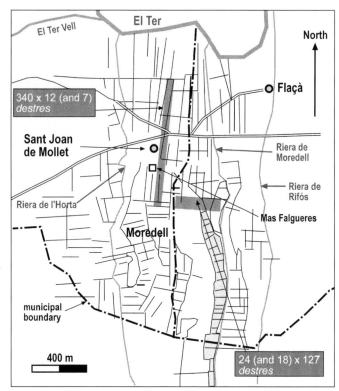

Figure 43. Fields of Sant Joan de Mollet (Gironès). According to documents from the tenth century, in this place, there were fields of about 33 m wide by about 959 m long.

the remains of which have not disappeared completely yet and were perhaps much more evident before 1000.

Castellar del Vallès (Vallès)

Pla de la Bruguera, located south of the current town of Castellar del Vallès and east of the mountain range crowned with a castle, was, about fifty years ago, one of the areas of the *comarca* of Vallès with the best-preserved plot division, coinciding with a centuriation (or perhaps a plot division network).[39] Currently, the entire plan that extends below the site of Castellar Vell lies underneath the Pla de la Bruguera industrial estate. For this reason, we need to go back to 1956 and try to understand what happened, judging by the aerial photographs taken at that time. At first, we realize the importance of the survival of the pre-medieval grid-patterned plots, fossilized in some roads and many field boundaries in the middle of the last century. Despite many coincidences, in this case, we must consider whether continuity of all the field boundaries is

---

39 Aguilar and others, 'Cadastres romans a Catalunya'; Flórez, 'Dinàmica del poblament i estructuració del territori a la Laietània interior', p. 275.

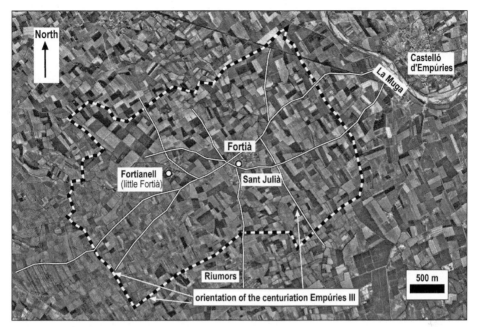

Figure 44. Village of Fortià (Alt Empordà). The territory that belongs to this village, an early medieval villa, has an almost rectangular shape. The orientation of its boundaries coincides with that of a centuriation. Source: © ICGC. Reproduced with permission.

possible — as the aerial photographs indicate — or if, instead, we must assume that they must have remained unchanged over the centuries, for example, in the case of roads, and perhaps only those older paths. Certainly, it is likely that in the modern period, plot division was reconstructed following the roads inherited from the Roman era. In the future, long-term studies will be required and, possibly, consider centuriations as not only a Roman reality.

Not far from Pla de Bruguera to the south is the municipality of Palau-solità i Plegamans where we find a similar case. Currently, there is also an industrial estate next to the Caldes stream. Throughout this area, judging by an aerial photograph from 1956, roads and fields were organized according to the Vallès C centuriation.[40] Moreover, even the boundary of the municipality, probably created in the Middle Ages, seems to follow this orientation. The importance of the road network — and perhaps sometimes also of boundaries — was probably fundamental to the perpetuation of the remains from the Roman era. Next to it, the district of Polinyà (Fig. 68) will be analysed in depth in Chapter 14, dedicated to boundaries.

---

40 Aguilar and others, 'Cadastres romans a Catalunya', p. 121.

198   CHAPTER 8

Fortià and Fortianell (Alt Empordà)

A document from 967 alludes to the villa *Fortuniano*, also called *Palaciolo*; in 974, the site of *Furtianellum minorem* was mentioned, a name that reflects the splitting of the settlement.[41] In Fortià, there was the church of Sant Julià. We also know that in 1282 there was a new town (*poblam novam*).[42] It should be noted that the name *Fortià* stems from the early Middle Ages and that, despite its Latin-looking ending, it does not correspond to a place name from the Roman period, which does not mean that the territory may not have coincided with a *fundus*, perhaps even from before the sixth century.[43]

Therefore, we infer that the territory of Fortià, a place that in the early Middle Ages was considered a *palol* or *palatiolum*, was plausibly a former fiscal estate, originating perhaps in the early medieval period (or before), and that during the years under Islamic rule, it was probably granted to someone trusted by the new authorities. Fortià is an interesting territory, organized according to the *Emporiae III* centuriation.[44] In this case, even the boundaries of the current municipality of Fortià coincide with the orientations of Roman plot division (Fig. 44). Likewise, many of the routes leading from the north-east to the south-west or from the north-west to the south-east have this same orientation. However, despite the regularity of the plot division in this area, there is also a road that goes from south to north, with an orientation like that of the *Emporiae II* centuriation. It should be remembered that the medieval landscape often had complex origins from the ancient past (and this is especially so with roads). Certainly, this complexity cannot be ignored, even if it breaks with the regularity that, supposedly, should prevail.

Vilallonga del Camp (Camp de Tarragona)

Vilallonga is a village located eleven kilometres north of Tarragona, a new town created in 1285 as a result of the transfer of people from another town that had been created a century before, in 1188, located next to the river Francolí, 1.6 kilometres east of this place.[45] This village in New Catalonia is far from the *comarca* of Empordà. Nevertheless, although this region was for several centuries under Islamic rule, we find here too substantial evidence of a pre-medieval past; Tarraco was a significant Roman city.

A close reading of the roads and the plot division in Vilallonga del Camp reveals the significance of elements inherited from conditions prior to the

---

41 *Catalunya carolíngia, vol. V: Els comtats de Girona, Besalú, Empúries i Peralada*, ed. by Sobrequés and others, docs. 381, 421.

42 *Colección diplomàtica del condado de Besalú*, ed. by Monsalvatje, pp. 262–64, doc. 1,204.

43 Coromines, *Onomasticon Cataloniae*, vol. IV, pp. 268–68.

44 Palet and Gurt, 'Aménagement et drainage des zones humides du littoral emporitain (Catalogne)'.

45 Español, 'Les cartes de població de Vilallonga'.

Middle Ages. Most fields in the western sector are organized according to the *Tarraco III* centuriation; there are also roads with an orientation coinciding with that of the *Tarraco II* and *Tarraco I* centuriations. However, in this case, when we look at boundaries, we find a reality slightly different from that in the *comarca* of Empordà. Some partitions coincide with orientations of centuriations, but there are also many orthogonal plots that, considering that these irregularities are medieval, lead us to conclude that, when this district was created, they were traced (and also remained undivided) according to pre-existing possessions. Therefore, we notice that, quite logically, the territory of Vilallonga was defined at the time when the new town was created during the high Middle Ages. Therefore, we notice in this place that there are some Roman precedents, especially in its roads, but the limits of the territory do not have clear-cut early medieval precedents, unlike the municipalities typical of Old Catalonia.

Talló (Cerdanya)

Talló, the capital of a *pagus* in the early Middle Ages, lies to the west of the Cerdanya plain. Here a church dedicated to Saint Mary is documented in the Carolingian period, although we know it was built earlier. Excavations have brought to light tombs from the fifth century to the tenth century. As for the plot division in this territory, as in most territories, the reality is highly intricate; the plot divisions for *Iulia Livica C* and *Iulia Livica B* are mixed up. The former predominates. In fact, it is the one best adapted to the topography of this *pagus* of Talló, bordered on the north by the river Segre and on the south by the mountains of Moixeró. This C centuriation not only organizes most of the fields in the vicinity of Santa Maria de Talló, but also, more importantly, it organizes the network of roads that go from west to east and from north to south.[46] Later, in studying the boundaries in Chapter 14, we will return to the *pagus* of Talló and the survival of its western border, which has remained fossilized over perhaps the last 1500 years.

Conclusions

As students of the medieval landscape, we consider ourselves fortunate because in the Roman period there were many changes in the territory and these transformations were, in principle, long-lasting. Before the sixth century, good foundations were laid on which the medieval landscape was built. This should make it easier to identify the transformations that took place over the next 1000 years and during the modern and contemporary eras.

---

46 Bolòs, 'Paisatge històric, cartografia i societat a l'alta edat mitjana: l'exemple de la Cerdanya', pp. 57–62.

However, we need to be aware of the pitfalls if we fail to realize that some mutations over centuries may mask and therefore distort evidence from the Roman period. For example, as seen in this chapter, while some roads may be very old, the arable land on both sides was created anew, following the same orientation, maybe in the medieval or more modern periods, since only the orientation was copied.[47] Even in territories whose link with the Roman world seems very clear, such as the Po plain in northern Italy, one must be very careful when making assumptions about the continuity of the landscape. On the other hand, as can be seen from some of the comments above, a few current realities reflect, surprisingly, a complexity of ancient influences that are difficult to delineate. Thus, for example, around a populated place, we often find roads that follow various orientations coinciding with the orientations of different plot divisions that, in principle, were organized in the Roman period. Research in many European countries shows this complex reality and often points to the benefits of interpreting the sources properly.[48] Thus, for example, a study carried out last century by Gérard Chouquer in the Burgundy-Franche-Comté region found with respect to large *villae* three main plot divisions as well as other minor ones created during the period of the late Roman Empire.[49] In Catalonia, we will surely find similar situations in many regions.

In this chapter we have described examples from the Gironès, Empordà, Camp de Tarragona, and Cerdanya. We could easily find others in most of the remaining Catalan *comarques*. Therefore, after studying these pre-medieval precedents, we can safely say that in almost all of Catalonia, there is evidence of an ancient landscape that requires in-depth study to interpret it adequately and thus be able to distinguish Roman from non-Roman remains. This same problem is true for much of Europe.[50] These pages have also confirmed the need for and the importance of doing long-term research on the historical landscape.

---

47 Chouquer, *L'étude des paysages*, pp. 146, 188.
48 Chouquer, 'Tissu archéologique en Bourgogne'.
49 Chouquer, *Entre Bourgogne et Franche-Comté*, p. 60.
50 Mennessier-Jouannet and Chouquer, 'Étude des formes paysagères de la région de Lezoux'.

CHAPTER 9

Coombs, Terraces, Concentric Forms, and Land Strips

Introduction

Studies over the last few years have revealed a set of landscape elements possibly dating back to the Middle Ages. Especially in New Catalonia, we find many coombs or small valleys that have probably existed at least since the first centuries of the Middle Ages. In many villages built on top of a hill or on steep slopes, we find such features as terraces, which are sometimes of medieval origin. Around some populated places, aerial photographs show radio-concentric shapes reminiscent of the early stages of new cultivation and the use of the land. Finally, many remains of early land strips have been discovered in recent years. They sometimes extend along a slope, sometimes along a plain, and at other times on either side of an old road or from one side of the valley to the other. Analysing these extant landscape elements marks an important step forward in understanding our current landscape. Recent studies carried out in the Vallès and Penedès *comarques* show the importance of interpreting the origin of these elements to understand the history of these regions near the city of Barcelona.[1] This chapter considers all these aspects.

What Do We Know About It?

While, as we have seen, learning about the origins of many lands cultivated and divided into plots before the Middle Ages is an essential requirement, we particularly need to study four components of the cultivated landscape that are medieval or modern: first *comes* (coombs) or cultivated flat valley bottoms; second, terraces, especially braided terraces. It is important to relate these to inhabited places that were already documented in the medieval period. Third, concentric shapes are usually the result of a process of clearing and deforestation. And fourthly, sloping strips, which are long strips of land parallel to each other, are often associated with the colonization processes. In this chapter, we will discuss these four components. In my opinion, some of the most important breakthroughs in research on the medieval landscape in the last few years have been related precisely to the work on these four.

The literature on these landscape components is not as abundant as that on other subjects. The most researched topic is terraced landscapes, characteristic

---

1 Bolòs, *El paisatge medieval del comtat de Barcelona.*

202   CHAPTER 9

of many European countries and a way of organizing the cultivated space around the world, from South America to China, via Africa.[2] Around the Mediterranean, many studies have shown that terraces were created long before the Middle Ages.

The exploitation of *comes* (in English, probably under the influence of French, often referred to as 'coombs') or flat and shallow valleys is very common in all the arid countries of the Mediterranean basin. A few years ago, Vita-Finzi studied the transformations on the banks of dryland watercourses over the centuries and the impact of human activity cultivating these spaces.[3] Recently, precise studies have been done on various *wadis* in North Africa, which are in fact quite similar to coombs, as we will discuss later.[4]

Lastly, the study of concentric shapes and strips of cultivated land has recently led us to point out the importance of aerial photographs as a source that allows us to deepen our knowledge. The list of books showing an interest in using them is extensive. Work undertaken using aerial photographs makes it possible to approach landscapes created in all periods.[5] In addition, in Chapter 16, we will analyse the use of LiDAR technology, which has enabled great strides forward in the interpretation of some landscapes.[6] Regarding the interpretation of concentric shapes and strips of land, there is in the next few pages a discussion of a few interesting contributions from recent years concerning other countries, such as Portugal.[7] In fact, in France, there are plenty of examples of this phenomenon, e.g. the village of Malicorne (Oc. Malicòrna) or the city of Bourges.[8]

Coombs

In Catalan, since the Middle Ages, the flat and cultivated valley bottoms have been known as *comes* (coombs), although, in the modern era, in some places, they have also been called *fondos*. On realizing their importance and dissemination in the medieval period and seeing that near these cultivated spaces, there were often old settlements, we inferred, while working on the PaHisCat project (see Chapter 16), that many of the coombs may have been cultivated at least since the beginning of the medieval period. Some may have been inhabited long before the Middle Ages.

---

2 Varoto and others, *World Terraced Landscapes*; Brown and others, 'Ending the Cinderella Status of Terraces and Lynchets in Europe'.
3 Vita-Finzi, *The Mediterranean Valleys. Geological Changes in Historical Times*.
4 Gilbertson and Hunt, 'Romano-Libyan Agriculture: Walls and Floodwater Farming'.
5 Agache and Bréart, *Atlas d'Archéologie aérienne de Picardie*; Beresford and St Joseph, *Medieval England: An Aerial survey*; Chevallier, *Lecture du temps dans l'espace*; Cowley and others, *Landscapes through the Lens*.
6 Crutchley and others, *Savernake Forest*.
7 Watteaux, 'La colonisation agraire médiévale en Alentejo'.
8 Chevallier, *Lecture du temps dans l'espace*, pp. 202–03.

It should be noted that coombs were important, especially in the drier and less humid parts of Catalonia, where they were often cultivated before irrigation systems were laid out, particularly during the tenth to thirteenth centuries in the Islamic era, and after the Christian conquest. However, we can also find them in eastern Catalonia (for example, at the foot of the Montseny Massif, Vallès Oriental) and even perhaps in some areas of the Pyrenees (such as Sant Julià de Cerdanyola, Berguedà).

One first aspect that should be noted concerning these elongated cultivated areas is that at the bottom of the small valley there is better sedimentary soil than that found on the slopes, usually with terraces created after flat and more fertile land has been used up.[9] It has been noted that in past phases of heavy erosion, such as at the beginning of the Middle Ages, these coomb plains may have filled up with alluvial soil.[10] Also, in rainy seasons, in the flat part of some of these valleys, a stream would flow. Now, we see these coombs cut transversely by dry-stone walls at the margins of a field or terrace or check-dams, which delimit the different *parades* or pieces of land. Many of these margins were probably built during the Middle Ages to prevent erosion, maintain soil moisture, and delimit properties.

It is worth distinguishing coombs, generally dry, from cultivated riverbeds, with a stream flowing, such as those found along the Riu Corb or in Vall Major, in Torrebesses.[11] It should be noted that there is a clear resemblance between these cultivated riverbeds and the *wadis* in North Africa or the eastern Mediterranean areas, which are close to the deserts.[12] In desert areas of Libya, along these *wadis*, large extensions of sidewalls as well as cross-*wadi* walls have been identified and studied. These walls may be dated to the Roman, medieval, or modern periods.[13] When they were investigated in the last century, a detailed typology was established. All the possible functions of these cross walls were also classified: the use of surface water, irrigation, erosion control, livestock movement, crop differentiation, setting property limits, etc.

In the Mediterranean Levant, in Palestine, we find similar situations. In Artas, near Bethlehem, there is the Rahhad *wadi*, which stretches for over two kilometres and is about forty metres wide. This *wadi* is divided into transversal strips, running from one bank to the other. Due to the presence

---

9 Regarding this difference in soil, it should be noted that this shows certain parallels with the dolines or the endorheic basins (Novaković and others, 'Karst dolinas'; Leveau, 'The Integration of Archaeological, Historical and Paleoenvironmental Data at the Regional Scale').

10 Sadori and others, 'Climate, Environment and Society in Southern Italy', p. 180.

11 Bolòs, 'Paisatges i transicions: canvis i continuïtats al llarg de la història', pp. 95–99; Aldomà ed., *L'aigua patrimoni de la Catalunya seca*.

12 Fenwick, *Early Islamic North Africa*, p. 90.

13 Gilbertson and Hunt, 'Romano-Libyan Agriculture: Walls and Floodwater Farming', p. 192.

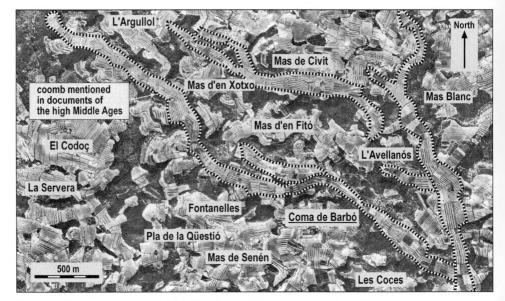

Figure 45. Coma de Barbó or Borbó (L'Espluga de Francolí, Conca de Barberà). This coomb was 2.5 km long. It was a fertile land granted to a knight at the time of the conquest by the count of Barcelona. It must have been cultivated long before. Source: © ICGC. Reproduced with permission.

of a watercourse, it was necessary to build a drainage channel at a higher level, to use the entire valley bottom.[14]

More comparisons can be made. When studying the plot division of irrigated areas in the Islamic era in Mallorca, it became evident that, in 8 per cent of cases, the margins ran crosswise to the valley bottom, an irrigated area. In addition, in 33 per cent of cases, there were margins running perpendicular to the course of the valley and terraces running parallel to the watercourse.[15] We will now turn back to the Catalan mainland and give a description of a few specific cases of coombs or valley bottoms.

Coma de Barbó (L'Espluga de Francolí, Conca de Barberà)

A land terrier from 1558 mentions the *Cavalleria de la Coma de Borbó* (now Coma de Barbó) that stood opposite Avellanós and the *Cavalleria de Les Coces*.[16] These *cavalleries* (or knight's fiefs), referred to in a sixteenth-century text, correspond to a phenomenon created in the eleventh century or perhaps the twelfth century, at the time of the conquest by the count of Barcelona

---

14 Ron, 'Sistemas de manantiales y terrazas irrigadas', pp. 395, 407.
15 Sitjes, 'Managing Slopes for Agricultural Purposes', pp. 206, 214.
16 Bolòs, 'PaHisCat: A Project to Discover the Landscape', pp. 387–88.

and the distribution of this area among its participants. In all likelihood, this coomb was cultivated before the count's conquest, in the Islamic period, and most likely during the years under Visigothic rule. This coomb is at least two and a half kilometres long and between ninety metres and one hundred and forty metres wide (Fig. 45). This elongated strip of farmland is now divided into plots (*parades*, in Catalan), bounded by dry stone margins separated by fifty-to-one hundred and thirty metres. Between the two ends of the coomb, upper and lower, there is a drop of about seventy-five metres. This case reveals not only that this land was cultivated throughout the medieval period, but also that it was a very attractive territory as it was deliberately seized by knights at the time of the conquest of Conca de Barberà, most likely in the eleventh century.

Comallonga (Castellví de la Marca, Alt Penedès)

A document from between 960 and 985 alluded to a place called Comallonga (*Choma Longa*).[17] This place still exists. It is close to the castle of Castellví de la Marca. To the east of the current farmhouse of Comallonga, as its Catalan place name indicates, there is a long and narrow coomb, with a length of about 1200 metres. Its width ranges from twenty-five to forty metres. The total area of cultivated land is about four hectares. Next to this fossilized evidence of a feature of the landscape dated to the early Middle Ages, well documented in the tenth century, we can identify, in the southernmost drylands and close to the farmhouse of Comallonga, other pieces of evidence from a remote past. Especially on the plain just south of this farmhouse, we find many field boundaries and, more importantly, paths following the orientation of the *Tarraco II* centuriation. It is also worth noting the proximity of this coomb to rock-cut graves which can be dated to the first centuries of the Middle Ages. This again confirms the early medieval dating we have proposed concerning the use of these coombs (although it cannot be ruled out that some may have already been cultivated before the Middle Ages).

Coma de la Vall del Barranc de Cabana (Ivars de Noguera, Noguera)

To the north of the village of Ivars de Noguera is a coomb whose characteristics help us understand a few more facts. First, it shows us the link between the coomb and this inhabited place which has a pre-Roman name that precisely recalls that there were small riverbanks, even irrigated in this place of Ivars.[18] Secondly, we see that this coomb of about 3.4 kilometres in length can be divided into two sections. The lower was probably irrigated (perhaps it even gave its name to the village of Ivars), while the upper 1.7 kilometres seem

17 *Catalunya carolíngia, vol. VII: El comtat de Barcelona*, ed. by Baiges and Puig, doc. 852.
18 Coromines, *Onomasticon Cataloniae*, vol. IV, p. 455.

206   CHAPTER 9

to have been drylands. The coomb, in its deep and flat part, is about fifty metres wide. There is, however, another aspect that we believe is even more important as regards its dating. This Cabana ravine, before draining into the river Noguera Ribagorçana, crosses a ditch and an irrigated area that extends to the left bank of this river.[19] This irrigated land is likely to date back to the Islamic era or from shortly after the conquest by the counts of Urgell. Be that as it may, we can say that the cultivated area of the coomb, at least this section, already existed before the irrigated lands on the banks of the river Noguera Ribagorçana were set up. This is common practice in a few other places, such as the left bank of the River Cinca, north of Monzón.[20] In a nutshell, this confirms that these coombs were already cultivated in the early medieval period, at least in the Visigothic era (and its pre-Roman place name gives away the origin of this settlement).

The Territory of Maldà and Maldanell (Urgell)

Around the village of Maldà, we find three valley bottoms sharing similar features, despite remarkable differences among them (Fig. 46). First, to the north of Maldà is the river Corb. We see a valley bottom furrowed by a stream. It is remarkably wide, at about 350 metres, and is crossed by numerous strips of land (which can be about thirty metres in length). There are areas, for example, near Sant Martí de Maldà, presumably with enclosed little *horts*, which may have originated in the late medieval period.

Secondly, to the south of Maldà and to the north of Maldanell is the Maldanell stream. The valley floor is just over five kilometres long and about 250 metres wide. It is also divided into crosswise strips, limited by margins of dry-stone walls. It was once furrowed by a watercourse, traces of which can now only be seen in aerial photographs.

Third, to the south of Maldanell, there is a coomb of about 1.7 km long and 150 m wide. Its morphology is similar to other valley bottoms, divided into transversal strips. In this case, however, we see no evidence of the existence of a watercourse.

The town of Maldà and the castles of Maldà and Maldanell can be dated to the second half of the eleventh century during the process of conquest and repopulation carried out by the Christian counts. However, studies show that this area was inhabited long before that. Under the castle of Maldanell, next to its coomb are several tombs cut into the rock, possibly from the early Middle Ages, very possibly from the Visigothic period.[21] The existence of a necropolis would indicate that there were also inhabited places very close by.

---

19 Bolòs, 'L'arqueologia del paisatge de la Catalunya medieval', p. 141.
20 Bolòs and Sànchez-Boira, 'Séquies i comes a la riba Esquerra del Cinca'.
21 Bolòs, 'Paisatges i transicions: canvis i continuïtats al llarg de la història', pp. 95–99.

COOMBS, TERRACES, CONCENTRIC FORMS, AND LAND STRIPS 207

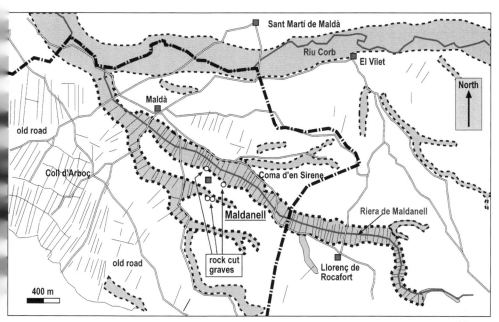

Figure 46. Comes de Maldà and Maldanell (Urgell). There was an intense use of the bottom of the valleys, whether or not a stream flowed through. Near the Maldanell coomb, there is a necropolis probably from the first centuries of the Middle Ages.

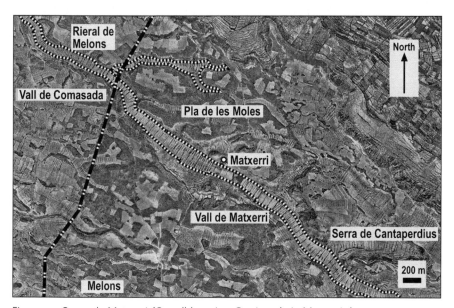

Figure 47. Coma de Matxerri (Castelldans, Les Garrigues). In Matxerri there was an Islamic era settlement. Next to it was a long coomb of over 3.5 kilometres long. Source: © ICGC. Reproduced with permission.

208   CHAPTER 9

This confirms the use of these flat and cultivated valley bottoms at least from the sixth or seventh centuries.

Matxerri (Castelldans, Les Garrigues)

To the east of Lleida, very close to Castelldans, we find a coomb next to a site from the Islamic era. Matxerri, where nowadays a farmhouse stands, is an interesting case (Fig. 47). Joan Coromines believes that its name is derived from the Latin name *maceries* (or rammed earth walls or masonry walls), a name coined by the Mozarabs.[22] In his doctoral thesis on Islamic Lleida and its periphery, Jesús Brufal says it may come from the word *majarr* (pastureland).[23] For our purposes, this place is interesting because the remains of walls have been found on the hilltop and the hill slopes, as well as several silos and numerous fragments of Islamic pottery. According to Brufal, this *almunia* was built in the second half of the tenth century.[24] Water was probably obtained by using wells, similar to other places in this region.[25]

Here our focus is the existence of a long coomb next to this site. The fragment of the coomb extending from the limit of the municipality of Artesa de Lleida to the west, where the territory of Castelldans began, to the east was about three and a half kilometres in length and must have extended over an area of about fifty hectares of good fertile land from the flat bottom of the valley of dryland. The archaeological site is located on the western side of the Mas de Matxerri on a hill next to several small coombs. All in all, the territory of Matxerri extended at least five square kilometres, perhaps a little more.

According to current findings, there is no evidence that this place was occupied before the tenth century. We think, however, that it is almost certain that this coomb was cultivated long before, probably in the Visigothic period. In addition, since this place name seems to have originated from *maceries* (rammed earth walls or masonry walls) we infer that when families settled there in the tenth century, there were already older walls in this place, perhaps half-collapsed. In a relatively recent study on the relationship between roads, boundaries, and orientations from the ancient period, Matxerri (and Mas de Melons) were noted for their continuity throughout the Middle Ages.[26]

This possible *almunia* could be included within a network of places inhabited since before the twelfth century, closely linked to the network of long and cultivated coombs or valley bottoms found throughout the *comarca*

---

22 Coromines, *Onomasticon Cataloniae*, vol. V, p. 238.

23 Brufal, 'L'espai rural del districte musulmà de Lleida'; Brufal, *El món rural i urbà en la Lleida islàmica*, p. 276; Groom, *A Dictionary of Arabic Topography and Placenames*, p. 166.

24 Brufal, 'L'espai rural del districte musulmà de Lleida', pp. 344, 395.

25 Aldomà, *L'aigua patrimoni de la Catalunya seca*.

26 Bolòs, *Els orígens medievals del paisatge català*, p. 408; Bolòs, 'Conèixer el paisatge històric medieval per poder planificar i gestionar el territori', p. 164.

of Les Garrigues. About three kilometres further south of Matxerri, there was another very similar survey site, Mas de Melons, next to another notable coomb. According to Coromines, the place name may well come from *Cumba Melonis*, the 'badger coomb' (badger, Meles meles).[27] Remains of walls, silos, a kind of cistern carved into rocks, and many fragments of pottery have also been found.[28] Its inhabitants probably worked mostly on the opposite coomb, which extended for at least two kilometres. The cultivated area of this valley bottom corresponded to about twenty hectares. The territory that depended on this possible *almunia* was also about five square kilometres; within this territory were smaller cultivated coombs, lands used for grazing cattle, and barren or rocky areas.

Coombs Close to the Village of Sanata (Llinars del Vallès, Vallès Oriental)

To the west of Sant Joan de Sanata, south of the Montseny Massif, there are three coombs oriented from north to south: that of Sanata, Can Diviu, and Les Valls. The longest furrow along the stream of Can Diviu is about two kilometres long. This place is in Old Catalonia, next to the road that has connected, since the Roman period, the cities of Barcelona and Girona. The name 'Sanata' is of Berber origin, which suggests that this is where members of the North African Zenata tribe settled to control this strategic spot at the time of the Islamic conquest (*c.* 713–719). The three coombs may well already have existed and been cultivated since before the eighth century.

This place was inhabited in the Muslim era (between 713–719 and 801), and it is there that we find other elements of the landscape taking us back to an even older past. These coombs, like the one in Comallonga, at the southern end, stand on plots of land dating to the Roman period. In addition, terraced plots of farmsteads were built after 1000, usually outside the space where the crops of the coomb were stretched along. Both chronological references, i.e., the Roman plot division and the farmsteads of the second millennium, take us back to the situations from before and after the early Middle Ages and surely date us chronologically to when these strips of fertile soil were first cultivated. In addition, the case of the *comarca* of Vallès Oriental also shows that we find coombs in Old Catalonia.

Medieval Terraces

Studies carried out in recent years in Galicia and the Basque Country have clarified the early medieval origins of some of the terraces in the Iberian Peninsula.[29] Archaeological excavations reveal that some terraces can be

---

27 Coromines, *Onomasticon Cataloniae*, vol. V, p. 248.
28 Brufal, 'L'espai rural del districte musulmà de Lleida'.
29 Ballesteros and Blanco-Rotea, 'Aldeas y espacios agrarios altomedievales en Galicia';

210 CHAPTER 9

dated to the early medieval period. Although there are much older terraces in some Mediterranean countries, these discoveries are significant because terraces are frequently thought to be modern. As for Catalonia, excavations have recently been carried out in the Cerdanya region, which have led to similar conclusions, as will be discussed later.[30]

In Catalonia, terraces are usually called *feixa*, as they resemble an elongated band-shaped (*faixa de terra*, in Catalan) strip of land. They are also sometimes referred to as *bancals*, perhaps because of their stepped structure (from *banc*, 'bench', in Catalan). The former predominates in Old Catalonia (and in the Occitan lands), the latter in New Catalonia and Valencia. We find terraces in many places, both inhabited by scattered populations (around farmsteads) and in areas of half-dispersed medieval villages and hamlets (for example, in Alt Berguedà or Ripollès), as well as, for example, in lofty hilltop castral villages. Now we will focus on some cases that will enlighten us about different situations and episodes in the Middle Ages.

Vilalta (Targasona, Alta Cerdanya)

In 2009, excavations were carried out at the site of the small, deserted village of Vilalta, at an altitude of 1650 metres.[31] Remains have been found of agricultural use from the middle Bronze Age and the beginning of the Iron Age. It was not until the Middle Ages, however, that remarkable changes occurred in Vilalta. Archaeological evidence shows that since the seventh century these lands were cultivated. Around the eighth century, it seems that there was a scattered settlement (the remains of a house were found), which probably led to the creation of the first terraces. The second half of the tenth century saw a concentration of settlements related to the existence of a system of small, stepped terraces. The village was not abandoned until the fourteenth or fifteenth century, at the beginning of a colder period and the demographic crisis of the late Middle Ages. Excavations have revealed, surprisingly enough, the reconstruction of the terrace system from just before the village was abandoned. It should be noted that the town of Targasona rises just over two kilometres to the east of the site of the hamlet of Vilalta. This site bears witness to the existence of terraces in Cerdanya in the Middle Ages, before 1000.

Ballesteros, 'La arqueología rural y la construcción de un paisaje agrario medieval: el caso de Galicia'; Quirós Castillo, 'Arqueología del campesinado altomedieval', p. 390; Quirós Castillo and Nicosia, 'Reconstructing Past Terraced Agrarian Landscapes in the Ebro Valley'.

30 We must also mention some excavations carried out in the farmstead L'Agustí, in the region of Vallès Oriental, municipality of Tagamanent: Retamero, 'Coping with Gravity: The Case of Mas L'Agustí'.

31 Rendu and others, 'Reconstructing Past Terrace Fields in the Pyrenees'.

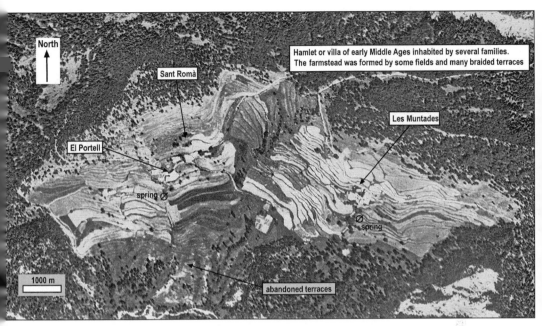

Figure 48. Terraces of Aranyonet (Gombrèn, Ripollès). In Aranyonet, a place already mentioned in documents from before 1000, we find a clearing of cultivated land, surrounded by forest, and covered with terraces. Source: © ICGC. Reproduced with permission.

Aranyonet (Gombrèn, Ripollès)

The history of this still inhabited place can be learned by reading medieval documents and through fieldwork. Aranyonet was a Carolingian *villa* with a parish church where several families lived. The settlement is documented in 982, although it cannot be ruled out that it is much older.[32] Around the Aranyonet farmstead, there are now large fields furrowed by stone-wall bench terraces around their outline (Fig. 48). This farmhouse is located on a sunny slope. There is a drop of about 140 metres between the upper and lower terraces. One may raise the possibility that initially there was a sloping crop area; very soon, however, to prevent its erosion, possibly around thirty stone-wall bench terraces were raised to create a stepped slope. Once some levelling was achieved on the terraces, deeper and wetter soils were possibly formed. However, in this case, the floor of each of the terraces was never too flat. This space had to be distributed among several family farms (one of which was Mas de les Muntades, to the east of the clearing in the crops).[33] Although without any excavation or OSL analysis no confirmation can be provided,

---

32 *Catalunya carolíngia, vol. II: Els diplomes carolingis a Catalunya*, ed. by Abadal, p. 172.
33 Bolòs, 'Paisatges i transicions: canvis i continuïtats al llarg de la història', pp. 75–76.

212   CHAPTER 9

it is likely that this cultivated space, surrounded by forest land, was already covered with terraces in the early Middle Ages, before 1000. The site recalls similar terraces elsewhere, e.g., Galicia or Asturias, dating to sometime in 'the long eighth century' (between 680 and 830) and is related to the restructuring of agriculture and the rural world.[34]

Llastarri (Tremp, Pallars Jussà; Sopeira, Ribagorça)

The town of Llastarri is 1.6 km from the Benedictine Monastery of Santa Maria d'Alaó. To the east of the river La Noguera Ribagorçana, between the abbey and the village, is the Clot del Vinyer, a large pit or depression. All three places were already recorded in the Carolingian period. Llastarri is documented in 851 (curiously, by mistake, it was called *suburbi Lastarre*). At that time some vineyards located in the Solà plot were sold. In 902, the castle of Llastarri is mentioned. The same document alludes to the plots of land in Vinyer (*Bingerum*).[35] Some vineyards surrounded by other vineyards were sold. Today on the Vinyer plot there is a fossilized traces of a set of terraces. To the west, there had been about thirteen of them, which stretched for about 3.8 hectares, with a difference in height between the highest and lowest of about one hundred metres. Further east, there are about seven stone-wall bench terraces within an area of about 3.2 hectares. Some margins of these terraces took advantage of natural rocks; others, according to what we now see, were probably partly refurbished fairly recently. However, we can affirm that in this place more than a thousand years ago (at least since the ninth century), there were already vineyards and perhaps terraces with margins. One of the functions of the terraces, apart from preventing erosion and ensuring the sowing quality of the soil, was clearance, removing the stones from the ground, and placing them around the edges.[36]

There is a very interesting document from a place near Llastarri that reports that to settle a conflict between Roda d'Isàvena and Güel, two villages in the Ribagorça region, around 1093 or 1094, it was agreed that people from Roda could have possessions in a nearby place, called Montoliu, provided that they did not break the *espones*, i.e., the margins of the terraces, which were probably made of stone (*spondas non frangant*). Likewise, they could graze their cattle and gather firewood as long as no harm was inflicted.[37]

---

34 Fernández Mier, 'Campos de cultivo en la Cordillera Cantábrica', pp. 52–56.
35 *Catalunya carolíngia, vol. III: Els comtats de Pallars i Ribagorça*, ed. by Abadal, doc. 282.
36 Torró, 'Terrasses irrigades a les muntanyes valencianes', p. 100.
37 *Col·lecció diplomàtica de l'Arxiu Capitular de Lleida. Segona part: Documents de les seus episcopals de Roda i de Lleida (anys 586–1143)*, ed. by Bolòs, doc. 131.

Vilalta (Cabanabona, La Noguera)

West of this village, also called Vilalta, and currently inhabited by twenty people, luminescence profiling and OSL dating were carried out in 2014. That enabled some field margins, which were made of finely chiselled dry-stone ashlars – typical of the land near the *comarca* of Segara, to be dated to the early thirteenth century.[38] The place of Vilalta, located at an altitude of 466 metres and, as the name suggests, situated in a privileged vantage position, is not documented until 1176, although the place had been occupied by the counts of Urgell, in all probability since the first half of the eleventh century. We cannot ascertain what existed here before this date, in the early Middle Ages. What seems to be clear is that to the west of the village there are several cultivated coombs or valley bottoms, and that, most notably on the eastern side, there are roads and field boundaries that seem to have an orientation that coincides with the Roman plot divisions of the city of Lleida.[39] Regardless, it is a remarkable achievement to have confirmed the dating of these margins to the thirteenth century, during a period of heavy demographic pressure and the dramatic expansion of cultivated lands.

In the context of Catalonia, we can establish a classification of terrace systems like that of other countries in the Mediterranean basin. There is evidence of braided terraces, which are certainly the oldest. We also find, sometimes not far away, terraces with parallel margins, which are often from the last few centuries. As reported, there are also check-dams, i.e. walls compartmentalizing the coombs. Finally, despite being scarcer and probably quite modern, we can also find examples of pocket terraces whose sole purpose was to hold the ground of a single tree, for example, an olive tree, or even perhaps box terraces (similar to those found in South America).[40] A fundamental aspect is figuring out how these terraces were built. Those cases that show not only *fill* but *cut and fill*, or whether an episodic sudden fill or a deposition fill occurred are worth noting. Similarly, it is important to consider whether the sites have retained their original soil.[41]

Finally, in the Mediterranean area, although terraces are normally made on non-irrigated land, there were also irrigated terraces, mostly in the Islamic period. They have been studied on the island of Mallorca and the region of

---

38 Turner and others, 'Changes and Continuities in a Mediterranean Landscape'; Turner and others, 'Canvis i continuïtats en un paisatge mediterrani'.

39 Bolòs, 'Paisatges i transicions: canvis i continuïtats al llarg de la història', pp. 99–102.

40 Crow and others, 'Characterizing the Historic Landscapes of Naxos'; Rackham and Moody, *The Making of the Cretan Landscape*, p. 141; Torró, 'Terrasses irrigades a les muntanyes valencianes', p. 86; Brown and others, 'Ending the Cinderella Status of Terraces and Lynchets in Europe'.

41 Ballesteros, 'La arqueología rural y la construcción de un paisaje agrario medieval: el caso de Galicia', p. 29; Brown and others, 'Ending the Cinderella Status of Terraces and Lynchets in Europe'.

Concentric Forms

From the air, on maps or orthophoto maps (or image maps), we can see that the edges of the fields or the paths produce rounded, circular, or oval shapes on the ground. It has been noted that these radio-concentric forms result from the processes of clearing land and its subsequent cultivation.[43] We can distinguish several types of forms, bearing in mind the possible causes behind their creation.[44] We will describe and illustrate them below.

Concentric Circles Caused by the Creation of a Village: Bellvei (Baix Penedès)

There are several examples of concentric shapes in Baix Penedès, in the lands conquered by the count of Barcelona in the tenth and eleventh centuries. The territory of Bellvei is a good example (Fig. 49) of this phenomenon. This place was first mentioned in a document from 1037; it is reported as 'ipsa turre qui fuit de Tedbert, que dicunt Belvizi'.[45] Around the village of Bellvei, about 700 or 800 metres away, there is a series of concentric lines, which coincide with paths or field boundaries.[46] Further on, the plot of the fields coincides mainly with orthogonal networks or Roman centuriations. Even a section of the municipal boundary between Bellvei and Santa Oliva is oriented in line with the *Tarraco I* centuriation. It should also be noted that the outward-bound road network from Bellvei seems to be radial. In fact, as with previous occurrences, we see that it was created by reusing older paths, plausibly before the Middle Ages, which often follow orientations that accord with those of various pre-medieval networks.

To the best of our knowledge, this concentric, almost circular shape is the result of the clearance that took place in the tenth century or early eleventh century when these lands were occupied by the counts of Barcelona. At this point we may wonder what was there before the occupation of this territory. Or a question with an even more difficult answer: why do we find in Bellvei marks that bear witness to a clearing or deforestation, while in many other

---

42 Kirchner and Navarro, 'Objetivos, métodos y práctica de la arqueología hidráulica', p. 179; Barceló and others, *El agua que no duerme*; Torró, 'Terrasses irrigades a les muntanyes valencianes', p. 103.

43 Deschamps and Pascal, 'Le cadastration antique de Rezé (*Ratiatum*, Loire-Atlantique)', p. 109.

44 González Villaescusa, *Las formas de los paisajes mediterráneos*, pp. 120–21.

45 *Cartulario de 'Sant Cugat' del Vallés*, ed. by Rius, vol. II, doc. 545.

46 Bolòs, 'Not So Dark Centuries: Changes and Continuities in the Catalan Landscape', p. 99.

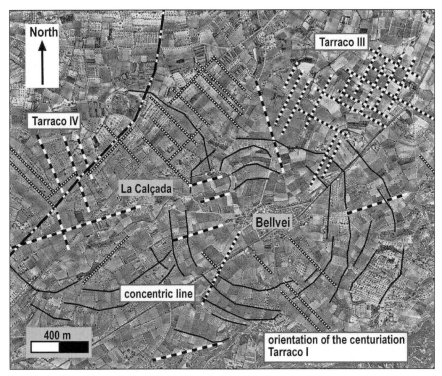

Figure 49. Bellvei (Baix Penedès). Around the village of Bellvei the aerial view shows some concentric circles created probably as a result of a clearance that took place around 1000. Source: © ICGC. Reproduced with permission.

places there is no such evidence? As for Bellvei, documents report that the Baix Penedès was a region around 1000 dedicated more to pasture than to agriculture. In 1012, a letter granted by the abbot of Sant Cugat del Vallès, claims — in a certainly far-fetched statement — that the adjacent place of Santa Oliva had been barren for over three hundred years, and only served as grazing land for onagers and deer.[47] The transformation of these pastures into cereal-growing fields may have led to the creation of these concentric shapes.

Vilajuïga (Alt Empordà)

As early as 982, the existence of Vilajuïga (*Villa Iudaica*) is recorded, although this villa had been created before then, perhaps even centuries ago.[48] Its church was dedicated to Sant Feliu. It had rather limited territory and, as its name suggests, in the early Middle Ages, a Jewish community lived there (probably

---

47 *Cartulario de 'Sant Cugat' del Vallés*, vol. II, ed. by Rius, doc. 449.
48 *Catalunya carolíngia, vol. II: Els diplomes carolingis a Catalunya*, ed. by Abadal, p. 243.

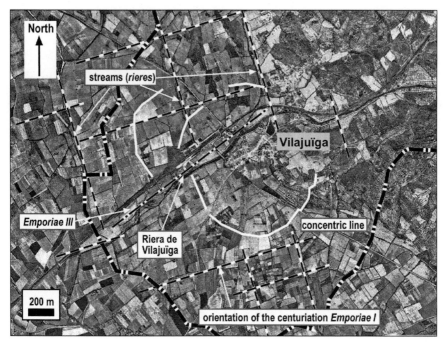

Figure 50. Vilajuïga (Alt Empordà). Around this village we see, from a bird's eye view, a concentric circle that must be related to clearance from the beginning of the Middle Ages. Source: © ICGC. Reproduced with permission.

from before 785, the date of the Carolingian conquest). One interesting aspect is the existence of concentric shapes around Vilajuïga, similar to those we see in another nearby town, Vilamalla (Alt Empordà) (Fig. 50). Especially on the southern, eastern, and western sides of the village, about 500 or 600 metres away, there are field boundaries with clearly rounded shapes. It must be said that, in Vilajuïga, during the same period, we find some lands basically oriented according to the *Emporiae I* centuriation. Likewise, the orientations of the outward-bound roads from the village coincide, in many cases, with those of some pre-medieval plots. Even the Vilajuïga stream has the same orientation as *Emporiae III*. Briefly put, the coincidence between watercourses and orientations of Roman centuriations is very common in many *comarques*. As for the circular shapes — the core of our research interest — they are much more difficult to date than in the case of Bellvei. Its historical circumstances are different from those found in Penedès. It would be very easy to conclude that they are from the eighth century, from a time when the Carolingians occupied the plain of Empordà. However, this would only be an assumption since they may be even older. Be that as it may, they must have originated at a time of reorganization of cultivated space close to the village, probably in the early medieval period. Actually, this circular shape has similarities with those found around settlements in the region of Lunel (Languedoc), in Dassargues, and in Lunel-Viel (Oc. Lunèl Vièlh), dated to the early Middle Ages, most probably in the sixth and seventh centuries. In this area, there is an accurately dated case, the *villa Campania* (Campagne, Oc. Campanha), documented in 640 and located to the south of Nimes (next to the airport); the site is currently enclosed within a circle of field boundaries and has a clear-cut radius ranging between 1200 and 2200 metres, from east to west.[49]

Candasnos (Fraga, Baix Cinca)

About twenty-five kilometres west of the city of Fraga, in an arid area, is the town of Candasnos (in the Middle Ages, called Campdàsens). The village stands at the centre of three rings. The first, next to the village, covers an area of about fifty hectares. The second ring, which coincides with a road, is approximately 1.2 kilometres from the village and comprises about 500 hectares, intended for *farraginals*, or land to cultivate grass for livestock. Inside, we find several transversal stripes. Further on, the third ring was created, enclosing an area of about 2000 hectares, intended for fields, also organized into radial plots. Then there was pastureland. According to Jacinto Bonales, these concentric forms could be related to an agricultural livestock farm from the Islamic Caliphate era or to a new thirteenth-century village.[50] The latter would be our choice, as we believe they coincide in time with the settlement charter granted in 1217 to thirty-seven families, by the Cistercian nuns of Sigena (Sixena, in the Middle Ages).[51] Similar forms have been found in other southern European countries.

In Beja, in the south of Portugal, we discover a very similar landscape. Concentric shapes, formed mainly by three rings that coincide with three roads, were initially related to a network of radial pathways. However, in-depth studies on this issue have concluded that they should be related to the occupation of this place and to the distribution of the agrarian space into plots (known as *sesmos*).[52]

Concentric Circles Caused by the Creation of a Hamlet or a Farmstead: Mas de Can Badia (Santa Pau, La Garrotxa)

We find rounded, concentric shapes in places where there were clearance of forest or pastureland. Above, we have focused on three villages. We find a similar situation, perhaps even more evident, in relation to hamlets created throughout the early Middle Ages, or new farmsteads built in the high Middle

---

49 Chouquer, *Dominer et tenir la terre dans le haut Moyen Âge*, pp. 336–39.
50 Bonales, *Traces d'un passat llunyà*, pp. 75–78, 249.
51 *Cartas de población del reino de Aragón en los siglos medievales*, ed. by Ledesma, doc. 163.
52 Watteaux, 'La colonisation agraire médiévale en Alentejo', pp. 63–65.

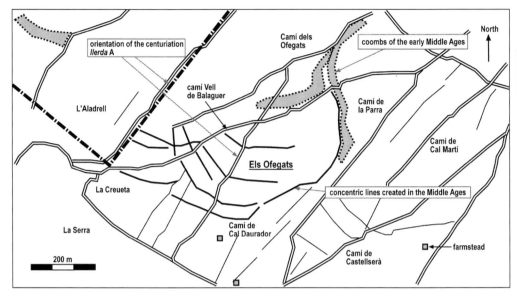

Figure 51. Els Ofegats (Agramunt, Urgell). In the plot of lands of Els Ofegats we see, from a bird's eye view, a half-circle that probably dates to the occupation of this place.

Ages, for example, in the middle of a forest. We will focus on Can Badia farmhouse (La Garrotxa) and then on the settlement of Els Ofegats (Urgell). In many other parts of Europe detached houses with circular or very often oval shapes can be found, for example, in French Brittany and regions near the lower stretch of the Loire River.[53]

Aerial photographs taken in 1956 of the farmstead of Can Badia indicate the process of deforestation that took place as a result of the creation first of an early medieval hamlet and then of the farmstead in the high Middle Ages (inhabited, perhaps, by more than one family). We see an oval-shaped area, located just below the house, with an area of 4.7 hectares. Then follows a second larger ring which encompasses the first ring and extends up to near the stream, with a total area of 11.4 hectares. Despite this, according to written documents, perhaps part of the income for this farmstead came from the fields below it, but another substantial part came from the firewood and the charcoal obtained from the forest around it.[54] The intensive use of the forest over the centuries has resulted in extensive flat rocky land (*codina*) without any vegetation due to erosion next to the farmhouse of Can Badia.

---

53 Pichot, *Le village éclaté*, pp. 201, 248; Pichot 'L'habitat dispersé dans l'Ouest de la France', pp. 83, 95.
54 Bolòs, *El mas, el pagès i el senyor*, p. 248.

Els Ofegats (Agramunt, Urgell)

As will be seen in Chapter 15, when studying landscape history, it is important to be familiar with previous and existing research on toponymy. According to Joan Coromines, the place name *Els Ofegats* must have come from the name *afocat*, a place that at some point in the Middle Ages had been inhabited.[55] By looking, as in the previous case, at the aerial photographs from the mid-twentieth century, we will describe what we see there.

From the air, on the southern side of the *partida* (several plots of land) of Els Ofegats, we find a hemispherical area with a radius of about 800 metres (Fig. 51). It must reflect a phase of land use that may have occurred in the second half of the eleventh century. Because of the county's conquest and still perilous situation, a tower was built at the centre of a *quadra* (a fief, perhaps owned by a knight). In addition, the 1956 orthophoto map shows fragments of a coomb, suggesting the existence of an even older settlement from the early Middle Ages. On the other hand, this territory is furrowed by several roads that almost certainly originated before the medieval period. There are remains of a road network (separated by about 1000 metres) that follows the orientation of *Ilerda A*, the most important centuriation of Lleida, a city located, however, about forty kilometres away. There is also a road with a different orientation, from south-west to north-east, which forms the northern limit of the space of Els Ofegats. The road follows an orientation created in ancient times, perhaps even before the Roman era.

Regarding the concentric shape of Els Ofegats, we discover similar features in many other places in this same *comarca* of Urgell, in Castellblanc, in Renant, or in Ca l'Escampa.[56] We can infer then that they must be related to the processes of colonization and land clearance from the time of the count's conquest, in the eleventh century.

Concentric Circles Caused by the Occupation of a Hilltop Village: Marcovau (Foradada, La Noguera)

In the lands colonized and repopulated between the tenth and twelfth centuries, in areas of the march or border which separated the Catalan counties from the lands controlled by the Muslims, population centres were often built on hilltops, often next to a fortification, one outstanding example of which is the village of Aguiló (Conca de Barberà) (Fig. 18). Sometimes the dry-stone walls of the terraces and fields around these hilltop settlements have, from

---

55 Coromines, *Onomasticon Cataloniae*, vol. VI, p. 16.
56 Bolòs, *Paisatge i història en època medieval a la Catalunya Nova*; Bolòs, *Els orígens medievals del paisatge català*, pp. 319–20; Bolòs, 'Processos de rompuda i d'ocupació de l'espai a l'època medieval', pp. 119–45.

an aerial perspective, circular shapes, which often coincide with the contour lines, as at Marcovau (La Noguera) and, for example, Erdao (Ribagorça).

The place name of Marcovau is of Germanic origin from an anthroponym probably attributed to its original settlers at the time of the conquest of the count of Urgell.[57] In this place, we discover a hilltop village (at an altitude of 433 metres) surrounded by terraces that extend along the slope. In this case, in the nearby fields, located about seventy-five metres below, we also see the fossilized evidence of concentric rings. The radius of the area of influence of this population was about 700 metres.[58] We see, therefore, that these concentric forms may be caused by the topography of the hill or may represent the reorganization of cleared ground, as seen in previous cases.

Radiocentric Forms Caused by Radial Roads: Alp (Cerdanya)

In some places, the radial network of outward-bound old roads may have led to the arrangement of fields in such a way that it now appears to be a concentric circular shape. An obvious example of this phenomenon is Alp, in Cerdanya, although, in this case, there is only half a ring because the southern part of the territory is a mountainous area.[59] If we look at the current fields facing the village of Alp, to the north-west, we find that they have a ring-like shape, concentric to the centre, located where the capital of the municipality stands. However, the limits of the municipal territory are formed by a series of straight sections, which really reflect more markedly their former position than the fields themselves. Many of the orientations of the lands facing the village of Alp are perpendicular to the six main outward-bound roads that enter the plain furrowed by the river Segre. Certainly, throughout the Middle Ages, the farmlands were organized on both sides of the roads; this process, described above, can be found in many other places.

Coaxial Slope Land Strips

On some mountain slopes we find farmland strips that begin in a watercourse (or a road), climb the slope, and eventually reach the mountain ridge (or a nearby location). Typically, these strips have a similar width. In general, we find them in repopulated lands in New Catalonia. One can only assume that these spaces were distributed, perhaps by lot, among the different inhabitants of the nearby village at the time when the Christian conquest took place. They

---

57 Coromines, *Onomasticon Cataloniae*, vol. V, p. 194.

58 Bolòs, 'Conèixer el paisatge històric medieval per poder planificar i gestionar el territori', pp. 215–16.

59 Bolòs, 'Paisatge històric, cartografia i societat a l'alta edat mitjana: l'exemple de la Cerdanya', pp. 77–79.

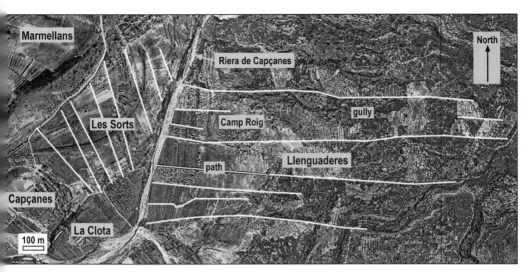

Figure 52. Llenguaderes (Capçanes, Priorat). Here we see a set of coaxial strips of cultivated land that extend along the side of the mountain from the bottom of the valley. They probably date to the twelfth century. Source: © ICGC. Reproduced with permission.

are often known as *parellades* and sometimes *sorts* (meaning, in Catalan, 'luck' or 'fates', distributed in batches, a name that reveals their origin and found too in northern Italy).[60] These dryland *parellades* should not be confused with irrigated *parellades* found, for example, near the city of Lleida, further discussed in Chapter 10. Similar colonization land strips have been found in flatter regions, most notably in Valencia, as described below.

Llenguaderes (Capçanes, Priorat)

Llenguaderes is a special case of a plot of land in the *comarca* of Priorat. This region was conquered by the count of Barcelona during the twelfth century. In the territory of Capçanes, we see a *partida* (several plots of land) formed by strips of cultivated land extending from a stream to the forest of the Tossal Redó mountain, in a tongue-like pattern (probably, hence, its name; *llengües*, tongues in Catalan). The land is divided into three sectors (Fig. 52). The first sector, closer to the watercourse and flatter, is about 170 metres long. The second sector, about 380 metres long and steeper, extends to the beginning of the forest. The third section, where the limits of the current properties stretch (as the cadastral maps reveal), follows the same orientations for about 700 metres more, in an area currently forested. The width of these strips of land ranges from eighty to one hundred and thirty metres. It should be noted

---

60 Mastrelli Anzilotti, 'Osservazioni in margine al lessico alpino', p. 57.

222   CHAPTER 9

that these strips are cut transversely by terrace margins made of dry stone to prevent erosion and contribute to the good health of the soil. On the other hand, a ditch often passes between the strips allowing rainwater to drain out. Incidentally, this is a well-organized plot of land, probably the result of planning by surveyors.

These sloping strips are related to the colonization process. Their giveaway name, Les Sorts (*sort* means distributed by drawing lots in Catalan), the name of a plot of land close to Llenguaderes with similar characteristics, illustrates its original position, determined by a draw among newcomers, perhaps during the second half of the twelfth century. However, we cannot rule out the possibility of earlier land use and that, when the settlers around 1154 arrived at this place called Llenguaderes, they found land that had already been cultivated and therefore took advantage of it. The village of Capçanes is just over 400 metres from this plot of land. Capçanes is a place name from Roman coinage, a fact that surely reflects the pre-medieval origin of this place and possibly continuity in the occupation of its lands.[61] Be that as it may, the current landscape is one of the main documents that bears witness to its past.

Coaxial Land Strips in Flat Areas

Often a large field was not owned by a single owner or was not held by a single farmer as a tenancy. Sometimes large extents of cultivated land are spread over elongated strips of field. As mentioned above, the term *feixa*, as far back as the Carolingian period, must relate to *faixes*, or strips of land. We have referred to strips of land when studying the case of Sant Joan de Mollet (Gironès), where they probably referred to land that had already been parcelled out, perhaps in the Roman period. In recent research on the *comarques* of Vallès and Penedès, I have found strips of land in fairly flat places, which may relate to plots created in the Roman period and, too, sometimes, to a land distribution resulting from the repopulation process of the ninth and tenth centuries.[62]

Related to these medieval coaxial land strips, beyond the southern border of Catalonia, in Valencia, a recent study analyses the granting in 1241 of the settlement charter of Vilafamés (Plana Alta).[63] An investigation of its landscape concluded that some of the current plots of land correspond to the land distribution made in the thirteenth century. In a very wide area of about 1260 hectares (i.e., over three kilometres long, from east to west), a series of long strips from south to north must have been distributed among

---

61 Coromines, *Onomasticon Cataloniae*, vol. III, p. 251.
62 Bolòs, *El paisatge medieval del comtat de Barcelona*, pp. 361–436.
63 Guinot, 'La construcción de nuevos espacios agrarios en el siglo XIII', pp. 148–52.

new settlers from the mid-thirteenth century. The reference measure used by surveyors to define the width of the strips was six *cordes* (*ropes*, in English), a former unit of measure; in total, they correspond to 244.62 metres.

Also in the territory of the former Kingdom of Valencia, in the *partida* (an area with several plots of land) of Les Alcuses, municipality of Moixent (La Costera), the existence of strips was also discovered a few years ago, with a very similar width. These strips of land were related to the settlement charter from 1303 which stated that Les Alcuses were to be divided 'inter ducentas partes et sortes' (i.e., into two hundred parts granted by a draw of lots).[64] Similar landscapes have also been studied in Beneixama (Alt Vinalopó) and Pego (Marina Alta).[65]

Sometimes, in not-so-flat lands, the processes of the subdivision and creation of terraces had similar characteristics. Josep Torró studied these processes at Plana de les Vinyes de Cocentaina (*comarca* of El Comtat), whose documentation also mentions the word *sort* (in this context, 'lot'), corresponding to each of the original blocks. Nearby, in Agres (El Comtat), we also found a *partida* called Les Sorts. Some of its plots of land were established and an irrigation system was built after the conquest of Valencia by King Jaume I.[66]

In other Mediterranean countries, similar cases to those of Vilafamés and Les Alcuses have been found, for example in the southern Portuguese region of Alentejo, in towns such as Marmelar, Serpa, and Monte do Trigo.[67] In Gascony, similar plots have been preserved around new villages created in the Middle Ages, such as Duhort (Oc. Dur Hòrt), Marmande (Oc. Marmanda), and in some of the lands of Trie-sur-Baïse (Oc. Tria de Baïsa).[68] Other studies have revealed coaxial field strips in the north of Italy, e.g., in Mola di Bari, Vilanova di Verona, and around the town of Pisa.[69]

Other Coaxial Strips Were Perhaps Older

The strips of Les Llenguaderes must, in principle, date back to the twelfth century, because of the conquest process. The same could be said of many of the coaxial strips in Valencia, dating from the thirteenth century. However, we believe that there may be older ones. When describing Sant Joan de Mollet, we have already pointed out that these were strips created in the early

---

64 González Villaescusa, *Las formas de los paisajes mediterráneos*, pp. 451, 467–68.
65 González Villaescusa, 'Centuriations, *alquerias* et *pueblas*', González Villaescusa, *Las formas de los paisajes mediterráneos*, p. 81; Torró, 'Les cartes de poblament i la colonització de Pego'.
66 Torró, 'Arqueologia de la conquesta'; Torró, 'Terrasses irrigades a les muntanyes valencianes'; Torró, 'Tierras ganadas'.
67 Watteaux, 'La colonisation agraire médiévale en Alentejo', pp. 56–61.
68 Lavigne, 'Parcellaires de fondation et parcellaires de formation à l'époque médiévale en Gascogne'.
69 Chouquer, *Les parcellaires médiévaux en Émilie et en Romagne*, pp. 226–38.

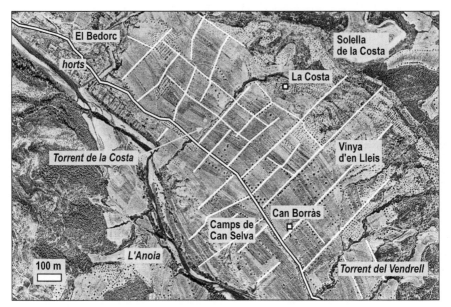

Figure 53. Between El Badorc and El Freixe (Piera, Anoia). Between these two villages we see a set of coaxial strips that extend along the side of a mountain range. The reorganization of this space must have taken place in the early Middle Ages. Source: © ICGC. Reproduced with permission.

Middle Ages based on Roman antecedents. They were, however, located in a flat place. Finally, we want to discuss other coaxial bands that, due to their characteristics, cast doubts on the accuracy of our dating.

Between El Bedorc and El Freixe (Piera, Anoia)

We know that in 954, Viscount Guitard gave some land to the place of El Freixe.[70] In the current aerial photographs, to the north of this place, we see a slightly sloping area that extends to the left bank of the Anoia, furrowed by paths or margins from the mountain range to a path near the river. They basically follow the orientation of the *Tarraco I* centuriation, perhaps in a casual way. There are about twelve coaxial strips, which reach the top of the mountain range and sometimes extend over more than 700 metres. At the top, the easternmost area is a set of terraces (Fig. 53). However, these terraces were built at a later stage when the longitudinal plots had already been defined. The footprints left by these sloping strips are deep: sometimes their limits, on both long sides, coincide with paths, or sometimes with furrows that

---

70 *Catalunya carolíngia, vol. VII: El comtat de Barcelona*, ed. by Baiges and Puig, doc. 345.

have survived to the present day. These furrows are used to prevent erosion and channel water in stormy weather. With the same orientation, there is the small stream of La Costa, which has a very straight route. In fact, these coaxial strips are a phenomenon found in many other places such as Serrabona (in the municipality of Sentmenat, Vallès Occidental).[71] This space may have been organized in the tenth century, although due to the orientation of the coaxial strips we cannot rule out earlier planning, perhaps related to the orientation of the road, which led to the channelling of a stream.

Conclusions

In this chapter, we have focused mainly on rainfed lands. We conclude that some changes in the landscape in the medieval period have left their imprint and are still visible on a country walk. We have described coombs, often located next to places whose medieval settlement dates from both the Visigothic and Islamic eras, and after the Christian conquest. We find coombs and riverbeds cultivated in much of Catalonia and in many of the countries surrounding the Mediterranean basin. We have also discussed the significance of terraces which gradually spread across the territory from the early medieval period to the late Middle Ages. This aspect, though, still needs further research as there may still be ancient, pre-medieval, or early medieval terraces hidden under the terraces made or rebuilt in the late Middle Ages (as seen in Cerdanya) or more recently (for example, shortly before the outbreak of phylloxera in the late nineteenth century). We have also seen the importance of circular, concentric shapes, which, through the use of aerial photographs, we discover in the limits of fields or on roads, and which usually reflect processes of deforestation or change in land use. They are frequently associated with the creation of settlements from the sixth to the eighth centuries,[72] the occupation of abandoned land (tenth to eleventh centuries), or the construction of new towns on repopulated land (possibly between the eleventh and thirteenth centuries). Finally, we have focused on cultivated strips of land that may reflect the way the land was distributed as a result of the processes of conquest and colonization that took place, for example, in the tenth, eleventh, and twelfth centuries. Often, the size and shape of these strips of land indicate the presence of surveyors in their planning. In the future, as more research is done, the chances of identifying the different components of the landscape created in the Middle Ages will increase, and so will the accuracy in dating them.

Being able to study the different components of the landscape separately and sometimes the ability to date them can make it easier to establish a stratification of this landscape based on comparing them. Certainly, we must

---

71 Bolòs, *El paisatge medieval del comtat de Barcelona*, pp. 561–642.
72 Chouquer, *Dominer et tenir la terre dans le haut Moyen Âge*, p. 338.

relate the elements studied in this chapter to those examined in the other chapters, such as the settlements, the buildings or spaces which generated the creation of a population nucleus, the fields, and the old roads. In this research to identify the phrases of the creation of these landscapes, it is very important to consult aerial photographs.[73]

---

73 Brogiolo, 'Some principles and methods for a stratigraphic study of historic landscapes'.

CHAPTER 10

Irrigated Land, Rivers, and Lakes

Introduction

Water is essential for the survival of any population and all villages and farmsteads had a place nearby where they could obtain it. In addition, in Mediterranean countries, it was especially important to be able to irrigate the *hortes*,[1] or the maximum extent of cultivated land. Irrigation marked the difference between having regular, predictable food production or going hungry every certain number of years (especially if there were no grains saved from previous years inside, for example, silos). Certainly, the knowledge that the Andalusian communities acquired was a breakthrough in the use of water and in increasing the number of plants that could be cultivated. However, despite our appreciation, we also need to assess the importance of previous stages or the changes and improvements that followed. Many Catalan *comarques* had little Islamic influence. In any case, it is important to emphasize the close link between the possibility of using water and the characteristics of the society that existed in each era. The peasant communities, the Islamic and Christian cities or towns, and the lords, before and after 1000, built ditches to irrigate *hortes* and sometimes to move mills. Water-related issues lead us, at the end of this chapter, to consider Catalonia's numerous lakes, often located near the coast, many of which dried up in the high Middle Ages.

What Do We Know About Medieval Irrigated Land

Numerous books have been published over the last few decades on irrigated areas in the Middle Ages. In the Balearic Islands, many of the hydraulic systems created during the Islamic era have been studied. After the publication by M. Barceló of *Les aigües cercades: els qanāt(s) de l'illa de Mallorca* (The waters sought: the qanāt(s) of the island of Mallorca), other works have followed making it possible to establish a methodology for researching irrigated areas, which, in the Balearic Islands, have been related to the Islamic conquest of the tenth century.[2] As regards Valencia, numerous studies have also been

---

1 To avoid confusion, I will use either the Catalan words *hort* or *horta*, or I will refer to 'irrigated land'. It should be noted that Catalan differentiates between an *hort* or piece of land that is often irrigated, and an *horta* or extensive irrigated land. It would be inappropriate to use the word *huerta* in Catalonia, as it is a term used in Spanish-speaking countries.

2 Barceló, *Les aigües cercades: els qanat(s) de l'illa de Mallorca*; Kirchner, *La construcció de l'espai pagès a Mayūrqa*; Kirchner, 'Original Design, Tribal Management and Modifications in Medieval Hydraulic Systems in the Balearic Islands'; Kirchner and Retamero, 'Becoming

CHAPTER 10

conducted, especially on the *hortes* of Valencia.[3] Recently, rigorous research work has been published on the *horta* near the city of Valencia.[4] The origin and changes made to the hydraulic system in this area after the Christian conquest has been studied.[5] These works are related to those carried out in Andalusia and other Mediterranean countries.[6]

There has always been a close relationship between irrigated lands and the Muslim era. As mentioned above, most contributions from recent years on this subject have focused on the time under Islamic rule. Although there is an undeniable link with the Muslim era, we believe that, before the arrival of the Muslims there must have been *horts*, vegetable garden areas, as we find them in Old Catalonia, well documented in the Carolingian era. In addition, in some regions of New Catalonia, it was not until the tenth and eleventh centuries that they saw a heavy increase in irrigated land areas, often near cities. In addition, we can say that, after the Christian conquests of the eleventh and twelfth centuries, these irrigated areas not only did not disappear but were consolidated and grew rapidly, promoted by the feudal lords who, along with the counts of Barcelona and Urgell, had conquered these territories.

In the coming paragraphs, we will zoom in on the *horts* in Old Catalonia and then the irrigated areas of New Catalonia, especially two territories that have been widely studied in recent years, the vicinity of the city of Lleida and the city of Tortosa which in the eleventh and twelfth centuries had been the capitals of their Islamic *taifas*.

The First *Horts*

We know little about what irrigated spaces looked like in the Roman period. Recently, some contributions have been made concerning the Tarragona area as well as the banks of the river Cinca.[7] As a working hypothesis, it has been suggested that there was already a ditch along this river before the Middle Ages and that the strip of irrigated land that extended to its right bank was distributed in line with the plots of land whose sizes matched those of the Roman centuriations.[8] This is an interesting proposal. These are complicated topics, which, in other cases, have been at the core of many discussions,

---

Islanders'; Glick and Kirchner, 'Hydraulic Systems and Technologies'; Kirchner, 'Arqueologia hidràulica i tipologia d'espais irrigats andalusins'.

3 Guinot and Selma, *Les séquies de l'Horta Nord de València*.

4 Esquilache, *Els constructors de l'Horta de València*; Esquilache 'Searching for the Origin'. On the difference between *horta* (like that of the city of Valencia) and *hort* (plot of irrigated land), see Guinot, 'El paisatge historic de les hortes medieval mediterrànies', pp. 60–62.

5 Guinot, 'Morphology of Irrigated Spaces in Late Medieval Mudejar Settlements'.

6 Cara and Malpica ed., *Agricultura y regadío en al-Andalus*.

7 Prevosti, 'Els estudis de paisatge al territori de la ciutat romana de *Tarraco*', pp. 206–11.

8 Bonales, *Traces d'un passat llunyà*, pp. 205–10.

notably whenever the origin of landscapes has been posited solely on the Roman period or, on the contrary, they are thought to have originated in the Islamic era. The reality is complex and, as seen in the case of terraces, recent changes may hide previous circumstances. As we have already said, as there is a constant use of the landscape, sometimes plots can be considered Roman and also medieval since they were used, maintained, and even transformed over the thousand years of the Middle Ages. However, a study by González Villaescusa on the *huerta* of Murcia concludes that despite its regular plot division, the irrigated land was created in the Islamic era.[9] On the other hand, recent research into the south of Valencia, the region of Xàtiva, shows that, according to the evidence, Roman centuriations on both sides of the Via Augusta, were adapted to the topography and hydrography of the territory.[10] Be that as it may, this case illustrates the importance of doing long-term research.

We will now shift our attention to the *horts* along watercourses in Old Catalonia, many of which must have been created in the early Middle Ages. These are small, irrigated areas with an original irrigation canal or ditch that allowed the watering of a few hectares of fertile land. In Vallès or Barcelonès, for example, these small *horts* have been dated to before 1000.[11] Next, we will describe the case of Sant Vicenç de Jonqueres, on the banks of the river Ripoll, near Sabadell. We have discovered similar small, irrigated areas next to other watercourses in various Catalan *comarques*, from Roussillon to Penedès.

Concerning some of these small, irrigated areas of the early Middle Ages, it is necessary to point out the existence of the so-called islands (*illes*, in Catalan, and *insulas*, in Latin).[12] These *insulas*, which have rarely survived unaltered to the present day, were areas irrigated perhaps only by capillarity, located on the banks of rivers, often near river meanders. Therefore, in the case of flooding, they could easily be destroyed. This was a situation which we also find in *comarques* that until the twelfth century remained under Islamic rule, where they were called *al-jazīra* or *algesira*, as will be explained when studying the *hortes* of the city of Tortosa. Likewise, along the river Ebro, above Tortosa are further *algesires* whose written documentation, made after the 1148 conquest, confirms their dating to the time of the Saracens. This may be the case in Benifallet, Som, or Xerta (Baix Ebre).[13]

---

9 González Villaescusa, *Las formas de los paisajes mediterráneos*, pp. 329–44; Chouquer, *Dominer et tenir la terre dans le haut Moyen Âge*, p. 140.

10 Ortega and others, 'El límite entre *Valentia y Saetabis*', pp. 162–64.

11 Vilaginés, *El paisatge, la societat i l'alimentació al Vallès Oriental*, pp. 96–101; Bolòs and Hurtado, *Atles del comtat de Barcelona (801–993)*.

12 Martí, 'Les *insulae* medievals catalanes'.

13 Negre, *En els confins d'al-Andalus*, pp. 285, 376; Virgili and Kirchner, 'The Impact of the Christian Conquest on the Agrarian Areas in the Lower Ebro Valley'.

230   CHAPTER 10

The Hortes *of Jonqueres (Sabadell, Vallès Occidental)*

The banks of the river Ripoll have been greatly transformed in recent decades. However, photographs of this river taken about seventy years ago still suggest a landscape that certainly had more similarities with what it may have been like in the Middle Ages. Through written documents and these contemporary images, we can try to know what was on the banks of the Ripoll about a thousand years ago (Fig. 54).

Sant Vicenç de Jonqueres is located on the right bank of the river Ripoll. Jonqueres derives its name from the presence of bullrushes, or *joncs* (*Scirpoides holoschoenus*) in Catalan. The construction of the settlement built next to the church and perhaps the creation of these *hortes* must have diminished the importance of bullrushes. Aline Durand, concerning Languedoc, has already pointed out that with the colonization of riverbanks, the area of bullrushes diminished considerably.[14]

Along this stretch of the river Ripoll, a deeply furrowed section has marked meanders. In this section, stretching along both sides of the river course, we see, thanks to the mid-twentieth-century aerial photographs, several sets of *horts*, probably with centuries of history, as confirmed by the Carolingian documents. There is evidence of a sale in 964 of an irrigated plot of land (*terra subreganea*), located in the villa of Jonqueres, with a length of ten *destres* (about 28.2 metres) and a width of only two *destres* (about 5.6 metres); it consisted of a strip of land within a medium-sized *horta*. In general, these *hortes*, around 1950, according to what we see in the aerial photographs, were only about two hectares, and, at most, about six hectares. We note that, next to this river, there were also mills, as evidenced by documents made before 1000. In 973, a man sold half of his right of use for a day and a night per week of a mill located 'intus in villa vocitata Goncheras' (inside the villa called Jonqueres).[15] On either side of the bed of the river Ripoll and the nearby irrigated lands, a deeply uneven margin of twenty or thirty metres served to separate this irrigable space from the dryland fields that extended above.

Nothing can be assured with full certainty; however, it is very likely that the origin of these small river *hortes* (currently destroyed) stems from the most remote early Middle Ages. These *horts* did not require large ditches but a few small dams (made of stones) or a few *paixeres* (made of branches) to divert the water and make it possible to irrigate a few hectares of land. The size of these Jonqueres *hortes* resembles those reported by Kirchner for other hydraulic systems in the *comarca* of Vallès.[16] Certainly, the yield of these irrigated lands, whether they were planted with *horta* products, cereals, or vineyards, was significantly larger than that obtained in drylands,

---

14   Durand, *Les paysages médiévaux du Languedoc*, pp. 355–56.
15   *Catalunya carolíngia, vol. VII: El comtat de Barcelona*, ed. by Baiges and Puig, doc. 609.
16   Kirchner, 'Hidráulica campesina anterior a la generalización del dominio feudal', p. 33.

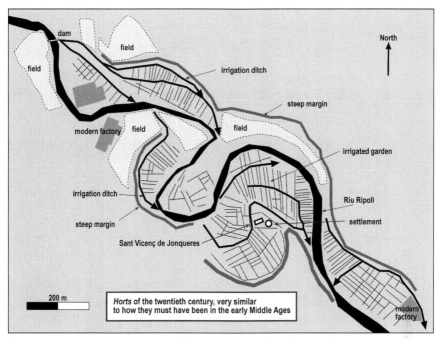

Figure 54. *Hortes* of Sant Vicenç de Jonqueres (Sabadell, Vallès Occidental). On both sides of the river Ripoll there were several small *hortes*, which are already mentioned in documents from the Carolingian period.

especially because at that time agricultural productivity across Europe was poor. These ditches, as mentioned above, also served to operate mills; in the tenth century, mills were small, their grindstones were small (less than ninety centimetres in diameter) and were possibly made largely of wood; we will discuss this in Chapter 11.

Irrigated Lands in Lleida

We cannot rule out or confirm the existence of ditches during the Roman period on the banks of the rivers Segre or Noguera Ribagorçana, as they seemed to have existed on the banks of the Cinca. On the other hand, recent studies suggest that during the early Middle Ages (perhaps even before 713–719), in valley bottoms or small valleys, there may have been not very long ditches that allowed the irrigation of small spaces, in a way similar to what was happening in the vicinity of Barcelona. Near Lleida, in the coombs and on the two banks of the so-called *reguers* and *clamors* there could have been irrigated lands since the ancient period. The sixth and seventh centuries were cold and rainy; then a drier and warmer phase began. The ditches of the

232   CHAPTER 10

early medieval period rarely took water from large rivers, such as the Segre, Noguera Ribagorçana, and Cinca.[17]

With the Arab-Berber conquest of what is now Catalonia between 713 and 719, came a period of growth in irrigated land. In Mallorca, from the tenth century onwards, as a result of the Islamic conquest (until then the island had been in the hands of the Byzantines), there was strong growth in the number of irrigated areas through the construction of *qanawat* (plural of *qanāt*) or mines and ditches.[18] Around Lleida in the eighth and ninth centuries, there were probably small *horts* connected with inhabited places; we can assume that there were old ones and maybe some new ones. However, it was in the tenth and eleventh centuries that Lleida, or the *medina Lārida*, became a relevant site, and various important hydraulic projects began to be promoted from this city, which we will describe briefly below.

The emergence of large urban hydraulic systems has been pointed out for years with respect to other Mediterranean cities, such as Orihuela (known as Oriola in the Middle Ages), whose *horta* space was designed in the second half of the tenth century and in the eleventh century.[19] In this case, this would have resulted in changes to the previous settlement dating to the Visigothic period that lived on the exploitation of wetlands, or *marjals*. The urban ditches of Orihuela were remarkable, many kilometres long (like those in Callosa or Alquibla). The various ditches dug on both sides of the river Segura have been associated with numerous *alquerias*. Additionally, as in the case of Tortosa (which we will discuss later), around the river Segura there is documentary evidence of the coexistence of ditches and drainage canals.[20]

Back in Catalonia, the city of Lleida was reconstructed and fortified between 883 and 901.[21] Around the Islamic *Lārida*, probably in the tenth and eleventh centuries, several large ditches were built (Fig. 55). The earliest ditch may have been the Alcarràs ditch which ran underneath the urban wall and set in motion a large vertical wheel mill, recently excavated, and watered the entire *horta* areas of Rufea and Butsènit where several settlements were located.[22] Further down the river Segre, the Remolins ditch was dug, which took water from near the village of Alcarràs, through Aitona, and then into the so-called *Séquia Major*, which rises in front of Torres de Segre, flows through

---

17   The case of Lleida, in relation to what we find in Old Catalonia, allows us to consider the problem of the dating of the first hydraulic spaces: how many were created in the eighth century and how many were a legacy of the small *horts* created before (which also found, for example, in Vallès or near Girona).

18   Barceló, *Les aigües cercades: els qanat(s) de l'illa de Mallorca*; Kirchner, *La construcció de l'espai pagès a Mayūrqa*.

19   Gutiérrez Lloret, 'El origen de la huerta de Orihuela', p. 87.

20   Azuar and Gutiérrez Lloret, 'Formación y transformación de un espacio agrícola islámico en el sur del País Valenciano'.

21   *De quan érem o no musulmans. Textos del 713 al 1010*, ed. and trans. by Bramon, pp. 113, 226.

22   Gil and Morán, 'Molí hidràulic de l'Avinguda Blondel, 94 de Lleida'.

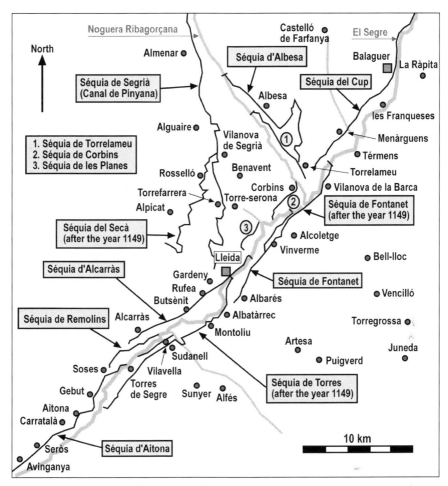

Figure 55. Ditches around Lleida. In the Islamic period, several ditches were dug near Lleida along the rivers Segre and Noguera Ribagorçana. After the conquest by the counts of Barcelona and Urgell in 1149, new ones were dug and the existing ones were enlarged.

the villages of Aitona and Serós, and into Massalcoreig.[23] At this point, it is worth noting the origin of these place names. Rufea must be related to *rīhā*, mill, while Butsènit and Massalcoreig must be connected with the Berber or Arab tribes of the Zenata and the Quraysh.[24] To the north-east of Lleida, upstream of the river Segre, there were several ditches, e.g. the Séquia de les Planes (after the Christian conquest, this is where the collegiate church of Sant

---

23 Monjo, 'Sarraïns d'Aitona, el tresor de la família Montcada', pp. 150–89.
24 Coromines, *Onomasticon Cataloniae*, vol. VI, p. 442; vol. III, p. 154; vol. V, p. 223.

Ruf was located), the Séquia de Corbins, and, on the other bank of the river Noguera Ribagorçana, the Séquia de Torrelameu and the Séquia d'Albesa.[25]

On the left bank of the river Segre, another ditch was dug called, after the Christian conquest in 1149, *Séquia de Fontanet*. It irrigated the entire *horta* in front of the city where we would probably have found small settlements until 1149. As we will see, this ditch was enlarged shortly after that date.

Finally, on the northern side of Lleida, it seems that before the Christian conquest a large ditch had already been created called *Séquia de Segrià* as it crossed from north to south the *comarca* of that name. This ditch made it possible to irrigate the lands located to the north of Lleida and those of northern urban suburbs. Immediately after the comital conquest documents reveal that this ditch reached as far as the outskirts of the city and passed by several 'towers' (*torres*, in Catalan; perhaps, as seen above, ancient Muslim *almúnies*), owned by nobles such as the Montcadas or the Boixadors who had given support to the counts of Barcelona and Urgell in the conquest of Lleida in 1149.

After the 1149 conquest, these Islamic canals were exploited and expanded. Thus, the Séquia de Fontanet, about ten kilometres long back then, was extended by another 7.6 kilometres. Before the end of the twelfth century, the Séquia de Segrià (now Canal de Pinyana), which was already about thirty kilometres long, was extended even further with a brand new branch or secondary canal (*braçal*, in Catalan). Shortly after the conquest, there is documentary evidence, for the area of Segrià, to the north of Lleida of the *cechia vetula* and the *cechia nova* (i.e., old and new ditch). On the other hand, early documents from the second half of the twelfth century refer to an official called the *çavaséquia*, heir of the officer who, during Islamic rule, was responsible for the proper functioning of ditches (known in Arabic as *sahib al-saquia*), as a sign of continuity of canal exploitation despite the break after the conquest.

The horta *of Menàrguens (La Noguera)*

The town of Menàrguens is halfway between Balaguer and Lleida, on the right bank of the Segre. Although Balaguer was conquered by the count of Urgell in 1105, it was not until 1149, the date of the siege of Lleida, that the rule over the territory of Menàrguens began. The settlement charter of this place, a document from 1163, alludes to the *cequia de Balaguerio*, which certainly must have existed before the conquest.[26] In the Islamic period there was certainly an irrigated area opposite Menàrguens, a name of Roman origin.[27] Nothing

---

25 Mulet and others, *Torrelameu. La nostra història*, pp. 78–79; Bolòs, 'Conèixer el paisatge històric medieval per poder planificar i gestionar el territori', p. 221.

26 *Cartas de población y franquicia de Cataluña*, ed. by Font Rius, vol. I, doc. 123.

27 Coromines, *Onomasticon Cataloniae*, vol. V, p. 249.

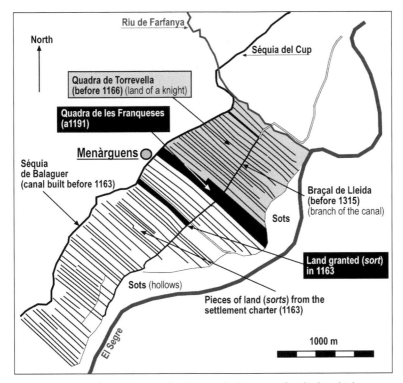

Figure 56. *Horta* of Menàrguens (La Noguera). Between the ditch, which already existed in the Islamic period, and the river Segre, is a set of narrow coaxial strips of land created after the Christian conquest.

is known about what the *horta* areas must have looked like before 1149, or what their shapes and sizes were. After the conquest, on the other hand, a landscape was created that, without much change, has survived to the present day (Fig. 56). According to its settlement charter, each villager received in the irrigated area plots of land measuring about fifty metres wide by about 700 metres long. Later this space was further expanded with the creation of a secondary canal that irrigated a new sector closer to the Segre. As mentioned above, it is still possible to make out the shapes of these irrigated pieces of land created in the middle of the twelfth century.[28]

In the *horta* of Menàrguens we find a layout similar to the that along the Séquia de Segrià (or Canal de Pinyana), where there was, after the count's conquest and the granting of many of the lands to the Templars, a distribution of the entire irrigated territory. *Parellades* (a *parellada* is the land worked by a pair of oxen) of about ten hectares were created, and distributed among

---

28 Bolòs, 'Paisatges i transicions: canvis i continuïtats al llarg de la història', pp. 102–04.

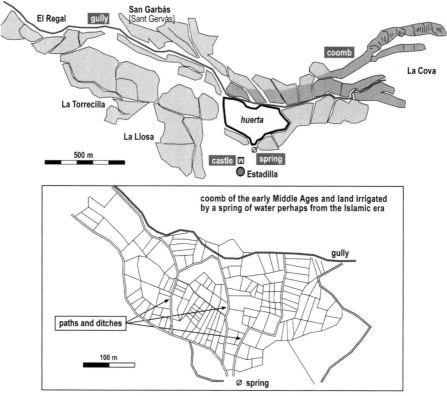

Figure 57. *Huerta* of Estadilla (Aragon). Between a spring and a coomb, we find a fragmented space made up of small *huertos* irrigated with spring water. It was probably organized in the Islamic period.

hereters (in this text, peasants with a land tenure) and their partners.[29] In this volume, there are previous references to this phenomenon, notably when alluding to the *torre* of Torrefarrera, in Chapter 6.

To finish this section out of Catalonia, we swing by the irrigated area next to Alcañiz el Viejo (near Alcañiz, in the south of Aragon), where we may see evidence of plot division, perhaps dating to the Islamic era. An old ditch stretches along the Guadalope River and is about thirty kilometres long. In the irrigated area we can distinguish a sector with a more irregular plot, perhaps similar to that which existed in the Islamic period, and a wide sector divided transversely by strips of land, in a manner similar to the division around the city of Lleida after the feudal conquest in the mid-twelfth century.[30]

---

29 Bolòs, 'Paisatge i societat al "Segrià" al segle XIII'.
30 Ortega, 'La agricultura de los vencedores y la agricultura de los vencidos', p. 126.

The *huerta* of Estadilla

On the left bank of the river Cinca stands the town of Estadilla (Estadella, in the Middle Ages), which was under Islamic rule until 1089. Subsequently, it came to belong to the county of Ribagorça, now in Aragon. Below the village, to the north, the landscape preserves traces of an interesting past.[31] A coomb stretches along the ravine and an irrigated area lies below a very large spring. The *huerta* area between the water spring and the ravine, with an area of 7.6 hectares, is made up of many small vegetable gardens crossed by three paths that coincide with several ditches (Fig. 57). Probably, the coomb dates to the early Middle Ages and the organization of this irrigated space was established in the Islamic period. We also believe that at some point in the past the irrigated area was more extensive; to the west, 1.5 kilometres away, there is still land known as *El Regal*, a clear reference to the Arabic name *ar-Riyād*, 'the gardens' or perhaps *raḥl*, 'country house'.

Irrigated Land in Tortosa

Recent research has allowed us to greatly increase our knowledge of what the Tortosa area was like around the twelfth century. We can distinguish three major sectors. To the north was the so-called Horta de Pimpí (irrigated land). It extended beyond the northern gate of the city.[32] The *horta* we would have found there, before the count's conquest, was not irrigated by using a ditch to take water from the river as in the city of Lleida, but rather with a system of *sínies* (*norias* in Spanish, waterwheels).[33] In general, in the Islamic period, to the north of the city of Tortosa, the cultivated strip of land ran farthest from the river to protect it from floods. However, near the city walls, according to documents after 1148, there was an *algesira*, an 'island' (or *insula*), located next to the river Ebro, obviously intended as a *horta*; after the conquest, it was ceded to the Jews of Tortosa.

To the south of Tortosa, the *partida* of Les Arenes did not require watering either; drainage pipes had to be fitted in. Studies show that between the seventh and tenth centuries these lands were becoming progressively drier, partly through human activity and also a climatic warm period.[34] In this case, therefore, the network of canals was intended to drain the water. According to documents written after the 1148 conquest, there was a Séquia Major and a Séquia Mitjana, located next to another *algesira* and the river. There were also

---

31   Bolòs, *Col·lecció diplomàtica de l'Arxiu Capitular de Lleida*, pp. 467–70.
32   Kirchner and Virgili, 'De Turṭûśa a Tortosa. La ciutat abans i després de la conquesta catalana'; Kirchner and Virgili, 'Espacios agrarios en el Bajo Ebro en época andalusí y después de la conquista catalana'.
33   Glick, 'Sistemes agrícoles islàmics de Xarq al-Andalus', p. 76.
34   Kirchner, Virgili, and Puy, 'Drainage and Irrigation Systems in Madīna Ṭurṭūša'.

238   CHAPTER 10

secondary canals, named after the sites, that they passed through or after the owners of the places.[35] By comparing and contrasting what the documentation indicates against what we now see, it is possible to reconstruct the layout of cultivated land from the mid-twelfth century and the changes, especially extensions, that it underwent over the next centuries. Prat de Tortosa began further south of Les Arenes and extended all the way to the sea; as the name implies, this space was most likely intended for cattle grazing.

According to documentation, on the right bank of the river Ebro, facing Tortosa, there were sections of ditches, probably used to drain heavily flooded land.[36] On the other hand, it was probably not until after 1148 that ditches were built to carry water from El Port Mountain to Molins del Comte (mills of the count), built on this bank of the river Ebro.

Medieval Canals, Towns, and Cities

In the early Middle Ages, there were already notable canals near some cities in Old Catalonia, such as the Rec Comtal in Barcelona or the Rec Monar in Girona, two cities which were created during the Roman period.[37] The Rec Comtal took water from the river Besòs, towards Montcada, and carried it to the city of Barcelona; it was over eleven kilometres long. Along its course, in the high Middle Ages, many mills were built.[38]

After 1000, canals were created in other towns such as Perpignan, Puigcerdà, and Manresa. As studied recently, the water supply for increasingly heavily populated medieval European cities was a major problem solved by the construction of wells, springs, canals, and even, sometimes, with the excavation of underground mines or wide underground conduits.[39] It should be borne in mind that in the cities, apart from the population, there used to be *horts* and flour mills, fulling mills, or tanneries for hides and skins, all of which required a lot of water. In Barcelona, for example, in 1356, running water arrived in Plaça de Sant Jaume, in the heart of the city, carried underground, from the mountain of Collserola. The mountain resources had been exploited for more than nine years, and mines with ventilation openings or wells had been excavated. The mine built to carry water from the natural springs of Collserola must have been similar to the Islamic *qanāt*.[40]

---

35   Kirchner and Virgili, 'Assentaments rurals i espais agraris al Baix Ebre i la ciutat de Tortosa en època andalusina i després de la conquesta catalana'.

36   Negre, *En els confins d'al-Andalus*, pp. 377–79.

37   Canal and others, *Girona, de Carlemany al feudalisme*, p. 414.

38   Bolòs, *Els orígens medievals del paisatge català*, p. 374.

39   Leguay, *L'eau dans la ville au Moyen Âge*.

40   Bruniquer, *Ceremonial dels Magnífics Consellers i Regiment de la Ciutat de Barcelona*, vol. IV, p. 268; Galindo, 'Anàlisi del paisatge històric a la zona nord del pla de Barcelona', p. 32.

Canals of Tuïr and Perpignan (Roussillon)

In Roussillon, there is evidence of small canals in the late ninth and tenth centuries; however, it is not until the eleventh and twelfth centuries that it is possible to find a significant number of well-documented ditches.[41] In the twelfth century, there is written evidence of Rec Comtal which carried water to Perpignan (Perpinyà, in Catalan), from the so-called Pas del Llop (passage of the wolf); the ditch was about twelve kilometres long. At the beginning of the fourteenth century, there was a significant breakthrough. The kings of Mallorca undertook the construction of the Rec de Tuïr (Thuir, in French) between 1308 and 1309. It was about thirty-four kilometres long and was to be used to irrigate fields and set in motion several mills on the Roussillon plain. It took water from near Vinçà and brought it to Tuïr, and from there to Palau dels Reis de Mallorca (palace of the Kings of Majorca), in the city of Perpignan.[42] In 1372, a strict regulation was established concerning this canal, regarding its exploitation and the assurance that the water reached the mills and the waterwheel in Perpignan, located next to the royal palace. After floods in 1408 and 1421, a new canal was built in the city of Perpignan in 1423, also promoted by the monarch, with the dam located towards the village of Illa; it was about twenty-five kilometres long.[43]

The King's Canal of Puigcerdà (Cerdanya)

The Puigcerdà canal was excavated after the construction of the new town of Puigcerdà, founded by the monarch of Catalonia and Aragon, Alfons I, in 1178 (Fig. 42). The canal was used to carry water from the river Aravó, mainly from a dam in Tor de Querol, over 9.1 kilometres, to a lake located near the capital of the Cerdanya region. The earliest evidence for the canal dates to the second half of the thirteenth century. This water was mainly used for powering the flour and fulling mills of the royal town of Puigcerdà and, secondarily, irrigating its *horts* and a few of its meadows.[44] For this reason, it was forbidden to use the water for irrigating meadows or fields along a route that crossed the territories of various villages.

---

41 Caucanas, *Moulins et irrigation en Roussillon du IXe au XVe siècle*.
42 When King Jaume I (James) died, in 1276, he bequeathed the Balearic Islands, Roussillon, and Cerdanya to his son also called Jaume. The rest of his kingdoms were passed on to his son, Pere II (Peter) the Great. This decision led to the creation of the so-called Kingdom of Majorca, which extended to the Balearic Islands, northern Catalonia, and the city of Montpellier. Subsequently, Pere III (Peter III) the Ceremonious conquered this kingdom in 1343, and incorporated it into the Catalan-Aragonese Crown.
43 Caucanas, *Moulins et irrigation en Roussillon du IXe au XVe siècle*, pp. 256, 267–78.
44 Kirchner and others, *Aigua prohibida. Arqueologia hidràulica del feudalisme a la Cerdanya*.

Canal of Manresa (Bages)

The Manresa ditch is much longer, at about twenty-six kilometres. It takes water from the river Llobregat, near Balsareny, and carries it to the city of Manresa. In 1339, the Catalan-Aragonese monarch granted this privilege, and, finally, in 1345, the bishop of Vic granted it too. In this case, the inhabitants of Manresa needed it for irrigation purposes. For this reason, in the Middle Ages, several secondary canals were constructed. The water went as far as the walls of Manresa.[45]

Canal of Vila-rodona (Alt Camp)

Apart from these urban ditches, others were built in smaller towns. Next to the river Gaià, south of Santes Creus, a ditch with a length of 8.8 kilometres was dug, which mainly watered the lands of the village of Vila-rodona.[46] This ditch was neither constructed in the Carolingian nor the Islamic era. It was re-dug in the last third of the twelfth century. In 1188, the bishop of Barcelona was granted by the abbot of Santes Creus the right to use the water of the river Gaià and authorization to run an irrigation canal through the lands of the abbey. Only two years later, in 1190, this bishop signed the settlement charter of Vila-rodona (or *Castelli Crescentis*).[47] This construction required mining work and the construction of an aqueduct. It would then be reasonable to assume the participation, during this complex work, of technicians who were knowledgeable about Islamic building techniques. This ditch was used to irrigate fields and power up a mill.

Dried-up Lakes and Ponds

In the early Middle Ages, in the Empordà and Roussillon, and also further north, in the Occitan lands, there were numerous lakes located very close to the coastline. Jean-Loup Abbé studied the process of drying up ponds in the Languedoc region.[48] Similar studies have been carried out with regard to the Roussillon area.[49] The monarchs of Catalonia and Aragon, in 1195 and 1205, granted the Templar order of El Masdéu the right to drain the Bages lake (Fig. 66). The Templars started draining other lakes, such as those of Bajoles, Sabadell, and Caraig. The process involved granting rights to lake users and landowners whose estates were crossed by drainage canals.

---

45 Bolòs, *Els orígens medievals del paisatge català*, p. 376.
46 Andreu and others, 'La sèquia de Vila-rodona'.
47 *Cartas de población y franquicia de Cataluña*, vol. I, ed. by Font Rius, doc. 184.
48 Abbé, *À la conquête des étangs*.
49 Caucanas, 'Assèchements en Roussillon'; *Diplomatari del Masdéu*, ed. by Tréton, pp. 76–77.

Further south, in the Empordà region, some larger lakes, such as Castelló or Ullastret, did not dry up until the modern era. In relation to that of Castelló, in the fifteenth century some small ponds and marshes were already dried up, but it was not until the seventeenth and eighteenth centuries that the work of draining the lake was undertaken with the creation of several drainage canals.[50]

The Importance of Fishing in Rivers, Lakes, and the Sea

Throughout the last few pages, we have talked a lot about the use of water, but we have not mentioned how important fishing was almost everywhere. Before 1000, especially in Carolingian precepts, the fishing rights that the monks of Ripoll had in the rivers Ter and Freser or those that the community of the abbey of Banyoles (Pla de l'Estany) had in the nearby lake are mentioned. The importance of the sea fishing rights of the monastery of Sant Pere de Rodes (Alt Empordà), which rises above the sea, is also referred to.[51] As for river fish, in 1151, the count of Barcelona was to receive forty trout (*xl truítes*) each year in Els Prats de Molló (Vallespir). In the documentation of the count of Barcelona or the king made throughout the twelfth century, very often fresh or salted fish are mentioned (*piscis fresc, salatus piscis*).[52] Finally, in relation to the end of the Middle Ages, numerous studies have recently been carried out on fishing on the Mediterranean coasts, especially in the Empordà, the Maresme, and Garraf.[53]

Conclusions

In Mediterranean countries land irrigation is of paramount importance, not only because it allows the planting of vegetables, but also cereals and sometimes even vineyards. From the beginning of the Middle Ages, we find small, irrigated areas located in coombs or next to watercourses, such as the river Ripoll in the *comarca* of Vallès. The value of irrigation is most evident

---

50 Romagosa, 'El procés històric de dessecació d'estanys a la plana empordanesa', p. 78; Saguer, 'Cultivar l'estany'.

51 *Catalunya carolíngia, vol. II: Els diplomes carolingis a Catalunya*, ed. by Abadal.

52 *Fiscal accounts of Catalonia under the early count-kings*, vol. 2, ed. by Bisson, pp. 18, 121, 129. These documents of the count-kings include a large amount of information about Catalonia in the twelfth century. For example, in the same document from Prats de Molló (1151) mention is made of salted trout and bears, chamois (*isárn, isard* in Catalan) or western capercaillies (*gallos silvaticos, galls fers* or *galls salvatges* in Catalan).

53 *Les Ordinacions de la pesquera de Calonge*, ed. by Alfons Garrido, Montse Pérez, Joan Lluís Alegret, and Montserrat Darnaculleta; *Llibre de la Cort de la Mar de Roses. Ordinacions, sentències i concòrdies sobre la pesca (segle xv)*, ed. by Pujol and Garrido; Ginot, 'Els drets sobre la pesca a l'Alt Maresme'; Muntaner, 'Terra de masos, vila de mar', pp. 279–306.

in the Islamic period when new plants from distant places were introduced and adapted to irrigated land.[54]

In the vicinity of Lleida, we have seen that after the construction of small ditches, possibly undertaken by early medieval rural communities, during a second stage close to 1000, urban ditches of a remarkable length were constructed to irrigate urban *hortes* and those of nearby *almúnies*, also used to power mills. This change certainly deeply affected the economy of this territory, and its impact has lasted until today. After the Christian conquest irrigated areas expanded, which allowed vegetables, cereals, vineyards, and even riverside trees to be planted on these lands. Given the characteristics of the terrain in Tortosa, the use of *norias* or *sínies* (waterwheels) and the construction of ditches to drain rather than distribute the water were widespread techniques.

It should be noted that over the last few decades, studies related to the use of water and the creation of irrigated areas have been of paramount importance, especially for the Balearic Islands and Valencia. In this chapter, we have described and illustrated the characteristics of irrigation systems in Catalonia in the Middle Ages, the importance of ditches and canals in Old Catalonia, and of dried-up lakes and ponds, particularly on land near the coast. The Roussillon lakes were largely dried up in the high Middle Ages, while the larger lakes of the Empordà region, such as the one next to Castelló d'Empúries, were not desiccated until the modern era or well into the eighteenth and nineteenth centuries.[55]

---

54 Watson, *Agricultural Innovation in the Early Islamic World*.
55 Romagosa, 'El procés històric de dessecació d'estanys a la plana empordanesa'.

CHAPTER 11

The Importance of Mills, Iron, and Salt

Introduction

In the rural landscape of the Middle Ages, several kinds of constructions were clearly visible, important to the people, and had an impact on the other surrounding elements. We will look into some of them in the next few pages, but first, we start with mills. There were water-powered flour mills everywhere. The mills must be related to inhabited places, cereal fields, roads, ditches, and society as a whole. The role of the mill in Andalusian, Carolingian, and feudal society has been widely discussed. We will not, however, refer to windmills, which we know existed but have not been studied in depth. We also skip fulling mills that we know were built near fabric-producing centres, for example, in Cerdanya or Lleida. The second topic covered here is metallurgical activities. Mining, smelting, and manufacturing were especially important in the Pyrenees, and metal was used in making tools and weapons. We also consider salt, an important ingredient in food preservation. It is necessary to connect the places containing salt with the road networks and centres of power. Finally, we will mention other constructions lost in the middle of fields or forests such as vats where grapes were crushed, wine presses, or charcoal piles, elements of the medieval landscape some of which survived until a few decades ago.

What Do We Know About Medieval Mills?

Across Europe, mills have attracted the attention of specialists and historians. For us, it is important to consider the relationship that has always existed between mills, society, and the economy. To demonstrate the interest in studies on mills and water use, I will emphasize three conferences whose core topics captured my attention. In 1999, a congress dedicated to *Moulins et meuniers dans les campagnes européennes* was held at the Gascon abbey of Flaran.[1] A few years later, in 2005, the fifth Ruralia Congress focused on *Water Management in Medieval Rural Economy*.[2] Finally, in 2011, a conference was held on the archaeology of watermills, animal-drawn mills, and windmills.[3] As we will see in this chapter, numerous studies and books on this subject

---

1 Mousnier, *Moulins et meuniers dans les campagnes européennes*.
2 Klápště, *Water Management in Medieval Rural Economy*.
3 Jaccottey and Rollier, *Archéologie des moulins hydrauliques, à traction animale et à vent*. Recently, Colin Rynne has made a synthesis of the discoveries and research that have taken place over the last decades. Rynne, 'Landscapes of Hydraulic Energy in Medieval Europe'.

244   CHAPTER 11

have been published in Catalonia and the Catalan countries as a whole in recent decades.[4]

A mill may just be a point on a map, as is a castle or a church. However, it is important to know its history and to see how its existence could alter its surrounding landscape. In addition, it is important to understand that each mill has certain features and was built in a certain place conditioned largely by the characteristics of the society that created it. For a long time, mills were one of the few sites inside which activity was carried out that could be considered proto-industrial, dedicated to the transformation of raw materials, i.e., grains of cereals, using machinery. In Catalonia, although we assume that there were mills in the Visigothic period, it is in the Carolingian period, i.e., in the ninth and tenth centuries, that we begin to find them documented. As for the Visigothic period, although there may have been many types, archaeological sites often reveal manual mills.[5] Possibly in Catalonia, the spread of small hydraulic mills reflects changes in society between the seventh and ninth centuries. It is also true that, for example, in eastern Languedoc, in the tenth and eleventh centuries, excavations have revealed the existence of grindstones powered by men or animals.[6] In this chapter, towards the end, we will also briefly refer to mines, forges, salt exploitation, wine presses, and charcoal piles.

Carolingian Mills

While working on the maps of *Atles dels comtats de la Catalunya carolíngia* (Atlas of the Counties of Carolingian Catalonia), to our surprise, we found a large number of flour mills registered before 1000.[7] In a few cases, these mills may have even been older. In 940, near Palau de Llierca (a former fiscal domain), there are references to a villa at Molivedre (*Molino Vetere*) meaning an old mill. Or when, not far from a place in Vallès Oriental called Monells, documented in 898 (*Mulinellus*), there was an inhabited place called Rifà (*Riffa*, year 941), a place named from the Arabic term *rīhā* for the *mill*. However, in most cases, we must assume that mills documented in the Carolingian period must have been built during the ninth and tenth centuries. Also, when reading about the thousands of mills from before 1000, we realize how widespread they were all over the counties of Old Catalonia.

---

4   Bolòs and Nuet, *Els molins fariners*; Bolòs, 'Mills, Landscape, and Society in Catalonia in the Middle Ages'; Selma, 'El molí hidràulic de farina i l'organització de l'espai rural andalusí'; Selma, *Els molins d'aigua medievals a Sharq al-Andalus*; Peris Albentosa, *Els molins d'aigua valencians (segles XIII–XIX)*.
5   Gibert, *La fi del món antic i els inicis de l'edat mitjana*, p. 43.
6   Maufras and others, '*Villae* — Villages du haut Moyen Âge en plaine du Languedoc oriental', p. 99.
7   Bolòs and Hurtado, 'Atles dels comtats de la Catalunya carolíngia' (ten volumes).

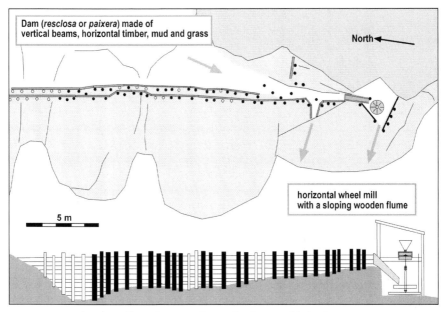

Figure 58. Carolingian mills in the Riera de Merlès (Berguedà). In this stream we can still see holes dug into the rock that bear witness to the existence of dams, ditches, and mills built around 1000.

Initially, there are two issues to be considered. First, many of the villages or rural communities of the ninth and tenth centuries had flour mills. This is the case, for example, of the mills in the county of Besalú.[8] In Old Catalonia, in some places, the members of the rural community apportioned the days and hours of the week during which individuals could use the mill for grinding purposes. This seems to be a different reality from that in northern Italy, where the increase in the number of mills (probably also those with a horizontal wheel) in the eighth and ninth centuries was related to the consolidation of the land ownership.[9] Also, this system differed from that of Neustria (northern Gaul), where mills (probably those with a vertical wheel) were mainly owned by great monasteries like Saint-Germain-des-Prés, Fontenelle, or Corbie, or in Austrasia, with the abbeys of Prüm or Montier-en-Der.[10] In Catalonia, the situation was very different; however, it soon changed dramatically, especially after 1000.

Secondly, we know what these mills looked like. They had a flume, and they were horizontal wheel mills, made of wood and built very close to a

---

8 Bolòs and Hurtado, *Atles del comtat de Besalú (785–988)*, pp. 44–45.
9 Gelichi, 'Agricoltura e ambiente nell'Italia tardo-antica e altomedievale', pp. 116, 121.
10 Lebecq, 'The Role of the Monasteries in the Systems of Production and Exchange of the Frankish World', p. 134.

watercourse, in other words, in an easily flooded place. They were fitted with small grinding millstones (about 90 cm). The most expensive parts in the mill, as the documents indicate, were the *ferramenta*, the iron pieces, i.e., spindle and rynd, embedded in the fixed grindstone and essential to transferring the power of the shaft of the mill to the runner millstone. A few years ago, while following the course of the Merlès stream, we found the remains of several sites fitted with mills, probably built around 1000. Evidence can still be seen of circular holes dug in flat rock, intended to support the beams of the dams, or *paixeres*, also the ditches through which water flowed, sometimes hollowed out in the rock, and it was even possible to see the cavities where the mill house was located.[11] These dams made of wood (*paxilli*) are also well documented in Languedoc, known as *moulins à paissière*, from the Occitan term *paissièra*.[12]

Mills of the Merlès Stream

Along over 30 km of the Merlès stream, which in the Middle Ages separated the counties of Berga and Osona, the evidence of mills built in the Carolingian period and later centuries abounds. As mentioned above, we can find many holes in the stony bed of the river, which remind us of the existence of wooden dams, made of beams, branches, and mud (Fig. 58). There is also evidence of small, not very long ditches, made of wood, or dug into the rock or into the ground, which often carried the water to the edge of a small waterfall, where there was a mill, also made of wood. The wheel must have been horizontal, given the small amount of water in it. Water fell on the wheel through a sloping channel or flume (then called *tudella*). No gear was needed to drive the waterpower from the wheel, through the shaft (with the metal spindle), into the iron rynd and the runner stone. The mills were inexpensive, and often belonged to peasant communities, and sometimes to a lord. There were dozens of them. They were, in many respects, like those found, for example, in Ireland, Scotland, England, and the Scandinavian countries.[13] They also abounded in many Mediterranean countries.

Therefore, it is very difficult for us to accept a supposed contrast between Mediterranean vertical wheel mills and horizontal wheel mills in northern Europe.[14] Even more so if we consider the number of horizontal wheel mills from the Roman period found in Gaul (Taradeau [Oc. Taradèu], La Croix de Fenouillé, La Calade [Oc. La Calada], etc.), even in Africa.[15] These adaptations of the mill relate to the material possibilities of the place (water flow, for

---

11 Bolòs, 'Les moulins en Catalogne au Moyen Âge'.

12 Durand, *Les paysages médiévaux du Languedoc*, pp. 253–54; Alibèrt *Dictionnaire Occitan-français d'après les parlers languedociens*, p. 520.

13 Rynne, 'Waterpower in Medieval Ireland'; Rynne, 'Water and Wind Power', p. 493; Kind, 'Fulda–Langebrückenstrasse', p. 282.

14 Benoit, 'Remarques sur les fouilles de moulins à eau médiévaux en Europe', p. 66.

15 Brun, 'Les moulins hydrauliques dans l'Antiquité', pp. 39–40.

example) and the economic status of its owner. Building a horizontal wheel mill was easier than gearing up a vertical wheel mill. Medieval horizontal wheeled mills can therefore also be a legacy of the Roman period in Catalonia.

Islamic Mills and Water Wheels or *Norias*

It has been pointed out in this volume that the toponym Rifà, located in Old Catalonia, recalls the existence of mills built during the years before 800 under Islamic rule. We know that there were also mills in the lands of New Catalonia, conquered by the Catalan counts, especially in the mid-twelfth century. A vertical wheel mill has recently been dug out in Carrer de Blondel, in the city of Lleida, next to where the Alcarràs canal passes (Fig. 55) and has been dated to before the Christian conquest of 1149.[16] This is not such an exceptional finding since, a few years ago, one was unearthed in the city of Valencia, also from the Islamic era, probably from the tenth century. The Valencian mill was, however, a horizontal wheel mill with a 110-centimetres diameter runner stone.[17]

Therefore, although the documents do not mention it, in Islamic Catalonia, in addition to vertical wheel mills (which need a regular and large flow), there were probably also tank (well-like) mills, which have also been found in North Africa (where the tank or well was called *maṣabb*).[18] Beginning in the twelfth century, we can find these tank mills (*molins de cup* in Catalan) throughout Catalonia, perhaps spreading from the Andalusian model. Islamic tank mills with a horizontal wheel have also been found in Mallorca and Valencia.[19] In addition, near Castelló de la Plana, possible pre-feudal ramp mills have also been discovered that bear a certain resemblance to Pyrenean canal or flume mills.[20]

In the lands of Muslim Catalonia, we would also have found waterwheels (*norias*) to lift underground water to the surface and irrigate *hortes*. As mentioned above, there is documentary evidence of *hortes* from the city of Tortosa, dating from before the count's conquest of 1148. The waterwheels (*sínies* in Catalan) of the Islamic period in Valencia have also been studied.[21] As regards the island of Mallorca, thorough studies are being carried out on medieval waterwheels, which have continued in use until today.[22]

---

16 Gil and Morán, 'Molí hidràulic de l'Avinguda Blondel, 94 de Lleida'.
17 Martí and Pascual, 'El Desarrollo urbano de *madīna Balansiya*', p. 514.
18 Selma, *Els molins d'aigua medievals a Sharq al-Andalus*, pp. 29, 31.
19 Argemí, 'El sistema de molinos andalusí del Guz de Yartan (Mayurqa)'; Glick, 'Sistemes agrícoles islàmics de Xarq al-Andalus', pp. 78–79.
20 Selma, *Els molins d'aigua medievals a Sharq al-Andalus*, pp. 59–61.
21 Bazzana and Montmessin, '*Nā'ūra* et *sāniya* dans l'hydraulique agricole d'al-Andalus à la lumière des fouilles de "Les Jovades" (Oliva, Valence)'.
22 Andreu, *Arquitectura tradicional de les Balears*, pp. 188–91.

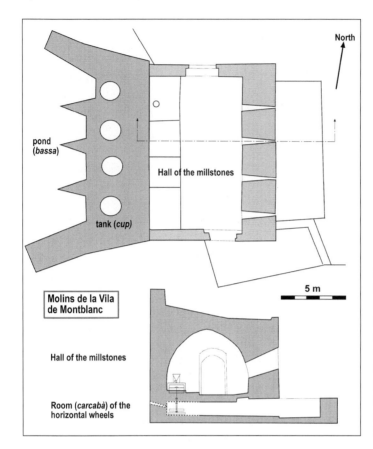

Figure 59. Molins de la Vila (Montblanc, Conca de Barberà). Mill constructed around 1300, with four tanks, which moved four millstones installed in a spacious hall. It depended on the town of Montblanc.

Mills from After the Christian Conquest

In the twelfth century, Catalonia saw a diversification of flour mills. Apart from sloping canal (or flume) mills, found mainly in the Pyrenees, people began to use vertical wheels (*molins roders* in Catalan) and, also, almost everywhere, tank mills (*molins de cup* in Catalan), often located along a pond where water was stored. In addition, around this time, fulling mills also spread, and, shortly afterwards, windmills began to be built.[23]

In medieval Catalonia, there were vertical wheel mills. These were uncommon and could only be found in places with a large and regular flow of water. Thus, for example, they abounded in large ditches in the vicinity of Lleida and Perpignan. This type of mill with a large wheel and a gear was common in the countries of central Europe, while, as we have said, in the most

---

23 Farías, *El mas i la vila a la Catalunya medieval*, pp. 235–36; Padilla, 'La construcció d'un enginy hidràulic'.

peripheral areas of the continent, horizontal wheel mills were predominant. This was the case throughout the Mediterranean area, both in Catalonia and in much of Occitania and Italy.

In Catalonia, perhaps the most important change that took place around the twelfth century was the appearance of tank mills (with a *cup* in Catalan), with a well several metres deep, which made it possible to significantly increase the power of the millstones. The appearance of tank mills is commonly associated with the existence of a pond, where water could be stored, and with the construction of a long irrigation canal or ditch, which made it possible to position the mill building far away from the river or stream. Hence, in mills built after 1000, possibly made of well-carved, square ashlars, often paid for by a feudal lord, there were several millstones and even a house where the miller and his family lived. In Vallès, the first reference to a miller is from the mid-eleventh century; in the twelfth century, they were already quite common.[24] The peasants had to pay for the *moltura*, a milling tax, to grind their grain and obtain flour from these seigneurial mills.

Molins de la Vila, Mills of a Town (Montblanc, Conca de Barberà)

Next to the river Anguera, one kilometre from the medieval walls of Montblanc, the new town of the Catalan-Aragonese king, there is a mill that is very different from those of the early Middle Ages (Fig. 59). It has a large room covered by an elaborate stone vault, inside which were four millstones. Underneath this room, four horizontal wheels had water pouring in from the four wells (or *cups*), still visible next to the pond. These deep wells, filled with water to the top, powered the water that spanned the wheel, the shaft, and the runner stone. This mill house, made of elaborate stone, was owned by the royal town of Montblanc. Most of the mills which shared these characteristics belonged to secular or ecclesiastical lords, who, after 1000, took ownership of the use of water and forced the peasants to grind the grain in their mills by paying, as mentioned above, a tax known as *moltura*. These mills in Montblanc, called *de la Vila* (from the town), were built in the late thirteenth century or early fourteenth century. They have now been turned into a museum and are considered part of the heritage of the town of Montblanc.

Mills of Empordà: Flour Mills and Fulling Mills

A doctoral thesis of 2013 presents a detailed study of the Empordà mills in the late Middle Ages.[25] What first captures our attention when reading this study is the large number of mills that existed in the thirteenth and fourteenth centuries in the county of Empúries and the viscounty of Rocabertí; as many

---

24 Farías, *El mas i la vila a la Catalunya medieval*, p. 85.
25 Gironella, *Els molins empordanesos baixmedievals*.

as 152 mills are documented (Fig. 60).[26] This research, apart from analysing who the owners were, inventoried the number of stone mills in each mill house; in most cases, there were two or more stone mills.

It is also interesting to know how many of these mills were flour mills or fulling mills; nineteen of them were used for stretching and beating cloth or textiles.[27] As stated above there were also fulling mills in other regions, such as Cerdanya, Berguedà, and Segrià. In relation to La Pobla de Lillet (Berguedà), for example, the contract signed between the lord and the miller has been preserved, or in Lleida the accounting for the construction of one of these fulling mills has come down to us.[28]

Mines and Forges

The production of metals, from Silesia to Scandinavia and the Iberian Peninsula, was highly valued throughout the Middle Ages, and had a significant impact on the environment.[29] In the Catalan counties, documents from before 1000 record the existence of places or valleys where iron could be extracted. This was the case, for example, in Andorra, where, in 860, there were references to tithes of iron (*decimis Andorrensis pagi ferri*);[30] in 2007, a metallurgical workshop was excavated in Sant Julià de Lòria, dated between the fifth and seventh centuries.[31] There was also evidence of metal working activity in the village of of Farrera (or Ferrera), and in Vallferrera, whose place name is already quite eloquent.[32] In this valley, metallurgical activity has been documented since the years AD 250–320.[33] One of the most important studies on the exploitation of iron in the Middle Ages was carried out as a result of the excavation of the Fabregada site in Pallars Jussà, especially after finding, next to a set of houses, the place where the forge was located, where ore was converted into iron and where metal was worked.[34]

In the early medieval period, there was already significant exploitation of minerals. Research carried out in recent years shows that Estanh Redon (Val d'Aran), a lake, was heavily polluted with lead during the late Roman and

---

26 Gironella, *Els molins empordanesos baixmedievals*, p. 73.

27 Gironella, *Els molins empordanesos baixmedievals*, p. 111.

28 We have evidence, for example, of the existence, in 1257, in Bagà (Berguedà) of a fulling mill, where two millers worked, one each week (Serra Vilaró, *Baronies de Pinós i Mataplana. Llibre segon*, p. 369). In relation to Lleida: Padilla, 'La construcció d'un enginy hidràulic' (The construction of a hydraulic device).

29 Hoffmann, *An Environmental History of Medieval Europe*, pp. 215–27.

30 *Catalunya carolíngia, vol. II: Els diplomes carolingis a Catalunya*, ed. by Abadal, p. 287.

31 Fortó and Vidal, 'En los orígenes de Sant Julià de Lòria (Andorra)', p. 256.

32 *Catalunya carolíngia, vol. III: Els comtats de Pallars i Ribagorça*, ed. by Abadal, doc. 108; Sancho, *Homes, fargues, ferro i foc*.

33 Davasse, *Forêts, charbonniers et paysans dans les Pyrénées*.

34 Sancho, *Ipsa Fabricata. Estudi de la farga medieval de Fabregada*.

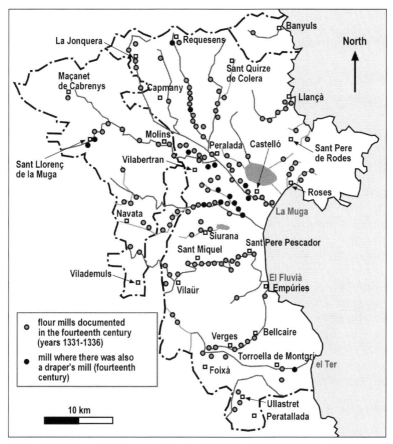

Figure 60. Mills of Empordà. In the fourteenth century there were 152 mills in the county of Empúries and the viscounty of Rocabertí. Source: Gironella, 'La mòlta de cereals i el batanatge de teixits al comtat d'Empúries', pp. 89, 253.

Visigothic periods. The highest point came in AD 600. It has been confirmed that this pollution came from mining operations located in the region of Ribagorça and perhaps also in the *comarca* of Val d'Aran.[35] Almost no written documents from the sixth and seventh centuries have been discovered, but nevertheless, fieldwork data indicates intensive activity.

These activities related to ironworking continued throughout the Middle Ages and we find them from one end of the Pyrenees to the other. In 2017, Catherine Verna published a study on the importance of metallurgical activities in the town of Arles (Fr. Arles-sur-Tech), in the region of Vallespir, in the fourteenth and fifteenth centuries.[36] The data obtained from the documentation

---

35 Esteban, 'El predominio de la acción antrópica', p. 149.
36 Verna, *L'industrie au village. Essai de micro-histoire*.

252   CHAPTER 11

enables a reconstruction of the people who worked there, their origins, and of the large amount of money that facilitated the remarkable businesses that were run there, even in this mountain territory.

Fabregada (Sant Esteve de la Sarga, Pallars Jussà)

In Fabregada, an excavation led by Marta Sancho found an eleventh-century forge.[37] This allowed us to know what the building was like, and where the oven, the bellows, the mallet (*mall* or *martinet* in Catalan) and the pond were. To fully understand the location of this forge, we need to know about its surroundings: the village and, above all, the land where ore was extracted from. Although the amount of ore extracted was low, its quality was high and it could be obtained in the open. In addition, in Fabregada, a place located in the woodlands of the Montsec range, coal was probably easily available, an essential element for operating the forge.

In recent years, other studies have been done on ironworks. Between the ninth and thirteenth centuries, Marta Sancho has already documented quite a few other places in Catalonia where iron was worked.[38] Véronique Izard has published her research work on the exploitation of iron in the northern Catalan *comarques* of Conflent, Vallespir, and Roussillon in the fourteenth century.[39] She points out the discovery of many so-called *molines de fer* (iron mills), which could be considered forges. She also notes that sometimes when a new forge was built, a community of workers with their families moved in. This must have generated hostility from the local communities. Thus, in 1330, the inhabitants of Prats de Molló (Vallespir), defending their interests, confronted the owners of *molines de fer* (forges) and also *molins serradors* (sawmills for sawing wood).[40]

In addition, Catalonia possessed mines where other metals were also obtained. Several documents from the twelfth century refer to iron and silver mines. In a book of accounts from 1151, it was indicated that there was a *menera de ferro* (an iron mine) in Cornellà de Conflent and *meneras argenti et ferri* in Escaró, also in Conflent.[41] In a document from 1227, there are references to possible *menis de ferro et argento* in Vallferrera (Pallars Sobirà).[42] In relation to the *comarca* of Priorat, in the south of Catalonia, a study has recently been carried out on the production of silver in *crosos* (i.e., holes made on the ground, as opposed to mines). This exploitation from the fourteenth

---

37 Sancho, *Ipsa Fabricata. Estudi de la farga medieval de Fabregada*.

38 Sancho, *Homes, fargues, ferro i foc*.

39 Izard, 'Cartographie successive des entreprises métallurgiques dans les Pyrénées nord-catalanes'; Izard, 'La "révolution industrielle" du xive siècle'.

40 Izard, 'La "révolution industrielle" du xive siècle', p. 60.

41 *Fiscal Accounts of Catalonia under the Early Count-Kings (1151–1213)*, ed. by Bisson, vol. II, pp. 20–21.

42 Oliver, 'Los paisajes del feudalismo', p. 260.

century, owned by Pere, count of Prades, has been studied.[43] These studies on mining can be related to others carried out, for example, in the Occitan lands, Alsace, or England.[44]

Other Rural Constructions

On the edges of some fields, we find evidence of constructions intended for transformation processes in relation to agricultural activities. These are constructions made in the Middle Ages and sometimes over the centuries. First, we can mention the vessels (Cat. *tines*) for grapes. Some may be dated to the high Middle Ages. In the municipality of Viver i Serrateix (Berguedà), on top of a rock, there are several vessels, which occupy the same space where tombs had been dug in the early Middle Ages.[45] These vessels are cylindrical tanks, with a depth of several metres. At the bottom was a hole through which the liquid could come out. Next to it, there would be a shallower container.[46] Vessels excavated in the rock have been found in several counties in central Catalonia and also further west, specifically in the regions of La Noguera or Pallars Jussà.[47]

Still, in relation to the production of wine, we can mention the preserved evidence of press or winepress (Cat. *trull*) bottoms. On the surface of a rock, quite flat, there is a recess of a few centimetres, sometimes of a circular or rectangular shape. Nearby, on the same rock, there are several holes for supporting the beams that supported the arm at the end of which was the counterweight, which allowed the grapes to be pressed. These have been found in several places.[48] They probably correspond to the winepresses (*torcularia*) recorded in many documents from the Carolingian period. We even see these presses depicted in iconographic sources from around 1000.

Kilns were also common in the medieval landscape. Mention should be made of the Casa-en-Ponç ceramic kilns, located near the city of Berga and dating from the late twelfth and thirteenth centuries. This was probably the first medieval site excavated in Catalonia (the excavations took place in 1959). Other sites, with a similar date have been studied, specifically in Cabrera d'Anoia.[49] Grey pottery was baked in these ovens. The pottery produced in Casa-en-Ponç must have been sold in the market of Berga, where it probably

---

43 Martínez-Elcacho, *Les argenteres de Falset (1342–1358)*.

44 Bailly-Maître, 'Paysages miniers médiévaux'; Bohly, 'Une mine de plomb au temps des châteaux forts'; Rippon and others, *Mining in a Medieval Landscape*.

45 Bolòs and Fàbregues, 'Sepultures excavades a la roca a les rodalies de Serrateix', pp. 156–60.

46 Roma, *Patrimoni existencial de la Catalunya rural*, p. 39.

47 Fité and Bertran, 'Una explotació vitivinícola altomedieval a Flix (la Noguera)'.

48 Roma, *Patrimoni existencial de la Catalunya rural*, pp. 47–53; Riu, *L'arqueologia medieval a Catalunya*, p. 103.

49 Travé, 'Producció i distribució d'una terrisseria medieval'.

254 CHAPTER 11

was bought by people from all over the *comarca*. In the medieval period, there must also have been lime and gypsum kilns, which were well documented in the late Middle Ages. Also, the toponymy reflects the existence of pitch kilns.[50]

Coal was also obtained during the Middle Ages. Some place names mentioned in documents from the Carolingian period bear witness to its existence (e.g., *Carboniles*, Carbonills, documented in 878).[51] Also, some documents from the high Middle Ages mention it. Charcoal piles were common landscape features until the last century. They have been studied in a systematic way in the Bosc de Virós (in Vallferrera, Pallars Sobirà), and they are mainly modern, although some of them belong to the fifteenth century or even to a much earlier era.[52]

Finally, it is worth noting the existence of ice wells. They must be connected with the climatic cooling experienced towards the end of the Middle Ages, as Chapter 12 explains, as well as possibly dating to the modern era. These are also probably related to new habits which emanated principally from urban environments in the sixteenth and seventeenth centuries.[53]

Salt

In the Middle Ages, salt was very important, especially for meat and fish preservation. Salt could be obtained from saltwater sources, such as those found in Gerri de la Sal, with salt beds where water coming from its springs was left to evaporate, and the resulting salt deposits could then be collected. In the Carolingian period, there are references to *eres* (*area*), *ipsas Murrarias* (place with brine), and *salectis*.[54] In the region of La Llitera, salt was obtained from other sources (towards Peralta de la Sal, Calassanç, or Jusseu). There is a very interesting document, written in 987, with references to salt beds in Aguilaniu (or Aguinaliu) and Jusseu, situated in an area where, in the late tenth century, despite being under Muslim rule, Christian communities lived.[55]

---

50 In modern times, pitch kilns (*pegueres*) were made up of three constructions: the well (*pou*), consisting of a cylindrical shape and a false dome, through which the resinous pine branches (*teia*) were inserted; the so-called pot (*olla*), where the tar was collected, and the *pastera*, where the pitch accumulated. Ferrer, *Eines i feines de pagès*, p. 93.

51 *Catalunya carolíngia, vol. II: Els diplomes carolingis a Catalunya*, ed. by Ramon d'Abadal, p. 35.

52 Most of these charcoal piles (Cat. *carboneres*) were made in the period between 1660 and 1950, although remains of coal from the Roman period and the late Middle Ages can also be found. Pèlachs, 'Els estudis del paisatge a Catalunya des de la Geografia', p. 182; Pèlachs and others, 'Changes in Pyrenean woodlands as a result of the intensity of human exploitation'. See too: Ferrer, *Eines i feines de pagès*, pp. 86–91.

53 Roma, *Patrimoni existencial de la Catalunya rural*, pp. 79–89. They have been studied mainly in relation to the Montseny mountain, although we also find them in other regions of Catalonia, Mallorca and the Valencian Country.

54 *Catalunya carolíngia, vol. III: Els comtats de Pallars i Ribagorça*, ed. by Abadal, docs. 16, 160, 200.

55 *Catalunya carolíngia, vol. III: Els comtats de Pallars i Ribagorça*, ed. by Abadal, doc. 270;

THE IMPORTANCE OF MILLS, IRON, AND SALT   255

Salt could also be obtained in mines, such as those in Cardona. It should be noted that places with salt reserves were very attractive to lay or ecclesiastical lords. While in Gerri there was an important Benedictine monastery, in Cardona a collegiate church was built, and its castle housed a family of viscounts. The so-called 'Cardona roads', even before 1000, allowed the passage of animals loaded with salt bags. Similar cases were also found in France and England.[56]

Finally, sea salt was also gathered. Documents from Roussillon from before 1000 already mention the existence of salt marshes in lakes close to the coast.[57] Later documents confirm the use and marketing of salt off the coast of Roussillon throughout the Middle Ages.[58] Sea salt was also obtained in Empordà and the Ebro delta.[59] In the late Middle Ages, there were salt beds in the municipalities of Tortosa (Baix Ebre) and Amposta. The so-called Vilafamés salt beds, located in the delta, in front of the town of Amposta (Montsià), have been thoroughly studied, thanks to documents from the fourteenth and fifteenth centuries.[60]

Conclusions

Mills were certainly the focus of attraction for many people. However, gradually fewer of them were preserved properly. When, in 1983, we published the book *Els molins fariners* (The flour mills), we were lucky enough to visit a fully operational mill where a miller showed us all of its parts and details.[61] This made us aware of the importance of the *ferramenta*, the valuable iron objects mentioned in medieval documents. That early study also allowed us to see why, even at the beginning of the twentieth century, in areas of scattered settlements, groups of farmsteads chose one of the mills along the course of a river, which sometimes was not the nearest. To us, this reality accounted for similar cases from the high Middle Ages, when the peasant of a farmhouse would choose a mill depending on his relationship with his lord.[62]

Then, the mills of the Merlès stream were studied, which allowed us to understand the constructions from around 1000. Other research has also been undertaken, such as Sylvie Caucanas's study of Roussillon mills, or archival

---

Col·lecció diplomàtica de l'Arxiu Capitular de Lleida. Segona part: Documents de les seus episcopals de Roda i de Lleida (anys 586–1143), ed. by Bolòs, doc. 10.

56 Gendron, *La toponymie des voies romaines et médiévales*, p. 92; Hooke, *The Anglo-Saxon Landscape. The kingdom of the Hwicce*, pp. 122–26. In relation to the importance of salt in England, also: Rowley, *Landscapes of the Norman conquest*, pp. 24–26.

57 Bolòs and Hurtado, *Atles dels comtats de Rosselló, Conflent, Vallespir i Fenollet (759–991)*, p. 64.

58 Tréton, 'Sel et salines en Roussillon au Moyen Âge'.

59 Farías, *El mas i la vila a la Catalunya medieval*, pp. 274–75.

60 Pitarch, *Les salines del delta de l'Ebre a l'edat mitjana*.

61 Bolòs and Nuet, *Els molins fariners*.

62 Bolòs, *El mas, el pagès i el senyor*, pp. 175–79.

research carried out by Josep M. Gironella on Empordà, or that by Francesc Roma on Collsacabra (Osona).[63] A few mills have also been restored and turned into museum spaces as at Montblanc (Fig. 59).

As regards settlements, in the preceding chapters, we have made a distinction, concerning Old Catalonia, between the transitional period that extended throughout the early medieval period (sixth and seventh centuries), the Carolingian stage (eighth–tenth centuries), the high Middle Ages, and the late medieval crisis (after 1348), which gave rise to the so-called modern age. In studying mills, we need to distinguish between the early Visigothic period, unfortunately poorly documented, the ninth and tenth centuries, in which there was a great construction boom in the mill sector, and, finally, the stage of intense monopolization in the construction of mills by feudal lords. There is a close link between the type of society, the number of hydraulic mills built, and their characteristics. Finally, it should be said that, although we believe in its importance, we do not know the actual impact of the Islamic period — less perceptible in Old Catalonia, more prolonged in New Catalonia — on mills. In other words, what does the place name Rifà (in the Vallès Oriental) tell us about the mills of the Islamic era? Or how were the mills from before the conquest of Lleida (Segrià) organized along the canal that brought water to this city and its *hortes*? Or how did these tank mills become widespread in the twelfth century throughout Catalonia?

With respect to forges, we should note the innovative research by Véronique Izard, especially on the Conflent *comarca*, or the excavations carried out by Marta Sancho in Fabregada, Pallars Jussà. Certainly, these medieval forges were a precedent for the great forges that spread across the Pyrenees in the modern era (especially in the seventeenth and eighteenth centuries). Finally, concerning salt and salt beds, the impact of salt extraction activities throughout the Middle Ages demonstrates not only the economic value of this activity but also the importance of communications that allowed its circulation everywhere.

---

63 Caucanas, *Moulins et irrigation en Roussillon du IXe au XVe siècle*; Gironella, *Els molins i les salines de Castelló d'Empúries al segle XIV*; Gironella, 'La mòlta de cereals i el batanatge de teixits al comtat d'Empúries i al vescomtat de Rocabertí; Gironella, *Els molins empordanesos baixmedievals*; Roma, *Molins del Collsacabra. Història i inventari*.

CHAPTER 12

Woodland and Pastureland

Changes in Vegetation and Environment

Introduction

Fields, pastures, and forests are fundamental parts of the landscape. Highly sensitive to changes caused by the people who use them, they also reflect changes in the environment and the climate. In this chapter, we will see the alterations of the layers of vegetation over the centuries in various places in Catalonia, especially those where pollen analyses have been carried out. We can see how complex this situation is. Change can be triggered by the actions of the people who live in a particular location or region; it can also be brought about by climate change or both. We will see surprising scholarly contributions that radically alter our traditional view of the landscape and the population that existed in some places. We will assess the importance of livestock throughout the Middle Ages, during the centuries of the great transhumance movements of herds, for example, those undertaken by the Cistercian monasteries, and also what was happening in the early Middle Ages. Finally, we look at the great climate changes: from around the sixth century, from 800, and in the fourteenth century. This is a topic of particular interest, given current climate change.

What Do We Know About the Plant Landscape?

Studying the historical landscape requires the use of various information sources, from written documents to pollen analysis, archaeological excavations, and toponymy. Pollen analysis makes it possible to clarify, for example, the great transformations of the early Middle Ages (a period for which we have very few written documents) and better understand the changes that took place around 1000.

For some years now, pollen analysis has been commonplace in historical landscape studies. It must always be accompanied by numerous ^{14}C dates that allow the major landscape changes to be dated and, as a result, enable us to relate them to the major historical stages. As will be seen in the coming paragraphs, concerning Catalonia, significant studies have been conducted by Santiago Riera, Francesc Burjachs, Andrés Currás, Ana Ejarque, and Didier Galop (Fig. 61).[1]

---

1   Riera, 'Natural Resources, Land uses and Landscape Shaping'; Burjachs, 'Paisatges i climes medievals de la façana ibèrica nord-occidental'; Currás, 'Estudio sobre la evolución de

The latter is the author of *La forêt, l'homme et le troupeau dans les Pyrénées* (The forest, man, and the herd in the Pyrenees), in which the author not only studies the landscape changes in the Catalan region of Cerdanya but also those that occurred in many areas on the northern side of the Pyrenees.[2] A shift in the focus of studies on the past landscape is reflected in a recent book on the forest during the Middle Ages, most notably in one of its chapters by Frédéric Guibal on the history of Mediterranean forests.[3] The book by Aline Durand on the medieval landscapes of Languedoc, which uses not only written documents but also anthracological work carried out through the analysis of charcoal, is also worth mentioning.[4] Finally, we must note a book that studies the forests around Toulouse and how the wood was used and the importance of its trade.[5] The forest and the use of wood and firewood was very important throughout the Middle Ages, as we will see in the next pages.

The Prominence of Mountains

Many of the previous chapters referred to the influence of mountains on the medieval landscape. As regards the counties of Old Catalonia, we have pointed out that often Carolingian documents noted a difference between mountain land and marchland (for example in relation to the county of Urgell). It has been pointed out that we can find hamlets and open villages, particularly in the Pyrenean *comarques*. In this chapter we will focus on pastures, and then Chapters 13 and 14 will look at mountain paths and valley boundaries.

Going through the mountains was dangerous both for people and beasts of burden, but they were never considered an insurmountable obstacle. However, toponyms include such place names as Llobera or Ossera, which often allude to dangerous animals like wolves or bears. In the fifteenth century, there were bears and wolves in the mountains of Alt Berguedà. Apparently, anyone who killed them would receive a reward in coins.[6] In the fourteenth century, some men from the Capcir *comarca* complained about the danger posed by wild boars and bears to the inhabitants of a village in that territory.[7] However, in the thirteenth century, shepherds who brought cattle along the

---

paisajes mediterráneos continentales en Lleida'; Ejarque, *La alta montaña pirenaica: génesis y configuración holocena de un paisaje cultural*.

2 Galop, *La forêt, l'homme et le troupeau dans les Pyrénées. 6000 ans d'histoire de l'environnement entre Garonne et Méditerranée*.

3 Bépoix and Richard, *La forêt au Moyen Âge*; Guibal, 'Les contrées méridionales', pp. 259–176.

4 Durand, *Les paysages médiévaux du Languedoc*.

5 Fabre, *Commerce et marchandisation du bois*.

6 For example, in 1495, seven wolves were killed near Bagà. For each dead wolf, the hunters received eight and a half *solidi*. Serra Vilaró, *Baronies de Pinós i Mataplana. Investigació als seus arxius*, p. 179.

7 Sabaté, 'La montagne dans la Catalogne médiévale', p. 186.

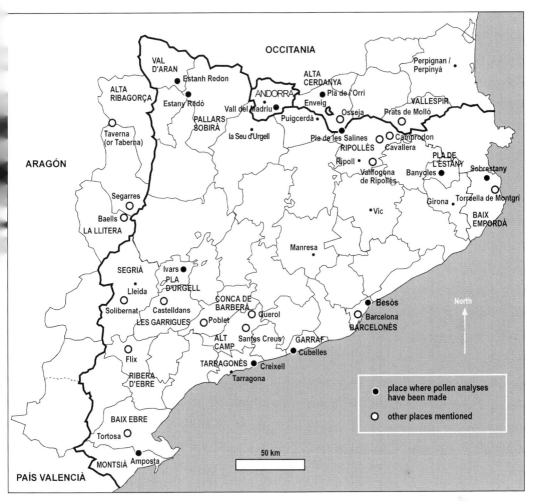

Figure 61. Map of historic Catalonia with the location of the places mentioned in this chapter.

roads crisscrossing Catalonia from north to south pointed out the absence of wolves, perhaps in comparison to the Gascon lands where they came from.[8]

In the mountains, there were woods and pastures, as we shall see later. As regards the former, it should be recalled that at the end of the Middle Ages, rivers were used to transport logs downstream, forming the so-called *rais* (rafts, in English), an uninterrupted activity until a few decades ago.[9] In the mountains, there were also forges and sawmills, as we saw in the last chapter.

---

8   Duvernoy, 'Activité pastorale et transhumance dans le domaine sud-occitan'.
9   Ferrer, 'Boscos i deveses a la Corona Catalano-aragonesa'.

260 CHAPTER 12

The need to protect forests led to the emergence of *forests* and *deveses* (land set aside for a particular purpose, from *defendre*, in medieval Catalan to defend or to prohibit), the right to afforest or use the forest, and *foresters*, men in charge of supervising it.[10] In addition, the mountain passes, or *ports*, had to be tightly controlled. Thus, in the fourteenth century, customs guards were employed; they were mainly responsible for ensuring that prohibited products did not cross the border.[11] On the other hand, hostels and sanctuaries were also built near these mountain passes, especially in the late Middle Ages.[12]

It should be noted that there were mountains and woods outside the region of the Pyrenees. There are other mountain ranges in many other places in the country, such as the Pre-Pyrenean or the Pre-Coastal Range. Thus, for example, in the north of the mountains of Prades, there was a forest that belonged to the Cistercian monastery of Poblet. This was a protected area in which felling trees was limited and collecting firewood was controlled. One fourteenth-century document specified what could be cut down and what was to be left untouched. With regard to firewood, it was established that branches of the same tree could not be cut down again unless at least four years had elapsed.[13] The Cistercians were aware of what needed to be done to avoid damaging the forest.

Pollen Analysis of the Pyrenees

A few years ago, while studying a pollen diagram from samples taken at the top of the mountain range that separates Cerdanya (Oceja district) and Ripollès (municipality of Toses), we noticed data that could be important for understanding the history of these *comarques*.[14] According to an analysis made in 1971, in Pla de les Salines (2200 metres high), around 800, there were important changes in the plant landscape. Unfortunately, at that time, not much ^{14}C dating was undertaken. However, it appears that around 600, there was a sudden increase in forest mass (50 per cent of pollens are from trees), followed by a sharp decline in the forest, which resulted in tree pollen accounting for only 6 per cent of the total by 800. In addition, around 800, there were other changes, such as the appearance, for the second time, of walnuts and an increase in cereals, as well as also the appearance of the first grapevine pollen (*Vitis*). Certainly, this must be related to the increase in temperature throughout Europe in these centuries, but also to a change in habits, perhaps linked to the arrival of clergymen and fugitives, possibly fleeing

---

10 Sabaté, 'La montagne dans la Catalogne médiévale', pp. 198–99; Ferrer, 'Boscos i deveses a la Corona Catalano-aragonesa'.

11 Sabaté, 'La montagne dans la Catalogne médiévale', p. 204.

12 Sancho and Soler, 'Balnearis, hospitals i santuaris al Pirineu català'.

13 Martínez, *El bosc de Poblet al llarg dels anys*.

14 Bolòs, 'Anàlisi pol·línica i història medieval', pp. 635–39.

WOODLAND AND PASTURELAND   **261**

from the southern plains, having committed themselves to Charlemagne's party in the last decades of the eighth century.

Subsequently, other analyses have been carried out in the same region of Cerdanya, for example in Pla de l'Orri (Enveig), at an altitude of 2150 metres. Around 1150, there was a notable decrease in forest land, possibly related to the arrival of transhumant cattle from the Cistercian monasteries of New Catalonia.[15] Earlier, these meadows of the Alta Cerdanya, between 100 BC and AD 1150, saw the arrival of pollen from vineyards, olive groves, and cereals. This enables us to date more specifically. At a nearby site, in Maurà (2220 metres high), vine pollen appears shortly before AD 900. In Maurà, in this Carolingian period, there was still a significant amount of forest land, which began to become less important around 1050 (this date coincides with the high level of charcoal as a result of forest fires) and reached its lowest point around 1300. Later, we will mention again the project studying the landscape of the mountain of Enveig, undertaken by Christine Rendu and published in 2003 (Fig. 63).[16]

In analyses carried out in *comarques* in the westernmost Catalan Pyrenees, such as Ribagorça, Pallars, or Val d'Aran, there are some differences. At Estany Redó (2114 metres above sea level, west of Espot, Pallars Sobirà), it has been noted that between AD 350 and 950, there was an increase in anthropogenic pressure. Numerous pollen grains from cereals grown in the nearby valleys of Pallars or Ribagorça appeared. Above all, however, there was an expansion in pastures and a decrease in forest land covered with mountain pine (*Pinus mugo* subsp. *uncinata*). A few kilometres away, at Estanh Redon (Val d'Aran), 2240 above sea level, a place hitherto perhaps less affected by human activities, we see a decrease in the early Middle Ages in oaks and a recovery of pine trees. Well into the high Middle Ages, between 950 and 1450, there was a significant increase in cereal pollens from the valley bottoms. In Estany Redó, pollen indicators reveal that the use of pastures was maintained, and the forest mass increased. In contrast, in Estanh Redon, located further north, the forests declined and the pastures increased.[17] In general, we do not see such intense changes as those caused by the arrival of large transhumant herds in Cerdanya, but we do see continuity throughout the early Middle Ages and a progressive strengthening of anthropogenic pressure.

The Valley of Andorra

The importance of research into the territory of Andorra deserves a separate section because while it confirms some of the aspects mentioned above, it

---

15   Galop, *La forêt, l'homme et le troupeau dans les Pyrénées*, pp. 67–71.
16   Rendu, *La montagne d'Enveig*.
17   Esteban, 'El predominio de la acción antròpica', pp. 146–47.

also shows that in the Middle Ages there could be significant differences between neighbouring valleys. In 2009, Ana Ejarque's doctoral thesis from 2009 presents the results of pollen analyses carried out in El Madriu valley and the neighbouring valleys of Perafita and Claror (Andorra). The altitude of the sampling points ranges from 2300 metres to 2531 metres. The results provide accurate information from which we will highlight the following three aspects: the growth or decline in pastures, forest production, and the arrival of crop pollen. Regarding the growth or decline in pastures, it should be noted that, after a period of stability, in the seventh through ninth centuries, there was an increase in livestock, with a significant increase in pasture areas. This is a change we find almost everywhere. And with the increase in livestock, the pressure on the landscape continued: dating to between the tenth and twelfth centuries, spores of coprophilic plants were found in El Madriu valley, and the remains of several huts, related to shepherds, were also excavated. In addition, microcarbons were discovered, suggesting the use of controlled fires to preserve or expand pastures.[18] Livestock pressure lasted until the end of the Middle Ages. In fact, in the thirteenth through fifteenth centuries, this issue was remarkable.

Regarding the forest, it should be noted that, between the fourth and seventh centuries, resin began to be exploited significantly; pitch kilns have even been found. This topic was dealt with in Chapter 11. The use of resin has been documented in several regions of Catalonia, from Ribagorça to Montseny and Montnegre (Vallès Oriental).[19] The place name Peguera must be related to the production of this product, since it means the pitch (*pega* in Catalan).[20] In Andorra, according to the findings of pollen from El Madriu, in the fifth and sixth centuries, there was a decrease in oaks, alders (*Alnus*), hazelnuts (*Corylus*), beeches (*Fagus*), firs (*Abies*), and birches (*Betula*).[21] From the ninth century and especially the tenth century, as pastures expanded, a decline in the number of pines occurred and, simultaneously, there was an increase in junipers (*Juniperus*), which spread across deforested areas. At the outset of the high Middle Ages, in some areas of El Madriu valley, the regeneration of the forest was no longer possible. At low altitudes, elms (*Ulmus*), beech trees, and lindens (*Tilia*) even disappeared, and there were virtually no firs, alders, or hazelnuts.[22]

---

18 Ejarque, 'Génesis y configuración microregional de un paisaje cultural de alta montaña', p. 283; Ejarque, *La alta montaña pirenaica*.

19 Ferrer, *Eines i feines de pagès*, pp. 91–93.

20 A document from 962, there is a written record of the *Peguera castrum*, located in the Berguedà, at an altitude of 1700 metres. 'Apèndix documental', ed. by Bolòs, doc. 18, p. 186.

21 Ejarque, 'Génesis y configuración microregional de un paisaje cultural de alta montaña', p. 274.

22 Ejarque, 'Génesis y configuración microregional de un paisaje cultural de alta montaña', p. 288.

WOODLAND AND PASTURELAND 263

Figure 62. Pollen analysis of Banyoles (Pla de l'Estany). Transformations took place throughout the Middle Ages in relation to grazing, cereals, forests, and also reedmace (*Typha-Sparganium*) that grew next to the lake. Source: Burjachs and others, 'Palinología holocénica y desertización', p. 381.

As for cereals, as in other Pyrenean lands, in the fifth and sixth centuries, there was an increase in rye pollen (*Secale*), which must have come from the lower areas of nearby valleys.[23] At the time, wine was produced on the hill where the Roc d'Enclar fortification was located at an altitude of 1250 metres.[24] Likewise, by the Carolingian era, in the ninth and tenth centuries, we find a growth in the production of cereals, especially rye. After 1000, between the eleventh and fourteenth centuries, in the valley of El Madriu, there is evidence of pollen of vines (*Vitis*), hemp (*Cannabis*), olive trees (*Olea*), walnuts (*Juglans*), and chestnut trees (*Castanea*). It has been noted that in some places in the valley of Andorra, in the thirteenth century, agricultural activities existed in areas above 1700 metres high.[25]

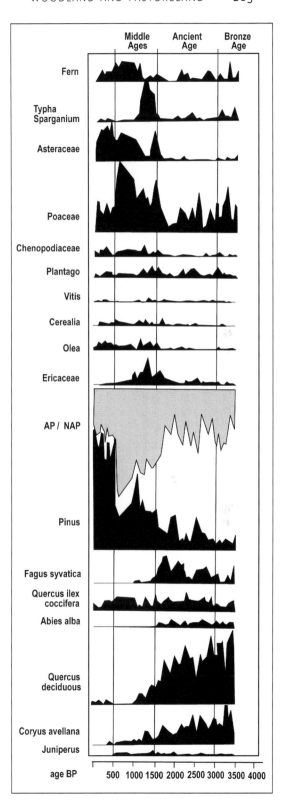

---

23 Ejarque, 'Génesis y configuración microregional de un paisaje cultural de alta montaña', p. 274.
24 Solé, 'L'explotació del baix Imperi (segle IV)', pp. 92–97.
25 Vela, 'Andorra entre els segles XII-XV', p. 148.

264   CHAPTER 12

Around Banyoles

Banyoles (Pla de l'Estany) is a town located between the plains of the Empordà and Girona and the most mountainous and humid lands of La Garrotxa. In Banyoles, at an altitude of only about 170 m, there is a large lake, next to which a Benedictine monastery was built before 822. In 1997, pollen analyses provided valuable data on the history of this place that allowed clarification of many aspects left unmentioned in written documents.[26]

As for the forest, between 500 and 1500, the medieval millennium, there was a sharp decline in the number of trees, which can be related to a gradual increase in the population and also to the widespread dispersal of inhabited places (Fig. 62). According to the analysis, there were other significant changes as well. First, there was an increase in pines, which became very numerous around 1000, a warm era in most parts of Europe. Surprisingly, fir pollen stopped spreading in Banyoles around 500, and beech pollen nearly vanished; these findings are consistent with a warm period, around 1000, but are incomprehensible in such a cold year such as 500. One can only assume that this was caused by human activity. As for common oaks, which had formerly been dominant and were found chiefly in cold places, their number fell sharply after 500, and almost disappeared around 1000; but on the contrary, evergreen oaks remained stable. All these events point to intense anthropogenic pressure throughout the Middle Ages, certainly much more intense than in the Roman period. Such pressure had already intensified even before the arrival of the Benedictine monks in the ninth century. The theory that monks settled in an abandoned place, as written documents can sometimes lead us to believe, seems to be disproved.

According to data obtained from the pollen analyses at Banyoles, there was an increase in livestock activity during the medieval period, as we can see almost everywhere. Throughout the early Middle Ages, there was a marked increase in plantain (*Plantago*) and *Poaceae* (evidence of an increase in cattle). The number of pollen grains from *Chenopodiaceae* and *Asteraceae* also grew. An expansion of *Ericaceae* during the early Middle Ages also reflects the marked degradation of forest lands, perhaps because the space dedicated to livestock expanded.

In the early medieval period, other important changes occurred. The number of cereal pollens increased, earlier than 800 (i.e., when the monastery was created), but around 500. The same phenomenon occurred with olive trees and vineyards. There was more pollen from *Vitis* in the early Middle Ages than after 1000. Finally, between the sixth and tenth centuries, there was a growth in reedmace (*Typha-Sparganium*), a plant that used to grow on the shores of the lake. This may be related to the use of this plant to make baskets, for example, or perhaps, to a sharp increase in wetlands, which disappeared

---

26 Burjachs and others, 'Palinología holocénica y desertización en el Mediterráneo occidental'.

precisely with the arrival of the Benedictine monks, who created drainage channels from the lake, and also the town of Banyoles was constructed, as we saw in Chapter 7.

To the South of Empúries

Pollen analyses carried out in Sobrestany, in the municipality of Torroella de Montgrí (Baix Empordà), allow us to perceive a slightly different situation.[27] We can differentiate the Visigothic from the Carolingian eras and the high Middle Ages. During the Visigothic period, there was a lot of deforestation, with a slight increase in agriculture and a significant growth in pastures. Evergreen oaks (*Quercus ilex*), which had been important throughout the Roman period, almost disappeared. Only the pines (*Pinus*) grew as the Carolingian era approached, which is commonly believed to have been warmer. There was, on the other hand, an increase in *Ericaceae*, especially *Calluna*, which reflects an increase in scrub. There was also some increase in *Cyperaceae* and *Poaceae* pollens. These plants, particularly plantain (*Plantago*), show the relevance of pastures and livestock. In general, too, the Visigothic period saw a slight increase in cereals and vines. Interestingly, after 500, the number of olive trees rose significantly.[28] We are unsure whether the changes in land ownership were exceptionally consequential before or after the fall of the Roman Empire, but still, we do see that the changes in the plant landscape were remarkable, indicating something far from a depopulated country but reflecting rather a pronounced increase in agricultural and especially livestock activities.

Interestingly, around the tenth century, the number of evergreen oaks, common oaks, and cork oaks (*Quercus suber*) increased. Overall, tree pollen rose significantly from this point onwards and did not decrease until later, as the twelfth and thirteenth centuries approached.[29] In these centuries, the impact of population growth is already noticeable. Only cork oaks and especially pines did not decline during the high Middle Ages. As for cultivated plants, the number of olive trees increased from the Carolingian period, as did the amount of pollen from vineyards and cereals.

---

27 Parra and others, 'Análisis palinológico y radiométrico del sondeo Sobrestany', pp. 38–39; Burjachs, 'Paisatges i climes medievals de la façana ibèrica nord-occidental', p. 235.

28 Burjachs, 'Paisatges i climes medievals de la façana ibèrica nord-occidental', p. 235.

29 Burjachs, 'Paisatges i climes medievals de la façana ibèrica nord-occidental', p. 235.

266   CHAPTER 12

The Lands of the River Besòs
and the Plain of Barcelona

The publication of a study on the pollen of ancient and medieval times around Barcelona has changed our views on the history of the plant landscape and the main economic activities of the early medieval period. A paper by Santiago Riera shows that for the coastal plains, fires, which occurred frequently in the fifth and sixth centuries AD, contributed to the expansion of deforested areas in the context of a relative expansion of agricultural activities.[30] Nevertheless, the decline in forest land was not linked to the growth of crops, but rather to the expansion of pastures in lands close to the sea. This phenomenon was also found in the region of Empordà. It was not until the second half of the eleventh century that a phase of clearing linked to a stage of agricultural expansion started around the city of Barcelona.[31]

On the other hand, this type of research has shown that in the fifth and sixth centuries, there was a stage of destabilization of the mountain slopes, for example, those in the north of the Barcelona plain, in the Coastal Range.[32] In many places, there was significant erosion, which led to the formation and consolidation of deltas, such as the delta of the river Llobregat.[33] Recent studies have consolidated the chronology of the different stages of the formation process of the Llobregat delta (Baix Llobregat), which makes it clear that its main formation process occurred during the early Middle Ages.[34]

In the transition between the ancient and medieval periods, there must have been an era of heavy rains and deforestation work which resulted in an increase in grazing land. The effects of erosion during the transition years between the Roman era and the Middle Ages are well known in northern Italy. The great floods that took place also left their traces, for example, those in 589.[35] This was not, however, the only rainy period during the Middle Ages. Although far from the era under analysis, in the last centuries of the Middle Ages, there was also an increase in rainfall, which caused severe flooding throughout Catalonia. This was the case in the Empordà and Roussillon. These floods often altered the course of rivers flowing through these plains.[36]

---

30   Riera, 'Natural Resources, Land Uses and Landscape Shaping in the Iberian Peninsula', p. 15. We must keep in mind that it has been stated that 'Romans and others cut trees but did not generally destroy woodlands, even in central Italy.' (Hoffmann, *An Environmental History of Medieval Europe*, p. 37).

31   Riera, 'Natural resources, land uses and landscape shaping in the Iberian Peninsula'.

32   Riera and Palet, 'Aportaciones de la Palinología a la historia del paisaje mediterráneo'; Riera and Palet, 'Una aproximación multidisciplinar a la historia del paisaje mediterráneo'.

33   Palet and others, 'Centuriación del territorio y modelación del paisaje en los llanos litorales de *Barcino*', p. 125.

34   Ferret, 'La Formació del Delta del Llobregat'; Esteban and others, 'El context deltaic: situació, origen geològic i història del poblament humà', p. 32.

35   Brogiolo and Chavarria, *Archeologia postclassica*, pp. 55–63.

36   Passarrius and others, *Vilarnau: un village du Moyen Âge en Roussillon*, pp. 289–92.

The Lands of Baix Penedès and Tarragonès

According to pollen analyses undertaken in Creixell, near Tarragona, there was a similar situation to that found in the lands near the city of Barcelona and in the Empordà. As early as the end of the Roman era, around the third century, there was a decline in cereals and olive trees and an increase in plants that reflected growth in livestock activities. This was a cold time and, near Tarragona, even pollen from firs and beeches was found (perhaps from the mountains of Prades). In the fifth century, there was still fir and chestnut pollen. During this century, the importance of livestock prevailed, and the amount of cereal and olive pollen did not decrease. On the other hand, in the eighth century, the cultivation of olive trees declined, but the pollen grains of cereals did not change. We then enter a warmer period, which led to the disappearance of firs, beech trees, and chestnuts after 1000.[37] Also, as concerns tree pollen, there was a clear increase in pine trees and a slight decrease in holm oaks. The same phenomenon applies to other coastal counties. In addition, one significant discovery found that during this time microcarbon levels increased remarkably, a clear sign of forest fires. Likewise, the number of plantain pollens (*Plantago*) increased gradually, which is linked to an increase in livestock, which must have been predominant, for example, in the half-flooded areas of the coast.[38] The increase in livestock must also have led to the consolidation of drovers' roads (*carrerades*), which may even have been drawn on maps, as we will discuss in Chapter 13.

These results are confirmed by pollen analyses carried out in Cubelles (Garraf), where between the third and the seventh or eighth centuries, there was an increase in forests, and also, in certain areas, crops, and, as almost everywhere, livestock. Likewise, in the seventh and eighth centuries, there were numerous fires, while vineyards, olive trees, and cereals diminished or almost disappeared, and, for example, plantains were maintained, reflecting the existence of pastures for livestock. After 1000, the cultivation of olive trees, vineyards, and cereals was restored. The conquest of these lands by the counts of Barcelona took place in the tenth and eleventh centuries. At this time there were seasonal coastal marshes where cattle could graze.[39] As for fires, it is difficult to know whether they should be related to the expansion of livestock, or the military campaigns launched between the eighth and tenth centuries. As for tree pollen, as in Empordà, there was after 1000 a remarkable increase in pine forests (*Pinus*) and a progressive decline in holm oaks and common oaks.[40]

---

37 Burjachs, 'Paisatges i climes medievals de la façana ibèrica nord-occidental' 2003: 233; Burjachs and Schulte, 'El paisatge vegetal del Penedès entre la Prehistòria i el Món Antic'.

38 Riera, 'Natural Resources, Land Uses and Landscape Shaping in the Iberian Peninsula', p. 16.

39 Esteban and others, 'Transformacions del paisatge i ramaderia a la costa catalana del Penedès i Garraf', p. 651.

40 Burjachs, 'Paisatges i climes medievals de la façana ibèrica nord-occidental', p. 238.

The Plain of Urgell

In 2012, an important doctoral thesis on continental Mediterranean landscapes was completed.[41] One of the excavation sites where pollen samples were extracted was the lake of Ivars, located about twenty-five kilometres east of Lleida. This lake, which temporarily dried up for a few decades in the twentieth century, is in the middle of the plain of Urgell, called Mascançà in the medieval period. The study has a broad chronological scope. However, the upper centimetres of the samples analysed allow us to gain knowledge of the plant landscape that existed in this place in the Middle Ages. We see the importance of the forest, crops, and pastures over the centuries. From 300 to 800, there was a loss of forest land: a decrease in the number of pine trees and, even more, in the number of evergreen oak pollens (*Quercus ilex*). This happened during the Visigothic period. Then came a stage of maintenance of the number of tree pollens with an extension of the pine groves towards the eleventh century; by 713–719, Islamic rule had begun. This study also states that in the early Middle Ages there were some birch trees (*Betula*), alders (*Alnus*), and hazelnut trees (*Corylus*), possibly near the lake. Their importance has diminished over time. This region was not conquered by the Christian counts until the twelfth century.

As for crops, since the end of the Roman era, there has been a certain increase in the production of cereals; in general, there has been an intensification in the number of cultivated species. There were no vineyards, but it was possible to find olive trees, which became more and more numerous as we approach the end of the Middle Ages. As for pastures, especially important in these lands, we find a certain continuity in the number of pollens that reflect cattle activity, like plantain (*Plantago lanceolata*), which over the early Middle Ages increased by 5 per cent.

For Lake Ivars, Currás differentiates between two stages, which roughly coincide with the early and high Middle Ages.[42] One of the distinguishing features of the former, i.e., before 1000, is that it shows numerous microcarbons. These fires were dated to around 700, the time of the Arab-Berber conquest, around 900, and about 1000. Perhaps the latter should be related to Christian armed campaigns (or perhaps to an expedition of Hungarians, documented in the summer of 942).[43]

It has been pointed out that, according to pollen analyses, the plain of Lleida saw a decline in agricultural activities in the eleventh century, while, on the other hand, in the twelfth and thirteenth centuries after the Christian conquest, these activities were resumed. Wars and military campaigns had an impact on the landscape. In the north of the plain of Lleida, in the Montsec

---

41 Currás, 'Estudio sobre la evolución de paisajes mediterráneos continentales en Lleida'.

42 Currás, 'Estudio sobre la evolución de paisajes mediterráneos continentales en Lleida'.

43 *De quan érem o no musulmans. Textos del 713 al 1010*, ed. and trans. by Bramon, p. 302.

WOODLAND AND PASTURELAND   269

Massif, in the Carolingian period (in the eighth and ninth centuries), there was also heavy deforestation caused by fires, most probably intentional. It seems that at the same time, there was an increase in the amount of pollen related to agriculture.[44]

Montsià

The last example in this chapter refers to Amposta (Montsià), next to the Ebro delta. Throughout the early Middle Ages, there was a decline in tree pollen, but perhaps not as evident as elsewhere. In this place, the pine groves, formerly of great importance, decreased, and instead, the evergreen oak forests thrived, while the common oak forests showed a scant increase. The riparian trees initially lost the importance that later, in the Islamic period, would be recovered, until the eleventh century when they lost that importance again. Like everywhere else, in the seventh and eighth centuries, there was a sharp increase in plantain (*Plantago*) and, hence, grazing. Also, since the eighth century, there has been an increase in cereals and olive trees.[45] Interestingly, in the seventh and eighth centuries, there was a remarkable growth in *Typha-Sparganium* pollen, which, as in Banyoles, may be related to the use of this plant or to a stage of abandonment and expansion of river wetlands. It should be noted that in the high Middle Ages there was a predominance of pine pollen among tree pollens. We also find a gradual increase in cereals and olive trees. After there had been, as we have said, a strong growth of plantain and pastures, the proportion of plaintain pollen remained the same throughout the rest of the Middle Ages.

Protecting Forests

There are some documents from the Carolingian period reporting on the existence of 'forests', which were probably forest lands where only the jurisdictional lord of the territory could hunt. In Gaul, the term *forestis* was first documented in the seventh century.[46] In Catalonia, *ipsa Foreste* was recorded in 962 in Vallfogona de Ripollès.[47] In the high Middle Ages in Catalonia, numerous documents provided for the protection of forests to guarantee that they could be used to obtain coal for forges, allow pigs to graze, provide wood for the sawmills, or especially get logs long enough for building ships.

---

44 Riera, 'Natural Resources, Land Uses and Landscape Shaping in the Iberian Peninsula'.

45 Burjachs, 'Paisatges i climes medievals de la façana ibèrica nord-occidental', p. 241.

46 Chouquer, *Dominer et tenir la terre dans le haut Moyen Âge*, p. 172. As is well known, in relation to England, the Anglo-Norman invasion had an impact on the spread of royal forests. Rowley, *Landscapes of the Norman conquest*, pp. 238–45.

47 *Catalunya carolíngia, vol. IV: Els comtats d'Osona i Manresa*, ed. by Ordeig, doc. 902.

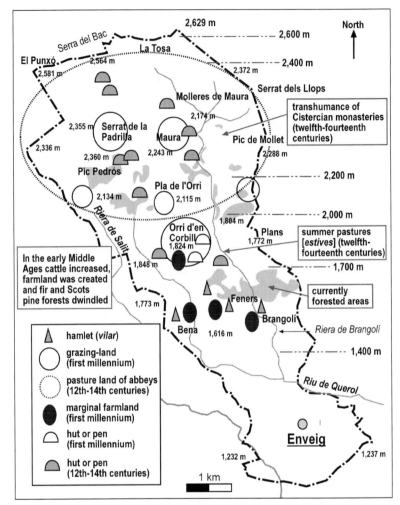

Figure 63. The pastures of Enveig (Cerdanya). In the mountain of Enveig, the changes in the use of pastures throughout the Middle Ages have been studied. Source: Rendu, *La montagne d'Enveig*.

Specifically, for example, in the regulations for Prats de Molló (Vallespir) from 1311, it was established that no one could cut down trees that could be used for making masts for boats and galleys.[48] The Catalan-Aragonese monarch, Pere III the Ceremonious, also established rules for the conservation and restoration of forests and, thus, in 1345, prohibited livestock and people from damaging forests that were recovering after logging and were in the process of regeneration. Nowadays, the same argument is firmly defended by botanists.

---

48 Izard, 'La forêt au Moyen Âge: enjeux, gestion et mutation d'un espace menacé', pp. 269–77.

The Pastures of Cerdanya

The main topic of the doctoral thesis by Christine Rendu was the study of the pastures of the municipality of Enveig, in Cerdanya (Fig. 63).[49] The study also revealed the changes this Pyrenean region experienced over the last millennia. To carry out this research, several sources were used: written documentation, archaeological excavations, and pollen analyses, already mentioned above (excavation sites of Pla de l'Orri and Maurà). It is worth noting some aspects of this research concerning the medieval period. In the early Middle Ages, livestock activities focused, as in the Roman era, on the lower part of the mountain, below 2000 metres. Some huts from the seventh through ninth centuries, located around 1900 metres, were excavated. However, since the eleventh century, huts have been set up above this altitude, and at the same time, to expand the land where livestock graze, the forests were burned. The maximum anthropogenic pressure was concentrated in the twelfth and thirteenth centuries. It should be noted that, between 1170 and 1180, the monastery of Santes Creus acquired the grazing rights for the mountains of Enveig. At this stage, the *cortals*, or huts, extended to the highest plains, even above 2200 metres. Over 10,000 sheep from the abbeys of Poblet and Santes Creus could graze there every summer.[50] From the fifteenth century onwards, sixty-metre-long enclosures have been found that served as milking parlours and shelters for storing cheese, also located in the high pasture plains. As the modern era approached, huts were consolidated and pastures and forests were increased, which must be related to changes in the way the mountainous terrain was exploited as well as a change in the society of nearby villages.[51]

Although there was mainly transhumance of sheep, one cannot rule out that, in some cases, horses grazed in the high mountain plains (*calmes*, in medieval Catalan). In Ripollès, we find written evidence of the Serra Cavallera, which in the tenth century was at the southern end of the county of Cerdanya. In Ribagorça, in the tenth century, a horse path (*via cavalar*) was mentioned.[52]

Livestock Transhumance

Twelfth-century documentation for the main Catalan Cistercian monasteries, Poblet and Santes Creus, shows that these abbeys received rights of passage and use of pastures on the *comarques* of Alt Berguedà and Cerdanya related

---

49 Rendu, *La montagne d'Enveig*.
50 Rendu, *La montagne d'Enveig*, p. 439.
51 Rendu, *La montagne d'Enveig*, p. 152.
52 Bolòs and Hurtado, *Atles dels comtats de Pallars i Ribagorça*, p. 72; Bolòs and Hurtado, *Atles dels comtats de Cerdanya i Berga*, p. 39.

to livestock transhumance.[53] In the high Middle Ages, the great Cistercian monasteries, the episcopal seats, and the military orders also must have used the transhumance routes that connected the central plains or the coastal lands of the country with the summer pastures of the Pyrenees.[54] According to documents, since the tenth century, Benedictine monasteries, such as that of Santa Maria de Lavaix (Alta Ribagorça), acquired summer pastures (*ipsas estivas*) in the nearby mountains.[55] In Languedoc, at least until the twelfth century, it was the ecclesiastical communities that organized the transhumance livestock movements.[56]

Subsequently, in the thirteenth century, there is written evidence of transhumance movements between the Pyrenees and the lands of the river Ebro and, also, of the lands to the north of Valencia from the Pyrenees (Ribagorça to Cerdanya) to Castelldans, Querol, Flix, Tortosa and also to Sant Mateu de Maestrat, Calig, or Peníscola. Some of the shepherds leading the animals were Gascons and Cathars.[57]

Let us step back in time a few centuries. There are certainly older precedents for these transhumance movements, dating back to the early Middle Ages. First, we must remember the importance of pastures in the Visigothic era, according to the results of pollen analysis and according to the laws then drafted by a kingdom of the Visigoths that extended from Portugal to the Rhône. In the next chapter, we will discuss the routes that were used for the movement of herds in the early medieval period.

In the Islamic era, which lasted only a few decades in Old Catalonia, but almost three and a half centuries in New Catalonia, the importance of livestock has been pointed out more than once. In Lleida, as mentioned above, next to many of the dry *almúnies* there was a drove road or *cabanera*. This was the case not only in the flatlands (for example in Solibernat or Vensilló) but also in *almúnies* located in La Llitera (for example in Baells) and in Baixa Ribagorça (in Segarres).[58] The frontier between Muslims and Christians could be more fluid for herds than some documents reveal with their continuous references to war and destruction. For example, at the end of the tenth century, the monastery of Taverna in Ribagorça was granted permission by the king to allow its sheep to graze on the lands of Al-Andalus.[59]

In the Carolingian period, there must have been a short-range transhumance movement within a single valley, and probably also a medium- or long-range

---

53 Riu, 'Formación de las zonas de pastos veraniegos del monasterio de Santes Creus'.

54 Ros, 'La ramaderia transhumant entre el Pirineu i el Pla de Lleida', pp. 165–91.

55 Oliver, 'Los paisajes del feudalismo', p. 242.

56 Durand, *Les paysages médiévaux du Languedoc*.

57 Duvernoy, 'Activité pastorale et transhumance dans le domaine sud-occitan', pp. 238–39.

58 Bolòs, *Col·lecció diplomàtica de l'Arxiu Capitular de Lleida*; Bolòs, *Els orígens medievals del paisatge català*, p. 87.

59 Bolòs and Hurtado, *Atles dels comtats de Pallars i Ribagorça*, p. 38; Gallon, 'Les monastères hispaniques dans les conflits entre chrétiens et musulmans', p. 241.

one. There are Catalan monasteries whose estates were distributed in such a way that leads us to infer the existence of transhumance, for example between summer pastures located in the *calmes* (highlands) of Ripollès and winter pastures in the *maresmes* (marshes) of the Empordà, specifically, the estates of the monastery of Sant Pere de Camprodon (built in the middle of the tenth century, in the county of Besalú). Visualizing the lands and rights granted to this Benedictine abbey on a map allows us to seriously consider this possibility.[60] In addition, studies carried out concerning the late medieval documentation also confirm the existence of this transhumance livestock movement between Empordà and Ripollès.[61] The seasonal movement at Camprodon Abbey could not have been an isolated case. Similar scenarios must have occurred in many other monasteries in Old Catalonia and Languedoc.

Human Activity and Climate Change

Many of the transformations we have described over the last few pages were due in part to human activity, but also to the way the climate changed during the Middle Ages. This is a subject that has been studied extensively in recent years.[62] According to recent studies, we can distinguish three major stages throughout the Middle Ages. During these stages, there were significant changes in temperatures and in rainfall, which obviously had an impact on the landscape in Catalonia and the rest of the European continent.

After the so-called Roman Climatic Optimum,[63] the decades of transition from the Roman era to the Middle Ages correspond to a first phase, which was, almost globally, colder and rainier.[64] Notable contributions have explored the reasons for this cold climate and its consequences.[65] As explained above, one of the most important consequences was severe erosion, which affected the slopes of the mountains and above all had an impact on the formation of

---

60 Bolòs and Hurtado, *Atles del comtat de Besalú (785–988)*. In fact, we find evidence of transhumance all around the Mediterranean and also in Atlantic lands, such as Wales. Hooke, 'Resource Management of Seasonal Pasture'.

61 Soldevila, 'L'élevage ovin et la transhumance en Catalogne nord-occidentale'.

62 See Hoffmann, *An Environmental History of Medieval Europe*; Aberth, *An Environmental History of the Middle Ages*; Thiébault, *Archéologie environnementale de la France*; Devroey, *La nature et le roi*; Unger, 'Introduction: Hoffmann in the Historiography of Environmental History'; Lagerås, *The Ecology of Expansion and Abandonment*. Research has also been done on the dangers caused by natural disasters (Gerrard and others ed., *Waiting for the End of the World?*) or on forests (Bépoix and Richard ed., *La forêt au Moyen Âge*) or grazing land.

63 Hoffmann, *An Environmental History of Medieval Europe*, p. 36.

64 It has been called, for example, 'Late Roman Little Ice Age' or 'Early Medieval Cold Period' (Hoffmann, *An Environmental History of Medieval Europe*, p. 67; Devroey, *La nature et le roi*, p. 45).

65 Büntgen and others, 2500 Years of European Climate Variability and Human Susceptibility'; Büntgen and others, 'Cooling and Societal Change during the Late Antique Little Ice Age'.

274 CHAPTER 12

the deltas. It probably also affected the filling-out of large plains, such as the plain of the river Po in Italy,[66] the banks of the Rhône in France, or many coombs. This has been analysed, for example, in relation to the creation of the Llobregat delta. The extent of firs, beeches, and chestnuts must have been much lower, as found, for example, in pollen analyses carried out in the Penedès. The same could apply to oaks.[67] This fact led to an increase in evergreen oaks in the interior plains, near Lleida.

A second phase centred on 1000 was warmer; this lasted from about 800 to after 1200, and is known as the Medieval Warm Period.[68] In many parts of Europe, this warming must have made it possible to work land that had not been used before.[69] In Catalonia, it caused changes in the vegetation cover and in the typology of cultivated plants. In the Pyrenees, there was an increase in cereal pollen, as we have seen, for example, in L'Estany Redó, linked to an increase in anthropogenic pressure.[70] In other nearby valleys, such as El Madriu, there was a sharp increase in grazing land between the seventh and tenth centuries.[71] Species such as beech or fir receded, while perhaps the pine gained ground, as is documented in relation to the lake of Banyoles or south of Empúries.[72] At the same time, we see that certain crops, such as vines, started spreading to altitudes where earlier it would have been very

---

66 Brogiolo and Chavarria, *Archeologia postclassica*, pp. 55–63.

67 In Languedoc (lake of Palavàs, for example), there was a sharp decline in oaks and beeches (*Fagus*) starting in the ninth century, while evergreen oaks have been maintained and pollen from olive trees (*Olea*) has increased. Guibal, 'Les contrées méridionales', p. 262.

68 Fagan, *The Great Warming*; Aberth, *An Environmental History of the Middle Ages*, p. 26; Hoffmann, *An Environmental History of Medieval Europe*, pp. 320–23. Jean-Pierre Devroey emphasizes the importance of local phenomena and the divergences of what we find in different places. However, he notes that, from 725 onwards, a stable period of solar activity and volcanic eruptions began. In addition, the eighth and ninth centuries were times of very low levels of erosion in the Rhone. Overall, it should be noted that there were differences: in the north of the Carolingian Empire there were cooler summer temperatures, while in the south they were more stable over these centuries (Devroey, *La nature et le roi*, pp. 42–43, 65, 68–69, 71–72).

69 This global warming has been considered to be one of the factors that favoured the economic growth of the early Middle Ages; it was not, however, the only reason. Leturcq and Mazel, 'Une dynamique d'expansion', p. 240.

70 Esteban, 'El predominio de la acción antròpica'.

71 Ejarque, 'Génesis y configuración microregional de un paisaje cultural de alta montaña'; Ejarque, *La alta montaña pirenaica*.

72 Burjachs and others, 'Palinología holocénica y desertización en el Mediterráneo occidental'; Parra and others, 'Análisis palinológico y radiométrico del sondeo Sobrestany', pp. 38–39; Burjachs, 'Paisatges i climes medievals de la façana ibèrica nord-occidental', p. 235. This process was widespread throughout Europe. Even in Sweden, we find that in some (not all) places, around 800, there was a decrease in the number of beeches (due to semi-deforested areas), which spread widely, from the fifteenth century. We must keep in mind the importance of human activity, which is clearly visible in countries such as Sweden, where the phases of colonization and abandonment can be clearly related to the results of pollen analysis (Lagerås, *The Ecology of Expansion and Abandonment*, pp. 222–23, 235).

difficult for them to survive. This was the case, for example, in many villages in Cerdanya, where the vineyards reached an altitude of about 1100 metres. After 1000, we also find vineyard pollen in El Madriu valley.[73] Even in the lowlands (such as Cubelles) there was an increase in olive groves, vineyards, and cereal land.[74]

The same phenomenon did not occur everywhere, which is probably due to different human activities. In some places near the coast, pastures increased, while in others there was growth in forest extent (for example in Cubelles). In general, in the Empordà or Garraf, around 1000, the pines increased, and the evergreen oaks and oaks fell.[75] The same can be said about the lands of western Catalonia, near Lleida.[76]

Finally, as we approach the end of the Middle Ages, we enter a third, very cold phase, which has been called the Little Ice Age lasting from around 1300 to the middle of the nineteenth century.[77] Certainly, the beginning coincided with the late medieval demographic crisis. Catalonia experienced a much colder period with spells of heavy rain. One of the most obvious aspects was a spate of large floods, for example in the Empordà or in Roussillon.[78] In many places, heavy rains caused the loss of crops. It has been pointed out that one of the indirect causes of the Black Death was precisely the malnutrition of the population due to these bad years, such as the so-called '*Mal any primer*' (the Bad First Year). We also notice that surprisingly in this same period, heavy flooding coexisted with extremely dry seasons.[79]

This situation in Catalonia continued throughout the following centuries: in the town of Olot, in the sixteenth century, there is written evidence that 'on Holy Saturday (March 31) which was the eve of Easter in 1579, at night, at eleven o'clock, a cold spell arrived of such severity that it killed all the grain

---

73 See also: Rama-Corredor, 'Reconstruction environnementale et climatique pendant l'optimum climatique médiéval', pp. 273–75.

74 Esteban and others, 'Transformacions del paisatge i ramaderia a la costa catalana del Penedès i Garraf'.

75 Burjachs, 'Paisatges i climes medievals de la façana ibèrica nord-occidental', p. 238.

76 Currás, 'Estudio sobre la evolución de paisajes mediterráneos continentales en Lleida'.

77 Fagan, *The Little Ice Age*; Aberth, *An Environmental History of the Middle Ages*, p. 49; Hoffmann, *An Environmental History of Medieval Europe*, pp. 323–29.

78 In 1445, 'the rivers Ter, Onyar, Güell and Galligants carried much water'; a church was flooded, a bridge was demolished, and several houses were flooded; it rained uninterruptedly for nine days (*Colección diplomàtica del condado de Besalú*, ed. by Monsalvatje, vol. XIII, doc. 1,894). A document from 1447, related to Roussillon, mentions the 'breaks' (*trencs*) caused —our literal translation from Catalan— by 'the great flood and deluge of water due to the rains' (Tréton, 'Crues et inondations dans les Pyrénées méditerranéennes', p. 226). These are just two examples. See also: Rama-Corredor, 'Reconstruction environnementale et climatique pendant l'optimum climatique médiéval', p. 281. There were also major floods in many other European countries. Hoffmann, *An Environmental History of Medieval Europe*, pp. 325–27.

79 Rama-Corredor, 'Reconstruction environnementale et climatique pendant l'optimum climatique médiéval', p. 282.

276 CHAPTER 12

and fruit on the trees, leaving walnuts looking as if they had been burned and scorched'. The document also states that the cold spread to Barcelona and western Catalonia and did not end until the spring of 1560.[80] To these other disasters must be added locust plagues and earthquakes.[81]

Conclusions

Years ago, Massimo Montanari in his book *L'alimentazione contadina nell'alto Medioevo* (Peasant nourishment in the early Middle Ages) revealed the importance of forest areas and uncultivated land in the diet of peasants from the early Middle Ages, especially in the north of Italy.[82] In Catalonia, the importance of livestock and forestry has also been demonstrated as regards hunting, obtaining wood, firewood, resinous wood, and wood to make charcoal. However, it is also clear that the Middle Ages were a time of constant struggle against the forest to create grazing land and, shortly after, increase cultivated land. Terraces, or *feixes*, with margins of dry-stone, were scattered throughout, even in places where the effort required to build them was barely offset by the potential gains. The constant destruction of forest land for household heating, making beams in the sawmills, or obtaining coal for forges made it necessary to establish protective measures for trees.

---

80 Translated from: Sala, *Dades històriques d'Olot*, pp. 75–76.

81 Regarding earthquakes, we mention that, for example, in 1428, some people of the city of Girona claimed that 'in many places in the mountains there has been an infinite number of damages with the death of many people, the loss of property and the destruction of towns and places in Catalonia'. They knew that in Puigcerdà, not only three hundred people died but, 'because the buildings are largely made of wood, the fire has destroyed the town'. The same phenomenon occurred in Camprodon because most of the houses are 'made of pine wood'. In addition, there is evidence that, in 'the town of Olot, which had been destroyed last May' by another earthquake, eighteen people died. The list of disasters is long (*Colección diplomática del condado de Besalú*, ed. by Monsalvatje, doc. 1,868; Olivera and others, *Els terratrèmols dels segles XIV i XV a Catalunya*, doc. 127). There are several studies on these and similar topics in Catalonia and the rest of Europe (Riera, 'El bisbat de Girona al primer terç del segle XV'; Gerrard and others, *Waiting for the End of the World?*). Thomas Labbé's book, *Les catastrophes naturelles*, is interesting for its research on natural disasters in the Middle Ages, which focused both on floods and earthquakes, as well as also on landslides, such as those in Andorra and in other regions of the Pyrenees throughout the Middle Ages (Planas and others, 'El substrat preromà en la toponímia relacionada amb inestabilitats de vessant').

82 Montanari, *L'alimentazione contadina nell'alto Medioevo*. We should also mention a more recent work that studies the importance of trees in Italy in the high Middle Ages. Cortonesi, *Il Medioevo degli alberi*. It should be noted that recently, using computer methods, it has been possible to make an accurate assessment, in relation to some territories, of the relationship that could exist between some human settlements and the environment that had to allow their sustainability (water, cultivated land, forests, pastures, and land with fruit trees). Citter, 'Landscapes, Settlements and Sustainability'. See also: Brogiolo, 'Some principles and methods for a stratigraphic study of historic landscapes', p. 369; Burri, 'Reflections on the concept of marginal landscape'.

Additionally, the value of livestock that all the peasant families had in their homes and also of the large herds that every year moved from the flatlands to the summer pastures in the high mountain *calmes* (highlands) is evident from medieval documents. Although written records fail to render sufficient data, it is impossible to understand the peasant and seigneurial economy without the contribution of domestic animals. For example, understanding life on the farmstead requires proper recognition, apart from agriculture, of the two remaining mainstays that complement the agricultural activities: livestock and forestry. This situation from the Middle Ages has continued into the modern period.

However, the most interesting piece of research revealed in this chapter has been the interpretation of pollen analyses conducted in recent years. This work has allowed us to learn about the early medieval period on account of the remarkable agricultural activity, more important than that in the Roman era, and especially because of the widespread and intense livestock herding activity. The data obtained, far from reflecting a decaying, depopulated, barren, and half-abandoned countryside, reveals an animated landscape, albeit with no large *villae*, but with numerous hamlets made of wood or rammed earth huts, with cereals, vineyards, and even olive trees, and numerous herds that, according to excavation results, must have consisted primarily of sheep and goats. In addition, we do not know what activity was carried out by the lords, lay or ecclesiastic, throughout the earlier medieval period.

Finally, it should be noted that the transformations of forests, fields, and pastures are related to the great climate changes that took place during the Middle Ages. This was a period of extremely cold and rainy seasons and also warmer and perhaps drier stages. This fact, as we have seen, certainly had a clear influence on the landscape, positive and at other times not. It was adversity that left more written testimonies. Especially in the late Middle Ages, many documents remind us of droughts, floods, earthquakes, plagues, etc. To these natural catastrophes must be added disasters caused by humans, such as wars. The walls of many towns remind us that they date back to the fourteenth century, the years of the war between the Catalan-Aragonese king and the monarch of the kingdom of Castile. Also, when we read about the trial of Count Hugh Roger III of Pallars, at the end of the fifteenth century, we realize how the systematic destruction of crops was a weapon of war.[83]

---

83 Bolòs, 'Un territori en temps de guerra', pp. 41–77.

CHAPTER 13

Roads and Pathways, the Network that Organizes the Landscape

Introduction

When we see a landscape, we must remember that roads are often among its oldest elements. Roads connected villages and towns but many were built before the medieval villages existed. It is also true that the route joining two points may change over the centuries. In addition, many boundaries or pieces of land use roads to demarcate their limits, organized, for example, across the way. With this in mind, we can talk about the shape of the roads (there are, for example, sunken ones), the locations they cross (e.g., through a gorge or a bridge), and the use that has been made of them (transhumance, for example). And, as said above, it is important to be aware that many medieval roads were created in relation to the network of settlements. Others, though, were set up before the Middle Ages; some have remained unaltered (except for paving) to the present. During the Middle Ages, the most important roads, as well as secondary routes, were public, as documents from the Carolingian era consistently state.

What Do We Know About How to Study Medieval Roads?

In 1989, Eric Vion published a paper in the first issue of the journal *Paysages découverts* dedicated to the study of communication routes. Through a methodological innovation, he sought to find new answers that would allow us to understand the organization of the road network. This proved to be a fruitful endeavour. Much of the methodology proposed for studying the Swiss roads has ever since been used in numerous papers published in France by Claude Marchand, Sandrine Robert, and Nicolas Verdier.[1] Vion emphasized the importance of studying not only communication routes but also analysing the entire network of roads in the territory. In this way, by focusing on a wider area, one can understand the changes in itineraries over the centuries.

In addition, as we will see over the next few pages, efforts have been made in other European countries to reconstruct the medieval road network.

---

1 Marchand, 'Réseau viaire et dessin parcellaire'; Robert and Verdier ed., *Dynamique et résilience des réseaux routiers.*

Recently, in England, there has been a notable attempt to identify the ways of the early Middle Ages in Wessex by conducting a detailed study of ten areas.[2]

Just as when studying fields we highlighted the importance of doing a long-term study on roads, it is also essential to trace their origins which often lie in the period before the early Middle Ages. The same principle applies to boundaries, another linear element of the landscape, which we will study in Chapter 14. One can safely state that most of the main roads in the early Middle Ages were created before the sixth century. Nevertheless, during the medieval period, new roads were built, others were abandoned, and still others were diverted, depending on the needs of each century. Later we will discuss as an example the Agramunt road (*camí d'Agramunt*), which will clearly show us its evolution over time.

Long-Distance Roads

Scholars of the Roman era have published several maps showing the network of main roads that connected cities across Catalonia. One of the most notable was the so-called *Via Augusta*, or, in Roussillon, the *Via Domitia*. In the early Middle Ages, most of the great Roman roads continued to be used. Often, in the Carolingian era, these roads (*viae* and *stratae*), some still stone-paved (*vias calciatas*, from vulgar Latin *calciata* [stone-paved], and referred to, in Catalan, as *calçades*), received a name of their own, which clearly distinguished them from other paths and roads. The documents allude, for example, to roads leading to the land of the Franks (*via francisca*) or of the Muslims, to the town of Cardona, or to the county of Razès (in Languedoc), or also a road of merchants crossing the Empordà (which would correspond to a section of the Via Augusta).

As for the ancient period, we can say that these main roads were only a small part of the roads crisscrossing the territory.[3] Certainly, apart these great roads, before the sixth century, many roads connected the *vici* or *villae* or delimited the centuriated plots of land or *fundi*. The *Ars Gromatica siue Geometria Gisemundi* text preserved in Ripoll, which is based on two manuscripts dating to the ninth century, differentiated between public roads, local roads, and common roads (*viae publicae, viae vicinales et viae communes*).[4] Local roads (*viae vicinales*) were managed by *magistros pagorum*, or officials of the *pagi* or countries, while the common roads (*viae communes*) served as boundaries between two properties. A map designed by Miquel Vives on the network of roads from the Roman period in Baix Llobregat and Alt Penedès reflects this reality: the map shows Via Augusta, several secondary roads, and

---

2 Langlands, *The Ancient Ways of Wessex*.
3 Soto and Carreras, 'Anàlisi de la xarxa de transport a la Catalunya romana'.
4 Andreu, 'Edició crítica, traducció i estudi de l'*Ars Gromatica sive Geometria Gisemundi*', p. 118.

ROADS AND PATHWAYS, THE NETWORK THAT ORGANIZES THE LANDSCAPE   281

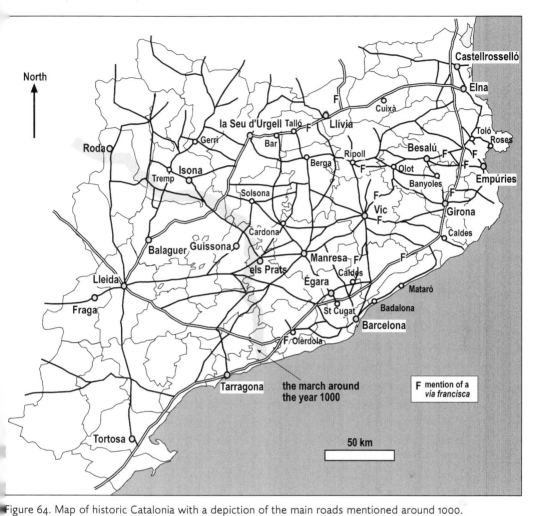

Figure 64. Map of historic Catalonia with a depiction of the main roads mentioned around 1000.

also numerous roads that coincided with the limits of the centuriation spread throughout the territory.[5]

On the other hand, even if it is more difficult to study, I believe that, in relation to the roads, we should not give up on going further back in time. I think that in the Roman era many times it was necessary to take advantage of a network of roads that already existed previously. It is certain that some of these pre-Roman roads, modified to varying degrees, have survived to the present day.

---

5   M. Vives, 'L'evolució històrica de la xarxa viària entre el Llobregat i el Foix des de l'època romana fins al tercer decenni del segle XX', map 5.1.

282   CHAPTER 13

In recent years, an effort has been made to map out the roads of the Carolingian era. The *Atles dels comtats de la Catalunya carolíngia* (Atlas of the Counties of Carolingian Catalonia) describes a county-by-county reconstruction of the main road network. Many of these roads are recorded in documents from before 1000 (Fig. 64). Lately, studies of the high Middle Ages have been conducted. For example, concerning the reign of the thirteenth-century Catalan King Jaume I (James I), I reconstructed the road network that this monarch passed along on his visits all over his kingdoms (i.e., Catalonia, Aragon, and the Kingdom of Valencia).[6]

As I mentioned, in 2007, Miquel Vives reconstructed the road network from the Roman period to the present between the rivers Llobregat and Foix; in other words, the *comarques* of Alt Penedès and Baix Llobregat. This study is interesting both because of the amount of data it provides, and the methodology used. It analyses how the Roman network was affected during the early Middle Ages and how this road network was transformed during the high Middle Ages. Research on the various historical stages is accompanied by accurate maps.

Roads Connecting Cities and Towns

There was a network of roads connecting the various main cities in the medieval period, basically, those capital cities of a county, those with a cathedral, or, in the high Middle Ages, cities hosting a market and (or) an important fair. Some of these roads are mentioned in the previous section, but in many other cases, this is not the case. Considering the organization of the network of communication roads, Vion suggests that by selecting the number of roads (*tri numérique*) meeting at a crossroads we find the importance of a settlement.[7] In making this selection, we often realize that the older and more important a population is, the greater the number of roads leading to (or leaving) it. Our main focus may be on county capitals from the Carolingian era, such as Girona, Barcelona, or Manresa, or cathedral towns, such as Elna, Vic, or La Seu d'Urgell. Whenever the city is located in the middle of a plain, as in the case of Vic, this radial network is even more evident.[8]

The same applies to other places that, for some reason, played an important role. This is the case of Cardona, a town that, because of its salt mines, was at the centre of a radial network of roads (the Cardona roads were mentioned in the documents of the Carolingian period) that led to Berga and Cerdanya,[9] Solsona and La Seu d'Urgell, and to Manresa and Barcelona; in addition, there

---

6   Bolòs, 'Els camins a Catalunya en temps de Jaume I', pp. 171–90.
7   Vion, 'L'analyse archéologique des réseaux routiers', pp. 82–83.
8   Bolòs and Hurtado, *Atles del comtat d'Osona (798–993)*, p. 44.
9   Obiols, 'El Camí Cardoner i el Camí Ramader'.

Roads and Villages

Generally, radiating from most villages is a network of roads leading to neighbouring towns. These radial networks were created according to the different settlements, whether they were villages, hamlets, or even farmsteads. From the reconstruction on a map of these local networks, Vion pointed out the interest in drawing anomalies that correspond to roads that are not integrated into the network of roads leading to settlements.[10] Checking a large number of fragments of anomalous roads led him to recognize the existence of successive phases of the formation of the road network, which made it possible to distinguish between various historical strata that have more or less left their imprint on the territory.

He also stressed that, over time, villages tended to attract all the main roads passing nearby, as we see, for example, in Catalonia, concerning the town of Santpedor (Bages).[11] Of course, in this case, when, in the eleventh century, an ecclesiastical village was created around the church of Sant Pere, there was already a much older road, which passed about 600 metres to the west.

In principle, we should think that this radial network, as mentioned above, was contemporaneous with the creation of different settlements. However, it must be borne in mind that, when studying the plot division networks first created in the Roman period, in many cases, some of these roads outside the population centres present orientations that coincide with pre-medieval plot divisions. Certainly, this raises a series of difficult questions to answer at the present moment.

In-depth studies of a territory, such as a *comarca*, are necessary, as they allow us to understand the transformations over the centuries and raise questions about irregularities and anomalies. Conducting a historical study drives us to find reasons behind the existence of territories with many roads as opposed to those with few roads, as well as explanations for the itineraries followed by communication routes. As said above, Bonales and Bailac carried out a thorough and in-depth study on the roads of Pallars Jussà which enabled them to pinpoint the differences between one place and another in terms of road network density and point out their causes.[12] Another significant aspect is being able to understand the itinerary that these roads follow, for example in mountainous lands. Jacinto Bonales points out that local roads

---

10 Vion, 'L'analyse archéologique des réseaux routiers', pp. 75–79.

11 Palet, 'Dinàmica territorial de l'antiguitat a l'edat mitjana a Catalunya'; Bolòs, *Els orígens medievals del paisatge català*, p. 401.

12 Bonales and Bailac, *Els camins històrics del Pallars Jussà*.

284 CHAPTER 13

going from village to village followed, in general, the most direct route, even when that meant overcoming steep slopes.[13] Later on in this chapter, we will look at the reasons why people going from the plains to the Pyrenees would choose to either go through a gorge or go over a mountain pass. Also, Chapter 16 points out the contributions made to the study itineraries using GIS, as this technique allows us to calculate the easiest route, the easiest way to get there. In the next few pages, we will focus our attention on specific cases that illustrate this introduction.

From La Granada to Sant Martí Sarroca (Alt Penedès)

This interesting nine-kilometre road (Fig. 65) connected two towns in the Penedès region. Both had castles built in the Middle Ages (the one in Sant Martí dates from the Carolingian period, the one in Granada from the feudal period). This road was first documented in a text written in 996.[14] It has been largely preserved and, in some sections, it is a hollow way. The road is very straight, and its orientation is far from accidental since it coincides with that of a Roman or perhaps pre-Roman orthogonal formation grid. The road is then an element of collective heritage, which has remained almost fossilized for over a thousand years.[15]

Roads of Vilanova de Raò (Roussillon)

There are several exceptional documents written in the tenth century that mention roads located in the municipality of Vilanova de Raò (Fr. Villeneuve-de-la-Raho). According to these documents, in the Carolingian period, there were roads from this villa to the Barrià lake, the villa of Pollestres, Bages, and toward Elna (Fig. 66). Roads that passed through the municipality of Vilanova and connected Vila-seca and Cornellà or Vila-seca and Elna were also mentioned.[16] This is an old landscape, where, in addition, the road to Narbonne and Les Cluses (or La Clusa) intersected with the one that, to the south of the municipality, connected Elna and the *comarca* of Conflent.[17] This municipality stretched over flat land, full of lakes and ponds, many of which dried up in the twelfth and thirteenth centuries, under the impetus of the Templar commandery of El Masdéu.[18]

Finally, it is worth alluding to the road connecting Vilanova de Raò with Bages ('via qui pergit de Villa Nova ad villa Baies'): a four-kilometre road

---

13 Bonales, 'L'estudi dels camins com a mètode d'anàlisi del paisatge històric', p. 166.

14 *Catalunya carolíngia, vol. VII: El comtat de Barcelona*, ed. by Baiges and Puig, doc. 1,351bis.

15 Bolòs, 'Història del paisatge i mapes de Caracterització del Paisatge Històric', p. 102.

16 *Catalunya carolíngia, vol. VI: Els comtats de Rosselló, Conflent, Vallespir i Fenollet*, ed. by Ponsich, docs. 228, 229.

17 Comps, 'De Roussillon en Conflent'.

18 *Diplomatari del Masdéu*, ed. by Tréton.

ROADS AND PATHWAYS, THE NETWORK THAT ORGANIZES THE LANDSCAPE 285

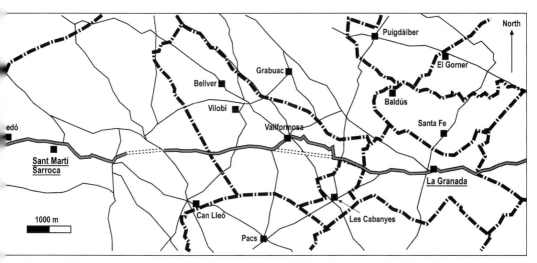

Figure 65. Road from La Granada to Sant Martí Sarroca (Alt Penedès), which is mentioned in a document from 996.

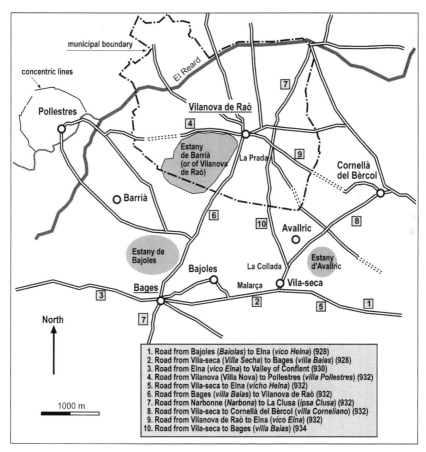

Figure 66. Paths of Vilanova de Raò (Roussillon). In an area with many lakes and remains from the Roman era, we find a network of paths documented in the Carolingian era.

286 CHAPTER 13

that coincides exactly with the orientation of the *Narbona* D centuriation (with 30 degrees deviation to the east).[19] Some of the other roads mentioned also seem to have had orientations reminiscent of pre-medieval plot division networks. I conclude that during the early Middle Ages, a network of settlements was created simultaneously with the creation of a network of roads, or rather, a consolidation of roads that joined all these settlements together. This humanized, medieval landscape was already outlined before the tenth century. Catalonia — like most countries — is a country with a long history.

The Road of Agramunt (Urgell and La Noguera)

This road is located to the west of the town of Agramunt and the north of the river Sió, with a south-east-north-west orientation. The road is then straight. Currently, despite its official name, the road does not start from the town of Agramunt and does not pass through any villages. In fact, on a closer look, we realize that its orientation coincides with that of a pre-medieval plot division network (*Ilerda G*); the same orientation coincides, for example, with the road from Castelló de Farfanya to Tornabous, and passes through Balaguer.[20] An analysis of the outline of this road reveals small deviations over the centuries. It was altered when another road was made from Butsènit (a name created in the Islamic period and probably related to the Zenata tribe, seen in Chapter 9).[21] Subsequently, the road was modified again with the creation of a radial network of roads from several towns located on the banks of the river Sió, such as Pradell or Montgai. This is probably a very old road, connecting Agramunt with Sant Llorenç de Montgai, a village located next to the river Segre.[22] In any case, this is a good example of an anomaly concerning the local road network, according to the terminology proposed by Eric Vion.[23]

Hollow Ways or Sunken Lanes

Hollow ways abound all over Europe and are very old. They may be sunken or hollow because of the wear and tear inflicted over the centuries by chariots and by the trampling of horses and people. Or maybe, in some cases, they were done in this way to avoid excessively steep slopes and level the ground beneath the track. It is also possible that, at times, they sank due to erosion caused by water or the need to delimit, on both sides, a path crossed by cattle, separating them from the fields and the former environment. Either way,

---

19 Chouquer and Comps, 'Centuriations et organisation antique de l'espace', p. 127.

20 Bolòs, 'Paisatges i transicions: canvis i continuïtats al llarg de la història', p. 91.

21 Coromines, *Onomasticon Cataloniae*, vol. III, p. 154.

22 Bolòs, *Els orígens medievals del paisatge català*, pp. 398–400.

23 Vion, 'L'analyse archéologique des réseaux routiers'.

ROADS AND PATHWAYS, THE NETWORK THAT ORGANIZES THE LANDSCAPE

many roads with these characteristics have been dated to the Roman period. In France, they have been associated with the place name *cavée*, from the Latin *cavata*.[24] Nor can we rule out that some are even older, from before the Roman era, or that some were created in the medieval period. In Catalonia, they have been found in Empordà, around Lleida, in Llitera, in Pallars, in Penedès (as explained in the previous section), in Vallès, near Girona, and in many other places.[25]

Drove Roads

To get closer to the study of drove ways, we basically have to look at maps made in the twentieth century. If we want to have an overview of the whole country, we must examine the map made by Vilà Valentí of the drove roads (*carrerades* or *cabaneres*, in Catalan) in Catalonia in the last century.[26] Surely, many contemporary transhumance roads have a long tradition, possibly dating to the Middle Ages. These roads were used to connect winter pastures with summer pastures. When studying the landscape and the organization of the territory, it is very important to know their characteristics and itineraries.

It is often necessary to relate these paths to formerly inhabited places. As we have mentioned, close to many Islamic habitats, located on rainfed land, we find drove tracks. Also, as we will discuss in the next chapter, very often the *carrerades* coincided with boundaries, or perhaps more likely, these drove paths went through these boundaries to prevent animals from trespassing and gaining access to the sown fields. The eighth book of the Visigothic *Liber iudiciorum*, written in the middle of the seventh century, had already established the penalties imposed if someone's cattle entered a field or another person's pastures.[27]

It should also be noted that, in recent years, the routes that some medieval drove roads followed have been drawn on maps; for example, roads that connected the lands of the Garraf with the plateaus of the Segarra, crossing the plain of Penedès.[28] As we have already mentioned, some roads in Old Catalonia, which made it possible to join the coastal plains and the pastures of the Pyrenees, must also have served as livestock roads. As indicated earlier, pollen analysis clearly shows that, in the early Middle Ages, livestock farming was fundamental to the economy.

---

24 Gendron, *La toponymie des voies romaines et médiévales*, p. 36.

25 Palet, 'L'organització del paisatge agrari al Penedès i les centuriacions del territori de Tàrraco', pp. 219–20; Mallorquí, *Cinquanta-cinc llegües de passos oblidats i xarrabascos*.

26 Vilà Valentí, *El món rural a Catalunya*, pp. 88–89; Bolòs, *Els orígens medievals del paisatge català*, p. 338.

27 *Llibre dels judicis. Traducció catalana moderna del* Liber iudiciorum, trans. by Bellés.

28 Palet, 'L'organització del paisatge agrari al Penedès i les centuriacions del territori de Tàrraco', p. 214.

288   CHAPTER 13

Drove roads should be studied more carefully and from a historical perspective. Despite efforts to prevent these memories from being lost, unfortunately, in many cases, they have disappeared, absorbed by fields or forests, and only a faint memory of their presence appears on old maps.

Gorges and Ridges

In Catalonia, to the south of the Pyrenees, there is a mountainous massif called the Pre-Pyrenees. This is the first mountain barrier one comes to when coming up from the south. The Pre-Pyrenees are criss-crossed by a series of rivers: from west to east, by the Éssera, Isàvena, Noguera Ribagorçana, Noguera Pallaresa, Segre, Cardener, Llobregat, and Ter, and beyond, further to the north-east, the Tec and Tet. These rivers, when cutting across the mountains, form deep gorges. This natural border became, around 800, especially in some western sectors, the southern boundary of the lands controlled by the Carolingian counts. For example, the gorge of Oliana, which was formed by the river Segre, was part of the southern boundary of the early county of Urgell with the castles of Castell-llebre (a 'castell vedre', an old castle) and Oliana, both documented in the Carolingian period. We should also note — as mentioned above — that, in most of these gorges, in the middle or even at the lower end, in the Carolingian era, it was common to find a monastery; for example, at the southern entrance of the gorge created by the river Noguera Ribagorçana, stands the great monastery of Santa Maria d'Alaó.

Along these narrow gorges, between the mountain cliffs and the watercourse, there are paths, many of which certainly existed in the early Middle Ages. This is the only explanation behind the monastery of Tresponts, located between bridges (*inter pontes*, in Latin) next to the river Segre, or that of Santa Maria de Gerri, built on the left bank of the river Noguera Pallaresa.[29] However, these paths were narrow, they had to overcome numerous difficulties, and were therefore very dangerous. So much so that, many times, there were other less flat, but possibly less exposed, paths, which ran parallel to these paths and rivers, and which either crossed the mountain passes of the transversal mountain ranges or ran along the ridges. Sometimes these passes were crowned with a castle. Thus, the castle of Sant Llorenç was built near the Coll d'Ares, a pass, in the Montsec, where, in 1046, the *strata maiore qui pergit de Ager a Pallares*, from the Àger valley to Pallars.[30] And, of course, drove roads almost always ran along the ridges, following paths that required more effort but were safer for a large herd of sheep than the narrow paths which dived into the gorges.

---

29   Coromines, *Onomasticon Cataloniae*, vol. VII, p. 349.
30   *Col·lecció diplomàtica de Sant Pere d'Àger fins 1198*, ed. by Chesé, doc. 19.

Roads and Boundaries

In the next chapter, we will focus on boundaries. However, here, it is worth noting the coincidence that sometimes exists between road itineraries and the itineraries of, say, municipal divisions. In general, whenever a boundary and a road follow the same route, we can assume that both of them are quite old. An example from the Vallès region: between Caldes de Montbui and Sentmenat there is an old road, and there is also a very old boundary; both settlements must certainly have existed in the early Middle Ages. In the Empordà, we discover a similar case between the municipality of Siurana and the districts of Fortià and Riumors (all of which are mentioned in Carolingian documents). We also find a magnificent example in the plain of Lleida, around the ancient Islamic *almúnia* of Vensilló (Fig. 34).

Bridges and Fords

On the Pont del Diable (devil's bridge) of Martorell, over the river Llobregat, marks recalling the Roman legion that built it originally are still visible. This bridge is also mentioned in the Carolingian period (perhaps in 795, even before Barcelona was conquered).[31] Before 1000, several documents mention other bridges spread across the various counties of Old Catalonia. Later, in the second half of the twelfth century, in the testaments and wills of Lleida, we find legacies for the construction or maintenance of bridges, such as the one in front of the city. With regard to north-eastern Catalonia, Victor Farias explains the existence of numerous stone and wooden bridges in documents from the high Middle Ages.[32] We know that guilds dedicated themselves to the maintenance of these constructions. Dozens of bridges built in the Romanesque or Gothic periods are still preserved today, as we can see in the volumes of *Catalunya Romànica* and other books.[33]

When a bridge could not be built, there was sometimes a ford, a place where, due to the characteristics of the riverbed, it was possible to cross the watercourse quite safely. In documents from the Carolingian period, we already find several examples in Roussillon (*guad de Tiraculs*, in 988, in La Tet), in Ribagorça (*vado Avellana*, in 974, in La Noguera Ribagorçana), and in the Baix Llobregat (*guado Bonamoca*, in 997, in the Llobregat).[34]

---

31 *Catalunya carolíngia, vol. II: Els diplomes carolingis a Catalunya*, ed. by Abadal, p. 310.

32 Farías, *El mas i la vila a la Catalunya medieval*, pp. 300–03.

33 Vigué and Pladevall ed., *Catalunya Romànica*; Maristany, *Els ponts de pedra de Catalunya*.

34 *Catalunya carolíngia, vol. VI: Els comtats de Rosselló, Conflent, Vallespir i Fenollet*, ed. by Ponsich, doc. 582; *Catalunya carolíngia, vol. III: Els comtats de Pallars i Ribagorça*, ed. by Abadal, doc. 50; *Catalunya carolíngia, vol. VII: El comtat de Barcelona*, ed. by Baiges and Puig, doc. 1413. In fact, the Gual de Tiraculs, as Joan Coromines points out (*Onomasticon*

290   CHAPTER 13

Understanding the Road Network

Understanding the communication routes of a region requires us to study the topography of the territory, to learn about its history, to relate its roads to its present and past settlement, and also to verify whether their orientations agree with those of the pre-medieval plot-divided networks (or perhaps just an orthogonal grid of tracks). In addition, it calls for comprehension of the changes that have taken place over the centuries and knowledge of why each road is the way it is. In some Catalan *comarques*, in-depth studies have been carried out on road networking: for example, in Cerdanya, Baix Llobregat and Penedès, Vallès, Empordà, La Selva, Segrià, Pallars Jussà, Anoia and Segarra, Priorat, etc.[35]

The Roads of Cerdanya

A study of the road network of Cerdanya allows us to clarify many aspects of the past of this Pyrenean region.[36] This is a flat territory, furrowed by the river Segre and surrounded by high mountains. It has a long history. For example, the town of Llívia (*Iulia Libica*) was built in the Roman period. Analysing the characteristics of the roads running through this plain, we were surprised at the persistence of the roads originally constructed in the Roman era and the close link between these roads and the network of inhabited places documented before 1000.[37] By investigating these two elements of the landscape, namely roads and settlements, we see that Cerdanya is a region whose long history can be explicated by reading its landscape on maps, aerial photographs, or even walking through the territory.

In the early Middle Ages, the central plain of Cerdanya was divided into two large *pagi*, namely one from Llívia and the other from Talló. Above, we alluded to the plot division around Talló (or Bellver de Cerdanya); we will now turn our attention to the eastern sector, where the Roman city of *Iulia Libica* once stood. From the Coll de la Perxa mountain pass located to the east, there was a road to Llívia, of which some sections can still be traced. To the west of this city, there were two roads that, following the orientations of two plot divisions of the Roman period, that connected Llívia and the Saig pass, the westernmost limit of the *pagus*. We are especially interested in these

---

Cataloniae, vol. VII, p. 276), must have been a dangerous place, where one could easily fall into the water.

35 Vives, 'L'evolució històrica de la xarxa viària entre el Llobregat i el Foix'; Flórez, 'Dinàmica del poblament i estructuració del territori a la Laietània interior'; Mallorquí, *Cinquanta-cinc llegües de passos oblidats i xarrabascos*; Bonales and Bailac, *Els camins històrics del Pallars Jussà*; Bolòs, 'Nous mètodes per a conèixer els camins medievals'; Bolòs and others, 'La Caracterització del Paisatge Històric (CPH) del Priorat'.

36 Bolòs, 'Paisatge històric, cartografia i societat a l'alta edat mitjana: l'exemple de la Cerdanya'.

37 Bolòs and Hurtado, *Atles dels comtats de Cerdanya i Berga (v788-v990)*.

routes because they were important for organizing medieval settlements. The upper route, which passes by the foot of the *solana* (literally, the sunny side of a mountain) of Cerdanya, goes below the settlements of Bolvir, Saga, Ger, All, and Isòvol. These place names are pre-Roman; in fact, along the way, we find other places with Roman names, such as Pedrinyà, Manyà, and Quart. The latter reminds us of a place within four miles of the western limit of the *pagus* of Llívia.[38] Indeed, understanding roads helps us to understand the history of territories.

Medieval Roads and Pre-Medieval Plot Divisions

The roads often follow orientations that coincide with centuriations, road networks, or grid patterns created before the Middle Ages. We have already seen some examples concerning various *comarques*. Sometimes these networks date back to the Roman period, while others are even pre-Roman. To understand the problems posed by these coincidences, in terms of centuriations, we must distinguish between the bare centuriate area itself, rather small, whose land was divided into regular plots, and which were ceded to Roman settlers (or those faithful to Rome), and a much larger territory, some of whose paths follow the same orientation. This is the case, although sometimes these areas are far from the centuriate area, and they are even located in areas where another centuriation predominates and therefore follows a different orientation.[39] This often results in roads heading out of the village with, as we have said, several orientations that coincide with the main pre-medieval networks of the region. Such a surprising situation, found in many places, deserves further in-depth analysis.

Conclusions

Understanding the medieval territorial landscape requires us to study the network of communication routes. In the prehistoric period, roads already existed, some of which we believe have survived to the present day. In the Roman period, of course, many were also built. They have been studied more carefully. Over the centuries, some roads fell into disuse while new ones were created as new uses emerged. Learning to understand the characteristics of the road network and the motives behind the creation and maintenance of

---

38 Bolòs, 'Paisatge històric, cartografia i societat a l'alta edat mitjana: l'exemple de la Cerdanya'.

39 We find that the main road and many of the fields in the village of Esparreguera (Baix Llobregat) have an orientation in line with the centuriation *Tarraco I*. The city of Tarragona is, however, located seventy kilometres away. Bolòs, *El paisatge medieval del comtat de Barcelona*, pp. 452–55.

these roads helps us to understand the history of any territory much better. Jacinto Bonales did so by approaching the knowledge of the roads of Pallars Jussà and Priorat. He discovered, for example, that sometimes where there was a sparsely knit road network, this was due to heavy depopulation at some point in the past (e.g., what happened after the demographic crisis of the fourteenth century).[40]

If we focus on the main roads, we can relate them to the major administrative or religious capital cities of the past. Next to them, however, was a tight network of roads that must have been related to the villages whose influence spread throughout the territory. Population centres often stood near the roads. Simultaneously, many roads serve to connect the various settlements. Assessing the anomalies of this network is one of the great contributions made in recent decades to the study of the past landscape which allows us to establish a relative date for the various roads. Studying the pathways also makes it possible to understand some of the boundaries, as we have seen and will continue to see in the next chapter. Finally, it should be recalled that old roads are also part of our heritage, regardless of the major modifications they have undergone over the centuries.

40 Bonales and Bailac, *Els camins històrics del Pallars Jussà.*

CHAPTER 14

Boundaries and Territories

A Country Full of Old Borders

Introduction

Drafting maps makes one realize the importance of studying boundaries: getting to know exactly where they are, when they were made, and then understanding why they follow a certain route. Over the next few pages, we will look at the boundaries of counties and bishoprics. In Old Catalonia, the network of bishoprics owes much to the ancient period. We will also discuss the boundaries of the Carolingian villas and those of the valleys. Sometimes we find territories belonging to a Carolingian villa that correspond to economic spaces used by a peasant community. In other examples, the boundaries are inherited from the pre-medieval past. We are also interested in parishes. Catalonia is one of the first European countries where the borders of parish churches were precisely defined in the document of the endowment of the church, in the ninth or tenth centuries. We also study castral districts, which we find along the march, the boundaries of seigneurial estates, the forms of the royal *vegueries*, created by the Catalan-Aragonese monarchs in the late Middle Ages, and even the boundaries of territories that depended on the various cities, such as Barcelona. Finally, we briefly comment on the evolution over the centuries of the borders of Catalonia itself.

What Do We Know About Medieval Boundaries?

In the Middle Ages, boundaries were everywhere. There were boundaries of counties and bishoprics, and also boundaries of towns and villages, of parishes, and certainly of lordly domains and estates. Nowadays, boundaries are quite invisible, they can only be seen either on maps or pointed out by locals. They constitute, however, an essential element of the landscape. Boundaries, like roads, must be the object of long-term studies; otherwise, an important part of the history of any particular territory is lost.

In Europe, there are very few studies of boundaries. Historians have too often failed to explore when they were created, why their routes went where they did, and whether they have changed much over the centuries. A few years ago, contributions were made in France that seemed interesting with regard to the formation of parishes.[1] However, many of those findings have

---

1   Aubrun, *La paroisse en France.*

294   CHAPTER 14

been disproved, as some of those statements were ill-founded. England is where the greatest efforts have been made to attempt to date territories and understand why they are the way they are.[2] One example of these studies is a publication on the boundaries of English parishes.[3] There have also been attempts to relate borderlines to other well-dated elements of the landscape.[4] It is also worth noting that in England since the seventh century, the custom of *perambulatio* ('beating the bounds') has meant annually walking the boundary.[5] This practice (also called *circumambulatio*, or moving around) is found in many other European countries and has a long tradition.[6] For example, in 993, in Roussillon, the oldest residents of the villages of Forques (Fr. Fourques) and Tàpies traced the old boundaries of an allod (*alou* in Catalan), described in great detail; when reading the document, one certainly is under the impression of walking around.[7] This was certainly not the first time this had been done in the Catalan counties.

In Catalonia, in recent years, efforts have been made to reconstruct, very often as a result of consulting written documents, the boundaries of villages, castral territories, parishes, counties, and royal *vegueries* (*vicariae*). In the next few pages, we will examine some of these examples. Before analysing them, one book is worth highlighting: *Andorra la Vella sense límits* (Andorra without limits), a careful reconstruction of the divisions of a Pyrenean parish from the Middle Ages to the present day.[8]

It should also be noted that recent studies on territories in the early Middle Ages that analyse how they were created have differentiated between those constructed from the ground up by farming communities, and those created from the top down, in line with the interests of counts or kings.[9] In Old Catalonia, these two realities coexist. In addition, however, to understand the outline of some territories, we must also consider the legacy received from before the early Middle Ages, as we will now see in the case of the boundary between two *pagi* of the Cerdanya. Next, we will describe the boundaries of counties, villas, and valleys. Often, these three origins mingle. For example, we can see some Carolingian villas as territories of peasant communities, created mainly as a result of ancient economic interests, and as manorial domains whose lords charged a census to peasants, dating perhaps from the most remote Middle Ages, or also as continuations of a remote past (e.g., the Roman period) and perhaps even sometimes heirs of some *fundi* of the late

---

2 Beresford, *History on the Ground*, pp. 23–62.

3 Winchester, *Discovering Parish Boundaries*.

4 Aston, *Interpreting the Landscape*, pp. 39–40.

5 Langlands, 'Local Places and Local People'.

6 Chouquer, *Dominer et tenir la terre dans le haut Moyen Âge*, p. 63.

7 *Catalunya carolíngia, vol. VI: Els comtats de Rosselló, Conflent, Vallespir i Fenollet*, ed. by Ponsich, doc. 620; Bolòs, *Els orígens medievals del paisatge català*, p. 15.

8 Bonales, *Andorra la Vella sense límits*.

9 Martín Viso, *La construcción de la territorialidad en la Alta Edad Media*.

Roman Empire (as asserted by Rouche, in his study of Visigothic Aquitaine).[10] Whether they were manorial or fiscal entities remains an unresolved issue.

Ancient Boundaries

Some boundaries following ridges or rivers are very old. Some boundaries coincide with roads that, as pointed out, may well also be many centuries old. There are still other boundaries with a surprising outline that can also have remote origins. These are, for example, straight boundaries. We are particularly interested in boundaries that coincide with the orientation of a pre-medieval centuriation or a grid pattern of roads (a formation network). There are many examples of those in many *comarques* of Catalonia, from coastal lands to inland plains, even in some Pyrenean areas, such as Cerdanya.

Between Baridà and the Territory of Talló (Cerdanya)

The municipal boundary that separates the villages of Bar, Barguja, and Ansovell (Baridà or formerly, *pagus* of Bar) and the area of Montellà, Víllec, and Bastanist (within the *pagus* of Talló) is a straight five-kilometres line. It stretches from near the river Segre, at 1565 metres, to the ridge of the Cadí range, at an altitude of 2568 metres. It follows no river or ridge. It is an orientation that coincides with the Roman-style plot division network around Talló (called *Iulia Livica C*). In the early Middle Ages, on either side of this line, two *pagi* or wide territories were created: that of Bar (*pago Baridano*) and that of Talló (*pau Tollonense*), both located within the county of Cerdanya. Of course, this limit must have had its origin at the time of the Roman Empire or, at the latest, the initial period of the early Middle Ages. Its long-lasting existence is a magnificent testimony to the continuity of these settlements, many of which bear a pre-Roman or Roman place name.

Counties and Dioceses

In the Carolingian period, Old Catalonia was divided into about fifteen counties, some of which were called *pagi* in their early days. Some were large, while some were small. They were generally smaller in size than those found in counties, for example, at the northernmost end of the Pyrenees. On the other hand, some of them had their own count while others never had a count of their own. Some of them had a cathedral. Our focus is on the boundaries of all these counties, which, before the publication of the ten volumes of the *Atles dels comtats de la Catalunya carolíngia* (Atlas of the Counties of

---

10 Rouche, *L'Aquitaine des Wisigoths aux Arabes, 418–781.*

Carolingian Catalonia), we knew little about.[11] However, even though the boundaries were well defined by 1000, we can find some areas where the county contours were not well defined or had changed, for example, along the ninth and tenth centuries. There are obvious cases in Ripollès and also in the western sector of Roussillon.

First off, it should be noted that, during the Carolingian era, the western or southern boundary of the counties of Barcelona, Manresa, Berga, Urgell, Pallars, and Ribagorça marked the border with the Islamic world. This boundary was not fixed. In 801, the river Llobregat was the border of the county of Barcelona. The border of this county, around 1000, was located about sixty kilometres to the west, beyond the river Gaià, near Tarragona. The same can be said about the other counties with a march border, as the border was almost always divided into castral districts, as will be seen below.

Many county boundaries followed mountain ridges or rivers. There are, however, boundaries that deserve special attention. First of all, the western border of the counties of Peralada and Empúries was the original Via Augusta, beyond which the county of Besalú began. We may then wonder when this boundary was first created. Perhaps it was the boundary of the old bishopric of Empúries, which existed in the Visigothic era, but which did not have continuity after the conquest of the Carolingian Franks

Moving westwards, we find the county of Besalú that stretched from the Via Augusta in the east, including Banyoles and the Fluvià basin, and the birth of the Ter basin. We might ask ourselves why this county offered this topography, allowing for diverse landscapes, from the Empordà plain to the high mountains of Ripollès. Perhaps, in an attempt to answer this question, we could relate it to the importance of livestock and the drove roads that connected the high valleys of the Ter (above the town of Camprodon) and the lands of the Empordà region. Faced with this scenario, one may wonder what or who had the upper hand: the daily reality of the shepherds, the interests of lords (who may have been the actual livestock owners), or a hypothetical pre-medieval tradition. We may ask ourselves a question similar to that posed concerning the origin of some Carolingian villas.

The relevance of sheep may also have affected other boundaries, such as those in the county of Cerdanya, as they did not follow the ridge surrounding the basin, but lay a few kilometres beyond. This allowed the county to extend through several nearby valleys, such as those of Bagà, Lillet, or Ribes de Freser (and at some point, also that of Gombrèn).[12] In fact, in a world where pastures could be more important than crop fields, rivers were probably more important when choosing a boundary than ridges. Therefore, we can understand that the county of Cerdanya extended above and beyond the mountain range

---

11 Bolòs and Hurtado, 'Atles dels comtats de la Catalunya carolíngia' (ten volumes, published between the years 1998 and 2018).

12 Bolòs and Hurtado, *Atles dels comtats de Cerdanya i Berga*, p. 106.

that goes from the Cadí range (2649 metres) to Puigmal (2909 metres). We could also assume, although this has a lesser probability, that this boundary was created between 788 and 798, when a Carolingian count controlled the Cerdanya, while the lands of Berguedà, Ripollès, and Osona were still under the rule of the Islamic authorities.

In the Carolingian period, there was not only confrontation with the Saracens, but also tension among the Christian counts. The count of Cerdanya expanded to the north, towards Capcir and even the Occitan lands (in the Donezan and the valley of Mérens). These Cerdanya counts imposed the creation of a March of Berga between the counties of Manresa and Urgell, in the hope of having land bordering the Muslim world into which they could expand. On the other hand, the count of Urgell spread his authority over a section of Pallars Jussà into the territory of the ancient Roman city of Isona, which in principle should have been the natural expansion path for the counts of Pallars.

In the ninth and tenth centuries, there were only the bishoprics of Barcelona, Girona, Vic, Elna, and Urgell. In the middle of the tenth century, the counts of Ribagorça managed to create their own bishopric at Roda d'Isàvena. The Visigothic bishoprics of Empúries and Ègara (Terrassa) were abandoned and absorbed by the episcopal seats of Girona and Barcelona, respectively. It should also be noted that in the twelfth century, as a result of the conquest process, the archbishopric of Tarragona and the bishoprics of Tortosa and Lleida were recovered (which led to the abandonment of the Pyrenean bishopric of Roda d'Isàvena in 1149).

Regarding New Catalonia, after the Islamic conquest, for a time, the territorial divisions from the Visigothic period survived. Urban constituencies, especially on the borderlands, in the *ṭaġr*, were called *aʾmāl*, often with the same boundaries as Visigothic-era bishoprics. There were also smaller ones called *aḥwāz* (plural of *ḥawz*).[13] Later, the *aʾmāl* were divided into smaller constituencies, the *aqālīm* (plural of *iqlīm*), which each had a *ḥiṣn*, a fortification in the centre.[14] In the eleventh century, two taifa kingdoms were created in New Catalonia, with the cities of Lleida and Tortosa as their capitals.

Carolingian Villas

In the Carolingian era in Old Catalonia, villages were known by the Latin name *villa*. The *villa* was not a manorial estate, as we find northwards, between the rivers Loire and Rhine.[15] The villa was a precedent for villages

---

13   In Vallès Oriental there is the place of Alfou, which must be related to the name *ḥawz*. See Coromines, *Onomasticon Cataloniae*, vol. II, p. 130.

14   Negre and Suñé, 'Territorio, fiscalidad y actividad militar en la formación de un espacio fronterizo', p. 730.

15   Verhulst, *Rural and Urban Aspects of Early Medieval Northwest Europe*; Chouquer, *Dominer et*

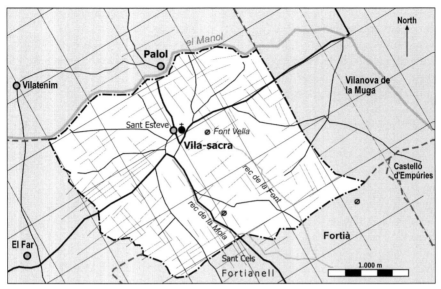

Figure 67. The parish of Vila-sacra (Alt Empordà). Territory organized in the early Middle Ages at the latest according to the orientations of the Roman centuriation.

of the high Middle Ages, made up of houses, often a church, and a territory whose resources provided their upkeep. The territory of Carolingian villas used to depend on a single jurisdictional lord, but the lands could be owned by several landlords (*seigneurs fonciers* in French) and also allodial peasants, who owned them. The large number of donations made, during the tenth and eleventh centuries by peasants to, for example, monasteries (such as the one in Sant Cugat del Vallès) or cathedrals (such as the one in Vic) prompts us to assume that there was a decline in the number of small properties, but also confirms the existence of a large number of owner peasants. On the other hand, in most counties, there were dozens of villas. These Carolingian villas had boundaries, some of which have sometimes survived to the present day.

Within a villa, there could be several hamlets, each with a territory, delimited with regard to the agricultural, pasture, or forest lands used by their inhabitants. It should be recalled that in the early Middle Ages, the population could be in many cases quite fluid and unstable. Contributions made in this respect to Roussillon or Languedoc have been instrumental for understanding this.[16]

---

tenir la terre dans le haut Moyen Âge, p. 287.

16 Kotarba, 'Les sites d'époque wisigothique de la ligne LGV'; Schneider, 'Dynamiques spatiales et transformations de l'habitat en Languedoc'; Schneider, 'Le territoire de l'archéologue et l'archéologie des territoires médiévaux'; Schneider, 'De la fouille des villages abandonnés à l'archéologie des territoires locaux'; 2005a, 2010; Schneider and others, 'Genèse d'une villa carolingienne de l'arrière-pays biterrois (vi^e-xe siècle), p. 112.

BOUNDARIES AND TERRITORIES 299

However, as we have seen in previous chapters, around 1000, settlements became polarized around a church or a castle (or were sometimes scattered around a large number of farmsteads).

References to villas leads us to parishes that often stretched across the same territory. We will get to them later. In Old Catalonia, often the territories of villas became the precedents of today's municipalities. However, on the southern and western borderlands of the Carolingian march, the castral districts are often the medieval antecedents of municipalities. It should be noted though that in documents from Carolingian Europe when locating a place, its county or *pagus* (for example in Cerdanya), valley or castle (corresponding to the Carolingian *vicaria*), villa, and sometimes hamlet or place is referred to. Until the eleventh century, the parish was seldom mentioned. This way of locating property is characteristic of the early Middle Ages and, in fact, connects with the late antique model.[17]

Below are some examples that describe the territories of some *villas* from the Carolingian period and discovering their origin.

Ultramort, Rupià, and Parlavà (Baix Empordà)

The will of Count Gausfred of Empúries, dated 989, mentions three villas handed over to a *fidelis* (who owed fealty to the count) named Guillem.[18] These three villages, Ultramort, Rupià, and Parlavà, are located next to each other. If we relate their data to the study of place names, the current municipal boundaries, and the orientation of Roman centuriation of this territory, we come to a few interesting conclusions. The place name Rupià corresponds to a name created in the Roman period. Parlavà is the name of an early medieval *palatium* (palace), probably fiscal land (therefore, in all probability, in the hands of the count). The boundaries of all three places basically coincide with the orientation of the Roman *Emporiae I* centuriation. It should also be noted that many of the roads that cross this territory have the same orientation as the centuriation. All this reflects a strong continuity in the occupation of this space, divided into three *fundi* from the beginning of the Middle Ages, that, with some changes, lasted throughout the early medieval period.[19] Surely, in other places as well, the boundaries of present-day municipalities are similar to those of the early Middle Ages.

---

17 Chouquer, *Dominer et tenir la terre dans le haut Moyen Âge*, pp. 429–30.
18 *Catalunya carolíngia, vol. V: Els comtats de Girona, Besalú, Empúries i Peralada*, ed. by Sobrequés, Riera and Rovira, doc. 519.
19 Bolòs, 'Conèixer el paisatge històric medieval per poder planificar i gestionar el territori', pp. 195–200; Bolòs, 'Aportació al coneixement de la morfogènesi dels pobles del comtat d'Empúries', p. 265; Bolòs, 'Not So dark Centuries: Changes and Continuities in the Catalan Landscape', p. 96.

Vila-sacra (Alt Empordà)

Moving further north, the municipality of Vila-sacra is a magnificent example of the territory created in the early Middle Ages which has survived without much change so far. In this municipality of Alt Empordà, the memory of the Roman *Emporiae III* centuriation has remained fossilized.[20] The Roman subdivision still affects three features of its landscape: roads, boundaries, and the plots of farmland, in this specific order (Fig. 67). The roads are very likely to be ancient, even pre-medieval. The extent of this place may have undergone changes, but such changes are, in all probability, quite old, at least from the early Middle Ages; many sections of the tracks follow accurately the orientation of the centuriation. It is plausible to assume that they originated in a *fundus* from the late Roman Empire. The margins of the plots in the fields could be just as old as they may well have formed over the centuries, copying the orientations of, for example, the roads running through this territory, which, as said above, appear to be quite old.

Luckily, there is plenty of data for this settlement. The site of Vila-sacra (*Villae Saccari*) is already documented in 974.[21] It had the same boundary as the parish of Sant Esteve. Furthermore, this borderline coincides with several centuriations (similar to what is found in other countries, such as Switzerland).[22] These coincidences, discovered a few years ago, lead us to infer that this territory originated before the Carolingian era, at least from the Visigothic era.[23] Subsequently, several excavations have confirmed this hypothesis. On the one hand, it has been shown that there was a Roman *villa*. On the other hand, near the place where the church was built, we have found graves dug into the soil from the seventh and eighth centuries. Some anthropomorphic tombs have also been excavated above these burials which can be linked to a pre-Romanesque church built around the ninth or tenth centuries. The excavations also revealed silos, possibly related to a *sagrera*. Finally, if we relate these findings with the first chapters of this book, from documents of around the fourteenth century, we learn that there were some cellars, within a *cellera* (synonymous with *sagrera*), as well as a *força* with some dry moats. Overall, this settlement, in the high Middle Ages, had characteristics very similar to those of many villages in the nearby region of Roussillon.[24]

---

20 Palet and Gurt, 'Aménagement et drainage des zones humides du littoral emporitain (Catalogne)', pp. 41–48.

21 *Catalunya carolíngia, vol. V: Els comtats de Girona, Besalú, Empúries i Peralada*, ed. by Sobrequés, Riera and Rovira, doc. 421.

22 Combe, 'La recherche des cadastrations antiques sur le plateau suisse', pp. 167–73.

23 Bolòs, *Els orígens medievals del paisatge català*, p. 98; Bolòs, 'Not So Dark Centuries: Changes and Continuities in the Catalan Landscape', p. 96.

24 Folch, 'Territorios y poblamiento en el noreste de la Tarraconense en época visigoda', p. 86; Moix, 'Excavació arqueològica a la necròpoli de Palau de l'Abat', pp. 511–15.

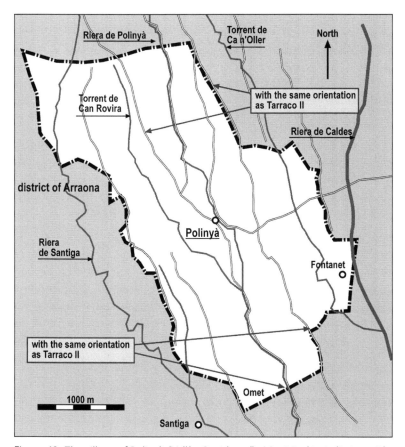

Figure 68. The village of Polinyà (Vallès Occidental). Municipal jurisdiction with the same boundaries as those of the Carolingian era.

Many territories of an inhabited place extend between the plain near a watercourse and a mountain slope, which makes them elongated in shape. We find this phenomenon in flatlands such as Roussillon and in mountainous regions such as Cerdanya.[25] The origin of this spatial distribution of the rural community probably dates back to the early Middle Ages, sometimes even before then. We find this in many nearby countries, such as the Occitan lands where it is related to the *fundi* of Late Antiquity, and even more distant lands, such as England, where it is related to the existence of common rights.[26]

---

25 Bolòs, *Els orígens medievals del paisatge català*, p. 105.
26 Rouche, *L'Aquitaine des Wisigoths aux Arabes, 418–781*; Banham and Faith, *Anglo-Saxon Farms and Farming*, p. 172.

302   CHAPTER 14

Polinyà (Vallès Occidental)

In 969, the villa of Polinyà (*villa que dicitur Pauleniano*) was sold by Count Borrell II to a man named Galí; in fact, as Pierre Bonnassie stated, what the count was selling was only jurisdiction, not land ownership.[27] The boundaries are mentioned in great detail (Fig. 68): to the north, *in terminio de Arraona vel de Canellas*, against the territory of Arraona (currently, Sabadell) and Canyameres; to the east, *in terminio de Palacio Zalatan vel de Figariolas*, bordering the territory of Palau-solità and 'Figueroles'; to the south, *in terminio de Olmedo vel de Sancta Maria*, the territories of Omet and Santiga, and finally, to the west, also against the district of Arraona. It was pointed out that within this territory there were houses, courtyards, *horts* with trees, lands, vineyards, springs, forests, and scrubland (or *garrigues*).

The current municipality of Polinyà is certainly not so different from what this territory was like in the Carolingian era.[28] It is now basically a rectangle of about 4.4 kilometres long by about two kilometres wide. The orientation of its watercourses, its main roads, and also part of the limits of its territory all coincide with the Roman network *Tarraco II*, which served to organize the lands of Camp de Tarragona, near the city of Tarraco, at a distance of ninety kilometres. This coincidence matches that of the southern side of the municipality (near Omet de Baix) and also that of the north-east; on the other hand, the boundaries of the north and north-west coincide with the *Vallès C* plot division system, which predominates in this region of Vallès.

As we approach Polinyà, we realize the importance of continuity in some places. Indeed, the origin of the current boundaries may well date back over a thousand years ago, despite minor changes over the centuries. We might even go further back, to the beginning of the Middle Ages, to the Visigothic era, using the seminal maps by Michel Rouche concerning several villas from the Visigothic period on the banks of the river Garonne as precursors of the current municipalities or *communes*.[29] On a hypothetical level, in this case, as in the previous one, we could even venture to posit its origins beyond the limits of the Middle Ages, perhaps in the *fundus* of a man named *Paulinus*. In fact, in the third century, Ulpian pointed out that each *fundus*, in *forma censalis*, had to be registered under its name, its *civitas*, and its *pagus*, its boundaries, and its main crops. Therefore, the *fundi* had clear-cut boundaries.[30] In this case, we need to picture it ourselves: a *fundus* belonging to Paulinus, in the *civitas* of Barcino, and in the *pagus* of Vallès or Ègara. The boundaries are well defined in the tenth-century document.

---

27 *Catalunya carolíngia, vol. VII: El comtat de Barcelona*, ed. by Baiget and Puig, doc. 555; Bonnassie, *Croissance et mutations d'une société*.

28 Bolòs, 'Història del paisatge i mapes de Caracterització del Paisatge Històric', p. 107.

29 Rouche, *L'Aquitaine des Wisigoths aux Arabes, 418–781*, p. 219.

30 Olesti, 'Héritage et tradition des pratiques agrimensoriques', p. 265.

The Outskirts of Girona

In 2003, an attempt was made to cartographically reconstruct the network of Carolingian villas around Girona from 1000.[31] The basis for this reconstruction was a donation charter, from 1018 that describes the territory surrounding Girona divided into *villas*. These Carolingian villas were, first and foremost, jurisdictional territories under the rule of a lord who held the ban, the public authority over it. However, these villas were inhabited by a community of people, some of whom were the owners, who were entitled to act collectively, if necessary, for example, during a trial. It should be noted that, for this region, the authors of the study searched for the origin of this organization in the *fundi* of the later Roman Empire and the *villae* of the early Middle Ages.[32] However, they point out that there were a few main villas, probably with a long tradition, which often had a parish church and corresponded to current municipalities, and villas within a smaller land piece, some of which have now become farmsteads. It is observed that when there was a church within the villa, the settlement and the church might be very close (possibly the church was older), while other times the church was located a few hundred metres from the settlement (perhaps the church was built afterward, as seen in open villages from the Pyrenees).

It should be noted that our examples of villas are located in flat counties where Roman remains frequently occur. Many of these Carolingian villas have clear precedents to the early *fundi*. The characteristics of Carolingian villas in more mountainous areas, for example, Berga (Vilosiu, Gavarrós, or Malanyeu), Urgell (Estamariu, Alàs, or La Freita), Pallars (Baén, Peramea, or Escós), or Ribagorça (Visalibons, Rallui, or Güel) were very different. Perhaps, in many cases, the origin of these Carolingian villas was not necessarily a *fundi* but an area used by a rural community living on agriculture and livestock.

Other Settlement Boundaries

All the examples hitherto described correspond to places in Old Catalonia. This might lead us to believe that the areas of Lleida or Tortosa have no evidence of ancient boundaries prior to the conquest of the counts of Barcelona and Urgell in the twelfth century. Far from it. In our previous reference to *almúnies*, we mentioned the case of Vensilló (Segrià) (Fig. 34), whose current boundaries coincide with drove paths and have the same orientation as some pre-medieval plot divisions. We have found the same coincidences, although they may not be as obvious as in this case, concerning other municipalities of New Catalonia.

---

31 Canal and others, *Girona, de Carlemany al feudalisme*, p. 369.
32 Canal and others, *Girona, de Carlemany al feudalisme*, pp. 370–71.

304   CHAPTER 14

Valleys

In the Pyrenees, territories in the early Middle Ages were organized into valleys. As far as we know, people living in these valleys had a very strong sense of belonging to a community. Within these valleys, we have found, in the Carolingian period, several churches and a large number of villas and small hamlets: for the county of Ribagorça, the valleys of Castanesa, Barravés, and Boí, in Pallars Sobirà, the valleys of Àneu, Cardós, Vallferrera, and Àssua. Out of these last four valleys, the one that preserved most of its own characteristics during the late Middle Ages was Àneu; we will discuss this case below. In the old county of Urgell, the valleys of Andorra, Castellbò, Cabó, and Lord are worth mentioning. Further east, we find the valleys of Bagà, Lillet, and Ribes (or Pedrera), which, despite not being located in the Cerdanya basin, also belonged to the county of Cerdanya. We have already mentioned the valleys of Ripoll, Sant Joan de les Abadesses, and Camprodon, which came under the control of three monasteries. Finally, in the county of Besalú, we find large valleys, such as Bianya, Santa Pau, and En Bas. The two latter, as mentioned above, show a displacement of an early medieval castle located on top of a mountain, towards a new feudal castle, located in the middle of the plain. In fact, in many of the other valleys mentioned, in the middle (or at one end of the valley) there was also an early medieval fortification. And, in the same way, there could be, in a central situation, a church that possibly maintained an ancestral religious tradition (as referred to above, for example, concerning Santa Maria d'Àneu or Santa Maria de Lord [Lord here refers to a place name]).

Andorra

Searching for a prime example of a Pyrenean valley from the early Middle Ages, Andorra could possibly be the best. Andorra is currently an independent state, although in the Carolingian era it belonged to the county and bishopric of Urgell. Its official language is Catalan. Within this valley, there were already, before 1000, six parishes, which ended up becoming the demarcations that organized the country (although now there are seven of them). Within each of these parishes we find, as seen above, a large number of hamlets (Fig. 32). The valley had some boundaries, the parishes also had them, and even the hamlets had a delimited space where their inhabitants could obtain the resources they needed. The boundaries have not changed much over the centuries. The changes are more noticeable in those areas whose lands intended for grazing were taken over by parishes; these *emprius* (from the Latin *ademprivium*) were often located beyond the strict limits of the valley.[33]

---

33   Bonales, *Història territorial de la vall d'Andorra*, pp. 190–275, especially map on page 273.

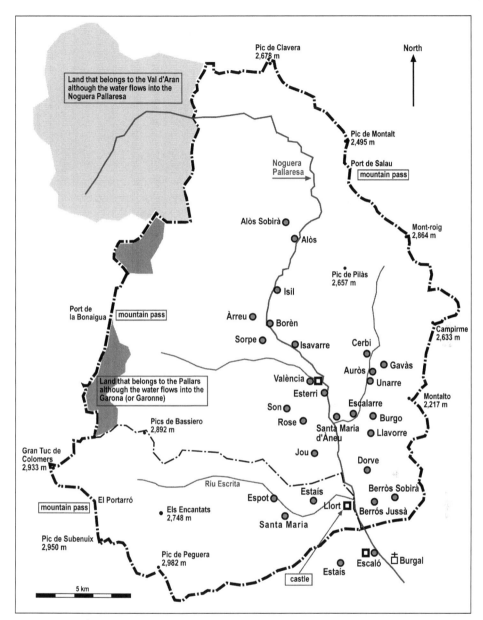

Figure 69. The Àneu valley (Pallars Sobirà). The extensive valley of the Pyrenees was inhabited by a community of peasants and shepherds who had their homes in the many villages and hamlets. There were several parishes and some castles.

This was a common feature in the Pyrenees. For example, in a quick overview of the southern limit of the Val d'Aran, we notice that it skips the mountains and reaches out, about 3.3 kilometres below the ridge, to the beginning of the course of the river Noguera Ribagorçana. The eastern limit of this Aranese valley, in Montgarri, also extends about eight kilometres beyond the basin of the river Garonne, following the basin of the Noguera Pallaresa to Pont de Marimanya, as we shall see below.

La Vall d'Àneu

The Àneu valley is located in Pallars Sobirà, to the west of Andorra. There were at least twenty-five settlements. In the eleventh century, we would have found about twenty-two churches (Fig. 69). Most place names are pre-Roman. There were several large sectors: the Isil valley, the Unarre valley, the central valley, around Santa Maria d'Àneu, and, surely, the Espot valley. In the centre of the valley was the castle of València d'Àneu. Further south, at the entrance of the Espot valley, stood the castle of Llort, documented before 1000.[34] It is interesting to note, concerning this valley, the splitting of some towns, such as Alòs or Berrós (with a lower [Jussà] site and an upper [Sobirà] site); in fact, the village of Espot itself was divided into two nuclei, the one in the shade and the one on the sunny side of the mountain (with the church between them) (Fig. 5). Finding the origin of all these settlements certainly takes us back to a few centuries before the Carolingian era, about which, unfortunately, no written documents have been preserved. Some privileges were preserved as late as the fourteenth century, which greatly limited the rights of the lord of the place, the Count of Pallars, over this valley. As pointed out in 1313, the count, who was the lord of the jurisdiction, would climb a rock, located in Segura (next to the castle of València), from where he had to swear freedom and exemptions (*llibertat* and *franquesa*) to the valley, and, in return, its inhabitants would pay homage to him.[35]

Parishes

After a few years of trying to date the origin of many parishes to the early Middle Ages, there is a widespread belief that, in these early centuries, parishes had a sparsely delimited, rather fluid territory, and that it was not until the high Middle Ages, after 1000, that their limits were defined, and have tended to remain unaltered to the present day.[36] However, we know that in Old Catalonia, before the turn of the millennium, some parish boundaries had already been clearly delimited; we will discuss this below with reference to some specific cases.

---

34 Bolòs and Hurtado, *Atles dels comtats de Pallars i Ribagorça (v806-v998)*, pp. 78–79.

35 Padilla ed., *L'esperit d'Àneu*, p. 125.

36 Zadora-Rio, *Des paroisses de Touraine aux communes d'Indre-et-Loire*.

BOUNDARIES AND TERRITORIES 307

In Chapter 3, regarding churches, it has been noted that parish churches, created by the bishop in the early Middle Ages, at first did not have a clear-cut territory. There were also churches founded by lay lords with chapels located on their estates; in this case, their area of influence probably coincided with the territories of the seigneurial *fundi*. Along with these religious buildings, over time, churches attached to monasteries were also created. The bishops of Vic and Barcelona consecrated the churches of Aiguafreda (898) and La Roca del Vallès (932), but they were dependent on the monastery of Sant Joan de les Abadesses.[37] And finally, there were churches created by parish communities. Even in the late Middle Ages, we find these diverse situations well documented, which, in all probability, had even more remote origins.[38]

In fact, many churches in the Pyrenees were built by local parishioners who kept custody of them. The churches in the Andorra valley were owned by the community, which had control over the rector's appointment and the collection of tithes.[39] In some Pyrenean valleys, such as those of Ribagorça, communities of ecclesiastics were headed by an abbot, closely linked to the local population. This was in line with the situation in Gascony with the so-called *fraternitates* or *fadernes*.[40] Catafau believes that these clerical groups could be a legacy of an early parish association linked to large parishes, which, in the Pyrenees, could coincide with valleys.[41]

Parishes of Olvan and La Quar (Berguedà)

In 899 the church of Santa Maria d'Olvan was consecrated and endowed.[42] The boundaries of the territory were set up. To the north, the parish reached the mountains of Escobet and Montsant. It included the nuclei of Olvan, Gironella, and Peraforn, a place that we believe corresponds to the pre-Romanesque church of Can Bassacs. This was a large territory, with an area of about forty-two square kilometres. The boundaries were well specified, as found in many of the endowments of churches in the Carolingian era.

That same year 899, eight days before, the bishop of La Seu d'Urgell, had consecrated the church of La Quar, a hilltop church on a prominent rock located about eight kilometres north-east of Santa Maria d'Olvan. In Olvan, according to the text of the endowment, there was a castle and a lord, but in La Quar it was its thirty-one inhabitants who promoted the creation of the church. The boundaries were established: from the Merlès stream to Montsant and Quadres, to the Pedret mountain range, the Masada villa,

---

37 *Les Dotalies de les esglésies de Catalunya (segles IX–XII)*, ed. by Ordeig, docs. 49, 17.
38 Bolòs and Piqué, 'Les parròquies: centres espirituals i demarcacions territorials', pp. 111–30.
39 Viader, *L'Andorre du IXe au XIVe siècle*; Catafau, 'Petites, nombreuses, isolées?', p. 76.
40 Poumarède, 'Les "Fadernes" du Lavedan', pp. 677–94.
41 Catafau, 'Petites, nombreuses, isolées?', p. 81.
42 *Les Dotalies de les esglésies de Catalunya (segles IX–XII)*, ed. by Ordeig, doc. 19.

308   CHAPTER 14

and the hamlet of Les Heures.[43] It covers an area of about thirty-eight square kilometres. Still in the ninth century, in the county of Berga we find several well-delimited parishes. The latter, La Quar, included various Carolingian villas and hamlets. A century later, around 1000, in La Quar, the social reality had already changed: next to the church and a new castle, the monastery of Sant Pere de la Portella was built.[44] In these cases, we are unsure whether, as proposed by Vigil-Escalera, the construction of a new church favoured the power of its local landowners.[45] Be that as it may, at the end of the Middle Ages, there were still churches of bishops, monasteries, lay lords, and rural communities.

Solsona (Solsonès)

The endowment of the church of Santa Maria de Solsona took place in 977.[46] Its document is highly interesting as it sets out in great detail the boundaries of this parish dedicated to the Virgin Mary. To a large extent, these boundaries coincide with the current municipal boundaries (Fig. 70). In 977, due to the precise delimitation of this territory, thirty-three places were located, of which we can accurately position thirteen. Thus, for example, *ipso Buxo* corresponds to the place of El Boix, *villa Maurone* in Vilamorós, *villa Palariense* in Pallarès or *Ciaresa* in Cirera. There is even a reference to a *Strata Cardonense*, which corresponds to the road that goes to Cardona, or a *Strata de ipsa Serra*, which must be the road that currently follows the ridge of the mountain range of L'Hostal de les Forques.[47] This way of delimiting this territory coincides with how the Roman *fundi* were delimited, especially during the Low Roman Empire.[48]

This document is also very interesting in other respects. On the one hand, it reflects a well-organized territory consisting of inhabited places, each of which bears its name. On the other hand, if we position these places on a map, we can discover that the orientation of the boundaries of the parish coincides with that of a plot division created in the Roman period, very common in Catalonia (*Tarraco II*, although Tarragona is located 100 kilometres south of Solsona). Much older territories were considered when establishing the boundaries of this Carolingian parish. This place in Solsona may have already been mentioned in a document from 522 (*Celsiasi*).[49] However, we need to go further back in

---

43 'Les Actes de consagracions d'esglésies del bisbat d'Urgell', ed. by Baraut, docs. 9, 10.
44 *Diplomatari del monestir de Sant Pere de la Portella*, ed. by Bolòs.
45 Vigil-Escalera, 'Meeting Places, Markets, and Churches in the Countryside', p. 193.
46 'Les Actes de consagracions d'esglésies del bisbat d'Urgell', ed. by Baraut, doc. 37.
47 Bolòs, 'Conèixer el paisatge històric medieval per poder planificar i gestionar el territori', pp. 208–11.
48 Andreu, 'Edició crítica, traducció i estudi de l'*Ars Gromatica sive Geometria Gisemundi*'; Olesti, 'Héritage et tradition des pratiques agrimensoriques'.
49 Tomás-Faci and Martín-Iglesias, 'Cuatro documentos inéditos del monasterio visigodo de

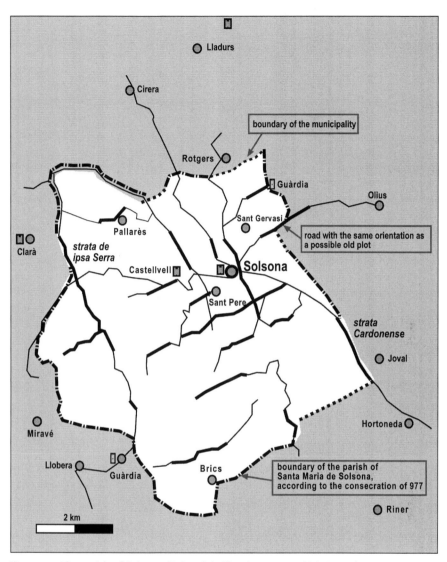

Figure 70. The parish of Solsona (Solsonès). The document which records the consecration of this parish in 977 refers to its exact boundaries.

time and assume that before the Middle Ages, this space had already been reorganized 'in the Roman way' and, to that end, an orientation that coincided with that of *Tarraco II* was used and, also (probably not coincidentally), with that of the river Negre, which runs from north to south from one side to the other of the municipality. At this point, it should be noted that Solsona was

---

San Martín de Asán', pp. 261–86.

310 CHAPTER 14

one of the few places, in the tenth century, which claimed to have both a
city and a castle (*civitate vel castro*) and that, therefore, it is not considered
to be only a villa. In addition, the endowed estates belonging to the church
of Santa Maria had been built in the ancient period, and it was consecrated
again in 977. Despite the wars and raids ravaging the area throughout the
tenth century, Solsona had a long history that was deeply imprinted on the
minds of its inhabitants.

The Outskirts of Girona

In 888, Bishop Teuter gave Santa Maria and Sant Feliu de Girona several
churches (*basilicas*), located to the west and south of the city.[50] Even though
no archaeological excavations confirm this, it is very likely that many of the
fourteen churches mentioned in the ninth century already existed before
the Frankish conquest (785).[51] To test this hypothesis, the authors of the
research refer to some pre-existing excavations as well as the analysis of the
distribution of churches throughout the territory and a study of dedications.
Certainly, except for the churches of Sant Gregori and perhaps Saint Martin
near Cassà de la Selva, the rest could correspond to churches that already
existed in the Visigothic period. This leads us to think that the plain of
Girona was a territory whose population had been fully Christianized since
the beginning of the Middle Ages. On the other hand, although in this case,
we could easily reconstruct the territories of these churches from the current
municipal boundaries, it is perhaps wiser not to do so and think that, in the
early Middle Ages, there must have been only a few areas of influence with
as yet blurred boundaries. It must be said, however, that it is very probable
that these municipalities showed many coincidences in their boundaries with
those of the villas, also documented in the year 1000. In addition, it should
be noted that the collection of tithes from the Carolingian period must have
gradually forced the definition of the territories of all these parish churches.

Castral Districts

In the Carolingian era, in much of Old Catalonia, when locating a place the
name of a county was indicated, perhaps that of a valley, and, very often, the
name of a villa. However, in the lands near the border, the name of a castle
within its district was taken as a reference. In a wide strip near the border
between the Christian counties and Al-Andalus, in the so-called *marca* (march,
in English), the whole territory was divided into castral districts. Within each

---

50 *Catalunya carolíngia, vol. V: Els comtats de Girona, Besalú, Empúries i Peralada*, ed. by
Sobrequés, Riera and Rovira, doc. 65.
51 Canal and others, *Girona, de Carlemany al feudalisme*, pp. 388–93.

castle, there was a fortification, a villa, a church, and perhaps several scattered hamlets. We find this form of organization on the plain of Vic, reorganized at the time of Guifré I el Pilós [Wilfred the Hairy] (870–897), and also in the region of Penedès, in the county of Manresa and in the southern parts of Berga, Urgell, Pallars, and Ribagorça. In recent decades, numerous examples of castral districts have been studied, such as that of the castle of Miralles, those of the plain of Vic, and those of Penedès; further research has also been done on all the marches of the different counties.[52]

Olèrdola

The district of the castle of Olèrdola was already documented in the tenth century (Fig. 71). This was a very large district, as it extended all over the Penedès region, conquered in the tenth century by the counts of Barcelona. Nevertheless, neither the fortification nor probably the boundaries of the castral territory were created at that time. Their origins go back to a distant past. The fortified town of Olèrdola has a long history, whose precedents are from the Bronze Age, the Iberian period, and the centuries under Roman rule. In the Islamic era, this place is supposed to have been the capital of Penedès. During the Carolingian period and until the twelfth century, Olèrdola was the most important town in this region.

As for the district of Olèrdola, there are two documents from 992, both of which contain a detailed account of its boundaries (*ipsas fronteras*).[53] Inside the district, in the early tenth century, we know that there were nine churches. Within the territory of Olèrdola, which initially extended all the way to the coast, in the tenth century two new districts were created around the castles of Olivella and Ribes. Possibly, the district of Olèrdola was more typically the territory of an early medieval city than that of a Carolingian castle.

Both documents offer a detailed description of the district and follow a procedure starting from the moment when places and domains (or *fundi*) ceased being located, taking centuriations as a point of reference (Chouquer used classical terminology and considered it a *finitio more arcifinio*).[54] There are other surprising findings when reading the boundaries of the castral district of Olèrdola. We can ask ourselves, for example, why the *calçada* (*ipsa calciata*, paved road), the Via Morisca dated to the tenth century, or the former Via Augusta, were not chosen as the northern limit of the territory of Olèrdola and the south of the castral districts of Castellví de la Marca, Sant Martí Sarroca,

---

52 Bolòs, 'Fortificacions frontereres situades entre els rius Anoia i Gaià'; Bolòs, 'El territori i els seus límits. El poble, la parròquia i el castell a l'edat mitjana', p. 49; Batet, *Castells termenats i estratègies d'expansió comtal*; Sabaté, *El territori de la Catalunya medieval*; Bolòs and Hurtado, collection of the ten volumes of 'Atles dels comtats de la Catalunya carolíngia'.

53 *Catalunya carolíngia, vol. VII: El comtat de Barcelona*, ed. by Baiget and Puig, docs 1,150, 1,181; Muntaner, *El terme d'Olèrdola en el segle X*.

54 Chouquer, *Dominer et tenir la terre dans le haut Moyen Âge*, p. 329.

Figure 71. The territory of Olèrdola (Alt Penedès). In the early Middle Ages, Olèrdola was the capital city of the *comarca* of Penedès. A document from 992 tracks its exact boundaries.

and Font-rubí. Instead, the district of the castle of Olèrdola was bordered to the north by a good number of fields, roads, trees (*ipso rovere, ipsa fighera, ipsa olcinia*), springs, pools (*gorgo nigro*), streams, inhabited places, ovens, and also, curiously, silos (*ipsa ciga*) and stone landmarks (*ipsa petra fita*) (Fig. 71). These were very complex boundaries that may not seem very logical to us, possibly because we are ignorant of the reason behind this decision. Although no evidence can be found to reinforce this statement, this very precise and complex delimitation can be understood only if we keep in mind that it is in line with an older tradition and if we assume that, when this was established, the districts of inhabited places possibly existed long before the tenth century. This very precise delimitation is reminiscent of those made in the Roman period to mark the boundary of properties with stones (*lapides*), mounds of stones (*congeries petrarum*), perhaps cisterns, or perhaps dolmens (*arcae finales*), silos or wells (*foveas*), and landmarks (*metas*). There is no need to go back centuries to find the possible origins of this terminology which we find in the surveying work of Gisemund, an inhabitant of Old Catalonia of the ninth century who had learned it from a text wrongly attributed to Boethius.[55]

Gelida (Alt Penedès)

In 945, a document mentioned the place of Gelida and also a mill below, on the banks of the river Anoia. The castle and its territory were also mentioned.[56] However, there is no doubt that this castle and its adjoining district already existed long before this date, as we will show below. In fact, as a result of the excavations carried out in the castle, numerous remains of houses carved in the rock from the early Middle Ages have been found, together with a fortification, possibly from the Islamic period, also documented.[57]

However, what discloses more information about the antiquity of this district is, curiously, the extent of its limits (Fig. 72). The north-eastern and south-western borders of the municipality of Gelida, along sections to the south of the river Anoia, are almost straight. First of all, it is very surprising that these two lines, about four and a half kilometres apart, run parallel to each other. The orientation of these parts coincides with that of the plot division network proposed by Miquel Vives as the centuriation of Alt Penedès (which, certainly, is very similar to that of Barcino).[58] The road from Gelida to Sant Llorenç d'Hortons follows the same orientation; in addition, other roads in the district also have a similar orientation.[59]

---

55 Olesti, 'Héritage et tradition des pratiques agrimensoriques', p. 267.

56 *Catalunya carolíngia, vol. VII: El comtat de Barcelona*, ed. by Baiget and Puig, doc. 264.

57 Macias and others, 'El castell de Gelida', p. 175; Guidi-Sánchez, 'El poblamiento del Penedès altomedieval', p. 116.

58 Vives, 'L'evolució històrica de la xarxa viària entre el Llobregat i el Foix'.

59 Bolòs, 'Història del paisatge i mapes de Caracterització del Paisatge Històric', p. 110.

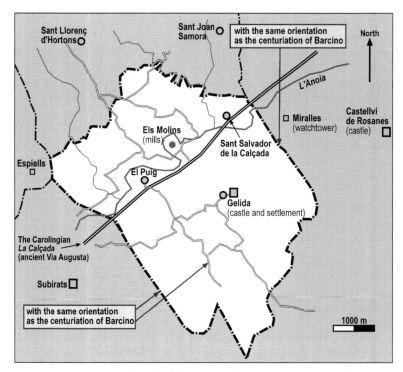

Figure 72. The municipality of Gelida (Alt Penedès). The boundaries of the town of Gelida, which contained an Islamic settlement and a castle, follow orientations created before the Middle Ages.

Further details concerning this site, the place name 'Gelida' may well come from the name of a Berber or Amazigh tribe.[60] This place, close to the confluence of the rivers Anoia and Llobregat, must have been given its name during the early years of Islamic rule. This may lead us to wrongly assume that no evidence of an earlier period has been left. As we have seen in other examples, this is not the case. The municipal boundaries of this territory have their roots in the pre-medieval period. This continuity can only be understood if we assume, on the one hand, the need, throughout the early Middle Ages, for well-defined boundaries (of a seigneurial domain, an economic space, or a fiscal district). On the other hand, this obviously required the continuity of at least part of its population, who kept the spatial memory alive throughout the sixth to tenth centuries.

---

60 Pérez, 'Toponímia d'origen islàmic a la Catalunya Vella', p. 82.

Seigneurial Estates

During the Middle Ages, there were many changes in lordship. The relations between the different members of the nobility, gradually increasing in frequency, varied over the centuries, and this affected the whole of society as well as the organization of the territory. The lords could have rights either over the land or jurisdictional (banal) rights, or perhaps both simultaneously. Enjoying jurisdictional sway meant being able to judge, impose monopolies (such as those on mills, blacksmithing, or ovens), and even impose the so-called 'evil customs' (legally legitimated abuses). It should be noted that these rights were often significantly fragmented. Therefore, it is very difficult to show lordships on a map. Lords of castles (castellans, *castlans* in Catalan) depended on and owed loyalty to members of the high nobility. Below them were sub-castellans (*sotscastlans* in Catalan) and numerous knights (*cavallers* in Catalan) who owned a manor or a fortified house with a district (a *quadra* or *cavalleria*, a land tenure). There were *quadres* in New Catalonia, but also in Old Catalonia, for example in the region of Vallès.[61] Some castral districts (such as Mediona, Penedès) could have as many as four levels in the feudal hierarchy, and others (such as Castellví de la Marca or Font-rubí, also in Penedès) could even have five.[62]

Moreover, rights for taxing the land were superimposed everywhere with jurisdictional rights, and even with what were originally ecclesiastical rights such as tithes. It was also common for a village to be under the jurisdiction of a secular or ecclesiastical lord, with its neighbouring village under the jurisdiction of a different lord. In addition, at the end of the Middle Ages, new lordships were created. Thus, in 1324, King Jaume II created the county of Muntanyes de Prades for his youngest son, Ramon Berenguer.[63] The capital of this newly created county was Falset. Part of this county had its origins in the castral district of Siurana, established in 1173, shortly after the conquest of its Islamic fortification (Fig. 16).

At present, there is no atlas depicting the lordships of the late Middle Ages; the best cartographic work done so far is the volume by Jesús Burgueño and Mercè Gras, concerning the seigneurial domains that existed in Catalonia around 1800.[64]

---

61 Canyameres, 'Les torres, propietats agrícoles grans amb orígens en alous i territoris de vil·les altmedievals'.
62 Dolset, 'La maîtrise du risque dans les marches catalanes', p. 68.
63 Martínez Elcacho, 'Organització senyorial i jurisdiccional del comtat de les Muntanyes de Prades i baronia d'Entença', pp. 226–81.
64 Burgueño and Gras, *Atles de la Catalunya senyorial*.

Quadres or Knight-Services

Beginning with the eleventh century, we find written references to knight-services (*quadres* and *cavalleries* in Catalan). A *quadra* was a seigneurial demarcation within a castral district, which, in principle, had been ceded to a knight. It included an agrarian and perhaps a livestock farm. At the same time, it served as a reinforcement in the defensive organization of the frontier or newly conquered lands. Thus, six *quadres*, or knight-services, can be found within the castle of Tàrrega (Urgell), which is located about forty kilometres from Lleida.[65] On the other hand, we have already seen the importance of *cavalleries* (which coincided with the most fertile coombs) as a result of the process of the conquest of the Conca de Barberà (Fig. 45). We have also seen that, around Lleida and Tortosa, documents from the twelfth and thirteenth centuries often allude to *torres* and *almúnies*, since the memory of the Islamic era was still very vivid. These *quadres*, *cavalleries*, and *torres* corresponded to a similar reality: feudal land tenure.

Royal Vegueries (*vicariae*)

Despite precedents in the thirteenth century, it was in 1301 when the King of Catalonia and Aragon, Jaume II, tried to establish *vegueries* as the mainstay of the territorial power of the monarchy. The *vegueries* would have a capital city, which was usually a royal city or town, extending its area of economic influence. Each *vegueria* was headed by a civil servant, the *veguer* (in Latin *vicarius*). Although the *veguers* had to deal with pressure from municipal authorities and the impossibility of exercising jurisdiction over lands controlled by the great lords, the *vegueria* system was consolidated. As a consequence, this continuity brought about, throughout the fourteenth and fifteenth centuries, changes in some boundaries of *vegueries* and, above all, the creation of new *vegueries* and sub-*vegueries*.[66]

Area of Influence of a Market Town

As seen in Chapter 5, in the high Middle Ages, many towns were created in an area allocated as a marketplace, where merchants gathered once a week.[67] These settlements sometimes depended on the monarch, or sometimes on an important lord, layman, or clergyman. Often, a community of artisans,

---

65 Sabaté, *El territori de la Catalunya medieval*, p. 94.
66 Sabaté, *El territori de la Catalunya medieval*, p. 172; Mestre and Hurtado, *Atles d'història de Catalunya*, pp. 108–09.
67 Batlle, *Fires i mercats, factors de dinamisme econòmic i centres de sociabilitat.*

merchants, and notaries settled in that area; there was a parish church, a lordly castle, and perhaps also a *call* (where the Jewish community lived). As we will see later, some market towns were originally ancient villages, documented as early as 1000; others were newly created, for example, at a crossroads or near a bridge.

Often, quite spontaneously, an area of economic influence for these settlements was created, involving people going to the market every week. At times, this area had already been defined by the privilege of the creation of the market, granted, for example, by the king. These areas often corresponded to current *comarques* or sub-*comarques*. In the high Middle Ages, in all the villages within this economic space, the same measuring tools were applied, which were possibly preserved in the town's marketplace, in a square, or in the main street. For example, in La Seu d'Urgell (Alt Urgell) and Monells (Baix Empordà), we can still see stone-made measures for cereals sheltered under the porches of the main street or in a square. This is also found, for example, in Monpazier (Oc. Montpasièr), in Gascony.[68]

The Territory of Cities

All the cities had territory that sometimes, in the high Middle Ages, could be well delimited with landmarks or boundary stones. The boundaries of the city of Barcelona were well defined, its territory covering an area of about 275 square kilometres, extending by sea from Montgat to Castelldefels and on the mountainside from Montcada to Molins de Rei, all crowned by Collserola mountain range. The territory included at least eighteen parishes. It was also thought that it extended to an area of twelve leagues into the sea.[69]

As for New Catalonia, there is an interesting document on the ancient territory of the city of Lleida. Made after the Christian conquest, this document must have served to justify the property rights of the inhabitants of the city immediately after the conquest of 1149, in marginal areas under competing demands with nearby towns or lords from neighbouring villages. It alludes to many places given names before the count's conquest and sets limits probably much wider than those of the urban *hawz* (or *alfoz* in Castilian) before 1149.[70] As pointed out above, when such precise boundaries were set, we assume the existence of people who knew the country very well. Certainly, these boundaries, sometimes made by walking through places, are, in certain cases, attempts to redefine the borders of a territory.[71]

---

68 Lilley, *Urban life in the Middle Ages*, p. 230.

69 Sabaté, 'Limites et villes dans la Catalogne médiévale', p. 189.

70 Garcia Biosca, *Els orígens del terme de Lleida*; Brufal, *El món rural i urbà en la Lleida islàmica*, p. 215.

71 Fernández Mier, 'La construcción de la territorialidad medieval', pp. 233–34; Lunven, 'Les actes de délimitation paroissiale', p. 40.

318   CHAPTER 14

The Borders of Catalonia

The form and the changes taking place on the borders of Catalonia have triggered the creation of numerous research projects. While the southern boundary has always been in La Sénia[72] and the eastern boundary is the sea, the western and northern boundaries have been constantly altered over the centuries. To the west, entire towns and *comarques* have alternated between the influence of Catalonia and Aragon. This was the case, for example, in relation to La Ribagorça.[73] The linguistic border between the Catalan-speaking lands, or the Aragonese, and Castilian was an important reference; it stretched along the Cinca River. However, political realities have not always coincided with the linguistic situation. Over the centuries, there has been a displacement of the western border of the Catalan language due to repopulation processes that took place in the modern era after the depopulation at the end of the Middle Ages (for example, in the east of the Cinca, in the *comarca* of Monzón, a town called Montsó in the Middle Ages).

The northern border, after the Treaty of Corbeil (1258), coincided with the boundary separating Catalan-speaking counties from Occitan-speaking counties. For example, after the wars waged during the first decades of the thirteenth century, this division between two states was fortified on both sides (for example, by strengthening many of the castles of Fenouillèdes or Fenolheda).[74] This reality did not change until the seventeenth century, following the Treaty of the Pyrenees (1659) by which the lands of the northern counties of Catalonia (Rosselló, Conflent, Vallespir, and part of Cerdanya) became dependent on the kingdom of France. The characteristics of this new, artificially created border in the north of Catalonia have motivated numerous studies.[75]

Conclusions

In Catalonia, the importance of studying boundaries has been traditionally underestimated. Studies conducted in England over the last few decades, as well as maps produced (e.g., the atlas of Partida, Hall, and Foard or the atlas of parishes by Cockin) have brought to the fore this gap in Catalan research.[76] The realization of this absence makes the atlas by Burgueño and Gras a very special production, as it shows modern seigneurial estates and parishes in

---

72 Also known, in the Middle Ages, as the Ulldecona River. Guinot, *Els límits del regne*, p. 31; Baydal, *Els valencians, des de quan són valencians?*, p. 30.

73 Bolòs, *Col·lecció diplomàtica de l'Arxiu Capitular de Lleida*.

74 Saguer, 'Consolidation ou disparition des frontières?'.

75 Sahlins, *Boundaries: The Making of France and Spain in the Pyrenees*; Pojada, *Viure com a bons veïns. Identitats i solidaritats als Pirineus*.

76 Partida and others, *An Atlas of Northamptonshire*; Cockin, *The Parish Atlas of England*.

Catalonia.[77] Some of its boundaries are very old, most of them dating from the Middle Ages.

Boundaries are not accidental features. They are related to other elements of the landscape, such as villages, roads, or old plot systems, which allow us to often date exactly the age of a borderline. Certainly, as in the case of roads, when studying limits, it is essential to know how to read and understand what might not seem logical, the anomalies, such as the fact that a limit is very straight and does not pass across a ridge, or that it does not match the course of a river or that of an old road. Boundaries, of course, also bring us closer to economic realities, to the knowledge of a society, and the understanding of political or administrative structures varied greatly throughout the Middle Ages, often faster than the actual drawing of boundaries.

Logically, the fact that there were boundaries in the territory of a village, parish, or castle did not prevent the people who lived there from surpassing them; this was the case throughout the Middle Ages.[78] As has been shown in this chapter, people related to those from neighbouring villages would go to the nearest market or graze their cattle in the *emprius* (rights of easement), which, as in the case of the valley of Andorra, could be located in another lordship, for example in Cerdanya or Gascony.[79] This does not imply a decrease, especially in the high Middle Ages, in the number of places, particularly at the borders where tolls were imposed on goods.

Studying the boundaries has led us to discuss the various territorial units found in Catalonia in the Middle Ages. Counties and bishoprics had boundaries, as did valleys. The territorial limits of castles with a district were well defined. The territories of Carolingian villas, villages, towns, and parishes have often been fossilized over the centuries. All this leads us to think that only if we accept that there was a certain continuity in settlement will we be able to understand that these ancient limits have lasted over the centuries, both in Old Catalonia and in other regions like Lleida and Tortosa.

---

77 Burgueño and Gras, *Atles de la Catalunya senyorial.*
78 Vigil-Escalera, 'Meeting Places, Markets, and Churches in the Countryside'.
79 Bonales, *Història territorial de la vall d'Andorra.*

CHAPTER 15

The Importance of Toponymy

Introduction

The creation of the *Atles dels comtats de la Catalunya carolíngia* (Atlas of the Counties of Carolingian Catalonia) has confirmed the importance of place names for studying territorial history. Recent research highlights the use of microtoponymy in understanding how people who lived in the Middle Ages looked at the surrounding landscape. For these reasons, we focus our particular attention on pre-Roman place names, those created in the Roman and Germanic periods, or created during the centuries under Islamic rule, as well as the Romanesque place names. We will also mention the importance of church dedications. Finally, based on some examples, we will evaluate the lessons of microtoponymy. In Catalonia, *capbreus* (land terriers) provide extensive information about fields, plots of land, and different woodland areas. In addition, this type of research brings together local history studies and work on the historical landscape.

Place Names and the Historic Landscape

Browsing through recent research in Europe regarding the validity of toponymy as a sound source of information to study the historic landscape, one can find profound differences among countries. While in France, some authors refer to a divorce between archaeology and toponymy,[1] in England, research focuses on the contributions of place names to the study of the landscape, for example, concerning the Anglo-Saxon period.[2] Also in England, recent studies emphasize the importance of minor toponymy when studying the landscape.[3] There is some truth in both positions. An analysis of these apparently opposing viewpoints leads us to conclude that, while the suspicious attitude of Elisabeth Zadora-Rio towards the inappropriate use of toponymy as a historical source seems quite reasonable, it is also true to say that the study of toponymy leads to a better understanding the past, as many scholars claim.

---

1 Zadora-Rio, Archéologie et toponymie: le divorce'; Bourin and Zadora Rio, 'Pratiques de l'espace: les apports comparés des données textuelles et archéologiques', p. 46.
2 Higham and Ryan, *Place-names, Language and the Anglo-Saxon Landscape*; Banham and Faith, *Anglo-Saxon Farms and Farming*.
3 Rippon, *Making Sense of an Historic Landscape*, pp. 69–84. Even, for example, Jones raises the interesting question of being able to know what the people of a territory (who spoke Old English) understood when they heard the toponyms of the territory where they lived. Jones, 'Place-names in Landscape Archaeology', p. 218.

322   CHAPTER 15

Just as boundaries are crucial elements of the landscape even if they are not visible from ground level, place names are also important in understanding past landscapes, despite seeing them only through maps and documents (or when asking locals). It should be noted that a place name is only alive if, from the time of its creation, many people have used it. Therefore, a fundamental assumption is that the oldest place names are those that, over the centuries, have been recognized as their own by more people.

Pre-Roman Toponyms

In Catalonia, 'pre-Roman place names' refers to different historical realities depending on the region under study, of which there are basically three. Some *comarques* stopped speaking their pre-Roman (Iberian) language during the centuries under Roman rule. This was the case in all the lands close to the coast or the lands of central and western Catalonia. By contrast, there were other *comarques* in which the loss of a pre-Roman language occurred later, at a time close to the transition to the Middle Ages, for example, in Cerdanya and perhaps in Alt Urgell (where there was an episcopal seat). Finally, in other areas, such as Pallars Sobirà, the disappearance of the pre-Roman language (in these Pyrenean lands, similar to Basque), occurred at a date close to 1000. Certainly, this has great importance for studying and dating many place names.

Indeed, there is a substantial difference between toponyms in, say, Osona, and those from the *comarca* of Pallars. While pre-Roman names in Osona correspond to central locations where there was often a fortified hill, in Pallars Sobirà or Alta Ribagorça, a significant percentage of current place names — villages and minor place names — are pre-Roman (Fig. 73). These pre-Roman place names were possibly being created until shortly before 1000 (when, obviously, the Roman Empire no longer existed). In the valleys of the westernmost Catalan Pyrenees, pre-Roman toponymy abounds. While working on the *Atles dels comtats de Pallars i Ribagorça (v806-v998)*, we included these names, which shared characteristics almost as if they had been written in a document of the Carolingian era.[4] Thus, in the Boí Valley, although no document mentions them before the turn of the millennium, we were able to include such villages as Irgo, Iran, Durro, or Taüll, whose names in Basque, according to Joan Coromines, translate as 'small village', 'large village', 'remote village', and 'village on a mountain pass'.[5]

---

4   Bolòs and Hurtado, ten volumes of 'Atles dels comtats de Pallars i Ribagorça' published during the years 1998–2018.
5   Coromines, *Onomasticon Cataloniae*.

THE IMPORTANCE OF TOPONYMY   323

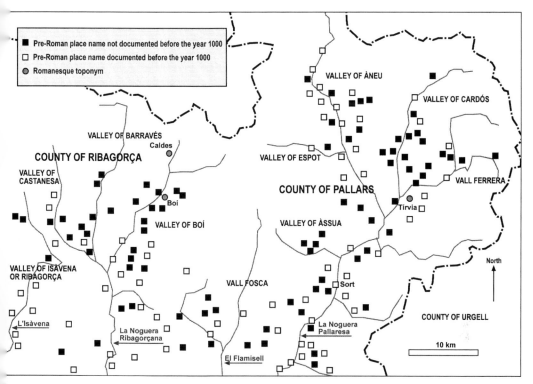

Figure 73. Pre-Roman place names in Pallars Sobirà and Ribagorça. Pre-Roman place names found in this region were established prior to 1000. Their study is an important source of information about the history of these valleys in the Pyrenees.

Pallars Sobirà

According to Joan Coromines, in Pallars Sobirà, a language related to Basque was spoken uninterrupted until around 1000.[6] It is of great interest to learn about its settlement in the early Middle Ages. For this *comarca*, in the documents written (and preserved) before 1000, only forty-two pre-Roman toponyms are mentioned (possibly many of them created in the medieval period). Along with these names documented in the Carolingian era, in these Pyrenean valleys we were able to locate about one hundred and twenty-five more current toponyms, also pre-Roman. These place names, as I have already said, certainly existed before the turn of the millennium.[7] Therefore, in this case, knowing and valuing place names allows us a better understanding of the early medieval history, population, and characteristics of this region.[8]

---

6   Coromines, *Estudis de toponímia catalana, volum I*.
7   Bolòs, 'Not So Dark Centuries: Changes and Continuities in the Catalan Landscape', p. 95.
8   Bolòs and Hurtado, *Atles dels comtats de Pallars i Ribagorça (v806-v998)*, pp. 52–53.

Roman Toponyms

In some *comarques* of Old Catalonia, we find a large number of place names created in the Roman period and ending in '-à' and '-ana', such as Cornellà and Cornellana, surely a sign of the existence of a Roman *fundus* or a pre-medieval *villa*. These place names are also an important source of information about the history of a territory. However, when dealing with toponyms, a certain amount of prudence is called for. It is common knowledge that place names can be moved from one location to another, carried by people. This transfer does not come from tens of kilometres away — certainly a highly unlikely but not impossible circumstance —, but we can assume as a probable force that, for example, in the early Middle Ages, a displacement within the same territory or *terroir* whereby it could be moved a few hundred metres or even move, for example, from a flat place to a steeper one.

Although one should be careful with toponyms, analysing the distribution and survival of place names created in the Roman period is of paramount importance. Surely, there may be cases of continuity between a Roman villa and one or more medieval villages or hamlets. Possibly they moved only a few hundred metres from the Roman remains, or perhaps at least within the same *terroir*.[9] This was the case in coastal *comarques* or regions; perhaps in the hinterland of Catalonia, the relationship between Roman *villae* and medieval hamlets was not so tight.[10]

Roussillon

In the territory of the ancient county of Roussillon (or Rosselló in Catalan) in the Carolingian period, there were about thirty-eight place names created in the Roman era (Fig. 74). Almost all of them were documented before the turn of the millennium.[11] They are predominantly along the main rivers, with five to ten kilometres between them. One interesting case is the place of Pesillà (*Pidiliano*, the *fundus* of a man named Pedilius, analysed above), where, in the Carolingian period, there was a villa and two churches. Around it we find, before 1000, place names that remind us of the *fundi* of Cornelius (*Corneliano*, nowadays Cornellà), Acutius (*Acuciano*, nowadays Agusà or Sant Esteve), Campilius (*Campiliano*), Palladius (*Pallagano*; now lost, perhaps Pallejà), Monnius (*Moniano*, nowadays Monyàs), Regulius (*Riliano*, nowadays Rellà) and Pollius (*Puliano*; now lost). It should again be noted that, in all these cases, the Roman *villa* did not necessarily have to be in the same place as the Carolingian villa or small settlement. However, as we saw in Chapter

---

9   Schneider, 'Dynamiques spatiales et transformations de l'habitat en Languedoc'.
10   Gibert, *La fi del món antic i els inicis de l'edat mitjana a la Catalunya Central*, p. 43.
11   Bolòs and Hurtado, *Atles dels comtats de Rosselló, Conflent, Vallespir i Fenollet (759–991)*, p. 47.

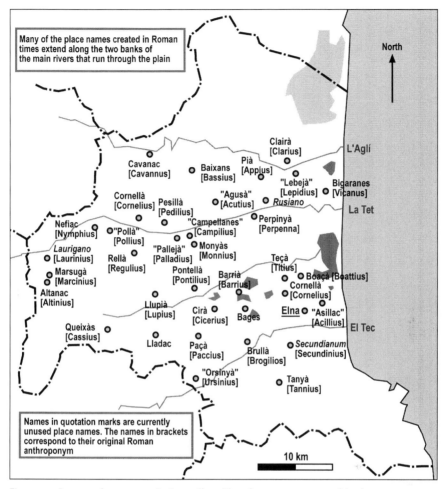

Figure 74. Roman place names in Roussillon. The place names created in the Roman period, which recall the existence of *villae* or *fundi*, abound. Although there may be transfers, they are an important source to learn about the history of this plain furrowed by the rivers Tet, Tec, and Aglí.

14, the municipalities of some of these places had a long tradition which is easily traceable to *fundi* established long before the Carolingian era. At least this was so in some of the municipalities of the *comarca* of Empordà — in the south of Roussillon, such as Rupià (Roman toponym), Parlavà (*palatium*), Vila-sacra, and Fortià (medieval toponyms) (Fig. 67).

Recent studies also point to the existence of several Greek names in Empordà.[12] Not only do places like Empúries (an ancient Greek colony)

---

12 Pérez, 'Topónimos catalanes de origen griego'.

326   CHAPTER 15

and Roses have this origin, but also towns like Calabuig (probably a person's name) or perhaps the place name *Armirodas*, documented in the early Middle Ages and now lost. These toponyms bear witness to the continuity of the settlement over the centuries.

Arabic Toponyms

One distinction between Old Catalonia and New Catalonia is clear. On the one hand, in Old Catalonia, there are very few Arabic place names, although we find some, especially in places of importance for ensuring control of the territory. On the other hand, in many counties of New Catalonia, a high percentage of place names were created during the Islamic era. Although a detailed account will not be provided here, a few significant clarifications will be made.

For Old Catalonia, in the county of Barcelona (conquered by the Carolingians in 801), knowledge and interpretation of the meanings of Arabic or Berber names can help us to understand how the country came under Islamic control. Following the Arab-Berber conquest, key places, such as castles, strategically located settlements, and the fiscal domains of the Visigothic kingdom, were targeted for domination. This is reflected in the toponymy after the Frankish conquest with such names as the castles of Gelida and Gallifa and names of settlements such as Vilatenim and Sanata, located next to main roads.[13] It is no coincidence either that many places designated as fiscal estates bearing Latin names such as *palatium* or *palatiolum*, during these years under Islamic rule, were accompanied by an Arabic name (such as Palau-solità, the palace of Sulayṭan, or *Palatio Auzido*, the palace of abū Zayd, now Ripollet).[14] Certainly, these fiscal palaces which were probably at least with a Visigothic origin, despite the same name with similar elements, they were just a little different from the *palatia*, and even the *palatiola* we find in Aquitaine, which were sometimes inhabited by Carolingian monarchs.[15]

As for New Catalonia, we find many names beginning with Vin- or Beni-, which recall that the place was 'from the son of' or 'from the descendants of'. One example could be Vensilló, seen in this volume (Fig. 34). We can easily make a list of them: Vinfaro, Vimbodí, Vinaixa, Vinallop, Vinaixarop, or also Benifallet and Benissanet. Another interesting example is that of the place name Massalcoreig, which reminds us of the migration of a member of the Quraysh tribe from the Arabian Peninsula. There are also place names related to the word *burǧ*, tower, such as Burjassénia, or the word *ribāṭ*, such

---

13   Bolòs and Hurtado, *Atles del comtat de Barcelona (801–993)*, pp. 64–65; Pérez, 'Toponímia d'origen islàmic a la Catalunya Vella', pp. 70, 76.

14   Pérez, 'Toponímia d'origen islàmic a la Catalunya Vella', pp. 74, 77.

15   Bourgeois and Boyer, 'Les palais carolingiens d'Aquitaine'.

THE IMPORTANCE OF TOPONYMY 327

as La Ràpita. The ribats were often fortified buildings where communities dedicated to the protection of the territory lived.[16]

Alongside these place names, there were also quite a few Mozarabic names as a sign of the language spoken before the arrival of the Muslims, which remained alive for some centuries after 713 or 714. An example worth noting is Vinatesa, which, according to linguists, should be interpreted as a *pinna tensa* 'extended rock'.[17] There are some Romanesque or even perhaps Roman or pre-Roman toponyms in the documents made immediately after the counts' conquest of the city of Lleida, which remained unchanged during the years under Muslim rule in a population that gradually became Arabic-speaking at the same time as it was Islamized, for example, Balaguer, Ivars, Gerb, perhaps Tabac and Mascançà, Tivenys, Xerta, and certainly Lleida and Tortosa.

Germanic Toponyms

Quite a few toponyms can be considered Germanic. It should be noted that almost all of them come from a person's name. Between the ninth and tenth centuries, approximately three-quarters of all anthroponyms of the people who lived in the Catalan counties were of Germanic origin.[18] In documents from the Carolingian period, we find some castles, some villas, and many hamlets with names of this linguistic origin: e.g., Rocabertí, Bao, Vilosiu, and Vilartolí. While in many *comarques* they do not represent a large percentage of toponyms, in others they correspond to a significantly high percentage.

Regarding Germanic place names, one should distinguish between Gothic-rooted anthroponyms (included in the toponym) and those of Frankish origin. We are aware that fashion was hardly a pivotal factor in medieval anthroponymy. Despite this, we believe that for places named after a person with a Frankish name, should the place have been created around 800, it is almost certain that this person came from the north, plausibly from Gaul, beyond the former province of Septimania (or Gothia, the Gothic March). This is important when assessing the processes of conquest and control of the territory, especially the dominance of the Carolingian monarchs.

Alt Berguedà

The northern sector of the *comarca* of Berguedà shows a high density of Germanic names, many of them Gothic or Frankish in origin. In the Alt Berguedà, there are places named Arderiu (and its plural genitive form,

---

16 Brufal, *Les ràpites. Proposta de definició conceptual*; Azuar, 'La Ràpita de Guardamar'; Varela and Varela, 'The Arrifana ribat (Algarve)', pp. 151–76; Negre, 'Espacios religiosos en el medio rural', pp. 115–34.

17 Turull, 'Sistematicitat i historicitat en la toponímia de les comarques de Ponent', p. 2,231.

18 Bolòs and Moran, *Repertori d'Antropònims Catalans (RAC) I*.

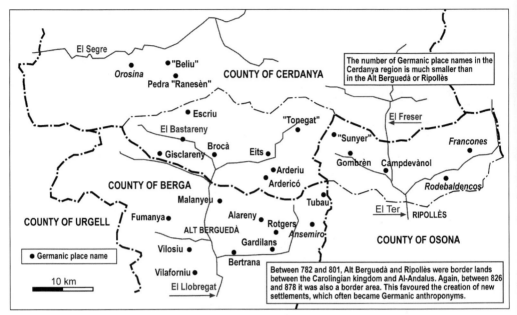

Figure 75. Germanic place names in the Alt Bergueda and Ripollès. The number of place names created from a Germanic, Gothic, or Frankish name is significant. These names often correspond to villages, hamlets, or farmhouses surrounded by forest.

Ardericó), Malanyeu, Castell de l'Areny (in fact, Alareny), Bastareny, Vilosiu, and Fumanya or Brocà (Fig. 75). This abundance of Germanic names points to the colonization of these mountainous lands, covered with forest, probably in the Carolingian period. Although, it cannot be denied that, in some cases, this process of occupation might have effectively begun before 788/798, when these lands came under the control of the Frankish monarchs and their representatives, the counts of Cerdanya.[19] Many of the Carolingian villas and hamlets bearing these names were settlements in clearings of fields and terraces surrounded by forest.

Romanesque Toponyms

The documents preserved to date report the existence of many Romanesque or Catalan place names. These place names reveal substantial information about what the territory was like. As said above, with reference to *Atles dels comtats de la Catalunya carolíngia*, the interest of toponymy in our knowledge of the fauna and flora of a county between the eighth and tenth centuries is essential. For example, there are dozens of place names that remind us that

---

19 Bolòs and Hurtado, *Atles dels comtats de Cerdanya i Berga (v788-v990)*, p. 48.

THE IMPORTANCE OF TOPONYMY   329

in a certain place, at a certain time before 1000, there were evergreen oaks, common oaks, pines, elm trees, ashes, etc. We also find references to eagles, crows, hawks, pigeons, etc.

Toponyms are especially relevant for learning about the history of the settlement. Some of them reflect cases of settlements being split into two. For example, in the *comarca* of Vallès, before 1000, we find a village named Lliçà d'Amunt and, two kilometres further south, one named Lliçà d'Avall (or 'de Vall'). There was also a villa named Corró d'Amunt, and five kilometres below, another one named Corró d'Avall. This phenomenon is in line with other European countries, for example, northern Italy.[20] It results from a transformation dating to the early Middle Ages, although it has also been pointed out that it could have precedents in the legislation from the late Roman period.[21] Other toponyms have made it possible to deepen our knowledge of the early medieval authorities' control of the territory, with place names containing the terms *palau* and *palol* (or *palou*) (in Latin, *palatium* and *palatiolum*). Other place names documented in the Carolingian era reveal a considerable amount of information and phenomena, such as Vilanova, Juïgues (*Iudaicas*), Vilajuïga (*Villa Iudica*), Fares (*Faras*), Ares (*Aras*), Pujafrancor (*Pugna Francorum*), Pau (from *pagus*), Quart (*Quarto*), La Clusa (*ipsa Clusa*), Caldes (*Calidas*), Ermedans (*Hermedanos*, from *eremitanos*), and Domeny (*Dominium*).

Place names can also reveal the origin of their settlers, e.g., the toponyms of the county of Osona were documented before 1000 with such names as *Tolosa* (hence Toulouse), *Carcases* (hence Carcassonne), *Gerundilia* (hence Girona), *Cerdanos* (hence Cerdanya), and *Francones* (from the country of the Franks).[22] Many names created in the Roman period and ending in '-ac' (e.g., Reixac, Gausac, or Pinsac) may well refer to those who came from the Occitan lands and settled in Old Catalonia around 800.

Dedications

In this chapter on place names, I will once again return to church dedications. During the process of creating *Atles dels comtats de la Catalunya carolíngia* we established a three-fold distinction between dedications from the early centuries of Christianity, those of Hispanic origin, and those from Frankish tradition. The years 759 (the conquest of Roussillon) to 801 (the siege of Barcelona by Charlemagne's army) marked a shift from an Iberian cultural area, including Septimania, to a new cultural area, influenced by Gallic tradition.[23] In this Carolingian period, Visigothic script was abandoned in

---

20 Settia, '*In Andisello et in Andego*. Couples toponymiques et peuplement rural', 647–70.
21 Olesti, 'Héritage et tradition des pratiques agrimensoriques', p. 265.
22 Bolòs and Hurtado, *Atles del comtat d'Osona (798–993)*, p. 37.
23 Bolòs and Hurtado, ten volumes of 'Atles dels comtats de Pallars i Ribagorça' published during the years 1998–2018.

330   CHAPTER 15

favour of Carolingian script, documents were dated according to the Frankish kings, and the monasteries imposed the rule of St Benedict. At the beginning of this volume, we noted the close link between Catalan and Occitan, which confirms the powerful link between Catalonia and the lands of southern Gaul. This strong bond can also be seen in the saints to whom churches were dedicated in those built during this new period of Carolingian rule. In the ninth and tenth centuries, many new churches were dedicated to Saint Martin, patron saint of the Franks. This trend, introduced in this case, especially by the Church, was more influential than we might think at first.

Microtoponymy

So far, I have talked about the names of inhabited places as well as the names of castles and churches. I have said little about microtoponymy. However, a close study of *capbreus* (land terriers) from the late Middle Ages provides in-depth information on the place names of uninhabited places, such as groups of fields (*partides* in Catalan). The *capbreus* of the late Middle Ages or early modern period form an interesting source for reconstructing the landscape of a territory. These documents were made by notaries and specified the peasants' possessions, as received from a lord in exchange for an annual rent. The documents described where the house was located, giving its boundaries, and where the lands that depended on it were situated, mentioning all of its boundaries as well. Obviously, the obligations of the peasant towards the lord concerning the property from which he enjoyed benefits were also described. This source of information is important because it not only tells us the names of the various land divisions, but it also tells us what was done with the land. However, being realistic, it would be fair to say that interpreting place names is not always an easy task as the names have been lost or transformed over the centuries.[24]

Jacinto Bonales analyses how place names in the municipality of Rocallaura (Urgell) have changed over time, from the fifteenth century to the present day.[25] He focuses on the evolution of such place names as Vilavella (now Esplanes), Farraginals (now La Bassa), Colomers (now La Plana), Les Feixes (now Camí del Tallat), L'Horta (equal), Coma de n'Arnau (equal), Comatorà (equal), Comellar (now Solans), Les Basses (lost), La Mata (now Obac del Carlà), La Sort (now Les Feixes), El Server (unidentified), etc. Therefore, the town of Rocallaura, inhabited since the Middle Ages, has a significant percentage of place names that have varied over the centuries. Also, the interest in fifteenth-century place names contributes to our understanding of the territory and realizing how it was perceived by its inhabitants. These

24   Lorcin, 'Microtoponymie et terroirs paroissiaux', p. 538.
25   Bonales, *Història de Rocallaura*, pp. 32–50.

names allude to an abandoned village (Vilavella), lands for obtaining grass for cattle (fodder) (*farraginals* in Catalan), pigeons, terraces, irrigated lands, several coombs, ponds (*basses*), a grove, fields randomly distributed among the settlers (*sorts*) of the place, and a sorb tree (*Sorbus domestica*).[26]

Certainly, many of these place names were given by the villagers themselves to distinguish the different groupings of fields (also known as *partides*). With respect to medieval England, it has been pointed out that this microtoponymy is of interest to see what peasants called everything they had around them and, in this way, being able to discover their perspective on the landscape.[27] In Catalonia, alongside the many names created by the peasants (perhaps the vast majority of them), there were also names inherited from a remote period (even pre-medieval) and place names that reflected precisely the link of some lands with the lord of the place (such as Domenge [demesme in English], Bovalar [pasture of cows] or Devesa [reserved space]).

L'Espluga de Francolí (Conca de Barberà)

A few years ago, we published a study of a *capbreu* (land terrier) of the Hospitaller commandery of L'Espluga de Francolí from 1558.[28] The number of place names mentioned in this municipality near Poblet is truly remarkable. The information contained in this land terrier allows us to understand many aspects of the history of this place following the eleventh-century conquest. We find fossilized names of numerous *cavalleries* (knights' fiefs), which corresponded to estates created at the time of the conquest (in the eleventh and twelfth centuries): for example, the *cavalleries* of Riupruners, En Roig, En Boixadors, Coma de Borbó (Fig. 45), and En Cervera, to name just a few. In addition, farmsteads (which must have spread mainly in the thirteenth century and the first half of the fourteenth century), and the names of other groupings of land, hills, plains, and forest lands are mentioned.

Conclusions

To sum up this chapter, two points are worth noting. First is the importance of using work done by linguists because of their knowledge of the origin and meaning of place names. For Catalan toponymy, the fundamental legacy is

---

26 We can point to other research, such as the one carried out by Elvis Mallorquí in relation to various land terriers (*capbreus*) of the monastery of Santa Maria de Cervià (Gironès), from the fourteenth, sixteenth and eighteenth centuries, and in relation to the minor toponymy of the place of Sant Mateu de Montnegre (Quart, Gironès). Mallorquí, 'Els noms de lloc i el temps'.

27 Kilby, *Peasant Perspectives on the Medieval Landscape*, pp. 89–119; Gardiner and Kilby, 'Perceptions of Medieval Settlement', p. 215.

28 Claramunt and Bolòs, *El capbreu de la comanda de l'Espluga de Francolí*.

the research by Joan Coromines.[29] Secondly, the current place names, mainly those mentioned in medieval documents, can provide us with substantial information about the history of places and their characteristics. Near La Seu d'Urgell, there are two separate villages 1.8 kilometres away from each other, one of which, the lowest, is called Cerc (at an altitude of 870 metres) and the other, the highest, Artedó (at 1130 metres). Both names refer to places with evergreen oak trees (*Quercus ilex*); however, one is written in a Romance language and the other in a language similar to Basque. Although both are documented as settlements from the Carolingian period, it is impossible to know whether these names existed before the houses were built in Cerc and Artedó. Therefore, it would be reckless to assume that in the early medieval period, when the two settlements were created, while a Romance language was spoken in the village below, the village above spoke a pre-Roman language. However, these place names reflect both a landscape and a history. And yet, both names reveal that both places — whether inhabited or not yet inhabited — have been referred to with the same place names uninterrupted for many centuries, plausibly at least from the early Middle Ages. Finally, we can confirm, after in-depth study, that place names are important sources of information for learning about the history of the landscape.

---

29 Coromines, *Onomasticon Cataloniae.*

CHAPTER 16

Mapping the Historical Landscape

Introduction

In Catalonia cartography has been of fundamental importance for several projects that have been carried out in recent years to learn about the past. In relation to the eighth to tenth centuries, everything mentioned in the thousands of documents preserved from this period has been transferred to maps. The toponymy referred to in texts from more than a thousand years ago, numerous economic data, and aspects related to the domination of the territory by secular or ecclesiastical lords have also been recorded. Ten volumes have been published on the different counties of Carolingian Catalonia. Various historical atlases of municipalities or *comarques* have also been compiled and published. Also, in 2010, three landscape units were studied in order to draft characterization maps of the historical landscape, similar to what has been undertaken by the English HLC (Historic Landscape Characterisation) project. With all this, and with many other published works, it has been shown that drafting maps is not just a way of illustrating research about history, but a way of knowing the past. In short, in order to study the history of the historical landscape, it is essential to create maps, a fundamental source of information.

The Importance of Historical Cartography

Mapping is important since it reflects what the country was like in the past and shows in visual form the historical realities recorded in written documents, brought to light by excavations, or even fossilized in current maps or orthophoto maps. Cartography is important for all disciplines focusing on historical studies, from those interested in events to those dealing with the arts from the past.[1] The present chapter will focus on a cartographic project developed over the last forty years, consisting of the reconstruction of Old Catalonia in the ninth and tenth centuries. At the end of the chapter, we will also consider another project, the PaHisCat.

Historical cartography has a long tradition in studies of the medieval past. H. C. Darby's *Domesday England*, first published in 1977, was by no means the first contribution in the field of historical cartography, but the book was remarkable in many respects. It should be noted that Darby was a geographer.[2] Mapping the eleventh-century English landscape, based on texts extracted

---

1 Bolòs, *Cartografia i història medieval.*
2 Darby, *Domesday England.*

from the *Domesday Book* (1086), was an exceptional feat. Although this work was not conceived as an atlas, it included hundreds of highly precise maps. In England, this tradition has been continued with in-depth studies such as Della Hooke's on the Kingdom of Hwicce, *An Atlas of Northamptonshire*, or the project *Historical Landscape Characterisation*.[3] Within this tradition, another study worth noting is *Landscapes, Documents, and Maps* as it emphasizes the importance of cartography for studying medieval settlements.[4]

As for France, there were a few significant contributions from Charles Higounet and the *Laboratoire de Cartographie Historique* in the city of Bordeaux, where, since World War II, dozens of maps were drawn that reflected different aspects of history. Another of the many works available on this topic is an atlas of France from 1000, which includes maps of religious communities (where the boundaries of dioceses were drawn), maps of fortified places (with no drawings of county boundaries), and even maps of economic aspects and pre-urban realities.[5] One of the areas represented in this atlas was the group of Catalan counties. The difference in the information preserved from the tenth century between the different areas of this Frankish kingdom is evident. Also, concerning France, mention should be made of the book coordinated by Sandrine Robert, about the sources and techniques of archaeogeography in which the interpretation of maps is of great importance.[6] Perhaps, however, the most notable recent releases is a book by Gérard Chouquer on *Les parcellaires médiévaux en Émilie et en Romagne*, in which cartography (115 maps) is a fundamental source of information.[7]

In Germany, historical cartography also has a long tradition that has made it possible to chart highly detailed maps of the great domains that existed in central Europe, as seen in the *Grosser Historischer Weltatlas* whose volume dedicated to the Middle Ages was published in 1979.[8] In this brief tour of European historical cartography, it is worth mentioning the *Atlas of the Irish Rural Landscape* which, despite devoting only a small part to the Middle Ages, is a good atlas that brings us closer to the rural landscape of this northern European country.[9] Yet there is further cartographic work offering a different outlook that reconstructs the landscape in the early Middle Ages of a series of noted sites in Tuscany, such as Scarlino, Montarrenti, or Miranduolo. These works chart map research on cereal fields, vineyards, olive groves, irrigated

---

3 Hooke, *The Anglo-Saxon Landscape: The Kingdom of the Hwicce*; Partida and others, *An Atlas of Northamptonshire: The Medieval and Early-Modern Landscape*.

4 Roberts, *Landscapes, Documents and Maps: Villages in Northern England*.

5 Parisse ed., *Atlas de la France de l'an mil*.

6 Robert ed., *Sources et techniques de l'archéogéographie*.

7 Chouquer, *Les parcellaires médiévaux en Émilie et en Romagne. Centuriations et trames coaxiales*.

8 Engel and others ed., *Grosser Historischer Weltatlas. II: Mittelalter*.

9 Aalen and others, *Atlas of the Irish Rural Landscape*.

lands, pastures, or forests (for example, chestnut trees).[10] This study shows the relevance of cartographic research with references to research about other sites, such as that of Montaillou (Oc. Montalhon).[11] It is therefore important to compare current research against past documentary and archaeological sources.

To cap off this introduction on map drafting, we provide a list of atlases released in the last few years in Catalonia. To begin with, there is the *Atles d'Història de Catalunya*.[12] Other recently published historical atlases are those by Víctor Hurtado.[13] There are also the *Atles dels comtats de la Catalunya carolíngia*, which we will discuss below, and several works on a specific topic, such as an atlas on Jews and an atlas on the lordships of Catalonia.[14]

The map should be the medium where historical information is represented but also an important source for researchers to better understand aspects of the past. This is what Elisabeth Zadora-Rio points out when approaching the work carried out by historians on cities and towns.[15] Certainly, we have always argued that maps should fulfil a dual purpose: shed some light on the past and, simultaneously, allow us to move forward and therefore discover and understand other aspects of the past centuries.

Atles dels comtats de la Catalunya carolíngia

In the Carolingian counties of Old Catalonia, an exceptional number of documents have been preserved in comparison with the rest of Europe before 1000. Thousands of documents were written and have been preserved. They were written by those who could compose them in every village or parish, mainly because they could be very useful (for example, in case anyone had to defend their interests in a trial). This wealth of documentation has made it possible to publish, between 1998 and 2018, a ten-volume atlas dedicated to representing the different Catalan counties from 759 to 1000 (the end of the Carolingian period). Many of the aspects dealt with in these volumes are of great interest for understanding the landscape during the eighth to tenth centuries.

---

10 Putti, 'Paesaggi e produzioni agricole nell'alto Medioevo', pp. 59–86.

11 Hallavant and Ruas, 'Pratiques agraires et terroir de montagne', p. 108.

12 Mestre and Hurtado ed., *Atles d'història de Catalunya*.

13 Hurtado, *Història. Política, societat i cultura dels Països Catalans. Cartografia històrica*; Hurtado, *Atles manual d'Història de Catalunya*.

14 Forcano and Hurtado, *Atles d'història dels jueus de Catalunya*; Burgueño and Gras, *Atles de la Catalunya senyorial*.

15 Zadora-Rio, 'Les approches morphologiques des agglomérations'.

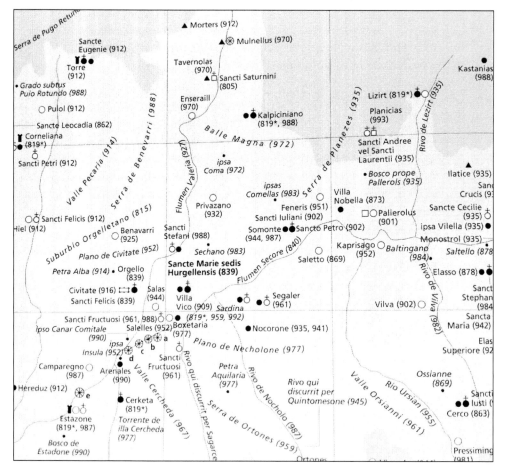

Figure 76. Fragment of a map of toponyms. Around La Seu d'Urgell, there is a city (Castellciutat) and numerous villas and hamlets, parish churches, inhabited places, towers, and mills. We also see rivers, valleys, and mountains. We have evidence of the name of all these places before 1000. Bolòs and Hurtado, *Atles del comtat d'Urgell (v788–993)*, p. 30.

Maps of Toponyms

Maps of toponyms may be the most important maps in an atlas (Fig. 76). In the ten volumes published, we have accurately located about 6,700 place names on maps at a scale of 1:100,000 (approximately 66 per cent of the place names mentioned in the documents written before 1000). These place names represent a sizeable percentage of the existing population centres. In addition, the maps include the names of watercourses and mountains. Certainly, this list of toponyms, each represented by a single point on the map, includes the toponyms of almost all castles and monasteries, and the names of many

MAPPING THE HISTORICAL LANDSCAPE   337

churches. The result, therefore, allows a fairly accurate reconstruction of what the fifteen counties in Old Catalonia were like more than a thousand years ago.

On the maps, each of these 6,700 place names is accompanied by the first date mentioned in the preserved documentation. Of course, knowing this date should not lead us to assume that the village, the castle, or the church could not be much older. The fact that some buildings are mentioned for the first time in a given year does not mean that they were finished at that time, as is commonly believed. On the other hand, it should also be noted that the name of an inhabited place may have existed long before its population settled down. This is important to keep in mind when, for example, the name is pre-Roman. Additionally, there is always the possibility that place names were transferred. Numerous place names, which were created during the Roman period, have been moved.

After a few initial doubts (involving the earliest volumes released), we soon realized that these maps of toponyms from before 1000 should also include all pre-Roman, Roman, and Arabic place names. This decision meant, for example, that, in the volume dedicated to the counties of Pallars and Ribagorça, many current places were included because they had a pre-Roman name, even though, perhaps and too often accidentally, they had not been mentioned in any document written before 1000.[16] In comparison, logically, there is far more information from places located near a monastery or a cathedral and from places where these institutions, which took great care of their archives, had their domains.

The Origins of Toponyms

Figuring out the linguistic origin of place names is of paramount importance and in Chapter 15 we dealt with this issue. At this point, it is worth stating that the ten volumes of the *Atles dels comtats de la Catalunya carolíngia* include thematic maps dedicated to pre-Roman place names, as well as those created under Roman rule, and also the Germanic and Arabic place names. The proportion of names with different origins varies greatly from county to county.

To minimize the possibility of leaving out important information, some maps in the *Atles* have been dedicated to place names of historical interest. In fact, there are many Romanesque (or Catalan) place names, documented more than a thousand years ago, which can provide remarkable data on the history of a place. For example, the place name 'arca' (*archa*) has sometimes been identified with a prehistoric monument, although it should, perhaps, normally be related to a landmark of the Roman past.[17] The place names *palatio* and *palatiolo*, which have been the focus of many studies lately, must be related to early medieval fiscal domains. The fact that the documents mention

---

16   Bolòs and Hurtado, *Atles dels comtats de Pallars i Ribagorça (v806-v998)*.
17   Chouquer, *L'arpentage romain*, p. 413.

a *Licano subteriore* (946) presupposes that there was also a *Lliçà d'Amunt*, or higher, and, therefore, leads us to assume that, in the Carolingian period, or even before, this site was split off from an earlier domain. This could be related to Roman laws that required the preservation of the *fundus* as a fiscal unit, which may have been maintained until the Visigothic era.[18] Before 1000, in many counties (Roussillon, Peralada, Cerdanya, Urgell, and Barcelona) the place name *vilanova* (in other words, 'new settlement') abounded. We believe that these places may correspond to villas created because of the process of Carolingian conquest, perhaps intended to facilitate territorial control.

Dedications

This topic was discussed in Chapter 15. It is important to represent on a map the dedications of all documented churches before 1000 which can help us find possibly older churches. Mapping also makes it possible to locate quite precisely churches built after the arrival of the Carolingians. Therefore, each of the ten volumes includes a map with churches dedicated to saints from the early Christian period (first and foremost, the Virgin and the apostles), churches with dedications to Hispanic saints, or even churches consecrated and dedicated to Frankish figures such as Saint Martin.

Forests and Cultivated Land

In documents from the eighth to tenth centuries, there are numerous references that, directly or indirectly, refer to forests and crops. Some documents mention forest areas, cultivated land, irrigated land, fruit tree land, or vineyards. There are even documents that mention place names that shed light on plants and animals that were (or had been) in a specific location. All this information, which allows us to learn about the landscape of the Carolingian period, has been transferred onto maps of the fifteen counties of Old Catalonia.

Roads and Mills

In each volume of the *Atles dels comtats de la Catalunya carolíngia* there is a map dedicated to representing the references to cultivated lands and forests found in documents, and another one representing roads, mills, mines, and forges. In the ten volumes of this atlas, we have drawn the roads mentioned in the documents and also those we know must have existed as an extension of a road alluded to in a document or because, for example, they served to connect two well-documented sites. The result allows for a fairly accurate reconstruction of the road networks of various counties. Chapter 13 of this book, dedicated to communication routes, owes much to research undertaken through drawing the maps of these atlases (Fig. 64).

---

18 Olesti, 'Héritage et tradition des pratiques agrimensoriques', pp. 265–66.

When making maps of mills, our expectations rose as we realized the large number of mills that existed more than a thousand years ago in the various counties. We have always assumed — although this assumption may be challenged — that when a list of goods is made about a property sold or given and one or several mills are included, it is because they existed. The first volume, published in 1998, of *Atles dels comtats de la Catalunya carolíngia* focused on Besalú county.[19] One of its most noticeable features was the abundance of mills on the main rivers and streams; most of its Carolingian villas had one. This fits perfectly with the type of society shown in Pierre Bonnassie's doctoral thesis, with smallholding peasants who sometimes possessed an allod and owned the land they worked on and, oddly enough, with the jurisdictional rights of their lands still in the hands of their sovereign (in fact, the count).[20] In general, in the Carolingian period, the great lords had not monopolized the right to use water, unlike what we find after 1000.

Case studies

The ten volumes of the *Atles dels comtats de la Catalunya carolíngia* include maps that act as case studies as we try to reinforce our knowledge of the landscape of a well-defined territory. These maps have sometimes been used either to publish the results of previous work or as catalysts for further analysis of a specific region.

Some examples will now be examined. In the volume dedicated to the county of Osona, we reconstructed on a map the parish of Sant Pere de Sora, based on the information recorded when the church was consecrated in 960. By doing so, we saw the opportunity to establish a link between the villas and hamlets mentioned in this document and the current cultivated spaces and farmsteads, probably created after 1000.[21] Additionally, in the same volume we created detailed maps of some settlements mentioned in the Carolingian era, such as Vilargonter (*Villare Gontario*, 937), the villa of Reixac (*Rexago*, 981), the villa of Albars (*Albas*, 905), Vilatemmar (*Villa Teudemar*, 956), and Sant Creu de Joglars (*Sancta Crucis Gugulares*, 984). In addition, we included the current cultivated spaces around them, surrounded by forests, which very often show concentric shapes, as seen in Chapter 9 of this volume.[22]

In the volume dedicated to the county of Urgell, we analysed the territory of Solsona, based on its consecration charter in 977, discussed above in Chapter 14, and accurately drew a map of the valleys of Andorra, Lord, Lavansa, and Castellbò.[23] In the volume on the counties of Cerdanya and Berga, the lands

---

19 Bolòs and Hurtado, *Atles del comtat de Besalú (785–988)*.

20 Bonnassie, *Croissance et mutations d'une société. La Catalogne du milieu du xe à la fin du xie siècle*.

21 Bolòs and Hurtado, *Atles del comtat d'Osona (798–993)*, p. 54.

22 Bolòs and Hurtado, *Atles del comtat d'Osona (798–993)*, p. 51.

23 Bolòs and Hurtado, *Atles dels comtats de Cerdanya i Berga (v788-v990)*, pp. 66–75.

340 CHAPTER 16

that depended on the county of Cerdanya, despite being in Ripollès, territories that were in theory included in the county of Osona were depicted on a map.[24]

Estates and Boundaries

The creation of boundary maps of the fifteen counties of Carolingian Catalonia made it easier to write Chapter 14, as it deals with valleys and castle districts. While it is hard to confirm, at the head of some of these demarcations there was probably a *veguer* or *vicarius*, supposedly appointed by the count. Whereas sometimes finding boundaries for Carolingian estates, especially in some counties, is quite an easy task, in other counties, this becomes a more intricate endeavour. It has been simple enough for some valleys, and particularly the castral districts of marchlands. It is, however, difficult to date them. Some of them belong to the Carolingian period, but some may have existed long before, perhaps from the early medieval period; this issue has been dealt with in previous chapters.

Cities

What we have learned about Carolingian cities or county capitals is still far too limited, as documents generally provide little information on this issue. We do know, though, that, at that time, there were very few important population centres. The largest inhabited areas were cities with a long-standing Roman heritage, such as Barcelona and Girona. Even in towns with an episcopal seat, such as Vic, Elna, La Seu d'Urgell, and Roda d'Isàvena, the actual population must have been very small. In other towns with a Roman past, such as Llívia, Mataró (Alarona), or Isona, where many remains are available, the number of inhabitants must have been low. Concerning such counties as Pallars, we have no confirmation on where the capital could have been, or where the counts had their residence, but we do know that by the late Middle Ages, their headquarters was established in the town of Sort. In the future, archaeological excavations will be very important, such as those carried out in the last few years in Elna, Girona, Llívia, and in L'Esquerda (*Rota Civitas*) or in Castellrosselló.

Estates of Lay and Ecclesiastical Lords

At the risk of digressing from the main subject, it should be noted that the third part of each volume of the *Atles dels comtats de la Catalunya carolíngia* was dedicated to creating a map, in a similar level of detail as in those maps on place names, of the documented domains of the counts, viscounts, and lay or ecclesiastical lords. Since most of the documentation comes from ecclesiastical

---

24 Bolòs and Hurtado, *Atles dels comtats de Cerdanya i Berga (v788-v990)*, p. 83.

sources, the best-represented manorial domains are those of bishoprics and monasteries. Nevertheless, hundreds of large and medium-sized domains, spread throughout the territory, are also represented.

Cartography and the Retrogressive Method

One of the best ways to carefully reconstruct the landscape is by using a retrogressive method. In Europe, there are a few interesting examples of such research, such as that carried out by Samuel Leturcq, about a territory located north of Orleans.[25] Also, despite using a slightly different method, Nicolas Poirier's research on a French territory 'through a magnifying glass' and in the *longue durée*, from prehistory to nowadays, has similar characteristics to the retrogressive method.[26]

In Catalonia, some research has also been conducted on the historical landscape using this approach. The retrogressive method requires us to approach the knowledge of the landscape and the social and economic organization of the territory by consulting contemporary documents and, from these, working our way backward, going back in time, for example, to the Middle Ages or the Roman period. Recently, this methodology has been applied to two municipalities near the city of Lleida: Menàrguens and Almacelles.

Atlas of the Municipality of Menàrguens (la Noguera)

In 2013, *Atles Històric de Menàrguens* (in English, Historical Atlas of Menàrguens) was published, a cartographic study of the changes in the historical landscape of this municipality in the *comarca* of Noguera over the last two thousand years.[27] After drawing the first maps of the PaHisCat project, we became aware of the need to deepen our knowledge of the historical landscape by consulting local studies, for example, of municipalities. Thanks to the support of the town council of Menàrguens, we succeeded in carrying out long-term research, from the Roman era to the present day, on this municipality located between the cities of Balaguer and Lleida. Using a retrogressive approach, we studied its properties and manorial domains, its main roads, its ditches, and its town planning. We differentiate between irrigated lands, created in the Islamic era, and possibly subdivided after the count's conquest, and drylands. We also took into special consideration the importance of livestock and animal roads.

---

25 Leturcq, *Un village, la terre et ses hommes. Toury en Beauce.*
26 Poirier, *Un espace rural à la loupe.*
27 Bolòs and Bonales, *Atles històric de Menàrguens. El paisatge històric d'un municipi de la comarca de la Noguera al llarg de dos mil anys.*

342   CHAPTER 16

Atlas of the Municipality of Almacelles (Segrià)

After our experience with the municipality of Menàrguens, a town next to the river Segre, we undertook on a similar project on Almacelles, a municipality also close to Lleida, but with a series of features of its own. Almacelles stands on unirrigated land.[28] Our book analyses its landscape from prehistoric times to the present. It describes the great changes that took place in the Roman and Islamic eras, the late Middle Ages as well the process of modern abandonment, and its contemporary repopulation and plot division.

Photographs from the Mid-Twentieth Century, GIS, and LiDAR

In an attempt to better understand what the landscape was like, for example, in the Middle Ages, aerial photographs taken in the mid-twentieth century (A-Series from 1945–1946 and B-Series from 1956–1957) have become an invaluable source of information. Photographs taken between 1956 and 1957 are generally a little more detailed than earlier ones. Certainly, the twentieth-century landscape differs from that of, say, the thirteenth century, or even more so, the sixth century. This is undeniable. However, since many counties of Catalonia have undergone profound transformations over the last fifty years, during which hundreds of suburbs, thousands of industrial buildings, and dozens of motorways have been constructed, it is essential to rely on these photographs to find elements of the medieval or ancient landscape that still existed in the 1940s or 1950s.[29] On the other hand, while some Catalan counties have undergone a harsh process of urbanization, others have seen a systematic process of depopulation, which has led to many farms and even entire villages being abandoned, and in turn, many fields, possibly cultivated since the Middle Ages, have turned into forested land.

Recently, geographic information systems (GIS) have been used not only to create the maps of the PaHisCat project, which will be explained later but also to conduct other research studies. The use of GIS was fundamental in the doctoral thesis by Marc Fernández Ferrer on settlements, fortifications, and communication routes located in the south of Montseny (Vallès Oriental).[30] The thesis undertook viewshed analysis for some castles and churches as well as catchment area analysis for various medieval inhabited places and cost path

---

28   Bolòs and Bonales, *Atles històric d'Almacelles. El paisatge històric d'un municipi de la comarca del Segrià des de la Prehistòria fins a l'actualitat.*

29   Bolòs, 'Història del paisatge i mapes de Caracterització del Paisatge Històric'.

30   Fernández Ferrer, 'Arqueologia del paisatge alt medieval al baix Montseny, segles VI–X. Una demostració pràctica dels sistemes d'informació geogràfica'.

analysis. These techniques have been used in similar ways in other European countries, such as in Liguria.[31]

Aerial photographs often show dark marks on cultivated land, reflecting abandoned buildings, field edges, or old waterways. Roger Agache's contribution to the study of Roman *villae* in northern France was highly remarkable and showed the importance of this photographic technique.[32] Recently, much research has been published in other countries, such as Denmark.[33] In Catalonia, recent studies have made it possible to discover, for example, the characteristics of extinct streams or the shapes of ancient fields, possibly medieval or perhaps, as has been proposed for example in France, even older.[34]

Shortly before, at the University of Lleida Antonio Porcheddu wrote his doctoral thesis on the use of LiDAR technology to gain a deeper insight into the medieval landscape of the Àger valley (La Noguera).[35] Certainly, this technology can help us to learn and better understand the historical landscape. For example, in central Europe, in forested lands, a few breakthroughs have been made on orthogonal or radial plots hidden in currently forested areas.[36] Therefore, the main priority is not so much using an innovative technique as achieving results that allow us to better understand the past and, in this case, discover what we cannot see either walking around or looking at aerial photographs.

Characterizing Historic Landscape

In 2010, at the University of Lleida, we set out to work on the PaHisCat (Historic Landscape of Catalonia) project. The project replicated the English project HLC (Historic Landscape Characterisation). The aim was to map the different landscape units established in the context of Catalonia by the Observatori del Paisatge, an advisory body of the Government of Catalonia. PaHisCat was funded by the then Catalan Ministry of Territorial Policy and Public Works (from 2010, the *conselleria* or ministry was renamed Ministry of Territory and Sustainability) of the government of the Generalitat.

The English HLC project sought to identify areas whose elements, such as field boundaries, roads, or farmhouses, were linked together due to their historic development, and by doing so, we would be able to identify the processes that had led to their creation.[37] The project was based on the assumption that the

---

31 Leonardi, '*Cost distance* e *viewshed analysis*'.
32 Agache and Bréart, *Atlas d'Archéologie aérienne de Picardie*.
33 Helles Olesen and others, *Luftfotoarkæologi i Danmark*; Helles Olesen and others, *Luftfotoarkæologi 2. Luftfotos, droner, laser og geofysik*.
34 Bolòs, *El paisatge medieval del comtat de Barcelona*, pp. 309–24.
35 Porcheddu, 'The Ager Valley Historic Landscape'.
36 Schwartz and others, 'Les paysages d'enclos médiévaux en Alsace', p. 171.
37 Turner, 'Historic Landscape Characterisation', p. 19.

whole landscape is historic, that everything is of interest in our search to learn about our past, and that, therefore, everything must also be well managed (although not everything needs to be preserved). For each plot of land, some consensus had to be reached as to what its predominant historic character was. To this end, a series of features or character types were established and adapted to the elements found in each region of England, depending on the current and historic characteristics of each landscape. In addition, thanks to the database, as the maps were being drawn using GIS, it was also possible to indicate their preceding types.[38] These types of landscapes could correspond to, for example, a field of medieval origin or an industrial estate from the second half of the twentieth century. This project was launched in 1993, and now the entire English landscape has been mapped. Comprehensive HLC work has also been done for Scotland, Wales, Ireland, and elsewhere.[39] More limited research have been conducted in Greece, Turkey, and Slovenia.[40] Numerous studies have recently been published that allow us to understand the characteristics of this HLC project.[41]

The PaHisCat Project

In line with the characteristics of the project, we first had to establish features or character types that would allow us to differentiate typologically and chronologically the various elements of the current landscape. We needed to consider both current and historical realities. Our focus was on areas or plots, without neglecting the elements represented as a point or a line on a map. To this end, we worked at a detailed scale that would allow us to characterize each plot of land. One of our main drawbacks was the lack of previous studies on Catalan historic landscapes as reliable as those carried out in England.

Having established the different types of landscapes (e.g., rainfed crops, irrigated areas, barren and forest areas, urban and industrial areas, etc.), the next step was to determine a possible date for their creation. To this end, we considered the great changes from the past. In the Roman period, these changes included the processes of organizing the territory into centuriations. In the Middle Ages, there was the creation of coombs, irrigated areas, terraces, farmsteads, and villages. An easier way of distinguishing the changes in recent decades has been by comparing aerial photographs from the mid-twentieth century with current orthophoto maps. The initial intention was to apply a

---

38 Clark and others, *Using Historic Landscape Characterisation*; Smith, *Patterns in the Landscape*.

39 Lambrick and others, *Historic Landscape Characterisation in Ireland*.

40 Crow and others, 'Characterizing the Historic Landscapes of Naxos'; Crow and Turner, 'Silivri and the Thracian Hinterland of Istambul'; Štular, 'Historic Landscape Characterisation: Kobarid'.

41 Turner, 'Historic Landscape Characterisation: an introduction to methods and applications'; Rippon, *Historic Landscape Analysis*; Smith, *Patterns in the Landscape*.

safe and simple methodology, given the need to analyse significant large areas in detail. This effort paid off and our knowledge of the historic landscape of the areas studied was broadened. It must be said, though, that, from the outset of the project, we always thought that our contribution would be much improved in the future; for this reason, corrections and amendments will be made in the future as we deepen our knowledge.

By way of examples, we offer a brief description of the characteristics of the three landscape units under study, for which maps were made and a study was published in two volumes published by the University of Lleida.

Horta de Pinyana

This landscape unit is north of the city of Lleida. The land is currently irrigated by the Pinyana canal and its different secondary ditches and it is crossed by numerous roads. This land has been inhabited uninterrupted for at least the last two thousand years. The creation of characterization maps drove us to differentiate between its different historic stages and focus on the great changes experienced in each of these past periods. To this end, we analysed its road network, the Roman centuriations and plot divisions, the fields in the narrow side valleys, perhaps, since the end of the Roman period, the creation of small ditches and the use of the so-called *reguers* (courses of drainage water) perhaps throughout the early Middle Ages, the creation of the Séquia Major de Segrià (Major canal of Segrià) and its influence on the development of the Muslim city (Fig. 55), the constitution or consolidation of different *almúnies*, the expansion of the number of branch canals (*braçals*) after the conquest in 1149, the creation of *torres* (often inherited from *almúnies*), the creation of a new town in 1231 (Castellnou or Vilanova de Segrià) and the growth of villages where a church was built (such as Benavent de Segrià and Torrefarrera). All these changes had to be represented graphically on a sufficiently detailed scale to define the characteristics of each plot of land. Many of these aspects have been discussed in this volume.

Choosing the characteristics of the landscape that could help us describe it typologically and chronologically, we drew a characterization map and several thematic maps, all of them georeferenced (GIS was used). To this end, previous studies were consulted.[42] Additionally, using maps to characterize the historical landscape allowed us to deepen our knowledge of the history of this territory.[43] The need to define a problem fosters creativity to find answers. In this case, our main endeavour consisted of figuring out the impact of the elements inherited from the Roman era on the current landscape and identifying these elements. Secondly, we aimed to characterize landscapes created before and after the Christian conquest of 1149.

---

42 Bolòs, 'Paisatge i societat al "Segrià" al segle XIII'.
43 Bolòs, 'Un paisatge complex d'un país molt vell'.

CHAPTER 16

MAPPING THE HISTORICAL LANDSCAPE 347

Figure 77. Historic Landscape Characterisation map. Part of the characterization map of the landscape unit of La Conca de Poblet (the Poblet Basin). There are different plots with strong pre-medieval survivals, coombs, terraces, orchards, dry fields, forests, wastelands, urbanized spaces from the medieval period, etc. Source: J. Bolòs and Observatori del Paisatge – PaHisCat.

348   CHAPTER 16

After publishing the maps, our findings on this landscape unit have progressed, especially as a result of the publication of a book on Torrefarrera and a study, currently in progress, on the links between ditches and secondary channels with the various *almúnies* that must have existed before 1149 to the north of the city of Lleida.[44] This research should make it possible to date more precisely the construction of the hydraulic network.

La Conca de Poblet

This landscape unit corresponds approximately to the Conca de Barberà region or *comarca*. This plain surrounded by mountains is endowed with the monastery of Poblet, the new town of Montblanc, and the castral town of L'Espluga de Francolí as well as many other villages (Fig. 77). Some of today's roads coincide with old ones. Unlike the previous landscape unit, most of the cultivated land is unirrigated. After studying the characterization maps, we concluded that there was a remarkable occupation of these flat lands in the Roman period. Then, in the early Middle Ages, many of the coombs may well have been exploited. It was precisely when trying to understand the landscape of this region that we realized the usefulness of identifying coombs as a means of understanding the population and the changes that took place in the early Middle Ages. After years under Islamic rule, in the eleventh century, this *comarca* was occupied by the count of Barcelona. As seen in previous chapters, the *cavalleries*, granted to feudal lords (some of them knights, *cavallers* in Catalan) who participated in the conquest, often extended along these elongated coombs, as they were the most fertile lands, cultivated for centuries. During the high Middle Ages, the Cistercian abbey of Poblet was built (Fig. 13), as well as several new towns, a few castral villages, and numerous scattered farmsteads.

Making the characterization map of the historic landscape gives us a better understanding of this territory and, first and foremost, an opportunity to interpret its changes over the centuries. For example, it allows us to discover the significance of transformations from the Roman period and the importance of the cultivation of coombs in the creation of the medieval landscape.

Other noted studies are those resulting from the documentation of Poblet, the commandery of Barberà, the town of Vimbodí, or the *capbreus* (land terriers) written by notaries in the late Middle Ages.[45] Thanks to the considerable amount of documentation preserved, it will soon be possible

---

44   Vicedo and others, *Les etapes de la construcció del territori a Catalunya: Torrefarrera*; Bolòs, 'El paisatge de Torrefarrera cap a l'any 1200 i als darrers segles medievals', pp. 45–67.

45   *Diplomatari de Santa Maria de Poblet. Volum I. Anys 960–1177*, ed. by Altisent; *Col·lecció diplomàtica de la casa del Temple de Barberà (945–1212)*, ed. by Sans Travé; Sans Travé, *La colonització de la Conca de Barberà després de la conquesta feudal*; Claramunt and Bolòs, *El capbreu de la comanda de l'Espluga de Francolí.*

to deepen our knowledge of the evolution of the landscape of this *comarca* over the last two thousand years.

La vall cerdana

Cerdanya is a natural region divided, after the Treaty of the Pyrenees in 1659, between the French and Spanish states in a random and harmful way for its population. This landscape unit includes only the part of the region dependent on the Catalan government. As reflected in its toponymy and archaeological excavations, Cerdanya is an 'old' country, inhabited for millennia. When studying this landscape unit, we first identified the lands whose orientations coincided with the plot division from the Roman period, regardless of whether these parallels were the result of a direct or indirect influence (e.g., because of the former orientation of some paths). We will also study the road network, the distribution of the population, and the impact of these inhabited places on their surroundings.

As in the previous landscape units, making the characterization map allowed us, in turn, to deepen our knowledge of the landscape of Cerdanya.[46] This work, resulting from the PaHisCat project, included the description and justification of the route of the main communication roads, which confirms the Roman precedents for most of these roads. The distribution of settlements, most of which are well documented in the Carolingian period, was also studied. Based on mid-twentieth-century aerial photographs, the shapes and orientations of the fields were analysed according to the characteristics of the toponymy, which allowed us to clarify aspects of the history of the landscape of this region. Shortly afterward, the *Atles dels comtats de Cerdanya i Berga (v788–990)* came out.[47]

Interestingly, in this case, differentiating between what was created in the Roman period and what was medieval was a more difficult task. One gets the impression that the onset of the Middle Ages saw the creation of a multitude of population centres (new towns and villages) willing to adapt the existing elements to their own needs. A very specific case is the village of Alp, a place where we discover the imprint of the Middle Ages on the radial network of roads leaving the village (partly inherited from the Roman era) and, above all, in the fields created on both sides of these roads (Chapter 9). On the other hand, it must be noted that we did not find evidence of the importance of livestock activity, which, as research carried out in the municipality of Enveig shows (Fig. 63), had always existed and, for a few centuries, had been especially important.[48]

---

46 Bolòs, 'Paisatge històric, cartografia i societat a l'alta edat mitjana: l'exemple de la Cerdanya'.
47 Bolòs and Hurtado, *Atles dels comtats de Cerdanya i Berga*.
48 Rendu, *La montagne d'Enveig*.

PaHisCat and Understanding Landscape History

These works have improved our understanding of landscape history. Certainly, the process of creating characterization maps of the historic landscape has triggered many questions whose answers have broadened our knowledge of the changes that have taken place in the landscape. For example, in the case of unexpected shapes or locations, their reason must always be sought. Finding the reason allows us to understand the puzzling and anomalous shape of certain paths and the location of some of these settlements and their changes over the centuries; similarly, it will enable us to understand why there are elongated fields known as *comes* (coombs), or even when some plots started to be irrigated and took on new shapes in line with social changes. However, the number of unanswered issues is endless. The need to come up with new questions and answers has been one of the great contributions made by the PaHisCat project.

Making characterization maps means giving up on studying isolated elements or components to start studying a type of landscape that can be found in more than one place and has similar features everywhere. As pointed out by Eric Vion, studying one individual road is less important than studying the whole network and we should refrain from considering only one specific and localized element of the landscape and try to learn about the territory as a whole, and determine where we can find similar elements and where there may also be other elements different from the one studied, yet created simultaneously.[49]

PaHisCat and Environmental Management

As pointed out by the authors of the English HLC project, the aims of the HLC should be both didactic and to improve the management of the territory. It is essential to try to disseminate results. People need to realize that a paved road can be built on earlier road with two thousand years of history. Public authorities and developers should be warned against destroying a communication route that already existed in the Roman period, was trodden on in the Islamic era, and has survived to the present day. A plot of land created during the Middle Ages, or perhaps even earlier, must be properly valued. Raising awareness is not an easy task everywhere, especially when we see what has happened in many regions of Catalonia, where old roads and historic fields have been systematically destroyed. In recent decades, urban developments and industrial estates have been randomly built, resulting in the destruction of landscapes with many centuries of history which can only be traced now by utilizing aerial photographs from the mid-twentieth century.

---

49 Vion, 'L'analyse archéologique des réseaux routiers'.

For all these measures to ensure the future management of our territory, profound knowledge of the history of the landscape around us is called for. Just as we value a Romanesque church, we must value the thirty-step *sagrera* space around it, although now we may only see a few modern houses. Also, we must value the roads crossing rainfed lands and reflect on the fact that they are many centuries old and must not be destroyed whenever there is a development project creating new irrigation ditches. There are countless examples. People should understand that a landscape has a long history and, therefore, is also part of the collective heritage, since, as we have seen throughout the pages of this book, it is also a living document that allows us to know our past.

New Projects

Within the PaHisCat project, two more landscape units were also partially studied: one located along the Segre River and another that extends to the north of Girona. Both studies remain, however, unpublished to date. Two books were subsequently published, dedicated to the municipalities of Menàrguens and Almacelles, as discussed above, as well as a study on the historical landscape of the region of Priorat and research on the landscape unit of the Cadí (Alt Urgell).[50] Later, a study on the terraces in western Catalonia led to the creation of different characterization maps of the historic landscape and, as we have said, became a breakthrough in the knowledge of this fundamental element of the Mediterranean landscape, studied in Chapter 9 of this volume.[51]

Conclusions

Recently, historians have begun to value cartography as an important complement for illustrating historical studies and even, as I have hoped, as a source of knowledge that allows us to reach out into the past. In addition, cartography has also become, in today's world where images play such a key role, an indispensable didactic tool. In a nutshell, in this chapter we have seen the importance of maps for understanding settlement changes, the distribution and evolution of place names, the shapes of fields and irrigated land, communication routes and ditches, and the outlines of boundaries.

---

50 Bolòs and Bonales, *Atles històric de Menàrguens*; Bolòs and Bonales, *Atles històric d'Almacelles*; Bolòs, 'La Caracterització del Paisatge Històric (CPH) del Priorat'; Bonales, *Atles històric del Cadí*. Recently, we have also published the first volume of the book *El paisatge medieval del comtat de Barcelona*, dedicated to the study of the landscape of the county of Barcelona. The second volume (to be published next year) will include a cartographic approach to the historical landscape units that we can find in this territory.

51 Turner and others, 'Changes and Continuities in a Mediterranean Landscape'.

The best way to relate all the realities of the landscape and perceive the transformations undergone over the centuries is by using maps.

Our study from 2010, consisting of an analysis of three landscape units, brought to light several points. First, there is the challenge of doing this kind of work. Having to deal with the uncertain realities of having to fill in all the spaces on a map drove us to ask ourselves many questions and struggle to answer them. Secondly, however, it also revealed some of the main difficulties that landscape studies must overcome. While there were collaborating historians who knew where to consult information, there were others who were not aware that we did not intend to explore a series of unrelated points, but rather what we were after was to understand the character of all the plots in a very large space and be able to represent them accompanied by a date. Thirdly, the task of communicating and disseminating our findings should be implemented with more emphasis. Although Catalonia is a country with many local and regional scholars, much work still needs to be done to make the population interested in studying the landscape from a historical perspective and for people to think of the landscape as part of our collective heritage.

Conclusion

Studying Historic Landscapes Bridges Gaps
Between the Past and the Present

When people walk around a place, most of them are incapable of dating the elements of the landscape they see. They do not know when a village was created or when a castle and a church were built, let alone how to date roads, or understand why they are the way they are. They find it difficult to tell when the various groupings of land around a settlement were organized. In a region with a predominance of dispersed settlements, the origin of farmsteads in a municipality is probably unknown to most people. They have no idea when the ditch was dug, even if it runs close to where they live. It is very possible that most people are ignorant of the layout of the boundaries of their municipality and why it is as it is. All of these are aspects that historic landscape studies can clarify. They correspond to questions raised in the various chapters of this volume. Work done in recent years has made it possible to answer some of these questions. However, we stand at the beginning of a long journey. Each step allows us to bridge the present and the past, and by so doing, get closer to the history of the landscape. The past has left its imprint on the landscape, as if it were an old document of sorts that we must know how to 'read'. Perhaps we cannot expect modern people to be able to notice the landscape of the Middle Ages, 'but experiencing that landscape directly is our best hope of doing so'.[52]

Studying Historic Landscapes is a Project of *Longue Durée*

Long-term research is essential in studying the historic landscape. If we take the Middle Ages as a point of reference, one needs to go back to the classical period. Learning about settlement distribution, understanding the shapes of roads, fields or boundaries requires knowledge of what was there from the Roman period and even in some cases it is necessary to discover possible precedents created in the stages before the Roman conquest.

But that alone is not enough. A full understanding of how the landscape has evolved over the last five centuries since the end of the Middle Ages is also necessary. To this end, we used a method of working towards an understanding of the past by an examination of the present, in other words, a *retrogressive*

---

52 Banham and Faith, *Anglo-Saxon farms and farming*, p. 12.

354 CONCLUSION

approach, as we did when working on the historical atlases of the municipalities of Menàrguens and Almacelles.[53] Keeping track of how the plots of land and roads either changed or persisted looking backwards from the first half of the twentieth century to the nineteenth and eighteenth centuries, or, going further back, the sixteenth or fifteenth centuries, is essential for understanding what the landscape was like back in the Middle Ages. This task is slow and therefore requires an enormous amount of documentary information about the settlement under study in the modern period. Additionally, this also requires access to maps or aerial photographs from the twentieth century as a means of distinguishing recent features, i.e., those from the last few decades, from those dating to prior times.

Studying Landscape History is a Multidisciplinary Endeavour

This is evident in the pages of this volume. Gaining an insight into past landscapes requires the consultation of written documents. It is also important to view old maps and, above all, current orthophoto maps and those made in the twentieth century. If we know how to accurately identify old elements in the landscape, aerial photographs from the mid-twentieth century can show us past remains, now gone. It is also important to create maps. Throughout the last pages, we have often mentioned *Atles dels comtats de la Catalunya carolíngia*. Archaeological excavations are also essential. We have mentioned some of them, such as that of Mas Vilosiu B, that of the Islamic houses in Lleida and Balaguer, or of those early medieval settlements. Fieldwork is also key, as a close study of the country we want to study is essential. A few years ago, an exceptional prospecting campaign was carried out in a small area of the burned mountain of Ropidera (Conflent).[54] Research in the mountains of Enveig (Cerdanya) has also been exemplary.[55]

In addition, archaeobotanists, geologists, and linguists have made important contributions to the study of the medieval landscape.[56] This volume has presented extensive explanations on the analysis of pollen, which have brought us closer to past vegetation, especially from the early Middle Ages, in the Pyrenees, in the plain of Lleida, in Banyoles, in the *comarca* of Empordà, in Barcelona, or near Tarragona. We have also assessed the contributions made through profiling and the use of Optically Stimulated Luminescence (OSL) and ^{14}C analyses. Other techniques mentioned have been GIS and

---

53 Bolòs and Bonales, *Atles històric de Menàrguens*; Bolòs and Bonales, *Atles històric d'Almacelles*.
54 Passarrius and Catafau, 'Ropidera: un poble medieval en els seus territoris'; Passarrius and others, *Archéologie d'une montagne brûlée*.
55 Rendu, *La montagne d'Enveig*.
56 Palet and others, 'Centuriación del territorio y modelación del paisaje en los llanos litorales de *Barcino*'.

CONCLUSION   355

LiDAR. We have devoted an entire chapter to toponyms as they yield valuable insights into past landscapes.

Three Interactions

Just as it is important to do long-term studies and multidisciplinary research, when studying the landscape from the Middle Ages, it is also important to assess three interactions. The first involves the society and the economy of the period under study. Such interaction has been illustrated in analysing the changes that have taken place over the centuries because of the different transitions. And, of course, the landscape is related to power and control of the territory, and the mindset and religion of the time. All these social and economic factors are interrelated, with dozens of examples that reinforce this statement. One of the most significant examples has been that of Sanata, in the *comarca* of Vallès Oriental, as it has enabled us to identify the existence of a road as well as the fertile coombs which extended to the south of Montseny; this is significant because this strategic location came under Berber control in the eighth century.

Another fundamental interaction seen in this volume has been that involving the different elements of the landscape. No study of villages would be complete without taking castles or churches into consideration, and no study of coombs and irrigated lands would be well-rounded without considering pre-medieval plot divisions. No analysis of roads would be comprehensive without the presence of the boundaries they crossed or overlapped along their way. Certainly, whenever the elements of the landscape coincide at a certain point in the past, they have an impact on each other. For example, in order to understand the road which connects La Granada and Sant Martí Sarroca, we need to look at its relationship with villages and castles, as well as its possible pre-medieval origin.

Finally, the third and last interaction is that which existed between countries. In this volume, constant consideration of other territories close to Catalonia, both on the shores of the Mediterranean and in Europe as a whole, has been crucial for analysing the historic landscape. Regarding such frequent elements as new towns (or *viles noves*), comparisons with other countries are simple. Concerning other elements and issues, this has not been the case. When studying coombs, consultation of the *wadi* in North Africa and the Eastern Mediterranean has been a logical step. Breakthroughs in recent decades in Catalonia about the different topics studied have been possible precisely because of comparisons and assessment of similarities and differences with other neighbouring countries. Examples of this are extraordinary works on house villages and open villages or on ecclesiastical villages. As we have pointed out more than once, to understand many aspects of the medieval landscape in Old Catalonia, it is necessary to know the history of the landscape in the Occitan lands.

The Landscape of Lords and the Landscape of Peasants

In recent years, notable research has been undertaken on how the peasants changed the landscape as well as attempts to find out how these farmers saw and valued the landscape around them.[57] It is difficult to speak of 'a landscape of lords' vs. a 'landscape of peasants', as if they were two separate realities. Having said that, in the Middle Ages, the view of the environment certainly varied according to the social situation of the observer. For example, the relationship between the farmer and the mill would certainly have been different if the mill belonged to the farmer or the community of peasants, or if the mill was the property of the lord and the peasants had to pay a tax (*moltura*) to use it. Villages created by peasants and towns created by lords, which might exempt settlers from some seigneurial rights and taxes, are another example. Also, there were churches built with the support of a rural community, and churches built by a lay or ecclesiastical lord, both of which have numerous examples in this volume. This was a complex reality that changed over the centuries. Going further back in time, even during the Islamic period, there were peasant communities that organized the land they worked and paid tribute and at the same time, elsewhere, there were lords owning extensive domains with peasants who ploughed and reaped their lands.[58]

The landowners were often the ones who set the boundaries of lordships, of castral districts, or parishes, but those who worked the land were the ones who, *de facto*, knew the land and its characteristics. Parallel to this reality, we, as historians, need to be interested in not only the landscape of the peasants but also the landscape of the lords. Simultaneously, we must try to distinguish their views of the landscape from each other.

What We Already Know and What Remains to Be Known

Recent advances in historical landscape studies in Catalonia and the rest of Europe are remarkable. It is worth noting the fact that in-depth knowledge of a wide range of diverse subjects has slowly been increasing. While years ago, villages were the focus of study, we now also have in-depth knowledge of roads or cultivated spaces. Below is a brief overview of the various issues analysed in this volume.

---

57 Mileson, 'The South Oxfordshire Project'; Mileson and Brookes, *Peasant Perceptions of Landscape*.

58 *De quan érem o no musulmans. Textos del 713 al 1010*, ed. and trans. by Bramon, p. 189.

Villages

Research into villages has been the area that has probably seen the most progress in recent decades. The study of *sagrera* villages has attracted a wide-range of historians. Following the key research by Aymat Catafau, several articles and books have been published.[59] There have been fewer contributions on castral villages and open villages. There have been remarkable studies on new villages in Valencia and the Balearic Islands.[60] In Catalonia, after the publication of research by Bolòs, *Els orígens medievals del paisatge català*, new studies have looked at how urbanism related to the society and economy, and how municipalities developed.[61] Hopefully, work on various types of towns and about the different Catalan *comarques* or regions will increase. It is certainly not enough to make a distribution map but we also need to look for the reasons for what we find. In the case of *sagreres*, this is obvious: after seeing their distribution, we have to consider why there are so many of them on the plain of Vic and so few in the Pallars.

Dispersed and Half-Dispersed Settlements

At present, it is possible to easily differentiate between *comarques* where dispersed settlements predominate, in farmsteads, and others where we find nucleated settlement in villages, and we can even find *comarques* established in half-dispersed settlements, in hamlets. Recent studies have allowed us to advance our knowledge of the formation and characteristics of dispersed settlements and have also made it possible to specify the *comarques* where they were (and still are) ubiquitous. Books, academic papers and conferences have also focused on farmhouses.[62] Research on hamlets will develop further in the future. In addition, there is a need for an analysis of the reasons behind the varying evolution of settlements in different regions, throughout the Middle Ages and after the year 1500. What impact did access to water, topography, or forests? Other factors considered include insecurity, tradition, as well as having a lord, a castle, or a church? And it will also be necessary to clarify, for example, whether there were hamlets that were a set of dispersed farmhouses, and whether there were farmsteads that were in fact small hamlets made up of a *mas* (farmhouse) and several clustered *masoveries*. The *masover*, who was the person living there, looked after the *masoveria* for another peasant.

---

59 Catafau, *Les celleres et la naissance du village en Roussillon*.

60 Rosselló, *Viles planificades valencianes*; Andreu, *L'Ordinació de Petra, any 1300* ; Mas, 'Les Ordinacions d'en Jaume II'.

61 Bolòs, *Els orígens medievals del paisatge català*; Soler, 'Feudalisme i nucleació poblacional'; Soler, 'Els espais d'intercanvi. El mercat en el procés de gènesi i consolidació del feudalisme al comtat de Barcelona'.

62 Ferrer and others, *El mas català durant l'edat mitjana i la moderna*.

358   CONCLUSION

Fields and Territorial Exploitation

Research on fields over the last few years has provided insights into a wide variety of *comarques*. Work on farmland from the Roman period in the Camp de Tarragona, Vallès, Empordà, and Pallars Jussà must be mentioned. In 2018, Jacinto Bonales published a study on the Baix Cinca region, which clarifies many aspects of the exploitation of the territory in this area, from prehistory to the Middle Ages. It is also worth noting the examinations of the lands of Tortosa in the Islamic era.[63] Studies have also been carried out in the vicinity of Lleida, where there was a process of colonization and, at the same time, a reorganization of space and where Christian and Muslim communities coexisted.[64] Contributions have also been made to the layout of fields in such *comarques* as Gironès, Vallès, Penedès, Cerdanya, Berguedà, Ribagorça, to name just a few.

To understand cultivated spaces and to be able to date them, it is essential to relate them to other elements of the landscape, such as roads, inhabited places, ditches, constructions, etc. As for terraces, an issue in Mediterranean lands, it is necessary to carry out archaeological excavations (such as those carried out in Cerdanya) and new analyses of the margins with the OSL technique.[65] Concerning hydraulic spaces, work started several decades ago in the Balearic Islands established a methodology to study them.[66] Research must continue on irrigated lands on the banks of the rivers Ebro, Cinca, or Segre and their tributaries, and also on the *hortes* found on the banks of the rivers running through Old Catalonia. In the future, it will be important to be able to precisely date some ditches and especially some irrigated spaces that could have been created at very different times in the early Middle Ages

The diversity and juxtaposition of landscapes with different historical origins is characteristic of the rural landscape of Catalonia. We concur with González Villaescusa that in some *comarques*, one can find evidence of a combination of centuriations, traces of a landscape created in the Islamic era, and strips of slope or repopulation from the high Middle Ages.[67] We see this in Valencia and New Catalonia. In Old Catalonia, there is a starker contrast between landscapes with strong Roman roots and those of medieval villages and farmsteads.

The plot division of territory that existed in the Roman period led to great transformations in the landscape of many Catalan regions. This is an essential principle if we want to understand the medieval landscape. At the same time,

---

63   Kirchner and Virgili, 'De Turṭûša a Tortosa. La ciutat abans i després de la conquesta catalana'; Negre, *En els confins d'al-Andalus*.

64   Bolòs, 'Paisatge i societat al « Segrià» al segle XIII'; Monjo, *Sarraïns sota el domini feudal*; Monjo, 'Sarraïns d'Aitona, el tresor de la família Montcada'.

65   Turner and others, 'Changes and continuities in a Mediterranean landscape'.

66   Barceló and others, *El agua que no duerme*.

67   González Villaescusa, *Las formas de los paisajes mediterráneos*, p. 458.

however, it should be noted that interpreting this Roman heritage, which mainly affects the network of roads and the organization of the fields, is often a difficult task. Certainly, the presence of the past remains in the landscape is not always as consistent as one might expect. Instead, we discover a mixture of inherited elements that are, however, difficult to understand. Hopefully, future research will make it possible to properly assess this diversity, which at times, although stubbornly obvious, may seem illogical.

The Organization of Territorial Boundaries

To find out where boundaries were set, maps are essential. Understanding the exact location of boundaries is very important in understanding the history of a region. There are economic boundaries related to the use of space by rural communities, domain boundaries, boundaries related to tax or jurisdictional rights, ecclesiastical boundaries of parishes, and so on. The boundaries of larger demarcations, such as counties, bishoprics, or kingdoms, must also be considered. In drawing up the *Atles dels comtats de la Catalunya carolíngia*, it was essential to outline the boundaries of not only the counties but also their various minor demarcations.[68] In Chapter 14 of this volume, we discussed the territories of villages and towns, parishes, valleys, and castles. We have discovered that, in some cases, these divisions were very old. Concerning this topic, in recent years, interesting contributions have been made, such as those by Carolina Batet and Flocel Sabaté.[69] Certainly, when studying boundaries, one needs to understand their layout to clarify when they were created and why they have been maintained over the centuries. We must start from the premise that, as we have said, there are current boundaries that may have originated in the Middle Ages and there are medieval boundaries that were possibly created before the year 500. There is much work to do as this is a subject that has attracted too little interest from historians, who are not yet aware of the relevance of studying them as a key element in learning the history of the country.

Roads

The contributions made in Europe to the study of the history of roads have been remarkable, especially the pioneering work by Eric Vion.[70] In France and England, notable research has also been conducted recently.[71] These are

---

68 Bolòs and Hurtado, 'Atles dels comtats de la Catalunya carolíngia'.

69 Batet, *Castells termenats i estratègies d'expansió comtal*; Sabaté, *El territori de la Catalunya medieval*.

70 Vion, 'L'analyse archéologique des réseaux routiers'.

71 Robert and Verdier, *Dynamique et résilience des réseaux routiers*; Langlands, *The Ancient Ways of Wessex*.

360   CONCLUSION

long-term studies. In Catalonia, research has been carried out on the road networks from the Carolingian period and the high Middle Ages.[72] Three methodologically interesting contributions should be noted. Jacinto Bonales and Miquel Bailac made a cartographic inventory of all the current paths of the Pallars Jussà.[73] Miquel Vives carefully reconstructed the road network of the *comarques* of Baix Llobregat and Alt Penedès, through a long-term study.[74] Elvis Mallorquí led an innovative study on the road network in the south of the city of Girona.[75] This study, despite its thoroughness, should be of interest to non-specialists; soon, following the methodology in many of these works, we will be able to study the road networks of all the *comarques* of Catalonia. The path to follow has been identified; we just need to set off on this research journey.

Cities and Towns

In the medieval period, it was sometimes difficult to draw a clear dividing line between the landscapes of cities and towns. Some of the settlements described in Chapter 5 could also have been studied in Chapter 7, or vice versa. This is why we have devoted an entire chapter to the urban world (although we are aware that this is not enough). It should be noted that, in recent years, insightful studies have been carried out on various medieval cities and towns in Catalonia. Research on Girona (in the Carolingian period and the fourteenth century), Barcelona, Perpignan, Tarragona, Lleida, or Tortosa deserves special mention.[76] In Chapter 7 we have tried to describe how cities were created and developed and how they survived in Catalonia throughout the Middle Ages, and we have emphasized the role played by walls, different streets or squares, and various buildings and central places. Obviously, we need to understand urban spaces in relation to societies found in each stage of our past. Certainly, it would be interesting to create atlases of the various Catalan cities, as is being done in the rest of Europe.

It should be recalled that, besides the most important cities, there were many medium-sized towns, which, on becoming centres where markets were held, were economically influential in neighbouring villages. Some of the

---

72   Bolòs, 'Aportacions al coneixement de les vies de comunicació'; Bolòs, 'Els camins a Catalunya en temps de Jaume I'; Bolòs, 'Paisatge històric, cartografia i societat a l'alta edat mitjana: l'exemple de la Cerdanya'.

73   Bonales and Bailac, *Els camins històrics del Pallars Jussà*.

74   Vives, 'L'evolució històrica de la xarxa viària entre el Llobregat i el Foix'.

75   Mallorquí, *Cinquanta-cinc llegües de passos oblidats i xarrabascos*.

76   Canal and others, *La ciutat de Girona en la 1ª meitat del segle XIV*; Canal and others, *Girona, de Carlemany al feudalisme (785-1057)*; Garcia and Guàrdia, *Espai i societat a la Barcelona pre-industrial*; Catafau and Passarrius, *Un palais dans la ville. Volume 2. Perpignan des rois de Majorque*; Bolòs, *Dins les muralles de la ciutat. Carrers i oficis a la Lleida dels segles XIV i XV*.

CONCLUSION 361

examples analysed have been Granollers, Vilafranca del Penedès, Cervera, Reus, Puigcerdà, and Balaguer. All of these towns are now *comarca* capitals.

Other Topics

Some topics have been left untouched in this volume. We have delved into elements of the landscape that are invisible, such as boundaries or place names. We have mentioned, perhaps in a marginal way, the impact of mentalities and beliefs on the landscape. No mention has been made, however, of what we might call the *soundscape*: for example, the sound of bells in the rural and urban world.[77] We know that in the cities when the bells rang, there was a pre-eminence of some bells over others. In the modern era, for example, various studies have been carried out on sounds in the city of Barcelona.[78] Nor have we mentioned, for example, the existence of *cornadors*, who, on behalf of a lord, were responsible for sounding the horn in certain places, at certain times. In La Garrotxa, in the castle of Mallol, in 1431, horns and smoke signals warned about danger.[79]

Studying the landscape allows us to learn about the space where people lived centuries ago. Places, now perhaps just cold witnesses to a remote past, were then meaningful realities for their inhabitants, spaces for work, leisure, and suffering. The environment has visually, and especially mentally, changed significantly over the years. Although we have alluded to city prisons, in the preceding pages there are no references to gallows. It should be remembered that at the entrance of the cities or in a prominent place of many lordships or jurisdictional districts, there was a place allocated for hanging criminals.[80] This place had to be clearly visible to everyone who entered the city or the lordship. Gallows too were elements of the landscape (which now we know about only if a place name has been preserved in memory of the people).

Current Research on Medieval Landscape History

The research agenda has been extensively mentioned in this volume. There are currently many places in Catalonia where research is being done on the history of the landscape. First, at various universities, scholars are working on the historical landscape: at the University of Barcelona (Imma Ollich, Marta Sancho or Maria Soler), the Autonomous University of Barcelona (Helena Kirchner, Antoni Virgili, Ramon Martí, Jordi Gibert, Cristian Folch, Joan Negre, Jesús Brufal), the University of Perpignan Via Domitia (Aymat

---

77 Mileson, 'Sound and Landscape'.
78 Knighton, *Els sons de Barcelona a l'edat moderna*; Pérez Samper, 'El patrimoni sonor de Barcelona: la veu de les campanes'; Raventós, 'Barcelona: paisatge sonor, cerimonial i festiu'.
79 Soler, 'Notes sobre el dret de cornar a Tortellà', p. 139; Castellet, 'Cartografia sonora de la comunicació castral', p. 6.
80 Cuadrada, 'El paisatge i l'organització del territori al Maresme medieval', pp. 124-25.

Catafau, Olivier Passarrius), the University of Lleida (Jordi Bolòs, Flocel Sabaté, Jacinto Bonales, Enric Vicedo) and the University of Girona (Lluís To, Elvis Mallorquí). There are also research centres, such as the Observatori del Paisatge (Landscape Observatory), based in Olot, or the ICAC (with the GIAP), based in Tarragona (Josep Maria Palet, Hèctor Orengo, Marta Prevosti), which mainly focus on the study of the Roman period. This is certainly an incomplete and short list. We must also keep in mind the work in study centres in Vic and L'Esquerda, Manresa, Mataró, Empordà, Perpignan, Puigcerdà, La Seu d'Urgell, Balaguer, Pallars, from the Penedès, etc. Nor can we forget the close relationship that exists with other universities, such as Valencia (Enric Guinot, Antoni Furió, Josep Torró, Ferran Esquilache) or the Balearic Islands (Antoni Mas, Jaume Andreu, Maria Barceló, Eugènia Sitges). And, certainly key contributions have been made in recent years in other neighbouring territories, such as Languedoc, Gascony, Aragon, the Basque Country, Galicia, Portugal, Castile, Andalusia, northern Italy, etc. Also, it is worth noting the methodological contributions that emerge from research carried out, for example, in England, France, Switzerland, Italy, and Germany.

Differences and Similarities

Catalonia is very diverse. This volume bears witness to this fact. Catalonia offers a wide variety of climates and vegetation. We discover this diversity by analysing the different forms of settlement and seeing the differences between *comarques* where farmsteads predominate, and those where we find mainly ecclesiastical or castral villages. We also notice a great interest in toponymy. We see it in the shapes of the fields or in the importance of ditches. This has led us to differentiate at least three major areas: Pyrenean Catalonia, Eastern and Central Catalonia, and New Catalonia. However, as we have seen, we must not forget that almost every region or *comarca* has its own history and has some distinctive features that differentiate it from others.

In these last pages, we would like to point out that, although we have tried to cover as many places as possible and, even though we have approached almost all the Catalan *comarques*, we may have left unmentioned places where perhaps remarkable research and findings have also been undertaken. Admittedly, plenty of research has been done on some issues, such as towns and cities, which has forced us to make a choice. In this volume, we have not intended to make a comprehensive synthesis, but a presentation of the various topics studied, on which, certainly, further research is needed. Much work remains to be done to advance the history of the medieval landscape and, of course, the history of Catalonia and Europe.

The North and the South

The study of the history of the landscape allows us to make comparisons and point out similarities and differences. If we look north, we can point out the existence of a common substrate with the lands located on the northern slope of the Pyrenees, especially in the Occitan lands of Languedoc and Gascony. This close link existed throughout the early Middle Ages, as we can see when we study Catalan's similarity to the Occitan dialects spoken in Septimania. Linguists point out that the similarities between these two languages are much greater than those with neighbouring languages, such as Spanish or French. If we look at the landscape, we see that this reality had a great impact on the shape of the villages and the characteristics of the population, apart from other aspects such as the delimitation of the territories or the way in which their resources were used. These ties were also fostered by political ties in the Visigothic era (when Languedoc was part of the Visigothic kingdom), during the Carolingian era, and until the Battle of Muret in 1213.

In addition, there were other influences, deriving from the fact that this land shared a border with Al-Andalus. This brought about two consequences. On the one hand, part of the country was organized as a frontier, which affected the territorial districts, the creation of numerous castles and the characteristics of the habitat. On the other hand, in many of the lands conquered between the tenth and twelfth centuries there was a process of colonization and, at the same time, the use by the new settlers of many of the components of the previously created landscape, such as ditches, irrigated areas and also the shape of the settlement. The study of the landscape often allows us to discover the changes that took place in each stage of the past. It should be noted that what happened in New Catalonia in the twelfth century was very similar to what happened in the new lands conquered by the Catalans in the thirteenth century, the Balearic Islands, and an important sector of Valencian territory. Understanding the landscape of Old Catalonia require us to examine the northern lands, while to comprehend the landscape of New Catalonia requires the study of the southernmost lands (Valencia), south of the La Sénia river.

Studying Landscape History Advances our Knowledge and Appreciation of a Country

There are several possible approaches to researching the history of the landscape. One approach is undertaking research which is primarily aimed at a university audience. The other approach is doing research aimed at people who are not professionally engaged in history, botany, geology, or toponymy. And there may be a third possibility, which is to try to reach both audiences by doing work that can be of interest to as many people as possible. In Catalonia, there are several examples of this type of approach that, while maintaining academic rigour, has managed to reach many a wide public. One example of this is the dense yet well-known work of Joan Coromines's *Onomasticon Cataloniae*.[81] Or the twenty-seven volumes of *Catalunya Romànica*, a research undertaking that nevertheless reached the shelves of thousands of Catalan homes.[82] The PaHisCat project is also another example of this endeavour to bring landscape history closer to society, as we believe in the importance of communicating research to wider society (as held by Jo Clark, John Darlington, Graham Fairclough and Cédric Lavigne).[83] Any piece of research should try to have an impact not only on specialist circles, but also on as many people as possible, since our work seeks to expand our knowledge of a country, its history, and help people to value their environment and, hopefully, by so doing, manage it better.[84]

---

81 Coromines, *Onomasticon Cataloniae*.

82 Vigué and Pladevall, *Catalunya Romànica*.

83 Clark and others, *Using Historic Landscape Characterisation*; Lavigne, 'L'archéogéographie, une expertise au service des politiques publiques d'aménagement'.

84 Watteaux, 'Paysage', p. 836.

Glossary

Advocació (cat). *See* Dedication.

Alfons I (Alfonso II of Aragon). King of the Catalan-Aragonese kingdom from 1164 to 1196.

Almúnia. From Arabic *al-munia*. Originally an irrigated piece of land, *horta* in Catalan. It became a settlement often linked to the ruling elite of the cities that owned it.

Alqueria. From Arabic *al-qarīa*. A small rural community.

Ashlar (Cat. *carreu*). Squared stone.

Peace and Truce of God (Cat. *Pau i Treva de Déu*). The goal of Peace and Truce of God was to limit the endemic violence in the western half of the former Carolingian Empire using spiritual sanctions. This movement began in Gaul in the late tenth century and soon reached the Catalan counties.

Block (Cat. *illa de cases*). A square group of houses with roads on each side.

Borda (Cat.). Small and secondary farmstead.

Braçal (Cat.). Secondary canal.

Burğ (plural *ʾabrāğ*) (Arabic) A tower, but also a small, defended settlement where several families lived, usually located on a hilltop and with a tower and probably a wall.

Call (Cat.). Jewish quarter.

Casa forta (Cat.; Fr. *maison forte*). Small castle owned by a knight.

Castell termenat (Cat.). Castle with a surrounding district. Found mostly in frontier lands.

Castlà (Eng. castellan). Governor or warden of a castle. In fact, a vassal enfeoffed with a castle by the lord and, therefore who enjoyed certain rights bestowed on a castle and on the territory that depended on it.

Castrum (Lt.). Stronghold. Extensive early medieval fortification, where lords could live and there might also be peasant houses, a church, and other buildings.

Cavalleria (Cat.). Territory ceded as a fief to a knight. Translated as knight's fief.

Cellera (Cat.). Space with cellars. Sometimes synonymous with *sagrera*. Sometimes also a space near a church (or a castle) where houses were built.

Centuriation (Cat. *centuriació*). A centuriation is characterized by the regular layout of a square grid traced using surveyors' instruments. Typical of the

Roman land organization, it may survive in the form of roads, canals, and agricultural plots. These plots, when formed, were allocated to Roman army veterans in a new colony, but they might also be returned to the indigenous inhabitants.

Charter of freedom and exemption (Cat. *carta de poblament i franquesa*). Grant by the sovereign or a lord of a settlement. A charter conferring privileges and exemption on inhabitants or prospective inhabitants.

Clearing (Cat. *rompuda*). An area of forest from which trees and bushes have been removed. An assart.

Coaxial strip (Cat. *franja coaxial*). It has two or more elements with the same axis. Applied often to long, narrow pieces of land with parallel sides.

Collegiate church (Cat. *canònica* or *col·legiata*). A church with an endowed chapter of canons and prebendaries attached to it.

Comarca (pl. *comarques*) (Cat.). Extension of territory, smaller than a region, defined in terms of certain natural conditions or common historical facts. Currently, in Catalonia, a local entity of a territorial nature formed by the grouping of contiguous municipalities.

Commandery (Cat. *comanda*). The smallest administrative division of a military order. It was also the name of the house where the knights lived.

Coomb (Cat. *coma*). Small valley with a flat cultivated bottom.

Corner tower (Cat. *torre d'angle*). Tower built at the corner of a castle or fortification.

Cuirassa (Arabic: *qawraya*). Jewish quarter of the city of Lleida.

Dam and **milldam** (Cat. *paixera* or *resclosa*). Wooden or stone wall that is made through a river to raise the water level and divert it to an irrigation canal or a mill.

Decastellamento (It.). The opposite of *incastellamento*. In the high Middle Ages, the process of abandonment by the population of the hilltop places, far from the fields. Word coined by Settia (1984) referring mainly to fortifications. This process could result in the creation of new towns or the growth of already existing towns.

Dedication (Cat. *advocació*). The name given to a church, a chapel, an altar, etc., dedicated to the Virgin Mary or a saint.

Devesa (Cat.). In the Middle Ages, often an enclosed piece of rural land. Often a small pasture. Some belonged to the lord or a monastery, while others were owned for the common good of a community of neighbours.

Ditch (Cat. *séquia* or *rec*). A long, narrow open hole dug into the ground, used especially for supplying water.

GLOSSARY **367**

Drive shaft (Cat. *arbre*). In the mill, wooden beam with an iron spindle at the top. At the bottom it fits the horizontal wheel and at the top it fits the rynd that carries the runner stone.

Drove track or **drove road** (Cat. *carrerada* or *cabanera*). Path for large groups of transhumance animals — sheep and cattle.

Early Middle Ages (Cat. *alta edat mitjana*). From the late fifth or early sixth century to the tenth century.

Encimbellament (Cat.). Transfer of the population from settlements located on flat ground to a hilltop location. It could be for security reasons or under pressure from a lord (*See incastellamento*).

Espluga (Cat.). Cave or cavern used as a place to live. Sometimes there are remains of buildings and even churches, castles, or monasteries.

Farmstead (Cat. *mas*). Traditional agricultural unit made up of the farmhouse, the fields, the stables, etc. A forest area also used to depend on it.

Farraginal (Cat.). Place where forage has been sown.

Feixa (Cat). See Terrace.

Fogatge (Cat.) A hearth tax. Imposition on the basis of an amount per fireplace or inhabited house.

Forge (Cat. *farga* and in the Middle Age *fàbrega*). Building where metallurgical materials were worked , especially one where iron was obtained through the direct reduction of the ore.

Franja de terra See land strip.

Fulling mill (Cat. *molí draper*). Mill where cloth was beaten with wooden hammers.

Grange (Cat. *granja*). A monastic grange was an outlying landholding held by a monastery. The first granges were owned by the Cistercians.

Grindstone (Cat. *mola*). Stone used to grind cereals in a mill. We can distinguish between the bed stone and the runner stone.

Guifré I el Pilós (Wilfred I the Hairy). Count of Urgell from 870 to 897 and of Barcelona from 878 until his death in 897.

Half tower (Cat. *bestorre*).

Hamlet (Cat. *vilar* or *llogaret*). A small settlement of five to ten families, usually within the boundaries of a village or parish.

Hearth tax (Cat. *fogatge*). The *fogatge* was a direct tax created during the reign of Pere III.

High Middle Ages (Cat. *edat mitjana central*). From the tenth century to the early fourteenth century.

Hilltop village (Cat. *poble encimbellat*). 'Perched' village located on top of a mountain or other elevated place. Related to an *encimbellament* or *incastellamento* process.

Hollow way or **sunken lane** (Cat. *camí enfonsat* or *enclotat*). A road or track that is significantly lower than the land on either side.

Hopper (Cat. *tremuja*). In a mill, a box in the shape of an inverted pyramid trunk that works like a funnel dropping materials that are thrown over the top through its lower opening.

Hort and **horta** (Cat; Sp. *huerto, huerta*). Irrigated land. Vegetable garden.

Illa (Cat.). See *Insula*.

Incastellamento (Italian; Cat. *encastellament*). Process of the concentration of the population next to the castles, related to the growth of feudalization that took place in the tenth and eleventh centuries. According to P. Toubert, it often involved the abandonment of a previous half-dispersed settlement and the construction of a new, concentrated village in a hilltop location ruled by a lord.

Insula (Lt.). Land irrigated with a ditch or by capillarity located next to a river. Name mentioned in early and high medieval documentation corresponding to the Arabic *al-jazīra*.

Irrigation channel. In a hydraulic system there is the main canal (*séquia* or *canal* in Catalan), which takes water from the river or stream, and secondary ditches (*braçals* in Catalan) that take water from this larger canal.

Jaume I el Conqueridor (James I the Conqueror). King of the Catalan-Aragonese kingdom from 1213 to 1276.

Jaume II el Just (James II the Fair). King of the Catalan-Aragonese kingdom from 1291 to 1327.

Keep (Cat. *torrassa*, Fr. *donjon*). Tower found from the twelfth century in some fortifications. This building could generally be used as a dwelling and included a hall.

Land registry or **cadastre** (Cat. *cadastre*). Registration of urban and rural properties made by the State to determine the extent of taxes.

Land strips (Cat. *franges de terra*). Pieces of coaxial farmland that often extend down the side of a mountain or along a road. Also known as *parellades*.

Land terrier (Cat. *capbreu*). Document containing the declarations made by the peasants of a lordship, and the charges they were obliged to pay. Usually drawn up before a notary appointed by the lord.

GLOSSARY 369

Llotja (auction market). Public place, usually a building, where merchants and traders meet to make their deals.

Lock (Cat. *resclosa*). See dam.

March (Cat. *marca*). Frontier/border territories.

Mas (Cat.). See farmstead.

Masoveria (Cat.). In the high Middle Ages, a farmstead occupied by peasants who paid rent to another farmer and to the lord.

Mercadal (Cat.) A market square. Space for holding the weekly market.

Mill (Cat. *molí*). A building where grain is ground into flour. There could be mills with a horizontal wheel (Cat. *molins de rodet horitzontal*), mills with a vertical wheel (Cat. *molins roders, de roda vertical*), tank mills (Cat. *molins de cup*), windmills (Cat. *molins de vent*), ship mills (Cat. *molins de nau*), etc.

Moat (Cat. *el vall* or *fossat*). Longitudinal excavation made in the ground, especially around a fortification.

Municipality (Cat. *municipi*). Modern administrative district of a city or town that has its own government.

New town (Cat. *vilanova* or *vila nova*). Town created by a lord with often the granting of a settlement charter. The lord's interest was often related to the control of territory in newly-acquired (sometimes frontier) lands. New towns frequently became economic centres.

Noria or **water wheel** (Cat. *sínia*). Water lifting machine, consisting basically of a vertical wheel driven by an animal or in some cases by the force of the water current.

Paer (Cat.). Town councillor. We find them mainly in western Catalonia (for example Lleida or Cervera). The building where they met was the Paeria.

Pagus (Lt). In the Carolingian period often synonymous with county (*comitatus*). Shortly before the year 1000 there was already a tendency to use that name to only refer to smaller sectors of a county, which generally had ancient origins, such as the *pagi* of Llívia, Talló or Bar (in the county of Cerdanya).

Palau or **palol**. Name of many documented places in the early Middle Ages. It comes from *palatium* or *palatiolum*. It was probably a fiscal domain created in the late Roman period or in the early Middle Ages. Many of these places were granted to the Islamic warrior elite who conquered the country around 713/714.

Parada (Cat.). Flat portion of arable land separated from the others by a margin (of earth or dry stone), a furrow or a crest. In the coombs, each of the plots of land.

Parellada (Cat.). Land worked by a pair of oxen. We find *parellades* on both dryland and irrigated land. The lands of *parellades* used to be coaxial strips.

Pariatge (Cat.). Sovereignty shared by two lords.

Partida (Cat.). Set of lands, group of fields.

Pere I el Catòlic (Peter II of Aragon). King of the Catalan-Aragonese kingdom from 1196 to 1213.

Pere II el Gran (Peter III of Aragon). King of the Catalan-Aragonese kingdom from 1276 to 1285.

Pere III el Cerimoniós (Peter IV of Aragon). King of the Catalan-Aragonese kingdom from 1336 to 1387.

Plan unit (Cat. *Unitat de pla*). Urban space that has a common internal organization and is different from the one around it, which allows us to assume that this space has a shared history.

Plot division (Cat. *Parcel·lació*). Division of the territory into plots. Sometimes these plots have orthogonal shapes (and can be related to a Roman centuriation), sometimes they are coaxial pieces of land or sometimes strips of land that stretch along a road or a river, or by the slope of a mountain.

Plot division network (Cat. *xarxa de parcel·lació*). We can talk about a plot network or a regular road network. There are also foundation networks (especially a centuriation) or formation networks (a cohesive, planned system).

Quadra (Cat.). Territory ceded as a fief to a knight. See *cavalleria*.

Rainfed agriculture (Cat. *agricultura de secà*). Farming that relies only on rainfall for water. It can be contrasted with irrigated agriculture and places with *horts* or *hortes*.

Rammed earth (Cat. *tàpia*). Wall made of kneaded earth pressed into moulds (*tapieres*). Usually about sixty centimetres high.

Ramon Berenguer IV. Count of Barcelona (1131–1162) and prince of Aragon. Conqueror of Tortosa (1148) and Lleida (1149).

Rampart or **wall** (Cat. *muralla*). A large wall built round a town or a castle to protect it.

Rec (Cat.). See Ditch.

Reguer (Cat.). Courses of drainage water. Sometimes they correspond to the original hydraulic network, before the time when the ditches or canals were built.

Ràpita (Cat.) (From Arabic *ribāṭ*). Small fortification built along a frontier during the first years of the Muslim conquest. Ribats were originally used to house those who fought to defend Islam.

GLOSSARY   371

Rompuda (Cat.). See Clearing.

Rynd or **rind** (Cat. *nadilla*). A piece of iron on which rests the runner stone of a flour mill. It fits with the spindle.

Sagrera (Cat.). Circular or rectangular space around a church and its cemetery. Those dwelling within the *sagrera* and their property were under the protection of the Peace and Truce of God enforced by the church. The limit was almost always thirty steps from the ecclesiastical building.

Secondary canal or **branch canal** (Cat. *braçal*) Secondary ditches branching off from main canals. They carry water to mills or drains that allow irrigation.

Secular lord (Cat. *senyor laic*). As opposed to ecclesiastical lords such as bishops or abbots.

Séquia (Cat.). See Ditch. From this canal there branched off canals or secondary canals.

Settlement (Cat. *poblament* or *hàbitat*). Subdivided as clustered settlement (villages and towns), a half-dispersed population (hamlets, *vilars*) and a dispersed settlement (farmsteads, *masos*).

Ship mill (Cat. *molí de nau*). A type of watermill built on a floating platform or ship.

Shipyard (Cat. *drassana*). A building where ships are built and repaired.

Silo (Cat. *sitja*). Spheroidal or prismatic tank intended for the storage and conservation of various products, especially cereals.

Sínia (Cat.). See noria.

Sitja (Cat., plural sitges). See Silo.

Spindle (Cat. *coll-ferro*). Iron bar nailed to the shaft of the mill, with the top fitting into the rynd hole.

Suburb (Cat. *raval* or *burg*). Part of a population located outside the first walls.

Suda (Cat.). Fortified space, citadel or kasbah, of many Catalan cities in the Islamic era.

Terrace (Cat. *terrassa, bancal,* or *feixa*). Flat piece of arable land, bounded by dry stone margins and usually located on a mountain slope

Tithe (Cat. *delme*). Tenth part of the harvest paid to the Church and sometimes to a lord.

Torre (Cat). Tower, related to a castle or by itself an isolated watchtower. Also applied to name settlements where families lived, in New Catalonia, inherited from the ʾ*abrāğ* (plural of *burğ*) of the Islamic era.

Valley (Cat. *la vall*). It can correspond to a topographic reality and to a space where a community lives that enjoys collective rights and privileges.

Vegetable garden (Cat. *hort, horta*). Irrigated space where mainly vegetables were grown.

Vegueria (Cat.; Lt. *vicaria*) Territory over which a veguer or vicar (*vicarius*) exercised power during the Carolingian era. Local authority delegated by the count and later, especially from the fourteenth century, the king. The Carolingian vicariae corresponded to the castral districts. The *vicariae* of the late Middle Ages had as their centre a city or town.

Vilar (Cat.). See hamlet.

Villa (Lt). It is necessary to distinguish the *villae* of the Roman era from the *villas* of the Carolingian era. In addition, Carolingian *villas* between the Rhine and the Loire were large estates, while the *villas* of Catalonia were villages often with numerous landowners.

Village (Cat. *poble*). A group of houses and other buildings smaller than a town or a city. If it was created next to a castle, we can refer to it as a castral village. If it was built around a church, we refer to it as an ecclesiastical village. If it was built anew, we can speak of a new town. And if it was only created with some houses, it is an open village of houses. We also find double villages (with the village above and the village below).

Well (Cat. *pou*)

Works Cited

Primary Sources

'Les Actes de consagracions d'esglésies del bisbat d'Urgell (segles IX–XII)', ed. by Cebrià Baraut, *Urgellia*, 1 (1978), 11–182

'Apèndix documental', ed. by Jordi Bolòs, in Jordi Bolòs and Montserrat Pagès, *El monestir de Sant Llorenç prop Bagà* (Barcelona: Edicions Proa, 1986), pp. 179–207

Bruniquer, Esteve Gilabert, *Ceremonial dels Magnífics Consellers i Regiment de la Ciutat de Barcelona* (Barcelona: Arxiu Municipal de Barcelona, 1915) <https://ajuntament.barcelona.cat/rubriques/bruniquer/#/>

Cartas de población del reino de Aragón en los siglos medievales, ed. by María Luisa Ledesma (Zaragoza: Institución Fernando el Católico, 1991)

Cartas de población y franquicia de Cataluña, vol. I, ed. by Josep M. Font Rius (Barcelona: CSIC, 1969)

Cartulario de 'Sant Cugat' del Vallés, vol. II, ed. by Josep Rius (Barcelona: CSIC, 1946)

Catalunya carolíngia, vol. II: Els diplomes carolingis a Catalunya, ed. by Ramon d'Abadal (Barcelona: Institut d'Estudis Catalans, 1926–1952)

Catalunya carolíngia, vol. III: Els comtats de Pallars i Ribagorça, ed. by Ramon d'Abadal (Barcelona: Institut d'Estudis Catalans, 1955).

Catalunya carolíngia, vol. IV: Els comtats d'Osona i Manresa, ed. by Ramon Ordeig (Barcelona: Institut d'Estudis Catalans, 1999)

Catalunya carolíngia, vol. V: Els comtats de Girona, Besalú, Empúries i Peralada, ed. by Santiago Sobrequés, Sebastià Riera and Manuel Rovira (Barcelona: Institut d'Estudis Catalans, 2003)

Catalunya carolíngia, vol. VI: Els comtats de Rosselló, Conflent, Vallespir i Fenollet, ed. by Pere Ponsich (Barcelona: Institut d'Estudis Catalans, 2006)

Catalunya carolíngia, vol. VII: El comtat de Barcelona, ed. by Ignasi J. Baiges and Pere Puig (Barcelona: Institut d'Estudis Catalans, 2019)

Catalunya carolíngia, vol. VIII: Els comtats d'Urgell, Cerdanya i Berga, ed. by Ramon Ordeig (Barcelona: Institut d'Estudis Catalans, 2020)

Col·lecció diplomàtica de l'Arxiu Capitular de Lleida. Segona part: Documents de les seus episcopals de Roda i de Lleida (anys 586–1143), ed. by Jordi Bolòs (Barcelona: Fundació Noguera, 2022)

Col·lecció diplomàtica de la casa del Temple de Barberà (945–1212), ed. by Josep M. Sans Travé (Barcelona: Generalitat de Catalunya, 1997)

Col·lecció diplomàtica de la Casa del Temple de Gardeny (1070–1200), ed. by Ramon Sarobe) Barcelona: Fundació Noguera, 1998)

Col·lecció diplomàtica de Sant Pere d'Àger fins 1198, ed. by Ramon Chesé (Barcelona: Fundació Noguera, 2011)

Colección diplomàtica del condado de Besalú, ed. by Francesc Monsalvatje (Olot: Joan Bonet, 1902, 1906)

WORKS CITED

Les Constitucions de Pau i Treva de Catalunya (segles XI–XIII), ed. by Gener Gonzalvo (Barcelona: Generalitat de Catalunya, 1994)

Diplomatari de Santa Maria de Poblet. Volum I. Anys 960–1177, ed. by Agustí Altisent (Barcelona: Generalitat de Catalunya and Abadia de Poblet, 1993)

Diplomatari del Masdéu, ed. by Rodrigue Tréton (Barcelona: Fundació Noguera, 2010)

Diplomatari del monestir de Sant Pere de la Portella, ed. by Jordi Bolòs (Barcelona: Fundació Noguera, 2009)

Diplomatari del monestir de Santa Maria de Serrateix (segles X–XV), ed. by Jordi Bolòs (Barcelona: Fundació Noguera, 2006)

'Els Documents, dels anys 1151–1190, de l'Arxiu Capitular de la Seu d'Urgell', ed. by Cebrià Baraut, *Urgellia*, 10 (1990–1991), 7–349

Les Dotalies de les esglésies de Catalunya (segles IX–XII), ed. by Ramon Ordeig (Vic: Estudis Històrics, 1993–1994)

Fiscal Accounts of Catalonia under the Early Count-Kings (1151–1213), ed. by Thomas N. Bisson (Berkeley: University of California Press, 1984)

Llibre de la Cort de la Mar de Roses. Ordinacions, sentències i concòrdies sobre la pesca (segle xv), ed. by Marcel Pujol and Alfons Garrido (Roses: Ajuntament de Roses, 2019)

Llibre dels judicis. Traducció catalana moderna del Liber iudiciorum, trans. Joan Bellés (Barcelona: Generalitat de Catalunya, 2008)

Les Ordinacions de la pesquera de Calonge (segles xv-xvii), ed. by Alfons Garrido, Montse Pérez, Joan Lluís Alegret, and Montserrat Darnaculleta (Palamós: Càtedra d'Estudis Marítims, 2010)

De quan érem o no musulmans. Textos del 713 al 1010, ed. and trans. by Dolors Bramon (Vic and Barcelona: Eumo editorial and Institut d'Estudis Catalans, 2000)

Tragó, Pere, *Spill manifest de totes les coses del vescomdat de Castellbò, ed. by* Cebrià Baraut (La Seu d'Urgell: Societat Cultural Urgel·litana, 1982)

Secondary Sources

Aalen, F. H. A., Kevin Whelan, and Matthew Stout, *Atlas of the Irish Rural Landscape* (Cork: Cork University Press, 1997)

Abbé, Jean-Loup, *À la conquête des étangs. L'aménagement de l'espace en Languedoc méditerranéen (XIIe-XVe siècle)* (Toulouse: Presses Universitaires du Mirail, 2006)

Abbé, Jean-Loup, Dominique Baudreu, and Maurice Berthe, 'Les villes neuves médiévales du sud-ouest de la France (XIe-XIIIe siècles)', in *Las villas nuevas medievales del suroeste europeo*, ed. by Pascual Martínez and Maria Urteaga (Irun: Arkeolan, 2006), pp. 1–33

Aberth, Hohn, *An Environmental History of the Middle Ages: The Crucible of Nature* (New York: Routledge, 2013)

Abulafia, David, and Nora Berend, ed., *Medieval Frontiers: Concepts and Practices* (London: Routledge, 2002)

Adell, Joan Albert, and Eduard Riu, 'La torre de l'alta edat mitjana de Ribes (Garraf)', *Quaderns d'Estudis medievals*, 2 (1980), 87–93

Agache, Roger, and Bruno Bréart, *Atlas d'Archéologie aérienne de Picardie. La Somme Protohistorique et Romaine* (Amiens: Société des Antiquaires de Picardie, 1975).

Aguilar, Àngels, Oriol Olesti, and Rosa Plana, 'Cadastres romans a Catalunya: Empordà i Gironès, Cerdanya, Vallès Occidental', in *Tribuna d'Arqueologia 1989–1990* (Barcelona: Generalitat de Catalunya, 1991), pp. 111–24

Aldomà, Ignasi, ed., *L'aigua patrimoni de la Catalunya seca. Passat i present en l'entorn de Torrebesses* (Lleida: Ajuntament de Torrebesses and Pagès Editors 2013).

Alegria, Walter, and Marta Sancho, 'Els Altimiris, enllaços i confluències entre la Tardoantiguitat i l'Alta Edat Mitjana', *Tribuna d'Arqueologia, 2008–2009* (2010), 221–36

Alessandri, Patrice, and Lucien Bayrou, 'Sur quelques fortifications de la frontière de 1258', in *Frontières et espaces pyrénéens au Moyen Âge*, ed. by Philippe Sénac (Perpignan: Université de Perpignan, 1992), pp. 151–79

Alibèrt, Loís, *Dictionnaire Occitan-français d'après les parlers languedociens* (Toulouse: Institut d'Etudes Occitanes, 1966)

Alòs, Carme, Anna Camats, Marta Monjo, and Eva Solanes, 'Les cases andalusines del Pla d'Almatà (Balaguer, Noguera)', in *Tribuna d'Arqueologia 2006* (Barcelona: Generalitat de Catalunya, 2008), pp. 273–90

Altisent, Agustí, *Història de Poblet* (Poblet: Abadia de Poblet, 1974).

Alturo, Jesús, and Tània Alaix, *Lletres que parlen: Viatge als orígens del català* (Barcelona: La Magrana, 2023)

Andreu, Ricard, 'Edició crítica, traducció i estudi de l'*Ars Gromatica sive Geometria Gisemundi*' (doctoral thesis, Universitat de Barcelona, 2012)

Andreu, Agustí, Marina Miquel, Josep Santesmases, and Dolors Saumell, 'La sèquia de Vila-rodona', *Quaderns de Vilaniu*, 9.30 (1996), 35–68

Andreu, Jaume, *L'Ordinació de Petra, any 1300. Teoria i realitat* (Petra: Ajuntament de Petra, 2000)

——, *Arquitectura tradicional de les Balears* (Pollença: El Gall editor, 2008)

Argemí, Mercè, 'El sistema de molinos andalusí del Guz de Yartan (Mayurqa)', in *Agricultura y regadío en al-Andalus. II Coloquio Historia y Medio Físico*, ed. by Lorenzo Cara and Antonio Malpica (Almería and Granada: Instituto de Estudios Almerienses and THARG, 1996 [1995]), pp. 259–71

Argilés, Caterina, 'Paisatge, societat i organització del territori a Rocallaura (Urgell) al segle XV', in *Paisatge i societat a la Plana de Lleida a l'edat mitjana*, ed. by Jordi Bolòs (Lleida: Publicacions de la Universitat de Lleida, 1993), pp. 83–114

Ariño, Enrique, Josep M. Gurt, and Josep M. Palet, *El pasado presente. Arqueología de los paisajes en la Hispania romana* (Barcelona: Universitat de Barcelona and Universidad de Salamanca, 2004)

Arizaga, Beatriz, *Urbanística medieval (Guipúzcoa)* (Donostia: Kriselu, 1990)

WORKS CITED

Assis, Yom Tov, *Els jueus de Santa Coloma de Queralt. Estudi econòmic i demogràfic d'una petita comunitat jueva a la fi del segle xiii* (Santa Coloma de Queralt: Associació Cultural Baixa Segarra, 2002) (original English edition: 1988)

Astill, Grenville, 'Understanding the identities and workings of local societies in Early Medieval England, AD 800–1100', in *Polity and Neighbourhood in Early Medieval Europe*, ed. by Julio Escalona, Orri Vésteinsson and Stuart Brookes (Turnhout: Brepols, 2019), pp. 39–56

Aston, Mick, *Interpreting the Landscape: Landscape Archaeology in Local Studies* (London: B.T. Batsford, 1985)

——, *Monasteries in the Landscape* (Stroud: Tempus, 2000 [first edition 1993])

Aston, Mick, and James Bond, *The Landscape of Towns* (London: J. M. Dent and Sons, 1976)

Aubrun, Michel, *La paroisse en France: Des origines au XVe siècle* (Paris: Picard, 2008)

Aurell, Martin, *Les noces du comte. Mariage et pouvoir en Catalogne (785–1213)* (Paris: Publications de la Sorbonne, 1995)

Austin, David, and Leslie Alcock, ed., *From the Baltic to the Black Sea: Studies in Medieval Archaeology* (London: Routledge, 1997)

Aventín, Mercè, *Vilamajor 872–1299. De la fi del sistema antic a la consolidació del feudalisme* (Sabadell: Editorial Ausa, 1990)

——, 'Le rôle du marché dans la structuration de l'habitat catalan au Bas Moyen Âge: l'exemple du Vallès Oriental', in *Villages pyrénéens. Morphogenèse d'un habitat de montagne*, ed. by Maurice Berthe and Benoôt Cursente (Toulouse: CNRS and Université de Toulouse-Le Mirail, 2000), pp. 273–82.

Azuar, Rafael, 'La Rápita de Guardamar (Alicante) y los otros Rībat/s, en el ámbito rural', in *Arqueologia medieval. Els espais sagrats*, ed. by Flocel Sabaté and Jesús Brufal (Lleida: Pagès editors, 2015), pp. 135–49

Azuar, Rafael, and Sonia Gutiérrez Lloret, 'Formación y transformación de un espacio agrícola islámico en el sur del País Valenciano: el Bajo Segura (siglos IX–XIII)', in *Castrum 5. Archéologie des espaces agraires méditerranéens au Moyen Âge*, ed. by André Bazzana (Rome/Madrid: Casa de Velázquez and École française de Rome, 1999), pp. 201–11

Bachelier, Julien, *Villes et villages de Haute-Bretagne (XIème–début XIVème siècle). Analyses morphologiques* (Rennes: Centre Régional d'Archéologie d'Alet, 2014)

Bailly-Maître, Marie-Christine, 'Paysages miniers médiévaux. Essai de restitution à partir des données de l'Archéologie et de l'Archéométrie', in *Marqueurs des paysages et systèmes socio-économiques*, ed. by Rita Compatangelo-Soussignan, Jean-René Bertrand, John Chapman, and Pierre-Yves Laffont (Rennes: Presses Universitaires de Rennes, 2008), pp. 89–98

Ballesteros, Paula, 'La arqueología rural y la construcción de un paisaje agrario medieval: el caso de Galicia', in *Por una arqueología agraria. Perspectivas de investigación sobre espacios de cultivo en las sociedades medievales hispánicas*, ed. by Helena Kirchner, BAR International Series, 2062 (Oxford: BAR, 2010), pp. 25–39.

Ballesteros, Paula, and Rebeca Blanco-Rotea, 'Aldeas y espacios agrarios altomedievales en Galicia', in *The Archaeology of early medieval villages in Europe*, ed. by Juan-Antonio Quirós (Bilbao: Euskal Herriko Unibertsitatea – Universidad del País Vasco, 2009), pp. 115–35

Ballesteros, Paula, and Felipe Criado, 'El paisaje agrario medieval en Galicia. Herramientas metodológicas', in *Poblament, territori i història rural. VI Congrés sobre sistemes agraris, organització social i poder local*, ed. by Jordi Bolòs and Enric Vicedo (Lleida: Institut d'Estudis Ilerdencs, 2009), pp. 599–612

Banks, Philip, 'The Topography of Barcelona and its Urban Context in Eastern Catalonia from the Third to the Twelfth Centuries' (doctoral thesis, University of Nottingham, 1980)

——, 'El marc històric', in *Catalunya Romànica, vol. XX: El Barcelonès, el Baix Llobregat, el Maresme*, ed. by Antoni Pladevall (Barcelona: Enciclopèdia Catalana, 1992), pp. 21–104

Banham, Deb, and Rosamond Faith, *Anglo-Saxon Farms and Farming* (Oxford: Oxford University Press, 2014)

Barbany, Carme, Cinta Cantarell, Jaume Dantí, M. Rosa Garcia, Pere Ribas, and M. Encarna Terrades, *De la balma a la masia. L'hàbitat medieval i modern al Vallès Oriental* (Granollers: Museu de Granollers, 1996)

Barceló, Miquel, *Les aigües cercades: els qanat(s) de l'illa de Mallorca* (Palma de Mallorca: Institut d'Estudis Baleàrics, 1986)

Barceló, Miquel, Helena Kirchner, and Carmen Navarro, *El agua que no duerme. Fundamentos de la arqueología hidráulica andalusí* (Granada: El legado andalusí, 1996)

Barceló, Miquel, and Pierre Toubert, ed., *L'incastellamento. Actes des rencontres de Gérone (26–27 novembre 1992) et de Rome (5–7 mai 1994)* (Rome: Ecole Française de Rome, 1998)

Barceló Crespí, Maria, and Guillem Rosselló, *La ciudad de Mallorca. La vida cotidiana en una ciudad mediterránea medieval* (Palma de Mallorca: Lleonard Muntaner editor, 2006)

Baron, Nacima, Stéphane Boissellier, François Clément, and Flocel Sabaté, ed., *Reconnaître et délimiter l'espace localement au Moyen Âge. Limites et frontières I.* (Villeneuve d'Ascq: Presses Universitaires du Septentrion, 2016)

——, *Ériger et borner diocèses et principautés au Moyen Âge. Limites et frontières II* (Villeneuve d'Ascq: Presses Universitaires du Septentrion, 2017)

Bartlett, Robert, *The Making of Europe: Conquest, Colonization and Cultural Change, 950–1350* (London: Penguin Books, 1994)

Bartlett, Robert, and Angus MacKay, ed., *Medieval Frontier Societies* (Oxford: Clarendon Press, 1989)

Barton, Thomas W., *Contested Treasure: Jews and Authority in the Crown of Aragon* (University Park: Pennsylvania State University Press, 2014)

——, *Victory's Shadow: Conquest and Governance in Medieval Catalonia* (Ithaca: Cornell University Press, 2019)

Batet, Carolina, *Castells termenats i estratègies d'expansió comtal. La marca de Barcelona als segles X–XI* (Vilafranca del Penedès: Institut d'Estudis Penedesencs, 1996)

Batlle, Carme, *Història de Catalunya, vol. III: L'expansió baixmedieval. Segles XIII–XV* (Barcelona: Edicions 62, 1988)

——, *Fires i mercats, factors de dinamisme econòmic i centres de sociabilitat (segles XI a XV)* (Barcelona: Rafael Dalmau editor, 2004)

——, *L'aljama de la Seu d'Urgell medieval. Una comunitat jueva del Pirineu català* (Barcelona: Rafael Dalmau editor, 2016)

Baudreu, Dominique, 'Une forme de villages médiévaux concentrés: le cas du Bas-Razès', *Archéologie du Midi médiéval*, 4 (1986), 49–73

Baudreu, Dominique, and Jean-Paul Cazes, 'Le rôle de l'église dans la formation des villages médiévaux. L'exemple des Pays Audois', *Heresis*, 2 (1990 [1992]), 139–58

Baydal, Vicent, *Els valencians, des de quan són valencians?* (Catarroja: Editorial Afers, 2016)

Bazzana, André, *Maisons d'al-Andalus. Habitat médiéval et structures du peuplement dans l'Espagne orientale* (Madrid: Casa de Velázquez, 1992)

——, 'Maison-bloc, maison-enclos et maison agglutinante: caractères de l'habitat rural dans Al-Andalus (IXe-XIIIe siècle)', in *Le village médiévale et son environnement. Études offertes à Jean-Marie Pesez*, ed. by Laurent Feller, Perrine Mane, and Françoise Piponnier (Paris: Publications de la Sorbonne, 1998), pp. 43–66

Bazzana, André, and Yves Montmessin, 'Nā'ūra et sāniya dans l'hydraulique agricole d'al-Andalus à la lumière des fouilles de "Les Jovades" (Oliva, Valence)', in *La maîtrise de l'eau en al-Andalus. Paysages, pratiques et techniques*, ed. by Patrice Cressier (Madrid: Casa de Velázquez, 2006), pp. 209–87

Bazzana, André, Patrice Cressier, and Pierre Guichard, *Les château ruraux d'al-Andalus. Histoire et archéologie des ḥuṣūn du sud-est de l'Espagne* (Madrid: Casa de Velázquez, 1988)

Benito, Pere, 'Casa rural y niveles de vida en el entorno de Barcelona a fines de la Edad Media', in *Pautes de consum i nivells de vida al món rural medieval.* (València: Universitat de València, 2008) <https://www.uv.es/consum/benito.pdf> [accessed 18 April 2015], <https://lleida.academia.edu/PereBenitoiMoncl%C3%BAs> [accessed 11 September 2021]

Benoit, Paul, 'Remarques sur les fouilles de moulins à eau médiévaux en Europe', in *Archéologie des moulins hydrauliques, à traction animale et à vent des origines à l'époque médiévale et moderne en Europe et dans le monde méditerranéen*, ed. by Luc Jaccottey and Gilles Rollier (Besançon: Presses Universitaires de Franche-Comté, 2016), pp. 51–72

Bensch, Stephen P., *Barcelona and its Rulers, 1096–1291* (Cambridge: Cambridge University Press, 1995)

Bépoix, Sylvie, and Hervé Richard, ed., *La forêt au Moyen Âge* (Paris: Les Belles Lettres, 2019)

Berdoy, Anne, and Ezéchiel Jean-Courret, 'Castelnaux du bassin de l'Adour (Landes et Béarn): morphologies et évolutions', in *Demeurer, défendre et paraître. Orientations récentes de l'archéologie des fortifications et des résidences aristocratiques médiévales entre Loire et Pyrénées*, ed. by Luc Bourgeois and Christian Remy (Chauvigny: APC, 2014), pp. 315–30

Beresford, Maurice W., *New Towns of the Middle Ages: Town Plantation in England, Wales and Gascony* (Struod: Sutton Publishing, 1988 [first edition 1967])

——, *History on the Ground: Six Studies in Maps and Landscapes* (London: Routledge, 2016 [first edition 1957; revised 1971])

Beresford, Maurice. W., and John Kenneth Sinclair St Joseph, *Medieval England: An Aerial Survey* (Cambridge: Cambridge University Press, 1979 [first edition 1958])

Berger, Jean-François, and Jacques Leopold Brochier, 'Paysages et climats en moyenne vallée du Rhône: apports de la géo-archéologie', in *Habitats, nécropoles et paysages dans la moyenne et la basse vallée du Rhône (VIIᵉ-XVᵉ s.). Contribution des travaux du TGV-Méditerranée à l'étude des sociétés rurales médiévales*, ed. by Odile Maufras (Paris: Maison des Sciences de l'Homme, 2006), pp. 163–208

Bernat i Roca, Margalida, *El call de ciutat de Mallorca a l'entorn de 1350* (Palma de Mallorca: Lleonard Muntaner editor, 2005)

Berthe, Maurice, and Benoît Cursente, ed., *Villages pyrénéens. Morphogenèse d'un habitat de montagne* (Toulouse: CNRS – Université de Toulouse-Le Mirail, 2001)

Bisson, Thomas N., *Tormented Voices: Power, Crisis, and Humanity in Rural Catalonia, 1140–1200* (Cambridge, MA: Harvard University Press, 1998)

Blair, John, Stephen Rippon, and Christopher Smart, *Planning in the Early Medieval Landscape* (Liverpool: Liverpool University Press, 2020)

Bocchi, Francesca, *Per antiche strade. Caracteristiche e aspetti delle città medievali* (Rome: Viella, 2013)

——, 'The Topography of Power in the Towns of Medieval Italy', in *Lords and Towns in Medieval Europe: The European Historic Towns Project*, ed. by Anngret Simms and Howard B. Clarke (London: Routledge, 2019), pp. 65–86

Bohly, Bernard, 'Une mine de plomb au temps des châteaux forts: le Donnerloch à Steinbach (Haut-Rhin)', in *Vivre dans la montagne vosgienne au Moyen Âge. Conquête des espaces et culture matérielle*, ed. by Charles Kraemer and Jacky Koch (Nancy: PUN-Éditions Universitaires de Lorraine, 2017), pp. 305–22

Boissellier, Stéphane, *Le peuplement médiéval dans le sud du Portugal. Constitution et fonctionnement d'un réseau d'habitats et de territoires XIIe-XVe siècles* (Paris: Centre cultural Calouste Gulbenkian, 2003)

Bolòs, Jordi, 'Anàlisi pol·línica i història medieval. Aportació al coneixement del paisatge pirinenc durant l'edat mitjana', *Quaderns d'estudis medievals*, 10 (1982), 635–39

——, 'Fortificacions frontereres situades entre els rius Anoia i Gaià. L'estructuració d'un territori el segle x', in *Arqueología Medieval española. II Congreso, tomo II:*

Comunicaciones (Madrid: Comunidad de Madrid and Asociación española de Arqueología medieval, 1987), pp. 113–22

——, 'Castell de Palau-sator', in *Catalunya Romànica, vol. VIII: L'Empordà I* (Barcelona: Enciclopèdia Catalana, 1989), pp. 231–32

——, 'Aportacions al coneixement de les vies de comunicació', in *Symposium Internacional sobre els orígens de Catalunya (Segles VIII–XI)* (Barcelona: Generalitat de Catalunya, 1991), pp. 409–36

——, 'La vila de Senet (Alta Ribagorça) al segle XII. Aproximació al coneixement del paisatge i de la societat d'un poble pirinenc', in *Miscel·lània. Homenatge a Josep Lladonosa* (Lleida: Institut d'Estudis Ilerdencs, 1992), pp. 147–63

——, 'Paisatge i societat al "Segrià" al segle XIII', in *Paisatge i societat a la Plana de Lleida a l'edat mitjana*, ed. by Jordi Bolòs (Lleida: Publicacions de la Universitat de Lleida, 1993), pp. 45–81

——, *El mas, el pagès i el senyor. Paisatge i societat en una parròquia de la Garrotxa a l'edat mitjana* (Barcelona: Curial, 1995)

——, 'Castell de Siurana', in *Catalunya Romànica. vol. XXI: El Tarragonès, el Baix Camp, l'Alt Camp, la Conca de Barberà, El Priorat* (Barcelona: Enciclopèdia Catalana, 1995), pp. 385–88

——, ed., *Un mas pirinenc medieval: Vilosiu B (Cercs, Berguedà). Estudi dels edificis i materials trobats durant les excavacions (1984–1986)* (Lleida: Publicacions de la Universitat de Lleida, 1996)

——, 'El territori i els seus límits. El poble, la parròquia i el castell a l'edat mitjana', in *Territori i Societat a l'Edat Mitjana, I*, ed. by Jordi Bolòs and Joan J. Busqueta (Lleida: Publicacions de la Universitat de Lleida, 1997), pp. 41–82

——, *Castells de la Catalunya central* (Manresa: Angle editorial, 1997)

——, 'Ciutat de Lleida', in *Catalunya Romànica, vol. XXIV: El Segrià, les Garrigues, el Pla d'Urgell, la Segarra, l'Urgell*, ed. by Antoni Pladevall (Barcelona: Enciclopèdia Catalana, 1997), pp. 131–38

——, 'Els pobles de Catalunya a l'edat mitjana. Aportació a l'estudi de la morfogènesi dels llocs de poblament', in *Territori i Societat a l'Edat Mitjana, II*, ed. by Jordi Bolòs and Joan J. Busqueta (Lleida: Universitat de Lleida, 1998), pp. 69–138

——, 'Le rôle du château et de l'église dans la structuration de l'habitat dans les Pyrénées catalanes. Les exemples du Pallars Sobirà et de la Garrotxa', in *Villages pyrénéens. Morphogenèse d'un habitat de montagne*, ed. by Maurice Berthe and Benoît Cursente (Toulouse: CNRS and Université de Toulouse-Le Mirail, 2000a [2001]), pp. 89–108

——, *Catalunya medieval. Una aproximació al territori i a la societat a l'edat mitjana* (Barcelona: Pòrtic and Enciclopèdia Catalana, 2000)

——, 'Changes and Survival: The Territory of Lleida (Catalonia) after the Twelfth-Century Conquest', *Journal of Medieval History*, 27 (2001), 313–29

——, *Cartografia i història medieval* (Lleida: Institut d'Estudis Ilerdencs, 2001)

——, 'Les moulins en Catalogne au Moyen Âge', in *Moulins et meuniers dans les campagnes européennes (IXᵉ-XVIIIᵉ siècle)*, ed. by Mireille Mousnier (Toulouse: Presses Universitaires du Mirail, 2002), pp. 53–75

—, 'Un territori en temps de guerra', in *Hug Roger III, senyor en les muntanyes. Procés al darrer comte del Pallars. 1491* (Lleida: Pagès editors, 2002), pp. 41–77

—, ed., *Paisatge i història en època medieval a la Catalunya Nova. Organització del territori i societat a la vila d'Agramunt (Urgell) i a la vall del Sió (segles V–XIX)* (Lleida: Publicacions de la Universitat de Lleida, 2002)

—, 'Fortificacions de la marca i organització del territori a Catalunya (segles VIII–XII)', in *Actes del Congrés Els castells medievals a la Mediterrània nord-occidental* (Girona: Museu La Gabella d'Arbúcies, 2003 [2004]), pp. 67–88

—, *Els orígens medievals del paisatge català. L'arqueologia del paisatge com a font per a conèixer la història de Catalunya* (Barcelona: Institut d'Estudis Catalans and Publicacions de l'Abadia de Montserrat, 2004)

—, 'Processos de rompuda i d'ocupació de l'espai a l'època medieval. Alguns exemples catalans', in *Les ressources naturelles des Pyrénées du Moyen âge à l'époque moderne. Exploitation, gestion, appropriation*, ed. by Aymat Catafau (Perpignan: Presses Universitaires de Perpignan, 2005), pp. 119–45

—, 'La implantació del Cister al territori: la formació del patrimoni i la transformació del paisatge', in *Actes del primer curs-simposi sobre el monaquisme cistercenc. El Cister: poder i espiritualitat (1150–1250)* (Santes Creus: Arxiu Bibliogràfic de Santes Creus, 2006 [2005]), pp. 35–74

—, 'Conèixer el paisatge històric medieval per poder planificar i gestionar el territori', in *Estudiar i gestionar el paisatge històric medieval. Territori i Societat a l'edat mitjana, IV*, ed. by Jordi Bolòs (Lleida: Publicacions de la Universitat de Lleida, 2007), pp. 145–226

—, 'Nous mètodes per a conèixer els camins medievals: la xarxa de vies a la Catalunya Central', in *El camí de Sant Jaume i Catalunya. Actes del Congrés Internacional celebrat a Barcelona, Cervera i Lleida* (Barcelona: Publicacions de l'Abadia de Montserrat, 2007), pp. 49–60

—, *Dins les muralles de la ciutat. Carrers i oficis a la Lleida dels segles XIV i XV* (Lleida: Ajuntament de Lleida and Pagès editors, 2008)

—, 'Aportació al coneixement de la morfogènesi dels pobles del comtat d'Empúries', in *Poblament, territori i història rural. VI Congrés sobre sistemes agraris, organització social i poder local*, ed. by Jordi Bolòs and Enric Vicedo (Lleida: Institut d'Estudis Ilerdencs, 2009), pp. 261–84

—, 'PaHisCat: A Project to Discover the Landscape of the Past and Manage the Countries of the Future', in *La caracterització del paisatge històric. Territori i Societat: el paisatge històric, V*, ed. by Jordi Bolòs (Lleida: Universitat de Lleida, 2010), pp. 371–407

—, 'Un paisatge complex d'un país molt vell. Els estudis d'història del paisatge per comprendre i valorar el territori', in *La caracterització del paisatge històric, Territori i Societat: el paisatge històric, V*, ed. by Jordi Bolòs (Lleida: Edicions de la Universitat de Lleida, 2010), pp. 82–147

—, 'L'estudi de les necròpolis medievals catalanes, entre l'arqueologia i la història', in *Arqueologia funerària al nord-est peninsular (segles VI–XII)*, ed. by Núria Molist and Gisela Ripoll (Barcelona: MAC, 2012), pp. 71–85

——, 'Els camins a Catalunya en temps de Jaume I', in *Jaume I. Commemoració del VIII centenari del naixement de Jaume I*, ed. by Maria Teresa Ferrer (Barcelona: Institut d'Estudis Catalans, 2013), vol. II, pp. 171–90

——, 'Pobles de sagrera i pobles castrals: dues realitats enfrontades?', in *La Corona Catalanoargonesa, l'Islam i el món mediterrani. Estudis d'història medieval en homenatge a la doctora Maria Teresa Ferrer i Mallol*, ed. by Josefina Mutgé, Roser Salicrú, and Carlos Vela (Barcelona: CSIC, 2013), pp. 109–19

——, 'El paisatge de Torrefarrera cap a l'any 1200 i als darrers segles medievals', in *Les etapes de la construcció del territori a Catalunya: Torrefarrera i la Catalunya occidental, segles VII a XX. Una proposta metodològica*, ed. by Enric Vicedo, Jordi Bolòs, José Ramon Olarieta, Ignasi Aldomà, and Miquel Aran (Lleida: Ajuntament de Torrefarrera and Pagès editors, 2013), pp. 45–67

——, 'Grottes habitées, ermitages troglodytiques et châteaux bâtis dans des grottes et des abris-sous-roche en Catalogne, durant le Haut Moyen Âge', in *Vivre sous terre. Sites rupestres et habitats troglodytiques dans l'Europe du Sud*, ed. by Monique Bourin, Marie-Élise Gardel, and Florence Guillot (Rennes: Presses Univeritaires de Rennes, 2014), pp. 131–49

——, 'L'arqueologia del paisatge de la Catalunya medieval', *Butlletí de la Societat Catalana d'Estudis Històrics*, 25 (2014), 101–70

——, 'Paisatge històric, cartografia i societat a l'alta edat mitjana: l'exemple de la Cerdanya', in *Poblament i societat als Pirineus els darrers dos mil anys, Territori i Societat: el paisatge històric, VI*, ed. by Jordi Bolòs (Lleida: Edicions de la Universitat de Lleida, 2014), pp. 37–146

——, 'Paisatges i transicions: canvis i continuïtats al llarg de la història', in *El paisatge en èpoques de transició al llarg dels darrers dos mil anys, Territori i Societat: el paisatge històric, VII*, ed. by Jordi Bolòs (Lleida: Edicions de la Universitat de Lleida, 2015), pp. 59–126

——, 'La Caracterització del Paisatge Històric (CPH) del Priorat', in *Caracterització històrica del paisatge del Priorat-Montsant-Siurana* ([Olot:] Diputació de Tarragona and Observatori del Paisatge, 2016), pp. 151–201 <http://www.catpaisatge.net/pahiscat/docs/CHPC_PRIORAT-MONTSANT-SIURANA.pdf> [accessed 10 December 2021]

——, 'Història del paisatge i mapes de Caracterització del Paisatge Històric (CPH): el Vallès i el Penedès (Catalunya)', in *Els caràcters del paisatge històric als països mediterranis. Territori i Societat: el paisatge històric, VIII*, ed. by Jordi Bolòs (Lleida: Universitat de Lleida and Pagès editors, 2018), pp. 65–146

——, 'Not So Dark Centuries: Changes and Continuities in the Catalan Landscape (6th-12th centuries)', in *Ruralia XII: Settlement Change across Medieval Europe; Old Paradigms and New Vistas*, ed. by Niall Brady and Claudia Theune (Leiden: Sidestone, 2019), pp. 91–101

——, 'Mills, Landscape, and Society in Catalonia in the Middle Ages', in *Hydraulic Heritage in Ibero-America*, ed. by Francisco Costa, António Vieira, José-Manuel Lopes-Cordeiro, and Jesús Raúl Navarro-García (New York: Nova Science Publishers Inc., 2020), pp. 257–84

———, *Col·lecció diplomàtica de l'Arxiu Capitular de Lleida. Primera part: Documents de les seus episcopals de Roda i de Lleida (fins a l'any 1143)* (Barcelona: Fundació Noguera, 2021)

———, *El paisatge medieval del comtat de Barcelona. Història del paisatge, documents i cartografia d'un país mediterrani. Volum I* (Lleida: Pagès editors and Universitat de Lleida, 2021)

———, 'Cartografiar el paisatge medieval de Catalunya (segles VIII–X). Segona part: A partir dels *Atles dels comtats de la Catalunya carolíngia*', in *Paisatge històric i cartografia. De l'època romana fins a l'actualitat, Territori i Societat: el paisatge històric, vol. IX*, ed. by Jordi Bolòs (Lleida: Universitat de Lleida and Pagès editors, 2021)

———, *El paisatge medieval del comtat de Barcelona. Història del paisatge, documents i cartografia d'un país mediterrani* (Lleida: Pagès editors, 2022)

Bolòs, Jordi, and Joan J. Busqueta, 'Castell de Lluçars', in *Catalunya Romànica, vol. XVI: La Ribagorça* (Barcelona: Enciclopèdia Catalana, 1996), pp. 492–94

Bolòs, Jordi, and Jacinto Bonales, *Atles històric de Menàrguens. El paisatge històric d'un municipi de la comarca de la Noguera al llarg de dos mil anys* (Lleida: Ajuntament de Menàrguens and Pagès editors, 2013)

———, *Atles històric d'Almacelles. El paisatge històric d'un municipi de la comarca del Segrià des de la Prehistòria fins a l'actualitat* (Lleida: Ajuntament d'Almacelles and Pagès editors, 2015)

Bolòs, Jordi, Jacinto Bonales, Marta Flórez, and Albert Martínez-Elcacho, *Caracterització històrica del paisatge del Priorat-Montsant-Siurana* ([Olot:] Diputació de Tarragona and Observatori del Paisatge, 2016) <http://www.catpaisatge.net/pahiscat/docs/CHPC_PRIORAT-MONTSANT-SIURANA.pdf> [accessed 11 September 2021]

Bolòs, Jordi, and Miquel Fàbregues, 'Sepultures excavades a la roca a les rodalies de Serrateix', *Acta Historica et Archaeologica Mediaevalia*, 3 (1982), 155–71

Bolòs, Jordi, and Víctor Hurtado, *Atles del comtat de Besalú (785–988)*, Atles dels comtats de la Catalunya carolíngia (Barcelona: Rafael Dalmau editor, 1998)

———, *Atles del comtat d'Osona (798–993)*, Atles dels comtats de la Catalunya carolíngia (Barcelona: Rafael Dalmau editor, 2001)

———, *Atles dels comtats de Rosselló, Conflent, Vallespir i Fenollet (759–991)*, Atles dels comtats de la Catalunya carolíngia (Barcelona: Rafael Dalmau editor, 2009).

———, *Atles dels comtats de Pallars i Ribagorça (v806-v998)*, Atles dels comtats de la Catalunya carolíngia (Barcelona: Rafael Dalmau editor, 2012)

———, *Atles dels comtats de Cerdanya i Berga (v788-v990)*, Atles dels comtats de la Catalunya carolíngia (Barcelona: Rafael Dalmau editor, 2015)

———, *Atles del comtat de Barcelona (801–993)*, Atles dels comtats de la Catalunya carolíngia (Barcelona: Rafael Dalmau editor, 2018)

———, 'Atles dels comtats de la Catalunya carolíngia' (Barcelona: Rafael Dalmau editor, 1998–2018). Ten volumes, each dedicated to a county or a set of counties.

———, *Poder, paisatge i societat a la Catalunya carolíngia. L'organització d'un país dins l'Europa de Carlemany* (Barcelona: Rafael Dalmau editor, 2020)

Bolòs, Jordi, and Lurdes Mallart, *La granja cistercenca d'Ancosa (La Llacuna, Anoia). Estudi dels edificis i dels materials trobats durant les excavacions (1981–1983)* (Barcelona: Generalitat de Catalunya, 1986)

Bolòs, Jordi, and Josep Moran, *Repertori d'Antropònims Catalans (RAC)* I (Barcelona: Institut d'Estudis Catalans, 1994)

——, *Abusos comesos a Lleida per Peire de Lobeira* (Barcelona: Institut d'Estudis Catalans, 2017)

Bolòs, Jordi, and Josep Nuet, *Els molins fariners* (Barcelona: Ketres editora, 1983)

Bolòs, Jordi, and Montserrat Pagès, *El monestir de Sant Llorenç prop Bagà* (Barcelona: Edicions Proa, 1986)

Bolòs, Jordi, and Joan-Ramon Piqué, 'Les parròquies: centres espirituals i demarcacions territorials', in *Arrels cristianes, vol. II: Temps de consolidació. La baixa edat mitjana. Segles XIII–XV* (Lleida: Pagès editors and Bisbat de Lleida, 2008), pp. 111–30

Bolòs, Jordi, and Imma Sànchez-Boira, 'Séquies i comes a la riba Esquerra del Cinca. La cartografia com a eina per a l'aprenentatge i el coneixement', in *Recs històrics: pagesia, historia i patrimoni. IX Congrés sobre sistemes agraris, organització social i poder local*, ed. by Enric Vicedo (Lleida: Institut d'Estudis Ilerdencs, 2018), pp. 669–98

Bolòs, Jordi, Rosa Maria Urpí, and Juan Antonio Resina, 'Els habitatges de Can Ximet', in *Catalunya Romànica, vol. XIX: El Penedès. L'Anoia* (Barcelona: Enciclopèdia Catalana, 1992), pp. 156–58

Bonales, Jacinto, *Andorra la Vella sense límits. Història de les afrontacions d'una parròquia del Principat (segles XIII–XXI)* (Andorra la Vella: Comú d'Andorra la Vella, 2011)

——, *Història territorial de la vall d'Andorra (dels orígens al segle XV)* (Andorra la Vella: Consell General, 2013)

——, *Història de Rocallaura* (Lleida and Rocallaura: EMD Rocallaura and Pagès editors, 2015)

——, 'L'estudi dels camins com a mètode d'anàlisi del paisatge històric. L'exemple del Pallars Jussà', in *El paisatge en èpoques de transició al llarg dels darrers dos mil anys, Territori i Societat: el paisatge històric, VII*, ed. by Jordi Bolòs (Lleida: Edicions de la Universitat de Lleida, 2015), pp. 155–74

——, *Traces d'un passat llunyà. El Baix Cinca (1200 aC–1149 dC)* (Fraga: Institut d'Estudis del Baix Cinca IEA, 2018)

——, *Atles històric del Cadí. El paisatge històric de la Unitat de Paisatge del Cadí des de la prehistòria fins a l'actualitat* (unpublished)

Bonales, Jacinto, and Miquel Bailac, *Els camins històrics del Pallars Jussà* (Tremp: Garsineu edicions, 2015)

Bonnassie, Pierre, *Croissance et mutations d'une société. La Catalogne du milieu du xe à la fin du xie siècle* (Toulouse: Presses Universitaires du Mirail, 1975–1976). Catalan version: *Catalunya mil anys enrere* (Barcelona: Edicions 62, 1979–1981)

——, 'Les sagreres catalanes: la concentration de l'habitat dans le "cercle de paix" des églises (xie s.)', in *L'environnement des églises et la topographie religieuse des campagnes médiévales*, ed. by Michel Fixot and Elisabeth Zadora-Rio (Paris: Éditions de la Maison des Sciences de l'Homme, 1994), pp. 68–79

——, 'Le littoral catalan durant le Haut Moyen Âge', in *Castrum 7. Zones côtières littorales dans le monde méditerranéen au Moyen Âge: défense, peuplement, mise en valeur*, ed. by Jean Marie Martin (Rome/Madrid: École française de Rome and Casa de Velázquez, 2001), pp. 251–71

Bonnet, Christian, and Christine Descatoire, *Les Carolingiens (741–987)* (Paris: Armand Colin, 2003)

Bourgeois, Luc, and Christian Remy, ed., *Demeurer, défendre et paraître. Orientations récentes de l'archéologie des fortifications et des résidences aristocràtiques médiévales entre Loire et Pyrénées* (Chauvigny: Association des Publications Chauvinoises, 2014)

Bourgeois, Luc, and Jean-François Boyer, 'Les palais carolingiens d'Aquitaine: genèse, implantation et destin', in *Demeurer, défendre et paraître. Orientations récentes de l'archéologie des fortifications et des résidences aristocratiques médiévales entre Loire et Pyrénées*, ed. by Luc Bourgeois and Christian Remy (Chauvigny: APC, 2014), pp. 67–118

Bourin, Monique, and Elisabeth Zadora-Rio, 'Pratiques de l'espace: les apports comparés des données textuelles et archéologiques', in *Construction de l'espace au Moyen Âge. Pratiques et représentations*, ed. by Régine Le Jan (Paris: Publications de la Sorbonne, 2007), pp. 39–55

Bowman, Jeffrey A., *Shifting Landmarks: Property, Proof, and Dispute in Catalonia around the Year 1000* (Ithaca: Cornell University Press, 2004)

Brigand, Robin, 'Les paysages agraires de la plaine venitienne: hydraulique et planification entre antiquite et renaissance', in *Medieval Europe Paris 2007. 4e Congrès International d'Archéologie Médiévale et Moderne* (2007) <https://halshs.archives-ouvertes.fr/halshs-01066424/document> [accessed 10 December 2021]

——, 'Centuriations romaines dans la plaine alluviale du Brenta (Italie)', *Études rurales*, 188 (2011), 21–38

——, 'Archaeogeography and Planimetric Landscapes', in *Detecting and Understanding Historic Landscapes*, ed. by Alexandra Chavarría Arnau and Andrew Reynolds (Mantua: SAP Società Archeologica, 2015), pp. 173–208

Brogiolo, Gian Pietro, 'Some principles and methods for a stratigraphic study of historic landscapes', in *Detecting and Understanding Historic Landscapes*, ed. by Alexandra Chavarría Arnau and Andrew Reynolds (Mantua: SAP Società Archeologica, 2015), pp. 359–75

Brogiolo, Gian Pietro, and Alexandra Chavarría, *Aristocrazie e campagne nell'Occidente da Costantino a Carlo Magno* (Firenze: Edizioni All'Insegna del Giglio, 2005)

——, *Archeologia postclassica. Temi, strumenti, prospettive* (Rome: Carocci editore, 2020)

Brogiolo, Gian Pietro, and Sauro Gelichi, *Nuove ricerche sui castelli altomedievali in Italia settentrionale* (Firenze: Edizioni All'Insegna del Giglio, 1996)

Brown, Antony G., Daniel Fallu, Kevin Walsh, Sara Cucchiaro, Paolo Tarolli, Pengzhi Zhao, Ben R. Pears, Kristofvan Oost, Lisa Snape, Andreas Lang, Rosa Maria Albert, Inger G. Alsos, and Clive Waddington, 'Ending the Cinderella Status of Terraces and Lynchets in Europe: The Geomorphology of Agricultural Terraces and Implications for Ecosystem Services and Climate Adaptation', Geomorphology, 379 (2021) <https://www.sciencedirect.com/science/article/pii/S0169555X20305523> [accessed 10 December 2021] (see under Fallu and others below)

Brufal, Jesús, Les ràpites. Proposta de definició conceptual a partir del cas del nord-est peninsular (Lleida: Publicacions de la Universitat de Lleida, 2007)

——, 'L'espai rural del districte musulmà de Lleida (segles XI–XII). Espais de secà meridonals' (doctoral thesis, Universitat de Lleida, 2008)

——, El món rural i urbà en la Lleida islàmica (segles XI–XII). Lleida i l'est del districte: Castelldans i el pla del Mascançà (Lleida: Pagès editors, 2013)

Brun, Jean-Pierre, 'Les moulins hydrauliques dans l'Antiquité', Archéologie des moulins hydrauliques, à traction animale et à vent des origines à l'époque médiévale et moderne en Europe et dans le monde méditerranéen, ed. by Luc Jaccottey and Gilles Rollier (Besançon: Presses Universitaires de Franche-Comté, 2016), pp. 21–50

Büntgen, Ulf, Willy Tegel, Kurt Nicolussi, Michael McCormick, David Frank, Valerie Trouet, Jed O. Kaplan, Franz Herzig, Karl-Uwe Heussner, Heinz Wanner, Jürg Luterbacher, and Jan Esper, '2500 Years of European Climate Variability and Human Susceptibility', Science, 331 (2011), 578–82

Büntgen, Ulf, Vladimir S.Myglan, Frederik Charpentier Ljungqvist, Michael McCormick, Nicola Di Cosmo, Michael Sigl, Johann Jungclaus, Sebastian Wagner, Paul J. Krusic, Jan Esper, Jed O. Kaplan, Michiel A.C. de Vaan, Jürg Luterbacher, Lukas Wacker, Willy Tegel, and Alexander V. Kirdyanov, 'Cooling and Societal Change during the Late Antique Little Ice Age from 536 to around 660 AD', Nature Geoscience, 9 (2016), 231–36

Burch, Josep, Excavacions arqueològiques de la muntanya de Sant Julià de Ramis (Girona: Universitat de Girona, 2006)

Burch, Josep, Pere Castanyer, Josep M. Nolla, and Joaquim Tremoleda, 'Formas de poblamiento y ocupación en el ámbito rural del Nordeste catalán desde el Bajo Imperio romano hasta la época visigoda', in Village and Domain at the End of Antiquity and the Beginning of Middle Age: How do Rural Societies Respond to their Changing Times?, ed. by François Réchin (Pau: Presses de l'Université de Pau et des pays de l'Adour, 2015), pp. 35–62

Burgueño, Jesús, and M. Mercè Gras, Atles de la Catalunya senyorial. Els ens locals en el canvi de règim (1800–1860) (Barcelona: ICGC and Rafael Dalmau editor, 2014)

Burjachs, Francesc, 'Paisatges i climes medievals de la façana ibèrica nord-occidental', in Actes del congrés Els castells medievals a la Mediterrània nord-occidental (Girona: Museu La Gabella d'Arbúcies, 2003 [2004]), pp. 231–46

Burjachs, Francesc, and Lothar Schulte, 'El paisatge vegetal del Penedès entre la Prehistòria i el Món Antic', in Territoris antics a la Mediterrània i a la Cossetània *oriental*, ed. by Josep Guitard, Josep M. Palet, and Marta Prevosti (Barcelona: Generalitat de Catalunya, 2003), pp. 249–54

Burjachs, Francesc, Santiago Giralt, Josep Ramon Roca, Guy Seret, and Ramon Julià, 'Palinología holocénica y desertización en el Mediterráneo occidental', *El paisaje mediterráneo a través del espacio y del tiempo. Implicaciones en la desertificación*, ed. by Juan José Ibáñez, Blas L. Valero, and Cristina Machado (Logroño: Geoforma, 1997), pp. 379–94

Burri, Sylvain, 'Reflections on the concept of marginal landscape through a study of late medieval incultum in Provence (South-eastern France)', *Post Classical Archaeologies*, 4 (2014), 7–38

Cabañero, Bernabé *Los castillos catalanes del siglo X. Circunstancias históricas y cuestiones arquitectónicas* (Zaragoza: Institución Fernando el Católico, 1996)

Campmajó, Pierre, Denis Grabol, Elisabeth Bille, Claude Raynaud, Marie-Pierre Ruas, Gilles Parent, and Christine Rendu, 'Un atelier de traitement du fer sur le site du Haut Moyen Âge de la Coume Païrounell à Angoutrine (Pyrénées-Orientales). Premiers résultats', *Domitia*, 8–9 (2007), 137–63

Canal, Josep, Eduard Canal, Josep M. Nolla, and Jordi Sagrera, *La ciutat de Girona en la 1ª meitat del s. xiv. La plenitud medieval* (Girona: Ajuntament de Girona, 1998)

——, *Girona, de Carlemany al feudalisme (785–1057). El trànsit de la ciutat antiga a l'època medieval* (Girona: Ajuntament de Girona, 2003)

Canyameres, Esteve, 'Les torres, propietats agrícoles grans amb orígens en alous i territoris de vil·les altmedievals (Vallès Occidental, segles xi–xix)', *Estudis d'Història Agrària*, 30–31 (2020 [2018–2019]), 93–136

Cara, Lorenzo, and Antonio Malpica, ed., *Agricultura y regadío en al-Andalus. II Coloquio Historia y Medio Físico* (Almería and Granada: Instituto de Estudios Almerienses and THARG, 1996 [1995])

Carreras, Antoni, *El monestir de Santes Creus, 1150–1200* (Valls: Institut d'Estudis Vallencs, 1992)

Casquete, Jacob, and Ivan Salvadó, 'Les balmes obrades de Can Ximet (Olèrdola). Un exemple d'hàbitat troglodític a l'Edat Mitjana', in *Actes del IV Congrés d'Arqueologia Medieval i Moderna de Catalunya* (Tarragona: Ajuntament de Tarragona and ACRAM, 2011), pp. 855–65

Casas, Montserrat, *Història de Cardona, vol. III: La canònica de Sant Vicenç de Cardona a l'edat mitjana* (Cardona: Patronat municipal de museus de Cardona, 1992)

Castanyer, Pere, Joaquim Tremoleda, Lídia Colominas, and Ferran Antolín, 'Després de les *villae*. La transformación del camp al nord-est català en els segles vi i vii a partir de l'exemple de Vilauba / *Villa Alba* (Pla de l'Estany)', *Estudis d'Història Agrària*, 27 (2015), 43–65

Castejón, Nativitat, *Aproximació a l'estudi de l'Hospital de la Santa Creu de Barcelona* (Barcelona: Fundació Noguera, 2007)

Castellanos, Carles, *Els cosins del català* (Argentona: Voliana edicions, 2019)

Castellet, Laura de, 'Cartografia sonora de la comunicació castral. La fonosfera del corn i del dret a cornar a la Catalunya medieval', *Summa*, 8 (2016), 4–25

Catafau, Aymat, *Les celleres et la naissance du village en Roussillon (x^e-xve siècles)* (Perpignan: Editorial El Trabucaire and Presses Universitaires de Perpignan, 1998)

——, 'Le rôle de l'église dans la structuration de l'habitat sur le versant français des Pyrénées. L'exemple du Conflent', in *Villages pyrénéens. Morphogenèse d'un habitat de montagne*, ed. by Maurice Berthe and Benoît Cursente (Toulouse: CNRS and Université de Toulouse-Le Mirail, 2001 [2000]), pp. 75–88

——, 'Les celleres du Roussillon, mises au point et discussions', in *L'Église au village. Lieux, formes et enjeux des pratiques religieuses. Cahiers de Fanjeux, 40* (Toulouse: Éditions Privat, 2006), pp. 17–40

——, 'Del poble al paisatge. Elements per a una historiografia recent del poblament medieval de l'Europa occidental', in *Poblament, territori i història rural. VI Congrés sobre Sistemes agraris, organització social i poder local*, ed. by Jordi Bolòs and Enric Vicedo (Lleida: Institut d'Estudis Ilerdencs, 2009), pp. 13–49

——, 'Petites, nombreuses, isolées? Les églises des vallées pyrénéennes. La spécificité du rôle de l'église dans la structuration du peuplement des montagnes, vallées et piémonts pyrénéens', *Domitia*, 12 (2011), 73–87

——, 'Le modèle de "village ecclésial" en Languedoc, Roussillon et Catalogne: les apports de l'archéologie et leur discussion', in *El paisatge en èpoques de transició al llarg dels darrers dos mil anys, Territori i Societat: el paisatge històric, VII*, ed. by Jordi Bolòs (Lleida: Publicacions de la Universitat de Lleida, 2015), pp. 19–58

——, 'Les cases dels eixamples medievals de Perpinyà als segles XIII–XV: aproximació des de les fonts escrites, la topografia i l'arqueologia', in *La casa medieval en Mallorca y el Mediterráneo. Elementos constructivos y decorativos*, ed. by Tina Sabater (Gijón: Ediciones Trea, 2021), pp. 189–220

Catafau, Aymat, and Olivier Passarrius, ed., *Un palais dans la ville. Volume 2. Perpignan des rois de Majorque* (Canet: Éditions Trabucaire, 2014)

——, '"Village ecclésial" et cellera en Languedoc-Roussillon: questions en débat et éclairages archéologiques', in *Le cimetière au village dans l'Europe médiévale et moderne. Flaran 35*, ed. by Cécile Treffort (Toulouse: Presses Universitaires du Midi, 2015), pp. 107–24

Català i Roca, Pere, ed., *Els castells catalans*, vols I–VI (Barcelona: Rafael Dalmau editor, 1967 1979)

Catalán, Raúl, Patricia Fuentes, and Juan Carlos Sastre, ed., *Las fortificaciones en la tardoantigüedad. Élites y articulación del territorio (siglos v–viii dC)* (Madrid: La Ergástula, 2014)

Catlos, Brian A., *The Victors and the Vanquished: Christians and Muslims of Catalonia and Aragon, 1050–1300* (Cambridge: Cambridge University Press, 2004)

Caucanas, Sylvie, 'Assèchements en Roussillon', in *Histoire et archéologie des terres catalanes au Moyen Âge* (Perpignan: Presses Universitaires de Perpignan, 1995), pp. 269–78

——, *Moulins et irrigation en Roussillon du ixe au xve siècle* (París: CNRS, 1995)

Chandler, Cullen J., *Carolingian Catalonia: Politics, Culture, and Identity in an Imperial Province, 778–987* (Cambridge: Cambridge University Press, 2019)

Chavarría Arnau, Alexandra, 'The Topography of Early Medieval Burials: Some Reflections on the Archaeological Evidence from Northern Italy (Fifth-Eighth Centuries)', in *Polity and Neighbourhood in Early Medieval Europe*, ed. by Julio Escalona, Orri Vésteinsson, and Stuart Brookes (Turnhout: Brepols, 2019), pp. 83–119

Chédeville, André, and Daniel Pichot, ed., *Des villes à l'ombre des châteaux. Naissance et essor des agglomérations castrales en France au Moyen Âge* (Rennes: PUR, 2010)

Chevallier, Raymond, *Lecture du temps dans l'espace. Topographie archéologique et historique* (Paris: Picard, 2000)

Chouquer, Gérard, 'Tissu archéologique en Bourgogne', *Paysages découverts. Histoire, géographie et archéologie du territoire en Suisse romande*, 2 (1993), 10–11

——, *Entre Bourgogne et Franche-Comté. Histoire d'un paysage de l'époque gauloise à nos jours* (Paris: Éditions Errance, 1993)

——, 'Etude morphologique du cadastre B d'Orange', in *Les campagnes de la France méditerranéenne dans l'Antiquité et le haut Moyen Âge. Études microrégionales*, ed. by François Favory and Jean-Luc Fiches (Paris: Editions de la Maison des Sciences de l'homme, 1994), pp. 56–72

——, 'La morphologie agraire et les paysages de la plaine des Tilles et de l'Ouche (Cote-d'Or)', in *Les formes du paysage. Tome 1. Etudes sur les parcellaires*, ed. by Gérard Chouquer (Paris: Éditions Errance, 1996), pp. 32–48

——, *L'étude des paysages. Essais sur leurs formes et leur histoire* (Paris: Éditions Errance, 2000)

——, *L'arpentage romain. Histoire des textes – Droit – Techniques* (Paris: Éditions Errance, 2001)

——, 'Glossaire', *Études rurales*, 167–68 (2003), 295–303

——, 'L'émergence de la planimétrie agraire à l'Âge du Fer', *Études rurales*, 175–76 (2005 [2006]), 29–52

——, *Cadastres et Fiscalité dans l'Antiquité tardive* (Tours: Presses Universitaires François-Rabelais, 2014)

——, *Dominer et tenir la terre dans le haut Moyen Âge* (Tours: Presses Universitaires François-Rabelais, 2020)

——, *Les parcellaires médiévaux en Émilie et en Romagne. Centuriations et trames coaxiales. Morphologie et droit agraire* (Paris: Éditions Publi-Topex, 2020) http://serveur.publi-topex.com/ EDITION/06ParcellairesMedievauxEmilieRomagne.pdf [accessed 11 September 2021]

Chouquer, Gérard, and Jean-Pierre Comps, 'Centuriations et organisation antique de l'espace: le point des connaissances et des incertitudes', in *Les Pyrénées-Orientales. 66, Carte Archéologique de la Gaule*, ed. by Jérôme Kotarba (Paris: Académie des Inscriptions et Belles-Lettres, 2007), pp. 124–28

Chouquer, Gérard, and François Favory, *Les paysages de l'Antiquité. Terres et cadastres de l'Occident romain (IVe s. avant J.-C. / IIIe s. après J.-C.)* (Paris: Editions Errance, 1991)

Chouquer, Gérard, and Cécile Jung, 'La dynamique du réseau: vers un autre objet', in *Le Tricastin romain: évolution d'un paysage centurié (Drôme, Vaucluse)*, ed. by François Favory (Lyon: Association de liaison pour le patrimoine et l'archéologie en Rhône-Alpes et en Auvergne and Publications de la Maison de l'Orient et de la Méditerranée, 2013), pp. 167–92

Christie, Neil, *The Fall of the Western Roman Empire: An Archaeological and Historical Perspective* (London: Bloomsbury, 2011)

Christie, Neil, and Hajnalka Herold, ed., *Fortified Settlements in Early Medieval Europe: Defended Communities of the 8th-10th Centuries* (Oxford: Oxbow, 2016)

Citter, Carlo, 'Landscapes, Settlements and Sustainability', in *Detecting and Understanding Historic Landscapes*, ed. by Alexandra Chavarría Arnau and Andrew Reynolds (Mantua: SAP Società Archeologica, 2015), pp. 253–72

Claramunt, Salvador, 'El bací dels pobres vergonyants de la parròquia del Pi de Barcelona medieval com atenuant de la crisi ciutadana del segle xv', in *Estudis dedicats a la doctora Josefina Mutgé*, ed. by Manuel Sánchez, Ana Gómez, Roser Salicrú, and Pere Verdés (Madrid: CSIC, 2013), pp. 203–13

Claramunt, Salvador, and Jordi Bolòs, *El capbreu de la comanda de l'Espluga de Francolí del 1558* (L'Espluga de Francolí: Casal de l'Espluga de Francolí, 1991)

Clark, Jo, John Darlington, and Graham Fairclough, *Using Historic Landscape Characterisation* (London: English Heritage and Lancashire County Council, 2004)

Cockin, Tim C. H., *The Parish Atlas of England: An Atlas of English Parish Boundaries* (Barlaston: Malthouse Press, 2017)

Codou, Yann, 'Dans les campagnes aussi, des monuments chrétiens', in *L'Antiquité tardive en Provence (ive-vie siècle). Naissance d'une chrétienté*, ed. by Jean Guyon and Marc Heijmans (Arles: Actes Sud, 2013), pp. 126–30

Colón, Germà, *El lèxic català dins la Romània* (València: Universitat de València, 1993)

Combe, Annette, 'La recherche des cadastrations antiques sur le plateau suisse', in *Les formes du paysage. Tome 2. Archéologie des parcellaires*, ed. by Gérard Chouquer (Paris: Éditions Errance, 1996), pp. 167–73

Comps, Jean-Pierre, 'De Roussillon en Conflent. La lente mise en place du réseau routier de l'Antiquité à nos jours', *Domitia*, 8–9 (2007), 21–42

Conzen, Michael Robert G., *Alnwick, Northumberland: A Study in Town-Plan Analysis* (London: George Philip & Son, 1960)

——, 'Morphogenesis, Morphological Regions, and Secular Human Agency in the Historic Townscape, as Exemplified by Ludlow', in *Urban Historical Geography: Recent Progress in Britain and Germany*, ed. by Dietrich Denecke and Gareth Shaw (Cambridge: Cambridge University Press, 1988), pp. 255–61

Coromines, Joan, *Estudis de toponímia catalana, volum I* (Barcelona: Editorial Barcino, 1965)

——, *Onomasticon Cataloniae. Els noms de lloc i noms de persona de totes les terres de llengua catalana*, vols II–VIII (Barcelona: Curial, 1994–1997) https://oncat.iec. cat/ [accessed 24 December 2021]

Cortonesi, Alfio, *Il Medioevo degli alberi. Piante e paesaggi d'Italia (secoli xi-xv)* (Roma: Carocci editore, 2022)

Costa, Xavier, 'Paisatges monàstics. El monacat als comtats catalans alt-medievals (segles IX-X)' (doctoral thesis, Universitat de Barcelona, 2019)

——, *Poder, religió i territori. Una nova mirada als orígens del monacat al Ripollès (segles ix-x)* (Barcelona: Edicions de la Universitat de Barcelona, 2022)

Cowley, David C., Robin A. Standring, and Matthew J. Abricht, ed., *Landscapes through the Lens: Aerial Photographs and Historic Environment* (Oxford: Oxbow, 2010)

Creighton, Oliver H., *Castles and Landscapes* (London: Continuum, 2002)

——, *Early European Castles: Aristocracy and Authority, AD 800–1200* (London: Bristol Classical Press, 2012)

Crow, James, and Sam Turner, 'Silivri and the Thracian Hinterland of Istambul: An Historic Landscape', *Anatolian Studies*, 59 (2009), 167–81

Crow, James, Sam Turner, and Athanasios K. Vionis, 'Characterizing the Historic Landscapes of Naxos', *Journal of Mediterranean Archaeology*, 24.1 (2011), 111–37

Crutchley, Simon, Fiona Small, and Mark Bowden, *Savernake Forest: A Report for the National Mapping Programme* (Swindon: English Heritage, 2009)

Cuadrada, Coral, 'El paisatge i l'organització del territori al Maresme medieval', in *Territori i Societat a l'Edat Mitjana I, ed. by* Jordi Bolòs and Joan J. Busqueta (Lleida: Universitat de Lleida, 1997), pp. 83–130.

Cubo, Adrià, Oriol Mercadal, Jordi Morera, Oriol Olesti, and Joan Oller, 'El Castellot de Bolvir. Un vilatge cerdà dels segles XI-XII', in *V Congrés d'Arqueologia Medieval i Moderna de Catalunya* (Barcelona: Ajuntament de Barcelona and ACRAM, 2015), pp. 687–700

Currás, Andrés, 'Estudio sobre la evolución de paisajes mediterráneos continentales en Lleida y Guadalajara durante los últimos 3.000 años a partir de las secuencias polínicas de Ivars, Somolinos y Cañamares' (doctoral thesis, Universitat de Barcelona, 2012)

Cursente, Benoît, *Les Castelnaux de la Gascogne médiévale. Gascogne gersoise* (Bordeaux: Fédération històriques du Sud-Ouest, 1980)

——, *Des maisons et des hommes. La Gascogne médiévale (xf^e-xve siècle)* (Toulouse: Presses Universitaires du Mirail, 1998)

——, 'Le village pyrénéen comme "village à maisons". Premières propositions', in *Villages pyrénéens. Morphogenèse d'un habitat de montagne*, ed. by Maurice Berthe and Benoît Cursente (Toulouse: CNRS and Université de Toulouse-Le Mirail, 2001 [2000]), pp. 157–69

Curtis, Daniel R., 'The Emergence of Concentrated Villages in Medieval Western Europe: Explanatory Frameworks in the Historiography', *Canadian Journal of History / Annales canadiennes d'histoire*, 48 (2013), 223–51

Czaja, Roman, 'Polish Town Plans as Expressions of Political and Economic Power', in *Lords and Towns in Medieval Europe: The European Historic Towns Project*, ed. by Anngret Simms and Howard B. Clarke (New York: Routledge, 2019), pp. 235–54

Daileader, Philip, *De vrais citoyens. Violence, mémoire et identité dans la communauté médiévale de Perpignan, 1162–1397* (Canet: Edicions Trabucaire, 2004 [Original version in English: 2000])

Dar, Henry C., *Domesday England* (Cambridge: Cambridge University Press, 1986 [first edition 1977])

Davasse, Bernard, *Forêts, charbonniers et paysans dans les Pyrénées de l'Est du Moyen Âge à nos jours: une approche géographique de l'histoire de l'environnement* (Toulouse: GEODE, 2000)

De Meulemeester, Johnny, 'Même problème, même solution: quelques réflexions autour d'un grenier fortifié', in *Le village médiévale et son environnement. Études offertes à Jean-Marie Pesez*, ed. by Laurent Feller, Perrine Mane, and Françoise Piponnier (Paris: Publications de la Sorbonne, 1998), pp. 97–112

Démians d'Archimbaud, Gabrielle, *Les fouilles de Rougiers: Contribution à l'archéologie de l'habitat rural médiéval en pays méditerranéen* (Paris: CNRS, 1981)

Denjean, Claude, *Juifs et Chrétiens. De Perpignan à Puigcerdà, xiiie-xive siècles* (Canet: Edicions Trabucaire, 2004)

Deschamps, Stéphane, and Jérôme Pascal, 'Le cadastration antique de Rezé (*Ratiatum*, Loire-Atlantique)', in *Les formes du paysage. Tome 1. Etudes sur les parcellaires*, ed. by Gérard Chouquer (Paris: Éditions Errance, 1996), pp. 104–10

Devroey, Jean-Pierre, *La nature et le roi. Environnement, pouvoir et société à l'âge de Charlemagne (740–820)* (Paris: Albin Michel, 2019)

Diarte-Blasco, Pilar, *Late Antique and Early Medieval Hispania: Landscapes without Strategy? An Archaeological Approach* (Oxford: Oxbow, 2018)

Dolset, Henri, 'La maîtrise du risque dans les marches catalanes, X^e-XIIe siècle', in *Les sociétés méditerranéennes face au risque. Espaces et frontières*, ed. by Christian Velud (Cairo: Institut Français d'Archéologie Orientale, 2012), pp. 53–70

Domergue, René-Pierre, 'La diversité morphologique des habitats du Sobrarbe, un témoin d'une frontière chrono-socio-spatiale médiévale? Description et hypothèses', in *Las fronteras pirenaicas en la edad media (siglos VI–XV)*, ed. by Sébastien Gasc, Philippe Sénac, Clément Venco, and Carlos Laliena (Zaragoza: Prensas de la Universidad de Zaragoza, 2018), pp. 441–71

Dominguez, Cécile, 'Les Espassoles', *Archéo 66. Bulletin de l'AAPO*, 31 (2016), 70–72

Du, Georges, *Guerriers et paysans, VIIe–XIIe siècle. Premier essor de l'économie européenne* (Paris: Editions Gallimard, 1973)

Durand, Aline, *Les paysages médiévaux du Languedoc (X^e-XIIe siècles)* (Toulouse: Presses Universitaires du Mirail, 1998)

Duvernoy, Jean, 'Activité pastorale et transhumance dans le domaine sud-occitan', *Heresis*, 2 (1990 [1992]), 229–41

Ejarque, Ana, 'Génesis y configuración microregional de un paisaje cultural de alta montaña durante el Holoceno: estudio polínico y de otros indicadores paleoambientales en el valle del Madriu-Perafita-Claror (Andorra)' (doctoral thesis, Universitat Rovira i Virgili / Institut Català d'Arqueologia Clàssica, 2009)

——, *La alta montaña pirenaica: génesis y configuración holocena de un paisaje cultural. Estudio paleoambiental en el valle del Madriu-Perafita-Claror (Andorra)* (Oxford: BAR International Series, 2013)

Elliott, John H, *The Revolt of the Catalans: A Study in the Decline of Spain (1598–1640)* (Cambridge: Cambridge University Press, 1984 [first edition 1963])

Engel, Josef, Wolfgang Mager, and Andreas Birken, ed., *Grosser Historischer Weltatlas. II: Mittelalter* (München: Bayerischer Schulbuch-Verlag Verlag, 1979)

Ennen, Edith, and Walter Janssen, *Deutsche Agrargeschichte vom Neolithikum bis zur Schwelle des Industriezeitalters* (Weisbaden: Steiner, 1979)

Enrich, Joan, Jordi Enrich, and Lluís Pedraza, *Vilaclara de Castellfollit del Boix (El Bages). Un assentament rural de l'Antiguitat tardana* (Igualada: Arqueoanoia edicions, 1995)

Eritja, Xavier, *De l'almunia a la* turris: *organització de l'espai a la regió de Lleida (segles XI–XIII)* (Lleida: Publicacions de la Universitat de Lleida, 1998)

Español, Francesca, 'Les cartes de població de Vilallonga', *Acta Historica et Archaeologica Mediaevalia*, 4 (1983), 87–106

Esquieu, Yves, *Quartier cathédral. Une cité dans la ville* (Paris: REMPART, 1994)

Esquieu, Yves, and Jean-Marie Pesez, *Cent maisons médiévales en France (du XIIe au milieu du XVIe siècle). Un corpus et une esquisse* (Paris: CNRS editions, 1998)

Esquilache, Ferran, *Els constructors de l'Horta de València. Origen, evolució i estructura social d'una gran horta andalusina entre els segles VIII i XIII* (València: Publicacions de la Universitat de València, 2018)

——, 'Searching for the Origin: A New Interpretation for the Horta of Valencia in the Time of al-Andalus', in *Agricultural Landscapes of Al-Andalus, and the Aftermath of the Feudal Conquest*, ed. by Helena Kirchner and Flocel Sabaté (Turnhout: Brepols, 2021), pp. 127–52

Esteban, Agustí, 'El predominio de la acción antrópica', in *La humanización de las altas cuencas de la Garona y las Nogueras (4500 aC-1955 dC)*, ed. by Agustí Esteban (Madrid: Ministerio de Medio Ambiente, 2003), pp. 146–54

Esteban, Agustí, Santiago Riera, Magí Miret, and Xavier Miret, 'Transformacions del paisatge i ramaderia a la costa catalana del Penedès i Garraf (Barcelona) a l'alta edat mitjana', in *IV Congrés d'Arqueologia medieval espanyola, Actes III* (Alacant: AEAM and Generalitat Valenciana, 1993), pp. 647–55

Esteban, Pau, Susana Laredo, Joan Pino, and Andrés Valverde, 'El context deltaic: situació, origen geològic i història del poblament humà', in *Els sistemes naturals del delta del Llobregat*, ed. by Josep Germain and Joan Pino (Barcelona: Institució Catalana d'Història Natural, 2018)

Fabre, Camille, *Commerce et marchandisation du bois à Toulouse à la fin du Moyen Âge* (Paris: Classiques Garnier, 2021)

Fabre, Guislaine, Monique Bourin, Jacqueline Caille, and André Debord, ed., *Morphogenèse du village médiéval (IXe-XIIe siècles)* (Montpellier: Association pour la connaissance du patrimoine du Languedoc-Roussillon, 1996)

Fàbregas, Marta, 'Sota l'enderroc: les restes del castell de Milany', *Ausa*, 179 (2017), 139–51

Fagan, Brian, *The Little Ice Age: How Climate Made History, 1300–1850* (New York: Basic Books, 2000).

——, *The Great Warming: Climate Change and the Rise and Fall of Civilizations* (London: Bloomsbury 2008).

Faith, Rosamond, *The Moral Economy of the Countryside: Anglo-Saxon to Anglo-Norman England* (Cambridge: Cambridge University Press, 2020)

Fallu, Daniel, Kevin Walsh, Sara Cucchiaro, Paolo Tarolli, Pengzhi Zhao, Kristof van Oost, Lisa Snape, Andreas Lang, Rosa Maria Albert, Inger Alsos, Clive Waddington, Francesco Ficetola, and Tony Brown, 'Ending the Cinderella Status of Terraces and Lynchets in Europe' (2020) <http://docplayer. net/190422888-Ending-the-cinderella-status-of-terraces-and-lynchets-in-europe.html> [accessed 10 December 2021] (see Brown and others above)

Farías, Víctor, *El mas i la vila a la Catalunya medieval. Els fonaments d'una societat senyorialitzada (segles XI–XIV)* (València: Publicacions de la Universitat de València, 2009)

Farías, Víctor, Ramon Martí, and Aymat Catafau, *Les sagreres a la Catalunya medi-eval* (Girona: Associació d'Història Rural de les Comarques Gironines and Universitat de Girona, 2007)

Fau, Laurent, 'Les monts d'Aubrac: approches d'un habitat médiéval montagnard', *Archéologie du Midi médiéval*, 21 (2003), 171–82

——, ed., *Les Monts d'Aubrac au Moyen Âge. Genèse d'un monde agropastoral.* Documents d'Archéologie Française 101 (Paris: Éditions de la Maison des Sciences de l'homme, 2006)

Favory, François, 'Les parcellaires antiques de Gaule médiane et septentrionale', in *Des hommes aux champs. Pour une archéologie des espaces ruraux du Néolithique au Moyen Âge*, ed. by Vincent Carpentier and Cyril Marcigny (Rennes: Presses Universitaires de Rennes, 2012), pp. 111–30

——, ed., *Le Tricastin romain: évolution d'un paysage centurié (Drôme, Vaucluse)* (Lyon: Association de liaison pour le patrimoine et l'archéologie en Rhône-Alpes et en Auvergne and Publications de la Maison de l'Orient et de la Méditerranée, 2013)

Fenwick, Corisande, *Early Islamic North Africa: A New Perspective* (London: Bloomsbury, 2020)

Fernández Ferrer, Marc, 'Arqueologia del paisatge alt medieval al baix Montseny, segles VI–X. Una demostració pràctica dels sistemes d'informació geogràfica' (doctoral thesis, Universitat de Barcelona, 2019)

Fernández Mier, Margarita, 'Campos de cultivo en la Cordillera Cantábrica. La agricultura en zonas de montaña', in *Por una arqueología agraria. Perspectivas de investigación sobre espacios de cultivo en las sociedades medievales hispánicas*, ed. by Helena Kirchner (Oxford: BAR International Series 2062, 2010), pp. 41–59

——, 'La construcción de la territorialidad medieval. Entre la documentación escrita y la arqueológica. La montaña centro occidental asturiana', in *La construcción de la territorialidad en la Alta Edad Media*, ed. by Iñaki Martín Viso (Salamanca: Ediciones Universidad de Salamanca, 2020), pp. 223–42

Ferrer, Llorenç, *Eines i feines de pagès* (Figueres: Brau edicions, 2013)

Ferrer, Maria Teresa, 'Boscos i deveses a la Corona Catalano-aragonesa (s. XIV–XV)', *Anuario de Estudios Medievales*, 20 (1990), 485–539

Ferrer, Maria Teresa, Josefina Mutgé, and Manuel Riu, ed., *El mas català durant l'edat mitjana i la moderna (segles IX–XVIII)* (Barcelona: CSIC, 2001)

Ferret, Joan Lluís, 'La Formació del Delta del Llobregat (nova versió) a càrrec de Joan Lluís Ferret i Pujol' (2014) <https://es.slideshare.net/amicsdelprat/la-formaci-del-delta-del-llobregat-a-crrec-de-joan-llus-ferret-i-pujol> [accessed 10 December 2021]

Fité, Francesc, *Reculls d'història de la Vall d'Àger. Període antic i medieval* (Àger: Centre d'Estudis de la vall d'Àger, 1985)

Fité, Francesc, and Prim Bertran, 'Una explotació vitivinícola altomedieval a Flix (la Noguera)', *Vinyes i vins: mil anys d'història. Actes i comunicacions del III Col·loqui d'Història agrària sobre mil anys de producció, comerç i consum de vins i begudes alcohòliques als Països Catalans*, ed. by Emili Giralt (Barcelona: Publicacions de la Universitat de Barcelona, 1993), vol, II, pp. 235–39

Fité, Francesc, and Jordi Bolòs, 'Vila d'Àger', in *Catalunya Romànica. vol. XVI: La Noguera* (Barcelona: Enciclopèdia Catalana, 1994), pp. 107–11

Fité, Francesc, and Eduard González, *Arnau Mir de Tost. Un senyor de frontera al segle XI* (Lleida: Universitat de Lleida, 2010)

Fité, Francesc, and Cristina Masvidal, 'Restes subsistents del recinte fortificat del castell d'Àger, d'època andalusina', *Revista d'Arqueologia de Ponent*, 25 (2015), 205–23

Fixot, Michel, and Elisabeth Zadora-Rio, ed., *L'église, le terroir* (Paris: Editions du CNRS, 1989)

——, ed., *L'environnement des églises et la topographie religieuse des campagnes médiévales* (Paris: Éditions de la Maison des Sciences de l'Homme, 1994)

Fleming, Andrew, *The Dartmoor Reaves:. Investigating Prehistoric Land Divisions* (Oxford: Windgather Press, 2008 [first edition 1988])

Flórez, Marta, 'Dinàmica del poblament i estructuració del territori a la Laietània interior. Estudi del Vallès oriental de l'època ibèrica fins a l'alta edat mitjana', *Butlletí de la Societat Catalana d'Estudis Històrics*, 21 (2010), 263–84

Folch, Cristian, 'Territorios y poblamiento en el noreste de la Tarraconense en época visigoda (siglos VI–VIII): una nueva aproximación al estudio de la organización territorial y de las formas de asentamiento', in *Las fronteras pirenaicas en la edad media (siglos VI–XV)*, ed. by Sébastien Gasc, Philippe Sénac, Clément Venco, and Carlos Laliena (Zaragoza: Prensas de la Universidad de Zaragoza, 2018), pp. 67–105

Folch, Cristian, and Jordi Gibert, 'L'ús de datacions radiocarbòniques en jaciments altmedievals de Catalunya (segles V–XI d.C.): estat de la qüestió i noves perspectives de recerca', in *Iber-Crono. Actas del congreso de Cronometrías para la Historia de la Península Ibérica*, ed. by Juan A. Barceló, Igor Bogdanovic, and Berta Morell (Barcelona: CEUR-WS, 2016), pp. 293–303

Folch, Cristian, and Ramon Martí, 'Excavacions arqueològiques al vilar de Montclús (Santa Maria de Merlès, Berguedà): un assentament rural del segle IX', in *III Congrés d'arqueologia medieval i moderna a Catalunya*, ed. by Marina Miquel and Josep M. Vila (Barcelona: Ajuntament de Sabadell and ACRAM, 2007), vol. II, pp. 506–13

Folch, Cristian, Jordi Gibert, and Ramon Martí, 'Les explotacions rurals tardoantigues i altmedievals a la Catalunya Vella: una síntesi arqueològica', *Estudis d'Història Agrària*, 27 (2015), 91–114

Forcadell, Toni, 'El rio Sénia: origen y fosilización de la frontera entre Cataluña y el reino de Valencia (ss. XII y XIII)', in *Las fronteras en la Edad Media hispànica, siglos XIII–XVI*, ed. by Manuel García, Ángel Galán, and Rafael Peinado (Granada: Universidad de Granada, 2019), pp. 271–308

Forcano, Manuel, and Víctor Hurtado, *Atles d'història dels jueus de Catalunya* (Barcelona: Rafael Dalmau editor, 2019)

Fortó, Abel, and Àlex Vidal, 'En los orígenes de Sant Julià de Lòria (Andorra). Las evidencias de ocupación durante la antigüedad tardía y la alta edad media del camp Vermell (ss. V–XII dC)', in *The Archaeology of Early Medieval Villages in Europe*, ed. by Juan-Antonio Quirós (Bilbao: Euskal Herriko Unibertsitatea – Universidad del País Vasco, 2009), pp. 253–62

Fournier, Gabriel, *Le château dans la France médiévale. Essai de sociologie monumentale* (Paris: Editions Aubier Montaigne, 1978)

Franceschelli, Carlotta, and Stefano Marabini, *Lettura di un territorio sepolto: la pianura lughese in età romana* (Bologna: Ante Quem, 2007)

Francovich, Riccardo, 'The Beginnings of Hilltop Villages in Early Medieval Tuscany', in *The Long Morning of Medieval Europe: New Directions in Early Medieval Studies*, ed. by Jennifer R. Davis and Michael McCormick (Farnham: Ashgate, 2008), pp. 55–82

Francovich, Riccardo, Enrica Boldrini, and Daniele De Luca, 'Archeologia delle terre nuove in Toscana: il caso di San Giovanni Valdarno', in *I borghi nuovi. Secoli XII–XIV*, ed. by Rinaldo Comba and Aldo Settia (Cuneo: Società per gli studi storici, archeologici ed artistici della provincia di Cuneo, 1993), pp. 155–94

Francovich, Riccardo, and Maria Ginatempo, ed., *Castelli. Storia e archeologia del potere nella Toscana medievale. Volume I* (Firenze: All'Insegna del Giglio, 2000)

Francovich, Riccardo, and Richard Hodges, *Villa to Village: The Transformation of the Roman Countryside in Italy, c. 400–1000* (London: Duckworth, 2003)

Freedman, Paul H., *The Diocese of Vic: Tradition and Regeneration in Medieval Catalonia* (New Brunswick: Rutgers University Press, 1983) (Catalan edition: 1985)

——, *The Origins of Peasant Servitude in Medieval Catalonia* (Cambridge: Cambridge University Press, 1991) (Catalan edition: 1994)

Furió, Antoni, *Història del País Valencià* (València: Edicions Alfons el Magnànim, 1995)

Gadot, Yuval, Uri Davidovich, Gideon Avni, and Naomi Porat, 'The Formation of a Mediterranean Terraced Landscape: Mount Eitan, Judean Highlands, Israel', *Journal of Archaeological Science: Reports*, 6 (2016), 397–417 <https://www.researchgate.net/publication/298327998_The_formation_of_a_Mediterranean_terraced_landscape_Mount_Eitan_Judean_Highlands_Israel> [accessed 10 December 2021]

Galindo, Esteban, 'Anàlisi del paisatge històric a la zona nord del pla de Barcelona, segles XV al XVIII: Bellesguard' (doctoral thesis, Universitat de Barcelona, 2020)

Gallon, Florian, 'Les monastères hispaniques dans les conflits entre chrétiens et musulmans: impacts d'une situation frontalière (VIIIe-XIe siècles)', in *Las fronteras pirenaicas en la edad media (siglos VI–XV)*, ed. by Sébastien Gasc, Philippe Sénac, Clément Venco, and Carlos Laliena (Zaragoza: Prensas de la Universidad de Zaragoza, 2018), pp. 225–75

Galop, Didier, *La forêt, l'homme et le troupeau dans les Pyrénées. 6000 ans d'histoire de l'environnement entre Garonne et Méditerranée* (Toulouse: Geode, Université de Toulouse II and Université Paul Sabatier, 1998)

Garcia Biosca, Joan Eusebi, *Els orígens del terme de Lleida. La formació d'un territori urbà (segles XI–XII)* (Lleida: Patronat Municipal Josep Lladonosa and La Mañana. 1995)

Garcia Espuche, Albert, and Manuel Guàrdia, *Espai i societat a la Barcelona pre-industrial* (Barcelona: Edicions de la Magrana and Institut Municipal d'Història, 1986)

García Marsilla, Juan Vicente, 'De la plaza a la tienda. Las infraestructuras del comercio al por menor en la Valencia medieval', in *Ciudades mediterráneas. Dinámicas sociales y transformaciones urbanas en el Antiguo Régimen*, ed. by Daniel Muñoz (València: Editorial Tirant, 2021), pp. 73–89

Garcia-Oliver, Ferran, ed., *El Císter, ideals i realitat d'un orde monàstic. Actes del simposi internacional sobre el Císter. Valldigna (1298–1998)* (València: Universitat de València and CEIC Alfons el Vell, 2001)

——, *The Valley of the Six Mosques: Work and Life in Medieval Valldigna* (Turnhout: Brepols, 2012) (Catalan version: *La Vall de les Sis Mesquites*, 2003)

——, *Els murs fràgils dels calls. Jueus i jueves dels Països Catalans* (Catarroja – Barcelona: Editorial Afers, 2019)

Gardiner, Mark, and Susan Kil, 'Perceptions of Medieval Settlement', in *The Oxford Handbook of Later Medieval Archaeology in Britain*, ed. by Christopher M. Gerrard and Alejandra Gutiérrez (Oxford: Oxford University Press, 2020), pp. 210–25

Gasc, Sébastien, Philippe Sénac, Clément Venco, and Carlos Laliena, ed., *Las fronteras pirenaicas en la Edad Media (siglos VI–XV)* (Zaragoza: Prensas de la Universidad de Zaragoza, 2018)

Gascón, Carles, 'Els acords de Pariatge al Bisbat d'Urgell (segles XII–XV)', *Quaderns d'Estudis Andorrans*, 10 (2017), 67–108

Gauthiez, Bernard, *Atlas morphologique des villes de Normandie* (Lyon: Éditions du Cosmogone, 1999)

——, 'La transformation des villes au Bas Moyen-Âge entre Valence et Pise', *Rodis. Journal of Medieval and Postmedieval Archaeology*, 1 (2018), 25–52

Gauthiez, Bernard, Élisabeth Zadora-Rio, and Henri Galinié, *Village et ville au Moyen Âge: les dynamiques morphologiques* (Tours: Presses Universitaires François-Rabelais, 2003)

Gelichi, Sauro, 'Agricoltura e ambiente nell'Italia tardo-antica e altomedievale. Una prospettiva acheologica', in *Agricoltura e ambiente attraverso l'età romana e l'alto medioevo*, ed. by Paolo Nanni (Firenze: Le Lettere and Accademia dei Georgofili, 2012), pp. 109–38

Gendron, Stéphane, *La toponymie des voies romaines et médiévales. Les mots des routes anciennes* (Paris: Editions Errance, 2006)

Gentili, François, 'L'archéologie au village en Île-de-France: quelques exemples d'études diachroniques', *Archéologie du Midi médiéval*, 36 (2018 [2020]), 81–101

Georges-Leroy, Murielle, Jérôme Bock, Etienne Dambrine, Jean-Luc Dupouey, Anne Gebhardt, and Jean-Denis Lafitte, 'Les vestiges gallo-romains conservés dans le massif forestier de Haye (Meurthe-et-Moselle). Leur apport à l'étude de l'espace agraire', in *Des hommes aux champs. Pour une archéologie des espaces ruraux du Néolithique au Moyen Âge*, ed. by Vincent Carpentier and Cyril Marcigny (Rennes: Presses Universitaires de Rennes, 2012), pp. 157–80

Gerrard, Christopher, Paolo Forlin, and Peter J. Brown, ed., *Waiting for the End of the World? New Perspectives on Natural Disasters in Medieval Europe* (London: Routledge, 2021)

Gerez, Pau, 'Ús i abús de l'aigua a la Girona baixmedieval', *Estudis d'Història agrària*, 23 (2010–2011), 219–29

Gibert, Jordi, *L'expressió material del poder durant la conquesta comtal. Esglésies, castells i torres a la Catalunya central (segles X–XI)* (La Pobla de Claramunt: Ajuntament de la Pobla de Claramunt, 2018)

——, *La fi del món antic i els inicis de l'edat mitjana a la Catalunya Central. Economia, societat i territori entre els segles V i VIII* (Tarragona: Institut Català d'Arqueologia Clàssica, 2018)

Gil, Isabel, and Marta Morán, 'Molí hidràulic de l'Avinguda Blondel, 94 de Lleida' (unpublished paper, *VI Congrés d'Arqueologia medieval i moderna a Catalunya*, Lleida, 2018)

Gilbertson, David D., and Chris O. Hunt, 'Romano-Lian Agriculture: Walls and Floodwater Farming', in *Farming the Desert: The UNESCO Lian Valleys Archaeological Survey. Volume One: Synthesis*, ed. by Graeme Barker (London: UNESCO, 1996), pp. 191–226

Ginot, Antoni, 'Els drets sobre la pesca a l'Alt Maresme (terme de Montpalau). Delme, castellatge i peix senyoriu (segles XIII-VI), *Estudis d'Història agrària*, 33 (2021), 161–88

Giralt, Emili, and Josep M. Salrach, eds, *Història agrària dels Països Catalans. II: Edat Mitjana* (Barcelona: Fundació Catalana per a Recerca and Universitats dels Països Catalans, 2004)

Gironella, Josep M., *Els molins i les salines de Castelló d'Empúries al segle XIV: la mòlta de cereals, el batanatge de teixits i l'obtenció de sal en una vila catalana baixmedieval* (Barcelona: Fundació Noguera, 2010)

——, 'La mòlta de cereals i el batanatge de teixits al comtat d'Empúries i al vescomtat de Rocabertí. Finals del segle XIII i primera meitat del XIV' (doctoral thesis, Universitat de Barcelona, 2013)

——, *Els molins empordanesos baixmedievals. Propietat, explotació i fiscalitat* (Girona: Associació d'Història Rural, 2014).

Glick, Thomas F., 'Convivencia: An Introductory Note', in *Convivencia: Jews, Muslims, and Christians in Medieval Spain*, ed. by Vivian B. Mann, Thomas F. Glick, and Jerrilynn D. Dodds (New York: George Braziller and The Jewish Museum, 1992), pp. 1–9

——, 'Sistemes agrícoles islàmics de Xarq al-Andalus', in *Història agrària dels Països Catalans. II: Edat Mitjana*, ed. by Emili Giralt and Josep M. Salrach (Barcelona: Fundació Catalana per a Recerca and Universitats dels Països Catalans, 2004), pp. 45–89

Glick, Thomas, and Helena Kirchner, 'Hydraulic Systems and Technologies of Islamic Spain: History and Archaeology', in *Working with Water in Medieval Europe: Technology and Resource-Use*, ed. by Paolo Squatriti (Leiden: Brill, 2000), pp. 267–329

González Villaescusa, Ricardo, 'Centuriations, *alquerias* et *pueblas*: éléments pour la compréhension du paysage valencien', in *Les formes du paysage. Tome 2. Archéologie des parcellaires*, ed. by Gérard Chouquer (Paris: Éditions Errance, 1996), pp. 155–66

——, *Las formas de los paisajes mediterráneos (Ensayos sobre las formas, funciones y epistemología parcelarias: estudios comparativos en medios mediterráneos entre la antigüedad y época moderna)* (Jaén: Universidad de Jaén, 2002)

——, 'Essai de définition d'un module agraire chez les Ibères', in *Métrologie agraire antique et médiévale*, ed. by François Favory (Besançon: Presses Universitaires Franc-Comtoises, 2003), pp. 15–25

Gonzalvo, Gener, 'La muralla de Poblet', in *L'Art Gòtic a Catalunya. Arquitectura III*, ed. by Antoni Pladevall (Barcelona: Enciclopèdia Catalana, 2003), pp. 277–78

Gort, Ezequiel, *Reus al segle XII* (Reus: Carrutxa and Migdia Serveis Culturals, 1998)

Graells, Raimon, 'Dues noves necròpolis del Segrià: Escalç (la Portella) i la Tossa de Baix (Rosselló)', in *La caracterització del paisatge històric. Territori i Societat: el paisatge històric, V*, ed. by Jordi Bolòs (Lleida: Universitat de Lleida, 2010), pp. 149–83

Grau, Ignasi, 'A Peasant Landscape in the Eastern Roman Spain. An Archaeological Approach to Territorial Organization and Economic Models', in *The Archaeology of Peasantry in Roman Spain*, ed. by Jesús Bermejo and Ignasi Grau (Berlin: De Gruyter, 2022), pp. 91–109

Grélois, Emmanuel, 'Pourtour et quartiers périphériques: forts villageois et transformations tardives des villages en Basse-Auvergne (XIIIe-XVIe siècles). Sur les pas de Gabriel Fournier', *Archéologie du Midi médiévale*, 36 (2018), 137–48

Groom, Nigel, *A Dictionary of Arabic Topography and Placenames* (Beirut/London: Librairie du Liban and Longman, 1982)

Guibal, Frédéric, 'Les contrées méridionales', in *La forêt au Moyen Âge*, ed. by Sylvie Bépoix and Hervé Richard (Paris: Les Belles Lettres, 2019), pp. 259–176

Guichard, Pierre, *Les musulmans de Valence et la Reconquête (XIe-XIIIe siècles)* (Damascus: Institut Français de Damas, 1990–91)

Guidi-Sánchez, José Javier, 'El poblamiento del Penedès altomedieval, siglos V–XI dC. Una aproximación a la problemática residencial', in *Família pagesa i economia rural. VII Congrés sobre Sistemes Agraris, Organització Social i Poder Local*, ed. by Jordi Bolòs, Antonieta Jarne, and Enric Vicedo (Lleida: Institut d'Estudis Ilerdencs, 2010), pp. 105–32

Guidoni, Enrico, *Storia dell'urbanistica. Il Duecento* (Rome: Editori Laterza, 1992)

Guilleré, Christian, *Girona al segle XIV* (Barcelona: Publicacions de l'Abadia de Montserrat, 1993)

Guillot, Florence, ed., *De la spelunca à la roca: l'habitat trglodytique au Moyen Âge* (Carcassonne: Amicale laïque de Carcassonne, 2006)

Guinot, Enric, *Els límits del regne. El procés de formació territorial del País Valencià medieval (1238–1500)* (València: Edicions Alfons el Magnànim, 1995)

——, 'El paisatge històric de les hortes medieval mediterrànies', *Estudis d'Història agrària*, 23 (2010–2011), 59–80

——, 'La construcción de nuevos espacios agrarios en el siglo XIII. Repartimientos y parcelarios de fundación en el Reino de Valencia: Puçol y Vilafamés', in *Trigo y ovejas. El impacto de las conquistas en los paisajes andalusíes (siglos XI–XVI)*, ed. by Josep Torró and Enric Guinot (València: Universitat de València, 2018), pp. 119–60

——, 'Morphology of Irrigated Spaces in Late Medieval Mudejar Settlements: The Canal of Lorca (Riba-roja de Túria, Valencia)', in *Agricultural Landscapes of Al-Andalus, and the Aftermath of the Feudal Conquest*, ed. by Helena Kirchner and Flocel Sabaté (Turnhout: Brepols, 2021), pp. 97–124

Guinot, Enric, and Sergi Selma, *Les séquies de l'Horta Nord de València: Mestalla, Rascanya i Tormos* (València: Generalitat Valenciana, 2005)

Gutiérrez Lloret, Sonia, 'El origen de la huerta de Orihuela entre los siglos VII y XI. Una propuesta arqueológica sobre la explotación de las zonas húmedas del Bajo Segura', *Arbor*, 593 (1995), 65–93

——, 'Ciudades y conquista. El fin de las *ciuitates* visigodas y la génesis de las *mudun* islámicas del Sureste de al-Andalus', in *Genèse de la ville islamique en al-Andalus et au Maghreb occidental*, ed. by Patrice Cressier and Mercedes Garcia-Arenal (Madrid: Casa de Velázquez and CSIC, 1998), pp. 137–57

——, 'Coming Back to Grammar of The House: Social Meaning of Medieval Households', in *De la estructura doméstica al espacio social. Lecturas arqueológicas del uso social del espacio*, ed. by Sonia Gutiérrez and Ignasi Grau (Sant Vicent del Raspeig: Universitat d'Alacant, 2013), pp. 245–64

Hallavant, Charlotte, and Marie-Pierre Ruas, 'Pratiques agraires et terroir de montagne: regard archéobotanique sur Montaillou (Ariège) au XIIIe siècle', *Archéologie du Midi médiéval*, 26 (2008), 93–129

Hansen, Inge Lyse, and Chris Wickham, ed., *The Long Eighth Century* (Leiden: Brill, 2000)

Hautefeuille, Florent, 'Limites, paroisses, mandements et autres territoires…', in *L'Église au village. Lieux, formes et enjeux des pratiques religieuses. Cahiers de Fanjeux, 40* (Toulouse: Éditions Privat, 2006), pp. 69–90

Helles Olesen, Lis, and Esben Schlosser Mauritsen, *Luftfotoarkæologi i Danmark* (Holstebro: Holstebro Museum, 2015)

Helles Olesen, Lis, Esben Schlosser Mauritsen, and Mathias Christiansen Broch, *Luftfotoarkæologi 2. Luftfotos, droner, laser og geofysik* (Holstebro: De Kulturhistoriske Museer i Holstebro Kommune, 2019).

Hernández Sesé, Ángel, *Mases y masoveros. Pasado, presente y futuro* (Zaragoza: Ceddad, 2005)

Higham, Nicholas J., and Martin Ryan, ed., *Place-Names, Language and the Anglo-Saxon Landscape* (Woodbridge: Boydell, 2011)

Higounet, Charles, *Paysages et villages neufs du Moyen Âge* (Bordeaux: Fédération històriques du Sud-ouest, 1975)

—— ed., *Châteaux et peuplements en Europe occidentale du Xᵉ au XVIIIᵉ siècle* (Auch: Centre Culturel de l'Abbaye de Flaran, 1980) <http://books.openedition.org/pumi/20972> [accessed 10 December 2021]

——, *Les Allemands en Europe centrale et orientale au Moyen Âge* (París: Aubier, 1989)

Hoffmann, Richard C., *An Environmental History of Medieval Europe* (Cambridge: Cambridge University Press, 2014)

Hooke, Della, *The Anglo-Saxon Landscape: The Kingdom of the Hwicce* (Manchester: Manchester University Press, 1985)

——, 'Resource Management of Seasonal Pasture: Some English/Welsh Comparisons', in *Living off the Land: Agriculture in Wales c. 400–1600 AD*, ed. by Rhiannon Comeau and Andy Seaman (Oxford: Windgather, 2019), pp. 37–56

Hurtado, Víctor, *Història. Política, societat i cultura dels Països Catalans. Cartografia històrica* (Barcelona: Enciclopèdia Catalana, 2000)

——, *Atles manual d'Història de Catalunya* (Barcelona: Rafael Dalmau editor, 2014, 2016, 2020)

Izard, Véronique, 'Cartographie successive des entreprises métallurgiques dans les Pyrénées nord-catalanes; support préliminaire à l'étude éco-historique des forêts charbonnées', *Archéologie du Midi médiéval*, 12 (1994), 115–29

——, 'La "révolution industrielle" du XIVᵉ siècle. Pouvoirs, enjeu, gestion et conflits autour d'un patrimoine minier, sidérurgique et forestier convoité (Pyrénées catalanes, France)', *Domitia*, 2 (2002), 43–62

——, 'La forêt au Moyen Âge: enjeux, gestion et mutation d'un espace menacé. Les forêts nord-catalanes du XIIᵉ au XIVᵉ siècle', in *Les ressources naturelles des Pyrénées du Moyen âge à l'époque moderne. Exploitation, gestion, appropriation*, ed. by Aymat Catafau (Perpignan: Presses Universitaires de Perpignan, 2005), pp. 255–87

Izdebski, Adam, Karin Holmgren, Erika Weiberg, Sharon R. Stocker, Ulf Büntgen, Assunta Florenzano, Alexandra Gogou, Suzanne A. G. Leroy, Jürgl Luterbacher, Belen Martrat, Alessia Masi, Anna Maria Mercuri, Paolo Montagna, Laura Sadori, Adam Schneider, Marie-Alexandrine Sicre, Maria Triantaphyllou, and Elena Xoplaki, 'Realising Consilience: How Better Communication Between Archaeologists, Historians and Natural Scientists can Transform the Study of Past Climate Change in the Mediterranean', *Quaternary Science Reviews*, 136 (2016), 5–22

Jaccottey, Luc, and Gilles Rollier, ed., *Archéologie des moulins hydrauliques, à traction animale et à vent des origines à l'époque médiévale et moderne en Europe et dans le monde méditerranéen* (Besançon: Presses Universitaires de Franche-Comté, 2016)

Jarrett, Jonathan, *Rulers and Ruled in Frontier Catalonia, 880–1010: Pathways of Power* (Martlesham: Boydell & Brewer, 2010)

Jiménez, Pedro, and Julio Navarro, 'El urbanismo islámico y su transformación después de la conquista cristiana: el caso de Murcia', *La Ciudad medieval: de la casa al tejido urbano*, ed. by Jean Passini (Cuenca: Ediciones de la Universidad de Castilla-La Mancha, 2001), pp. 71–129

Jones, Richard, 'Place-names in Landscape Archaeology', in *Detecting and Understanding Historic Landscapes*, ed. by Alexandra Chavarría Arnau and Andrew Reynolds (Mantua: SAP Società Archeologica, 2015), pp. 209–24

Juan-Villanueva, Jordi, 'Hidraulisme històric del monestir de Poblet i del seu hinterland immediat' (Monestir de Poblet, 2010) <http://poblet.cat/pfw_files/cma/Content/Fundaci_/Hidraulisme_historic_del_monestir_de_Poblet_i_els_seu_hinter.pdf> [accessed 10 December 2021]

Jusué, Carmen, *Poblamiento rural de Navarra en la Edad Media. Bases arqueológicas. Valle de Urraul Bajo* (Pamplona: Gobierno de Navarra, 1988)

Jusué, Carmen, and Mercedes Unzu, 'Villas nuevas en Navarra (siglos XII–XIV). Proceso urbanitzador', in *Las villas nuevas medievales del suroeste europeo*, ed. by Pascual Martínez and Mertxe Urteaga (Irun: Arkeolan, 2006), pp. 139–62

Kil, Susan, *Peasant Perspectives on the Medieval Landscape: A Study of Three Communities* (Hatfield: University of Hertfordshire Press, 2020)

Kind, Thomas, 'Fulda – Langebrückenstrasse: the first excavated early medieval watermill in Europa', in *Archéologie des moulins hydrauliques, à traction animale et à vent des origines à l'époque médiévale et moderne en Europe et dans le monde méditerranéen*, ed. by Luc Jaccottey and Gilles Rollier (Besançon: Presses Universitaires de Franche-Comté, 2016), pp. 277–87

Kirchner, Helena, *La construcció de l'espai pagès a Mayūrqa: les valls de Bunyola, Orient, Coanegra i Alaró* (Palma: Universitat de les Illes Balears, 1997)

——, 'Original Design, Tribal Management and Modifications in Medieval Hydraulic Systems in the Balearic Islands (Spain)', *World Archaeology*, 41.1 (2009), 151–68

——, 'Arqueologia hidràulica i tipologia d'espais irrigats andalusins', in *Arqueologia medieval. La prospecció i el territori*, ed. by Flocel Sabaté and Jesús Brufal (Lleida: Pagès editors, 2010), pp. 129–46

——, ed., *Por una arqueología agraria. Perspectivas de investigación sobre espacios de cultivo en las sociedades medievales hispánicas* (Oxford: Archaeopress, 2010)

——, 'Hidráulica campesina anterior a la generalización del dominio feudal. Casos en Cataluña', in *Hidráulica agraria y sociedad feudal. Prácticas, técnicas, espacios*, ed. by Josep Torró and Enric Guinot (València: Universitat de València, 2012), pp. 21–50

Kirchner, Helena, and Carmen Navarro, 'Objetivos, métodos y práctica de la arqueología hidráulica', *Arqueología y territorio medieval*, 1 (1994), 159–82

Kirchner, Helena, Jaume Oliver, and Susanna Vela, *Aigua prohibida. Arqueologia hidràulica del feudalisme a la Cerdanya. El Canal Reial de Puigcerdà* (Bellaterra: Universitat Autònoma de Barcelona 2002)

Kirchner, Helena, and Fèlix Retamero, 'Becoming Islanders: Migration and Settlement in the Balearic Islands (10th-13th centuries)', *Agricultural and Pastoral Landscapes in Pre-Industrial Society. Choices, Stability and Change*, ed. by Fèlix Retamero, Inge Schjellerup, and Althea Davies (Oxford: Oxbow, 2016), pp. 57–78

Kirchner, Helena, and Antoni Virgili, 'De Turțûša a Tortosa. La ciutat abans i després de la conquesta catalana (1148)', in *V Congrés d'Arqueologia Medieval i Moderna de Catalunya* (Barcelona: ACRAM, 2015), pp. 117–43

——, 'Espacios agrarios en el Bajo Ebro en época andalusí y después de la conquista catalana (siglos XI–XIII)', in *Trigo y ovejas. El impacto de las conquistas en los paisajes andalusíes (siglos XI–XVI)*, ed. by Josep Torró and Enric Guinot (València: Universitat de València, 2018), pp. 15–49

——, 'Assentaments rurals i espais agraris al Baix Ebre i la ciutat de Tortosa en època andalusina i després de la conquesta catalana (segles X–XIII)', in *Tribuna d'Arqueologia 2016–2017* (Barcelona: Generalitat de Catalunya, 2020), pp. 84–102

Kirchner, Helena, Antoni Virgili, and Arnald Puy, 'Drainage and Irrigation Systems in Madīna Țurțūša (Tortosa, Spain) (Eight-Twelfth Centuries), in *Agricultural Landscapes of Al-Andalus, and the Aftermath of the Feudal Conquest*, ed. by Helena Kirchner and Flocel Sabaté (Turnhout: Brepols, 2021), pp. 153–72

Klápště, Jan, ed., *Water Management in Medieval Rural Economy. Les usages de l'eau en milieu rural au Moyen Âge* (Turnhout: Brepols, 2005)

Knighton, Tess, ed., *Els sons de Barcelona a l'edat moderna* (Barcelona: MUHBA – Ajuntament de Barcelona, 2016)

Kosto, Adam J., *Making Agreement Medieval Catalonia: Power, Order, and the Written Word, 1000–1200* (Cambridge: Cambridge University Press, 2008)

Kotarba, Jérôme, 'Les sites d'époque wisigothique de la ligne LGV. Apports et limites pour les études d'occupation du sol de la plaine du Roussillon', *Domitia*, 8–9 (2007), 43–70

Koziol, Geoffrey, *The Peace of God* (Leeds: Arc Humanities Press, 2018)

Kremer, Dieter, 'Zur Urkunde A. 913 des Archivo Condal in Barcelona', *Beiträge zur Namenforshung. Neue Folge*, 9 (1974), 1–82

Labbé, Thomas, *Les catastrophes naturelles au Moyen Âge, XIIe-XVe siècle* (París: CNRS éditions, 2017)

Lagerås, Per, *The Ecology of Expansion and Abandonment: Medieval and Post-Medieval Land-Use and Settlement Dynamics in a Landscape Perspective* (Stockholm: National Heritage Board – Riksantikvarieämbetet, 2007)

Lambrick, George, Jill Hind, and Ianto Wain, *Historic Landscape Characterisation in Ireland: Best Practice Guidance* (Dublin: An Chomhairle Oidhreachta / The Heritage Council, 2013)

Langlands, Alexander, *The Ancient Ways of Wessex: Travel and Communication in an Early Medieval Landscape* (Oxford: Windgather Press, 2019)

——, 'Local Places and Local People: Peasant Agency and the Formation of the Anglo-Saxon State', in *Polity and Neighbourhood in Early Medieval Europe*, ed. by Julio Escalona, Orri Vésteinsson, and Stuart Brookes (Turnhout: Brepols, 2019), pp. 381–405

Lauwers, Michel, 'De l'*incastellamento* à l'*inecclesiamento*. Monachisme et logiques spatiales du féodalisme', in *Cluny. Les moines et la société au premier âge féodal*, ed. by Dominique Iogna-Prat, Michel Lauwers, Florian Mazel, and Isabelle Rosé (Rennes: Presses Universitaires de Rennes, 2013), pp. 315–38

Lauwers, Michel, Magali Watteaux, and Isabelle Catteddu, 'Lieux et dynamiques du peuplement rural', in *Nouvelle Histoire du Moyen Âge*, ed. by Florian Mazel (Paris: Seuil, 2021), pp. 85–98

Lavaud, Sandrine, 'The Atlas històriques de Bordeaux: A Newcomer to the Series Atlas històriques des villes de France', in *Lords and Towns in Medieval Europe: The European Historic Towns Project*, ed. by Anngret Simms and Howard B. Clarke (London: Routledge, 2019), pp. 87–98

Lavigne, Cédric, 'Parcellaires de fondation et parcellaires de formation à l'époque médiévale en Gascogne; clefs de lecture et problèmes d'interprétation', *Les formes du paysage. Tome 3. L'analyse des systèmes spatiaux*, ed. by Gérard Chouquer (Paris: Éditions Errance, 1997), pp. 149–58

——, *Essai sur la planification agraire au Moyen Âge: les paysages neufs de la Gascogne médiévale (XIIIᵉ-XIVᵉ siècles)* (Pessac: Ausonius, 2002)

——, 'L'archéogéographie, une expertise au service des politiques publiques d'aménagement: L'exemple de la commune de Bègles (Gironde)', *Les Nouvelles de l'Archéologie*, 125 (2011), 47–54

Lebecq, Stéphane, 'The Role of the Monasteries in the Systems of Production and Exchange of the Frankish World between the Seventh and the Beginning of the Ninth Centuries', in *The Long Eighth Century*, ed. by Inge Lyse Hansen and Chris Wickham (Leiden: Brill, 2000), pp. 121–48

Leclerc, Sabine, 'Les églises fortifiées du Roussillon', in *Etudes roussillonnaises offertes à Pierre Ponsich / Estudis rossellonesos dedicats a en Pere Ponsich*, ed. by Marie Grau and Olivier Poisson (Perpignan: Le Publicateur, 1987), pp. 223–33

Leguay, Jean-Pierre, *La rue au Moyen Âge* (Rennes: Editions Ouest-France, 1984)

——, *L'eau dans la ville au Moyen Âge* (Rennes: Presses Universitaires de Rennes, 2002)

Leonardi, Micaela, '*Cost distance* e *viewshed analysis* per un modello ricostruttivo dei percorsi in Alta Val Tanaro', in *Un paesaggio medievale tra Piemonte e Liguria. Il sito di Santa Giulitta e l'Alta Val Tanaro*, ed. by Paolo Demeglio (Sesto Fiorentino: All'Insegna del Giglio, 2019), pp. 71–83

Leturcq, Samuel, *Un village, la terre et ses hommes. Toury en Beauce (XIIᵉ-XVIIᵉ siècle)* (Paris: Comité des travaux historiques et scientifiques, 2007)

Leturcq, Samuel, and Florian Mazel, 'Une dynamique d'expansion. VIIIᵉ-XIᵉ siècle', in *Nouvelle Histoire du Moyen Âge*, ed. by Florian Mazel (Paris: Seuil, 2021), pp. 229–43

Leveau, Philippe, 'The Integration of Archaeological, Historical and Paleoenvironmental Data at the Regional Scale: The Vallée de Baux, Southern

France', in *Environmental Reconstruction in Mediterranean Landscape Archaeology*, ed. by Phillipe Leveau, Frédéric Trément, Kevin Walsh, and Graeme Barker (Oxford: Oxbow, 1999), pp. 181–91

——, 'Compte rendu de: Gérard Chouquer, L'étude des paysages. Essais sur leurs formes et leur histoire, Paris, Errance, 1999', *Histoire et Sociétés Rurales*, 15–1 (2001), 238–43

Lieberman, Max, *The Medieval March of Wales: The Creation and Perception of a Frontier, 1066–1283* (Cambridge: Cambridge University Press, 2010)

Lilley, Keith D., 'Mapping the Medieval City: Plan Analysis and Urban History', *Urban History*, 27(1) (2000), 5–30

——, *Urban Life in the Middle Ages, 1000–1450* (Basingstoke: Palgrave, 2002)

——, 'Urban Landscapes and their Design: Creating Town from Country in the Middle Ages', in *Town and Country in the Middle Ages: Contrasts, Contacts and Interconnections, 1100–1500*, ed. by Kate Giles and Christopher Dyer (Leeds: Maney Publishing, 2005), pp. 229–49

——, 'Overview: Living in Medieval Towns', in *The Oxford Handbook of Later Medieval Archaeology in Britain*, ed. by Chistopher M. Gerrard and Alejandra Gutiérrez (Oxford: Oxford University Press, 2020), pp. 275–96

Lladonosa, Josep, *L'Estudi General de Lleida del 1430 al 1524* (Barcelona: Institut d'Estudis Catalans, 1970)

Llovera, Xavier, Josep M. Bosch, Maria Àngels Ruf, Cristina Yáñez, Xavier Solé, and Antoni Vila, ed., *Roc d'Enclar. Transformacions d'un espai dominant (segles IV–XIX)* (Andorra la Vella: Govern d'Andorra, 1997)

López Elum, Pedro, *La alquería islámica en Valencia. Estudio arqueológico de Bofilla, siglos XI a XIV* (València: self-publication, 1994)

López, Alberto, Àlvar Caixal, and Xavier Fierro, 'Difusión de las cerámicas grises/oxidadas medievales en las comarcas de Barcelona (siglos IX–XIII)', in *IV Congrés d'Arqueologia Medieval Espanyola. Societats en transició* (Alacant: AEAM and Generalitat Valenciana, 1993), vol. II, pp. 1027–1033

López, Tomàs, *La Pia Almoina de Barcelona (1161-1350). Estudi d'un patrimoni eclesiàstic català baixmedieval* (Barcelona: Fundació Noguera, 1998)

Lorcin, Marie-Thérèse, 'Microtoponymie et terroirs paroissiaux. Quelques réflexions sur le Lyonnais de la fin du Moyen Âge', in *Le village médiévale et son environnement. Études offertes à Jean-Marie Pesez*, ed. by Laurent Feller, Perrine Mane, and Françoise Piponnier (Paris: Publications de la Sorbonne, 1998), pp. 537–49

Lorentz, Philippe, and Dany Sandron, *Atlas de Paris au Moyen Âge. Espace urbain, habitat, Société, religion, lieux de pouvoir* (Paris: Parigramme, 2006)

Loriente, Ana, *L'horitzó andalusí de l'antic Portal de Magdalena* (Lleida: Ajuntament de Lleida, 1991 [1990])

Loriente, Ana, and Anna Oliver, *L'antic Portal de Magdalena* (Lleida: Ajuntament de Lleida, 1992)

Luault, Noémie, 'Angoustrine-Villeneuve-des-Escaldes (Pyrénées-Orientales). Coume Païrounell', *Archéologie médiévale*, 48 (2018), 196–97

Lunven, Anne, 'Les actes de délimitation paroissiale dans les diocèses de Rennes, Dol, et Saint-Malo (XIe-XIIIe siècles)', in *Reconnaître et délimiter l'espace localement au Moyen-âge. Limites et frontières vol. I*, ed. by Nacima Baron-Yelles, Stéphane Boisselier, Clément François, and Flocel Sabaté (Villeneuve d'Ascq: Presses Universitaires du Septentrion, 2016), pp. 35–54

Macias, Josep M., Josep Anton Remolà, and Mireia Mestre, 'El castell de Gelida: l'excavació arqueològica de l'any 1991', in *Miscel·lània Penedeseca 1993* (Vilafranca del Penedès: Institut d'Estudis Penedesencs, 1993), pp. 168–88

Mallorquí, Elvis, 'Els noms de lloc i el temps: la toponímia des de la història', in *Toponímia, paisatge i cultura. Els noms de lloc des de la lingüística, la geografia i la història*, ed. by Elvis Mallorquí (Girona: Associació d'Història Rural de les Comarques Gironines, 2006), pp. 101–26

——, 'Els veïnats: orígens i evolució d'una demarcació territorial a l'interior de les parròquies del bisbat de Girona, segles X-XIV', in *Poblament, territori i història rural. VI Congrés sobre Sistemes agraris, organització social i poder local*, ed. by Jordi Bolòs i Enric Vicedo (Lleida: Institut d'Estudis Ilerdencs, 2009), pp. 363–96

——, 'Les celleres medievals de les terres de Girona', *Quaderns de la Selva*, 21 (2009), 117–48

——, *Cinquanta-cinc llegües de passos oblidats i xarrabascos. Els camins històrics de la plana selvatana (la Selva i el Gironès)* (Santa Coloma de Farners: Centre d'Estudis Selvatans, 2015–2016)

Malpica, Antonio, and José María Martín, 'Las villas nuevas medievales del reino de Granada (siglo XV-comienzos XVI)', in *Las villas nuevas medievales del suroeste europeo*, ed. by Pascual Martínez and Mertxe Urteaga (Irun: Arkeolan, 2006), pp. 371–92

Mann, Vivian B., Thomas F. Glick, and Jerrilynn D. Dodds, ed., *Convivencia: Jews, Muslims, and Christians in Medieval Spain* (New York: George Braziller and The Jewish Museum, 1992)

Marchand, Claude, 'Réseau viaire et dessin parcellaire: étude morphologique de la région du Gâtinais Oriental', in *Les formes du paysage. Tome 3. L'analyse des systèmes spatiaux*, ed. by Gérard Chouquer (Paris: Éditions Errance, 1997), pp. 66–77

Maristany, Manuel, *Els ponts de pedra de Catalunya* (Barcelona: Generalitat de Catalunya, 1998)

Martí, Javier, and Josefa Pascual, 'El Desarrollo urbano de *madīna Balansiya* hasta el final del califato', in *Ciudad y territorio en al-Andalus*, ed. by Lorenzo Cara (Granada: Athos-Pérgamos, 2000), pp. 500–36

Martí, Ramon, 'Les *insulae* medievals catalanes', *Bolletí de la Societat Arqueològica Lul·liana*, 44 (1988), 111–23

——, 'L'ensagrerament: l'adveniment de les sagreres feudals', *Faventia*, 10.1/2 (1988), 153–82

——, 'L'ensagrerament: utilitats d'un concepte', in *Les sagreres a la Catalunya medieval* (Girona: Associació d'Història Rural de les Comarques Gironines, 2007), pp. 85–204

Martí, Ramon, and Joan Negre, 'Assentaments i espais agraris medievals al Baix Ebre i al Montsià: una anàlisi diacrònica', *Estudis d'Història agrària*, 27 (2015), 67–89

Martín Viso, Iñaki, '¿Datar tumbas o datar procesos? A vueltas con la cronología de las tumbas excavadas en roca en la Península Ibérica', *Debates de Arqueología Medieval*, 4 (2014), 29–65

——, 'Espacios funerarios e iglesias en el centro peninsular: una relación compleja', in *Arqueologia medieval. Els espais sagrats*, ed. by Flocel Sabaté and Jesús Brufal (Lleida: Pagès editors, 2015), pp. 81–114

——, 'Ancestors and Landscape: Early Medieval Burial Sites in the Central-Western Regions of the Iberian Peninsula', in *Polity and Neighbourhood in Early Medieval Europe*, ed. by Julio Escalona, Orri Vésteinsson, and Stuart Brookes (Turnhout: Brepols, 2019), pp. 121–46

——, ed., *La construcción de la territorialidad en la Alta Edad Media* (Salamanca: Ediciones Universidad de Salamanca, 2020)

Martínez, Manel, *El bosc de Poblet al llarg dels anys* (Montblanc: Centre d'Estudis de la Conca de Barberà, 2001)

Martínez, Pascual, and Mertxe Urteaga, ed., *Las villas nuevas medievales del suroeste europeo* (Irun: Arkeolan, 2006)

Martínez-Elcacho, Albert, 'Organització senyorial i jurisdiccional del comtat de les Muntanyes de Prades i baronia d'Entença a mitjan segle XIV: el paradigma del desmembrament de l'antic terme castral de Siurana', in *Estudiar i gestionar el paisatge històric medieval. Territori i Societat a l'edat mitjana, IV*, ed. by Jordi Bolòs (Lleida: Universitat de Lleida, 2007), pp. 226–81

——, *Les argenteres de Falset (1342–1358). Gestió, control i registre de l'explotació minera i metal·lúrgica de la plata a la Catalunya medieval* (Barcelona: Fundació Noguera, 2019)

Mas, Antoni, 'Les Ordinacions d'en Jaume II (1300): la segona colonització del reialenc de Mallorca', in *Els caràcters del paisatge històric als països mediterranis. Territori i Societat: el paisatge històric, VIII*, ed. by Jordi Bolòs (Lleida: Universitat de Lleida and Pagès editors, 2018), pp. 147–88

Mastrelli Anzilotti, Giulia, 'Osservazioni in margine al lessico alpino: idiomi a confronto', in *Le Alpi medievali nello sviluppo delle regioni contermini*, ed. by Gian Maria Varanini (Napoli: Liguori editore, 2004), pp. 53–65

Mataró, Montserrat, Imma Ollich, and Anna M. Puig, 'Santa Creu de Rodes (el Port de la Selva, Alt Empordà)', in *Actes del IV Congrés d'Arqueologia Medieval i Moderna a Catalunya* (Barcelona: ACRAM and Ajuntament de Tarragona, 2012), vol. II, pp. 719–26

Maufras, Odile, Mathieu Ott, Claude Raynaud, Marie Rochette, and Liliane Tarrou, '*Villae* – Villages du haut Moyen Âge en plaine du Languedoc oriental. Maillage, morphologie et économie', *Archéopages*, 40 (2014 [2015]), 92–103 <https://journals.openedition.org/archeopages/620?lang = es> [accessed 10 December 2021]

Mazzoli-Guintard, Christine, *Ciudades de al-Andalus. España y Portugal en la época musulmana (siglos VIII–XV)* (Granada: ALMED, 2000 [French edition: 1996])

McCrank, Lawrence J., *Medieval Frontier History in New Catalonia* (Aldershot: Variorum, 1996)

Menchon, Joan Josep, 'Algunes fortificacions (islàmiques?) al sud de Catalunya. Reflexions, dubtes i provocacions', in *L'empremta de l'Islam a Catalunya. Materials, tècniques i cultura*, ed. by Pilar Giràldez and Màrius Vendrell (Barcelona: Patrimoni 2.0, 2013), pp. 57–105

——, 'Dos torres y un relato histórico en revisión: Santa Perpètua de Gaià (Tarragona) y Vallferosa (Lleida)', *Treballs d'Arqueologia*, 22 (2018), 107–34

——, 'Una torre, dues anelles i unes analítiques impertinents: Vallferosa (Torà, La Segarra, província de Lleida)', in *Arqueologia medieval IX. Fortaleses a la Vall de l'Ebre (segles VII–XI)*, ed. by Jesús Brufal, Joan Negre, and Flocel Sabaté (Lleida: Pagès editors, 2020), pp. 255–304

Menchon, Joan, and Lluís Piñol, 'La ciutat de Tarragona', in *L'art gòtic a Catalunya. Arquitectura III. Dels palaus a les masies*, ed. by Antoni Pladevall (Barcelona: Enciclopèdia Catalana, 2003), pp. 63–67

Mennessier-Jouannet, Christine, and Gérard Chouquer, 'Étude des formes paysagères de la région de Lezoux', in *Les formes du paysage. Tome 1. Etudes sur les parcellaires*, ed. by Gérard Chouquer (Paris: Éditions Errance, 1996), pp. 111–25

Mercadal, Oriol, and Sebastià Bosom, 'La vila de Puigcerdà', in *L'art gòtic a Catalunya. Arquitectura III. Dels palaus a les masies*, ed. by Antoni Pladevall (Barcelona: Enciclopèdia Catalana, 2003), pp. 88–91

Mestre, Jesús, and Víctor Hurtado, ed., *Atles d'història de Catalunya* (Barcelona: Edicions 62, 1995)

Milanese, Marco, *Alghero. Archeologia di una città medievale* (Sassari: Carlo Delfino editore, 2013)

Mileson, Stephen, 'The South Oxfordshire Project: Perceptions of Landscape, Settlement and Society, *c.* 500–1650', *Landscape History*, 33.2 (2012), 83–98.

——, 'Sound and Landscape', in *The Oxford Handbook of Later Medieval Archaeology in Britain*, ed. by Christopher M. Gerrard and Alejandra Gutiérrez (Oxford: Oxford University Press, 2020), pp. 713–24

Mileson, Stephen, and Stuart Brookes, *Peasant Perceptions of Landscape: Ewelme Hundred, South Oxfordshire, 500–1650* (Oxford: Oxford University Press, 2021)

Milton, Gregory B., *Market Power: Lordship, Society, and Economy in Medieval Catalonia (1276–1313)* (New York: Palgrave Macmillan, 2012)

Miró, Climent, 'Territoris i economia als monestirs del comtat d'Urgell (800–1100)' (doctoral thesis, Universitat de Barcelona, 2022)

Moix, Elisenda, 'Excavació arqueològica a la necròpoli de Palau de l'Abat (Vila-sacra, Alt Empordà)', in *X Jornades d'Arqueologia de les Comarques de Girona* (Barcelona: Generalitat de Catalunya, 2011), pp. 511–15 <https:// tribunadarqueologia.blog.gencat.cat/2011/10/14/actes-de-les-x-jornades-darqueologia-girona-2010/> [accessed 10 December 2021]

Moner, Jeroni, 'La vila de Banyoles', in *L'Art Gòtic a Catalunya. Arquitectura III*, ed. by Antoni Pladevall (Barcelona: Enciclopèdia Catalana. 2003), pp. 91–93

Monjo, Marta, *Sarraïns sota el domini feudal. La Baronia d'Aitona al segle XV* (Lleida: Universitat de Lleida, 2004)

———, 'Sarraïns d'Aitona, el tresor de la família Montcada. Estudi de l'aljama al segle XV: el treball agrícola, els sistemes hidràulics i les rendes senyorials' (doctoral thesis, Universitat de Lleida, 2015)

Monjo, Marta, Carme Alòs, and Eva Solanes, 'El Pla d'Almatà (Balaguer, La Noguera): vint anys de recerca arqueològica', in *Arqueologia medieval. La transformació de la frontera medieval musulmana*, ed. by Flocel Sabaté and Jesús Brufal (Lleida: Pagès editors, 2009), pp. 177–90

Montanari, Massimo, *L'alimentazione contadina nell'alto Medioevo* (Napoli: Liguori editore, 1979)

Montón, Félix J., *Zafranales. Un asentamiento de la frontera hispano-musulmana en el siglo XI, Fraga, Huesca* (Huesca: Diputación de Huesca, 1997)

———, 'El poblamiento de la frontera hispano-musulmana en al-Andalus durante el siglo XI: Zafranales (Huesca)', *Archéologie islamique*, 7 (1997), 45–60

Morelló, Jordi, 'La vila de Reus', in *L'art gòtic a Catalunya. Arquitectura III. Dels palaus a les masies* (Barcelona: Enciclopèdia Catalana, 2003), pp. 115–17

———, 'Singularitats (o no) d'un fenomen "català": l'ensagreramentt. Primers resultats d'una recerca en curs' (dissertation, CSIC in Barcelona, October 14, 2020)

Mousnier, Mireille, ed., *Moulins et meuniers dans les campagnes européennes (IXe-XVIIIe siècle)* (Toulouse: Presses Universitaires du Mirail, 2002)

Mulet, Marta, Javier Escuder, and Jacinto Bonales, *Torrelameu. La nostra història* (Torrelameu: Ajuntament de Torrelameu, 2019)

Muntaner, Carme, 'Terra de masos, vila de mar. Vida, economia i territori al castell de Sitges i el seu terme entre els segles XIV i XV (1342-1418)' (doctoral thesis, Universitat de Barcelona, 2013)

Muntaner, Ignasi Maria, *El terme d'Olèrdola en el segle X segons el document de dotació de l'església de Sant Miquel* (Vilafranca del Penedès: Institut d'Estudis Penedesencs, 1995)

Negre, Joan, 'Espacios religiosos en el medio rural: rábidas, mezquitas y necrópolis en el ḥawz de Ṭurṭūša', in *Arqueologia Medieval. Els espais sagrats*, ed. by Flocel Sabaté and Jesús Brufal (Lleida: Pagès editors, 2015), pp. 115–34

———, *En els confins d'al-Andalus. Territori i poblament durant la formació d'una societat islàmica a les Terres de l'Ebre i el Maestrat* (Benicarló: Onada edicions, 2020)

Negre, Joan, and Josep Suñé, 'Territorio, fiscalidad y actividad militar en la formación de un espacio fronterizo. La consolidación de Tortosa como límite extremo del Al-Andalus omeya', *Anuario de Estudios Medievales*, 49/2 (2019), 705–40

Nolla, Josep M., and Jordi Sagrera, 'Girona a l'edat mitjana. L'urbanisme', *Rodis. Journal of Medieval and Postmedieval Archaeology*, 1 (2018), 53–69

Novaković, Predrag, Helene Simoni, and Branko Mušič, 'Karst Dolinas: Evidence of Population Pressure and Exploitation of Agricultural Resources in Karstic Landscapes', in *Environmental Reconstruction in Mediterranean Landscape*

Archaeology, ed. by Phillipe Leveau, Frédéric Trément, Kevin Walsh, and Graeme Barker (Oxford: Oxbow, 1999), pp. 123–34

Obiols, Lluís, 'El Camí Cardoner i el Camí Ramader, camins històrics de llarg recorregut a la cara nord del Cadí', *Ker. Revista del Grup de Recerca de Cerdanya*, 2 (2009), 30–34

Olesti, Oriol, 'Héritage et tradition des pratiques agrimensoriques: l'Ars Gromatica de Gisemundus. La pervivencia de la Agrimensura romana durante la Antigüedad tardía y la Alta Edad Media en Hispania: preservando el "paisaje en orden"', *Dialogues d'histoire ancienne*, 43.1 (2017), 257–74

Oliver, Jaume, 'Los paisajes del feudalismo', in *La humanización de las altas cuencas de la Garona y las Nogueras (4500 aC-1955 dC)*, ed. by Agustí Esteban (Madrid: Ministerio de Medio Ambiente, 2003), pp. 143–266

Olivera, Carme, Esther Redondo, Jérôme Lambert, Antoni Riera, and Antoni Roca, *Els terratrèmols dels segles XIV i XV a Catalunya* (Barcelona: Institut Cartogràfic de Catalunya, 2006)

Ollich, Imma, Montserrat Mataró, and Anna M. Puig, 'Dos exemples d'urbanisme medieval a Catalunya: L'Esquerda de Roda de Ter (Osona) i Santa Creu de Rodes al Port de la Selva (Alt Empordà)', *Rodis. Journal of Medieval and Postmedieval Archaeology*, 3 (2020), 85–118

Ollich, Imma, Montserrat de Rocafiguera, Oriol Amblàs, Albert Pratdesaba, and M. Àngels Pujol, 'Visigots i carolingis a Osona. Novetats arqueològiques des del jaciment de l'Esquerda', in *III Jornades d'Arqueologia de la Catalunya central* (Barcelona: Generalitat de Catalunya, 2015), pp. 14–22 <http://calaix.gencat. cat/handle/10687/119226#page = 1> [accessed 10 December 2021]

Ollich, Imma, Montserrat de Rocafiguera, and Maria Ocaña, 'The Southern Carolingian Frontier in *Marca Hispanica* along the River Ter: *Roda Civitas* and the Archaeological Site of L'Esquerda (Catalonia)', in *Fortified Settlements in Early Medieval Europe: Defended Communities of the 8th-10th Centuries*, ed. by Neil Christie and Hajnalka Herold (Oxford: Oxbow, 2016), pp. 205–17

Oosthuizen, Susan, *Landscapes Decoded: The Origins and Development of Cambridge-shire's Medieval Fields* (Hatfield: University of Hertfordshire Press, 2006)

Ortega, M. Julián, Josep M. Palet, and Hèctor A. Orengo, 'El límite entre *Valentia* y *Saetabis*: un paisaje cultural de origen romano al sur de los ríos Xúquer y Magre (Xàtiva, Valencia)', *Agri Centuriati. An International Journal of Landscape Archaeology*, 12 (2015 [2016]), 153–74

Ortega, Julián, 'La agricultura de los vencedores y la agricultura de los vencidos: la investigación de las transformaciones feudales de los paisajes agrarios en el valle del Ebro (siglos XII–XIII)', in *Por una arqueología agraria. Perspectivas de investigación sobre espacios de cultivo en las sociedades medievales hispánicas*, ed. by Helena Kirchner (Oxford: BAR International Series 2062, 2010), pp. 123–45

Ortí, Pere, 'La primera articulación del estado feudal en Cataluña a través de un impuesto: el bovaje (ss. XII-XIII)', *Hispania*, 209 (2001), 967–98

Padilla, J. Ignacio, 'La construcció d'un enginy hidràulic. Els comptes d'un molí batan de Gardeny (Lleida, 1290–91)', *Ilerda. Humanitats*, 49 (1991), 105–27

——, ed., *L'esperit d'Àneu. Llibre dels Costums i Ordinacions de les valls d'Àneu* (Esterri d'Àneu: Consell Cultural de les Valls d'Àneu, 1999)

Paio, Alexandra C. R., 'As novas vilas medievais portuguesas, 1248–1325', in *Las villas nuevas medievales del suroeste europeo*, ed. by Pascual Martínez and Mertxe Urteaga (Irun: Arkeolan, 2006), pp. 309–46

Palahí, Lluís, and Josep M. Nolla, *Entre l'hospici i l'hospital. Evolució urbanística d'un sector de Girona: el carrer de Savaneres (Girona, Gironès)* (Barcelona: Generalitat de Catalunya, 2007)

Palet, Josep Maria, *Estudi territorial del Pla de Barcelona. Estructuració i evolució del territori entre l'època íbero-romana i l'altmedieval, segles II–I aC - X–XI dC* (Barcelona: Ajuntament de Barcelona, 1997)

——, 'Dinàmica territorial de l'antiguitat a l'edat mitjana a Catalunya: arqueomorfologia i estudi de casos', in *Territori i Societat a l'Edat Mitjana, III*, ed. by Jordi Bolòs and Joan J. Busqueta (Lleida: Universitat de Lleida, 1999–2000), pp. 75–110

——, 'L'organització del paisatge agrari al Penedès i les centuriacions del territori de Tàrraco: estudi arqueomorfològic', in *Territoris antics a la Mediterrània i a la Cossetània oriental*, ed. by Josep Guitard, Josep M. Palet, and Marta Prevosti (Barcelona: Generalitat de Catalunya, 2003), pp. 211–29

——, ed., *Paisatge històric a la muntanya de Montjuïc. Resultats del projecte La Satalia* (Barcelona: Ajuntament de Barcelona, 2021)

Palet, Josep M., and Josep M. Gurt, 'Aménagement et drainage des zones humides du littoral emporitain (Catalogne): une lecture diachronique des structures agraires antiques', *Méditerranée. Archéologie et paléopaysages*, 90 (1998), 41–48

Palet, Josep M., and Hèctor A. Orengo, 'Les centuriacions de l'*Ager Tarraconensis*: organització i concepcions de l'espai', in *Ager Tarraconensis, 1: Aspectes històrics i marc natural*, ed. by Marta Prevosti and Josep Guitart (Tarragona: Institut d'Estudis Catalans and ICAC, 2010), pp. 121–54

Palet, Josep M., Hèctor A. Orengo, and Santiago Riera Mora, 'Centuriación del territorio y modelación del paisaje en los llanos litorales de *Barcino* (Barcelona) y *Tarraco* (Tarragona): una investigación interdisciplinar a través de la integración de datos arqueomorfológicos y paleoambientales', in *Sistemi Centuriali e opere di asseto agrario tra età romana e primo medioevo. Aspetti metodologici, ricostruttivi e interpretativi. Agri Centuriati 7*, ed. by Pier Luigi Dall'Aglio and Guido Rosada (Pisa: Fabrizio Serra Editore, 2011), pp. 113–29

Palol, Pere de, ed., *Del romà al romànic. Història, art i cultura de la Tarraconense mediterrània entre els segles IV i X* (Barcelona: Enciclopèdia Catalana, 1999).

Papell, Joan, 'El domini del monestir de Santes Creus. Un exemple d'organització del territori en època medieval (1150–1233)', in *Territori i Societat a l'Edat Mitjana, III (1999–2000)*, ed. by Jordi Bolòs and Joan Busqueta (Lleida: Universitat de Lleida, 2000), pp. 191–53

Parisse, Michel, ed., *Atlas de la France de l'an mil: État de nos connaissances* (Paris: Picard, 1994)

Parra, Igor, Elise Van Campo, and Thierry Otto, 'Análisis palinológico y radio-métrico del sondeo Sobrestany. Nueve milenios de historia natural e impactos humanos sobre la vegetación del Alt Empordà', *Empúries*, 54 (2006), 33–44

Partida, Tracey, David Hall, and Glenn Foard, *An Atlas of Northamptonshire: The Medieval and Early-Modern Landscape* (Oxford: Oxbow, 2013)

Passarrius, Olivier, and Aymat Catafau, 'Ropidera: un poble medieval en els seus territoris', in *Poblament, territori i història rural. VI Congrés sobre sistemes agraris, organització social i poder local*, ed. by Jordi Bolòs and Enric Vicedo (Lleida: Institut d'Estudis Ilerdencs, 2009), pp. 285–334

——, 'Trois décennies d'archéologie à Perpignan. 1985–2011', in *Un palais dans la ville. Volume II: Perpignan des rois de Majorque*, ed. by Aymat Catafau and Olivier Passarrius (Canet: Trabucaire, 2014), pp. 21–47

——, 'Autour de quelques villages du Roussillon: le cadastre et les textes à l'épreuve de l'archéologie', *Archéologie du Midi médiéval*, 36 (2018 [2020]), 253–65

Passarrius, Olivier, Aymat Catafau, and Michel Martzluff, ed., *Archéologie d'une montagne brûlée* (Canet: Trabucaire, 2009)

Passarrius, Olivier, Richard Donat, and Aymat Catafau, *Vilarnau: un village du Moyen Âge en Roussillon* (Canet: Trabucaire, 2008)

Passini, Jean, 'Habitat villageois médiéval le long du chemin vers Saint-Jacques de Compostelle', in *Castrum 6. Maisons et espaces domestiques dans le monde méditerrannéen au Moyen Âge*, ed. by André Bazzana and Étienne Hubert (Rome/Madrid: École française de Rome and Casa de Velázquez, 2000), pp. 219–31

——, *Casas y casas principales urbanas. El espacio domestico de Toledo a fines de la Edad Media* (Toledo: Universidad de Castilla-La Mancha, 2004)

Pèlachs, Albert, Jordi Nadal, Joan Manuel Soriano, David Alejando, and Raquel Cunill, 'Changes in Pyrenean woodlands as a Result of the Intensity of Human Exploitation: 2,000 Years of Metallurgy in Vallferrera, Northeast Iberian Peninsula', *Vegetation History and Archaeobotany*, 18.5 (2009), 403–16

——, 'Els estudis del paisatge a Catalunya des de la Geografia: l'exemple de la Vall Ferrera', *Butlletí de la Societat Catalana d'Estudis Històrics*, 25 (2014), 171–90

Pérez, Santiago, 'Toponímia d'origen islàmic a la Catalunya Vella', *Societat d'Onomàstica. Butlletí Interior*, 110 (2008), 64–87

——, 'Topónimos catalanes de origen griego', *Real Acadèmia de Cultura Valenciana: Sección de estudios ibéricos 'D. Fletcher Valls'. Estudios de lenguas y epigrafía antiguas* — ELEA, 9 (2009), 431–60

Pérez Samper, Maria-Àngels, 'El patrimoni sonor de Barcelona: la veu de les campanes', in *Els sons de Barcelona a l'edat moderna*, ed. by Tess Knighton (Barcelona: MUHBA and Ajuntament de Barcelona, 2016), pp. 47–66

Peris Albentosa, Tomàs, *Els molins d'aigua valencians (segles XIII–XIX)* (València: Institució Alfons el Magnànim, 2014)

Pichot, Daniel, 'L'habitat dispersé dans l'Ouest de la France (Xᵉ-XIIIᵉ siècle): état de la question', in *L'habitat dispersé dans l'Europe médiévale et moderne*, ed. by Benoît Cursente (Toulouse: Presses Universitaires du Mirail, 1999), pp. 65–95

——, *Le village éclaté. Habitat et société dans les campagnes de l'Ouest au Moyen Âge* (Rennes: Presses Universitaires de Rennes, 2002)

Piera, Marc, and Joan Menchon, 'El castell de Siurana (Cornudella de Montsant, el Priorat). Treballs arqueològics dels anys 2009–2010', in *Actes del IV Congrés d'Arqueologia Medieval i Moderna a Catalunya* (Tarragona: ACRAM and Ajuntament de Tarragona, 2010), pp. 867–78

Pitarch, Josep, *Les salines del delta de l'Ebre a l'edat mitjana* (Barcelona: Columna edicions, 1998)

Pladevall, Antoni, *Taradell. Passat i present d'un terme i vila d'Osona. I. Dels orígens a finals del segle XVIII* (Vic: Eumo and Ajuntament de Taradell, 1995)

—— ed., *L'Art Gòtic a Catalunya. Arquitectura III* (Barcelona: Enciclopèdia Catalana, 2003)

Planas, Xavier, Àurea Ponsa, and Ánchel Belmonte, 'El substrat preromà en la toponímia relacionada amb inestabilitats de vessant en l'àmbit geogràfic nord-oriental de la Península Ibèrica i zones properes', *Fontes Linguae Vasconum (FLV)*, 109 (2008), 481–509

Poirier, Nicolas, *Un espace rural à la loupe. Paysage, peuplement et territoires en Berry, de la préhistoire à nos jours* (Tours: Presses Universitaires François-Rabelais, 2010)

Pojada, Patrici, *Viure com a bons veïns. Identitats i solidaritats als Pirineus (segles XVI–XIX)* (Catarroja: Editorial Afers, 2017) (original edition in French: Poujade, Patrice, *Identité et solidarités dans les Pyrénées: essai sur les relations humaines (XVIe-XIXe siècle)* [Aspet: PyréGraph, 2000])

Porcheddu, Antonio, 'The Ager Valley Historic Landscape: New Tools and Quantitative Analysis. Architecture and Agrarian Parcels in the Medieval Settlement Dynamics' (doctoral thesis, Universitat de Lleida, 2017)

——, 'Archeologia del paesaggio e fortificazioni medievali in una montagna mediterranea', in *Arqueologia medieval IX. Fortaleses a la Vall de l'Ebre (segles VII–XI)*, ed. by Jesús Brufal, Joan Negre, and Flocel Sabaté (Lleida: Pagès editors, 2020), pp. 381–99

Poumarède, Jacques, 'Les "Fadernes" du Lavedan: associations de prêtres et société de crédit dans le diocèse de Tarbes (XVe-XVIIIe siècles)', in *Mélanges offerts à Jean Dauvillier.* (Toulouse: Presses de l'Université des Sciences Sociales, 1979), pp. 677–94

Pozo, Indalecio, 'La alquería islámica de Villa Vieja (Calasparra, Murcia)', in *Castrum 6. Maisons et espaces domestiques dans le monde méditerrannéen au Moyen Âge*, ed. by André Bazzana and Étienne Hubert (Rome/Madrid: École française de Rome and Casa de Velázquez, 2000), pp. 165–75

Prata, Sara, 'Post-Roman Land-Use Transformations: Analysing the Early Medieval Countryside in Castelo de Vide (Portugal)', in *Ruralia XII: Settlement Change across Medieval Europe; Old Paradigms and New Vistas*, ed. by Niall Brady and Claudia Theune (Leiden: Sidestone, 2019), pp. 65–71

Pratdesaba, Albert, *El procés de fortificació i reocupació del territori a Catalunya entre els rius Ter i Llobregat en època visigòtica i carolíngia. El cas de l'Esquerda (segles VIII-X)* (Barcelona: Societat Catalana d'Arqueologia, 2021)

Prevosti, Marta, 'Els estudis de paisatge al territori de la ciutat romana de *Tarraco*', *Butlletí de la Societat Catalana d'Estudis Històrics*, 25 (2014), 191–223

Puig, Anna Maria, 'La vila de Castelló d'Empúries', in *L'art gòtic a Catalunya. Arquitectura III. Dels palaus a les masies*, ed. by Antoni Pladevall (Barcelona: Enciclopèdia Catalana, 2003), pp. 75–78

Puigferrat, Carles, *Sant Julià de Vilatorta després de la Pesta Negra de 1348. Mortaldats, fams i altres tribulacions d'una parròquia osonenca* (Vic: Patronat d'Estudis Osonencs, 2004)

Puigvert, Xavier, *L'època medieval* (Girona: Ajuntament d'Olot and Diputació de Girona, 1996)

——, *La reconstrucció de la vila d'Olot després dels terratrèmols (1427–1433)* (Olot: Arxiu Històric Comarcal d'Olot and Museu Comarcal de la Garrotxa, 1996)

Pujol, Marcel, *La vila de Roses (segles XIV–XVI). Aproximació a l'urbanisme, la societat i l'economia a partir dels capbreus del monestir de Santa Maria de Roses (1304–1565)* (Figueres: Brau edicions and Ajuntament de Roses, 1997)

——, 'L'urbanisme de la vila de Roses (segles XI–XVIII). La complementarietat de les fonts d'informació', *Rodis. Journal of Medieval and Postmedieval Archaeology*, 1 (2018), 71–94

Putti, Manuele, 'Paesaggi e produzioni agricole nell'alto Medioevo', *Archaeologia e storia dei paesaggi senesi. Territorio, risorse, commerci tra età romana e medioevo*, ed. by Stefano Bertoldi, Manuele Putti, and Edoardo Vanni (Sesto Fiorentino: All'Insegna del Giglio, 2019), pp. 59–86

Quirós Castillo, Juan-Antonio, 'Arqueología del campesinado altomedieval: las aldeas y las granjas del País Vasco', *The Archaeology of Early Medieval Villages in Europe*, ed. by Juan-Antonio Quirós (Bilbao: Euskal Herriko Unibertsitatea – Universidad del País Vasco, 2009), pp. 385–403

Quirós Castillo, Juan-Antonio, and Cristiano Nicosia, 'Reconstructing Past Terraced Agrarian Landscapes in the Ebro valley: The Deserted Village of Torrentejo in the Basque Country, Spain', *Geoarchaeology*, 34.6 (2019), 1–14 <https://doi.org/10.1002/gea.21730> [accessed 10 December 2021]

Rackham, Oliver, and Jennifer Moody, *The Making of the Cretan Landscape* (Manchester: Manchester University Press, 1996)

Rama-Corredor, Eduard, 'Reconstruction environnementale et climatique pendant l'optimum climatique médiéval à partir des sources documentaires. Le cas de la Catalogne', in *Histoire et nature. Pour une histoire écologique des sociétés méditerranéennes (Antiquité et Moyen Âge)*, ed. by François Clément (Rennes: Presses Universitaires de Rennes, 2011), pp. 267–83

Raventós, Jordi, 'Barcelona: paisatge sonor, cerimonial i festiu', in *Els sons de Barcelona a l'edat moderna*, ed. by Tess Knighton (Barcelona: MUHBA and Ajuntament de Barcelona, 2016), pp. 67–90

Remacle, Claudine, 'Les maisons rurales en pierre au Val d'Aoste: diversité fonctionnelle et caractères architecturaux (XVe-XVIe siècle)', in *Le village médiévale et son environnement. Études offertes à Jean-Marie Pesez*, ed. by Laurent Feller, Perrine Mane, and Françoise Piponnier (Paris: Publications de la Sorbonne, 1998), pp. 203–19

Rémy, Isabelle, and Aymat Catafau, 'Maisons urbanes à Perpignan dans les lotissements du XIIIe siècle', *Rodis. Journal of Medieval and Postmedieval Archaeology*, 3 (2020), 57–84

Rendu, Christine, *La montagne d'Enveig. Une estive pyrénéenne dans la longue durée* (Canet: Trabucaire, 2003)

——, 'Pistes et propositions pour une archéologie de l'estivage, à partir d'une expérience dans les Pyrénées de l'Est', *Archéologie du Midi médiéval*, 21 (2003), 147–57

Rendu, Christine, Olivier Passarrius, Carine Calastrenc, Ramon Julià, Murie Llubes, Pauline Illes, Pierre Campmajo, Clara Jodry, Denis Crabol, Elisabeth Bille, Marc Conesa, Delphine Bousquet, and Véronique Lallemand, 'Reconstructing Past Terrace Fields in the Pyrenees: Insights into Land Management and Settlement from the Bronze Age to the Early Modern Era at Vilalta (1650 masl, Cerdagne, France)', *Journal of Field Archaeology*, 40.4 (2015), 461–80 <https://www.researchgate.net/publication/279188481_Reconstructing_past_terrace_fields_in_the_Pyrenees_Insights_into_land_management_and_settlement_from_the_Bronze_Age_to_the_Early_Modern_era_at_Vilalta_1650_masl_Cerdagne_France> [accessed 10 December 2021]

Retamero, Fèlix, 'Coping with Gravity: The Case of Mas L'Agustí (Montseny Mountains, Catalonia, Spain, ca. 15th-18th Centuries', in *Agricultural and Pastoral Landscapes in Pre-Industrial Society. Choices, Stability and Change*, ed by Fèlix Retamero, Inge Schjellerup, and Althea Davies (Oxford: Oxbow Books, 2016), pp. 173–85

Revilla, Víctor, 'On the Margins of the *Villa* System? Rural Architecture and Socioeconomic Strategies in North-Eastern Roman Spain', in *The Archaeology of Peasantry in Roman Spain*, ed. by Jesús Bermejo and Ignasi Grau (Berlin: De Gruyter, 2022), pp. 169–200

Rich, Anna, *La comunitat jueva de Barcelona entre 1348 i 1391 a través de la documentació notarial* (Barcelona: Fundació Noguera, 1999)

Riera Melis, Antoni, 'El bisbat de Girona al primer terç del segle XV. Aproximació al context sòcio-econòmic de la sèrie sísmica olotina (1427–1428)', *Anuario de Estudios Medievales*, 23 (1992), 161–204

Riera, Santiago, 'Natural Resources, Land Uses and Landscape Shaping in the Iberian Peninsula from Roman to Medieval Times: Historical Paleoenvironmental Records', in *Archaeology of Farming and Animal Husbandry in Early Medieval Europe (5th–10th centuries). Vitoria-Gasteiz, 15th–16th November 2012. Abstract Book* (2012), pp. 12–16 <https://www.academia.edu/2128962/natural_resources_land_uses_and_landscape_shaping_in_the_iberian_peninsula_from_roman_to_medieval_times_historical_palaeoenvironmental_records>

Riera, Santiago, and Josep M. Palet, 'Aportaciones de la Palinología a la historia del paisaje mediterráneo: estudio de los sistemas de terrazas en las Sierras Litorales Catalanas desde la perspectiva de la Arqueología Ambiental y del Paisaje', in *Una aproximació transdisciplinar a 8.000 anys d'història dels usos de sòl – Transdisciplinary Approach to a 8,000-yr History of Land Uses*, ed. by Santiago Riera and R. Julià Brugués (Barcelona: Universitat de Barcelona, 2005), pp. 55–74

——, 'Una aproximación multidisciplinar a la historia del paisaje mediterráneo: La evolución de los sistemas de terrazas con muros de piedra seca en la sierra de Marina (Badalona, Llano de Barcelona)', in *El paisaje en perspectiva histórica. Formación y transformación del paisaje en el mundo mediterráneo*, ed. by Ramon Garrabou and José Manuel Naredo (Zaragoza: SEHA and Prensas Universitarias de Zaragoza, 2008), pp. 47–90

Rippon, Stephen, *Historic Landscape Analysis: Deciphering the Countryside* (York: Council for British Archaeology, 2012 [first edition 2004])

——, *Making Sense of an Historic Landscape* (Oxford: Oxford University Press, 2012)

——, 'Historic Landscape Analysis: Understanding the Past in the Present', in *Detecting and Understanding Historic Landscapes*, ed. by Alexandra Chavarría Arnau and Andrew Reynolds (Mantua: SAP Società Archeologica, 2015), pp. 158–72

——, *Kingdom,* Civitas, *and County: The Evolution of Territorial Identity in the English Landscape* (Oxford: Oxford University Press, 2018)

Rippon, Stephen, Peter Claughton, and Chris Smart, *Mining in a Medieval Landscape: The Royal Silver Mines of the Tamar Valley* (Exeter: University of Exeter Press, 2009)

Rippon, Stephen, Chris Smart, and Ben Pears, *The Fields of Britannia: Continuity and Change in the Late Roman and Early Medieval Landscape* (Oxford: Oxford University Press, 2015)

Riu, Eduard, *L'arqueologia i la Tarragona feudal* (Tarragona: Museu Nacional Arqueològic de Tarragona, 1987)

Riu, Manuel, 'Formación de las zonas de pastos veraniegos del monasterio de Santes Creus en el Pirineo durante el siglo XII', *Santes Creus*, 14 (1961), 137–53.

——, *Excavaciones en el poblado medieval de Caulers. Mun. Caldes de Malavella, prov. Gerona* (Madrid: Ministerio de Educación y Ciencia, 1975)

——, *L'arqueologia medieval a Catalunya* (Sant Cugat del Vallès: Els Llibres de la Frontera, 1989)

Robert, Sandrine, ed., *Sources et techniques de l'archéogéographie* (Besançon: Presses Universitaires de Franche-Comté, 2011)

Robert, Sandrine, and Nicolas Verdier, ed., *Dynamique et résilience des réseaux routiers: archéogéographes et archéologues en Île-de-France* (Paris: FERACF, 2014)

Roberts, Brian K., *The Making of the English village: A Study in Historical Geography* (Burnt Mill: Longman, 1987)

——, *Landscapes of Settlement: Prehistory to the Present* (London: Routledge, 1996)

——, *Landscapes, Documents and Maps: Villages in Northern England and Beyond* AD *900–1250* (Oxford: Oxbow, 2008)

Roberts, Kathryn, ed., *Lost Farmsteads: Deserted Rural Settlements in Wales* (York: Council for British Archaeology, 2006)

Roca, Guillem, *Pobresa i hospitals a la Lleida baixmedieval* (Lleida: Pagès editors, 2020)

Rodrigo, Esther, 'L'estructuració del territori de *Iesso* en època romana', in *Iesso I. Miscel·lània Arqueològica*, ed. by Josep Guitart and Joaquim Pera (Barcelona-Guissona: Patronat d'Arqueologia de Guissona, 2004), pp. 171–86

Roig, Albert, 'Despoblat d'Esplugallonga', in *Catalunya Romànica*, vol. XV: *El Pallars* (Barcelona: Enciclopèdia Catalana, 1993), pp. 440–41

Roig, Jordi, 'Asentamientos rurales y poblados tardoantiguos y altomedievales en Cataluña (siglos VI al X)', in *The Archaeology of Early Medieval Villages in Europe*, ed. by Juan-Antonio Quirós (Bilbao: Euskal Herriko Unibertsitatea / Universidad del País Vasco, 2009), pp. 207–51

——, 'Vilatges i assentaments pagesos de l'Antiguitat tardana als *territoria* de *Barcino* i *Egara* (Depressió Litoral o Prelitoral): caracterització del poblament rural entre els segles V-VIII', in *Actes del IV Congrés d'Arqueologia Medieval i Moderna a Catalunya* (Tarragona: ACRAM, 2011), vol. I, pp. 227–50

——, 'Formas de poblamiento rural y producciones cerámicas en torno al 711: documentación arqueológica del área catalana', in *711, Arqueología e Historia entre dos mundos* (Alcalá de Henares: Museo Arqueológico regional, 2011), vol. II, pp. 121–46

——, 'Silos, poblados e iglesias: almacenaje y rentas en época visigoda y altomedieval en Cataluña (siglos VI al XI)', in *Horrea, Barns and Silos: Storage and Incomes in Early Medieval Europe*, ed. by Alfonso Vigil-Escalera, Giovanna Bianchi, and Juan-Antonio Quirós (Bilbao: Euskal Herriko Unibertsitatea / Universidad del País Vasco, 2013), pp. 145–70.

Roig, Albert, and Jordi Roig, 'L'ocupació del territori de muntanya: l'urbanisme i els despoblats al Pallars (Pirineu Central)', in *IV Congrés d'Arqueologia Medieval Espanyola. Societats en transició* (Alacant: AEAM and Generalitat Valenciana, 1993), vol. II, pp. 325–30

Roma, Francesc, *Patrimoni existencial de la Catalunya rural* (Valls: Cossetània edicions, 2017)

——, *Molins del Collsacabra. Història i inventari* (Valls: Cossetània edicions, 2018)

Romagosa, Francesc, 'El procés històric de dessecació d'estanys a la plana empordanesa', *Documents d'Anàlisi Geogràfica*, 53 (2009), 71–90

Ron, Zvi Y. D., 'Sistemas de manantiales y terrazas irrigadas en las montañas mediterráneas', in *Agricultura y regadío en al-Andalus. Síntesis y problemes*, ed. by Lorenzo Cara and Antonio Malpica (Almería-Granada: Instituto de Estudios Almerienses and THARG, 1996 [1995]), pp. 383–408

Ros, Ignasi, 'La ramaderia transhumant entre el Pirineu i el Pla de Lleida. Una aproximació diacrònica', *Estudis d'Història Agrària*, 18 (2005), 165–91

Rosselló, Vicenç M., *Viles planificades valencianes medievals i modernes* (València: Publicacions de la Universitat de València, 2017)

Rouche, Michel, *L'Aquitaine des Wisigoths aux Arabes, 418–781: naissance d'une région* (Paris: EHESS and Éditions Jean Touzot, 1979)

Rovira, Jordi, Àngels Casanovas, Joan-Ramon González, and Josep-Ignasi Rodríguez, 'Solibernat (Lleida). Un asentamiento rural islámico con finalidades militares de la primera mitad del siglo XII', *Archéologie islamique*, 7 (1997), 93–110

WORKS CITED

Rowley, Trevor, *The Welsh Border: Archaeology, History and Landscape* (Stroud: Tempus, 2001)
——, *Landscapes of the Norman Conquest* (Barnsley: Pen and Sword books, 2022)
Ryder, Alan, *The Wreck of Catalonia* (Oxford: Oxford University Press, 2007)
Rynne, Colin, 'Waterpower in Medieval Ireland', in *Working with Water in Medieval Europe. Technology and Resource-Use*, ed. by Paolo Squatriti (Leiden: Brill, 2000), pp. 1–50
——, 'Landscapes of Hydraulic Energy in Medieval Europe', in *Detecting and Understanding Historic Landscapes*, ed. by Alexandra Chavarría Arnau and Andrew Reynolds (Mantua: SAP Società Archeologica, 2015), pp. 225–52
——, 'Water and Wind Power', in *The Oxford Handbook of Later Medieval Archaeology in Britain*, ed. by Christopher M. Gerrard and Alejandra Gutiérrez (Oxford: Oxford University Press, 2020), pp. 491–510
Sabaté, Flocel, *El territori de la Catalunya medieval. Percepció de l'espai i divisió territorial al llarg de l'edat mitjana* (Barcelona: Fundació Vives i Casajuana, 1997)
——, 'La montagne dans la Catalogne médiévale. Perception et pouvoir', in *Montagnes médiévales. XXXIVᵉ Congrès de la SHMES* (Paris: Publications de la Sorbonne, 2004), pp. 179–218
——, *Història de Catalunya. Volum 2: Catalunya medieval* (Barcelona: L'Esfera dels Llibres, 2006)
——, 'Limites et villes dans la Catalogne médiévale', in *Reconnaître et délimiter l'espace localement au Moyen-âge. Limites et frontières vol. I*, ed. by Nacima Baron-Yelles, Stéphane Boisselier, Clément François, and Flocel Sabaté (Villeneuve d'Ascq: Presses Universitaires du Septentrion, 2016), pp. 161–90
——, 'Catalan Identity Discourse in the Late Medieval Mediterranean. Creation and Contrast with Neighbouring Identities', in *Memories in Multi-Ethnic Societies: Cohesion in Multi-Ethnic Societies in Europe from c. 1000 to the Present*, I, ed. by Przemyslaw Wiszewski (Turnhout: Brepols, 2020), pp. 349–68
Sabaté, Flocel, and Jesús Brufal, ed., *Arqueologia medieval IV: Els espais de secà* (Lleida: Pagès editors, 2011)
Sabaté, Mireia, and Cristian Folch, 'El castell de Vilademàger (La Llacuna, l'Anoia): arqueologia d'una fortificació comtal (segles x–xv)', *Treballs d'Arqueologia*, 22 (2018), 135 54. <https://revistes.uab.cat/treballsarqueologia/article/view/v22-sabate-folch/80-pdf-ca> [accessed 11 December 2021]
Sadori, Laura, Carlo Giraudi, Alessia Masi, Michel Magny, Elena Ortu, Giovanni Zanchetta, and Adam Izdebski, 'Climate, Environment and Society in Southern Italy during the Last 2000 Years: A Review of the Environmental, Historical and Archaeological Evidence', *Quaternary Science Reviews*, 136 (2016), 173–88
Saguer, Enric, 'Cultivar l'estany. Un assaig d'avaluació del dessecament de l'estany d'Ullastret durant la segona meitat del segle xix', *Estudis d'Història agrària*, 23 (2010–2011), 175–92
Saguer, Romain, 'Consolidation ou disparition des frontières? Les comtés de Roussillon et de Cerdagne après la chute de la couronne de Majorque

(seconde moitié du XIVe siècle)', in *Frontières spatiales, frontières sociales au Moyen Âge* (Paris: Editions de la Sorbonne, 2021), pp. 195–209

Sala, Carme, *Dades històriques d'Olot. Segle XVI* (Olot: Edicions Municipals, 1985).

Sales, Jordina, *Las construcciones cristianas de la* Tarraconensis *durante la Antigüedad Tardía. Topografía, arqueología e historia* (Barcelona: Universitat de Barcelona, 2012)

Sales, Jordina, and Marta Sancho, 'Monastic Networks and Livestock Activity: Relationships and Contacts at Regional Level in the Southern Slopes of the Pyrenees (6th–9th centuries)', in *Les mobilités monastiques en Orient et en Occident de l'Antiquité Tardive au Moyen Âge (IVe-XVe siècle)*, ed. by Olivier Delouis, Maria Mossakowska-Gaubert, and Annick Peters-Custot (Rome: École Française de Rome, 2019), pp. 197–220

Sahlins, Peter, *Boundaries: The Making of France and Spain in the Pyrenees* (Berkeley: University of California Press, 1989)

Salrach, Josep Maria, *Història de Catalunya, vol. II: El procés de feudalització. Segles III–XII* (Barcelona: Edicions 62, 1987)

——, 'El mercat de la vila, mercat de productes', in *Història agrària dels Països Catalans. II: Edat Mitjana*, ed. by Emili Giralt and Josep M. Salrach (Barcelona: Fundació Catalana per a Recerca and Universitats dels Països Catalans, 2004), pp. 433–64

——, ed., *Història Agrària dels Països Catalans. Edat Mitjana* (Barcelona: Fundació Catalana per a la Recerca, Universitat de Barcelona, UAB, UdG, Universitat de les Illes Balears, Universitat Jaume I, UdL, Universitat Pompeu Fabra, URV, Universitat de València, 2004)

Sánchez-Pardo, José Carlos, Emmet H. Marron, and Maria Crîngaci Ţiplic, ed., *Ecclesiastical Landscapes in Medieval Europe: An Archaeological Perspective* (Oxford: Archaeopress, 2020)

Sancho, Marta, *Ipsa Fabricata. Estudi de la farga medieval de Fabregada (s. XI–XIII). Tres anys de recerques arqueològiques (1992–1994)* (Barcelona: Universitat de Barcelona, 1997)

——, *Homes, fargues, ferro i foc. Arqueologia i documentació per a l'estudi de la producció de ferro en època medieval: les fargues dels segles IX–XIII al sud del Pirineu català* (Barcelona: Marcombo and Enginyers Industrials de Catalunya, 1999)

——, *Mur, la història d'un castell feudal a la llum de la recerca històrico-arqueològica.* (Tremp: Garsineu edicions, 2009)

Sancho, Marta, and Maria Soler, 'Balnearis, hospitals i santuaris al Pirineu català: identificació i definició de les àrees d'assistència a l'edat mitjana', in *Els caràcters del paisatge històric als països mediterranis. Territori i Societat: el paisatge històric VIII*, ed. by Jordi Bolòs (Lleida: Universitat de Lleida and Pagès editors, 2018), pp. 233–72

Sans Travé, Josep Maria, *La colonització de la Conca de Barberà després de la conquesta feudal. El cas de Vimbodí (1149?/1151–1200)* (Valls: Cossetània edicions, 2002)

Schneider, Laurent, 'Villes et villages du Languedoc central: le cas du bassin moyen de l'Hérault', in *Village et ville au Moyen Âge: les dynamiques morpho-*

logiques, ed. by Bernard Gauthiez, Elisabeth Zadora-Rio, and Henri Galinié (Tours: Presses Universitaires François-Rabelais, 2003), pp. 111–30

——, 'Dynamiques spatiales et transformations de l'habitat en Languedoc méditerranéen durant le Haut Moyen Âge (VIe-IXe s.)', in *Dopo la fine delle ville: la campagne dal VI al IX secolo*, ed. by Gian Pietro Brogiolo, Alexandra Chavarría, and Marco Valenti (Màntua: SAP Società Archeologica, 2005), pp. 287–312

——, 'Le territoire de l'archéologue et l'archéologie des territoires médiévaux', in *Les territoires du médiéviste*, ed. by Benoît Cursente and Mireille Mousnier (Rennes: Presses Universitaires de Rennes, 2005), pp. 309–28

——, 'De la fouille des villages abandonnés à l'archéologie des territoires locaux. L'étude des systèmes d'habitat du haut Moyen Âge en France méridionale (V^e-Xe siècle): nouveaux matériaux, nouvelles interrogations', in *Trente ans d'archéologie médiévale en France* (Paris: Publications du CRAHM, 2010), pp. 133–61

Schneider, Laurent, Pierre Rascalou, Guilhem Colomer, and Agnès Bergeret, 'Genèse d'une villa carolingienne de l'arrière-pays biterrois (VIe-Xe siècle). La *villa plaxano* du cartulaire d'Aniane et la fouille des Termes à Plaissan (Hérault)', *Archéologie du Midi médiéval*, 32 (2014), 93–121

Schwartz, Dominique, Marc Grodwohl, Boris Dottori, and Frédéric Staut, 'Les paysages d'enclos médiévaux en Alsace: nouvelles avancées', in *Vivre dans la montagne vosgienne au Moyen Âge. Conquête des espaces et culture matérielle*, ed. by Charles Kraemer and Jacky Koch (Nancy: PUN and Éditions Universitaires de Lorraine, 2017), pp. 165–84

Segura, Joan, *Història de Santa Coloma de Queralt* (Santa Coloma de Queralt: Ajuntament de Santa Coloma de Queralt, 1984)

Selma, Sergi, 'El molí hidràulic de farina i l'organització de l'espai rural andalusí. Dos exemples d'estudi arqueològic espaial a la serra d'Espadà (Castelló)', *Mélanges de la Casa de Velázquez*, 27.1 (1991), 65–100

——, *Els molins d'aigua medievals a Sharq al-Andalus. Aproximació a través de la documentació escrita dels segles X–XIII (IV–VII H.)* (Onda: Ajuntament d'Onda, 1993 [1994])

Semple, Sarah, 'In the Open Air', in *Signals of Belief in Early England: Anglo-Saxon Paganism Revisited*, ed. by Martin Carver, Alex Sanmark, and Sarah Semple (Oxford: Oxbow, 2014), pp. 21–48

Sénac, Philippe, *La frontière et les hommes (VIIIe – XIIe siècle). La peuplement musulman au nord de l'Ebre et les débuts de la reconquête aragonaise* (Paris: Maisonneuve et Larose, 2000)

——, *Un 'village' d'al-Andalus aux alentours de l'an Mil. Las Sillas (Marcén, province de Huesca)* (Toulouse: Université de Toulouse-Le Mirail, 2009)

Serra Vilaró, Joan, *Baronies de Pinós i Mataplana. Investigació als seus arxius. Llibre segon* (Barcelona: Biblioteca Balmes, 1947)

Settia, Aldo A., *Castelli e villagi nell'Italia padana. Popolamento, potere e sicurezza fra IX e XIII secolo* (Napoli: Liguore Editore, 1984)

——, '*In Andisello et in Andego*. Couples toponymiques et peuplement rural', in *Le village médiévale et son environnement. Études offertes à Jean-Marie Pesez*, ed. by

Laurent Feller, Perrine Mane, and Françoise Piponnier (Paris: Publications de la Sorbonne, 1998), pp. 647–70

Settis, Salvatore, ed., *Misurare la terra: centuriazione e coloni nel mondo romano* (Modena: Franco Cosimo Panini Editore, 2003)

Shideler, John C., *A Medieval Catalan Noble Family: The Montcadas, 1000–1230* (Berkeley: University of California Press, 1983 [Catalan edition: 1987])

Simms, Anngret, and Howard B. Clarke, ed., *Lords and Towns in Medieval Europe: The European Historic Towns Project* (New York: Routledge, 2019)

Sitjes, Eugènia, 'Managing Slopes for Agricultural Purposes: Terrace Morphology in Andalusi Hydraulic Systems', in *Agricultural and Pastoral Landscapes in Pre-Industrial Society. Choises, Stability and Change, ed. by* Fèlix Retamero, Inge Schjellerup and Althea Davies (Oxford: Oxbow, 2016), pp. 201–19

Slukan Altić, Mirela, 'The Medieval Planned Towns in Croatia', in *Lords and Towns in Medieval Europe: The European Historic Towns Project*, ed. by Anngret Simms and Howard B. Clarke (New York: Routledge, 2019), pp. 305–20

Smith, Nigel, *Patterns in the Landscape: Evaluating Characterisation of the Historic Landscape in the South Pennines* (Oxford: Archaeopress, 2014)

Soldevila, Xavier, 'L'élevage ovin et la transhumance en Catalogne nord-occidentale (XIIIe-XIVe siècles)', in *Transhumance et estivage en Occident des origines aux enjeux actuels. Flaran XXVI*, ed. by Pierre-Yves Laffont (Toulouse: Presses Universitaires du Mirail, 2006), pp. 109–18

Solé, Xavier, 'L'explotació del baix Imperi (segle IV)', in *Roc d'Enclar. Transformacions d'un espai dominant (segles IV–XIX)*, ed. by Xavier Llovera, Josep M. Bosch, Maria Àngels Ruf, Cristina Yáñez, Xavier Solé, and Antoni Vila (Andorra la Vella: Govern d'Andorra, 1997), pp. 86–97

Soler, Maria, 'Feudalisme i nucleació poblacional. Processos de concentració de l'hàbitat al comtat de Barcelona entre els segles X i XIII', *Acta historica et archaeologica mediaevalia*, 23/24 (2002), 69–101

——, 'Els espais d'intercanvi. El mercat en el procés de gènesi i consolidació del feudalisme al comtat de Barcelona (segles IX a XIII)' (doctoral thesis, Universitat de Barcelona, 2006)

Soler, Santi, 'Notes sobre el dret de cornar a Tortellà (terme del castell de Sales). Segles XIV-XVII', in *IX Assemblea d'Estudis sobre el comtat de Besalú* (Olot: Amics del comtat de Besalú, 2003), pp. 137–55

Soto, Pau de, and Cèsar Carreras, 'Anàlisi de la xarxa de transport a la Catalunya romana: alguns apunts', *Revista d'Arqueologia de Ponent*, 16/17 (2006–2007), 177–91

Štular, Benjamin, 'Historic Landscape Characterisation: Kobarid, Staro Selo, Drežnica, Ladra', (2009). <https://www.academia.edu/348782/Historic_Landscape_Characterization_Kobarid_Staro_Selo_Dre%C5%BEnica_Ladra> [accessed 11 December 2021]

Taylor, Christopher, 'Polyfocal Settlement and the English Village', *Medieval Archaeology*, 21 (1977), 189–93

——, *Village and Farmstead: A History of Rural Settlement in England* (London: George Philip, 1983)

Taylor, Griffith, 'Environment, Village and City: A Genetic Approach to Urban Geography; with Some Reference to Possibilism', *Annals of the Association of American Geographers*, 32.1 (1942), 1–67

Thiébault, Stéphanie, *Archéologie environnementale de la France* (Paris: La Découverte, 2010)

To, Lluís, 'Le mas catalan du XIIᵉ s.: genèse et évolution d'une structure d'encadrement et d'asservissement de la paysannerie', *Cahiers de Civilisation Médiévale*, 36–142 (1993), 151–77

To, Lluís, Jeroni Moner, and Berta Noguer, ed., *El mas medieval a Catalunya* (Banyoles: Centre d'Estudis Comarcals de Banyoles, 1998)

Tomás-Faci, Guillermo, and José Carlos Martín-Iglesias, 'Cuatro documentos inéditos del monasterio visigodo de San Martín de Asán (522–86)', *Mittellateinisches Jahrbuch*, 52.2 (2017), 261–86

Torró, Josep, *El naixement d'una colònia. Dominació i resistència a la frontera valenciana (1238–1276)* (València: Universitat de València, 1999)

——, 'Arqueologia de la conquesta. Registre material, substitució de poblacions i transformació de l'espai rural valencià (segles XIII–XIV)', in *El feudalisme comptat i debatut. Formació i expansió del feudalisme català*, ed. by Miquel Barceló, Gaspar Feliu, Antoni Furió, Marina Miquel, and Jaume Sobrequés (València: Universitat de València, 2003), pp. 153–200

——, 'Les cartes de poblament i la colonització de Pego (1279–1300)', in *Carta de poblament de Pego, 1279*, ed. by Enric Guinot, Josep Torró, and Javier Martí (Pego: Ajuntament de Pego, 2004), pp. 23–32

——, 'Terrasses irrigades a les muntanyes valencianes: les transformacions de la colonització cristiana', in *Estudiar i gestionar el paisatge històric medieval. Territori i Societat a l'edat mitjana, IV*, ed. by Jordi Bolòs (Lleida: Universitat de Lleida, 2007), pp. 81–143

——, 'Tierras ganadas. Aterrazamiento de pendientes y desecación de marjales en la colonización cristiana del territorio valenciano', in *Por una arqueología agraria. Perspectivas de investigación sobre espacios de cultivo en las sociedades medievales hispánicas*, ed. by Helena Kirchner (Oxford: BAR International Series 2062, 2010), pp. 157–72

Torró, Josep, and Enric Guinot, 'De la *madīna* a la ciutat. Les pobles del sud i la urbanització dels extramurs de València (1270–1370)', *Saitabi. Revista de la Facultat de Geografia i Història*, 51/52 (2001/02), 51–103

Toubert, Pierre, *Les structures du Latium médiéval: Le Latium méridional et la Sabine du IXᵉ siècle à la fin du XIIᵉ siecle* (Roma: École Française de Rome, 1973)

Travé, Esther, 'Producció i distribució d'una terrisseria medieval: Cabrera d'Anoia' (doctoral thesis, Universitat de Barcelona, 2009)

Treffort, Cécile, ed., *Le cimetière au village dans l'Europe médiévale et moderne* (Toulouse: Presses Universitaires du Midi, 2015)

Tréton, Rodrigue, 'Sel et salines en Roussillon au Moyen Âge' (maîtrise, Université Paul Valéry-Montpellier III, 1999) <https://www.academia.edu/10109378/Sel_et_salines_en_Roussillon_au_Moyen_Age?auto = download> [accessed 10 December 2021]

——, 'Crues et inondations dans les Pyrénées méditerranéennes aux xive et xve siècles: état des sources et perspectives de recherches', *Domitia*, 8–9 (2007), 213–26

Turner, Sam, 'Historic Landscape Characterisation: An Introduction to Methods and Applications for Historical Research', *La caracterització del paisatge històric. Territori i Societat: el paisatge històric, V*, ed. by Jordi Bolòs (Lleida: Edicions de la Universitat de Lleida, 2010), pp. 17–40

Turner, Sam, Jordi Bolòs, and Tim Kinnaird, 'Changes and Continuities in a Mediterranean Landscape: A New Interdisciplinary Approach to Understanding Historic Character in Western Catalonia', *Landscape Research*, 43.7 (2017), 1–17 <https://doi.org/10.1080/01426397.2017.1386778> [accessed 11 December 2021]

——, 'Canvis i continuïtats en un paisatge mediterrani: una nova aproximació interdisciplinària al coneixement dels caràcters del paisatge històric de la Catalunya occidental', in *Els caràcters del paisatge històric als països mediterranis. Territori i Societat: el paisatge històric, VIII*, ed. by Jordi Bolòs (Lleida: Universitat de Lleida and Pagès editors, 2018), pp. 23–64

Turull, Albert, 'Sistematicitat i historicitat en la toponímia de les comarques de Ponent' (doctoral thesis, Universitat de Lleida, 2001)

Taylor, Christopher C., 'Polyfocal Settlements and the English Village', *Medieval Archaeology*, 21 (1977), 189–93

Unger, Richard W., 'Introduction: Hoffmann in the Historiography of environmental History', in *Ecologies and Economies in Medieval and Early Modern Europe: Studies in Environmental History for Richard C. Hoffmann*, ed. by Scott G. Bruce (Leiden: Brill, 2010), pp. 1–21

Urteaga, Metxe, 'Censo de las villas nuevas medievales en Álava, Bizkaia y Gipuzkoa', in *Las villas nuevas medievales del suroeste europeo*, ed. by Pascual Martínez and Mertxe Urteaga (Irun: Arkeolan, 2006), pp. 37–98

Vaccaro, Emanuele, 'Il popolamento rurale tra fine v e inizi x nella Maremma Grossetana: indagini di superficie tra la valle dell'Alma e la valle dell'Osa', in *Dopo la fine delle ville: le campagne dal vi al ix secolo*, ed. by Gian Pietro Brogiolo, Alexandra Chavarría, and Marco Valenti (Mantua: SAP Società Archeologica, 2005), pp. 179–92

Valor, Magdalena, and Avelino Gutiérrez, *The Archaeology of Medieval Spain, 1100–1500* (Sheffield: Equinox Publishing, 2014)

Varela, Rosa, and Mário Varela, 'The Arrifana ribat (Algarve): Sacred Space and Ideological Context (12th century)', in *Arqueologia medieval. Els espais sagrats*, ed. by Flocel Sabaté and Jesús Brufal (Lleida: Pagès editors, 2015), pp. 151–76.

Varoto, Mauro, Luca Bonardi, and Paolo Tarolli, ed., *World Terraced Landscapes: History, Environment, Quality of Life* (Cham: Springer, 2019)

Vela, Susanna, 'Andorra entre els segles xii-xv', in *Història d'Andorra. De la Prehistòria a l'edat contemporània*, ed. by Ernest Belenguer (Barcelona: Edicions 62, 2005), pp. 105–51

Verdés, Pere, and Max Turull, 'La vila de Cervera', in *L'art gòtic a Catalunya. Arquitectura III. Dels palaus a les masies* (Barcelona: Enciclopèdia Catalana, 2003), pp. 96–99

Verhulst, Adriaan, *Rural and Urban Aspects of Early Medieval Northwest Europe* (Aldershot: Variorum, 1992)

Verna, Catherine, *L'industrie au village. Essai de micro-histoire (Arles-sur-Tech, xive et xve siècles)* (Paris: Les Belles Lettres, 2017)

Viader, Roland, *L'Andorre du ixe au xive siècle. Montagne, féodalité et communautés* (Toulouse: Presses Universitaires du Mirail, 2003)

Vicedo, Enric, Jordi Bolòs, José Ramon Olarieta, Ignasi Aldomà, and Miquel Aran, *Les etapes de la construcció del territori a Catalunya: Torrefarrera i la Catalunya occidental, segles vii a xx. Una proposta metodològica* (Lleida: Ajuntament de Torrefarrera and Pagès editors, 2013)

Vicens Vives, Jaume, *El gran sindicato remensa (1488–1508): La última etapa del problema agrario catalán durante el reinado de Fernando el Católico* (Barcelona: CSIC, 1954)

Vigil-Escalera, Alfonso, 'Meeting Places, Markets, and Churches in the Countryside between Madrid and Toledo, Central Spain (*c.* AD 500–900)', in *Polity and Neighbourhood in Early Medieval Europe*, ed. by Julio Escalona, Orri Vésteinsson, and Stuart Brookes (Turnhout: Brepols, 2019), pp. 173–202

Vigué, Jordi, and Antoni Pladevall, ed., *Catalunya Romànica*, vols I–XXVII (Barcelona: Enciclopèdia Catalana, 1984–1998)

Vilà Valentí, Joan, *El món rural a Catalunya* (Barcelona: Curial, 1973)

Vila, Josep M., and Ainhoa Pancorbo, 'La topografia urbana de Granollers entre els segles x i xvi. Estat de la qüestió i hipòtesi de configuració', *Lauro. Revista del Museu de Granollers*, 30 (2009), 10–32

Vilaginés, Jaume, *El paisatge, la societat i l'alimentació al Vallès Oriental (segles x–xii)* (Barcelona: Publicacions de l'Abadia de Montserrat, 2001)

——, *La gent i el paisatge. Estudis sobre el Vallès medieval* (Barcelona: Publicacions de l'Abadia de Montserrat, 2006)

Vinyoles, Teresa, 'Veus i sensacions dels mercats medievals', in *El mercat. Un món de contactes i intercanvis*, ed. by Flocel Sabaté (Lleida: Pagès editors, 2014), pp. 77–97

Vion, Eric, 'L'analyse archéologique des réseaux routiers: une rupture méthodologique, des réponses nouvelles', *Paysages Découverts*, 1 (1989), 67–99

Virgili, Antoni, and Helena Kirchner, 'The Impact of the Christian Conquest on the Agrarian Areas in the Lower Ebro Valley: The Case of Xerta (Spain)', in *Ruralia XII: Settlement Change across Medieval Europe; Old Paradigms and New Vistas*, ed. by Niall Brady and Claudia Theune (Leiden: Sidestone, 2019), pp. 413–20

Vita-Finzi, Claudio, *The Mediterranean Valleys: Geological Changes in Historical Times* (Cambridge: Cambridge University Press, 1969)

Vives, Miquel, 'L'evolució històrica de la xarxa viària entre el Llobregat i el Foix des de l'època romana fins al tercer decenni del segle xx' (doctoral thesis, Universitat de Barcelona, 2007) <https://www.tdx.cat/handle/10803/2604#page = 1> [accessed 29 November 2021]

Watson, Andrew, *Agricultural Innovation in the Early Islamic World: The Diffusion of Crops and Farming Techniques, 700–1100* (Cambridge: Cambridge University Press, 1983)

Watteaux, Magali, 'Archéogéographie de l'habitat et du parcellaire au haut Moyen Âge', in *L'Austrasie. Sociétés, économies, territoires, christianisation. Actes des XXVIᵉ Journées Internationales d'Archéologie Mérovingienne*, ed. by Edith Peytremann (Nancy: Presses Universitaires de Nancy, 2009), pp. 109–20

——, 'La colonisation agraire médiévale en Alentejo (Portugal)', *Études rurales. Archéogéographie et disciplines voisines*, 188 (2011), 39–72

——, 'Archéogéographie morphologique de la plaine sud-vendéenne', in *Des hommes aux champs. Pour une archéologie des espaces ruraux du Néolithique au Moyen Âge*, ed. by Vincent Carpentier and Cyril Marcigny (Rennes: Presses Universitaires de Rennes, 2012), pp. 275–87

——, 'Le bocage. Un paysage rural à la lumière des études archéologiques et archéogéographiques', *Archéopages*, 34 (2012), 64–73

——, 'Paysage', in *Nouvelle Histoire du Moyen Âge*, ed. by Florian Mazel (Paris: Seuil, 2021), pp. 829–36

Wickham, Chris, 'Overview: Production, Distribution and Demand, II', in *The Long Eighth Century*, ed. by Inge Lyse Hansen and Chris Wickham (Leiden: Brill, 2000), pp. 345–77

——, *Framing the Early Middle Ages: Europe and the Mediterranean, 400–800* (Oxford: Oxford University Press, 2005)

Williams, David H., *The Cistercians in the Early Middle Ages* (Leominster: Gracewing, 1998)

Winchester, Angus, *Discovering Parish Boundaries* (London: Bloomsbury, 2000)

Wolff, Philippe, *Regards sur le Midi médiéval* (Toulouse: Privat, 1978)

Zadora-Rio, Elisabeth, 'Archéologie et toponymie: le divorce', *Les petits cahiers d'Anatole*, 8 (2001) <http://citeres.univ-tours.fr/doc/lat/pecada/F2_8.pdf> [accessed 11 September 2021]

——, 'Les approches morphologiques des agglomérations: essai d'historiographie', in *Village et ville au Moyen Âge: les dynamiques morphologiques*, ed. by Bernard Gauthiez, Elisabeth Zadora-Rio, and Henri Galinié (Tours: Presses Universitaires François-Rabelais, 2003), pp. 13–27

——, *Des paroisses de Touraine aux communes d'Indre-et-Loire. La formation des territoires* (Tours: FERACF, 2008)

——, 'Early Medieval Villages and Estate Centres in France (*c.* 300–1100)', in *The Archaeology of Early Medieval Villages in Europe*, ed. by Juan Antonio Quirós (Bilbao: Euskal Herriko Unibertsitatea / Universidad del País Vasco, 2009), pp. 76–98

Index of Personal Names

Abbé, Jean-Loup: 240
Agache, Roger: 343
Alfons I, king of Catalonia and
    Aragon (reigned 1164–1196): 115,
    123, 239
Alfonso I, king of Aragon (reigned
    1104–1134): 72
al-Ḥimyarī (fifteenth century): 165,
    170–71
Andreu, Jaume: 362
Arnau Mir de Tost, Viscount
    (c.1000–1072): 88–90, 130
Aston, Mick: 50, 162
Augustus, reign of (27 BC–AD 14): 193
Aventín, Mercè: 151

Bailac, Miquel: 283, 360
Barceló, Maria: 362
Barceló, Miquel: 228
Bartlett, Robert: 108
Barton, Thomas: 19
Batet, Carolina: 359
Baudreu, Dominique: 22, 33, 92
Bensch, Stephen: 18
Bisson, Thomas: 18
Boethius (c. 480–524): 313
Bolòs, Jordi: 357, 362
Bonales, Jacinto: 149, 192–93, 217, 283,
    292, 330, 358, 360, 362
Bond, James: 162
Bonnassie, Pierre: 18, 33, 62, 302, 339
Borrell I, count of Cerdanya
    (c. 798): 154

Borrell II, count of Barcelona and
    Urgell (966–988): 302
Bowman, Jeffrey: 19
Brigand, Robin: 192
Brogiolo, Gian Pietro: 33
Brufal, Jesús: 148, 208, 361
Burgueño, Jesús: 315, 318
Burjachs, Francesc: 257

Castillo, Albert del: 155
Catafau, Aymat: 32, 33, 49, 50, 54, 57,
    59, 60, 62, 96, 100, 135, 307, 357, 361
Catlos, Brian: 19
Caucanas, Sylvie: 255
Chandler, Cullen: 19
Charlemagne, king of the Franks and
    emperor (reigned 768– 814): 14,
    16, 67, 108, 134
Chavarría-Arnau, Alexandra: 33
Chouquer, Gérard: 189, 191, 200, 311,
    334
Christie, Neil: 78
Christine, Rendu: 261
Clark, Jo: 364
Cockin, Tim C. H: 318
Conzen, Michael Robert G.: 32, 162
Coromines, Joan: 40, 208–09, 219,
    322–23, 332, 364
Creighton, Oliver: 21, 78
Currás, Andrés: 257, 268;
    see also pollen analyses
    in Index of Subjects
Cursente, Benoît: 21, 33, 36, 43, 126

INDEX OF PERSONAL NAMES

Darby, Henry Clifford: 333
Darlington, John: 364
Duby, Georges: 193
Durand, Aline: 230, 258

Ejarque, Ana: 257, 262; *see also* pollen
  analyses *in* Index of Subjects
Elisabeth Zadora-Rio: 335
Elliott, John: 18
Esquieu, Yves: 162
Esquilache, Ferran: 362

Fairclough, Graham: 364
Farias, Víctor: 289
Favory, François: 189
Fernández Ferrer, Marc: 342
Fixot, Michel: 21, 33, 50
Foard, Glenn: 318
Folch, Cristian: 361
Font Rius, Josep M.: 108
Freedman, Paul: 18, 29
Furió, Antoni: 362

Galí, owner of a villa (tenth
  century): 302
Galop, Didier: 257
Garcia-Oliver, Ferran: 182
Gausfred, count of Empúries and
  Roussillon (931–991): 299
Gauthiez, Bernard: 162
Gibert, Jordi: 361
Gironella, Josep M.: 256
Gisemund, author *Ars Gromatica sive
  Geometria*: 193, 313
González Villaescusa, Ricardo: 229, 358
Gras, Mercè: 315, 318
Guibal, Frédéric: 258
Guifré el Pilós, count of Barcelona
  and Urgell (Wilfred the Hairy)
  (870–897): 28, 64, 66, 88, 311
Guillem, *fidelis* (989): 299
Guilleré, Christian: 18

Guinot, Enric: 362
Guitard, Viscount (954): 224

Hall, David: 318
Herold, Hajnalka: 78
Higounet, Charles: 334
Hooke, Della: 334
Hug Roger III, count of Pallars Sobirà
  (1451–1491): 40, 277
Hurtado, Víctor: 335

Izard, Véronique: 252, 256

Jarrett, Jonathan: 19
Jaume I, king of Catalonia and Aragon
  (James I) (reigned 1213–1276): 17,
  28, 85, 90, 144, 163, 174, 178, 223, 282
Jaume II, king of Catalonia and
  Aragon (James II) (reigned
  1291–1327): 315–16

Kirchner, Helena: 230, 361
Kosto, Adam: 19

Lauwers, Michel: 44
Lavigne, Cédric: 191, 364
Leturcq, Samuel: 341
Lilley, Keith: 167

Mallorquí, Elvis: 154–55, 360, 362
Marchand, Claude: 279
Martí, Ramon: 21, 361
Mas, Antoni: 362
Milton, Gregory: 19
Montanari, Massimo: 276

Negre, Joan: 361

Oliba, Abbot and Bishop
  (971–1046): 53–54
Ollich, Imma: 361
Orengo, Hèctor: 362

INDEX OF PERSONAL NAMES 429

Palet, Josep Maria: 362
Partida, Tracey: 318
Passarrius, Olivier: 362
Passini, Jean: 162
Paulus, Favius, Visigothic duke
  (seventh century): 80
Pere I, king of Catalonia and
  Aragon (or Peter I) (reigned
  1196–1213): 90
Pere III, king of Catalonia and Aragon
  (or Peter III), the Ceremonious
  (1336–1387): 71, 126, 163–64,
  174–75, 177, 178, 270
Pere, count of Prades (1341–1381): 253
Pesez, Jean-Marie: 162
Poirier, Nicolas: 341
Porcheddu, Antonio: 343
Prevosti, Marta: 362

Ramon Berenguer IV, count of
  Barcelona and prince of Aragon
  (1131–1162): 16. 71, 110
Ramon Berenguer, count of Prades
  (son of Jaume II) (1324–1341): 315
Ramon Sunifred, lord of Rubí
  (eleventh century): 62
Rendu, Christine: 271
Riera, Santiago: 257, 266
Riu, Manuel: 91, 155
Robert, Sandrine: 279, 334
Roig, Albert: 91
Roig, Jordi: 34, 91
Roma, Francesc: 256
Rouche, Michel: 295, 302
Ryder, Alan: 19

Sabaté Carrové, Mariona: 29
Sabaté, Flocel: 359, 362
Sànchez-Boira, Imma: 29
Sancho, Marta: 252, 256, 361
Sénac, Philippe: 83
Settia, Aldo A.: 102
Shideler, John: 18
Simon de Montfort (thirteenth
  century, crusade against the
  Cathars): 90
Sitges, Eugènia: 362
Soler, Maria: 361

Taylor, Griffith: 32
Teuter, bishop of Girona (888): 310
To, Lluís: 362
Torró, Josep: 223, 362
Toubert, Pierre: 33, 77, 99

Ulpian, jurist (c.170–228): 302

Verdier, Nicolas: 279
Verna, Catherine: 251
Vicedo, Enric: 362
Vicens Vives, Jaume: 23
Vigil-Escalera, Alfonso: 308
Vilà Valentí, Joan: 287
Vilar, Pierre: 18
Vion, Eric: 27, 279, 282–83, 286, 350,
  359
Virgili, Antoni: 361
Vita-Finzi, Claudio: 202
Vives, Miquel: 280, 282, 313, 360

Wickham, Chris: 36

Zadora-Rio, Elisabeth: 21, 30, 50, 321

Index of Place Names

This place name index includes only those toponyms studied in detail in the book. Where applicable, the municipality, the *comarca* (or region), or the country is provided in parentheses. Place names from the department of the Pyrénées-Orientales are written in Catalan with the French equivalent in parentheses. Place names from Occitania are written in French with the Occitan equivalent in parentheses.

Abbreviations
Ar. Arab
Ct. Catalan
La. Latin
Fr. French
It. Italian
Oc. Occitan
Sp. Castilian or Spanish

Àger (Noguera): 109, 130
  collegiate church: 68, 130
  valley: 288, 343
Agramunt (Urgell): 109–10, 286
  road (Ct. *Camí d'Agramunt*): 280
Aguilaniu (or Aguinaliu)
  (Ribagorça): 254
Aguiló (Conca de Barberà): 92, 94, 219
Aiguacuit, L', archaeological site
  (Terrassa, Vallès Occidental): 34, 35
Aitona (Segrià): 47, 232–33
Al-Andalus: 18, 27, 65, 85, 104, 133, 142, 272, 363
Albesa, Séquia d': 234
Alcarràs (Segrià): 232
  Séquia d': 166, 232, 247
Alcuses, Les (Moixent, La Costera, Valencia): 223
Aldea, L' (Baix Ebre): 144
Alguer, L' (It. Alghero) (Sardinia, Italy): 18
All (Cerdanya): 291
Almacelles (Segrià): 341–42, 351, 354
Alós d'Isil (Pallars Sobirà): 306

Alp (Cerdanya): 220, 349
Alt Berguedà: 210, 258, 271, 327;
  see also Berguedà
Alt Empordà, *comarca*: 13, 300;
  see also Empordà
Alt Penedès, *comarca*: 27, 280, 282, 360; *see also* Penedès
Alt Urgell, *comarca*: 13, 37, 322
Alta Cerdanya, *comarca*: 13, 261;
  see also Cerdanya
Alta Ribagorça, *comarca*: 322;
  see also Ribagorça
Altimiris, Els, archaeological site
  (Pallars Jussà): 74; *see also* Santa
  Cecília d'Altimiris
Aluderia, L' (Carrer del Carme, Lleida): 178
Amposta (Montsià): 255, 269
  Hospital commandery: 72
Ancosa, monastic grange, archaeological site (La Llacuna, Anoia): 71
  horts: 71
  pipes of: 71
Andalusia (Spain): 120, 228, 362

INDEX OF PLACE NAMES   431

Andorra: 13, 37, 80, 139, 250, 262–63,
304, 306–07
valley of: 261, 304, 319, 339
Andorra la Vella (Andorra): 81
Àneu, valley of (Pallars Sobirà): 304,
306
Anglesola (Urgell), lords of: 94
Anoia, *comarca*: 290
Anoia, River: 224, 313–14
Aragon: 13, 16, 17, 47, 82, 83, 110, 134,
237, 282, 318, 362
Kingdom of: 17, 88
Aranyonet (Gombrèn, Ripollès): 211
Arboç, L' (Baix Penedès): 112
Arderiu (Berguedà): 327
Ardèvol, castle, archaeological site
(Solsonès): 85–86
Àreu (Alins, Pallars Sobirà): 42, 100
Arles (Fr. Arles-sur-Tech)
(Vallespir): 124, 251
monastery: 67; *see also* Santa Maria
d'Arles
Arraona (Sabadell, Vallès
Occidental): 302
Artedó (Alt Urgell): 332
Artés (Bages): 74, 155
necropolis: 44
Auditorium of Lleida (or Portal
de Magdalena), archaeological
site: 165, 171

Baells (La Llitera): 272
Baén (Pallars Sobirà): 303
Bagà, valley of (Berguedà): 296, 304
Bages, *comarca*: 57, 98, 142, 190
Bages de Rosselló (Roussillon): 60,
134, 284
lake: 240
Baix Cinca, *comarca*: 358
Baix Ebre, *comarca*: 190
Baix Empordà, *comarca*: 13, 120;
see also Empordà

Baix Llobregat, *comarca*: 27, 61, 280,
282, 289–90, 360
Baix Penedès, *comarca*: 214, 267;
see also Penedès
Baix Segre (Segrià): 182;
see also Segrià
Baixa Ribagorça, *comarca*: 144, 272;
see also Ribagorça
Bajoles (Roussillon): 240
Balaguer (Noguera): 47, 109, 111, 122,
132, 128, 165, 170, 180, 234, 286, 327,
341, 354, 361–62
madīna Balagī: 170
Séquia de Balaguer (*Séquia del
Cup*): 234
Balearic Islands (Ct. *Illes Balears*): 16,
18, 25, 107, 144, 227, 242, 357–58,
363
Balsareny (Bages): 90, 240
Banyoles (Pla de l'Estany): 66, 67,
124, 241, 264–65, 269, 296, 354
lake of: 63, 274
monastery: 74; *see also* Sant Esteve
de Banyoles
town of: 265
Banys d'Arles, Els (Fr. Amélie-les-
Bains) (Vallespir): 74
Bao (Fr. Baho) (Roussillon): 327
Bar (Alt Urgell): 295
pago Baridano: 295; *see also pagus*
Barberà (Conca de Barberà): 74
Templar commandery of: 72, 348
Barcelona (Barcelonès): 11, 13, 15,
16, 17, 19, 65, 70, 85, 108, 115, 163,
178–82, 189, 209, 231, 238, 266–67,
276, 282, 289, 293, 317, 326, 340,
354, 360–61
bishopric or diocese: 49, 54, 61, 88,
240, 297, 307
count of: 15, 16, 17, 18, 147, 165, 204,
214, 221, 228, 234, 267, 303, 311, 348
County of: 88, 99, 102, 247, 296, 338

plain of: 266
siege of: 329
see also monarchs and counts
Barcelonès, *comarca*: 229
Barguja (Alt Urgell): 295
Bas (or En Bas), valley of (Vall d'en Bas, Garrotxa): 104, 304
Basque Country: 37, 115, 120, 209, 362
Bearn (Gascony, France): 43
Bedorc, El (Anoia): 224
Bellvei (Baix Penedès): 214, 216
Bellver (Cerdanya): 112, 176, 290
Berga (Berguedà): 127, 154, 253, 282
County of: 13, 28, 246, 296, 303, 308, 311, 339
market of: 253
Berguedà, *comarca*: 13, 53, 73, 82, 127, 133–34, 250, 297, 358
Besalú (La Garrotxa)
County of: 13, 61, 64, 103, 245, 296, 304, 339
Beseit (Matarranya): 112
Besòs, El, River: 238, 266
Blondel, Carrer de, archaeological site, mill (Lleida, Segrià): 247
Boí, valley of (Alta Ribagorça): 74, 304, 322
churches: 11
Bolvir (Cerdanya), archaeological site: 92, 291
Borriana (Plana Baixa, Valencia): 118
Bovalar, El, archaeological site (Seròs, Segrià): 35, 74
Buars (Fraga, Baix Cinca): 192
Butsènit (Lleida, Segrià): 232–33
Butsènit (Noguera): 286
Butsènit (Valencia): 184

Ca l'Estrada, archaeological site (Canovelles, Vallès Oriental): 35
Cabó, valley of (Alt Urgell): 73, 304
Cabrera, castle (L'Esquirol, Osona): 82

Cabrera d'Anoia, archaeological site (Anoia): 253
Cadí range (Alt Urgell): 295, 297, 351
Calassanç (La Llitera): 254
Calders (Moianès): 44, 45
Caldes de Montbui (Vallès Oriental): 289
Cambrils (Baix Camp): 110, 112
Camp de Tarragona: 16, 74, 189, 200, 302, 358
Camprodon (Ripollès): 296
monastery: 64; *see also* Sant Pere de Camprodon
valley of: 304
Camps, necropolis (Fonollosa, Bages): 44
Can Gambús, archaeological site (Sabadell, Vallès Occidental): 35
Can Ximet, archaeological site, cave (Alt Penedès): 157–58
Candasnos (Fraga, Baix Cinca): 217
Canigó, El, mountain (Conflent): 74
Capçanes (Priorat): 221–22
Capcir, *comarca*: 258, 297
Cappont (Lleida, Segrià): 168–69, 180
Carcassonne (Oc. Carcassona) (France): 108, 117
County of: 16
Cardona (Bages): 74, 108, 154, 255, 280, 282, 308
collegiate church: 68, 75, 255
roads: 255
viscounts of: 255
Casa-en-Ponç, kilns, archaeological site (Berga, Berguedà): 127, 253
Casserres, *castrum*, archaeological site (Berguedà): 82
Castell Formós, Islamic fortification (Balaguer, Noguera): 82
Castellar del Vallès (Vallès Occidental): 196
Plaça Major, archaeological site: 34

INDEX OF PLACE NAMES   433

Castellar Vell, archaeological site: 35
Castellbò (Alt Urgell)
  valley of: 304, 339
Castelldans (Garrigues): 110, 208, 272
  Islamic fortification: 82
Castelldefels (Baix Llobregat): 317
  monastery: 65; see also Santa Maria
  de Castelldefels
Castellnou de Segrià (now Vilanova
  de Segrià) (Segrià): 112, 345
Castelló d'Empúries (Alt
  Empordà): 53, 107, 131, 180, 242
  lake of: 241
Castellrosselló, archaeological site
  (Roussillon): 189
Castellví de la Marca, archaeological
  site, castle (Alt Penedès): 80, 82,
  205, 311, 315
Castile, Kingdom of: 18, 71, 107, 277,
  362
  Crown of: 20
Catalan-Aragonese Crown (or Crown
  of Aragon): 20
  King, monarch: 17, 90, 122–23, 174,
  240, 249, 270, 277, 293
  Kingdom of: 18, 61
Catalunya del Nord, see Pyrénées-
  Orientales
Caulès, archaeological site (Caldes de
  Malavella, La Selva): 35, 91
Cerc (Alt Urgell): 332
Cerdanya, region and basin: 13, 25,
  13, 27, 37, 38, 73, 92, 143, 190, 200,
  210, 225, 239, 243, 250, 258, 260–61,
  271–72, 275, 282, 290–91, 294, 297,
  301, 304, 318–19, 322, 349, 358
  count of: 328
  County of: 13, 92, 271, 295–96, 304,
  338–40
  plain of: 199, 290
Cervera (Segarra): 109, 132, 175, 180, 361

Cinca, River: 17, 147, 206, 228, 231–32,
  237, 318, 358
Clairvaux, Cistercian abbey
  (France): 70
Claror, valley of (Andorra): 262;
  see also Madriu
Cluses, Les (or La Clusa)
  (Vallespir): 189, 284, 329
Coaner, castle (Sant Mateu de Bages,
  Bages): 85
Coastal Range (Catalonia): 266
Collserola mountain range
  (Barcelonès): 238, 317
Conca de Barberà, comarca: 70, 72,
  123, 190, 205, 316, 348
Conflent, comarca: 13, 36, 37, 252, 256,
  284, 318
  County of: 13
Corb, river (or Riu Corb): 203, 206
Corbie, monastery (France): 193, 245
Corbières Massif (Occitania,
  France): 21
Córdoba (Spain): 17
  Caliphate of: 17, 85, 170, 217
  Emirate of: 15, 18, 85, 108
Cornellà de la Ribera (Fr. Corneilla-
  la-Rivière) (Roussillon): 54, 324
Cornellà del Bèrcol (Fr. Corneilla-del-
  Vercol) (Roussillon): 284, 324
Cortsaví (Fr. Corsavy) (Vallespir): 93,
  99–102, 104–05
Cotlliure, castrum (Fr. Collioure)
  (Roussillon): 80
Crown of Aragon, see Catalan-
  Aragonese Crown
Cruïlles (Baix Empordà): 62, 89, 155
Cubelles (Garraf): 267, 275
Cuixà, monastery (Fr. Cuxa)
  (Codalet, Conflent): 11, 29
Curullada, La (Granyanella,
  Segarra): 101

Devil's Bridge, *see Pont del Diable* (Martorell)

Domeny (from La. *dominium*) (Gironès): 329

Durro (Alta Ribagorça): 322

Ebro, River (Ct. L'Ebre): 16, 72, 144, 170, 182, 229, 237–38, 272, 358
delta: 144, 255, 269

Ègara (Terrassa, Vallès Occidental), bishopric of: 297, 302

Eixalada, monastery (Canavelles, Conflent): 64

Elna (Fr. Elne) (Roussillon): 163, 282, 284, 340
bishopric, diocese: 49, 54, 57, 297

Empordà, region: 13, 62, 74, 94, 122, 189, 198–99, 200, 216, 240–41, 249, 255–56, 264, 266–67, 273, 275, 280, 287, 289, 296, 325, 354, 358, 362; *see also* Alt Empordà, Baix Empordà
Empordà plain: 296

Empúries (Alt Empordà): 163, 265, 274, 325
bishopric: 296–97
County of: 13, 131, 249, 296
Emporiae: 189
necropolis: 44

England: 28, 36, 73, 107, 120, 128, 133, 153, 191, 193, 246, 253, 255, 280, 294, 301, 318, 321, 331, 334, 344, 359, 362

Enveig (Alta Cerdanya): 261, 271, 349, 354
mountain of: 261, 271

Espaçoles, Les, archaeological site (Tuïr, Roussillon): 135, 142

Esparreguera (Baix Llobregat): 155

Espluga de Francolí, L' (Conca de Barberà): 109–10, 204, 331, 348

Esplugallonga, L', archarological site, cave (Pallars Jussà): 157–58

Esplús (or Esplucs) (La Llitera): 144

Espot (Pallars Sobirà): 40, 60, 98, 261, 306
Espot, valley of: 306
Espot Obago: 42

Esquerda, L', archaeological site (Roda de Ter, Osona): 78, 80, 81, 91, 175

Estanh Redon (Val d'Aran): 250, 261

Estany Redó, L' (Pallars Sobirà): 261, 274

Estany, L', collegiate church (Moianès): 68

Europe: 26, 49, 50, 65, 69, 78, 79, 90, 92, 99, 107, 108, 114, 117, 120, 127, 132, 135, 138, 151, 155, 185, 189, 200, 202, 218, 231, 264, 274, 286, 293, 321, 329, 335, 341, 343, 355–56, 359–60, 362
central: 248
eastern: 108
southern: 18, 33, 217

Fabregada, archaeological site (Pallars Jussà): 250, 252, 256

Fals, castle (Fonollosa, Bages): 85

Falset (Priorat): 315

Farners (Santa Coloma de Farners, La Selva): 89

Farrera (or Ferrera) (Pallars Sobirà): 250

Fenouillèdes, *comarca* (Oc. Fenolheda) (France): 318

Fenouillet, castle (Oc. Fenolhet) (Fenouillèdes): 90

Figueres (Alt Empordà): 111–12

Finestres, castle (Sant Aniol de Finestres, Garrotxa): 103, 104, 123

Fluvià basin (Garrotxa): 296

Foixà (Baix Empordà): 100

Fondespatla (Matarranya): 112

INDEX OF PLACE NAMES

Fontfroide, Cistercian abbey
(Oc. Fontfreja) (France): 71
Fontjanina (Montanui, Ribagorça): 73
Fontova, castle (Sp. Fantova)
(Ribagorça): 82
Font-rubí (Alt Penedès): 313, 315
castle: 85
Forques (Fr. Fourques)
(Roussillon): 294
Fortià (Alt Empordà): 198, 289, 325
Fortianell (Alt Empordà): 198
Fraga (Baix Cinca, Aragon): 15, 31, 50,
109, 147, 165, 192, 217
France: 25, 28, 33, 37, 44, 46, 50, 59, 90,
153, 162, 189, 191, 194, 202, 255, 274,
279, 287, 293, 321, 334, 341, 359, 362
Kingdom: 98
France, northern: 135, 193, 343
Francolí, River: 198
Freixe, El (Piera, Anoia): 224
Fumanya (Berguedà): 328

Gaià, River (Catalonia): 70, 71, 108,
240, 296
Galicia: 209, 212, 362
Gallifa, castle (Vallès Occidental): 326
Gardeny (Lleida, Segrià): 74, 89, 90, 168
commandery, Templar castle: 72, 148
Garraf, *comarca*: 241, 275, 287
Garrigues, Les, *comarca*: 209
Garrotxa, La, *comarca*: 13, 56, 133–34,
153, 264, 361
Gascony (France): 16, 21, 25, 36, 37, 43,
126, 188, 191, 223, 259, 307, 317, 319,
362–63
Gaul: 53, 246, 269, 327
northern: 245
southern: 24, 330
Gelida (Alt Penedès): 313–14
castle of: 326
Ger (Cerdanya): 291
Gerb (Os de Balaguer, Noguera): 110

Germany, Germanic countries: 25,
107, 334, 362
Gerri de la Sal (Pallars Sobirà): 74,
124, 254
monastery: 11, 64, 66, 255
Girona (Gironès): 11, 17, 19, 65, 82, 111,
161, 163, 178, 180–82, 184, 189, 195,
209, 238, 282, 287, 303, 310, 340,
351, 360
archdeaconry: 155
bishopric, diocese: 49, 54, 55, 57,
155, 297
cathedral: 131
plain of: 264, 310
Gironella (Berguedà): 307
Gironès, *comarca*: 56, 73, 74, 134, 200,
358,
Gombrèn (Ripollès): 112, 296
Granada, La (Alt Penedès): 284, 355
Granollers (Vallès Oriental): 127,
172–73, 180, 361
Granyena de Segarra (Segarra): 110
Guàrdia, La (Castell de Mur, Pallars
Jussà): 99, 102
new town: 103
Güel (Ribagorça): 212, 303
Guissona (Segarra): 53, 109, 163, 190
Gurri, hamlet (Taradell, Osona): 134,
153

Heures, Les, farmstead (La Quar,
Berguedà): 134, 140–41, 308
Hispania: 14, 19, 188
Citerior: 189
Hispanic March, *see* territories and
districts
or Al-Andalus: 85

Iberian Peninsula, Iberia: 16, 17, 24,
44, 171, 189, 209, 250, 329
Iesso: 190; *see also* Guissona
Ilerda: 190; *see also* Lleida

INDEX OF PLACE NAMES

Illa (Roussillon): 239
Iran (Alta Ribagorça): 322
Irgo (Alta Ribagorça): 322
Isàvena, River (Ribagorça): 64, 288
Isil, valley of (Pallars Sobirà): 306
Isona (Pallars Jussà): 163, 190, 192, 340
    Roman city (*Aeso*): 297
Isòvol (Cerdanya): 291
Italy, Italian state. Italian regions: 18,
    22, 34, 46, 78, 92, 99, 107–08, 115,
    117, 120, 127, 133, 192, 194, 249, 274
    northern: 135, 191, 200–21, 223, 245,
    266, 276, 329, 362
Iulia Lybica: 190; *see also* Llívia
Ivars, lake (Pla d'Urgell): 268
Ivars de Noguera (Noguera): 205

Jonqueres (Sabadell, Vallès
    Occidental): 230
Jusseu (Ribagorça): 254

Languedoc (France): 16, 18, 19, 22, 46,
    90, 123, 126, 135, 140, 149, 230, 240,
    244, 246, 258, 272–73, 298, 362, 363
Lavansa (or La Vansa), valley of (Alt
    Urgell): 339
Lillet, valley of (Berguedà): 296, 304
Llacuna, La (Anoia): 103, 105, 128
    Benedictine priory: 103
Llastarri (Tremp, Pallars Jussà;
    Sopeira, Ribagorça): 212
Lleida (Segrià): 13, 15, 17, 19, 25, 31, 47,
    70, 72, 74, 83, 100, 108–10, 115, 126,
    144, 146–48, 163, 165, 167, 170–71,
    178–84, 190, 213, 219, 221, 228,
    231–34, 236–37, 242–43, 247–48,
    250, 256, 268, 272, 274–75, 287, 289,
    297, 303, 316–17, 319, 327, 341–42,
    345, 348, 354, 358, 360;
    conquest of (1149): 17, 234
    diocese, bishopric: 94, 146, 297
    madīna Lārida: 165, 232

    plain of: 16, 189, 268, 289
    region of: 54; *see also* Segrià,
      comarca
    taifa of: 17, 85, 165, 170, 297
Llenguaderes, Les (Capçanes,
    Priorat): 221–23
Lliçà d'Amunt (Vallès Oriental): 329,
    338
Lliçà d'Avall (or Lliçà de Vall) (Vallès
    Oriental): 329
Llimiana (Pallars Jussà): 82, 91
Llitera, La, *comarca*: 144, 254, 272, 287
Llívia (*Iulia Libica*) (Cerdanya): 143,
    163, 190, 290, 340
    castrum: 80
    pagus: 290–91
Llobera (Solsonès): 258
Llobregat, River (Catalonia): 15, 19,
    63, 64, 90, 108, 128, 240, 266, 282,
    288–89, 296, 314
    delta (Baix Llobregat): 266, 274
Llordà (Pallars Jussà): 21, 88, 90
Lluçars, castle (Tolba, Ribagorça): 21,
    88, 89
Lord, valley of (Solsonès): 73, 304, 339
Lòria (Andorra): 139; *see also* Sant
    Julià de Lòria

Madremanya (Gironès): 65, 73
Madriu valley (Andorra): 262–63, 274–75
Maella (Matarranya): 111–12
Malanyeu (Berguedà): 303, 328
Maldanell (Urgell), castle: 206
Maleses, Les, monastery, troglodytic
    (Pallars Jussà): 157
Mallol, El (Vall d'en Bas, Garrotxa): 104
    castle of: 361
Mallols, Els, archaeological site
    (Vallès Occidental): 35
Mallorca (or Majorca): 17, 204, 213,
    227, 232, 247; *see also* Majorca
    kings of: 239

INDEX OF PLACE NAMES   437

Manresa (Bages): 238, 240, 282, 362
County of: 13, 28, 54, 100, 102,
    296–97, 311
walls: 240
Marcovau (Foradada,
    Noguera): 219–20
Maresme, *comarca*: 13, 190, 241
Marqueixanes (Fr. Marquixanes)
    (Conflent): 73
Martorell (Baix Llobregat): 127–28,
    132, 172, 289
Mas de Bondia (Montornès,
    Segarra): 112, 114
Mas de Melons (Castelldans,
    Garrigues): 148, 208–09
Mascançà (Urgell, Pla d'Urgell): 268,
    327
Masdéu, El, Templar commandery
    (Roussillon): 72, 74, 240, 284
Massalcoreig (Segrià): 233, 326
Mataró (old: Alarona, Maresme): 340,
    362
Matxerri (Castelldans,
    Garrigues): 145, 148, 208
Maurà (Enveig, Alta Cerdanya): 261,
    271
Menàrguens (Noguera): 110, 146, 234,
    341, 351, 354
Meritxell, sanctuary (Andorra): 74
Merlès stream: 141, 246, 255, 307
Milany, castle (Vidrà, Osona): 104–05
Miralles, castle (Santa Maria de
    Miralles, Anoia): 86, 311
Miravet, Templar castle (Ribera
    d'Ebre): 72, 74
Molins de Rei (Baix Llobregat): 317
Molivedre, old mill (Garrotxa): 244
Monells (Baix Empordà): 317
Monells (Vallès Oriental): 244
Montblanc (Conca de Barberà): 98,
    111–12, 122–23, 128, 132, 172, 175,
    249, 256, 348

walls of: 249
Montbui, castle (Santa Margarida de
    Montbui, Anoia): 85–86
Montcada (Vallès Occidental): 238, 317
Montclar (Berguedà): 91
Montclús, hamlet, archaeological
    site (Santa Maria de Merlès,
    Berguedà): 136, 140, 143, 156
Montfalcó Murallat (Les Oluges,
    Segarra): 98
Montgarri (Val d'Aran): 306
Montmell, castle (Baix Penedès): 108
Montnegre (Vallès Oriental,
    Maresme): 262
Mont-rebei gorge (Pallars Jussà,
    Ribagorça): 64
Montsec, mountain range (La
    Noguera, Pallars Jussà): 74, 130,
    252, 268, 288
Montseny, massif (Catalonia): 127,
    203, 209, 262, 342, 355
Montserrat, mountain range
    (Catalonia): 74
Montsià, *comarca*: 117, 269
Monzón (Montsó in medieval times)
    (Aragón): 206, 318
Mosoll (Cerdanya): 73
Muig, hamlet (Sant Joan de les
    Abadesses, Ripollès): 137, 139
Muntanyes de Prades, county
    (since 1324): 315
Mur (Pallars Jussà)
    castle, archaeological site (Pallars
    Jussà): 21, 88, 89
    collegiate church, Santa Maria de
    Mur: 68, 89
Murcia (Spain): 47, 229
Muret (Occitania, France): 17, 90
    battle of (1213): 363

Narbonne (Oc. Narbona)
    (France): 16, 190, 284

INDEX OF PLACE NAMES

Nèfol (Bellver de Cerdanya,
 Cerdanya): 73
New Catalonia (Ct. *Catalunya
 Nova*): 16, 18, 19, 24, 26, 32, 47, 71,
 72, 93, 94, 99, 104–05, 107–10, 144,
 149, 181, 198, 201, 210, 220, 228, 247,
 256, 261, 272, 297, 303, 317, 326, 358,
 362–63; *see also* Old Catalonia
Nimes (France): 189, 217
Noguera, *comarca*: 253, 341
Noguera Pallaresa, River: 64, 66, 130,
 288, 306
Noguera Ribagorçana, River: 40, 64,
 130, 206, 212, 231–32, 234, 288–89,
 306
Núria, sanctuary (Ripollès): 74

Obiols, necropolis (Avià, Berguedà): 44
Occitania, Occitan lands, region: 16,
 17, 20, 22, 78, 90, 107, 110, 115, 117,
 120, 126, 132–33, 140, 192, 210, 240,
 249, 253, 297, 301, 329, 355, 363
Oceja (Alta Cerdanya): 260
Ofegats (or Els Ofegats)
 (Urgell): 218–19
Old Catalonia (Ct. *Catalunya
 Vella*): 15, 16, 18, 19, 53, 64, 72, 74,
 99, 104, 110, 134, 149, 151, 182, 199,
 209–10, 228–29, 238, 242, 244–45,
 247, 256, 258, 272–73, 287, 289, 293,
 297, 299, 303, 306, 310, 313, 319, 324,
 326, 329, 333, 335, 337–38, 355, 358,
 363; *see also* New Catalonia
Olèrdola, *oppidum*, castle,
 archaeological site (Alt
 Penedès): 80, 82, 157, 311
 district of: 311
Oliana (Alt Urgell), castle: 108, 288
 gorge of: 288
Olopte (Isòvol, Cerdanya): 38
Olot (Garrotxa): 13, 112, 114, 120, 275, 362

Olvan (Berguedà): 307
 castle: 307
 parish: 307
Ordino (Andorra): 151
 parish: 139
Organyà (Alt Urgell): 69, 74, 112, 114
 collegiate church, Santa Maria
 d'Organyà: 68, 75, 113–14
Orihuela (Oriola in Middle Ages)
 (Valencia): 232
Oroners, settlement inside a cave
 (Camarasa, Noguera): 157
Orriols (Tamarit de Llitera,
 Aragon): 146
Osona, *comarca*: 13, 57, 62, 82, 133–34,
 190, 258, 297, 322
 County of: 13, 88, 246, 329, 339–40
Ovarra, monastery (Ribagorça): 64;
 see also Santa Maria d'Ovarra

País Valencià, see Valencia
Palamós (Baix Empordà): 112, 120
Palau de Llierca (Garrotxa): 244
Palau dels Reis de Mallorca
 (Perpignan, Roussillon): 239
Palau-sator (Baix Empordà): 92, 94
Palau-solità i Plegamans (Vallès
 Occidental): 197, 302
 palace of *Sulayṭan*: 326
Pallars, region: 37, 62, 82, 261, 287–88,
 322, 340, 357, 362
 count of: 306
 County of: 54, 88, 97, 99, 102, 296,
 297, 303, 311, 337
 feudal wars: 54
Pallars Jussà, *comarca*: 27, 88, 190, 192,
 250, 253, 283, 290, 292, 297, 358, 360
Pallars Sobirà, *comarca*: 40, 97, 261,
 322–23
 valleys of: 304
Palma de Mallorca (Mallorca): 165, 180

Parlavà (Baix Empordà): 299, 325
Pau (from *pagus*) (Alt Empordà): 329
Peguera (Berguedà): 262
Penedès, region: 54, 70, 82, 157, 190,
    201, 222, 229, 274, 284, 287, 290, 311,
    358, 362; *see also* Alt Penedès, Baix
    Penedès
Peralada (Alt Empordà): 131, 173, 180
    County of: 13, 296, 338
Peralta de la Sal (La Llitera): 254;
    see also salt *in* Index of Subjects
Perpignan (Ct. Perpinyà)
    (Roussillon): 11, 13, 16, 20, 180, 181,
    183, 184, 238–39, 248, 360, 362
Pertegàs, necropolis, archeological
    site (Calders, Moianès): 44
Pertús, El (Vallespir): 189
Perxa, Coll de la, mountain pass
    (Conflent, Alta Cerdanya): 290
Pesillà de la Ribera (Fr. Pézilla-la-
    Rivière) (Roussillon): 29, 44, 54,
    57–59, 324
Peyrepertuse, castle (Oc.
    Pèirapertusa) (Fenouillèdes): 90
Pinyana, Canal de (or *Séquia de
    Segrià*): 234, 345
Pla d'Almatà, archaeological site
    (Balaguer, Noguera): 170–71
Pla de l'Orri (Enveig, Alta
    Cerdanya): 261, 271
Pla de les Salines (Ripollès, Alta
    Cerdanya): 260; *see also* pollen
    analyses *in* Index of Subjects
Po River plain (Italy): 188, 194, 200, 274
Pobla de Lillet, La (Berguedà): 112, 250
Pobla de Segur, La (Pallars Jussà): 112,
    123
Poblet, Cistercian monastery (Conca
    de Barberà): 11, 69–71, 74, 260, 271,
    331, 348; *see also* Santa Maria de
    Poblet
    inner court: 71

Polinyà (Vallès Occidental): 197, 302
Pollestres (Roussillon): 284
Pont del Diable (devil's
    bridge) (Martorell, Baix
    Llobregat): 128, 289
Ponts (La Noguera)
    castle: 85
    collegiate church: 68
Porqueres, necropolis (Pla de
    l'Estany): 44
Port, El, mountain of (or Els Ports de
    Tortosa-Beseit): 171, 238
Portugal: 136, 202, 223, 272, 362
    Kingdom of: 18, 107
Prada de Conflent (Fr. Prades)
    (Conflent): 54
Prades, mountain (Baix Camp,
    Priorat): 260, 267
Prats de Molló (Vallespir): 241, 252, 270
Pre-Pyrenean mountain range
    (Catalonia): 260, 288
Priorat, *comarca*: 221, 252, 290, 292, 351
Provence (France): 16, 133
    County of: 16
Puig Rom, *castrum*, archaeological
    site (Roses, Alt Empordà): 80
Puigcerdà (Cerdanya): 13, 112, 132, 172,
    176–77, 180, 238–39, 361–62
    canal of: 239
Pyrenees, Pyrenean lands, region: 16,
    19, 21, 22, 31, 37, 40, 85, 94, 140, 153,
    188, 190, 203, 243, 247–48, 251, 256,
    258, 260–61, 263, 271–72, 274, 284,
    287–88, 290, 294–95, 303–05, 307,
    323, 354, 363
Pyrénées-Orientales (Ct. *Catalunya
    del Nord*) (France): 13, 29

Quar, La (Berguedà): 308
    parish: 307
Quart (Bolvir, Cerdanya): 291, 329

INDEX OF PLACE NAMES

Ràpita, La (Montsià, Noguera, Alt Penedès): 327

Reixac (Vallès Occidental): 329

Reus (Baix Camp): 112, 172, 176, 361
castle: 176

Rhône, River: 272, 274
valley: 188, 194

Ribagorça, region: 19, 36, 37, 82, 85, 212, 237, 261–62, 271–72, 289, 307, 318, 358
count of: 297
County of: 13, 88, 296, 303–04, 311, 337

Ribes, castle (Garraf): 88, 311; see also Sant Pere de Ribes

Ribes de Freser, valley of (Ripollès): 296, 304

Rifà (Ar. *rīhā*, mill) (Vallès Oriental): 244, 247, 256

Riner, castle (Solsonès): 90

Ripoll (Ripollès): 64, 111, 124
benedictine monastery: 11, 74, 120, 188, 193, 241; see also Santa Maria de Ripoll
valley of: 304

Ripoll, River (Vallès): 229–30, 241

Ripollès, *comarca*: 36, 37, 210, 260, 271, 273, 296–97, 340

Ripollet (Vallès Occidental): 326

Roc d'Enclar, *castrum*, archaeological site (Andorra): 80, 81, 263

Roc de Pampeluna, archaeological site (France): 78

Roc de Sant Urbici (Serrateix, Berguedà): 65

Roca d'Albera, La (Fr. Laroque-des-Albères) (Roussillon): 63, 122–23
castle: 96, 97

Rocabertí (Alt Empordà): 327
Viscounty of: 249

Rocallaura (Vallbona de les Monges, Urgell): 149, 330

Roda d'Isàvena (Ribagorça): 212, 340

bishopric, diocese: 28, 54, 297
castle: 82

Ropidera (Conflent): 98, 354

Roses (Alt Empordà): 66, 326
monastery: 124; see also Santa Maria de Roses

Rosselló (France), see Roussillon

Rosselló (Segrià): 148

Roussillon, *comarca* (Ct. *Rosselló*): 13, 17, 19, 33, 48, 50, 53, 57, 62, 74, 90, 135, 189, 229, 240, 242, 252, 255, 266, 275, 280, 289, 294, 296, 298, 300–01, 318, 329
County of: 13, 324, 338
mills: 255
plain: 239

Rubí (Vallès Occidental): 62

Rufea (Lleida, Segrià): 232–33

Rupià (Baix Empordà): 299, 325

Ruscino: 189; see also Castellrosselló (Roussillon)

Sabadell (Vallès Occidental): 229

Safranals, Els, archaeological site, Islamic *burğ* (Fraga, Baix Cinca): 47, 83, 147

Saig, mountain pass of (Cerdanya): 290

Sallent, El (Santa Pau, Garrotxa): 153–54, 159

Salses (Roussillon): 17

Sanata (Llinars del Vallès, Vallès Oriental): 209, 326, 355

Sant Andreu de Lleida (Segrià), parish: 165–66, 169, 178; see also Lleida

Sant Andreu de Sureda, monastery (Roussillon): 63, 65

Sant Boi de Llobregat (Baix Llobregat): 62

Sant Corneli and Sant Cebrià d'Ordino (Andorra): 139

INDEX OF PLACE NAMES 441

Sant Cugat del Vallès, monastery
(Vallès Occidental): 11, 63, 66, 74,
215, 297
Sant Esteve d'Arles (Vallespir), parish
church: 67
Sant Esteve d'en Bas (Garrotxa): 56
Sant Esteve de Banyoles, monastery
(Pla de l'Estany): 66, 264;
see also Banyoles
Sant Esteve de Granollers (Vallès
Oriental): 173; see also Granollers
Sant Esteve de Vila-sacra (Alt
Empordà): 300; see also Vila-sacra
Sant Feliu de Girona: 182
Sant Feliu de Guíxols (Baix
Empordà): 120, 124, 128
monastery: 65, 112, 125
necropolis (Baix Empordà): 44
Sant Feliu de Pesillà (Roussillon): 57, 59
Sant Feliu de Sort (Pallars Sobirà): 97
Sant Feliu de Tanyà (La Roca
d'Albera, Roussillon): 97
Sant Feliu de Vilajuïga (Alt
Empordà): 215; see also Vilajuïga
Sant Fruitós de Bages (Bages): 57
Sant Genís de Fontanes, monastery
(Roussillon): 63
Sant Genís de Torroella (Torroella de
Montgrí, Baix Empordà): 120
Sant Jaume de Cortsaví (Vallespir): 101
Sant Jaume de Perpinyà
(Roussillon): 183–84
Sant Joan d'Àger (Noguera): 130;
see also Àger
Sant Joan de les Abadesses, female
monastery (Ripollès): 64, 66, 74,
111–12, 115, 124, 128, 307
valley: 134–36, 304
Sant Joan de Lleida (Sant Joan de la
Plaça): 165–67; see also Lleida
Sant Joan de Mollet (Gironès): 195,
222–23

Sant Joan de Perpinyà (Roussillon): 183
Sant Joan de Pladecorts (Fr. Saint-
Jean-Pla-de-Corts, Vallespir): 100,
105, 111–12
Sant Julià de Cerdanyola
(Berguedà): 203
Sant Julià de Lòria, archaeological site
(Andorra): 140, 250
Sant Julià de Ramis, castrum,
archaeological site (Gironès): 82
Sant Julià de Vilatorta (Osona): 56
Sant Julià del Mont, monastery
(Garrotxa): 65
Sant Llorenç, castle of (Àger,
Noguera): 288
Sant Llorenç de Lleida
(Segrià): 165–66, 168;
see also Lleida
Sant Llorenç de Morunys
(Solsonès): 111–12
Sant Llorenç del Munt, monastery
(Vallès Occidental): 65
Sant Llorenç prop Bagà, monastery
(Berguedà): 64
Sant Lluc d'Ulldecona
(Montsià): 117–18;
see also Ulldecona
Sant Martí de Cortsaví (Fr.
Corsavy) (Vallespir): 62, 101;
see also Cortsaví
Sant Martí de Lleida, parish
(Segrià): 165–66; see also Lleida
Sant Martí del Canigó, monastery
(Conflent): 65
Sant Martí Sarroca (Alt
Penedès): 284, 311, 355
Sant Mateu de Maestrat (Baix
Maestrat, Valencia): 272
Sant Mateu de Perpinyà
(Roussillon): 183–84;
see also Perpignan

Sant Menna (Sentmenat, Vallès Occidental): 74

Sant Miquel de Cuixà, monastery (Conflent): 27, 63; *see also* Cuixà

Sant Pau del Camp, monastery (Barcelonès): 65

Sant Pau of Lleida, parish (Segrià): 166; *see also* Lleida

Sant Pere d'Àger, collegiate church (Noguera): 130

Sant Pere d'Eixalada (Conflent): 64; *see* Eixalada

Sant Pere d'Olopte (Isòvol, Cerdanya): 38

Sant Pere de Camprodon (Ripollès): 273; *see also* Camprodon

Sant Pere de Casserres, monastery (Osona): 63

Sant Pere de Galligants, monastery (Gironès): 65, 182

Sant Pere de la Curullada (Segarra): 101

Sant Pere de la Portella, monastery (Berguedà): 308

Sant Pere de les Puelles, feminine monastery (Barcelona): 65

Sant Pere de Ribes (Garraf): 88, 108 castle: 85

Sant Pere de Ripoll (Ripollès): 66; *see also* Ripoll

Sant Pere de Roda (L'Esquerda, Osona): 81; *see also* Esquerda, L'

Sant Pere de Rodes, monastery (Alt Empordà): 11, 65, 66, 241

Sant Pere de Sant Cugat del Vallès (Vallès Occidental): 66; *see also* Sant Cugat del Vallès

Sant Pere de Sora, parish (Osona): 339

Sant Pere of Santpedor (Bages): 283

Sant Pol de Mar, monastery (Maresme): 65

Sant Ruf, collegiate church (Segrià): 233

Sant Sadurní de Pesillà, necropolis (Roussillon): 44, 58; *see also* Pesillà de la Ribera

Sant Urbici, rock of (Berguedà): 73

Sant Vicenç d'Àger (Noguera): 130; *see also* Àger

Sant Vicenç de Cardona, collegiate church (Bages): 68; *see also* Cardona

Sant Vicenç de Jonqueres (Vallès Occidental): 229–30

Sant Vicenç del Sallent, parish (Santa Pau, Garrotxa): 140, 153, 159

Sant Vicenç dels Horts (Baix Llobregat): 61, 62

Santa Cecília d'Altimiris, archaeological site (Sant Esteve de la Sarga, Pallars Jussà): 64; *see also* Altimiris

Santa Cecília de Montserrat, monastery (Bages): 64; *see also* Montserrat

Santa Cecília de Senet (Vilaller, Alta Ribagorça): 40

Santa Coloma, church (Andorra): 81

Santa Coloma d'Àger (Noguera): 130 *see also* Àger

Santa Coloma de Queralt (Conca de Barberà): 94, 107, 129–30

Santa Creu de Llagunes, archaeological site (Soriguera, Pallars Sobirà): 35, 91, 142

Santa Creu de Rodes (or Santa Helena), archaeological site (Alt Empordà): 66

Santa Cristina d'Aro, necropolis (Baix Empordà): 44

Santa Llogaia d'Espot (Pallars Sobirà): 41

INDEX OF PLACE NAMES 443

Santa Magdalena de Lleida
(Segrià): 165–69, 178
Santa Margarida de Martorell,
archaeological site (Baix
Llobregat): 52
Santa Maria d'Alaó, monastery
(Ribagorça): 11, 64, 212, 288
Santa Maria d'Àneu (Pallars
Sobirà): 304, 306
Santa Maria d'Arles (Vallespir): 66,
67; see also Arles
Santa Maria d'Olvan (Berguedà): 74,
307
Santa Maria d'Organyà, collegiate
church (Alt Urgell): 69;
see also Organyà
Santa Maria d'Ovarra, monastery
(Ribagorça): 64
Santa Maria de Castelldefels,
monastery (Baix Llobregat): 65
Santa Maria de Castelló
d'Empúries (Alt Empordà): 13;
see also Castelló d'Empúries
Santa Maria de Gerri (Pallars
Sobirà): 288; see also Gerri
Santa Maria de Lleida, cathedral
(Segrià): 165, 178; see also Lleida
Santa Maria de Lord (Solsonès): 73,
304
Santa Maria de Mijaran (Val
d'Aran): 73
Santa Maria de Montblanc (Conca de
Barberà): 123; see also Montblanc
Santa Maria de Poblet (Conca de
Barberà): 70; see also Poblet
Santa Maria de Ripoll, monastery
(Ripollès): 64, 66; see also Ripoll
Santa Maria de Roses, monastery (Alt
Empordà): 66
Santa Maria de Serrateix,
monastery (Berguedà): 63, 154;
see also Serrateix

Santa Maria de Solsona
(Solsonès): 308–10
Santa Maria de Talló, archaeological
site: 199; see also Talló
Santa Maria de Valldigna, Cistercian
abbey (La Safor, Valencia): 70
Santa Maria de Vilagrassa
(Urgell): 115; see also Vilagrassa
Santa Maria de Vilosiu (Cercs,
Berguedà): 156; see also Vilosiu
Santa Maria dels Turers (Banyoles,
Pla de l'Estany): 66;
see also Banyoles
Santa Oliva (Baix Penedès): 214
Santa Pau (La Garrotxa): 63, 111–12,
122–23, 128, 132
castle: 103, 104
valley of: 304
Santa Perpètua de Gaià (Pontils,
Conca de Barberà): 21
castle: 85–87
Santes Creus, Cistercian monastery
(Alt Camp): 11, 69–71, 74, 240, 271
Santiga, archaeological site (Santa
Perpètua de Mogoda, Vallès
Occidental): 35, 302
Santpedor (Bages): 59, 283
Segarra, comarca: 86, 101, 213, 283, 287,
290
Segarres (or Sagarres) (Baixa
Ribagorça): 272
Segre, River: 64, 165, 170, 180, 199, 220,
231–35, 286, 288, 290, 295, 351, 358
Segrià, comarca: 72, 144, 146, 148, 234,
250, 290
plain of: 72
Séquia de Segrià (or Canal de
Pinyana): 234–35
Segura, rock of (Pallars Sobirà): 306
Selva del Camp, La (Baix Camp): 98,
112, 115–16

Selva, La, *comarca*: 35, 89, 91, 155, 290
   archdeaconry: 155
Senet (Vilaller, Alta Ribagorça): 40
Sénia, La, River (Catalonia,
   Valencia): 17, 318, 363
Sentmenat (Vallès Occidental): 225,
   289
   Can Palau, archaeological site: 35
   necropolis: 44
Septimania (or Gothia, the Gothic
   March): 327, 329, 363
Serradar, El, archaeological site (Sant
   Pere Pescador, Alt Empordà): 35
Serrateix (Berguedà): 73, 154;
   see also Santa Maria de Serrateix
Seu d'Urgell, La (Alt Urgell): 163, 282,
   307, 317, 332, 340, 362
Seu Vella of Lleida: 166–67, 179;
   see also Santa Maria de Lleida
   cathedral: 167
Siurana, Islamic fortification
   (Priorat): 82–84, 110, 315
Sobrestany (Baix Empordà): 265
Solana, La, archaeological site
   (Cubelles, Garraf): 35
Solibernat, archaeological site, Islamic
   burǧ (Torres de Segre, Segrià): 47,
   83, 147, 272
Solsona (Solsonès): 86, 282, 308, 310, 339
Solsonès, *comarca*: 134, 155, 190
Sort (Pallars Sobirà): 97, 340
Sorts, Les (Capçanes, Priorat): 222
Subirats, castle (Alt Penedès): 85

Tabac (Segrià): 148, 327
Talló (Cerdanya): 199, 295
   pagus: 290, 295
Talteüll, castle (Fr. Tautavel)
   (Roussillon): 90
Tamarit de Llitera (La Llitera): 146
Tarabau (Baronia de Rialb,
   Noguera): 80, 82

   castrum: 81
   Tarabald, Frankish name: 82
Taradell (Osona): 56, 151–52, 154
Targasona (Alta Cerdanya): 210
Tarragona (Tarragonès): 11, 13, 70,
   108–11, 116, 163, 179, 184, 189, 198,
   228, 267, 296, 354, 360, 362
   archdiocese: 116, 297
   chamberlain of the church of: 176
   region: 54
   Tarraco: 189, 198, 302
Tàrrega (Urgell): 109–11, 115, 132, 316
Taüll (Alta Ribagorça): 322
Tec, River (Conflent, Roussillon): 67,
   288
Ter, River (Catalonia): 63, 64, 66, 81,
   195, 241, 288, 296
   basin: 296
Tet, La, River (Roussillon): 64, 288–89
Timorell (Castelldans, Garrigues): 148
Tivenys (Baix Ebre): 327
Toló, castle (Gavet de la Conca,
   Pallars Jussà): 82
Toluges (Fr. Toulouges)
   (Roussillon): 53, 62
Tona, castle (Osona): 87
Torre Bofilla, archaeological
   site (Bétera, Camp de Túria,
   Valencia): 47
Torre de la Força, Islamic tower
   (Torre del Caragol, Artesa de
   Segre, Noguera): 82
Torre Pallaresa (now Torre-serona,
   Segrià): 148
Torrefarrera (Segrià): 146, 148, 236,
   345, 348
Torregrossa (Pla d'Urgell): 148
Torrelameu (Noguera): 148
   Séquia de: 234
Torres de Segre (Segrià): 232
Torroella de Montgrí (Baix Empordà): 112,
   120, 122, 128, 132, 265

INDEX OF PLACE NAMES 445

Tortosa (Baix Ebre): 13, 15, 17, 19, 25, 26, 47, 83, 108–10, 144, 161, 165, 180, 182, 228–29, 232, 237–38, 242, 247, 255, 272, 297, 303, 316, 319, 327, 358, 360
  bishopric of: 297
  conquest of (1148): 17
  Madīna Ṭurṭūša: 170
  region: 54
  Taifa of: 17, 85
Tossa de Dalt, archaeological site, necropolis (Rosselló, Segrià): 46
Toulouse (Oc. Tolosa) (Occitania, France): 36
Tresponts, monastery (Alt Urgell): 64, 288
Tuïr (Fr. Thuir) (Roussillon): 61, 135, 239
Tuscany (Italy): 92, 120, 334

Ullastret (Baix Empordà), lake of: 241
Ulldecona (Montsià): 111–12, 117
  castle: 117
Ultramort (Baix Empordà): 299
Ultrera, *castrum* (Roussillon): 80
Urgell (Alt Urgell)
  bishopric, diocese: 54, 139, 297, 304
  count of: 165, 170–71, 206, 213, 220, 228, 234, 303
  County of: 13, 81, 87, 88, 132, 258, 296–97, 303–04, 311, 338–39
Urgell, *comarca*: 219
  plain of: 268
Val d'Aran, *comarca*: 73, 251, 261, 305

Valencia
  city of: 85, 146, 173, 180, 184, 192, 228, 247
  Kingdom of: 223, 282
  Valencia (Ct. *País Valencià*): 14, 16, 18, 25, 47, 70, 82, 107, 117–18, 132, 144, 182, 210, 214, 221–23, 229, 242, 247, 272, 357–58, 363

València d'Àneu (Pallars Sobirà): 306
Vall d'Uixó, La (Plana Baixa, Valencia): 47
Vallbona de les Monges, female Cistercian monastery (Urgell): 69
Valldaura (Vallès Occidental): 71
Valldigna, Cistercian abbey of Santa Maria Valldigna (La Safor, Valencia): 182
Vallès, region: 34, 48, 61, 74, 127, 142, 190, 201, 222, 229–30, 241, 249, 287, 289–90, 302, 315, 329, 358;
  see also Vallès Oriental
Vallès Oriental, *comarca*: 62, 133, 203, 209, 244, 355
Vallespir, *comarca*: 13, 252, 318
  County of: 13
Vallestàvia (Fr. Baillestavy) (Conflent): 101
Vallferosa, castle (Torà, Segarra): 21, 85–87, 104
Vallferrera valley (Pallars Sobirà): 42, 250, 252, 304
Vallfogona de Ripollès (Ripollès): 101, 104–05, 269
Vedella, La, monastery (Berguedà): 64
Vensilló (Els Alamús, Segrià): 145, 272, 289, 303, 326
Verdú (Urgell): 99, 102, 111–12
Viacamp (Ribagorça): 21, 88, 89
  castle: 82
Viana (Navarre): 115
Vic (Osona): 53, 62, 81, 87, 88, 122, 152, 163, 180, 282, 297–98, 340, 362
  bishopric, diocese: 28, 49, 54, 56, 93, 94, 240, 307
  plain of: 56, 311, 357
  see also Osona, County
Vilabertran, collegiate church (Alt Empordà): 53, 68, 74
  Santa Maria de Vilabertan (Alt Empordà): 68, 75

INDEX OF PLACE NAMES

Vilaclara, hamlet, archaeological site (Castellfollit del Boix, Bages): 35, 142

Vilademàger, castle, archaeological site (La Llacuna, Anoia): 85, 99, 102–05

Vilademuls (Pla de l'Estany): 62

Vilafamés (Plana Alta, Valencia): 222–23

Vilafamés, salt beds (Amposta, Montsià): 255

Vilafranca de Conflent (Conflent): 112, 114

Vilafranca del Penedès (Alt Penedès): 98, 112, 127–28, 132, 172, 174–75, 361

Vilagrassa (Urgell): 112, 114–15

Vilajuïga (*Villa Iudica*) (Alt Empordà): 215, 329

Vilallonga del Camp (Tarragonès): 112, 198

Vilalta, OSL analyses (Cabanabona, Noguera): 213

Vilalta, archaeological site (Targasona, Alta Cerdanya): 210

Vilamitjana (Alt Urgell): 91

Vilanova d'Alpicat (now Alpicat) (Segrià): 112

Vilanova de la Barca (Segrià): 100, 112

Vilanova de Raò (Fr. Villeneuve-de-la-Raho) (Roussillon): 284

Vilanova de Segrià (Segrià): 98, 100, 126

Vilanova i la Geltrú (initially Vilanova de Cubelles, Garraf): 111–12, 131–32

Vilarnau, archaeological site (Canet de Rosselló, Roussillon): 44

Vila-rodona (Alt Camp): 240

Vilartolí (Alt Empordà): 134, 327

Vila-sacra (Alt Empordà): 28, 300, 325

Vila-seca (Tortosa, Baix Ebre): 170, 284

Vilatenim (Torre dels Frares, Montcada i Reixac, Vallès Occidental): 326

Vilauba, archaeological site (Camós, Pla de l'Estany): 35

Vilaür (Alt Empordà): 55, 56

Villa Fortunatus, archaeological site (Fraga, Baix Cinca): 50, 74

Vilosiu, farmsteads, archaeological site (Cercs, Berguedà): 143, 149, 157, 303, 327–28

Vilosiu A, *mas*: 155–56

Vilosiu B, *mas*: 155–56, 354

Vimbodí (Conca de Barberà): 110, 326, 348

Vinaixa (Garrigues): 110, 326

Vinallop (Baix Ebre): 326

Vinatesa (Lleida, Segrià): 327

Vinçà (Conflent): 239

Vinfaro (Segrià): 148, 326

Virós, Bosc de, forest (Vallferrera, Pallars Sobirà): 254

Viver, castle (Berguedà): 85

Xerta (Baix Ebre): 229, 327

Index of Subjects

almúnies and alqueries
    'abrāǧ (pl. of *burǧ*): 47, 83, 126, 144, 146–48, 159; *see also* hamlets
    alqueries: 47, 133, 144, 232
    almúnies: 46, 72, 126, 133, 144–48, 159, 208–09, 234, 242, 272, 289, 303, 316, 345, 348
        and drove roads: 272
        in dryland: 144
        irrigated: 72, 144, 146
    rafals: 133, 144
animals, domestic
    cows: 331
    goats: 173, 277
    horses: 271, 286
    oxen: 146, 235
    pigeons: 329, 331
    pigs to graze: 269
    sheep: 156, 271–72, 277, 288, 296
animals, wild
    badgers (*Meles meles*): 209; *see also* Mas de Melons *in* Index of Place Names
    bears: 258
    boars: 258
    crows: 329
    eagles: 329
    fish, fresh: 241
    fish, salted: 241
    fishing: 65, 241; *see also* Sant Pere de Rodes *in* Index of Place Names
    hawks: 329
    hunting: 276
    wolves: 258, 259; *see also* Capcir *in* Index of Place Names
archaeological sites
    castles and *castra*: 21, 34, 78, 80, 81, 82, 85–86, 88, 157, 189, 205, 263, 311
    caves: 157
    churches: 35, 52, 74, 199
    farmsteads: 155–56, 354; *see also* Vilosiu *in* Index of Place Names
    forges: 250, 252, 256; *see also* Fabregada *in* Index of Place Names
    granges: 71

Islamic sites: 47, 83, 147, 170–71

kilns: 127, 253; *see also* Casa-en-Ponç *in* Index of Place Names

mills: 247

monasteries: 64, 74

necropolis: 46, 80, 81, 135, 142, 199

terraces: 210

towns and cities: 165, 170–71

villages and hamlets: 34, 35, 44, 66, 74, 80, 81, 91, 92, 135–36, 140, 142–43,
156, 291

borders: 17, 65, 69, 80, 84, 85, 87, 90, 98, 100, 102–04, 108, 130, 142, 150, 219,
222, 288, 296, 310; *see also* boundaries

linguistic borders: 90, 318

marches, marchland: 14, 18, 19, 54, 57, 77, 80, 84, 85, 87, 88, 100–01, 103, 108,
129, 142, 219, 258, 293, 296, 297, 299, 310–11, 327, 340

of Catalonia: 318

ṭaġr, borderlands: 297

boundaries: 27, 28, 198–99, 214, 279, 293, 307, 319, 340, 356, 359

borders and ridges: 288

circumambulatio: 294

fronteras, ipsas: 311

frontiers: 14, 15, 17, 22, 27, 57, 85, 99, 272, 316

a new frontier: 90, 363

immunitatis signum (Arles, Vallespir): 67

landmarks (La. *metas*): 313

monoliths: 73

mounds of stones (*congeries petrarum*): 313

perambulatio (En. beating the bounds): 294;
see also Forques *in* Index of Place Names

stone landmarks (*ipsa petra fita*): 313

stones (*lapides*): 313

buildings in the countryside

balmes: 157; *see also* caves

barns: 54, 89, 158

bridges (rural): 180, 288–89, 317

caves or *esplugues*: 157–58; *see also* Esplugallonga, L'
in Index of Place Names

cisterns: 84

arcae finales, cisterns or possibly dolmens: 313

carved into rocks: 209

cortals, huts: 271

domus, farmstead: 149, 159

INDEX OF SUBJECTS 449

esplugues (La. *speluncas*): 157–58, *see also* caves
espones, margins of terraces: 212
forges, *see* metallurgical activities
huts: 35, 61, 262, 271, 277
ice wells: 254
kilns

    ceramic, pottery (Casa-en-Ponç, Cabrera d'Anoia): 127, 253
    gypsum: 254
    lime: 254
    pitch: 254, 262

manse (La. *mansus*): 159; *see also* farmsteads
mansiones: 51
mas (pl. *masos,* La. *mansus*): 149–57, 357; *see also* farmsteads
masos torre, tower-shaped farmhouses: 155
masoveries (farmsteads that depended on another peasant and the
   lord): 140, 150–51, 154, 159, 357
    masovers (peasants who live in a *masoveria*): 141, 357
neighbourhoods (La. *vicinati,* Ct. *veïnats*): 154–55
wells (La. *foveas*): 166, 249, 313
rammed earth (Ct. *tàpia*): 34, 98, 171, 277
pit-houses (Ge. *Grubenhauser*): 34
vici: 51, 280
vilanova, new settlement before 1000 (not to be confused with the new
   towns of the high Middle Ages): 284, 338
silos (Ct. *sitges*): 20, 34, 35, 81, 84, 135, 209, 313
villas, Carolingian: 122, 134, 211, 293–94, 296, 298, 303, 308, 319, 324, 328, 339
winepresses (La. *torcularia,* Ct. *trulls*): 20, 35, 243–44, 253
vessels (Ct. *tines*): 253

Carolingian
   abbeys: 27, 157; *see also* abbeys, monasteries
   castle and *castrum*: 82, 311; *see also* castles and fortifications
   cities: 340; *see also* settlement patterns
   conquest: 141, 216, 296, 338
   counties, counts: 15, 18, 74, 88, 282, 288, 297, 335, 340
   documents: 143, 159, 230, 258, 289, 330
   Empire: 14, 15, 18, 19, 52, 85, 108, 193, 280
   estates: 340; *see also* medieval society
   hamlets, *vilar*: 139–41, 143, 151, 155, 195, 308; *see also* hamlets
   lords: 91; *see also* medieval society
   mansus: 134, 159; *see also* farmsteads
   marches: 87; *see also* borders

450   INDEX OF SUBJECTS

mills: 244; *see also* mills

monarchs, kings: 16, 63, 326–27, 338

parish: 308; *see also* churches

precepts: 241

script: 330

villas, *see* buildings in countryside

castles and fortifications: 78–90

albacar, enclosed space: 47, 83

castella or strongholds: 52, 82; *see also castra*

castle-palace: 77, 104

castles of the March: 84–88, 89; *see also* Vallferosa *in* Index of Place Names

castra or *oppida*: 60, 79, 80–82, 83, 87, 89, 92, 104

    Roman *castrum*: 63

castral villages, *see* villages

celòquia (Ar. *salūqiya*): 83; *see also husun*

dry moats (Ct. *valls* or *fossats*, La. *valla*): 60, 67, 123–24, 300

feudal castles: 21, 77, 82, 88–90, 104, 304

força (La. *fortitudo*), castral village: 42, 57, 60, 61, 98, 100, 300

fortalicium, fortified places: 97

fortified houses (La. *domus fortis*, Fr. *maison forte*): 37, 315

ḥiṣn, ḥuṣūn: 83, 297

keeps (Fr. *donjons*, Ct. *torrasses*): 89, 90

manor (Ct. *casa forta*): 37, 62, 101, 104, 155, 315

ramparts: 93, 98, 124, 177–78; *see also* villages and urban landscape

scaffolds, wooden (hoardings or *bretèches*): 86, 89

towers

    corner towers (Ct. *torres d'angle*): 98

    half towers (Ct. *bestorres*): 98

    watchtowers (Ct. *torre de guaita*): 85, 89

changes in settlement and in the landscape

central places: 23, 81, 127, 179, 185, 360

decastellamento: 102–03, 117

depopulation: 292, 318, 342; *see also* Sallent, El *in* Index of Place Names

desencimbellament or descent from the top of a hill: 118

emmasament, diffusion of new farmsteads: 149–51

encimbellament, creation of a hilltop settlement: 22, 104;

ensagrerament: 21

hilltop buildings

    churches: 307

    monasteries: 64–65

    villages, hamlets, settlements: 31, 34, 35, 42, 61, 90–92, 94, 98–105, 142, 147, 208, 210, 219, 220

INDEX OF SUBJECTS   451

incastellamento (Ct. *encastellament*): 22, 42, 63, 77, 92, 93, 99, 100–02, 104, 123

inecclesiamento: 44, 49

isoclinie, displacement of form with the same orientation: 194

isotopie, transmission of form in the same place: 194

polyfocal settlements: 107, 113, 128– 32; *see also* Santa Coloma de Queralt
    in Index of Place Names

charters

consecration charters: 339

donation charters: 303

of franchise: 22, 125

of freedom and exemptions (*llibertat i franquesa*): 306

population charters (Ct. *carta de poblament*): 23, 98, 108, 110

privilege charters: 22, 111, 124, 177

settlement charters: 88, 100, 115–16, 118, 126, 122–24, 126, 132, 176, 217,
    222–24, 235, 240

churches: 11, 21, 31–33, 35–46, 48–63, 66–69, 72–75, 81, 82, 84, 85, 87, 90,
    93–101, 103–05, 111, 115, 118, 120, 122–23, 128–31, 134, 135, 148, 151, 155, 157,
    161, 163, 168, 173–77, 179–80, 182–84, 193, 198–99, 230, 233, 283, 293, 299,
    300, 303–11, 317, 321, 324, 329–30, 337–39, 345, 355–57

consecration of a church: 52, 67, 135, 155, 307, 339

dedications: 41, 310, 321, 329–30, 338

ecclesias incastellatas or fortified churches: 54, 62, 98

endowment of a church: 293, 307–08

formation of parishes: 293

Gothic period: 289

Hispanic saints: 338

location of the churches: 37, 40

number of churches: 51

paleo-Christian church: 63

parish churches: 28, 50, 66, 67, 94, 134, 139, 155, 294, 306–10

pre-Romanesque church: 87

Romanesque: 38, 39, 40, 75, 81, 84, 87, 89, 90, 92, 98, 289, 351

saints from the early centuries: 338

saints from the Franks: 338

separation from the castle: 94

St Martin: 330, 338

climate changes and natural disasters

Black Death (1348): 150, 153, 159, 174, 181, 275

climate: 13, 15, 23, 257, 273, 362

coombs, *see* shape and use of farmland

droughts: 72, 277

earthquakes: 120, 276, 277; *see also* Olot *in* Index of Place Names

environment: 26, 50, 69, 150, 161, 250, 254, 257, 286, 356, 361, 364
    management: 350
erosion: 194, 203, 211–12, 218, 222, 225, 266, 273, 186
    rocky land (*codina*): 218
fires, rural and urban: 177, 181, 261–62, 266–69
floods: 237, 239, 266, 275, 277
Little Ice Age (since the fourteenth century): 264, 275
locust plagues: 276
Mal any primer, Lo (the Bad First Year) (1333): 275
Medieval Warm Period (AD 800 to 1200): 264, 274
phylloxera (second half of the nineteenth century): 225
plagues: 276–77
rainfall: 13, 24, 266, 273
Roman Climatic Optimum (250 BC to AD 400): 273
sedimentation: 194
communities
    Berber or Amazigh tribes: 47, 209, 233, 314, 355;
        see also Sanata *and* Gelida *in* Index of Place Names
    Christian communities under Muslim rule: 130, 254
    coexistence between Christians and Muslims: 182, 358
    Jewish communities: 181, 215, 317
    Muslim or Andalusian: 47, 181, 227, 243, 247, 358
    parish communities: 74, 307
    peasant: 91, 227, 293–94, 356
    rural, local: 21, 79, 242, 245–46, 252, 301, 303, 308, 356, 359
    valleys: 304
    village communities: 21
convents: 49, 122, 166, 168, 175, 177, 180, 183
    Dominican: 175, 180
    Franciscan: 175, 177, 180
    Order of St Anthony: 168
craftsmen, tradesmen, and other jobs
    artisanal activities: 179–81
    bakers: 166, 179–80
    belt makers: 180
    blacksmiths: 181, 315
    boilermakers: 180
    butcher shops; 97, 166, 181
    çabaséquia (Ar. *sahib al-saquia*), who take care of the ditch: 234
    cornadors, who sound the horn: 361
    merchants: 23, 161, 166, 172, 176, 185, 280, 316–17
    millers: 249–50, 255

INDEX OF SUBJECTS 453

notaries: 172, 317, 330, 348
ovens, one who works at: 142, 166, 179–80
potters: 45, 127, 143, 148, 180, 208–09, 253; *see also* kilns
saddlers: 180
shoemakers: 180
silversmiths: 180
tanners: 166, 238
weavers: 180

farmsteads (Ct. *masos*): 18, 19, 23, 35, 54, 56, 133, 140, 149, 151, 154–55, 158, 210,
211, 217–18, 255, 299, 331, 344, 348, 357–58, 362; *see also* buildings in the
countryside
   bordes (secondary farmsteads): 140, 149, 151, 153, 159;
    see also Sallent, El *in* Index of Place Names
   capmàs (pl. *capmasos*; La. *caput mansus*), farmhouses of a village: 40, 159
   empty, deserted (Ct. *mas rònec*): 140
   farmhouses: 35, 45, 133–34, 139, 141, 150–51, 155–59, 205, 208, 211, 218, 255,
    343, 357
   masoveries, farmhouse of a *masover*: 150
   splitting of: 153; *see also* Gurri *and* Sallent, El *in* Index of Place Names
forests: 26, 260, 262, 264, 269–70, 328, 338, 357
   clearings or deforestation: 214, 269, 328
   conservation and restoration: 270, 276
   fires: 261–62, 266–69
   foresters, forest supervisors: 260
   hunting: 269, 276
   pitch (Ct. *pega*): 254, 262
   production: 262
   protection of forests: 260, 269
   see also plants, woods

graves, tombs: 87, 199
   burials: 20, 43–46, 49, 62, 74, 93, 135, 300
   cist tombs: 95
   cut into the rock, rock-cut graves: 43, 46, 81, 154, 205–06, 253
   necropolises: 31, 43, 44–46, 62, 81, 84, 142, 206
   sarcophagi: 43
   slab tombs: 43, 44
   tegulae graves, tombs: 43, 58, 95

454 INDEX OF SUBJECTS

hamlets (Ct. *vilars*, Fr. *hameaux*): 20, 22, 35, 43, 133–35, 150–51, 155, 158, 210,
217, 277, 298–99, 328, 357
fragmented into farmsteads: 141, 152
torres: 46, 72, 126, 144, 148 159, 236, 316, 345; *see also almúnies and alqueries*
vilars (La. *villares*) or hamlets: 20, 22, 34–35, 48, 61, 134, 136–37, 139–42,
154–55, 159

irrigated land and ditches
algesira, (Ar. *al-jazīra*), islands (Ct. *illes*, La. *insulas*): 229, 237
ditches (Ct. *séquies*): 11, 46, 71–72, 148–49, 166, 177, 206, 222, 227–40,
232–34, 237, 240, 242–43, 246, 248–49, 341, 345, 348, 351
drainage canals, pipes: 232, 237, 240–42
hortes, irrigated land area: 18, 26, 103, 227–30, 232, 234–35, 237, 242, 247,
256, 358
of Valencia: 228
horts, irrigated lands: 115, 156, 206, 228–30, 238–39, 302
huertas: 229, 237
qanawat (plural of *qanāt*): 227, 232, 238
secondary canals, branch canals (Ct. *braçal*): 148, 234–35, 237, 240, 345
sínies (Sp. *norias*, En. water wheels): 237, 239, 242, 247
Islamic period, Al-Andalus
'abrāğ (pl. of *burğ*): 47, 83, 126, 144, 146–48, 159; *see also torres*
a'māl: 297
ahwāz (pl. of *hawz*): 297
Al-Andalus: 18, 27, 65, 85, 104, 133, 142, 272, 363
aljames (Muslim and Jewish quarters): 181–82
aqālīm (pl. of *iqlīm*): 297
burğ: 133, 147–48, 326; *see also 'abrāğ*
butchers (*carnizeria sarracenorum*): 181
Caliphate: 17, 85, 170, 217
castles, *husūn*: 82–84, 315; *see also* castles and fortifications
cities: 165–71
conquest (*c.* 713–719): 171, 209, 227, 232, 297, 326
Emirate: 15, 18, 85, 108
Islamization: 17, 19, 20, 327
kasbah (*al-qaṣabah*) or citadels: 165, 167, 170; *see also Suda*
medina or *al-madīnah*: 165, 167, 170, 182, 232
Mozarabs: 208, 327
Muslims: 11, 17, 22, 25, 64, 77, 83, 85, 103, 161, 272, 280; *see also* communities
pottery: 148, 208–09
qanawat (plural of *qanāt*): 227, 232, 238
quarter: 47, 166, 181–82

INDEX OF SUBJECTS 455

Quraysh, Arab tribe: 233, 326
ribāṭ (or Ràpita): 326–27
rule: 16, 36, 147, 159, 247, 268, 297, 321, 326–27, 348
Saracens (Ct. *sarraïns*): 17, 65, 181, 229, 297
Suda: 165, 167, 169–70, 183
taifas: 17, 85, 109, 165, 170, 228, 297
Zenata, Berber tribe: 209, 233, 286; *see also* Sanata, Butsènit *in* Index of
Place Names

Jews, Jewish
aljames (Jewish and Muslim quarters): 181–82
quarter (Ct. *call*): 122–23, 126, 131, 161, 165, 167–68, 170, 174, 177, 181–83, 215,
237, 317
Cuirassa (Ar. *qawraŷa*), Jewish quarter (Lleida): 165–67, 181
synagogues: 166, 170, 181
jurisdictional rights
'bad' or 'evil' customs (Ct. *mals usos*, La. *malos usaticos*): 101, 315
banal rights: 315
mills: 315
blacksmithing: 315
ovens: 315
fiscal units, land, domains, estates: 159, 198, 244, 295, 199, 314, 326, 337–38
gallows: 361
see also medieval society

language
Arabic: 144, 327
Basque (*euskara*): 38, 322–23, 332
Catalan: 16, 18, 19, 69, 90, 132, 328, 330–31, 363
Homilies d'Organyà: 69
Iberian: 322
Latin: 193
Occitan: 16, 19, 90, 246, 330, 363
Occitan-Catalan linguistic space: 19
Romance languages: 17, 332
livestock: 257, 262, 264, 267, 272, 276–77
bovalar (pasture of cows): 331
carrerada, cabanera: 144; *see also below* drove roads
deveses (forbidden space): 260, 331
drove roads, livestock paths, tracks: 38, 87, 144, 267, 272, 287–88, 296, 303
and boundaries: 289
and ridges: 288

456   INDEX OF SUBJECTS

emprius (La. *ademprivium*), rights of easement: 304, 319
herds (cattle): 272, 277
horse paths (La. *via cavalar*): 271
horse pastures: 271
meadows: 239
milking parlours: 271
pastures: 259, 262, 265, 268, 271
rights of passage and use of pastures: 271
sheep: 156, 271–72, 277, 288, 296
shelters for storing cheese: 271
shepherds: 262, 272
short-range transhumant movement: 272
summer pastures (*ipsas estivas*): 272
transhumance: 27, 64, 261, 271–73, 279, 287
     of sheep: 271
     routes: 272
calmes, highlands, high mountain plains: 271, 273, 277

medieval society, lords, and estates
allod (Ct. *alou*): 113, 136, 294, 339
     allodial peasants: 298
bordarius (En. bordar or boarder): 153
cabalers, younger sons: 56
capbreu (La. *caput breve*, En. land terrier): 66, 97, 149, 153, 330–31, 348
castellans (or chatelains) (Ct. *castlans*): 130, 315; *see also* Santa Coloma de
     Queralt *in* Index of Place Names
cavalleries (knights' fiefs): 204, 315–16, 331, 348
demesme (Ct. *domenge*): 159, 331
estates, seigneurial estates: 69, 72, 144, 148, 159, 161, 196, 198, 240, 273, 293,
     297, 307, 310, 315, 318, 326, 331, 340
     and boundaries: 340
'evil' customs (Ct. *mals usos*): 101, 315; *see also* jurisdictional rights
feudal lords: 32, 34, 40, 46, 91, 97, 103, 228, 249, 256, 348
feudal society: 150, 243
fogatge (hearth tax): 174
focs (hearths or inhabited houses): 174–75
fundi: 28, 58, 69, 190, 193, 198, 280, 294, 299, 300–03, 307–08, 311, 324–25, 338
heirs (Ct. *hereus*): 56, 72. 294
hereters (peasants with a land tenure, Segrià): 236
knights (Ct. *cavallers*): 148, 204–05, 219, 315–16, 331, 348
land surveyors (Ct. *agrimensor*): 25
landlords (Fr. *seigneurs fonciers*): 298

llevador de comptes (En. rental): 154

palatiolum (Ct. *palol* or *palou*): 198, 326, 329, 337

palatium (Ct. *palau*) 299, 325–26, 329, 337

pariage agreement (Ct. *pariatge*): 69

poor (Ct. *pobres de solemnitat* and *vergonyants*): 183

quadra (a fief owned by a knight): 219, 315–16

slaves: 35

sub-castellans (Ct. *sotscastlans*): 315

sub-establishment: 154

teloneum: 87

tenure: 236, 315–16

tithes: 94, 307, 310, 315

    of iron (*decimis ferri*): 250

metallurgical activities: 143, 243, 250–51

  blacksmiths: 181, 315

  crosos (holes made on the ground): 252

  forges (Ct. *fargues, fàbregues*): 244, 250, 252, 256, 259, 269, 276

    bellows: 252

    coal: 269

    mallet (Ct. *mall* or *martinet*): 252

    molines de fer, iron mills: 252

  lead: 250

  mines: 244, 250, 252

    menera de ferro (iron mine): 252

    meneras argenti (silver mine): 252

  silversmiths: 180

methodology, projects and research centers

  aerial photographs (A-Series from 1945–46 and B-Series from 1956–57): 342–43, 350

  anthracological work: 258

    micro carbons: 262, 267–68

  anthroponyms: 137, 220, 327

    Frankish: 137, 327

    Gothic: 327

  archaeobotany, archaeobotanists: 354

  archaeogeography: 334

  archaeology: 33, 155; *see also* archaeological sites

    and history: 32

  botany, botanists: 363

  cartography: 28, 333, 351

    historical cartography: 333

  fieldwork: 211, 251, 354

458 INDEX OF SUBJECTS

geography: 354
geology, geologists: 354, 363
GIS (Geographic Information Systems): 284, 342, 344, 354
heritage: 11, 14, 163, 249, 284, 292, 340, 351–52, 359
Historic Landscape Characterisation, project (HLC): 14, 28, 333–34, 343, 350
ICAC (with the GIAP): 362
Laboratoire de Cartographie Historique (Bordeaux): 334
LiDAR technology: 202, 342–43, 355
linguistics, linguists: 19, 137, 318, 327, 331, 337, 354, 363
longue durée: 341, 353
morphogenesis of villages: 32, 57
multidisciplinary research: 354
Observatori del Paisatge (Olot): 343, 362
Optically Stimulated Luminescence (OSL): 24, 211, 213, 354, 358
PaHisCat (*Paisatge Històric de Catalunya*): 14, 28, 190, 202, 333, 341–42, 343–44, 349–51, 364
peasant perspectives, peasants changed the landscape: 356
personal names, *see above* anthroponyms
place names: 22, 28, 29, 73, 134, 140, 145, 154, 198, 205–06, 208–09, 219–20, 233, 244, 250, 254, 256, 258, 262, 287, 291, 295, 299, 304, 306, 314, 321–32, 336–38, 340, 351, 361; *see also below* toponymy
plan units: 23, 162
post-mortem inventories: 155
radiocarbon dating, Carbon-14 dates: 46, 85, 86, 257, 260, 354
retrogressive method: 341, 353
soundscape: 361
toponymy: 28, 29, 74, 219, 254, 257, 321–29, 333, 349, 362–63; *see also above* place names
  microtoponymy: 321, 330–31
transition period: 20, 193
military orders
commanderies: 49, 71–72, 75
  Order of the Hospital, Hospitallers
    commandery: 331
    knights: 71
  Order of the Temple, Templars: 72, 74, 235, 240
    commandery: 148, 284, 348
    knights, lords: 71, 100
mills (Ct. *molins*): 26, 141, 230, 238–39, 242–44, 249, 255–56, 338–39
boat mills (on the riverbank): 166
built by a feudal lord: 249, 256
Carolingian: 244

INDEX OF SUBJECTS 459

dams, made of stones: 230
 made of branches (Ct. *paixeres*): 230, 246
 ferramenta (especially the spindle and the rynd): 246, 255
 flour mills: 250
 flumes (Ct. medieval: *tudella*): 245, 247
 fulling mills: 238–39, 243, 249–50
 Islamic mills: 247
 manual mills: 244
 millstones, grindstones: 246: 249
 powered by men or animals: 244
 moltura, mill tax: 249, 356
 number of stone mills in each building: 250
 ponds of a mill: 248–49
 rīhā, mill in Arabic: 233; *see also* Rifà, Rufea *in* Index of Place Names
 rynd (Ct. *nadilla*): 246
 sawmills (Ct. *molins serradors*): 252, 259, 269, 276
 spindle (Ct. *arbre*): 246
 tank (Ct. *cup*, North Africa: *maṣabb*): 247, 249
 windmills: 243, 248
 with a horizontal wheel: 26, 245–47, 249
 with a sloping channel or flume: 246, 248
 with a tank (Ct. *molins de cup*): 26, 248
 with a vertical wheel (Ct. *molins roders*): 26, 245–48
monasteries, abbeys: 63, 64
 and gorges: 64
 and valleys: 64
 Benedictine monasteries: 49, 63–65, 67, 74, 124, 212, 255, 264–65, 272–73
  priories: 103
 Cistercian abbeys: 27, 49, 69–71, 75, 182, 257, 260–61, 271–72, 348
  nuns: 217
  precinct walls: 70
 granges: 69
 hilltop monasteries: 64
 maritime monasteries: 65
 monastic allod: 136
 urban: 65

new towns and new quarters
 along one or more lengthwise road axes: 110
 at a crossroads: 132
 bastides: 22, 107, 110, 115, 117, 132
 castellnous and castelnaux (or *castèthnaus*): 126

460 INDEX OF SUBJECTS

colomines, new quarters (Perpignan): 184
establiments (En. settlements), new quarters: 184
irregular shapes: 111, 123
monastic new town: 124
new towns (Ct. *viles noves*): 22, 31, 32, 107, 198, 355
orthogonal grid pattern: 111
pobles (Valencia): 184
with a main axis: 110, 114
with a square: 122
with rectangular-shaped blocks of houses: 120
with square-shaped blocks of houses: 117

pagan survivals, pagan background: 73
cult of trees: 73
holy stones or monoliths (Mijaran stone, Val d'Aran): 73
Sant Urbici (Berguedà): 65
Jana, Diana goddess (Fontjanina, Ribagorça): 73
Mater magna or Cybele (Madremanya, Gironès): 73
mausoleum (Mosoll, Cerdanya): 73
mother-oaks (Marqueixanes, Conflent): 73
nymphs of the forest (Nèfol, Cerdanya): 73
Nempetano, pagus (Cabó, Alt Urgell): 73
place of the church: 37
sacred mountains: 74
sanctuaries (Meritxell, Montserrat, Núria): 74
place names: 28, 29, 208–09, 208–09, 219–20, 321–32, 336–38
Arabic: 326, 337
beginning with 'Vin-' and 'Beni-': 326
Berber: 326
ending in '-à' and '-ana': 324; *see also* Cornellà *in* Index of Place Names
Germanic: 327–28, 337
Greek: 325
Mozarabic: 327
pre-Roman: 40, 73, 139, 205, 291, 295, 321–23, 327, 337
Roman: 292, 295, 324, 327
Romanesque: 321, 327–28
plants and groves, cultivated
barley (*Hordeum vulgare*): 143
cereals: 260–61, 263, 265, 267, 269, 277
pollen: 261, 264
farratge, grass for cattle: 331
grapevines, vines (*Vitis*): 260, 263, 274

INDEX OF SUBJECTS   461

hemp (*Cannabis*): 263
olive trees, groves (*Olea*): 261, 263–65, 267–69, 277, 331
pulses: 143
rye (*Secale cereale*): 143
    pollen: 263
vineyards: 212, 261, 264–65, 267, 275, 277
wheat (*Triticum aestivum/durum/turgidum*): 143
see also pollen analyses
plants and groves, wild
alders (*Alnus*): 262, 268
ashes (*Fraxinus*): 329; *see also* Freixe, El *in* Index of Place Names
Asteraceae, family of plants: 264
beeches (*Fagus sylvatica*): 13, 262, 267, 274
birches (*Betula*): 262, 268
bullrushes (Ct. *joncs*) (*Scirpoides holoschoenus*): 230
Calluna, common heather: 265
Chenopodiaceae (or Amaranthaceae), family of plants: 264
chestnuts (*Castanea*): 263, 267, 274, 335
coprophilic plants: 262
cork oaks (*Quercus suber*): 265
Cyperaceae, family of plants, 265
elms (*Ulmus*): 262, 329
Ericaceae, family of plants, heath family: 264, 265
evergreen oaks (*Quercus ilex ssp. ilex*): 13, 140, 265, 264–65, 275, 329, 332
firs (*Abies alba*): 13, 262, 267, 274
forests, groves: 267, 269
hazelnuts (*Corylus*): 262, 268
holm oaks (*Quercus ilex*): 267; *see also above* evergreen oaks
junipers (*Juniperus*): 262
lindens (*Tilia*): 262
mountain pines (*Pinus mugo* subsp. *Uncinata*): 261
oaks (*Quercus pubescents, Quercus robur*): 13, 261–62, 264–65, 267, 269, 274–75, 329; *see also* pollen analyses
pines (*Pinus*): 261–62, 265, 267–68, 274–75, 329
plantain (*Plantago lanceolata*): 264, 267–69
Poaceae, family of plants, grasses: 264–65
Quercus ilex rotundifolia: 13; *see also above* holm oaks
Quercus ilex: 13; *see also above* evergreens oaks, holm oaks
Quercus pubescens: 13; *see also above* oaks
reedmace (*Typha-Sparganium*): 264, 269;
    see also Banyoles *in* Index of Place Names
riparian trees: 269

462 INDEX OF SUBJECTS

scrub, scrubland (Ct. *garrigues*): 265, 302
sorb trees (*Sorbus domestica*): 331
Typha-Sparganium: 269; *see also above* reedmace
vegetation: 13, 23, 26, 149, 218, 257, 274, 354, 362
walnuts (*Juglans*): 260, 263, 276
pollen analyses: 26, 257, 260, 262, 268, 271, 274, 277, 354
Amposta (Montsià): 269
Banyoles (Pla de l'Estany): 264
Besòs, Coastal Range (Barcelonès): 266
Creixell (Tarragonès): 267
Cubelles (Garraf): 275
El Madriu, Perafita, Claror (Andorra): 261–62
Enveig, Pla de l'Orri, Maurà (Alta Cerdanya): 261
Ivars, Vila-sana (Pla d'Urgell): 268
Pla de les Salines (Alta Cerdanya, Ripollès): 260
radiocarbon dating, 14th century dates: 257, 260
Sobrestany (Baix Empordà): 265
previous periods, precedents of the Middle Ages: 143
Bronze Age: 91, 210, 311
Byzantines: 232
Greek colony: 325
Iberian period: 13, 81, 91, 192, 311
Iron Age: 143, 210
Late Antiquity (fourth-sixth centuries): 59, 91, 301
Roman period
cadastre, Roman: 193
cardo: 178, 190, 193; *see also below decumanus*
centuriations, *see* shape and use of farmland
cities: 189–90, 290
conquest: 353
decumanus: 178, 190; *see also above cardo*
Empire: 36, 43, 191–92, 193, 265, 280, 295, 308, 322
fall: 77
Late: 36, 63, 178, 190, 200, 250, 300, 303, 329
Western: 24
heritage: 359
laws: 338
legions (*Pont del Diable*): 289
plot divisions, *see* shape and use of farmland
roads: 187, 280, 311; *see also* roads, ways, and tracks
temples, Roman: 179
toponyms: 324–26; *see also* place names

villae, Roman: 20, 34, 48, 79, 158, 190, 200, 277, 280, 303, 324, 343

walls: 163, 178

Religion and the Christian Church

Cathars, Catharism: 132, 272

crusade against the Cathars: 108

Benedict, rule of St: 63, 330

Benedictine and Cistercian monasteries, *see* monasteries, abbeys

Christian conquest: 25, 26, 46, 47, 83, 130, 144–46, 165, 167–68, 170, 179, 184, 203, 220, 225, 228, 233–34, 242, 247–48, 317, 345

Christianization: 50, 65, 73–74, 163

collegiate churches: 49, 67–69, 75, 89, 113–14, 130, 233, 255

Institutio canonicorum (816): 67

Rule of St Augustine, 68

hermits: 64

Peace and Truce of God: 44, 49

assemblies: 53, 62; *see also* Toluges *in* Index of Place Names

sanctuaries (near mountain passes): 260

see also communities, churches, convents, monasteries, pagan survivals

roads, ways, and tracks: 27, 194, 279–92, 338, 349–51

anomalous roads: 283

cavée (La. *cavata*): 287; *see also* hollow ways

crossroads: 63, 100–01, 132, 175, 282, 317

fords (Ct. *guals*): 289

hollow ways or sunken lanes: 284, 286–87

long-distance roads: 280–82

mountain passes or *ports*: 260, 284, 288, 322

network of roads: 24, 197, 199, 214, 280–83, 286, 290–92

number of roads (*tri numérique*): 282

pre-Roman roads: 191, 281

radial network: 217, 220

roads connecting cities and towns: 282–83

roads and villages: 283–84

stratae: 280

Strata Cardonense: 308; *see also* Cardona *in* Index of Place Names

through a gorge: 284

viae: 280; *see also* livestock

Via Augusta: 189, 229, 280, 296, 311

Via Domitia: 189, 280

Via francisca: 280

Via morisca: 311

viae communes, common roads: 280

viae publicae, public roads: 280

464   INDEX OF SUBJECTS

viae vicinales, local roads: 280

vias calciatas, stone-paved: 280

calçada (La. *ipsa calciata,* paved road): 311

salt: 243–44, 254–56

salt beds (Vilafamés): 255

salt mines (Cardona): 68, 282

saltwater sources (Gerri de la Sal, Calassanç, Jusseu): 254

settlement patterns

'abrāǧ (pl. of *burǧ*): 47, 83, 126, 144, 146–48, 159; *see also torres*

aldea: 144

cities: 15, 19, 23, 109, 161–71, 179–85, 340, 360–61; *see also* urban landscape

civitas: 81, 302

Islamic cities: 165, 170–71

Roman heritage: 163

concentrated: 19, 25, 77, 133

dispersed or scattered: 23, 40, 47, 48, 56, 83, 134–35, 143, 149–54, 157, 159, 353, 357; *see also* farmsteads

half-dispersed: 23, 134–35, 140, 144, 151, 159, 210, 357; *see also* hamlets, *almúnies* and *alqueries*

towns (Ct. *viles*): 23, 42, 47, 66–69, 92, 97, 109–32, 161–70, 172–78, 180–85, 360–61; *see also* new towns

troglodytic: 157; *see also* buildings in the countryside

unstable: 43, 48, 135, 158, 298

shape and use of farmland

bancals: 210; *see also* terraces

centuriations: 146, 178, 187–90, 195, 197–99, 205, 214, 216, 219, 228–29, 281, 291, 295, 299, 300, 302, 311, 313, 345, 358

coaxial field strips, slope land strips, bands, strips of farmland: 25, 146, 149, 189, 191–92, 194, 202, 220–25, 236

comes, see below coombs

concentric shapes: 195, 201–02, 214–20

coombs (or combes), valley bottoms (Ct. *comes*): 18, 24, 201–04, 206, 208–09, 213, 219, 225, 237, 274, 331, 344, 348, 355

check-dams (in the coombs): 203, 213

farraginals, land to cultivate grass for livestock: 217, 331; *see also* plants and groves

feixa: 210, 222, 276; *see also* terraces

faixes (strips of land): 210, 222

finitio more arcifinio: 311

forma censalis: 302

formation networks (Fr. *réseaux de formation*): 188, 191

foundation networks (Fr. *réseaux de fondation*): 188, 191

irrigated land (*terra subreganea*): 25, 26, 29, 32, 72, 146, 148, 194, 206, 213, 227–40, 242, 331, 341, 355; *see also* irrigated land and ditches

maresmes, marshes: 273

marjals, wetlands: 232

orthogonal plots (in the countryside): 188, 190, 192, 199, 214, 284, 290, 343

parades or pieces of land: 203, 205

parellades (land worked by a pair of oxen): 72, 146, 148–49, 221–22

 dryland: 72, 221–22; *see also* Llenguaderes, Les *in* Index of Place Names

 irrigated: 72, 148–49, 221, 235

partides (sets of plots of land): 149, 219, 221, 223, 237, 330–31

plot division: 25, 188, 192, 194, 195–96, 198–99, 229, 345, 355, 358

 Islamic: 236

 Roman period: 146, 188–90, 198–99, 200, 209, 213, 286, 290–91, 295, 302–03, 308, 313, 345, 349

 post-Roman: 192–94

 pre-Roman: 192

radio-concentric shapes: 195, 201, 214; *see also above* concentric shapes

sorts, fields randomly distributed among the settlers: 221, 222–23, 331

terraces: 24, 139–41, 150, 201–04, 209–14, 219–20, 223–25, 328, 331, 344

 braided terraces: 139, 201, 213

 or *feixes*: 210, 272, 276

 pocket terraces: 213

three rings (Baix Cinca): 217

territories and districts

 a'māl: 297

 aḥwāz (pl. of *ḥawz*): 297, 317

 aqālīm (pl. of *iqlīm*): 297

 archbishoprics: 179, 297

 archdeaconries: 155

 castells termenats, castles with a *terme*, a district: 54, 85, 88

 castral districts: 27, 77, 293, 296, 299, 310–15, 340, 356

 counties: 13–19, 27, 28, 85, 88, 108, 293–97, 318, 335–40, 359

 dioceses, bishoprics: 27, 28, 54, 293–97, 334, 359

 districts: 22, 27, 28, 54, 77, 85, 88, 103, 197, 293, 298–99, 310–16, 340, 356

 marca: 100, 310; *see also below* march

 march or frontier territory, marchlands: 14, 18, 19, 54, 57, 77, 80, 84–88, 100–01, 103, 108, 129, 142, 219, 258, 293, 296, 310–11, 340

  castles of the March: 84–88

  Gothic March: 327

466   INDEX OF SUBJECTS

Hispanic March (border country with al-Andalus or Hispania): 14, 85, 299

March of Berga: 297

municipalities (modern): 299

pagus (pl. *pagi*): 199, 280, 290, 294–95, 299, 302, 329

of Andorra (*Andorrensis pagi*): 250

of Bar (Alt Urgell): 295

of Llívia (Cerdanya): 291

of Talló (Cerdanya): 199, 295

pagus Nempetano: 73; *see also* pagan survivals

parishes, *see* churches

sub-*vegueries*: 316; *see also vegueries*

ṭaġr, borderlands, march: 297

taifa kingdoms: 17, 85, 109, 165, 170, 228, 297

territories of cities: 317

terroir (Ct. *terrer*), agricultural economic space: 46, 324

vegueries (La. *vicariae*), *veguers* of the king: 293–94, 316

vegueries, veguer of the count (La. *vicarii*, En. viguiers): 103, 340

villas, *see* buildings in countryside

urban landscape: 23, 161; *see also* new towns and new quarters

Almshouse (Ct. *Almoina*): 183

almodí (building for cereal storage and sale): 166

arcades (Ct. *porxos, arcades*): 104, 111, 122, 166, 180

Assoc (Muslim market): 166

auction markets (Ct. *llotges*): 180

bakeries: 166, 179–80

baths: 47, 166, 170

bridges: 56, 180

Lleida: 166

Pont del Diable (Devil's Bridge): 128

brothels: 166, 180

butcher shops (Ct. *carnisseries*): 97, 166

Muslim butcher: 181

cathedrals: 49–50, 122, 163, 165, 166–67 (Seu Vella), 178–79, 183, 282, 295, 298, 337

Aryan cathedral: 163

cemeteries of Christians, Jews, and Muslims: 166

of Jews (Lleida): 166, 181

of Muslims: 166, 181

ecclesiastical quarter: 183

INDEX OF SUBJECTS   467

episcopal palace: 183
    of Lleida: 166, 179, 183
façades of houses: 185
fairs: 128, 174, 176, 282
gates, portals: 97, 130, 166, 168, 173, 175, 177–78
hospitals: 123, 177, 179, 180, 183
    Lleida: 166, 168, 183
hostels: 166, 179, 180
Islamic quarters: 168; *see also below Vila dels sarraïns*
kasbah (*al-qaṣabah*) or citadel: 165, 167, 169, 170, 183
markets, marketplaces: 22, 23, 66, 67, 69, 103–04, 111, 123, 126–28, 130, 132,
   151, 162–63, 166, 172–78, 180, 253, 282
    area of influence: 316–17
medina or *al-madīnah*: 165, 167
mercadals or market squares: 111, 122–23, 125, 173, 179, 182
    forum (Martorell): 128, 173
mines (like a qanat): 238
mosque: 161, 165–67, 170, 181
ovens: 142, 166, 179–80
places, land without housing (Lleida): 169, 184–85
port cities: 180
prisons: 166, 180, 361
royal palaces and castles of the King: 122, 124, 139, 163, 165–67
shipyards (Ct. *drassanes*): 170, 180; *see also* Tortosa *in* Index of Place
   Names
slaughterhouses (Ct. *maell*): 166
squares: 34, 124, 130–31, 173, 175, 177, 179, 181
suburbs (Ct. *ravals, burgs*): 65, 130, 163, 165, 175, 178, 182–83, 234
synagogues: 166, 170, 181
tanneries: 166, 238
taverns: 166
topography of power: 179
town halls (*Consell de Cent*, Paeria): 166, 175, 179
universities (*Estudi General* of Lleida): 166, 183
urban planning
    deliberate: 162
    spontaneous: 162
Vila dels sarraïns (*Villa Sarracenorum*) (Lleida, Segrià): 181
walls: 122, 161, 163, 165–67, 169, 173–74, 177–78, 180–81, 183
weighing, places of: 180
    Pes de la llana (wool weighing) (Lleida): 166
    Pes de l'oli (oil weighing) (Lleida): 166

468 INDEX OF SUBJECTS

villages
   à maisons: 21, 31, 33; *see also* open villages
   Carolingian villas (in the Catalan counties): 122, 155, 211, 293–94, 296–303, 319, 324, 328, 339
   casaliers: 36; *see also below* open villages
   castral villages: 22, 31, 32, 35, 42, 49, 53, 54, 77–105, 111, 149, 348, 357, 362
   cellera: 50, 52, 56–58, 60–62, 100, 183, 300; *see also below* sagreres
      in a castral village: 96, 100, 122–23
   cellers (En. cellars): 44, 57; *see also* sagrers
   dry moats: 60, 67, 123–24, 300
   ecclesiastical villages: 19, 21, 31, 32, 49–61, 94, 96, 107, 283, 355
      transformations of: 62, 63
   encastellats, near a castle: 105; *see also* changes in settlement
   hilltop villages: 31, 34, 35, 42, 90, 91, 94, 99, 102–03, 205, 219–20
   neighbourhoods (La. *vicinati*, Ct. *veïnats*): 154–55
   open villages: 21, 31, 36, 37–43, 48, 50, 128, 258, 355
   Pyrenean villages: 32; *see also above* open villages
   sagreres (*sacraria*): 21, 32, 44, 50, 52–63, 97, 100, 101, 128–29, 159, 173, 300, 351, 357
   sagrers (La. *sacrarii*, plots of land): 44, 56, 62, 101
   walls: 35, 40, 58, 61, 65, 67, 91–94, 98, 117–18 124–25, 130–31, 142, 147
violence, riots, and wars
   colonization: 18, 22, 72, 105, 108, 110, 201–02, 221–22, 225, 328, 358, 363
   conquest
      Christian conquest, conquest of a county: 17, 25, 26, 46, 47, 72, 83, 85, 105, 108–10, 126, 130, 144–46, 148–49, 165, 167–68, 170–71, 178–79, 182, 184, 203–06, 219–20, 223, 225, 228–29, 233–37, 242, 247–48, 256, 267, 297, 303, 315–17, 327, 329, 331, 341, 345, 348
      Carolingian conquest: 141, 216, 296, 310, 329, 338
      Islamic conquest, Arab-Berber conquest: 171, 209, 227, 232, 268, 297, 326
      crusade against the Cathars: 108
      of Catalonia by the King of France (1285): 126
      of the county of Pallars: 40
   crops, destruction of: 277
   feudal wars of Pallars: 54
   fighting among feudal lords: 97
   fitna: 17
   Hungarians, expedition of: 268
   remences, war of (fifteenth century): 23
   Treaty of the Pyrenees (1659): 20
   War of the Two Peters: 277

INDEX OF SUBJECTS 469

watercourses, springs, and lakes
    clamors (watercourse that sometimes makes noise): 145, 231
    deltas: 144, 255, 266, 269, 274
    drying up lakes and ponds: 240
    fords (Ct. *guals*): 289
    fountains: 65, 166
    gorge (Ct. *congost*): 64, 288; *see also* monasteries
    lakes: 63, 66–67, 177, 227, 239–42, 250, 255, 261, 264–65, 268, 274, 284
    ponds (Ct. *basses*): 240–42, 252, 284, 177, 331; *see also* mills
        salt ponds: 66
        pond of a mill: 248–49
    rafts (Ct. *rais*): 259
    reguers (old streams, courses of drainage water): 145, 231, 345
    riverbanks: 166, 230
    riverbeds: 225
    springs: 71, 103, 140, 142, 150, 214, 254, 302, 313
        urban: 237–38
    streams: 45, 139, 141, 195, 206, 225, 246, 255, 307,
    wetlands: 232, 264; *see also* shape and use of farmland
woods: 259, 276–77; *see also* forests, plants
    charcoal, coal: 243–44, 252, 254, 276
        analysis of charcoal: 258
        charcoal piles: 243–44, 254
        for forges: 269
    firewood: 212, 218, 258, 260, 276
    for shipbuilding: 269
    masts for boats and galleys: 270
    resinous wood: 276

The Medieval Countryside

All volumes in this series are evaluated by an Editorial Board, strictly on academic grounds, based on reports prepared by referees who have been commissioned by virtue of their specialism in the appropriate field. The Board ensures that the screening is done independently and without conflicts of interest. The definitive texts supplied by authors are also subject to review by the Board before being approved for publication. Further, the volumes are copyedited to conform to the publisher's stylebook and to the best international academic standards in the field.

Titles in Series

The Rural History of Medieval European Societies: Trends and Perspectives, ed. by Isabel Alfonso (2007)

Eva Svensson, *The Medieval Household: Daily Life in Castles and Farmsteads, Scandinavian Examples in their European Context* (2008)

Land, Power, and Society in Medieval Castile: A Study of Behetría Lordship, ed. by Cristina Jular Pérez-Alfaro and Carlos Estepa Díez (2009)

Survival and Discord in Medieval Society: Essays in Honour of Christopher Dyer, ed. by Richard Goddard, John Langdon, and Miriam Müller (2010)

Feudalism: New Landscapes of Debate, ed. by Sverre Bagge, Michael H. Gelting, and Thomas Lindkvist (2011)

Scale and Scale Change in the Early Middle Ages: Exploring Landscape, Local Society, and the World Beyond, ed. by Julio Escalona and Andrew Reynolds (2011)

José Ramón Díaz de Durana, *Anonymous Noblemen: The Generalization of Hidalgo Status in the Basque Country (1250–1525)* (2011)

Settlement and Lordship in Viking and Early Medieval Scandinavia, ed. by Bjørn Poulsen and Søren Michael Sindbæk (2011)

Britons, Saxons, and Scandinavians: The Historical Geography of Glanville R. J. Jones, ed. by P. S. Barnwell and Brian K. Roberts (2012)

Ferran Garcia-Oliver, *The Valley of the Six Mosques: Work and Life in Medieval Valldigna* (2012)

Town and Countryside in the Age of the Black Death: Essays in Honour of John Hatcher, ed. by Mark Bailey and Stephen Rigby (2012)

Town and Country in Medieval North Western Europe: Dynamic Interactions, edited by Alexis Wilkin, John Naylor, Derek Keene, and Arnoud-Jan Bijsterveld (2015)

Crisis in the Later Middle Ages: Beyond the Postan–Duby Paradigm, ed. by John Drendel (2015)

Alasdair Ross, *Land Assessment and Lordship in Medieval Northern Scotland* (2015)

Power and Rural Communities in Al-Andalus: Ideological and Material Representations, ed. by Adela Fábregas and Flocel Sabaté (2015)

Peasants and Lords in the Medieval English Economy: Essays in Honour of Bruce M. S. Campbell, ed. by Maryanne Kowaleski, John Langdon, and Phillipp R. Schofield (2015)

Eline Van Onacker, *Village Elites and Social Structures in the Late Medieval Campine Region* (2017)

Yossef Rapoport, *Rural Economy and Tribal Society in Islamic Egypt: A Study of al-Nābulusī's 'Villages of the Fayyum'* (2018)

The Villages of the Fayyum, a Thirteenth-Century Register of Rural, Islamic Egypt, ed. and trans. by Yossef Rapoport and Ido Shahar (2018)

Peter Hoppenbrouwers, *Village Community and Conflict in Late Medieval Drenthe* (2018)

Polity and Neighbourhood in Early Medieval Europe, ed. by Julio Escalona, Orri Vésteinsson, and Stuart Brookes (2019)

Agricultural Landscapes of Al-Andalus, and the Aftermath of the Feudal Conquest, ed. by Helena Kirchner and Flocel Sabaté (2021)

In Preparation

Conflict, Language, and Social Practice in Medieval Societies: Selected Essays of Isabel Alfonso, with Commentaries, ed. by Julio Escalona Monge, Alvaro Carvajal Castro, and Cristina Jular Pérez-Alfaro